The Elizabethan Puritan Movement

The Elizabethan Puritan Movement

Patrick Collinson

METHUEN
London & New York

First published 1967
This edition published by
arrangement with
Jonathan Cape Ltd
in 1982 by Methuen & Co. Ltd
11 New Fetter Lane, EC4P 4EE
Published in the USA by
Methuen & Co.
in association with Methuen, Inc.
733 Third Avenue, New York, NY 10017

Printed in Great Britain
by J. W. Arrowsmith Ltd., Bristol

British Library Cataloguing in Publication Data

Collinson, Patrick
The Elizabethan puritan movement.—
(Methuen library reprints)
1. Puritans — England — History
I. Title
285'.9'0942   BX9334.2

ISBN 0-416-34000-8

Contents

CONTENTS

For my mother

'For to collect all that is to be known, to put the discourse in order and curiously to discuss every particular point, is the duty of the author of a history.'

(2 *Maccabees* ii 31)

'Some men divide generally all Protestants into Puritans and Antipuritans; but I shall admit of subdivisions in both, for all men are not alike, which either affect or disaffect, either Puritans or Antipuritans.'

(HENRY PARKER [?], *A discourse concerning Puritans*, 1641, p. 4)

'I think our studies ought to be all but purposeless. They want to be pursued with chastity, like mathematics.'

(Lord Acton to Richard Simpson, January 22nd, 1859; F. A. GASQUET, *Lord Acton and his Circle*, p. 57)

Preface

THE APPEARANCE of yet another study of early English puritanism calls for an apology and an explanation. They are best made by referring to a slim volume published for the Royal Historical Society in 1905, *The Presbyterian Movement in the Reign of Queen Elizabeth*.* Under this title, the American scholar Roland Green Usher edited two important documentary sources which together contained, as he thought, the 'essential truth' and the 'ultimate knowledge' now available to us about that lost cause. Such a judgment might be thought needlessly pessimistic if it were not for Usher's evident distaste for his subject. They provided, for him, a narrative 'as full as could be wished'. Since then, the assumption that little more of significance would be uncovered about the organized and militant puritanism of Elizabeth's reign has happily proved to lack foundation. Since the early years of this century, other valuable bodies of information have come to light, or have been made more accessible. There has been, for example, an immeasurable advance in the care and understanding of ecclesiastical and other local records, many of which are rich in the raw material of the religious history of the later sixteenth century. During the same half-century, the progress of Elizabethan historical studies, and especially Sir John Neale's reconstruction of the parliamentary history of the reign, has heightened our sense of the importance of puritanism and has provoked new questions. Yet the puritan movement, as distinct from puritanism more broadly conceived, has remained only a little less obscure than it was some sixty years ago.

* Camden Socy, 3rd ser., viii.

PREFACE

What I have written is no more than a history of the quest by the Elizabethan puritans for what some of them called 'a further reformation', the logical completion of the process of reconstituting the national Church, which in their view had been arrested halfway. Although the activities of the more extreme, presbyterian puritans, especially in the 1580s, provide the justification for this study, I have set that episode in the wider context of Elizabethan church history (without which it cannot be understood), but yet with many self-denying ordinances suggested as much by the prior claims staked by other, learned authors as by the limitations of my own theme. This is no attempt to replace the magisterial description of puritan dissent and the puritan ethos provided a generation ago by Marshall Moon Knappen in his *Tudor Puritanism* (1939). Nor have I tried to emulate those distinguished American exponents of the puritan mind and its expression, William Haller and Perry Miller.* Still less do I concern myself with the moral and material advantages of the puritan ethos for the rising and accumulating classes with which Mr Christopher Hill has been so profitably absorbed, especially in his recent book, *Society and Puritanism in Pre-Revolutionary England* (1964). I make no contribution to the current interest in the relation of puritanism to the diversification of education and the dissemination of useful knowledge.† Thomas Cartwright, the ideological leader of the Elizabethan presbyterians, makes fewer appearances in my narrative than he might have done if the late Dr A. F. Scott Pearson had not made an exhaustive exploration of his career in his *Thomas Cartwright and Elizabethan Puritanism* (1925). Moreover, the separatist groups which excluded themselves from the fellowship of the national Church find no place in my story in their own right. Somewhat like the continental anabaptists, they believed not in reformation, properly understood, but in the creation or restitution of a totally alien, select Christian society. Their scattered writings are now undergoing systematic publication,‡ the necessary pre-condition for the modern, comprehensive history of their movements which we still lack, although the late Dr Albert Peel looked towards it, and spent his life clearing the ground in numerous articles and monographs.

This is a study of church puritanism as a movement, and as a political and ecclesiastical organism; of its membership, structures and internal

* Haller, *The Rise of Puritanism* (1938); Miller, *Orthodoxy in Massachusetts, 1630–50* (1933), and *The New England Mind: The Seventeenth Century* (1939).
† See Christopher Hill, *Intellectual Origins of the English Revolution* (1965); Joan Simon, *Education and Society in Tudor England* (1966).
‡ In the series *Elizabethan Nonconformist Texts* inaugurated by Dr Albert Peel and continued by Professor Leland H. Carlson.

contradictions; and of the effort to redeem what Elizabethans understood by the 'outward face' of religion, the institutions, discipline and worship of the Church. For the most part events have been allowed to speak for themselves according to what may be thought a rather old-fashioned plan. This has seemed the wisest course, in view of the uncertain definition of the categories in which any analytical discussion of the subject has to be conducted. Certainly I make no apology for declining to enter at any depth into the debate over the meaning and the very existence of the concepts of puritanism and Anglicanism,* terms which are heavily loaded with later associations, and anachronistic when applied too rigidly to the Elizabethan age. I have tried to remember that Elizabethans rarely used words ending in 'ism', and hardly at all to describe principles in the abstract. 'Isms' were more often parties and factions inseparable from the people who led or composed them – for example, 'Brownism' and 'Martinism' – and it is with this understanding that the word 'puritanism' can be most safely employed in its Elizabethan setting. Puritanism, that is to say, should be defined with respect to the puritans, and not vice versa. 'Anglicanism', which was a term unknown to the sixteenth century, and, as an indication of a distinct system of divinity, an invention of the nine-teenth, is best avoided altogether. If this can be said of what is primarily an essay in church history, I have provided a political narrative, dealing with personalities, alliances and conflicts, and reflecting the pragmatic spirit which was characteristic of the period. If the story is told in what may sometimes seem excessive detail, my excuse is that much of it has never been told before, and that it is drawn very largely from unpublished manuscripts and other primary sources.

'Further reformation' is a phrase which can be associated with the Elizabethan puritan movement in two ways. In that they were organized to secure reform in the whole body of the Church, and by means of public authority, the puritans intended to complete the English Reforma-tion. Their campaign was successfully deflected by the queen and Archbishops Whitgift and Bancroft, and in this sense there was no further reformation. But the organization and the methods which were employed, and which, against less determined opposition, might well have prevailed, are of the greatest interest and importance. This is in the first place a study of the politics of the attempt, and of the failure. But public authority was not the sole arbiter of what took place in the Elizabethan Commonwealth;

* But see C. H. and K. George, *The Protestant Mind of the English Reformation, 1570–1640* (1961); J. F. H. New, *Anglican and Puritan: The Basis of their Opposition, 1558–1640* (1964); Basil Hall, 'Puritanism: the Problem of Definition', *Studies in Church History*, ii (1965), 283–96.

and, to borrow the jargon of sixteenth-century Calvinism, the puritans were not disposed to 'tarry for the magistrate' in all respects and for ever. In fact they were already fulfilling the further reformation within their own brotherhood, and in those parishes, households and other communities where their influence was not resisted. Consequently puritanism was more than a movement: it was already an institution, a church within the Church, with its own standards and nascent traditions, and even its own discipline and spiritual government. The conferences of puritan ministers which managed the campaign for further reform were at the same time the co-ordinating bodies for that potentially sectarian society. This characteristic ambivalence gives the elusive concept of puritanism its validity, at least for this period. In many respects the Elizabethan puritans constituted a sect, with all that that implies of the solidarity of 'known men'. Yet this was a sect saved from introspection by its belief in an established church coterminous with society as a whole, and devoting much of its effort to the attempt to impose the reformed conception of religion on a whole nation. This paradoxical and somewhat untidy combination of what Ernst Troeltsch differentiated as the 'church type' and 'sect type' of Christian societies was the hallmark of early puritanism.

It is only with the sense of a continuous, further reformation which is acquired from contact with the puritan movement that the Elizabethan history of the Church of England can be seen in correct perspective. Viewed from a distance, the settlement of religion at the beginning of the reign appears definitive, and it is easy, especially for members of the Anglican Church, to regard all subsequent attempts to advance beyond or diverge from that standard as mere dissent and aberration. This cannot have been the contemporary view. Rather, as a learned German observer, Dr A. O. Meyer, remarked long ago in his masterly study of Elizabethan England in its relations with the Catholic Church, Reformation and Counter-Reformation synchronized in England and reached their climax together as mutually exacerbating forces. Far from being limited to or dependent upon the settlement of a state Church, English protestantism was a gathering force from the mid-sixteenth century far into the seventeenth.* That the reign of Elizabeth was as much or more an age of movement as of conservation was very largely due, on the one side, to those fervent protestants whose enemies called them puritans. In this sense, the further reformation was not a failure, and it put a lasting mark on some parts of England and some sections of the population. The result – the

* A. O. Meyer, *England and the Catholic Church under Queen Elizabeth*, English tr. 1916, pp. 1–8; see also pp. 122–222.

puritan civilization of the seventeenth century and its bequests to later generations and other countries – is a matter of familiar knowledge. But for much of England the process of conversion itself, which is simply the local history of the Reformation in its secondary, enduring phase, has never been adequately described and is only imperfectly known. Since the agencies were not, for the most part, those of government, either spiritual or temporal, and have left only accidental traces in the public records, there is much that will probably never be recovered. But my hope is that this necessarily general survey may help to stimulate further local studies of what was, for many of England's provinces, the real, rather than the merely formal and constitutional Reformation. These will certainly correct some of the unguarded generalizations of my own work.

* * *

Memories of an American musical comedy of the early 1950s, 'Wonderful Town', include the girl from Ohio whose typewriter lost the use of its capital W soon after she had completed her Master's dissertation on Walt Whitman. By the same token the small p of my ageing machine should show signs of wear after thirteen years of devotion to the Elizabethan puritans. During this time I have incurred many debts. The first and greatest is to Sir John Neale, who introduced me to Elizabethan studies and supervised the London doctoral thesis out of which this book has grown. The latest of his many kindnesses was to give my typescript a most careful and critical reading. Professor Joel Hurstfield has been characteristically generous of his time, and in one way and another has helped to form what little understanding I have of Elizabethan civilization. To have worked under the guidance of Neale and Hurstfield is to have tapped the accumulated experience of the mid-Atlantic circle of scholars and researchers who pass in and out of the Monday evening seminar at the Institute of Historical Research of the University of London. I should mention particularly the inspiration and help received from Dr M. Claire Cross, Miss N. M. Fuidge, Mr R. C. Gabriel, Miss K. M. Longley, Fr A. J. Loomie, s.j., Miss Carolyn Merion, Professor Carl S. Meyer, Miss Helen Miller, the late Dr H. Gareth Owen (a sad loss, and not least to Elizabethan ecclesiastical studies), Mr J. C. Roberts, Dr A. Hassell Smith, Dr A. L. Smith and Professor Wyndham M. Southgate. I am especially indebted to Professor Leland H. Carlson, who read the whole book in typescript and spotted innumerable blunders and infelicities; and to Professor Wallace T. MacCaffrey, who read the first three parts at the same stage and made some helpful suggestions. I must further acknowledge the stimulus, correction or information freely imparted at various times by Professor S. T. Bindoff, Dr John Bossy, Professor Ian Breward, the Rev. Dr S. J. Cuming, Professor Gordon Donaldson, Dr A. M. Everitt, the Rev. Basil Hall, Professor William Haller, Mr Christopher Hill, Mr E. L. C. Mullins, the Rev. Dr J. S. Newton, the Rev. Dr Geoffrey Nuttall, Dr H. C. Porter, the late Rev. Dr Norman F. Sykes, Mr N. R. N. Tyacke and the Rev. Professor George Yule. I owe more than can easily be expressed to my colleagues at King's College, London, and my seniors in reformation studies, the Rev. Professor C. W. Dugmore and Professor A. G. Dickens. Professor Dickens was good enough to read the whole book in page-proof, and made numerous comments and corrections. Professor Dugmore read and offered advice on Chapter III of Part Seven, as did the Rev. Dr R. C. D. Jasper. My thanks are due for permission to refer to a number of unpublished theses: those of Professor Donaldson, Dr Everitt, Mr Gabriel, Dr R. A. Marchant, Dr Owen, Dr Newton, Mr Roberts, Dr Hassell Smith and Fr F. X. Walker, s.j. What I have gained from the published works of others is not adequately conveyed in my footnotes. But Dr Knappen's *Tudor Puritanism* has been a constant guide, and this should not go unacknowledged. One further obligation of a somewhat unusual kind must be honoured. When I first began to work on Elizabethan puritanism, Professor Neale allowed me to make use of the papers of the late Miss Edna Bibby, whose own work on the puritan *classis* movement was cut short by her premature death more than thirty years ago. Although I never met Miss Bibby, we have as it were worked in partnership, and my thanks are due to her father, whose thoughtful generosity made this material available. I need hardly add that I retain sole responsibility for the many errors of judgment and fact which are sure to have persisted to the end, in spite of the contributions to this book, direct and indirect, of so many whose competence exceeds my own.

I am grateful to the librarians and custodians of archives for permission and facilities to consult manuscripts and early printed books in the possession of the Bodleïan Library, the British Museum, the Cambridge University Library, the Essex Archaeological Society, the City Corporation Library, Guildhall, Dr Williams's Library, the Inner Temple Library, the Ipswich Public Library, the John Rylands Library, Lambeth Palace Library, the National Register of Archives, the Principal Probate Registry Somerset House, the Public Record Office, the Seckford Library, Woodbridge (Redstone Papers), the Sheffield City Library and Sion College; and at the local record offices of Essex, Greater London

(London Division), Hertfordshire, Ipswich and East Suffolk, Kent, Norfolk and Norwich, and West Suffolk. I am grateful to the governing bodies of the following colleges for permission to consult manuscripts in their possession: Corpus Christi, Gonville and Caius, Magdalene and Pembroke Colleges, Cambridge; and Corpus Christi, Queen's and University Colleges, Oxford. In thanking the staff of all these institutions and societies for their patient assistance, I must mention especially the friendly offices of Mr E. G. W. Bill of Lambeth Palace Library, Mr F. G. Emmison and his colleagues of the Essex Record Office, Mrs Dorothy Owen for her expert introduction to the Ely Diocesan Records, now deposited in the Cambridge University Library, and Dr Roger Thomas and his assistants at Dr Williams's Library.

My mother first typed my thesis, then indexed it, and finally typed the successive drafts through which this book has gestated. I hope that to see it finally in print may prove some consolation for so much tedious labour. My own labours were undertaken at the expense of my wife and children, who deserve my grateful apologies.

* * *

Spelling, punctuation and capitalization have been modernized in all quotations, except for those which stand as mottoes at the head of some chapters, but not in the titles of early printed books as given in the footnotes. Most references have been gathered into composite footnotes, attached where it has been feasible to the end of a paragraph, and corresponding in order to the arrangement of material in the text. Dates are given in New Style. I should perhaps explain that I have not made myself independent of the voluminous eighteenth-century compilations of the Rev. John Strype, although I have based my work on original manuscripts, even when these are printed in extenso in his works. To have mentioned every occurrence of a document in Strype would have needlessly overloaded an already ponderous critical apparatus. The substance of Part Three, Chapter III was delivered in a different form to the winter meeting of the Ecclesiastical History Society in January 1964 and appears in *Studies in Church History*, vol. iii. Part Seven, Chapter III was read to the Cambridge Theological Society in November 1965.

PATRICK COLLINSON

University of London, King's College
November 1966

Part I

Puritanism and the Elizabethan Church

1 The Church of England and the English Churches

'To the true and faithful congregation of Christ's universal Church, with all and singular the members thereof, wheresoever congregated or dispersed through the realm of England.'

(Dedicatory address in JOHN FOXE's *Acts and Monuments*, 1570 edition)

IN THE THIRD YEAR of the reign of Queen Elizabeth I, a certain William Ramsey, a preacher then residing at Chard in Somerset, addressed himself to a collection of old friends in and around the little market town of South Molton, on the southern edge of Exmoor. His letter was quaintly modelled on St Paul, an Epistle to the 'Moltonians' which conveyed pious exhortation and messages of personal encouragement to leading members of the local community by name. Ramsey's adoption of an apostolic style was not altogether incongruous, for he seems to have been one of the 'apostles' or roving preachers who first carried the protestant gospel to this obscure corner of the West Country. 'Early and late, privately and openly, as cause required and occasion served,' he had shepherded and taught the scattered protestants of north Devon in the 'perilous time' of Mary's reign. Now, in happier days, his letter was not only intended for the people of South Molton, where it was to be read 'to all your holy congregation'; copies were to be distributed to the 'other congregations dispersed here and there abroad', where the preacher's apostolate had taken him.[1]

John Wesley might have written such a letter two centuries later, rejoicing, like Ramsey, at the news of a sinner 'lately turned to the Lord'. But the 'Epistle to the Moltonians' opens an unsuspected window into the religious world of Elizabethan England. At this time, or so we are told, no one, or almost no one, supposed that the Church of God was constituted by the congregation of fervent Christians in gathered companies, 'here and there'. Rather it was understood to take in the whole of society, for, as Hooker understood the matter, 'there is not any man of the Church of England but the same man is a member of the Commonwealth, nor a member of the Commonwealth which is not also a member of the Church of England.' If we can reconcile that celebrated pronouncement with the impression left by Ramsey's Epistle, we may succeed in providing what must be basic to any history of the Elizabethan puritan movement: a definition of what is meant by a puritan.

With the repudiation of foreign, papal government, the Church of England had no distinct existence apart from the political community of England. In an age which could describe Christ Himself as 'a godly nobleman',[2] that community was conspicuously hierarchical in form, consolidated by differences of degree and the mutuality of privileges and responsibilities. Even William Ramsey's correspondents were named in descending order of rank, headed by Sir John Chichester, a substantial gentleman whose staunch protestantism counted for more in north Devon than the opinions of hundreds of lesser fry. For centuries yet to come, Chichester's kind would be, in William Wilberforce's words, 'the nerves and ligatures of your political body',[3] and the mainstay of the Church as well. It was more significant still that Chichester's friend and patron, Francis Russell, earl of Bedford, was a sincere adherent of the new religion, for Bedford's standing in the West Country was all but viceregal. In an age of volatile opinion, the ownership of land on a large scale by such 'nurses of religion'[4] as a Bedford could stabilize the religion of half a shire, both directly, through the right of presenting the parish clergy which the nobility and gentry exercised in so many churches, and indirectly in a hundred less definable ways. When the central government maintained the old faith, in Mary's reign, it enabled the protestant religion to survive the persecution, just as under Elizabeth it would retain for catholicism whole tracts of Lancashire and sizeable enclaves in such counties as Sussex and Hampshire.

If the 'natural' leadership of the nobility still counted for much in the sixteenth century, the Tudor monarchy discovered a far greater potentiality to determine the religious allegiance, and even the religious persuasion of the whole nation. In the 1530s, Henry VIII and his chief minister, Thomas Cromwell, had given precise, legislative expression to the claim that the government of spiritual, no less than of temporal, affairs was the exclusive concern of the Crown. In the ensuing decades, Henry and his children, in association with Parliament, and, to a lesser extent, with their clergy represented in the Convocations, had employed this enlarged sovereignty to dictate the forms of religion which their people were to practise and even the doctrines which they were to profess. When those who governed the country in the name of Edward VI publicly embraced protestantism and enjoined the universal use of new forms of service, there was a sense in which the Reformation was enacted, and England became protestant by a constitutional process; by the same power of statute, the country was brought back to the old religion under Mary, only to undergo yet another upheaval with the accession of her half-sister Elizabeth. To an extent, the formula *cuius regio, ejus religio* applied to the English scene, where acts of parliament controlled the direction and pace of religious change, although royal policy could never be insensitive to private initiatives.

For the most part, the country adjusted itself to these successive 'settlements' with a resilience which historians have found remarkable. But alongside and among those who merely acquiesced in religious change, protestantism was performing its own work. Lively, rather than formal faith was generated by preaching, regarded by protestants as 'the ordinary means of faith', and by the printing presses which dispersed the new English versions of the Bible and a variety of other, more pointed protestant propaganda; as well as by the personal persuasion of one man by another, of husbands by wives, of whole households by their masters. No sixteenth-century government could hope to have these spontaneous forces wholly at its command, and in England they were gathering strength throughout and beyond the years conventionally assigned to the Reformation by the textbooks. 'I beseech God bless my good Uncle Brent,' wrote an Elizabethan preacher, forty years after Henry's Act of Supremacy, 'and make him now to know [that] which in his tender years he could not see ... And the Lord open His gracious countenance ... unto my aunt, that she may also make a blessed change.'[5] No account of the English Reformation will suffice which is so confined by statutes and prayer books that it ignores the 'blessed change'.

Left to itself, and without respect for tradition and existing institutions, the reception of the new gospel might have led to the birth of a new kind of Christian church. 'All men do know by experience', wrote a group of Leicestershire ministers, 'that sticks of fire scattered can give no such piercing heat as when they are laid together, neither yet lights, far dissevered and separate, have the like power as near joined.'[6] It was the experience of all the early protestants as they came together for the exposition of 'the word of God' from the Bibles of Tyndale and Coverdale, and, presently, the new Bible from Geneva; and to receive the mutual encouragement and correction of which they read in the New Testament. On the engraved title-page of John Foxe's famous 'Book of Martyrs' we see them sitting under the preacher with Bibles open on their laps: these are the godly-minded Elizabethans who are the subject of this book.

Every godly protestant who knew what it was to exercise a lively faith must have felt the inclination to define the Church in a sense which excluded the more formal profession of those he knew as 'the common sort of Christians'. Catholics who complained of the low standards of protestant behaviour were told that none were accounted 'true friends of the gospel but such as do yield and show their obedience thereunto, and express the doctrine thereof in their conversation. How small so ever the number of such seem unto your bleared eyes for to be ... they are the true Church of God ... '[7] In the days of popery there was no doubt that the true Church existed as leaven in an otherwise evil lump. When the prince was not 'godly', and the parish churches were given over to popish masses, 'Christ's approved churches' were to be sought among those whom Foxe called 'the secret multitude of true professors'. Under Mary, as in the France of Francis I, sincere protestants separated themselves in 'privy churches', of which William Ramsey's congregation at South Molton may have been an example. In a rare account of the organization of the secret congregations in Marian London, we are told that they admitted to communion only those who 'were kept pure from popery' and from evil conduct, or who repented in the presence of the assembly. Unlike the inchoate lollard conventicles of pre-Reformation days, these were fully organized churches whose members kept themselves apart from the parish churches and ministered their own sacraments.[8] Others with the requisite means went abroad into a voluntary exile. There, in the reformed cities of Switzerland and the Rhineland, from Emden, through Frankfort and Strasbourg to Basle, Aarau, Zürich and Geneva, the future leaders of English protestantism gathered their churches and enjoyed the rare and exhilarating experience of inventing and quarrelling over liturgies and church constitutions. In the course of five years, many of the habits and attitudes that belonged to life in an established Church – the habits of centuries – were temporarily discarded.

But the accession of protestant Elizabeth at once revived deeply-rooted notions of the Church as a great public corporation, one with the Commonwealth, and presided over by royal governors. 'Wherefore now is our season if ever any were of rejoicing', wrote Catharine Bertie, the dowager duchess of Suffolk, as she returned from her own remarkable

travels. 'For if the Israelites might joy in their Deborah, how much more
we English in our Elizabeth, that deliverance of our thralled conscience.'
At once, the imaginations of protestants were transported from the
conditions of apostolic Christianity to the godly Commonwealth of
Israel. As the separatist Henry Barrow would later complain: 'All this
people, with all these manners, were in one day, with the blast of Queen
Elizabeth's trumpet, of ignorant papists and gross idolators, made faithful
Christians, and true professors.' But for most, that day was a source of
deep gratification, not merely on account of the deliverance of their own
'thralled consciences', but in the universal establishment of true worship
and, presently, of sound doctrine. Laurence Humphrey, an original leader
of Elizabethan nonconformity, congratulated the queen 'for tender
cherishing and renewing the Church, by God's singular mercy and
providence; for restoring religion from exile (as it were) to her ancient
sincerity and primitive pureness; for the merry quiet and clear calm,
ensuing the tossings and troublesome storms of later times.' John Foxe
believed Elizabeth to be a second Constantine, the inaugurator of the last,
peaceful age of the Church, and the image was conveyed to a wide
audience through his vast and schematic panorama of Christian history,
Acts and Monuments of the Church. [9]

Elizabethan protestants might distinguish between the public, visible
Church and the invisible company of God's elect, concealed within it.
But election itself was more commonly an inclusive than an exclusive
concept. By a kind of charitable assumption, the whole nation, however
ignorant, however lacking in faith, was deemed to be 'the people of the
Lord'. For the Church was constituted, not by the Christians of whom it
was composed, nor by the sincerity of their profession, but by the purity
of the doctrine publicly preached and upheld by authority, and by the
sincere administration and reception of the sacraments, safeguarded by the
exercise of church discipline. The Church of Rome was false, not because
all or any of its members stood outside God's grace, but because the
tyranny of the papacy had perverted its doctrine, sacraments and discipline. Where these essential 'marks' or 'notes' were to be found, the
presence of any number of what the puritans called 'cold statute protestants' could not invalidate the Church. For religion was a public duty,
not a private opinion or a voluntary profession. The gospel was good
news of salvation; but it was also to be obeyed, and obeyed universally.
Consequently, when the puritans attacked the imperfections of the
Elizabethan religious settlement, it was not so much to request a toleration
of their own consciences as to demand the imposition of true reformation,

as they understood it, on the whole Church and nation, by public authority. Their complaint was not that religion was made a matter of compulsion, but that the law failed to conform to the pure model which they had set before the queen's eyes. For as the separatist Barrow noted: 'These men still would have the whole land to be the Church, and every parish therein a particular congregation of the same.'[10]

Yet while the comprehensive, established Church was not in itself offensive to protestant opinion, no one, friend or foe, was likely to confuse the minority of convinced and fervent protestants with the general mass of those who merely conformed to the queen's religion. The difference was apparent between 'the godly', 'the scripture men', 'such as run to hear preaching', and those characterized by the preachers as 'neuters', such as 'quietly enjoy the world, they care not what religion come', commonly supposed at the time to make up the bulk of the population.[11] Although the godly for the most part attended their own parish churches and rubbed shoulders with the not so godly, they were united among themselves by a closer bond. Their preachers, and at first only a minority of the Elizabethan clergy were preachers, were equally conscious of their membership of a select brotherhood. Among the puritan ministers it would later be common doctrine that only parishes supplied with an acceptable preaching ministry were in any proper sense churches at all. Certainly sincere, instructed protestants constituted the Church 'more fully'. 'If God have any Church or people in the land, no doubt the title is given them.'[12] In Elizabeth's reign, the godly only rarely and in exceptional circumstances carried their implicit dissent to the point of open separation. Yet to their neighbours they were men of 'singularity', marked by the voluntary religious exercises to which they were addicted, as well as by peculiarities of moral and social behaviour. Both were soon to be branded without discrimination as points of 'puritanism': 'Oh, say the scorning railers, now this holy man will go to heaven in a hay-barn, now these *puritans* flock together.'[13]

So far it has been suggested that the puritans were identified by all that separated real from merely formal protestants, and that the distinction was as much sociological as theological. But what, it may be objected, of the real protestants, many of them men of learning and responsibility, who were in no sense puritans, and who on occasions directly opposed the puritans? Something must be now said about the ideological differences which arose between English puritanism and what we are almost forced, in spite of the anachronism, to call Anglicanism. These were differences of degree, of theological temperature so to speak, rather than of fundamental principle. 'The hotter sort of protestants are called puritans', explains an Elizabethan pamphleteer,[14] innocent of the sophistication of later discussions of the problem. Consequently the terms puritan and Anglican are elusive and intangible, limited in their usefulness to interpret the complexities of English church history between the Elizabethan Settlement and the Civil War. The English Church of this age was a spectrum, in which the ultimate extremes of colour are clear enough, but the intermediate tones merge imperceptibly; or, to change the image, it resembled the French Chamber rather than the English House of Commons, with almost imperceptible gradations towards the left and the right, but no sharp polarity of government and opposition.

But a polarity there was on those occasions, not necessarily very frequent, when those in authority made demands with which the more extreme or, to use the parlance of the time, 'precise' protestants felt unable to comply. Like Luther at the Diet of Worms, these 'precisians' in their lesser causes withheld conformity on the grounds that their consciences were constrained by the word of God. At such times it would appear that something more fundamental than the relative intensity of their protestant convictions divided the nonconformists from conformable Anglicans. The Bible, either in its explicit teaching or in what one puritan divine calls 'the constant sense of the general tenor of scripture' and Tyndale 'the whole course of the scripture'[15] – this was the only authority which the puritan acknowledged in matters of religion. Where human authority failed to conform with even the general implication of scripture, as expounded and applied by the preacher, it must be resisted. Within eight years of Elizabeth's accession it was said that 'the authority that princes have over the churches is a service to defend it, and to seek the profit thereof, rather than a prerogative to burden it with superfluous and hurtful ceremonies at their pleasure.'[16] The queen was executrix of a law which she could neither make nor unmake, which she could not even interpret, but which was known to any of her simple Christian subjects, instructed and armed from scripture: here was the political potency of puritanism.

Conformists, on the other hand, if they were no mere time-servers, drew a philosophical distinction between the essentials and the non-essentials of religion, the invariable and the variable, and taught that, in all 'indifferent' matters, human reason and human authority had the power to devise and enforce policy. This concept of the *adiaphora* of God's service, which had a notable influence on the affairs of the Lutheran churches of Germany, formed the corner-stone of Anglicanism, if by Anglicanism we mean the claim made on behalf of a national Church to develop its own forms of church order. 'The Bible, I say, the Bible only is the religion of protestants,' wrote Chillingworth. His aphorism belongs more properly to those protestants called puritans.

To anyone familiar with the later, fissiparous history of English protestant dissent, and with the principles which would later differentiate presbyterians and independents, baptists and quakers, this attempt to convey the essential quality of early puritanism may seem to be less than adequate in its concealment of many diverse tendencies. More than a century later, Archbishop Tenison would complain that 'these may associate in a *Caravan*, but cannot join in the communion of a Church.'[17] But I believe that I have attached to the name of puritan as much precision as it possessed for those who first applied it. The original puritans were defined by what they appeared to hold in common, not by their differences, which were the consequences as much as the cause of conflicts in the English Church which still lay in the future. The wise observer of Elizabethan religion will resist the temptation to impose on a confused scene the clear-cut pattern of denominations not yet born. He will be equally on his guard against the tendency to treat early puritanism as a monolith, as if, in the words of a shrewd seventeenth-century observer, 'all puritans were alike to be embraced.' Rather he will use the expression 'cautiously, as if that difference and contrariety might happen amongst puritans in England as did once amongst the disciples in our Saviour's own school.'[18]

2 'But Halfly Reformed'

'For your Majesty hath so insufficientlie heard, believed, and taken to hart what God hath commaunded you, and so weakelie and coldlie obeied, and folowed the same ... that but halflie by your Majesty hath God bene honoured, his Church reformed and established, his people taught and comforted, his enemies rejected and subdued, and his lawbreakers punished.'

> (WILLIAM FULLER in his 'Booke to the queene'; *The Seconde Parte of a Register*, ii. 52)

WHAT HAS ALREADY BEEN SAID may have served to explain the presence of a loosely defined and widely dispersed 'puritanism' in Elizabethan England. But to account for the activity of a 'puritan movement' organized to realize a programme of further reformation requires a closer examination of the aspirations of 'the hotter sort of protestants' against the character imposed on the Church of England in the Elizabethan settlement of religion.

Queen Elizabeth's church policy was not unaffected by her private religious opinions, which seem to have been those of a moderate protestant, held with the independence of a mind which was not possessed by any of the current orthodoxies. Her conservative tastes might well have found their most appropriate satisfaction in a church of Lutheran faith and practice, although her abiding objection to clerical marriage was as much out of tune with the Augsburg Confession as with the teaching of any other evangelical community. But with Elizabeth, the queen often obscures the believer as well as the woman, and her conduct of church affairs was above all an act of statesmanship. She succeeded to a kingdom which contained sharply opposed religious interests which, for all that they were both minority interests, threatened political division and social disturbance. Moreover the country was so weak externally that its viability as an independent state was open to question. In these circumstances expediency dictated a religious policy which would cause the minimum of offence to a Europe where the great powers had rejected

29

the Reformation, and one which would hold out some hope of healing rather than exacerbating domestic divisions. Historians have always agreed that these considerations governed Elizabeth's approach to a church settlement rather than those which the returning exiles commended to her attention. More recently Sir John Neale's persuasive reinterpretation of the policies of the religious settlement has suggested that the outlook for protestants was even dimmer than had been supposed.[1] For Professor Neale believes that the queen's true intentions may have been conveyed to the Spanish ambassador when she said that she was 'resolved to restore religion as her father left it'; that is, to exclude the pope and assume supreme powers over the Church, but to do nothing, at least for a time, to define its doctrine and worship in a protestant sense.

Elizabeth can scarcely have needed the warning she received from the diplomatist Armagil Waad 'of how dangerous it is to make alterations in religion, specially in the beginning of a prince's reign.' Her sister bequeathed a war with France, an empty treasury and an excessive dependence upon the patronage of Spain. With insecurity on both the Scottish and Channel frontiers there was small scope for the pursuit of an independent policy. Elizabeth must have known that liturgical and doctrinal definition could not be avoided for long, but she seems to have hoped that it could be postponed beyond these early and perilous months, if not years. Accordingly, she proposed to dissolve her first Parliament before Easter 1559, when it had passed a bill restoring ecclesiastical supremacy to the Crown but had done nothing else to satisfy protestants beyond conceding the communion in both kinds in a clause of the Supremacy bill. As Neale plausibly suggests, her motives may well have included the intention to delay the revision of worship until after the deprivation of the more rigid papists among the higher clergy, so that Convocation could contribute to the settlement what she would have regarded as its proper contribution. The queen was perhaps already on her guard against the dangerous pretensions of the House of Commons to make and revise religious settlements.

The fears of some protestants overseas, partly aroused by reports from England, tend to confirm Professor Neale's hypothesis. In January Rodolph Gualter of Zürich warned the queen to beware of those who would obtrude on the churches 'a form of religion which is an unhappy compound of popery and the gospel, and from which there may at length be an easy passage to the ancient superstition.' To another correspondent he revealed his fears of 'a form of religion of a mixed, uncertain and doubtful character'. Early in March the duchess of Suffolk, still out of the country, complained to the new secretary, Sir William Cecil, of the backwardness of the queen's counsellors, and of her correspondent in particular, asking with the prophet Elijah: 'How long halt ye between two opinions?' In Geneva, when it was observed that the queen was crowned with traditional rites 'and did still many other grievous things', some resolved to continue in exile until directed by Calvin himself to return, with the chilly encouragement that at least 'the extreme persecution was ceased.'[2]

News of the conclusion of peace at Cateau-Cambrésis which reached London on March 19th may have helped to change the queen's mind. Certainly this event coincided with her decision to prolong the parliamentary session, and this allowed the passage of a bill replacing the mass with Prayer Book worship. But the reversal of policy which this decision implies had already been commended by the precision and vigour of both catholic and protestant opinion, especially as they were voiced in the parliamentary proceedings before Easter. Professor Neale therefore believes that the Act of Uniformity and the Prayer Book of 1559 are a measure of the extent to which Elizabeth was unwillingly driven in a protestant direction by the opposition to her original proposals offered both by the Marian higher clergy, who resisted her assumption of ecclesiastical supremacy in Convocation as well as in the House of Lords, and by a vigorous and apparently dominant protestant phalanx in the Commons, which was insistent on an immediate and thorough reformation. Until recently, the composition of this first Elizabethan House of Commons was partly unknown, although it was sufficiently clear that of the active members a majority must have been decided protestants who found their leadership among the returned exiles. The recent discovery of a full list of the members has revealed an impressive concentration of godly protestant gentlemen, many of whom owed their places to the patronage in a large number of West Country boroughs of a nobleman widely recognized, even overseas, as the aristocratic leader of the reformed party in England: Francis Russell, earl of Bedford.[3]

'We are moving far too slowly,' wrote Sir Anthony Cooke, himself an émigré, of the parliamentary proceedings in February,[4] and his party expressed their impatience with official policy by attempting to amend the government Supremacy bill, and even to intrude their own protestant Uniformity measures. In all probability they were advised by the clerical exiles, many of whom remained expectantly in London after their arrival.[5] These efforts, together with the intransigence of the Marians, exposed the worthlessness of Henrician Anglo-Catholicism as a mediating formula.

Unless the queen was prepared to recognize the papal pretensions so confidently asserted from Convocation, she would be almost compelled to commit the leadership of her Church to ecclesiastics of definitely protestant views. Even before her crucial decision was made, there were signs that the queen could no longer control the pace of events. The Lenten preachers at Court were all recently-arrived exiles, with the sole exception of the archbishop-designate, Matthew Parker. The same group, substantially, was chosen as early as March 20th to defend their cause in a disputation with the leading catholic divines which could only have been intended by its sponsors as a public demonstration of the justice of the protestant cause. John Jewel told his mentor Peter Martyr on that date that 'though the beginnings have hitherto seemed somewhat unfavourable, there is nevertheless reason to hope that all will be well at last.' A month later he reported that in many places the mass had 'of itself fallen to the ground, without any laws for its discontinuance.' When Parliament reassembled after Easter, the Westminster Disputation was manipulated to discredit the catholic cause, while a Uniformity bill establishing Prayer Book worship and originating from the government was introduced into the Commons and proceeded with relative smoothness to the royal assent.[6]

The queen, however, was far from having made over her prerogative rights in matters of religion to a faction. The settlement which emerged in its essentials at the end of this Parliament reflected both her conservative taste for decency and order and her statesmanlike rather than zealous intention to maintain a church respectable in the eyes of the non-protestant world and inoffensive to that unmeasured element among her own people which was still attached to the old ways.

Elizabeth may well have thought that these purposes would be best served by a re-enactment of the first Edwardine Prayer Book of 1549, with those structural affinities to the Latin mass and the studied ambiguities which had enabled Bishop Stephen Gardiner to describe it as 'not distant from catholic faith'. What was perhaps more to the point was the even greater proximity of 1549 to the religion of the Augsburg Confession, at least in appearances. As Maitland pointed out long ago, a settlement which tended in that direction would have associated England with what was by then widely regarded as a mediating creed. In France in 1561 many hopeful persons – including the queen-regent – would try to make use of it, in the late H. O. Evennett's phrase, as 'a kind of theological sticking-plaster' to attach the catholic and reformed faiths.[7] To appreciate how unacceptable such a proposal would have been in England we have first to remember that by the shibboleth of their doctrine of the Lord's supper, English protestants were generally considered to belong to the Swiss reformed camp rather than to have any kinship with the Lutherans, still less to hold a mediating position of their own. We then have to take into account the liturgical and ceremonial tendencies of the exiles in the course of their stay overseas. At the time of their departure few, so far as we know, stood to the right of the second Edwardine Book of 1552, which embodied a simplified, not to say dislocated version of the communion service and of some of the other offices, and came close to the memorialism of the Zwinglians in its eucharistic doctrine. But even the 1552 Book retained too strong a memory of the old rites for some of the exiles, who took advantage of their new and voluntary circumstances to reform Cranmer's liturgies still further (which, they reported, Cranmer himself would have done, granted the opportunity) and even to throw off the restraint of an English pattern of worship altogether.

At Frankfort there was strife between the radical following of William Whittingham and John Knox and those who were with Richard Cox, later the Elizabethan bishop of Ely, in demanding 'the face of an English Church'; a quarrel which divided the congregation, sent the Knoxians to a more congenial environment at Geneva, and anticipated the alignment of puritans and conformists in the Elizabethan Church.[8] These celebrated troubles were far from typical of the congregational life of the Marian exiles, yet the same division was later reproduced at Basle, where John Bale wrote bitterly in 1556 of 'our new Catharites', erecting 'their church of the purity' and slandering the Prayer Book as if it bore 'the face of a popish mass'.[9] But even the Coxians were willing to discard many of the ceremonies of the second Edwardine Book, including private baptism and confirmation, kneeling at the communion, the surplice and the sign of the cross, 'not as being impure and papistical', but to avoid offence. It is reasonable to suppose that after four more years the more conservative of the exiles had lost the habit of strict conformity to English formularies, and that on their return they would favour some advance on the state of religion as they had known it at the end of Edward VI's reign. Edmund Grindal, a Coxian in 1554, assured Bullinger that, at the beginning of Elizabeth's reign, he and his friends from Strasbourg, Basle and Zürich 'contended long and earnestly' for a Prayer Book without vestments and other ceremonies.[10] The queen for 1549: the radical protestants for 1552 at the very least. This is the equation which seems to explain the nature of the 1559 compromise: a Prayer Book which was substantially that of 1552 with a number of conservative amendments.

The significant alterations which were specified in the Act of Uniformity included the excision of the bishop of Rome from the Litany and the somewhat ambiguous addition of the formula which accompanied the administration of the communion in 1549 to that of 1552, so balancing the memorialist emphasis of the later service with a phrase which could be construed as an affirmation of the real presence in the consecrated elements. A gesture in the same direction was the suppression of the rubric, attached at the eleventh hour in 1552 by the mere authority of the Council, which had explained that to kneel for the reception of the sacrament as the Prayer Book directed need not imply adoration of the 'real and substantial' presence. But more immediately offensive to precise consciences was the ornaments proviso, clause twelve of the Act, which led to the contentious ornaments rubric of the Elizabethan Prayer Book. No doubt sensing that what Bishop Jewel was to call 'the scenic apparatus' of worship would impress both her more ignorant subjects and foreign observers at least as much as its doctrine, the queen ambiguously required the use of the eucharistic vestments which were in use in the second year of Edward VI. (The surplice, the major cause of offence, was in any case required by the 1552 Book.) The first puritans were to find nothing more intolerable than this demand to array themselves in garments which identified them with the popish priesthood rather than with the ministry of the best reformed churches overseas. Moreover, the new Prayer Book as printed proved to contain a number of additional minor alterations which the Act had not specified, and these too were all in a conservative direction. When the queen issued the Royal Injunctions which were to amplify the programme of the Prayer Book, they were found to require the use of wafers in the communion – another calculated gesture towards simple catholics – where the Prayer Book spoke of 'common bread'. When Convocation completed the religious settlement by revising the doctrinal articles (in 1563) Archbishop Parker here and there tempered the doctrine of the Forty-two Articles of Edward's reign. For this reason the Elizabethan Thirty-nine Articles were only barely acceptable to minds schooled in continental reformed theology.

The celebrated *via media* which characterized all these formularies was a note sounded by the queen for pragmatic reasons but which, with the passage of time, would seem a faithful expression of reformed catholicity and of a characteristic Anglican centrality and moderation. The Elizabethan Settlement would appear to bear all the marks of design rather than of accident, so that a member of the House of Commons four centuries later could suggest that the Church of England should be defined with respect to its supposed 'duty', under the Act of Uniformity (of 1662), 'to keep the mean between the two extremes.'[11] Sir John Neale has restored what must surely have been the contemporary view of these somewhat fortuitous arrangements. The settlement was a compromise in the lively political sense that it was the outcome of manœuvres in which both the queen and the protestants were forced to yield some ground. The result must have seemed precarious and provisional, not a settlement to last for four hundred years. Admittedly the queen implied by her subsequent pronouncements on religious questions that she regarded the measures of her early years as definitive; that she had 'resolved to be still *semper eadem*, and to alter nothing which she had once settled', as the bishops informed her successor.[12] Sir John Neale's hypothesis helps to explain the fixity of her mind. But no constancy could yet have been discerned in Elizabeth's actions, and her prevarications in 1559 explain why protestants had as yet no sense of security.

This was the significance of the crisis provoked by a small silver cross or crucifix which appeared in the Chapel Royal in October, together with two burning candles on the table, 'standing altar-wise'. By February 1560 some of the new bishops were even prepared to resign their places rather than reconcile themselves to this 'offendicle', or so they assured their old hosts at Zürich. The modern reader might be excused for suspecting a storm in a teacup, but he would be wrong. The clue to the crisis is contained in a dispatch from Sir Nicholas Throckmorton, Elizabeth's ambassador in Paris. The ultra-catholic Guise party in France 'made their advantage of the cross and candles in your chapel, saying you were not yet resolved of what religion you should be.' The Chapel Royal was an example to the whole Church, and the queen's gesture implied a reversal of the vigorous instructions with which the royal visitors had been sent out in the summer of 1559, and which they had interpreted by the systematic removal and destruction of rood-lofts, crucifixes and vestments. It is in the light of this episode that we should view all 'relics of popery' entertained in the early Elizabethan Church. It was no doubt the way that Elizabeth intended they should be taken, at least by catholics, foreign and native. Thomas Lever reported from Coventry that 'the multitude' was so fascinated by the vestments prescribed for the clergy that they persuaded themselves either that the popish doctrine was still retained, or that it would soon return.[13]

Another reason why the new church settlement must have seemed no more than provisional is to be found in the general expectation that the queen would marry. Whether she elected to marry a foreign prince or a subject, a papist or a true protestant, the details of her initial religious and political settlement could not be expected to survive her change of state. As for the radical protestants whose efforts in 1559 had secured more than they might have gained but less than they had hoped for, they were the last people to regard the Church as 'settled' by these measures.

But supposing that a permanent settlement of the Church had in fact been made (and eventually some awareness of this would begin to dawn); what was its character and where did it stand? In its provision for preaching and prayer, as radical protestants would complain, the Reformation had proceeded 'but halfly forward and more than halfly backward'.[14] Judged by a narrow scripturalism, the Prayer Book was still 'papistical' in form and in many of its ceremonies cherished popish superstition. Apart from the vestments, the surplice and the outdoor dress of the clergy, the first and most prominent of their *gravamina*, the puritans would object with monotonous consistency to signing with the cross and addressing interrogatories to the infant in baptism, baptism by midwives, the rite of confirmation, kneeling at the communion and the use of wafer-bread, the giving of the ring in marriage, the purification of women after childbirth, the retention of such terms as 'priest' and 'absolution', the observation of saints' days, bowing at the name of Jesus and 'exquisite singing in parts' and organs. More radically, some of them would complain of the liturgical forms themselves and of the 'longsomeness of the service' which seemed out of proportion in a reformed Church and implied a subordinate place for the sermon. For all these reasons, the puritans could not regard the Prayer Book as sacrosanct. They would demand a further reform for which the word of God as interpreted by 'the best reformed churches' supplied the model, and which they hoped to achieve by the same means of organized agitation which had been employed with some success at the time of Elizabeth's first Parliament.[15]

It has often been said that the Elizabethan puritan protest was concerned only with subsidiary matters of ceremony and church order and had nothing to do with doctrine: except (presumably) in the sense that its basis was a relatively greater insistence on the distinctive protestant doctrines of God's sovereignty, man's impotence and the all-sufficiency of scripture. The suggestion has been made that the explicit content of controversy in the Elizabethan Church was not theological, and in particular that Calvin's doctrines of grace and predestination went almost unchallenged, even by most of the bishops, until the rise of English 'Arminianism' at the end of the century. So it may seem if we restrict our view of the matter to the Cambridge theology which was so much in the ascendant throughout these years. Even so, as Dr H. C. Porter has rightly insisted, the label 'Calvinist' has often been used without proper discrimination, and it by no means accurately describes the doctrine of grace taught in the Thirty-nine Articles, or even its treatment in Archbishop Whitgift's Lambeth Articles of 1595, invariably cited as proof of their author's Calvinist orthodoxy. Did not Whitgift say (with deliberate exaggeration) that 'the doctrine of the Church of England doth in no respect depend upon' Calvin, Beza or Peter Martyr?[16] Implicit theological differences there were among the learned Elizabethan divines and they will repay investigation, although there was no clear theological polarity, and it is another question whether these issues served neatly to differentiate puritanism and Anglicanism.[17]

But if we attempt to discover what the Elizabethans believed, not from the pronouncements of recognized theologians but at the popular level, then it may well appear that the differences between the puritans and their opponents were overtly theological. Richard Kitchen, rector of the Essex parish of Stisted, was a country parson who liked to do things in the traditional way; he valued the old rogationtide custom of beating the parish bounds, and he preferred to say service in the chancel, facing what he still called the high altar. In 1564 he was complaining of the neighbouring clergy with some bitterness as 'these bold rude English preachers and doctors' who insisted so much on predestination, and he had publicly attacked their 'daily deep stirring and high wading in this secret doctrine'. Essex puritans, for their part, had many harsh things to say about 'the country divinity' which such men as Kitchen encouraged, 'the religion which is among the common sort of Christians'. 'I mean well, I hurt no man, nor I think no man any hurt. I love God above all and put my whole trust in Him. What would ye have more? They preach and teach, they can tell us no more but this when they have all said what they can.' As for election and predestination, 'what should such matters be spoken of among the people? They make men worse.' A Kentish minister would recall at the end of the reign that in all his experience of questioning those who came into his village from elsewhere he could remember scarcely any who came from a parish lacking a resident preaching ministry that had any knowledge of justification by faith. This rustic Pelagianism could derive at least some comfort from the Prayer Book, and it was there that parsons like Kitchen would find their theology: in the ceaseless round of the Church's year, in the laconic and repetitive petitions of the collects, and in the prayer which any Calvinist was bound to find objectionable, that all men might be saved. For as long as the mass of the population, and even the majority of their teachers, were ignorant of the proper ground of salvation, no puritan could regard the Church as thoroughly reformed in doctrine. Moreover, in a majority of parishes there was, in a sense, no doctrine, since there was an almost entire absence of preaching.[18]

Even if the worship and doctrine of the Elizabethan Church had left nothing to be desired, the more earnest protestants would have considered the Reformation incomplete so long as there was no fundamental reform of the Church in the institutions of its ministry and government. The doctrinaire objection to a ministry ordained and ruled by bishops lay in the future, but it was already a source of embarrassment to many of the hotter protestants that their Church bore small resemblance to the drastically reconstituted churches which they had encountered overseas. In substance the government of the Elizabethan Church was royal, in form episcopal, and it could boast few if any of the attributes of a reformed polity. Without congregational participation, spiritual government was ordinarily conducted at the diocesan and archidiaconal levels. Henry VIII's creation of six new bishoprics had done nothing to alter the essential character of late medieval ecclesiastical administration, and by reformed standards the English dioceses were too large. Pastoral care meant, in effect, the impersonal judicial processes of the church courts, where the bishop was represented by officials who in the post-Reformation period were more often than not laymen, civil lawyers whose attitude can be described without prejudice as professional rather than evangelical and pastoral.

The jurisdiction of these courts, provincial, diocesan and archidiaconal, was not seriously impaired by the Reformation, although its source and sanction were now understood very differently. Not even the content of the law administered in the courts had been radically changed, except, of course, where events had rendered the *Corpus Juris Canonici* otiose, as with the chapters relating to the pope, or to the conduct of religious houses. A succession of Henrician and Edwardine statutes had provided for a total revision of the Canon Law of the Church, but the project was stillborn. In Edward's reign a commission had indeed drafted a code known as the *Reformatio Legum Ecclesiasticarum*, which Cranmer and later Parker revised and perfected. But few things were of less interest to Northumberland's government than the modernization of the Church's laws for its own self-government. Later attempts to procure statutory recognition for the *Reformatio Legum* in the Elizabethan Parliaments of 1559 and 1571 were to come to nothing. To be sure, from a variety of sources a mass of legislation accumulated for the guidance of the reformed

Church, much of it in the spirit of the Reformation: the canons approved from time to time in Convocation (but rarely confirmed by the queen and never in Parliament), the royal injunctions and other royal mandates, and the numerous metropolitan and episcopal articles and injunctions. But the legal standing of many of these documents was uncertain and until 1603 there was no attempt to knit them together in a coherent code. Their capacity to excite the loyalty and obedience of clergy and laity was not great.

Meanwhile the Henrician Act for the Submission of the Clergy had left it in no doubt that if the officially-inspired project to rewrite the Canon Law should fail, then such existing canons and constitutions 'which be not contrarient or repugnant to the law, statutes and customs of this realm, nor to the damage or hurt of the king's prerogative' were to remain in force. As a later statute implied, and as ecclesiastical judges came to understand the situation, much of the ancient ecclesiastical law, whether derived from papal legislation or from domestic constitutions or mere convention, was part and parcel of the customary law of the realm by virtue of its long acceptance. But precisely how much has never been defined from that day to this, so that common lawyers and 'parliament men' would be prone to attack the constitutional validity of all canons which were not expressly confirmed by statute. Although the study of Canon Law was by now extinguished in the universities, so that the degrees held by judges in the church courts were likely to be in Civil Law, knowledge of the traditional jurisprudence of the Church was preserved and even furthered and advanced by the civilians, judges and advocates who belonged to that curious society known as Doctors' Commons, which from early in Elizabeth's reign occupied the premises in Knightrider Street where it was still to be found in Dickens's day. In no other English courts did the judges enjoy such wide discretion to interpret and apply, and almost by judicious selection to create the law, and outside their own rare experience the situation could only appear to be one of great confusion. The puritan view was thus tersely reported to Zürich by Thomas Lever: 'No discipline is as yet established by any public authority.'[19]

Discipline! We have now used that potent word for the first time. The extensive exercise of jurisprudence could scarcely be avoided in a large national church of the sixteenth century, still less the multifarious processes of ecclesiastical administration. But 'discipline', which, according to reformed thinking, embraced both, should have as its guiding principles only biblical, evangelical sources. The *Jus Civile* of the Roman Empire and the pope's law were equally out of place in the Church of God. The

39

correction of faults, discipline in its narrower sense, ought to be solemn and yet fraternal in the manner of its application, and restorative in intention, for, to quote the Ecclesiastical Ordinances of Geneva, 'all corrections are but medicinal, to bring back sinners to our Lord.' Whether exercised by magistrates or by ministers and church elders, it should be inspired by the moral purpose of preserving the communion of true believers from contamination. But its use should only follow brotherly admonition. However basic such principles were to the law which the Church had always known, they seemed to the puritans to have been all but forgotten in the Church of England. The courts dealt impersonally with those who came before them, after the manner of secular justice, and they were ineffective in debarring from the communion the truly scandalous. Excommunication was lightly pronounced, often by a single layman, and for 'twelve-penny' matters, in marital, testamentary and other civil suits, or in matters of petty discipline. Most commonly it was invoked as the mere 'pain of contumacy', for those who failed to present themselves in court, or who neglected to pay their fees or fines.

To be sure, there was need of some sanction to protect the church courts from the contempt of the public. Generalizations are dangerous in such a relatively unexplored field, and it may yet appear that the credibility of ecclesiastical discipline varied widely between one diocese and another, and as between northern and southern England. However, the diocese of Gloucester provides a notorious and perhaps extreme example of rusty machinery. Under the rule of Bishop Cheyney, the proportion of contumacious defendants was as high as two out of three or even five out of seven. On one exceptional court day, there were thirty-four absentees in thirty-seven cases. In this diocese offenders were often represented – at a price – by proxies who were the very apparitors responsible for securing their corporal attendance! And, for all its social inconvenience, there is evidence that excommunication itself was held in very general despite. Among the Elizabethan records of the diocese of Ely there is a register of excommunications in the consistory court, running from 1571 to 1584. It contains the details of three hundred and forty-six cases, of which only one hundred and six have been scored through to indicate the subsequent alleviation of the ban. Of two hundred and twenty-five persons suspended or excommunicated in the diocese of Gloucester in a period of twelve months beginning in November 1569, only forty-two are noted as having received absolution. In these two dioceses the great majority of excommunicates apparently never gained – nor, presumably, sought – restoration to the full communion of the Church. By issuing a formal *significavit* to

Chancery, an ecclesiastical judge could indeed secure a writ *de excommunicato capiendo*, which required the sheriff to imprison the recalcitrant offender. Yet this procedure was so hamstrung by delays and the non-cooperation of the secular courts that it was invoked with increasing rarity in the later sixteenth century.[20]

Another major cause of scandal existed in the archbishop's Court of Faculties, dealing in those dispensations, licences and faculties which might enable a man to hold two or more incompatible benefices at once, to be non-resident, to be ordained at less than the canonical age, or married outside the canonical seasons, or within the prohibited degrees of consanguinity. The puritans complained that by the Henrician statute which transferred to this institution powers previously exercised only by the Roman *curia*, the archbishop was made 'as it were a pope', and that almost every enormity now had its price in England 'as formerly at Rome'. The Geneva pastors thought such abuses 'nearly incredible' in a Church professing purity in doctrine.[21]

One should not suppose that the ecclesiastical courts were in decline in the second half of the sixteenth century, even if they lacked efficacy as instruments of 'discipline'. As the multiplication of their act-books suggests, many of these institutions shared in the general expansion of business and the resulting administrative sophistication which was a by-product both of rising prosperity and security, and of the attendant growth of both government and litigation. In the civil suits known as 'instance' causes, the laity made use of the church courts to protect their rights in marital, testamentary and tithe disputes. Yet to sue or to be sued in these courts was, or so we are told, both vexatious and expensive. In the criminal or 'office' causes, on the other hand, the courts offended the puritans with their officialdom and their lack of moral purpose, while the lay Englishman with a Common Law training (often the same person) objected to the foreign procedures of self-incrimination, and to the prosecution by the judge of his own case. The prominence of these issues in the religious and legal conflicts of the period can perhaps be accounted for by saying that the ecclesiastical courts came to the height of their development at the time of their greatest unpopularity.[22]

The regulation of the ministry of the Church seemed to the puritans equally faulty. The clergy were ordained indiscriminately into the priestly order (itself a questionable concept for any protestant) and were not called to serve a specific vocation in a particular congregation, according to reformed practice. Neither presbytery nor congregation had any say in their appointment to a parish. Their examination, either before ordination or before collation to a benefice, was often perfunctory, and the standards expected by the examiners distressingly low. In the early years of the reign, especially, a high proportion of those ordained were incapable of anything more than a 'bare reading ministry' and lacked the minimal qualifications for the reformed pastor. No part of the puritan programme would carry more weight than the incessant plea for a 'learned preaching ministry'.

We are now gaining in our understanding that in many parts of Western Europe Reformation and Counter-Reformation alike represented an attempt to rationalize what Mr Christopher Hill has called 'the chaos of ecclesiastical economics' in the later medieval Church.[23] The situation was one in which the distribution of endowment bore little logical relation to spiritual needs and pastoral considerations. Clerical absenteeism whereby the revenues of benefices were in effect diverted to serve another function; pluralism; the appropriation of tithes to some other purpose than the maintenance of the parochial ministry; corrupt presentations with simoniacal contracts whereby part of the income of a living might be secured to the lay patron: the English Reformation had as yet done little to control these familiar evils. On the contrary, it had aggravated some of them by dispersing among countless lay proprietors the impropriate tithes formerly held by religious houses and much other church property besides, and by making the Church generally vulnerable to lay spoliation. If material weakness was not the root-cause of the unlearned and unworthy ministry, it was a nearly inescapable obstacle to its reform, as Archbishop Whitgift never tired of reminding his critics. The practical failures of the Church had deeper and more technical causes than the puritans cared to penetrate; often the puritan laymen who complained most hotly were themselves direct contributors to the Church's debility. But as soon as the more forward protestants lost confidence in the sincerity of the government's reforming intentions, they found it easy to lay the blame for all these anomalies on the ill-will of the authorities and the corruption of the bishops. The gravity of the organizational and economic confusion of the Church gave to the puritan cause a moral intensity and a plausibility which it would otherwise have lacked.

The returned exiles and other protestant idealists found it difficult to accommodate themselves to the measure of wealth and dignity which still adhered to the higher offices of the English Church. In May 1559 John Parkhurst, soon to be bishop of Norwich, told Bullinger, with evident satisfaction, that 'the bishops are in future to have no palaces, estates or country seats'. But of course he was wrong. In spite of serious dilapidations, many of the Elizabethan bishops were to enjoy incomes which set them alongside the wealthier gentry and nobility in the social scale, barely recognizable as reformed pastors to eyes grown accustomed to the bourgeois values of the Swiss and Rhineland ministers. A young German protestant who visited Bishop Jewel at Salisbury was astonished – and gratified – to find him living in a spacious palace fit to receive the queen on progress, to be entertained by the bishop's young gentlemen with hunting and a visit to Stonehenge, escorted by a retinue, and to receive 'a beautiful and valuable horse' as a present from Bishop Sandys of Worcester. As we shall see, many of the exiles were hesitant to accept a prelatical status which they had so recently equated with sinful pride, and they were inclined to be critical of their friends who succumbed to these temptations.[24]

When Theodore Beza of Geneva had the English situation explained to him by an embittered puritan, he concluded that 'the papacy was never abolished in that country, but rather transferred to the sovereign.'[25] And one sees that the essential rock of offence for the radical conscience was the large measure of continuity with the immediate past which persisted in the ministry and government of the Church as well as in its liturgy and to some extent in the fabric and furnishings of the churches. Towards the end of his life Archbishop Parker drew gratuitous attention to this Anglican continuity in his *Lives of the Archbishops of Canterbury*, an account of the unbroken succession beginning with St Augustine and culminating in Parker himself, the seventieth archbishop. A glance at the later biographies in this work – Warham, Cranmer, Pole – would not suggest that there had been any major disturbance in the even flow of English church life in their times. Pirating the official account of Parker's own life, which the archbishop was modest enough not to have included in the earliest edition of his *De antiquitate*, an anonymous puritan author attacked with hostile glosses the very concept of a succession from 'this hellish Austen'. What good could come to the Church of God by 'raking together' out of the medieval chronicles 'and such authentic writers the wicked lives and gross blindness of Dunstan, Cuthbert, Becket and other their fellows of latter times? Or what godly estimation to the Christian Church of England to have the lives of such not men but monsters recorded in this time, as though they were to be reckoned good workmen in the Church?' Parker had furnished a list of all the Elizabethan bishops, recording amongst other data their original vocations, 'priest regular' or 'priest secular'. 'Why did he not at least in the behalf of those godly men and preachers of the truth set out withal this truth also: that is, how sorry they are and ashamed of that their former priesthood, and how loathsome those disorderly orders are to them?'[26]

Enough has perhaps been said to introduce some of the principal planks in the puritan platform and to explain why few earnest protestants at the time could have shared the assumption of an eminent church historian that 'the English Reformation attained its goal in the Elizabethan Settlement (1563).'[27]

3   The Beginnings of a Party

THESE IMPERFECTIONS WERE SUFFICIENT to deter a number of the most
forward protestants from identifying themselves unreservedly with the
new dispensation, even after the 1559 Parliament had settled the Church
on a recognizably protestant basis; while some of the most radical spirits
were to find that they had small hope of preferment or even of a welcome
in the Church of the Elizabethan *via media*. From the earliest months of
the reign there were signs of the beginnings of future puritan associations,
if not of a coherent party, among those repatriated exiles who, whether by
choice, or of necessity, remained on the periphery, devoting themselves
to the pursuit of an ideal which differed materially from the official policy
of the Church.

Amongst these potential dissenters were several leading members of
the English congregation in Geneva who lingered abroad, uncertain
whether to support the new regime or to wait for a still more favourable
day. These included the translators of the Geneva version of the Bible,
William Whittingham and his collaborators. Their continued absence
would be amply justified by all that English protestantism would owe to
that compact, serviceable volume with its apparatus of 'profitable annotations' and its modern type and format. But others remained in Geneva
out of mere pessimism, believing that 'there was no hope of such reformation ... as was before hoped for.' In October 1559 Knox was still advising
his intimates that 'we ought not to justify with our presence such a
mingle-mangle as now is commanded in your kirks', while censuring

those who stayed away 'only for negligence'. When they did reach England, the men of Geneva found that the advocacy of active resistance to an ungodly ruler in those political tracts of Knox and Christopher Goodman which had appeared from Geneva in 1558 had deprived them of any hope of influence under Queen Elizabeth. Whittingham had contributed a preface to Goodman's tract on *How superior powers oght to be obeyed*, and on his arrival in the summer of 1561 he found that he was not allowed to preach. The ban was lifted only in the following January, by which time he was preparing to leave again for France. Goodman came to London, but conducted himself like a fugitive before going off into what was, in effect, a second exile in Scotland. From there he assured Calvin that England was overtaken with ungodliness, pride, avarice and luxury, the inevitable fruits, as he thought, of female government. But he chose to see this as a salutary time of trial for those who had shared the joys of Calvin's 'blessed city of God'. Meanwhile in London a rump of Knox and Goodman's congregation retained something of its disciplined identity, a nucleus in the years to come for the English presbyterian movement.[1]

Not only the Genevans but many of the more forward men from other centres of exile were at first inclined to stand aloof from the Church, or at least to avoid incurring major responsibilities within it. Thomas Sampson was the government's first choice for the bishoprics of Hereford and Norwich, but he told Peter Martyr at Zürich (who had advised him to accept): 'Let others be bishops; as to myself, I will either undertake the office of a preacher, or none at all.' Miles Coverdale was considered for Exeter where he had been bishop under Edward VI, but if he was offered the see he must have refused. Alexander Nowell, later dean of St Paul's, was put down for Coventry and Lichfield but seems to have rejected it. David Whitehead is rumoured to have had first refusal of the arch-bishopric of Canterbury itself, and he certainly turned down the mastership of the Savoy. Apologizing to Cecil, he explained that he would gladly accept the living 'if I thought or could be persuaded to further true religion and God's holy word in so doing', but that he was prevented by 'things of some weight and importance, at least with me'. After White-head's death, the puritan leader John Field would write of him 'as a man that would have all well first, and then he would labour that all should be well.' This, it is not unjust to say, was the attitude of many incipient puritans in 1559.[2]

Some of those who eventually accepted bishoprics, notably John Parkhurst of Norwich, yielded only after a period of indecision, and through persuasion that no good could be served through allowing the leadership of the Church to fall into wrong hands. Edmund Grindal, soon to be bishop of London and a future archbishop of both York and Canterbury, was not without his doubts, although these were set aside in the course of 1559. In January 1560 Peter Martyr wrote: 'I vehemently approve your opinion not to desert the Church, or to refuse the functions which you have been offered ... What you then say about external things seeming to you not to be occasions for contention or for renouncing your vocation appears to me to be godly and rightly said.' The prospect would be much worse if he and others were to yield their places to Antichristian wolves. 'We who are now bishops', Grindal later informed Martyr's colleague, Henry Bullinger, 'on our first return, and before we entered on our ministry, contended long and earnestly for the removal of those things that have occasioned the present dispute; but as we were unable to prevail, either with the queen or the Parliament, we judged it best, after a consultation on the subject, not to desert our churches for the sake of a few ceremonies, and those not unlawful in themselves, especially since the pure doctrine of the gospel remained in all its integrity and freedom.'[3]

Although scarcely one of these émigré churchmen entertained a dogmatic objection to episcopacy, they were fresh from the invigorating poverty and simplicity of the exile, and in the past they had often denounced what John Jewel called the 'royal pomp and courtly bustle' of the catholic prelates. It should not surprise us that they hesitated to fill the same offices which their popish enemies had so recently vacated. 'Let others have their bishoprics,' wrote Parkhurst, back in his old Gloucestershire parish; 'my Cleeve is enough for me. Many of the bishops would most willingly change conditions with me; though one or two perhaps, a little ambitious, might decline doing so.' When Laurence Humphrey asked Cecil for promotion, he felt bound to explain that he was 'moved of necessity and not for profit or pleasure; of a care of my family, and not for love of having much.' After Humphrey had been rewarded with the presidency of Magdalen College, John Foxe the martyrologist, who accepted no preferment, sent a jocular rebuke: 'Come now, tell me, my friend, have you really deserted our flock and order?'[4]

Most of those who paused on the brink of new responsibilities must have felt some at least of the puritan scruples with which Thomas Sampson continually harried Peter Martyr. They doubted whether they could accept high office in a church which retained popish ceremonies and which was faulty in discipline.[5] But there were other, more tangible reasons for

47

the *nolo episcopari* of some. By a statute of her first Parliament, Elizabeth received authority to appropriate bishops' lands in exchange for property of a (nominally) equivalent value in the form of impropriate tithes in royal possession, tithes which a careful conscience would feel should be devoted to the maintenance of the parochial ministry for which they were originally intended.[6] These unfavourable and embarrassing exchanges were made a condition of episcopal appointment. Five of the bishops-elect, headed by Parker, protested against the 'inconveniences' of the transaction, and their consecrations were delayed while they overcame their objections; while James Pilkington, later bishop of Durham, forfeited the bishopric of Winchester rather than accept these terms. In late August 1559 Peter Martyr addressed Richard Cox prematurely as 'Domino Ricardo Coxo Anglo, Dei gratia episcopo', only to be forced to apologize for the embarrassment which he had caused. The new bishops were to be left in no doubt that it was by the grace of Queen Elizabeth that they were what they were.[7]

Among those whose doubts were not overcome and who continued to be at odds with the new establishment there were the makings of a party. This is suggested by a list of names presented to Lord Robert Dudley no later than 1564, and perhaps as early as 1561, which informed him of twenty-eight 'godly preachers which have utterly forsaken Antichrist and all his Romish rags', to be contrasted with 'the lord bishops and others that for worldly respects receive and allow them.'[8] By the time that this document was drawn up it was as if the concepts of 'government' and 'opposition' had already emerged in the reformed English Church. The list can serve to introduce us to some of the names which will occur again and again in association in the early part of our story. They include old Miles Coverdale, *'quondam episcopus'*, a father of the English Bible who now bore the mark of Geneva; and, also from Geneva, Whittingham, Anthony Gilby, like Coverdale respected as a 'father' of the reformed English Church, and William Cole. All four had contributed to the translation of the Geneva Bible. Percival Wiburn, who would later head a Calvinist reformation in the east Midlands, had spent the last year of Mary's reign at Geneva, while Laurence Humphrey and Thomas Sampson, the original intellectual leaders of Elizabethan puritanism, had made shorter visits to Calvin's city. William Turner had spent his time of exile gathering plants in different parts of Germany, for he was the founder of systematic botanical studies in this country, an early representative of the link between protestant liberalism and scientific inquiry. Also on Dudley's list were Robert Crowley, the preacher-printer who first published *Piers Plowman*, and Thomas Lever, with Crowley and Latimer the social conscience of Edwardine England. All but seven of the twenty-eight had been on the Continent, at least nine of them in settled residence at Geneva.

Few of those mentioned in this list were left without any preferment. Three became heads of Oxford colleges: Humphrey president of Magdalen, Sampson dean of Christ Church, and Cole, after eight more years in limbo, the first married president of Corpus Christi and, according to legend, the ruin of the college. Turner recovered the deanery of Wells which he had enjoyed under Edward VI. Lever was made archdeacon of Coventry. And several others of the group were rewarded with cathedral prebends or parochial benefices. Yet some notable names among them, Coverdale, Foxe and Gilby, received scant recognition (if, indeed, they looked for it), and only one became a bishop – Pilkington of Durham.[9]

The failure or reluctance of many of the most forward protestants to secure the higher ecclesiastical positions was an important factor in the formation of the puritan mentality, and specifically of the anti-prelatical, even presbyterian temper of the party. By the time the new bishops were obliged to conform to unpopular royal policies, other more radical protestants were choosing to forget the admirable motives with which they had incurred these responsibilities. As early as 1567 it was said that they had been moved by worldly motives and 'against their conscience', while the reader of a puritan tract published at almost the same time took up his pen and spattered the margins with such comments as these: 'They rather serve their bellies, that are papists in outward show, to please men and maintain their kitchens' – 'worldly greatness more sought than God's glory' – 'ear-rings the devil's badge'. Later a veteran of the Geneva Church would assure Dudley – by then earl of Leicester – that the schism in the Church need never have arisen if the bishops 'had at the beginning sought a full reformation according to God's word.' Instead, 'everyone sought how to catch a wealthy and rich bishopric, some paying well for it ... and thus, neglecting God's glory, they sought their own, and therefore God never blessed their doings to this day, nor never will so long as they continue in this pomp and great wealth.' Nor was this exclusively a puritan sentiment. Burghley himself could write, when this generation of bishops had given place to another: 'I see such worldliness in many that were otherwise affected before they came to cathedral chairs, that I fear the places alter the men.' It could hardly have been otherwise.[10]

For as long as they escaped preferment, the godly ministers devoted themselves to itinerant preaching, for which the royal visitation of the

Church in the summer of 1559 provided both stimulus and opportunity. Thomas Lever told Bullinger of Zürich that after his return to England he 'travelled through a great part of it, for the sake of preaching the gospel.' One is irresistibly reminded of the orders of friars of the medieval church, and so were the preachers themselves, Foxe writing humorously of 'the mendicant brothers, or, if you will, the preaching brothers'. For these 'brethren' the Elizabethan dispensation was an opportunity to proclaim the protestant gospel freely, not an invitation to assume a static ecclesiastical responsibility. Jewel told Peter Martyr that his old friends were 'entirely scattered – not for the dispersion, but, as I hope, for the gathering of nations.'[11]

When the preachers settled down, it was often under private patronage, rather than in beneficed positions. Coverdale found a niche in the pious menage of the duchess of Suffolk. Foxe preached in Norwich for a year or two, enjoying the personal patronage of Bishop Parkhurst, before settling in London as a dependant of the duke of Norfolk. Thereafter he combined the labours of authorship with free-lance preaching. William Cole preached to the English merchants in Antwerp, and when he returned to England in 1564, it was to serve in another salaried preaching post, at Colchester.[12] Anthony Gilby became the earl of Huntingdon's pensionary at Ashby-de-la-Zouch.[13]

This was the quiet beginning of the great age of puritan lectureships, salaried preaching appointments in parish churches which offered a reasonable livelihood and freedom from the restraint of the Prayer Book. At the city church of St Antholin's, where the oldest of the London lectureships had been planted in Edward's reign, early morning sermons were now preached six days a week by three preachers to a congregation which assembled to sing metrical psalms after the Geneva fashion for an hour before the sermon.[14] In market towns in the country, the magistrates were already engaging their own preachers, or in some other way providing themselves with regular weekday sermons, serving all the parishes of the town. This happened early in the reign at Coventry, Colchester, Ipswich and (at the earl of Huntingdon's instigation) at Leicester. By the end of the second Elizabethan decade, Ipswich often found employment and stipends – which might approach a total of more than a hundred pounds yearly – for two preachers. At Colchester in 1564, the preacher's wages were found by 'free and voluntary contribution' of the governing body, together with some forty other inhabitants, presumably all sound gospellers. Three years later a larger body of burgesses subscribed a little more money. At Ipswich, the money was to be raised partly from the town treasury, partly from a rate levied – not without difficulty – on householders, under an Act of Parliament procured in 1571, primarily to provide for the maintenance of the parish clergy.[15]

Where such preachers combined learning and reputation with the good favour of the weightier inhabitants, they were often the apostles of the towns they served, men of an almost episcopal standing, as was Lever already in Coventry, and, a few years later, Wiburn in Northampton and John More in Norwich. In some of these centres the preachers took the initiative in the early 'sixties in establishing 'exercises of prophesying'. These were conferences of the preaching clergy devoted to systematic Biblical exposition. By the popular interest which they attracted and the indoctrination and homiletical training which they offered to the more ignorant clergy, the prophesyings did more than any other agency to propagate and establish the new religion in Elizabethan England. We shall hear more of them at a later stage in our story.

None of these activities owed much to the initiative of the ecclesiastical authorities, and they were not, so far as the queen and Archbishop Parker were concerned, part of the official programme of the established Church. Although Lever acquired regular ecclesiastical standing as archdeacon of Coventry, the strength of his position derived from his appointment as town preacher. 'After I had discovered', he wrote, 'by the experience of some weeks, that vast numbers in this place were in the habit of frequenting the public preaching of the gospel, I consented to their request, that I should settle my wife and family among them; and thus, now for nearly a whole year, I have preached to them without any hindrance, and they have liberally maintained me and my family in this city. For we are not bound to each other, neither I to the townsmen, nor they to me, by any law of engagement, but only by free kindness and love.'[16] In the ranks of the 'roving apostles', the parish lecturers and the town preachers, in their sermons, prophesyings and psalm-singing, one can already trace the outline of a 'church within the Church', even before these activities attracted the unfavourable attention of those in authority.

The early puritan movement has often been described as if it were nothing but a clerical and academic coterie. Canon Dixon, for example, represented Elizabethan nonconformity as 'of ministerial origin' and not 'likely in itself to arouse partisan feelings in the community'.[17] But the patronage which the preachers enjoyed is in itself sufficient indication that influential persons in the early Elizabethan Court and in society at large were more aware of the need to forward the gospel than of any duty to maintain a religious *via media*. No more than the preachers were they able to entertain the idea of a 'mediocrity' between the old and new faiths. Coverdale wrote from the duchess of Suffolk's household to inform Gilby, Whittingham and Cole that his patron shared their abhorrence of popish ceremonies, and so one would expect from her scolding of Cecil's conservatism in 1559.[18]

If the radical protestant cause in England had a single potential leader at this time it was Whittingham, and what little we know of his movements suggests that he and his friends already commanded support in the highest places. Whittingham spent the early months of 1561 in France, attached to a mission of the earl of Bedford. Later in the same year we learn that the earl of Huntingdon has been 'good to him', setting him up to preach in Leicester and underwriting the salary which the earl's servants were set to collect from the reluctant Leicestershire clergy. In the following year it was the earl of Warwick who was Whittingham's patron and commander, when he went over as preacher to the expeditionary force at Le Havre. There he joined his old Genevan companions: William Kethe, author of the metrical version of the 'Old Hundred', and Thomas Wood, an elder of Knox's congregation and now clerk to Warwick's Council of War. If Warwick had had his way, Christopher Goodman and Percival Wiburn would have been there as well, a real anticipation of the puritan militancy of a later age. At 'Newhaven' Whittingham's talents as a diplomatist may have proved just as serviceable as his spiritual leadership. Here, evidently, was the man who might have been the Francis Hotman or the Philippe Marnix van Sint Aldegonde of English Calvinism, the intermediary between the clerical rank and file and the princely patrons of the reform. From Le Havre, Warwick used his brother Lord Robert Dudley to pull the strings that made Whittingham, layman from Geneva though he was, dean of Durham. In that remote and affluent refuge his ties with international Calvinism seem to have loosened, and eventually he was estranged from his radical friends in the south.[19]

Of the 'inferior magistrates' of England, one nobleman at first stands out from the rest as the aristocratic leader of the reformed party: Francis Russell, earl of Bedford. He was the mainstay of protestantism in the West Country, the patron of those closely interrelated families which we met in William Ramsey's 'Epistle to the Moltonians'. 'There wanteth nothing but preachers', he was told by Sir John Chichester, writing from north Devon in August 1559. But Bedford's influence was more than provincial, as the Swiss reformers well knew. He had spent a Marian winter at Zürich, and in Elizabeth's reign he continued to correspond with his old hosts, and with Calvin, who clearly regarded him as a personage of special potentialities. To the French pastor in London, Nicolas des Gallars, who was a close colleague of Calvin, he was the 'most powerful and most noble earl', a great source of comfort. Bedford's deep interest in reformed theology is revealed in his library, which at his death consisted very largely of religious books, including numerous works of Calvin and Beza as well as the writings of most of the prominent English puritan divines. In 1561 he seemed to Cecil the most suitable person to send to France on a mission which would enable contact to be made with the leading huguenots and to dissuade France from involvement in the Council of Trent, and, as we have seen, Whittingham went with him.[20]

Bedford was one of the most reliable and sincere friends of the gospel in England, but he was not the most useful. The greater potential to help the cause lay in the hands of Lord Robert Dudley, whose religious position in these early years was more ambiguous, reflecting the instability of the great favourite, the man who had to play every card in aiming at the highest prize.[21] Yet as earl of Leicester, Dudley would emerge in Izaak Walton's phrase as 'cherisher and patron-general' of the puritans, and there are signs that he was already committed to that side. Within a few years Lever would testify that 'heretofore I and many others have by your means had quietness, liberty and comfort to preach the gospel of Christ.'[22] In 1568 the French ambassador had to report to Charles IX that Leicester was 'totally of the Calvinist religion' and that to prove it he had recently taken communion with the French protestant refugees in London, the first prominent courtier to be seen in these circles.[23] Who can doubt that in their own more orderly political context and by less overt means these English magnates were public defenders of the reformed religion as fully as were the prince of Condé or Admiral Coligny in France, or Regent Moray in Scotland? Only Elizabeth's capacity to out-live all the successive crises of her reign has concealed the political implications of their faith. For if the queen had succumbed to the smallpox in October 1562, as for a time it seemed that she would, the arm of flesh of English Calvinism would have come into play to defend the protestant succession of Lady Catherine Grey, or of the earl of Huntingdon himself.[24]

Among the leading gentlemen of the Court there were not a few staunch friends of the radical preachers. Some, like Sir Francis Knollys, a cousin by marriage to the queen, and Sir Anthony Cooke, the father-in-law of Cecil and Sir Nicholas Bacon, had been exiles themselves in Mary's reign and are known to have led the effective protestant agitation in the 1559 Parliament. Other key figures, Bacon himself and Sir Nicholas Throckmorton, and above all Cecil, the future Lord Burghley, occupied a somewhat different position, *politiques* all of them rather than *dévots*, as indeed all courtiers were obliged to be for at least some of the time, in virtue of their office. But the interest of policy itself, as these statesmen interpreted it, told on the side of the godly, and increasingly so as the reign matured and gathering dangers seemed to indicate a strong hand with papists at home and the advancement of protestant causes in Europe. From the beginning the catholics themselves had virtually no representation in the inner circles of government.

We shall gain a similar impression if we look out from the centre to the peripheral but all-important world of local government and to those microcosms of the Elizabethan Commonwealth which were the English shires. The most significant political achievement of the English Reformation, and one accomplished very largely in Elizabeth's reign, would be the recruitment of the class of country gentry, or at least of a sizeable and energetic section, to a serious, informed puritan piety. In the early 'sixties this process still had far to go. But many heads of land-owning families were now sending their sons to the universities, where many of them would be deeply affected by the influence of their puritan tutors. In 1565 Laurence Humphrey excused himself from appearing in London to answer for his nonconformity with the plea that he was responsible at Magdalen for the care of 'divers noblemen's sons'.[25] These included Huntingdon's younger brother, Francis Hastings, who became an erudite theologian and one of the most reliable political supports for the puritan ministers in Parliament, throughout the Midlands, and in Somerset where he settled later in the reign.[26] In Humphrey's opinion, whoever made a nobleman a more learned or a better man, 'causeth not that one or a few become more healthful; but that many, yea, the whole Commonwealth, is the better and more sound.'[27] Already the early Elizabethan Parliaments provide impressive evidence of the strength of religious radicalism in national politics, and so by inference in local affairs as well. To read Sir John Neale's account of these Parliaments is to conclude that the hotter protestants were already strongly placed in the social hierarchies of many shires, and that they were singularly intolerant of half-measures in God's causes. Evidently in local affairs, at least in the relatively protestant counties of East Anglia, the South-East, the Midlands and the West Country, political and religious 'soundness' favoured the advancement of zealous protestants into the inner circles of the hardest-worked and most responsible magistrates. Certainly many of the opposite, conservative party were excluded from the commissions of the peace at the beginning of the reign, and again in 1564, at about the time that the bishops were invited to report on the religious sympathies of the justices. In Norfolk alone, these purges removed at least twenty members of suspect families from the Commission.[28]

It may be thought anachronistic to attach the name of 'puritan' to these protestant noblemen and gentlemen in the years before the name had come into common currency, and a full generation before it would be applied to persons of such consequence. But it would be still more misleading to call them 'Anglicans' with any of the modern associations of that ascription. The formularies of the Elizabethan settlement were no delimitation of their religion, and like the preachers whose interest they advanced, they must have regarded that settlement as imperfect and provisional. Their outlook was international, and increasingly so as the ideological struggle of the later sixteenth century intensified. Consequently only two religions were recognized in most places in Elizabethan England and 'Anglicanism' was not one of them.

Part 2

The Breach Opens

1 So many Learned and Religious Bishops

'There is a report brought unto us, and the same is confyrmed by certaine mennes letters both out of Fraunce and out of Germany, that in your countrie, many Ministers of gods worde, (who otherwise wer faultlesse as well in life as in doctrine) were put out of offyce by the queenes maiestie, even with the consent of you Bishops, bicause they refused to subscribe to some certaine Ceremonies ... I wrote agayne to those freendes of mine, That the church of God did perswade it selfe farre other wise, bothe of the queenes maiestie, and also of so many learned and religious bishops ... '

(THEODORE BEZA TO BISHOP GRINDAL, June 5th, 1566;
contemporary translation, *Puritan Manifestoes*, p. 45)

SO FAR WE HAVE TRACED the beginnings of future puritan associations if not of a puritan party in the brotherhood of preachers who stood aside from the main stream of the Elizabethan Church. But this is a very partial impression of the Elizabethan situation. It could be argued, and not inconsistently, that the 'main stream' of Anglicanism was not so certainly identified with the 'mediocrity' of the queen and Archbishop Parker that it might not yet flow in the direction set by the more advanced protestantism of the repatriated exiles. Puritanism was to take root within the established Church and within its beneficed ministry, not to any significant extent outside it. And this too was determined by the manner in which the Church was resettled in Elizabeth's early years.

For every returned exile who remained on the periphery, there were perhaps five who were offered and accepted preferment, moved by the simple need of a livelihood, or by the loftier persuasion that they could do more good by accepting places of influence themselves than by allowing them to fall into the hands of 'wolves and antichrists'. Within their dioceses, archdeaconries and parishes they were often free to apply a generously protestant interpretation to the queen's ecclesiastical policy and to obscure what may seem to us the true essence of Anglicanism as the Elizabethan settlement had defined it. Preaching went forward – far more of it than Elizabeth ever thought desirable – and the Prayer Book was allowed to become the vehicle of a simplified puritan worship. For much of the time and in many localities it must have seemed that puritan aspirations would be satisfied without schism and even without conspicuous conflict. Not until the rise of Archbishop Laud and his episcopal colleagues in the reign of Charles I were these tendencies radically reversed. If it were not something of a contradiction in terms, one could speak of sixty or seventy years of puritan government in some of the most populous areas of England. Some dioceses – York, Lincoln, Norwich – enjoyed a succession of radically protestant bishops. Their indulgence and the many anomalies and inadequacies of sixteenth-century administration gave the Church enough latitude to contain puritanism throughout the years of its strongest growth.

From what has already been said it will be clear that Elizabeth's deeply conservative views on religious and ecclesiastical questions were very far from finding expression in a constant and vigilant care over her Church. Elizabeth's personal contribution to the government of her Church was one of occasional intervention, prompted by an angry reaction to the reports which reached her, as often as not, unofficially and spasmodically. Such an intervention occurred in 1565, when the bishops were scolded for their inaction and commanded to treat all nonconformity with uncompromising severity. At once, and indeed whenever that demand was repeated in the years to come, a painful division was created among protestants who might seem to be in substantial agreement on almost all other matters of religion but who differed on the crucial question of whether the queen was in all circumstances to be obeyed. This initial difference, narrow as it seemed at first, was to widen, revealing a substantial divergence of opinion on the nature of the Church and its proper relationship to the Commonwealth and the magistracy; and leading, ultimately, to the emergence of protestant dissenting bodies irrevocably separated from the national Church. It will not surprise us to find that this acid test tended to divide the governors from those who lacked high preferment and its accompanying responsibilities. Whatever their sympathies and their views before they were elevated, the bishops rarely refused to execute royal policy when the necessity was unavoidable. Only one Elizabethan prelate – Grindal as archbishop of Canterbury – ever dared to explain to the queen's face that as a bishop of Christ's Church he was subject to a higher power, and the result was suspension from office and the irretrievable loss of her favour. It was in these recurrent crises of conscience that the concealed isolation of the puritan 'church within the Church' became from time to time apparent. Here we have to trace the first of these crises, which was also the most important. For it was in the vestments controversy of 1563–7 that 'puritanism', name if not thing, was born, and thereafter it remained in fairly constant currency. After this episode the English Church and English protestants could never again pretend to be entirely at peace.

The story begins with the appointment to many of the leading bishoprics of returned exiles who shared in varying degrees the puritan desire to see a progressive reformation. At least eight of the bishops promoted in the first two and a half years of the reign were themselves progressives, if not puritans: Thomas Bentham of Coventry and Lichfield (a contributor to the Geneva Bible), Edmund Grindal of London (later of York and Canterbury), Robert Horne of Winchester, John Parkhurst of Norwich, James Pilkington of Durham (like Bentham for a short time a member of Knox's congregation at Geneva), Edwin Sandys of Worcester (born in the same Cumberland parish as Grindal and his successor at both London and York), and Edmund Scambler of Peterborough and later of Norwich (not an exile, but for a time a pastor to the secret protestant congregation in Marian London, as was Bentham). John Scory of Hereford, while somewhat lacking in godly zeal in his later years and by general consent not a 'good bishop', should be included in the same group. Moreover, if we are inclined to place John Jewel of Salisbury in a class of his own, it must be with the recognition that his officially sponsored *Apology of the Church of England* erected all its defences on one flank only and allowed not so much as a suspicion that the English church settlement could be threatened from a protestant quarter: a disappointment for those who already saw in the moderate position of the English Church a pointer to a middle way which others might be persuaded to follow.[1] The remaining bishops were all more conservative than those so far named: some, like Cox of Ely, more in temperament and policy than on principle, although Cheyney of Gloucester held the Lutheran doctrine of the Lord's Supper and Edmund Guest of Rochester tended in the same direction. But most of the larger and wealthier sees were in the hands of what Sandys called 'Germanical natures'.[2] If all those who were originally considered for bishoprics had accepted them, an episcopate which included Sampson, Coverdale and Nowell would have been still more radical and 'continental'.

A familiar fact of history they may be, but these appointments are not to be taken for granted. They amounted to little less than the surrender of the Church to an émigré government potentially out of tune with the queen's own conservative instincts. 'Surrender' is perhaps an inappropriate expression, for Elizabeth surrendered nothing to her servants, least of all to her bishops. But that she committed episcopal responsibility to men of conviction rather than time-servers, to men whose outlook was in many ways so unlike her own, is a conundrum which underlies much of the ecclesiastical conflict of the reign. It may be argued from the intransigence of virtually all the surviving Marian prelates that the more distinguished of the new bishops appointed themselves, especially since the field of choice was restricted by the loss under Mary of so much of the potential leadership of a protestant Church. Again, it is clear that Edwardine reputations were not forgotten. Grindal, for example, as the only survivor of the preaching prebendaries whom Ridley brought from Pembroke Hall to London, had assumed his master's mantle and was his natural successor, at least in the eyes of a protestant city which revered the memory of Rogers and Bradford. Yet the promotion of these scholars and exiles (some of them, like Jewel, totally lacking in administrative experience) surpassed their earlier expectations.[3] Patronage there must have been in the disposal of livings worth well over twenty thousand pounds a year, and the absorbing question remains: whose patronage?[4]

To such a question there can be only speculative answers, since the transactions at Court through which a new bishop emerged have mostly gone unrecorded, or else the records have been lost. But one need not assume that the queen concerned herself directly with the quality and opinions of men who were for the most part unknown to her personally and who were to be her commissioners rather than free agents. At a rather later date both Cecil and Archbishop Parker took a careful interest in the supply of vacant sees. And Cecil was the 'principal procurer' of Grindal's successive preferments, or so Grindal himself acknowledged at the end of his life. But neither secretary nor archbishop had the queen's church patronage in his pocket, and others undoubtedly had a share: Sir Nicholas Bacon, for example, the new lord keeper, who was persistent in wearing down Parker's own very real reluctance to be 'intruded into such room and vocation.' Bacon's responsibility in church affairs is thought to have been considerable. He was, of course, a convinced protestant, and his second wife Ann, whom he married in 1557, was a most ardent puritan and sister of Cecil's equally godly partner.[5]

We should not overlook the possible intervention in some of these appointments of Lord Robert Dudley, the future earl of Leicester, Elizabeth's favourite and, as rumour would have it, her lover. 'The cock that sitteth next the hen' never sat nearer than in the eighteen months from the spring of 1559 to the autumn of 1560, when at times even Cecil's standing was precarious. It was within this period that most of the episcopal appointments which interest us were made. Between late May and mid-July 1559 the first batch was chosen, all exiles: Grindal, Jewel, Sandys and Scory with Pilkington (abortively for Winchester) as well as Cox (at first for Norwich and then for Ely) and Barlow for Chichester. In this early summer of 1559 it also seems to have been intended that Miles Coverdale should return to Exeter, and that Sampson should have Norwich, Nowell Coventry and Lichfield, and Horne Durham (where he was already restored as dean, but where the aged Tunstall was as yet undisturbed as bishop). Bentham was chosen by late November, Parkhurst (in place of Sampson) by April 1560, Horne for Winchester by November of that year (by which time it was known that Pilkington would be transferred to Durham) and Scambler by February 1561.[6]

Even if, as most authorities agree, Dudley was of no constant religion at this time, his good offices may have been employed by some of his allies whose radical protestant sympathies are not in doubt: these might have included his brother Ambrose (soon to be earl of Warwick) and the earls of Huntingdon and Bedford. Dudley's correspondence for these early years contains a number of requests for preferments in the queen's gift, some of them addressed by the real patrons to whom the queen was not so accessible. Amongst them is a request from Lady Jane Grey's old tutor John Aylmer asking for the deanery of Durham, 'since Mr Horne is sped of his bishopric.' Two years later the combined influence of both the Dudleys secured the same deanery from a reluctant queen for Whittingham, the acknowledged leader of the Geneva party. At a time when most of the original Elizabethan bishops were still living, Leicester would invite the puritans to consider the quality of 'all the bishops that can be supposed that I have commended to that dignity since my credit any way served.' And there is evidence both in their correspondence and in the sinecures with which Leicester was rewarded within their diocesan establishments to suggest that Grindal, Horne, Sandys, Pilkington and Scambler all felt themselves to be under some particular obligation to him. Thomas Young, the first Elizabethan archbishop of York to be consecrated – no puritan but possibly an exile – was commonly thought to have owed his promotion to the earl.[7]

The preferment of these bishops and the deprivation of so many of the higher Marian clergy ensured that a large number of church appointments of the second rank went in the same direction. In the diocese of London, Grindal secured four out of the five archdeaconries, the chancellorship and a number of minor official appointments for repatriated exiles. Moreover, with the dean of St Paul's – Alexander Nowell – and seven of the canons drawn from the same group, the extensive patronage of the chapter ensured the bestowal of a good proportion of city livings on the more radical protestants. At the other end of the country a group of exiles, some of them from Geneva, acquired a strong interest in the diocese of Durham through the influence first of Horne as dean and later of Bishop Pilkington and Dean Whittingham.[8]

These bishops of the *Zurich Letters* can scarcely be called 'Anglicans' if by Anglican we mean to conjure up Newman's *via media* or even what Parker meant when he spoke approvingly of 'reverent mediocrity'. But such a conception of the Anglican position was exceptional among the clerical elite of the Elizabethan and Jacobean Church. Jewel spoke contemptuously of some who were 'seeking after a *golden*, or as it rather seems to me, a *leaden* mediocrity; and are crying out, that the half is better than the whole.' With many of his episcopal colleagues, the bishop of Salisbury had as dualistic a view of the religious conflict of his times as any puritan. In spite of the continuity with the past which so many Anglican institutions conserved, succession through the Roman Church was the last thing that he wanted to emphasize. The Church of England in doctrine and achievement was the true successor of the Church of the apostles and fathers, but it succeeded the unreformed Church in quite another way. 'The doctrine of Christ this day, Mr Harding,' he told his opponent, 'succeedeth your doctrine, as the day succeedeth the night; as the light succeedeth darkness; and as the truth succeedeth error.' How unlike Parker, who could repeat with pleasure the compliment of a French ambassador that 'we were in religion very nigh to them'! As for the foreign reformed churches, for Jewel and his friends it was a matter of *pas d'ennemi à gauche*. Jewel could assure Peter Martyr of the substantial affinity in doctrine of England and Zürich: 'We have pared everything away to the very quick, and do not differ from your doctrine by a nail's breadth.' 'Vestiges of popery', including what he called the 'theatrical habits', Jewel hoped to see 'extirpated, even to the lowest roots'.[9] If there was a difference between his position and that of many less moderate protestants, in England and overseas, it concerned the 'formal' principle of religious authority rather than what Jewel, in common with all other protestants, held to constitute the essential matter of true religion. Only in his understanding of what constituted religious authority did Jewel, like Cranmer before him, tread a middle way.

It was with the most progressive of intentions that the émigré bishops assumed their burdens. 'Remember, my lord,' Leicester later reminded Scambler of Peterborough, 'how before you were bishop you would find fault with negligence of bishops, how much you cried out to have preachers and good ministers to be increased and carefully placed. And so did you all almost that be now bishops.' While they were gratified by what was gained in the Elizabethan settlement they were far from satisfied, and they expected to be the agents of further reforms, especially in the field of ceremonies. Observing that the ornaments clause of the Act of Uniformity was to remain in force until 'other order' should be taken by the queen with the advice of her Ecclesiastical Commissioners, Sandys assured Parker that 'our gloss upon this text is, that we shall not be forced to use them', interpreting the clause as a precaution to ensure the physical survival of the vestments and other valuable ceremonial furniture until the queen should take charge of them. But when in the summer of 1559 the enthusiasm of the royal visitors ran away with them and in many parishes the eucharistic vestments went into the bonfire with all other 'monuments of idolatry and superstition', the bishops made an informal and unauthorized decision to require no more than the cope for the communion and the surplice for all other administrations.[10]

Throughout the 'sixties the more radical of the bishops hoped for 'better times', when the ceremonies and other embarrassments such as the archbishop's Court of Faculties would be swept away. A preacher at Paul's Cross – one of Bishop Horne's chaplains – would tell his auditory in September 1566 that 'the fathers of England did not at the first pluck out all abuses, thinking at the length they should loose the root with more ease, and therefore they began with some things and did let other some alone.' But in the preacher's opinion 'how much they be deceived you see.' Five years later still his master could advise Bullinger that with Elizabeth holding the helm, 'it would be very dangerous to drag her on, against her will, to a point she does not yet choose to come to, as if we were wresting the helm out of her hands.' Yet it was their daily prayer that God would 'turn at length our sails to another quarter.' At the end of his life, Archbishop Sandys could still record his conviction that though ceremonies must be observed 'for order and obedience sake', they were 'not so expedient' that they might not 'better be disused by little and little, than more and more urged.'[11]

When the first Convocations of the reconstituted Church met in 1563, the extent to which its leading echelons had been penetrated by radical protestants was apparent. Among the many reformatory *gravamina* commended by members of the Lower House of Canterbury Convocation, there were three proposals for important changes in the Prayer Book which would discourage kneeling at the communion, suppress 'all curious singing and playing of the organs', restrict baptism to ministers, abolish the sign of the cross in that sacrament and sweep away the observance of saints' days and all liturgical and other distinctive dress for the clergy. Among the subscribers to this motion were the dean of St Paul's and prolocutor, Alexander Nowell, four out of the five archdeacons of the diocese of London, and four deans and eight archdeacons from other dioceses. A second programme differing from the first only in the retention of the surplice was defeated by the narrow margin of one vote. The more forward of the bishops were evidently favourable to some at least of these proposed reforms. Parkhurst had told Bullinger a year before that he hoped for 'an improvement at the approaching Convocation', and Sandys moved on his own initiative to abolish the cross in baptism and baptism by midwives.[12]

Frustrated in Convocation, the radicals were bound to look to Parliament. Once again there were bishops who approved of their initiative, Horne assuring Zürich that they 'certainly hoped' to repeal the ornaments clause in the parliamentary session expected in 1565. When the third Elizabethan Parliament met a year later, a majority of the bishops morally supported – if they did not secretly sponsor – an unofficial Commons bill which proposed to give statutory confirmation to the Thirty-nine Articles. Whatever view may be taken of the theology of the Articles, there can be no doubt that their parliamentary enactment at this time would have served to range England less equivocally with the Swiss and South German churches. Moreover, the bill proposed to make the Articles a test by which to purge the ministry of lurking papists. It was not until 1571, after the publication of the papal bull of excommunication against the queen, that the Articles were given a limited statutory recognition in an act imposing clerical subscription. The quashing of the 1566 bill by the queen over the protest of the archbishop and thirteen other prelates is an indication of how far the bishops could find themselves out of line with royal ecclesiastical policy and associated with elements which would soon be driven into open opposition.[13]

Meanwhile, the reformist bishops proved reluctant to enforce the Act of Uniformity against fellow protestants. Thomas Sampson later told Burghley of a bishop who had remarked in a public sermon that 'the law was not made to forbid one man to do better than the law prescribed, but that no man should do worse', while the puritans spread the report overseas that some bishops had promised their more precise brethren 'free liberty in the government of their churches, and for some years they kept this promise.' Grindal of London was the most prominent of perhaps half a dozen bishops who were prepared on occasions of insurmountable prejudice to grant an informal, verbal licence to minister without the surplice. Not surprisingly, the example proved contagious in the strongly protestant towns of north Essex. 'I was contented to bear with Mr Upchire for the surplice,' wrote Grindal, 'and upon that three or four more took upon them the like liberty, without licence.' Later, when London was distracted by the vestments controversy, Parker told Cecil that its bishop was but reaping the fruits of his own earlier laxity. Not that Grindal had been unaware of the dangers of his policy. 'Therefore I require you to look well about,' he had warned the archdeacon of Colchester in 1560, 'and not to suffer ministration of the communion in gowns without surplices to spread and creep forward ... You may not relent at every persuasion in this matter.' Yet it was characteristic of Grindal to recognize that in such a situation mere repression would only increase the likelihood of schism.[14]

Grindal's own liturgical liberalism seems to be revealed in a letter of advice sent in 1564 to the preacher to the English merchants at Antwerp, who came under the bishop of London's jurisdiction. For common prayer the preacher – William Cole – was to use the English Book and none other, but he was to take as much or as little of it as he and the elders of the congregation thought fit. To use the entire Prayer Book order, Grindal implied, would leave too little time for the sermon if the service were to be of reasonable length. Cole was to follow the Book for baptism and the Lord's supper, but to adapt the ceremonial to that of the local reformed churches. 'Place the table as theirs is. If they receive the sacrament standing, kneeling or sitting, do you the like. Neither need you use any surplice, whether they use it or no, for they know that the high Almayne churches [i.e. in Switzerland and South Germany] use none.' No predilection here for 'the face of an English church'![15]

Bishop Bentham treated conscientious nonconformists with no less indulgence and in 1565 was censured 'from above' for his laxity. When the curate of a small mining village near Ashby-de-la-Zouch was cited before him for the surplice 'as he had been oft before', we are told that 'two ancient old men above three score years apiece' went with him to testify to their recent conversion through the preacher's 'painful travail'. 'Wherewith the bishop, being as it was astonied, turned his back and slipped away and so, God be praised, they enjoy their minister still to their great comfort.' This possibly apocryphal tale relates to the early 'seventies, but Bentham can never have found it easy to subject the godly to the full rigour of the law. On another occasion he told a Shropshire minister: 'Mr Axton, you shall yield somewhat unto me, and I will likewise yield unto you what I can. For the cross in baptism, I will never require it of you, and for the surplice, if you will wear it but sometimes, or but twice or thrice, or if you will wear it but once, I will urge you no further.' Scory of Hereford tolerated the only nonconformist in his backward diocese 'because of the good service that otherwise he hath done and doeth.'[16]

Some radicals in authority showed even less restraint in their encouragement of nonconformity. Parkhurst, once 'king' in his own parish of Cleeve, now administered his diocese of Norwich without much reference to his episcopal colleagues. In 1570 Jewel told their common Zürich friends that he had not seen his old tutor for six years. 'A surplice may not be borne here' was Cecil's complaint after the Court had been on progress in Suffolk. In Essex, the archdeacon, Thomas Cole, was himself a flagrant nonconformist, while in the archbishop's peculiar jurisdiction of Bocking in the same county the dean put his own radical interpretation upon Parker's visitation articles.[17]

In these ways confidence and peace among protestant brethren was precariously preserved. But by the same token a severe strain was imposed on the unity of the Church at large. No puritan would be content with a toleration for himself. The more liberty he enjoyed, the readier he would be to disparage the conformity of others. From Bocking a plaintive conformist warned Parker of the provocations of 'the English doctors' who denounced those of their neighbours who failed to preach the Calvinist doctrines of election and predestination or who loyally observed the legal ceremonies. 'I depend upon them that have authority to alter ceremonies, not upon the lewd brethren that seem and would be thought to have authority, and have none.' There followed this pregnant comment: 'Sir, truly, I write as other men talk.' Parker was already exercised by the wider implications of the problem which this letter brings to life. As early as 1561 he had cause to complain that his own efforts in 'moderating some things indifferent' had earned him 'the foul reports of some protestants'. These perhaps did not exclude his episcopal colleagues, for Sandys of Worcester had to beg him not to 'utterly condemn all Germanical natures.'[18]

By 1563 the chief bone of contention was acknowledged to be the surplice and the outdoor clerical dress prescribed in the royal injunctions. (The ornaments rubric was virtually a dead letter, so that the vestments controversy, strictly speaking, is a misnomer, the anachronistic echo of nineteenth-century 'ritual' prosecutions which turned on the interpretation of the ornaments clause.) Already the two most distinguished protestants in the university of Oxford, the president of Magdalen and Regius professor of divinity, Laurence Humphrey, and the dean of Christ Church, Thomas Sampson, were the recognized leaders of the opinion which rejected out of hand these all-too-visible 'vestiges of popery'. In the late summer of that year they pressed the pastors of Zürich for a ruling in the matter: 'To the pure ... can all these things be pure, and matters of indifference?'[19] Humphrey and Sampson had no more doubt of the answer than that Anglo-Züricher, John Hooper, who as bishop-elect of Gloucester in Edward's reign had scrupled to wear the prescribed vestments for his consecration. The traditional clerical attire conjured up images of the Roman, and ultimately of the Jewish priesthood, clean contrary to the gospel and to the general tenor of scripture; they were therefore snares for the simple, not matters of indifference, and no human authority could require their use; but if, for the sake of argument, they were indifferent, why wound a godly conscience and deny Christian liberty by enforcing them with a kind of popish tyranny?[20] Late in 1564, Parker drew some of the bishops and commissioners into a private negotiation with the Oxford leaders. They were confronted with an episcopal *propositio* to the effect that for the sake of decency a difference of apparel could be legitimately enjoined by public authority without implying false doctrine. Not all Parker's advisers were able to set their names to this document without qualification, and Humphrey and Sampson were only willing to subscribe it with the Pauline proviso that if all things were lawful, all things were not expedient. In so doing they remained judges of what was expedient, and Parker's initiative had failed.[21]

It remains an open question whether Parker himself or Cecil or the queen launched the general and less fraternal assault on nonconformity which started in January 1565. On the twenty-fifth of that month Elizabeth wrote a letter to the archbishop which expressed alarm at the growing 'diversity of opinions and specially in the external, decent, and lawful rites and ceremonies to be used in the churches'. Parker and his fellow bishops and commissioners were scolded for their neglect of this dangerous and creeping abuse. 'Varieties, novelties and diversities' were to be investigated and certified forthwith, and no one was in future to be admitted to any ecclesiastical office without a formal promise to observe 'such order and uniformity in all the external rites and ceremonies' as were established. Any 'superior officers' who failed to carry out these orders were to be delated to the queen, and for the purpose of this inquiry no jurisdiction was exempt, the universities and colleges being explicitly included.

The letter was drafted by Cecil who was to be reminded by Parker that he was the initiator of these proceedings and blamed by some of the puritans on the same score. But there is no reason to doubt that Elizabeth's own sense of order was offended by what she had heard of the increasing 'singularity' of many of the clergy, or that she had sound diplomatic reasons for wishing to preserve a dignified and semi-catholic appearance in the Church, of which uniformity in the vestments was an essential part. It was all one with other, studied gestures which followed in Lent: shouting down the unfortunate Dean Nowell in the midst of an attack on images, and reviving the traditional foot-washing rites of Maundy Thursday. She certainly strengthened Cecil's draft in her own hand to order the bishops to use 'all expedition' rather than their 'good discretion'. Yet neither she nor Cecil gave the archbishop much direct support, or any increased authority to execute the new policy. The possibility remains that it was Parker in the first instance who asked for the royal letter to strengthen his hand. We know that Cecil sent him the draft to approve, and it is not impossible that even the queen's sharp amendment of the letter may have been at his own request.[22]

Within a week of receiving his orders, Parker issued instructions through Grindal to all the bishops of the province, requiring them to certify the disorders in their jurisdictions and to use the censures of the Church against all offenders. By early March he and four other bishops had perfected a new standard of uniformity: a book of articles largely compiled from earlier and unofficial resolutions of the bishops for which Parker hoped to secure royal confirmation as an example of 'other order' within the meaning of the Act of Uniformity. No such sanction was ever forthcoming, and when Parker printed and circulated the new articles in March 1566 it was with the unprepossessing title of 'Advertisements', which barely concealed their doubtful constitutional validity as the basis for judicial procedure. So far as it concerned 'the habits', the new code discarded the unrealistic requirement of the eucharistic vestments, except for the cope and that only in cathedral and collegiate churches. But it insisted most explicitly on the surplice and on every detail of clerical outdoor dress. For minds disposed to compromise, this was not an unreasonable standard. But the 'precisians' were in no such mood.[23]

2 That Comical Dress

BARROW. And if it be indifferent, as yow say it is, then doe I wel in not using it.

ARCHBISHOP. Nay, yow doe not wel in refusing it, for therin yow shew yowr self disobedient to the higher powers set over yow by God.

BARROW. Even now yow said it was a thing indifferent; if it be so, ther is no power can bringe me in bondage to my libertie.

(*The Writings of Henry Barrow, 1587-90*, ed. Carlson, Eliz. Nonconformist Texts, iii. 94)

THE QUEEN'S LETTER of January 1565 opened a new chapter. As early as July 1560 the minister of the French church in London had reported a 'great controversy' over the ceremonies which 'grew greater every day.'[1] But here for the first time was an ultimatum, a day of reckoning. Unless they were prepared to abandon their offices to 'Lutherans and semi-papists', as Grindal put it, the émigré bishops could not openly refuse to execute the queen's command against their precise brethren. In the Elizabethan Commonwealth, bishops were not so much fathers of their churches and fellow-ministers of the gospel as 'superior officers' (to use Elizabeth's expression), commissioners for the queen's supreme authority. Their acceptance of episcopal office itself implied the admission that the supreme magistrate had discretionary power to regulate the affairs of the Church, at least in all 'indifferent' matters which were not of the substance of religion. By contrast, those who had evaded these responsibilities could afford to take a different view. The controversy which now began was essentially a debate about the limits of public authority in the sphere of 'things indifferent' – *adiaphora* – and about the definition of the *adiaphora* themselves. On account of what some of the bishops held to be trivia, 'that comical dress', 'these ridiculous trifles',[2] fundamental questions of religious liberty and authority which had troubled English protestants in the past were reopened, and with lasting consequences.

In 1550 John Hooper's consecration as bishop of Gloucester had been delayed while he refused to assume the vestments which the Ordinal required. In explaining himself to the Council Hooper had reduced to almost nothing the discretionary powers of the magistrate in matters of religion. Even things indifferent required general confirmation from the word of God and proof of their evangelical utility. Any religious institution which lacked these credentials was lacking in indifference. For the liberty of a Christian man was simply his duty to be ruled in all things by God's word. Bishop Ridley, on the other hand, who answered Hooper's 'notes', stood in the Anglican tradition established by the Cromwellian publicists of the 1530s when he insisted that such extravagant biblicism destroyed altogether the fruitful and necessary domain of human policy. If anything threatened to take away Christian liberty and to add to the word of God, it was this.[3]

The debate was continued, in effect, in the celebrated 'troubles of Frankfort' during the Marian exile. The Knoxians had based the worship and order of the Frankfort congregation upon their understanding of scripture, whereas Cox's faction pleaded the duty of the congregation to respect a form of service confirmed by public authority and hallowed by its use in Edward's reign. 'They would do as they had done in England; and ... they would have the face of an English Church' – an ungodly preference, in the Knoxian view, for a book whose contents rested only on the warrant of human authority 'and no ground in God's word for the same'. Although by 1559 few of the exiles were still strongly attached to the ceremonies of the 1552 Book, an ominous echo of the old dispute still sounded in the letters which the English congregations exchanged on hearing of Elizabeth's accession. Geneva, seizing the moment with characteristic opportunism, proposed the burying of old contentions over 'superfluous ceremonies ... from the which God of His mercy hath delivered us', and appealed for all good protestants 'to hold fast together.' While Thomas Lever led the Aarau congregation in welcoming this initiative, Frankfort qualified its enthusiasm with the advice that 'as we purpose to submit ourselves to such orders as shall be established by authority, being not of themselves wicked, so we would wish you willingly to do the same.' It was as if they foresaw precisely the situation which would arise in 1565.

The queen's letter to Parker necessarily revived the conflict between those who held with Knox that 'in the Lord's action nothing ought to be used that the Lord Jesus hath not sanctioned neither by precept nor practice' and those who could claim even Calvin on their side in the politic excuse that 'certain things though not positively approved must be tolerated.' A threat to any of the essentials of their religion would have found English protestants united in its defence. The assault on this marginal issue might have been calculated to confound them.[4]

According to the Spanish ambassador, certain of the bishops openly opposed the new orders in a rancorous encounter with Cecil which ended 'to the small satisfaction of some of them, indeed of most'. The report is no doubt exaggerated and out of focus. Yet three bishops – Parkhurst, Sandys and Pilkington – were later praised by the puritans for their 'kind forbearance' in avoiding the enforcement of the Advertisements. In the case of Parkhurst's diocese this restraint was notable, for there must have been scores of nonconformists in Norfolk and Suffolk, even as early as this. But some other diocesans evidently shared the outlook of Archbishop Young of York, who assured the queen that her firmness would be 'a very great comfort to many good subjects that now stand amazed and much discouraged.'[5] Parker himself, Jewel, Cox, Berkeley of Bath and Wells and eventually a reluctant Grindal pursued the cause of uniformity with some vigour. At Oxford, Humphrey and Sampson were threatened with deprivation and in due course Sampson was forced out of his deanery of Christ Church, a sad blow for protestantism in a university where much land remained to be possessed. In March 1566, thirty-seven London ministers were suspended, and some of these were later deprived. There was some action elsewhere. The puritan botanist William Turner was evicted from his deanery of Wells, where, as legend has it, he had trained a pet dog to leap up and snatch the square caps from the heads of conforming clerics. Meanwhile Cecil, as chancellor, had insisted on the strict enforcement of vestiarian uniformity in the university of Cambridge, brushing aside the apprehensions of the vice-chancellor Robert Beaumont (an old Geneva man) and a number of other heads and seniors. The story of the academic *furor* which ensued, and which concerned Cecil's own college of St John's especially, has been told once and for all in Dr H. C. Porter's *Reformation and Reaction in Tudor Cambridge*.[6] For the general history of the controversy, of which only certain aspects are treated here, there is as yet no substitute for the somewhat lapidary periods of the sixth and final volume of Canon Dixon's monumental *History of the Church of England from the Abolition of the Roman Jurisdiction*.[7]

In an apology addressed to the Zürich pastors, who by general consent were expected to umpire this dispute, Grindal and Horne explained that they disliked the vestments as much as anyone and deplored 'these unseasonable contentions'; but that they were persuaded that these were indifferent things which the queen had the right to impose for order's sake and which were not *per se* 'impious, papistical and idolatrous' as their opponents insisted. 'You see me wear a cap or a surplice in Paul's,' Grindal told a group of London puritans. 'I had rather minister without those things, but for order's sake and obedience to the prince.' In Cambridge Beaumont protested to his critics that if he refused to wear the cap and surplice he would not be suffered to preach. 'I wish with many more godly brethren that they may speedily be taken away: the which should shortly be brought to pass if I were the public person for such matters, lawfully authorized. But now my hands are tied.' Grindal and Horne suggested to Bullinger of Zürich that to side with the puritans might alienate the unpredictable mind of the queen from true religion altogether. The Erastianism of Elizabethan Anglicanism was now nakedly revealed.[8]

The split in the Church was no less real or painful for these fraternal regrets. Horne informed Zürich that 'our little flock has divided itself into two parties.' 'And so', echoed an obscure London clergyman who kept some record of these events, 'the gracious knot of Christian charity is broken.' When the bishops frustrated a move to have the cause of the nonconformists debated at the Convocation of 1566, the puritan who sponsored the motion retorted: 'We thought the queen was the author of this business, but we now perceive that you yourselves are.'

At first the nonconformists had been as eager as the bishops to treat the affair as a regrettable difference of opinion among friends, 'evangelical not papistical, fraternal, not fratricidal'.[9] On March 20th, 1565, twenty of them submitted an appeal to the Ecclesiastical Commissioners requesting their forbearance. Until recently, this letter was known only from the copy in Cecil's papers, ascribed in Cecil's endorsement to Humphrey and Sampson alone. The discovery of the original has revealed that the left wing of the Church was already acting as a coherent party.[10] Besides the two Oxford leaders, the signatories included Whittingham and Lever together with a number of leading men from the diocese of London: Nowell, the dean of St Paul's; the three archdeacons of London, Essex and Middlesex, Mullins, Cole and Calfhill; old Miles Coverdale with John Foxe and Percival Wiburn; and three incumbents who would presently emerge as leaders of militant dissent in the city, Robert Crowley, John Philpot and John Gough. Thirteen of the twenty names had appeared on the list of hotter protestants recommended to Lord Robert Dudley four or five years before, and all but three had been exiles. But the tone of the letter was mild. The subscribers begged to be excused from the necessity of conforming, much as Beaumont and his Cambridge colleagues would soon plead an exemption for the university. But their implication was that resistance would not be prolonged if the Commissioners should refuse their modest request. This was not the voice of puritanism, and although we may count these progressives of the exile as the original puritan party, it was not to them that the label was to stick. Only three of the twenty, Coverdale, Sampson and Wiburn, remained staunch to the radical cause until their deaths, and Coverdale was dead within three years. For more than half of the suppliants conformity seems to have followed almost at once. This was the end rather than the beginning of their dissent.

The real crisis came in London a year later.[11] London churches tended to set the tone for the whole Church of England and nonconformity was nowhere more strongly entrenched or more ably led. In Parker's opinion, 'a few in London rule over this matter.' Yet as Bishop Cox had assured him, 'if London were reformed, all the realm would soon follow.' It was a case of *purga Romam, purgatur mundus*. As for London's bishop, Grindal was so reluctant to forfeit the confidence and goodwill of 'the godly' that he would not apply effective remedies without a very direct and personal charge from the queen, reducing his own responsibility. But the Court was silent (to Parker's disgust) and Grindal correspondingly inactive, so that the puritans were soon boasting that 'my lord of London is their own ... and is but brought in against his will.' At Easter 1565 both Humphrey and Sampson were appointed to preach at Paul's Cross, presumably by Grindal, at the very time when the archbishop was making plans for their deprivation. Grindal's visitation of the following month led to the temporary suspension of a few ministers but was no credible deterrent for the more intransigent nonconformists. Robert Crowley, their leader and organizer, later claimed that the vestments had been attacked from the pulpits in Grindal's diocese 'without any great contradiction'.

So one can imagine. In the autumn of 1565 Crowley himself 'took occasion to inveigh against the popish ceremonies' in more than one Paul's Cross sermon, and to inform his audience that it was not 'sober apparel for the prophets to use the apparel of the priests of the ethnics.' Paul's Cross continued to ring with a puritan note throughout the winter. The new year began with an attack on Christmas 'because it was made rather a feast of Bacchus than a true serving of the memory of Jesus Christ.' The preacher was John Gough, rector of St Stephen's, Cornhill, and one of Crowley's lieutenants. He attacked the decking of the churches with holly, over-eating and card-playing 'and to do also what we lust, because it is Christmas.' Lawful, healthy games were, of course, tolerable, 'but give an inch and they will take an ell.'[12]

All this time Grindal was charting a course of his own. No doubt he thought, and with justification, that he understood the precisians better than Parker did. At a meeting with his clergy which seems to have taken place early in 1566, he successfully commended a compromise by which all but a few Marians agreed to adopt the surplice and a novel form of outdoor dress which was distinctive but lacked either popish or foreign protestant associations. But Parker could tolerate no deviation from the programme of the Advertisements – nor, it appears, would the queen, though she still withheld overt support – and in March the archbishop wrote with some bitterness of 'other men' who slipped their heads 'out of the collar, and convey the envy otherwise.' This was the end of Grindal's non-cooperation. By March 20th he had toed the line, and when one hundred and ten London clergy obeyed a summons to Lambeth on the 26th they faced both their diocesan and the metropolitan, though not the senior privy councillors whom Parker and Grindal had hopefully invited to assist them. The clergy were confronted with a clerical mannequin and a peremptory demand to subscribe their willingness to assume the same costume: 'Be brief: make no words.' According to a puritan report they were asked besides whether they were willing to acquiesce in the royal proceedings in matters of religion 'ordained and to be ordained'. Thirty-seven declined and were at once suspended from their functions. The fruits of their benefices were sequestered and they were threatened with deprivation within three months if they remained obdurate. These did not include Miles Coverdale, who had absented himself. One of the non-subscribers was surprised that he had so few supporters: 'Behold, the inconstancy of man in trial.' Yet they seem to have included such distinguished divines as James Calfhill, Thomas Becon and John Foxe.[13]

It was an odd time of year in which to strike. Some churches were deprived of all ministrations a mere fortnight before Holy Week, and on the three Sundays of the Easter season there were serious disturbances in a number of parishes, either because there was no minister to serve the cure at all, or because the puritans organized noisy demonstrations against the conforming clergy who were intruded to fill their places. The High Commissioners sat daily to deal with 'brabbling matters', unsupported by queen or Council. By the end of April Parker was an exhausted and despondent man. The Advertisements were now in print, but their title only thinly disguised the fact that they lacked royal authority.[14]

To the godly mind, the most serious aspect of this dislocation was the silencing of the pulpits. In an angry letter to Cecil, the old Genevan elder

Thomas Wood made the pointed claim that among those suspended were many 'that travailed in preaching of the word with more zeal and diligence than many others of greater calling', so that almost all the regular preaching exercises in the city were 'utterly overthrown'. Wood complained particularly of the interruption of the daily lectures at St Antholin's, where all three lecturers had been suspended, and of the suspension of a weekly exercise of 'prophesying' held on Thursdays at 'St Peter's' (St Peter's, Cornhill or St Peter-le-Poer). But according to John Stow, some of these preachers defied the ban and in their sermons openly attacked the queen, the Council and the bishops. In these turbulent weeks, puritanism was given definition by 'the ministers of London', and it was these preachers who first took the significant step of publicizing their cause in print. The leaders of what their opponents called 'this small rout' were the three St Antholin's lecturers: Robert Crowley, the printer of *Piers Plowman* and a noted preacher of the school of Latimer, John Philpot and John Gough. All three had parishes elsewhere in the city and Crowley, incongruously enough, was a considerable pluralist, vicar of St Giles Cripplegate, rector of St Peter-le-Poer, prebendary of St Paul's and archdeacon of Hereford. The parish lecturer at St Giles, John Bartlett, completed the militant leadership.

These were 'the greatest animators of all the whole city to do the like, upon whom the greatest number of other ministers did depend.' Stow tells us that besides preaching against the bishops they distributed 'at their morning congregatings' two printed tracts. One of these was the famous *Briefe discourse against the outwarde apparell*, the earliest puritan manifesto. Crowley had set this tract in its final order, but Stow says that the materials were supplied by the 'whole multitude of London ministers, every one of them giving their advice in writing.' The *Briefe discourse* argued that the habits were things indifferent in themselves, but that by leading 'simple Christians' into idolatry they had ceased to be indifferent. The ministers thought it their duty 'utterly to refuse' to conform and were willing to suffer 'whatsoever punishment the laws do appoint in this case', an echo of Hooper's truculence sixteen years before. This marked the end of merely fraternal disagreement. In its concluding paragraphs the tract insinuates that 'the earnest solicitors of this matter ... are not, neither were at any time protestants: but when time would serve them they were bloody persecutors, and since time failed them they have borne back as much as lay in them', which seems to be a cruel and unjustified slur on Parker's reputation and perhaps on Cecil's as well. An official reply was prepared, possibly by Parker himself, *A briefe examination ... of a certaine declaration*. This accepted the new bitterness of invective and replied in the same coin, speaking of the 'superfluous brawlings of men perverse in heart, from whom the truth is withdrawn.' Crowley at once retorted with *An answere for the tyme to the examination*.[15]

From the puritan side there were further salvoes, including *Two short and comfortable epistles* addressed to 'my loving brethren that is troubled about the popish apparel', and printed abroad, possibly at Emden. The first of these was written by Anthony Gilby from the security of the earl of Huntingdon's patronage at Ashby-de-la-Zouch to Coverdale, Turner, Whittingham, Sampson, Humphrey, Lever, Crowley and others, 'who being in authority are first called to the battle to strive for God's glory.' In print these names were discreetly suppressed, as were some of the epistle's more intemperate expressions. It appeared under a separate cover in the same year as the preface to a tract called *The hunting of the fox and the wolfe, because they make havocke of the sheepe of Christ*. This was nothing else but a reprint of William Turner's *Huntyng of the Romyshe vuolfe*, first printed at Zürich in 1554. The implication was unmistakable. Turner's attack on the Marian prelates as 'false prophets, wolves, thieves and murderers' was now held to be applicable to their Elizabethan successors. (Those who had read the earlier 'animal' pamphlets by John Bale and Turner would know that the fox symbolized covert popery.)

Gilby's epistle later appeared as the preface to his own *Pleasaunt dialogue betweene a souldior of Barwicke and an English chaplaine*, an early puritan exercise in the art of 'pleasant' badinage which would one day give birth to Martin Marprelate. One smells the true tang of puritan satire in the description of the conforming cleric who 'didst jet up and down so solemnly in the church, and so like an old popish prelate', and who boasts that though unlearned he is now 'no more of the lewd laity, but of the holy spirituality, and I have gotten a good benefice or twain, and am called Master Parson, and may spend with the best man in our town.' One finds, too, the bitterest attack yet made upon the 'lordly bishops', maintainers of 'this filthy ware': 'Repent ye proud prelates, and join hands once again with your poor persecuted brethren, to root out all popery, or else your fall will be perilous.' Gilby struck at more than the vestments, 'this bloody beast's gear': an appendix lists 'an hundred points of popery yet remaining, which deform the English reformation.' Although written in 1566, the dialogue was suppressed until 1573 'of charity', and because until then the author still hoped to see the bishops relent. Others were less restrained. Crowley's tracts are spattered with contemptuous references to 'these prelates', and Thomas Wood, reporting a practical joke played on the vice-chancellor by the Cambridge undergraduates, comments: 'If they had served all our bishops ... in like sort, they should never be accused for me.'[16]

The two parties were still more sharply differentiated in their rival efforts to gain the support of the leading centres of continental reform. Humphrey and Sampson had written to Bullinger, ostensibly for resolution of their difficulties, in reality to enlist the Zürich pastors on their side. In an age when so much correspondence was of a semi-public character, this was an accepted polemical manœuvre. But Bullinger had already assured Bishop Horne of his conviction that it was not expedient to abandon the ministry to 'wolves' for a matter in which only public order and no superstition was involved. [17] He now offered the same advice to the nonconformists themselves in the course of a detailed reply to all their questions, and warned them against concealing 'a contentious spirit under the name of conscience'.[18] Bullinger thought it improper to have private dealings with two inferior ministers, and saw to it that copies of this letter reached all the bishops known to him personally, and Grindal. Grindal at once had his copy printed in Latin and English, without the author's knowledge or consent. According to the bishops the document had a steadying effect, and deterred many who might otherwise have left the ministry. But there was a sharp reaction from the more intransigent puritan circles, where the Zürich pastors were denounced as at worst deviationists and at best deluded dupes of the bishops.

Hoist with their own petard, Humphrey and Sampson complained to Bullinger and broke into recriminations against their oppressors: 'We have always thought well of the bishops; we have put a candid interpretation upon their display of grandeur: why cannot they endure us who formerly bore the same cross with them? ... Why do they cast us into prison? Why do they persecute us on account of the habits?' They were now stung into the claim that far more was at stake than vestments, so magnifying the issues by which the Church was divided. They complained, among other things, of 'a kind of popish superstition' pervading all Anglican worship, of the utter lack of discipline, and even of the inadequate eucharistic doctrine of the Articles. Joined by Coverdale, they now turned to Geneva and sent Farel, Beza and their colleagues a sensational report of events which spoke of the bishops turning their houses into prisons for preachers and 'raging against their own bowels.' 'Thus you have the image and representation, such as it is, of our Church.'[19]

These letters were accompanied by a delegation to the Swiss churches. In the summer of 1566 one of the London ministers, Percival Wiburn, travelled to Geneva with two puritan gentlemen, one of them Andrew Kingsmill, an Oxford lawyer and lay theologian and brother of two puritan M.P.s who had sat in the Parliament of 1563. Theodore Beza, Calvin's Elisha, accepted their extravagant indictment and sent Wiburn on to Zürich with the strongest recommendation and the proposal that Rodolph Gualter, a name to conjure with in England, should himself visit the scene of the dispute. The Zürichers received the puritan emissary with diffidence, but proved open to persuasion that there was more amiss with England than a few vestiarian trifles. They now wrote a number of letters which redressed the balance of their earlier advice. Grindal and Horne were reproached for their underhand dealing and Coverdale was offered an apology.[20]

Gualter, always more sympathetic to the puritans than Bullinger, was particularly unguarded in a letter to Parkhurst, an old friend from Oxford days, which, while congratulating him on refusing to deprive any ministers in his own diocese, censured most of his colleagues, comparing them to the faithless steward in the parable. 'For I do not see much difference between his conduct and theirs, who so readily give their sanction to the crotchets of superstitious courtiers, and treat godly ministers with so much cruelty.' When Cox came across Gualter's letter five years later, he sent the writer an angry reproof: 'These imputations are very hard, and very far from the truth.' But worse was to follow, for Parkhurst had allowed copies of the letter to fall into the wrong hands. It was tit for tat when, in the summer of 1572, the puritans pressed it into service as an appendix to the infamous *Admonition to the Parliament*. All this placed a severe strain on the sentimental bridges which linked the émigré bishops to Zürich. But by 1572 English puritanism had taken a still more radical turn and was associated with trends in the continental reformed churches which Zürich itself deplored, so that Gualter was by then eager to explain his letter to Parkhurst as a passing aberration. 'Since that time we have certainly had nothing to do with those vain brawlers, who neither at any time wrote to us, nor had it in their power to boast of any letters from us.' He now repaired the damage by dedicating his homilies on First Corinthians to Grindal, Sandys, Horne, Cox, Parkhurst and Pilkington, with an epistle which extolled the unity in diversity of the true churches of God and was intended, as he told Cox, for a 'public attestation of my regard for yourselves and the Anglican churches'. But when John Whitgift published Gualter's letter to Cox in his *Answer to the admonition* the Züricher was again understandably vexed. The Swiss were out of their depth in this English quarrel which had moved far beyond the kind of fraternal difference in which they felt competent to intervene.[21]

In the summer of 1567 two more puritan ambassadors had appeared on the Continent: John Bartlett, the lecturer at St Giles Cripplegate, and George Withers, a Cambridge man who was now to play a significant part in the establishment of a severe Calvinist discipline in the Palatinate. Bartlett and Withers conducted themselves like exiles. In an appeal to the Elector Palatine, Frederick III, the rising hope of the Genevan party throughout Europe, they spoke of 'the Church of England now lying prostrate and ... on the very brink of destruction', virtually without ministry or discipline. The bishops were said to have acted against conscience in accepting their dignities and to have 'excited the hatred of all, and especially of the godly, against them.' The elector was asked to write to Elizabeth and to take 'especial care to transfer all the blame from the queen unto the bishops.' Here were all the ingredients of the extreme, presbyterian puritanism of the immediate future.[22]

Geneva, as might be expected, proved more susceptible to these frenzied appeals than Zürich or even Heidelberg. To be sure Beza trod somewhat delicately in his correspondence with England. He was reluctant to believe what was told him of the bishops, and even to the puritans continued to speak of them with evident respect. Moreover, he valued such small influence as Geneva possessed with the English authorities, and which might evaporate altogether if he appeared as an open partisan of the nonconformists. Yet he was prompted by Wiburn's visit in 1566 to write a very plain letter to Grindal which the puritans were later happy to print as a further appendix to the *Admonition*. 'I must needs confess that I am astonished and amazed so often as I think of these things,' he wrote in conclusion of a lengthy review of the shortcomings of the English Church. A year later he responded to many urgent requests with a letter of advice for the puritans themselves, which Bartlett probably took home with him. The English aberrations in ceremonies and polity were roundly condemned: Beza and his colleagues thought it 'almost incredible that such a perverse abuse' should still exist in a reformed church as the English manner of excommunication. They themselves would not dream of exercising their ministry under such conditions. The puritans, however, were advised to bear with what they could not alter and above all not to found their own sects. 'It is better to have something than nothing.' But if they were asked positively to approve these abuses by subscription, they must refuse, even at the cost of their ministry. 'But we prophesy better things for England than these extremities.' Only in his letters to Zürich did Beza allow his feelings full rein. 'What good can be expected in

England, while things remain as they are? ... If the case is as I know it to be (and indeed these things can scarcely be invented) where did such a Babylon ever exist?'[23]

Radical and precocious the nascent puritan party had shown itself to be in both thought and action, yet the suspended and deprived ministers made no concerted effort to challenge the dubious legality of the proceedings taken against them. At this stage we are not witnessing the alliance with the lawyers which was to be so marked a feature of the puritan movement in the 'eighties and in the early seventeenth century. Parker and the Commissioners for their part dealt with the London ministers with rather more determination than even Archbishop Whitgift was able to summon up twenty years later. The ringleaders were sent out of town: Gough and Philpot to Horne in the diocese of Winchester where they were beneficed. Their departure over London Bridge was celebrated by two or three hundred women laden with bags and bottles full of all kinds of comforts, and 'animating them most earnestly to stand fast in the same their doctrine.' Crowley and Bartlett remained for a time in London, Crowley boasting that he had 'friends enough to have set the whole realm together by the ears.' He probably meant the earl of Leicester, who was Bartlett's patron as well. But for all that Crowley was soon sent to the custody of Bishop Cox at Ely.[24]

With the removal of the militant leadership, the resistance of those left behind soon crumpled, undermined by financial exigency. Married clergy could not lightly contemplate the loss of a hardly-won living, and Parker showed that he would not hesitate to proceed to deprivation when he ordained (as one of the suspended men complained) 'quisque and quibuscunque to place in our rooms.' By July 1566 only eight London incumbents, three parish lecturers and three or four curates still held out. The rest were lost to the radical cause, many of them for ever. The implacable nonconformist incumbents were all deprived: they included Crowley, Philpot, Gough and Wiburn. Coverdale resigned his living in the same year and Bartlett was among the lecturers now permanently silenced. But Philpot returned from Winchester in the early autumn a subscriber, sold up his goods and retired to Rye in Sussex. There he found a living worth thirty pounds a year where there was no need to wear a surplice. He even recovered his former benefices in the city. Not all the London nonconformists found so realistic and cynical a solution to their problem. Philpot was 'much rebuked of his brethren.' Yet even Crowley later conformed and was rewarded with another London parish and the scorn of the next generation of radicals. The rest either left London behind them (for example Wiburn, who was soon preaching drastic reformation in Northampton) or scattered into the ecclesiastical wilderness of roving, unbeneficed preachers. It is there that we must now follow them, and the puritan movement.[25]

3 London's Protestant Underworld[1]

'It is no great inconvenience though some parishes want in London. London is no grange. They may go elsewhere. But these precise men, for all their brag of six hundred communicants, do profess openly, that they will neither communicate nor come in the church where either the surplice or the cap is, and so I know is practised.'

(ARCHBISHOP PARKER TO CECIL, Good Friday, April 12th, 1566, *Parker Correspondence*, p. 279)

THE EVENTS OF 1566 for ever dissociated the beneficed parish clergy of London from the clerical leadership of the puritan movement. Parker and Grindal had done their work so effectively that few truly radical incumbents were left, and it was not until the following century that the Anglican church polity was again seriously threatened from the relative respectability of the London parsonages. The record of preachers at Paul's Cross provides one useful index of the change that now came over the ecclesiastical scene. Before March 1566 the nonconformists were the most regular preachers at the Cross: Crowley appeared there at least eight times and Coverdale six. Of twenty sermons preached between June 1565 and the following March, nine were by subscribers of the anti-vestiarian petition of March 1565, and their tone was militantly protestant. But thereafter almost all the preachers were clergy who had conformed.[2] This is not to say that London now lost its importance as a puritan centre. On the contrary, in the 'seventies and even more in the 'eighties, the capital would serve as the nerve-centre of an organized clerical agitation for further reformation. But the London preachers whose strategically central position made them natural leaders of this movement would not be incumbents, unlike the majority of their correspondents in the country on whom they would strive to impose their generally more inflexible policies.

When the puritans spoke of 'the church in London' they meant, in effect, a group of unbeneficed stipendiary curates and preachers, some of them lecturers in the parish churches or in the inns of court, others lacking even that measure of settled responsibility. There were many ways in which a preacher could pick up a living in Elizabethan London, almost as many as when the careless colleague of Chaucer's poor parson 'ran to London, un-to seynt Poules, to seken him a chaunterie for soules.' The standing of these hirelings might seem at first glance to be precarious, lacking as they did the proprietary security which enabled a Robert Crowley to boast that he was master of his own parish. A licence to preach or serve a cure was no freehold. But it was not easy to drive such men out of London altogether. Some niche always remained, if only in a private household. As the queen herself once had occasion to complain, London was a city 'where every merchant must have his schoolmaster and nightly conventicles, expounding scriptures and catechizing their servants and maids', so that servant-girls were heard 'to control learned preachers and say that such a man taught otherwise in our house.'[3] The casual preacher had less to lose than the incumbent, even if he lost it more easily, and he could afford the extremism which his relatively irresponsible situation encouraged. So although they might minister in parish churches, the small army of salaried lecturers and curates who were attracted by the teeming religious life of the capital had a much more tenuous connection with the institutional Church than the beneficed clergy. They were dependent directly upon their auditories for both appointment and remuneration, and lecturers could set the Prayer Book entirely aside and even plead ignorance of its contents. These were the natural successors of the preaching friars, and many of them observed an old tradition in their disregard of episcopal discipline. Here was the 'church within the Church' par excellence, and it was a disturbing consequence of Parker's spring offensive that they were henceforth able to assume control of the puritan movement at its very heart.

Among this circle were two of the ex-incumbents deprived in 1566: Nicholas Standon and Edward Saintloe (or Sinclair). But the future leaders came into London after 1566 and were never in a beneficed ministry in their lives. There was a hint of this development at the time of the Lambeth proceedings, when Thomas Wood reported that the St Antholin's lecture was temporarily sustained by 'such godly young men as having no spiritual livings were not called before the Commissioners.'[4] These new preachers probably included two Oxford graduates who would later seize the initiative with the publication of their explosive manifesto, An admonition to the Parliament: John Field and Thomas Wilcox.

Field was a Londoner born and bred, supported at Oxford by the

Clothworkers' Company,[5] and he seems to have been ordained priest by Grindal (although aged only twenty-one) on March 25th, 1566, the day before the fateful meeting at Lambeth. It was an appropriate start to the career of the organizing secretary of Elizabethan presbyterianism. By April 12th Parker had silenced these 'new coming preachers to London' and Field probably returned to Oxford, where one of his name proceeded M.A. in 1567. But if so he was back in London within a year, preaching in the parish of Holy Trinity Minories and acting as curate at Crowley's old parish of St Giles Cripplegate. The experience of the next five years would strengthen Field's naturally pugnacious qualities, and would turn him into a dedicated revolutionary, a militant Calvinist whose capacity for leadership was acknowledged internationally as well as within English puritan circles. In speaking of him, we are introducing the principal character in the drama. 'As God hath his Moses,' he would say, 'so he hath his Elijah'; and 'it is no time to blench, nor to sew cushions under men's elbows, or to flatter them in their sins.' 'Brother Wilcox', at this time curate in the parish of All Hallows Honey Lane, was the younger man, and tended to be Field's subordinate. He, to be sure, was no Elijah, but rather one of the earliest of the 'affectionate, practical' puritans, the spiritual directors of Calvinism. For this reason, his collected works were edited and appreciated in the seventeenth century and his 'comfortable' letters preserved at a time when Field was all but forgotten. The list of his correspondents – the letters are no longer extant – suggests the nature of Wilcox's contribution to the cause of further reformation: it included those interrelated puritan worthies Peter Wentworth, the parliament man, Robert Beale, clerk of the Council, and his wife, and Lady Walsingham, the wife of the secretary; besides Lord and Lady Zouche, Sir Fulke Greville, Lady Ann Bacon, Lady Mary Grey, Sir John Brocket, Sir John Cutts, Charles Morrison, the countess of Sussex and others.[6]

The liberty of the Minories, where both Field and Wilcox preached, Field for a short time as curate, was the original home of puritanism in the sense that it seems to have been with 'the godly' who frequented its parish church that the name was first associated. There can be little doubt that the sobriquet originated in London, and John Stow, writing in 1567, says that a group 'who called themselves puritans or unspotted lambs of the Lord ... kept their church in the Minories without Aldgate.' (These would almost certainly be opprobrious labels attached to them, not what they called themselves.) No earlier use of the term in English has been recorded, although John Bale had written from Basle in 1556 of 'our new Catharites', and of 'their church of the purity'.

The Minories was a liberty for purposes of civil administration, with closely-guarded privileges. Moreover, the Sisters of St Clare had bequeathed a legacy of independence from the ordinary arrangements of ecclesiastical government. The newly-created parish of Holy Trinity Minories at this time successfully claimed exemption from the bishop's jurisdiction, and independence in the appointment of its ministers. As a donative curacy, the parishioners themselves possessed the right to appoint their curate, without any process of presentation or ecclesiastical institution and induction, and to support him from the rectorial dues which they themselves collected. In addition the parish hired lecturers, apparently more than one. At the time of which Stow writes, their choice of both curate and preachers seems to have been virtually confined to tested and radical puritans. If Field and Wilcox preached some of their first sermons from this pulpit, it was here that almost the last words were heard from Coverdale (himself an ex-Augustinian friar!). Coverdale's patron, the duchess of Suffolk, owned property in the parish and her chaplains, Browne and Pattenson, both preached there. Almost all the preachers associated in the inception of the weekly conferences organized by Field and Wilcox from about 1570 were to be seen and heard in this church. It is unlikely that their auditory was genuinely parochial; in all probability it was composed of godly-minded persons from all parts of the city and its suburbs. As Parker remarked on one occasion, 'London is no grange', and Londoners had their pick of churches. As for the preachers, Pattenson was not afraid to tell the authorities that he was in the habit of preaching 'wheresoever I do meet with a congregation that are willing to hear the word of God preached at my mouth.' But the Minories was probably the home of the puritan congregation in a special sense. One of its preachers, one Seth Jackson, refers to it in his last testament as the 'congregation of Christ', and he gave the church a residuary interest in his estate. Perhaps we shall not be far wrong if we identify the Minories congregation with the puritan 'chapel' referred to in an anti-puritan pamphlet of 1566: 'Resort to your chapel in London, and let me see in the whole form of your secret service one prayer for any that is in authority.'[7]

It was in the radical nexus of preachers and hearers who gathered in the Minories, amongst other places, that a new and more extreme puritanism was nourished. It is hardly worth discussing whether its character was or was not 'separatist' or even 'congregationalist', although these are problems to which the historians of congregationalism, Dexter, Burrage, Peel and others, have devoted much attention. At this primitive stage these groups were not identified with any very definite or exclusive church principle. Preachers like Field were later to overcome any leanings they may have had towards separatism, rejecting any notion of dissolving the comprehensive, national Church, or of departing from it. Yet Stow calls the puritans of the Minories 'anabaptists', by which he presumably means that they were sectaries with a bent to break away from their parish churches and to establish congregations of their own. He almost equates the Minories church with a succession of ephemeral conventicles, 'many congregations of the anabaptists', which in the early months of 1568 met at various times on a lighter in St Katherine's Pool, in a house in Thames Street, in Pudding Lane, in Mountjoy Place (apparently with Grindal's connivance) and in a goldsmith's house in the Strand. Such transient congregations were probably a recurrent element in Elizabethan London life. Twenty years later the separatists met in private houses in the winter, and in summer in the fields around the city and in one of the 'summer houses' in the gardens outside Bishopsgate, close by Bedlam and Moorfields.[8]

In June 1567 about a hundred of these godly Londoners were apprehended by the sheriff after hiring Plumbers' Hall, ostensibly for a wedding. In the following March six of the eight spokesmen for this group reappear in a list of seventy-seven persons arrested on premises near the Savoy belonging to the goldsmith James Tynne. Their homes were in no less than forty-two separate streets and localities, as various as Aldgate, Southwark, St Martin's in the Fields, Holborn, Islington and Smithfield. Two of their preachers, Nicholas Crane and William Bonham, were later employed in the Minories as lecturers after the release of these puritans from Bridewell in 1569. It seems reasonably clear that in all these places and on all these occasions we are coming across what was essentially the same congregation, created by the stimulating experience of persecution which, as the separatists told John Knox, 'brought many a hundred to know one another that never knew before.'[9]

Fortunately we possess an authentic account of the aspirations and doings of these people in the examination of the Plumbers' Hall leaders, held before Grindal and the Commissioners in June 1567 and carefully 'registered' by the puritans.[10] On this occasion 'the ancientest of them' explained that he and his friends had not separated from their parish churches or assembled in private houses so long as they had preaching and the administration of the sacraments 'without the preferring of idolatrous gear about it ... But when it came to this point, that all our preachers were displaced by your law, that would not subscribe to your apparel and your law, so that we could not hear none of them in any church by the space of seven or eight weeks, except Father Coverdale, of whom we have a good opinion, and yet (God knoweth) the man was so fearful, that he durst not be known unto us where he preached, though we sought it at his house – and then were we troubled and commanded to your courts from day to day, for not coming to our parish churches – then we bethought us what were best to do.' They recalled that there was 'a congregation of us in this city in Queen Mary's days; and a congregation at Geneva, which used a book and order of preaching, ministering of the sacraments and discipline, most agreeable to the word of God.' So they revived the Marian 'privy churches', using (as the Marian congregations had not) the book and order of Geneva. No other record that we possess tells us more about the origins and motivation of Elizabethan separatism than this.

Our preachers! Your law, your courts and your apparel! It is clear that these puritans were already virtual sectarians before the crisis of 1566. Their attachment was to their preachers (though it was scarcely an un-critical attachment), not to the parish church. But we may perhaps call them 'circumstantial separatists' since there is no evidence in their testi-mony that they had consciously made an irrevocable act of secession. On the contrary, their apology implied that they would return to their parishes when they could hear sound preachers who were not obliged to wear 'idolatrous gear'. Meanwhile they had taken no steps to elect their own officers or otherwise to set up an independent sectarian organization. Yet the recollection of the Marian precedent is most significant. The puritans now found themselves in prison, and the fact that they kept a record of their examination, evidently modelled on the accounts of Marian trials in Foxe's 'Book of Martyrs' (it is the earliest surviving puritan document of this kind), implies that they saw themselves in an analogous situation. Some of them later wrote of their handling by 'the popish court' and 'in popish excommunication and imprisonment'.[11] Under questioning, the Plumbers' Hall men rated the strict observance of the Prayer Book little higher than the mass, and condemned 'a great company' of London clergy as unrepentant papists whose churches they would not enter; and yet 'you thrust out the godly.' Clearly they counted ✓ as true churches of God those congregations of the Church of England where godly preachers had banished popish ceremony and preached true doctrine. Any articulate group of puritan laymen, pressed to locate the true Church, might well have revealed the same opinion.

It was probably after their release from Bridewell in April 1569 that some members of this puritan society went beyond this position and deliberately separated themselves from the establishment. Their gathered church was now supplied with a form of covenant, subscribed by the members on their admission, and with elected officers and the discipline of excommunication. By about 1570 there seems to have been more than one of these sects, the sequel to schism. For Browne, the duchess of Suffolk's chaplain, writes of 'four or five churches divided one from another, so that one of them either cannot or will not join, one with another.' Alas, we know precious little about what Dr Albert Peel boldly identified as the first congregational churches, and nothing at all about Richard Fitz, who evidently provided the intellectual leadership for the separation. But we have the names of twenty-five members of Fitz's church; seven were among those taken at Tynne the goldsmith's in 1568 and one of their preachers was Pattenson, another of the duchess of Suffolk's protégés. A deacon, Thomas Bowland, had been a spokesman for the Plumbers' Hall group at their examination, while one of the elders, John Bolton, is probably to be identified with a weaver who spent the last two years of Mary's reign in Geneva. Later Bolton recanted, suffered excommunication from the rest of the congregation, and finally hanged himself, providing fertile material for anti-separatist pamphleteers.[12] Some members of these congregations remained in prison at least until 1581, at which time they still preserved the text of their covenant. This document, of which more than one version survives,[13] binds to the true Church of Christ those who have separated from Antichrist and 'the church of the traditioners'. These 'anabaptists' did not symbolize their restitution of the true Church by undergoing rebaptism, but they did partake of the communion 'for ratification of their assent', as Parker tells us in an endorsement of a copy of the covenant. Among the motives for secession, the covenant lays emphasis on the necessity for true discipline in the body of Christ. 'For in the church of the traditioners there is none other discipline, but that which hath been ordained by the Antichristian popes of Rome.'

Grindal reports that Humphrey, Sampson, Lever and other prominent nonconformists refused to condone this separation, and that the puritans responded by repudiating them as semi-papists and banning attendance at their sermons. The historical 'register' of puritan documents amassed by Field contains a number of letters which confirm the disagreement between the separatists and such preachers as Lever, Turner, Browne and John Knox, who was drawn into the controversy when Grindal sent some of the leaders up to Scotland in 1569. All these relatively conservative puritans expressed faith in the Church of England, with or without ceremonies, as a valid part of the body of Christ. Knox, for example, in condemning the separation, pointed out that 'it condemneth the public ministry of England.' On the other hand, 'a certain brother, a minister' wrote from Geneva encouraging the separatists 'to begin the work of building in an other place ... leaving these men's sermons and preachings ...'[14]

Yet these differences were not so sharply defined as they may appear to the modern observer, and it is in no exclusive sense that any of the modern free churches can claim to have found its ultimate forebears in Plumbers' Hall or even in Fitz's church. The over-enthusiastic pursuit of denominational genealogy may well distort the blurred image that we have of these sects, which in its very indistinctness possesses a certain validity. The quarrel of the separatists with the more conservative preachers was about the attitude to be adopted towards the 'traditioners', not about the constitution of the ideal church, and presbyterianism and independency were not yet defined in mutual contradistinction. The leading separatists desired to associate themselves with the French and Dutch congregations in London and with the Scottish Church and told John Knox: 'We desire no other order than you hold.'[15]

4 The People and the Pope's Attire

'John Sharp sayd when he did se the minister wer the surplice that the fole had gotten on his fooles cote, and did axe [ask] the minister yf he wolde have yt to kepe him warme?'

(Court proceedings, archdeaconry of Colchester, 1585;
Essex Record Office, D/ACA/13, fol. 161ᵛ)

WHAT LITTLE WE KNOW of these sects and semi-sects provides ground on which to challenge the unwarranted assumption that the earliest tensions and conflicts in English protestantism aroused only clerics and intellectuals. Admittedly we are not yet witnessing that concerted agitation by lawyers and country gentlemen which was to be a formidable armament of dissent in the 1580s and the early years of James I. The political overtones of those later struggles would owe a great deal to the dangers, real and imagined, of resurgent, post-Tridentine catholicism, which were not strongly felt in the 'sixties. Yet it was in the midst of the vestments controversy that the earl of Leicester first showed his colours as the best friend that the radicals possessed. Thomas Wood, an old dependant of the Dudleys, later acknowledged that the earl had deserved well of the nonconformists in the beginning of their troubles, when he was 'their chiefest and in manner their only patron'. At about this time Humphrey, Sampson, Lever, Whittingham, Coverdale, Bartlett and, probably, Crowley, all looked in his direction for support. He would soon go out of his way to help even that unfortunate Calvinist pariah, Christopher Goodman. It was the earl who persuaded Grindal to appoint Humphrey and Sampson to preach at Paul's Cross in the very month when Parker was arranging for their deprivation. And at this time the rumour went around that 'my lord of Leicester ... shall move and obtain the queen's majesty, and this thing is now done in his absence.' Elizabeth's insistence on ceremonial uniformity had its political and even its diplomatic implications. No less, it may yet appear, did Leicester's subversion of her policy.[1]

Parker's actions were probably viewed with little enthusiasm by most of the committed protestants in positions of central or local authority. He would later be told by the Privy Council that there was no question of dealing with the preachers 'as in popish time', notorious nonconformists though they might be. They must be given a fair hearing, and, it was implied, the benefit of the doubt.[2] This may well explain why the bishops found the Court so unhelpful in the moment of crisis, and why the ceremonial standards of Parker's *Advertisements* were not widely imposed outside London and the universities. If there was no outcry from the protestant gentry in 1565–7, this was because in counties like Essex and Suffolk very few preachers were disturbed. In London, of course, it was another matter. There the riotous events and later the schisms which accompanied the enforcement of uniformity suggest that perhaps four or five hundred citizens objected to the 'popish ceremonies' more stridently than the ministers themselves.

We have said 'citizens', but we might with more accuracy have spoken of citizens' wives, since it was the women of London who occupied the front line in defence of their preachers, and with a sense of emotional engagement hardly exceeded by the suffragettes of three and a half centuries later. This should not surprise us, since not only in England but in the whole of Reformation Europe the supposedly weaker sex demonstrated what Lucien Romier called 'un zèle enflammé et une inflexible ténacité' which were a major source of strength to repressed minorities, whether protestant or catholic. The case of John Bartlett, the suspended lecturer of St Giles Cripplegate, was defended by sixty women who descended on Grindal in his own house. The bachelor bishop retreated before this monstrous imposition with the suggestion that they send 'half-a-dozen of their husbands, and with them I would talk.' A month later Grindal informed Cecil of another 'womanish brabble'. A Scottish preacher who had deserted the cause was physically assaulted by 'a certain number of wives', and Grindal himself was 'hooted at' in another parish with cries of 'ware horns ... especially the women'. When Gough and Philpot were conducted over London Bridge to their exile in the country, the occasion was fêted by two or three hundred women with exhortations and all kinds of creature comforts. There were more women than men among the separatists imprisoned in Bridewell in 1568.[3] All this was but a foretaste of the later efflorescence of female religious enthusiasm in the sects of the mid-seventeenth century.[4]

The vestiarian disturbances are a reminder that puritanism, in this respect strikingly unlike catholic dissent, was not excessively reliant upon either clerical or aristocratic leadership. Protestantism was at least potentially a levelling principle, with those marked anti-hierarchical and anti-clerical tendencies which were displayed by the obscure John Smith when he damned even a Coverdale with the faintest of praise. 'Father Coverdale, of whom we have a good opinion, and yet ... ' In the context of an apology and encomium for nobility, Laurence Humphrey was forced to concede that 'in Christ Jesus, I deny not, all are of equal right ... For with Him is no account of persons.' It was 'in Christ Jesus' and with no account of persons that Thomas Wood could sharply inform the earls of Leicester and Warwick that those who served as Satan's instruments had a heavy account to make, 'of what calling so ever they be.' It should be noted that when Elizabethans spoke of 'the godly' they usually meant neither the preachers nor the protestant nobility and gentry but the more zealous of the rank and file. They also used that deceptive expression 'the people', which is scarcely valid in the discussion of Tudor political history but which already has some meaning in the context of protestant affairs.[5]

All the evidence of contemporary observation would suggest that those identified in this way were a minority in Elizabethan society, even in those parts of southern England where the influence of protestantism had been most pervasive, even in London itself. But modern experience has taught us that at times of revolutionary dissolution, history is made by minorities. If the nineteenth century believed in the native protestant patriotism of the people of the northern Netherlands, the twentieth century, finding the authentic reflection of its own history, has discovered that the destiny of large and of themselves relatively inert Dutch communities could rest in the hands of Calvinists who were to be counted in hundreds or even scores rather than in thousands.[6] These insurgents shared the beliefs and the aims of the Elizabethan 'godly'. For all the important political and social differences of the English environment, it will be a gravely deformed account of the puritan movement which ignores the potentialities of our native Calvinists, or which represents them as an amenable 'following'. Those who challenged the puritans in their own time never made such a mistake. It was a charge which they constantly repeated that the preachers were too responsive to 'the folly of the people, calling it charity to feed their fond humour.'[7]

On few issues did lay prejudice find such forceful expression as in the rejection of the surplice and the square cap. All the indications are that, contrary to the impression of some historians, the scandal of the 'popish rag' was felt more strongly by the godly than by their ministers. This is perfectly understandable. However much they might detest the old ceremonial, men of learning could preserve a measure of detachment towards the more incidental trappings of popish worship, distinguishing between the thing itself and its superstitious use. For Grindal these were 'things of no importance', for Jewel abuses chiefly because those in authority insisted on taking them seriously. 'Those very things which you and I have so often laughed at', he told Peter Martyr, 'are now seriously and solemnly entertained by certain persons ... as if the Christian religion could not exist without something tawdry.' But for 'simple gospellers' (as the London ministers describe them) the symbols themselves were a concrete, visible offence. Their emotional reaction reminds Dr T. M. Parker of the attitude of the revolutionary sans-culottes to the knee-breeches of the *ancien regime*, and even of the sartorial principles of the first Socialist Cabinet ministers of 1924. The comparison is not strained, for Elizabethan protestants regarded the surplice and the square cap as the uniform of an oppressive class. Unlike the new bishops and many of the preachers, they were witnesses of the Marian burnings, and they were well aware that many hangers-on of these cruel proceedings continued to hold office in the Elizabethan Church, and that it was for them that the English ministry was still saddled with some portions of 'the pope's attire'.[8]

The point is well made in a dialogue 'of square caps and certain abundant vestures' which may have been the work of William Turner. The nonconformist is made to ask of the conformist: 'Have you forgotten those cruel and popish butchers which not long ago burned so many Christian martyrs, which had on their heads such woollen horns? ... Why therefore wear ye not a cap like unto an honest citizen or preacher of Germany, rather than like unto a mass-monger?' His opponent replies with the stock defence of his position. Granted a free choice he would 'rather be like the godly than the ungodly', but he obeys the prince, 'seeing that in a cap is neither life nor death.' He is not allowed to get away with that. 'If ye had been so conversant among the gospellers in the time of Queen Mary's persecution as I was, ye would recant; for then all shavelings, known tormentors and masking priests only ware such caps. And would ye not think that all such as hid themselves in Queen Mary's time would have judged all such cap-men as you are to have been of the number of those tormentors and mass-mongers; ... and do ye think that that opinion is yet taken out of the people's heads?' 'Therefore my heart ariseth in my body,' protested Gilby's soldier of Berwick, 'when I see thee and thy fellows clothed like [the pope's] chaplains, that burned the blessed Bible, and our faithful Fathers and dear brethren in our eyes.' Of course there was room to argue that, of the principal victims, Cranmer and Ridley had not only worn the offending habits but had stoutly defended their use against Hooper in Edward's reign. Might not their deaths have sanctified a dignified attire, as Cranmer's ashes for some were to hallow episcopacy? But readers of John Foxe learned that, at his degradation, even Ridley refused to associate himself with his persecutors by wearing a surplice. Not for nothing would Bancroft speak of the puritans as English Donatists. It was the persecution which gave an edge to their protest which Hooper's earlier dissent had lacked.[9]

When a nonconformist baulked at the surplice, it was often not so much his own scruples which deterred him as fear of the catastrophe which might overtake his ministry if he were to appear before his people in the offensive garment. When Grindal allowed an Essex incumbent to dispense with the surplice, it was with a realistic respect for an unusually prejudiced congregation. The minister was asked 'privately to exhort the godly so to frame their judgments that they conceive no offence if it be altered hereafter by authority.' George Withers as preacher at Bury St Edmunds wrote to Parker of 'the townsmen of Bury, whose offence I chiefly feared.' And in Cranbrook, an industrial community in the Kentish Weald where protestantism overlaid an older lollard tradition, there were protests from the congregation and interruptions, 'open challenges ... pens walking at sermons', when the vicar began to commend the necessity and dignity of ceremonies which he had earlier condemned. Some of the local people attributed their conversion to his ministry, 'but those very parties do now also affirm that [he] hath run headlong, to the eversion of many consciences.'[10]

Where the surplice and other ceremonies were forced on to a congregation of this quality, it might be at the expense not merely of everted consciences but of the repulsion of the godly into actual schism, as happened in London in the aftermath of 1566. We may well wonder whether it was not in similar circumstances that every early movement of separation had its origin. In Norfolk the puritan ministers would later explain that they had 'much ado' to keep their people from the Brownists even when there was 'reasonable plenty of preaching'. But where an unacceptable ministry had been intruded 'we fear the unruly sort will make that rent in the Church which we had rather be dead (if God so please) than live to behold.' They were told by the separatist leader Robert Harrison that though they might claim the spiritual parentage of their flocks, the children would prove 'forwarder than their father'. But the truth was that 'the chief begetters of these children' were not the ministers at all but the people themselves 'by fruitful edifying of gracious speech and godly conference'. How astonished both Browne and Harrison and their distracted opponents would have been to find that in many of the histories 'puritan' is taken to be practically coterminous with 'puritan minister'![11]

Part 3

The First Presbyterians

1 A New Dogma

'Notes might plentifullie be drawen and manie weightie arguments framed ... to shew the excellencie, amenitie, pleasantness, comliness, congruence, utilitie, necessity, perpetuity, of Christ's pastorall government of his church.'

(HENRY BARROW, *A briefe discoverie of the false church* in *The Writings of Henry Barrow, 1587–90*, ed. Carlson, Eliz. Nonconformist Texts, iii. 574)

'WHAT SAY YOU to a seignory or eldership? Were it not good for the state of the Church at this day that the same were established in every congregation as it was in the apostles' days?' – 'What is your judgment, ought there to be any bishops in the churches of Christians?' – And granted there ought, 'yet in this I would very gladly be absolved, whether they may lawfully vindicate or challenge to themselves superiority and primacy above their fellow brethren of the ministry or no? for some hold that there ought to be equality in the ministry, and no superiority at all. How say you?'[1]

These questions – opened for us by the popular moralist Philip Stubbs – were to prove fascinating for generations of British people in the sixteenth and seventeenth centuries, and they are still emotive in some parts of these islands today. These, not ornaments and ceremonies, were the real issues in the protest against the half-measures of the Elizabethan Church, or so according to the new and more radical puritans of the early 'seventies. 'A great reproof it is to all the learned,' wrote the twenty-six-year-old John Field of his elders, 'who have made some ado about shells and chippings of popery, but that which beareth up Antichrist chiefly, they have said little or nothing of it.' The foundation of popery, in Field's opinion, was the unreformed English polity, which obstructed 'the awful ministry of the word and the right government of the Church, ... matters of far greater weight and importance than ceremonies, and therefore more earnestly to be sought for and quickly pursued after.'[2]

A decade later, Stubbs's questions were an echo of this new and disturbing voice. But the answers which Stubbs supplied were not Field's answers. Rather they represent that moderate view of church polity to which the whole protestant world would have subscribed in the mid-sixteenth century. To anticipate the argument of much that will follow, it can be said that this would continue to be the opinion of most Anglicans and even of most puritan Anglicans for the remainder of Elizabeth's reign and far beyond it. For that reason it deserves to be stated before we examine the novel and doctrinaire position of the early presbyterians.

According to Stubbs's understanding, it was essential for the well-being of a church to enjoy some good 'discipline', a conception which embraced the ordination and regulation of the ministry as well as the correction of faults. It was assumed that in a national church these needs were to be best met through the subordination of many ministers to the government of a few, and therefore by the provision of bishops. Bishops, in Stubbs's view, were even a necessity, but they were not a separate species of minister, at least not in respect of the essentials of their ministerial office, 'for therein the poorest pastor or shepherd that is is coequal with them.' Episcopal office was a superiority of 'dignity, authority, honour', conferred by the only source of rule in a well-ordered kingdom, the prince. It was not easy for the sixteenth-century mind to dissociate spiritual government from its traditional hierarchical forms, but for Stubbs these had no basis in divine law. As for the rule of lay elders in every congregation, this was a polity which had fitted the circumstances of the proscribed apostolic Church, but the 'several estates and conditions' of churches were 'divers and much different one from another', and 'under Christian princes it is not so needful.'

Stubbs was popularizing a view of the ministry and government of the Church which was shared by most of the founding-fathers of the English Reformation.[3] The Edwardine Ordinal in its preface finds it 'evident' that there has been a threefold ministry of bishops, priests and deacons 'from the apostles' time' and declares the intention that they shall be 'continued, and reverently used and esteemed.' But modern Roman Catholic polemicists are no doubt justified in their contention that those who composed and first employed the Ordinal did not share the pre-Reformation doctrine of the priesthood, or of its transmission through the episcopate.[4] Indeed, to pursue the problem into the massive corpus of writings edited by the Parker Society is to emerge with the clear impression that few of the English reformers regarded the precise form of the Church's ministry and government as having any dogmatic quality at all.

Cranmer's mature (if ambiguous) view can be deduced from the code of reformed church law composed late in the reign of Edward VI, the *Reformatio Legum Ecclesiasticarum*. If bishops are here described as exercising authority over the 'inferior orders of the clergy', their own office is called a *gradus ac dignitas*, not an *ordo*. Cranmer's position probably approximated to that of the seminal Strasbourg reformer, Martin Bucer, then resident in Cambridge, who insisted that no bishop could fulfil his office without the counsel of 'the rest of the presbyters'. Bucer envisaged one form of ordination for all grades of the ministry, except that when 'any superintendent, that is bishop,' was to be ordained, everything should be 'somewhat more fully and gravely done and finished'.[5] This was Jewel's view of the matter. Against Thomas Harding, he placed great weight on certain convenient patristic texts – from Jerome, Chrysostom and Augustine – to suggest that the distinction of bishop and presbyter was an order and custom of the Church rather than a divine prescription. His radical episcopal colleague, Pilkington of Durham, merely sharpened the same argument when he insisted that the privileges and superiorities of his own office were 'rather granted by man for maintaining of better order and quietness in commonwealths, than commanded by God in his word ... God's commission and commandment is like and indifferent to all, priest, bishop, archbishop, prelate, by what name soever he be called.'[6]

When the first presbyterians claimed on scriptural authority that there must be a strict parity of pastors and congregations, they were rebuffed with no stronger weapons than these. Even Archbishop Whitgift conceded an equality of all ministers 'touching the ministry', and reserved the superiority of bishops to their jurisdiction. 'For we acknowledge that there is one equal power and function of all ministers, but yet superiority also to be among them for order's sake.' Where there was no Christian magistrate there might be no bishops either, and then the Church would be well governed by elders and elected assemblies. Such a polity was suited to free cities and commonwealths such as Geneva, but not to a Christian monarchy. Similarly, the last will and testament of Archbishop Sandys recorded the conviction that 'the state of a small private church and the form of a learned Christian kingdom neither would long like nor can at all brook one and the same ecclesiastical government.' Nevertheless, the Anglican mind of Jewel, Whitgift and Hooker expressed a strong and growing predilection for episcopacy and a sense of its normative place in Christian tradition, and this would provide a foundation for the high Caroline doctrine of episcopacy.[7]

John Keble, in a different age, was disappointed with the Elizabethans.[8]

Careless of the historic episcopate which their Church retained, they taught a doctrine of the ministry not conspicuously different from that of other reformed churches which had discarded it. For if Jewel and Whitgift were no episcopalians, neither were the Swiss reformers presbyterians. The Second Helvetic Confession of 1566, which united Geneva and Zürich on this among other questions, distinguished bishops from other pastors and elders as 'superintendents and watchmen in the Church'. Calvin identified bishop, priest, pastor and minister as one office and order, but even he acknowledged the long tradition that lay behind the subordination of some ministers to others for the sake of order; and in his correspondence with the reformed kingdoms of England and Poland he raised no objection to diocesan government, provided its form was, as we should say, constitutional rather than monarchical. When Whitgift invoked Calvin against the English presbyterians, Cartwright could only reply that they did not believe something to be true merely because Calvin had said it. 'Calvin herein grants more than I would grant' was the marginal comment of an English student of the *Institutes* who read that the bishop of Rome had enjoyed a measure of primacy in the early Church.[9] As for the leaders of Zürich and Strasbourg, the flattering address which they paid to the Elizabethan bishops is sufficient indication that they found nothing incongruous in the government of a reformed church by superior pastors occupying the old catholic sees.

Practice, not principle, was the concern of this generation in almost everything that they wrote about church polity. The very fact that Calvin devoted scores of pages to the abuses of episcopacy in the unreformed Church implied some commendation of what our English reader of the *Institutes* called 'the holy and charitable use of good bishops'.[10] In England the Reformation schism was frequently justified by a highly-coloured comparison of the true with the false bishop, which drew its inspiration partly from the new appreciation of the pastoral epistles of the New Testament, partly from the Book of Revelation and the medieval apocalyptic tradition. The man who did the work of a true bishop had gone most of the way to establishing his title to the office. For apostolic succession, as Jewel chose to emphasize it, was a succession of doctrine, not of sees. Jewel told Josiah Simler in 1559 that the popish bishops, 'those oily, shaven, portly hypocrites' had been 'sent back to Rome from whence we first imported them; for we require our bishops to be pastors, labourers and watchmen.' He would know that Ponet, the Edwardine bishop of Winchester, had suggested substituting the Latin form of 'superintendent' for the Greek of 'bishop', to emphasize that the reformed bishop was a different creature, a preacher and a true father in God, free from the sins of prelacy and worldly preoccupation, instant in season and out of season.[11] This ideal was old before the Reformation. It inspired the exiles who accepted bishoprics in 1559 and numbers of Elizabethan writers paid tribute to it.[12] But a mere ideal it remained, a standard by which to judge the drabber reality of the actual episcopate of the time, but always exercising a fascination warmer and more comprehensible than the dialectic of the presbyterians.

It was with this pragmatic outlook and in terms of the godly reformed bishop that the first Elizabethan puritans attacked the abuses still inherent in the episcopal office; and the complaint was addressed as if to brethren who once shared, and had not yet entirely lost, the same ideal conception of a pastor's office. Anthony Gilby and his fellow Leicestershire ministers reproached Bishop Cooper of Lincoln that 'you yourselves that be great bishops would not join with Christ's poor ministers, either for your great affairs which you commonly allege, or for your great travail or great charges, that cannot come without some great troop of horses.' 'Come amongst us sometimes in Christian humility,' Cooper was told, 'laying aside all popish lordliness, and so exercise your good gifts amongst your brethren that we of your great light may receive some light.' 'As for the bishops,' Gilby had written in 1566, 'they are not all so far gone, I trust in God.' How could he say otherwise? Bentham of Coventry and Lichfield, once a colleague at Geneva and now his neighbour at Eccleshall Castle, addressed him at this time as his 'very loving friend and brother in Christ' and meekly accepted Gilby's 'friendly admonition'.[13]

The presbyterians replaced pragmatism with dogma. Many protestants had for long agreed that spiritual and moral discipline could be usefully furnished in the local church by means of the congregational consistory: a court composed of the pastor and the lay officers called elders, in some measure representative of and responsible to the congregation. The presbyterians insisted on the absolute necessity of this institution, as alone embodying New Testament discipline, for them an indispensable mark of a true church. To quote an English presbyterian manifesto, discipline 'cometh from God and is therefore unchangeable and perpetual and common to all churches.'[14] Hitherto congregational discipline had not been thought incompatible with the higher government of the Church by Christian magistrates or bishops. The presbyterians condemned both out of hand. The rule of magistrates was excluded by the distinction of Church and Commonwealth as two separate, if interdependent spheres of authority. The rule of bishops was dismissed by claiming on biblical authority the parity of both congregations and pastors. The subordination of one church or of one minister to another was condemned by arguments closely related to those which the first generation of protestants had deployed against the primacy of the bishop of Rome.

In practice presbyterianism differed from other polities not so much at the congregational level as in the method it prescribed for the federation of individual congregations in the fabric of the wider Church. In place of the rule of magistrates or bishops it provided a graduated series of representative assemblies: a meeting called a *classis*, composed of the ministers and elders of the churches of a convenient division (the *colloque* of French and the presbytery of Scottish Calvinism), and – above the *classis* – synods, provincial, national and, ultimately and ideally, universal. The distinguishing marks of presbyterianism are the *classis*, and the rotation of the presiding office of moderator within its membership. These institutions preserve the principle of parity and so distinguish the system from any kind of episcopal or quasi-episcopal polity. On the other hand, the power of the *classis* over the local churches, an authority residing in the ordained ministry, separates presbyterianism from the purely congregational form of church order.

To define the political arrangements characteristic of presbyterianism is not adequately to convey its quality, but this will reveal itself in later chapters. Its ethos was that of matured Calvinism: the application to the constitution of the Christian society of the great Calvinist theological emphases on the sovereignty and unfailing providence of God, the eternal decrees of salvation conveyed to the elect by the preaching of the word, and obedience to the law of the Gospel enforced by godly discipline. Since preaching was both 'the ordinary means of faith' and the declaration of divine law, the presbyterians had an exalted view of the ministerial office as 'of greater weight than the strongest back can bear, of wider compass than the largest hands can fathom.' 'The true minister', wrote Edward Dering, drawing on nothing but biblical imagery, 'is the eye of the body, the workman of the harvest, the messenger that calleth unto the marriage, the prophet that telleth the will of the Lord, the wise man that teacheth to discern between good and evil, the scribe that doth expound the law ... the dispensers [*sic*] of the mysteries of God ... the minister by whom the people do believe.'[15] Consequently there was a progressive tendency in all presbyterian churches to elevate the pastor above his people, the *classis* above the congregation, and to convert the elders from elected representatives of the laity into permanent clerical officials, non-preaching presbyters.

Here in fact was an incipient clericalism, old priest writ large. One does not have to be told that these notions were deeply subversive of the Erastian, monarchical constitution of the Elizabethan Church and of the political structure of the Tudor State. 'Teach her', wrote John Field of the queen, 'to be humble under thy hand, to kiss the rod, and to profit under thy corrections, which thou hast or shall hereafter in mercy lay upon her. Teach her to hearken unto thy word, and to be ruled by it, as by the only rule and square, both of her life and government.' This was in the context of a published collection of family prayers, in which heads of households were instructed to pray that their prince might learn to 'acknowledge in truth that it was thine arm that did advance her, hath preserved and kept her against so many conspiracies and enemies from time to time.'[16] What has to be insisted on with equal force is that the presbyterian claims ran counter to the anticlerical self-assertion of the laity as a whole, undermining as it did all established hierarchies. With a truly remarkable presumption for the age in which he lived, Field could assure his patron the earl of Warwick and the countess of his fervent prayer 'that always you may show your obedience to the ministry.'[17] This was to strike out against one of the strongest of all the confused tides running in the Reformation, and it is not to be wondered at that presbyterianism never succeeded in dominating the English protestant tradition. But against all the resentment they inevitably aroused, the presbyterians could pit the resources derived from a tightly organized cellular structure, invested at every level with group discipline. In favourable political circumstances these weapons might, and occasionally did, gain the mastery.

The details of the presbyterian system were elaborated only in the course of time and were a matter for controversy throughout the Calvinist world. The English presbyterians disputed endlessly the distribution of power as between the whole congregation and the consistory, and whether, once elected, the officers of a church remained answerable to the membership; this, after all, was nothing less than the issue of oligarchy against democracy. Similarly there was fertile ground for disagreement in determining the responsibility of the local church to *classes* and synods; and here the New Testament offered very little guidance. In the first definitive treatment of presbyterian government, *Ecclesiasticae disciplinae … explicatio*, translated as *A full and plaine declaration of ecclesiastical discipline* (1574), Walter Travers was neither full nor plain in his treatment of this problem, and virtually left it on one side, either because his own tendencies were congregationalist, or because it was still too much in dispute. After many pages devoted to the congregational consistory, the question of higher assemblies was briefly touched, of which 'many things might be said'; but with the excuse that others had dealt adequately with the topic, Travers thereupon returned gratefully to the eldership. But whatever the nature of his views on the wider government of the Church, Travers was an unashamed aristocrat when it came to the distribution of power within the congregation. He defined the rule of the consistory as 'aristocracy: that is, that government and state wherein a few of the best do bear the rule; or rather, theocracy, that is, the government of God.' William Fulke, who wrote his *Briefe and plaine declaration* of presbyterian principles a year or two earlier, in 1572, was more insistent than Travers on the representative character of government by consistory, and allowed the reference of all weighty decisions to the 'whole multitude'. It was perhaps for this reason that his tract was withheld from publication for twelve years. 'You know there are certain things in it not agreed upon, and those of weight,' wrote Laurence Tomson to Anthony Gilby.[18]

These internal contradictions aside – and we shall hear more of them – what mattered at first were the primary assertions of presbyterianism: the separation of 'ministry and magistracy' and the particular slant given to the word 'discipline', linked with the demand for parity. In England the last of these principles was the first to make an impression, because of its obvious threat to episcopacy. 'One thing that I do principally dislike is this,' the authors of the *Admonition to the Parliament* were told by the archbishop's chaplain, hastily summoned to question them; 'you would have in the Church, so far as I can gather by your writings, equality of ministers.'[19]

2 The Circumstances of its Assertion

IF THE NEO-CALVINISM encased in the presbyterian system had a single progenitor it was Theodore Beza, professor at the Geneva Academy and Calvin's successor. Presbyterianism was perhaps implicit in the teaching of Beza's master, but like that other secondary product of his thought, the Calvinist doctrine of active political resistance, it remained to less conservative temperaments to draw the final and radical conclusions. Moreover, the narrow dogmatism of the new line was foreign to the mind of a reformer who was more concerned with transmitting the spirit than the form of his achievements. The responsibility for elevating polity to the rank of a protestant dogma and for anathematizing episcopacy, name and thing, lies with Calvin's successor.

Beza's views were clarified with specific reference to affairs in England and Scotland, where the reformed churches were peculiar in their retention of forms of diocesan government. In his popular catechism, *A brief and pithy sum of the Christian faith*, episcopacy was still afforded some recognition. And in correspondence with Grindal in 1566 Beza could write respectfully enough of 'your reverend fellow officers' and of 'so many learned and religious bishops'. But at this time he failed – or refused – to understand the true position of the English prelates. He believed, or professed to believe, that they could stand on their own spiritual authority as if England accepted the Calvinist dichotomy of minister and magistrate. It never occurred to him, until disquieting reports reached Geneva in 1566, that their superintendency excluded the proper contribution to discipline of their fellow pastors and of the elected representatives of congregations. When he learned the truth, he asked what could be more 'abominable' and 'extravagant' than the arbitrary powers of the English bishops. The admirable Grindal was now admonished on the necessity of following the doctrine of the apostles in all points, and a letter of 1568 reviewed a damaged relationship.[1]

Not even Beza was so impolitic as to suppose that the reformed churches could dispense with protestant England, bishops and all, and there were to be other, more cordial letters in the future. His honest, matured opinions on the matter were revealed only to Scotland, where the preservation of an effete episcopacy could be of no possible benefit to the Calvinist cause. In a letter of 1572 which became a kind of charter for the Scottish presbyterians, Beza warned Knox of the evils which the Church would suffer if it entertained 'pseudepiscopi', the dregs of the papacy. This letter and Beza's earlier correspondence with Grindal were in circulation among the English puritans as soon as they were published in Beza's *Epistolae* in 1573. Three years later, Beza attacked diocesan episcopacy more directly and offensively in a letter to the Scottish chancellor, Lord Glamis, which went under the title *De triplici episcopatu* and which John Field would later publish in England. There was 'not one syllable' in the New Testament to justify the setting of one pastor above his brethren, so that the institution of episcopacy was entirely 'of man'. But only the devil could be held responsible for a regime in which the bishops separated themselves from the eldership and challenged to themselves 'and I know not to what officials' the authority to elect, depose and excommunicate. This was to call the Elizabethan episcopate devilish.[2]

Beza's doctrine was absorbed at the Geneva Academy by an international band of scholars, which in 1571 included the Englishmen Thomas Cartwright and Walter Travers and the Scot Andrew Melville. Cartwright taught in the Academy and even attended – by special leave – sessions of the Geneva Consistory 'to see the order they kept and to profit from it.' Cartwright and Melville returned to their respective churches to assume the inspirational leadership of kindred presbyterian movements.[3]

Bishop Sandys later named Cartwright as 'the author of these novelties, and after Beza the first inventor'. He was told by Gualter of Zürich that on the contrary the same errors were very widely dispersed, and were present wherever Geneva was held to be '*orbis Christiani oraculum*'. But in this international ideological movement there is no need to think of English developments as merely peripheral. It was an English student at the University of Heidelberg, George Withers, who in 1568 argued the presbyterian case in a famous disputation with the professor of medicine, Dr Thomas Erastus, who chose to defend the contrary doctrine of the sole and unitary authority in a Christian state of the godly magistrate. In his treatise on excommunication, *Explicatio gravissimae quaestionis*, Erastus later acknowledged that the great debate which gave to our civilization the concept of 'Erastianism' had begun in this confrontation with 'Anglus quidem'. And Gualter, who sympathized with Erastus against the Genevans, named Withers and his fellow-tourist John Bartlett as 'the chief authors of those changes in the Palatinate, which have inflicted such a blow upon the churches in that quarter.'[4]

In the early 'seventies an urge to confer and to organize possessed all the reformed churches under the influence of the Genevan *oraculum*; it was felt in France, the Netherlands and the Rhineland, as well as in Scotland and England.[5] National synods were held which adopted or revised confessions of faith and forms of discipline, and which issued instructions for the distribution of local churches among *classes* and provincial meet-ings. There was little local spontaneity in this activity, and yet it owed nothing to the initiative of governments. Here was no 'tarrying for the magistrate', to use a meaningful separatist cliché. These developments were not unconnected with the threat which seemed to hang over all the reformed churches, especially after the fateful meeting of the ruling families of France and Spain at Bayonne in 1565, an event which was widely supposed to have inaugurated a conspiracy of Europe's leading powers against the gospel. For the French and the Dutch churches the danger and the conflict were real enough, and even in England there was sufficient to alarm the godly: the Ridolfi plot, the northern rebellion, Pius V's excommunication of the queen. Viewed against this ripening crisis, the English episcopate which ten years before had seemed a credible instrument of reform appeared as at best a tiresome anachronism, as a puritan M.P. would put it some years later, 'a northern wind that seldom bloweth good to the Church of God.'[6]

If the presbyterian doctrine and its implementation was in part a response to the pressures of the Counter-Reformation, its introduction in particular situations depended much upon other more local circumstances. On the face of it, Beza's teaching needed no other justification than its claim to be apostolic, for 'nothing at all should be added to the simplicity of the apostolic Church.' But Calvinists were not noticeably immune from the perennial tendency to find in the Bible what one has good reason to look for, and there was a strong element of pragmatism in the presby-terian programme. In Scotland, the new system commended itself as a convincing remedy for the chaos of ecclesiastical economics.[7] And in England, the new tones were first heard, not in an intellectual or academic vacuum, but in response to particular conditions of conflict. These conditions were not constant, and presbyterianism was not to be a constant or typical expression of the English protestant mind.

The doctrine is usually said to have made its first appearance in the academic detachment of a series of lectures on the Acts of the Apostles delivered in Cambridge in the spring of 1570 by Thomas Cartwright, then newly-elected Lady Margaret professor of divinity. At thirty-five Cartwright was much younger than the 'fathers' of the English Reformation, but senior by a decade to the generation of Field and Wilcox. He came up to Cambridge from Royston in Hertfordshire in 1547 and held a scholarship at St John's in the years of Thomas Lever's mastership. This seniority helps to account for the prestige enjoyed in a movement of young radicals through thirty years not overfilled with achievement; this and his undoubted intellectual and rhetorical gifts which are manifest from his impact on Cambridge, even if we reject as apocryphal the pious stories of men running like boys to be sure of a place at his sermons, and the sexton of Great St Mary's fearful for his windows in the crush. In the early years of the reign, Cartwright was fellow successively of St John's and Trinity; a forward scholar and a prominent participant in the academic contests staged for the queen's entertainment on the occasion of the famous royal visit of 1564. A year later he seems to have led the agitation in Trinity against the surplice, before retiring discreetly to Ireland, where for two years he served Archbishop Loftus of Armagh as domestic chaplain. A somewhat unheroic tendency to withdraw from the scene of conflict would always be characteristic of Cartwright, and it hampered his capacity for decisive leadership.[8]

The controversial material in Cartwright's 1570 lectures was contained in his exposition of the model of the primitive Church from the first two chapters of Acts. To apply these standards to the contemporary situation was to call for the abolition of the names and offices of archbishops, bishops, deans and archdeacons, and for the reduction of the ministry to the apostolic offices of pastor and deacon; and to suggest that the government of the Church should be restored from the usurpation of bishops' and archdeacons' officials to the minister and presbytery of every local church, and that a minister should be elected by his congregation and subsequently linked to it indissolubly. It is not easy to tell how pointed these strictures were, how far on the other hand mere academic observation, for we are very far from possessing a full text of the lectures.[9] But it is certain that their topicality aroused an enthusiastic response from the younger element in the university, and a marked reaction from the university authorities and the government which led to a 'hurly-burly and shameful broil' between two opposed factions, dividing the university between them and threatening to split the Church. In the midst of the furore Cartwright was ejected from his chair (at the end of 1570) and withdrew to Geneva, where his reception implies recognition of the representative and leading English neo-Calvinist.

The Lady Margaret professor's discoveries were not quite so novel as they have sometimes been represented. First Luther and then Tyndale had taught that bishops, priests and elders were essentially one order of the ministry, deacons another, and that both should be elected by the people. And it was now sixteen years since the veteran puritan reformer William Turner had concluded from the same texts in Acts that unless they were joined to the function of preaching and teaching, the offices of bishop, dean, provost, canon, parson and vicar were inadmissible human inventions; and that 'in the primitive Church the whole congregation choosed the pastors, and that by voices, and sometimes by lots.' Accordingly, Turner already looked for the day when there would be 'no such bishops as we now have, and that all pastors should be alike, none above another.' But the dean of Wells had indulged in no empty theorizing. His remarks were directed against the particular episcopal regime of Gardiner and Bonner. As we have seen, the effect of the conflict over ceremonies in the early Elizabethan Church was to attach only a slightly lesser degree of obloquy to the protestant successors of these popish prelates, and old arguments against episcopacy were now refurbished. Turner, about to be deprived of his deanery, demanded of the bishops: 'Who gave them authority more over me than I over them, either to forbid me preaching or to deprive me? unless they have it from their holy father, the pope.' Evidently, the presbyterian movement derived its energy not so much from intellectual originality as from the pressures under which such extreme positions came to be occupied. For this reason, Cartwright's Cambridge lectures were hardly as significant as certain more obscure developments at the storm-centre, in London.[10]

The London puritans had no need to be ignorant of the principles of reformed church order. Their number included several veterans of the English congregation at Geneva who knew Calvin's system at first hand. For others there was a constant opportunity to observe and even to share in the affairs of self-governing congregations organized on the Calvinist pattern. These were the London churches of the French and Dutch protestant refugees, and the rather less successful and enduring Italian and Spanish congregations.[11] The history of these 'stranger churches' began in the reign of Edward VI, when the Polish reformer, John à Lasco, obtained generous privileges from the government and provided one of the earliest versions of a reformed church order. Early in Elizabeth's reign the leading personality in the foreign congregations was the French pastor, Nicholas des Gallars, sieur de Saules. Des Gallars was a Calvinist of the highest international reputation, and, what the bourgeois republic of Geneva with its plebeian reformer valued so much, an aristocrat. In sending him to London, Calvin cannot have intended that his influence should be restricted to the small community of French refugees. He preached once a week in Latin, probably for the benefit of the London clergy, and as early as 1560 his advice was sought by the English non-conformists. Des Gallars was responsible for a revision of the discipline of the French church on lines much closer to the Ecclesiastical Ordinances of Geneva, and this constitution in its Latin text was in the possession of John Field himself; his is the only surviving copy. More than that, members of the inner, Genevan circle of English puritanism took an active part in the life and even in the government of these foreign Calvinist communities.

Under the Elizabethan dispensation, the stranger churches were required to accept the bishop of London as their superintendent, and this restricted their full participation in the developing organization of their home churches. But under a superintendent as 'continental' in his outlook as Grindal, little restriction was placed on their local autonomy, and none on their freedom to follow their own reformed orders of worship and assembly. The status of the refugee churches was a constant reminder for the London puritans that the superintendency of a bishop need not exclude self-government by the congregation or the use of an order of worship far more godly than the English Prayer Book. No wonder that one of the incumbents suspended in 1566 wrote wistfully: 'It seemeth rightful that subjects natural [should] receive so much favour as the churches of national strangers have here with us. But we cannot once be heard so to obtain. This with them: they an eldership, we none; they freely elect the doctor and pastor, we may not; they their deacons and church servants with discipline, and we not.' Moreover, the strangers provided a convenient and confidential link with the reformed churches overseas. Beza sent his letters by way of the French church in London, 'very frequently' according to Percival Wiburn. So that it was with more than a distant knowledge of developments in other churches that the first *Admonition* could demand: 'Is a reformation good for France? and can it be evil for England? Is discipline meet for Scotland? and is it unprofitable for this realm? Surely God hath set these examples before your eyes to encourage you to go forward to a thorough and a speedy reformation.' Here was one advantage among many which favoured the pretensions to national leadership of the young and radical London preachers.[12]

We are now ready to look for the circumstances under which some London puritans applied these examples to their own situation. What made England fertile soil for Beza's new dogma was the combination of irregularities unusual in a supposedly reformed church and the suppression by the bishops of unauthorized attempts to remedy the situation. Many schemes of practical reform had been and would be proposed which fell far short of the doctrinaire remedies of the presbyterians. But the continual frustration of these moderate proposals itself nourished extremism. Episcopacy on the Elizabethan pattern turned sour in Beza's mouth when the state of the English Church was explained to him in some detail. But it took the reaction of 1565-7 to bring these shortcomings to his notice. In England, equally, it was the repressive role which the bishops were at that time obliged to assume which first persuaded some puritans that the bishops themselves and the system for which they stood constituted the main obstacle to progress. Presbyterianism was to be destructive of the peace and unity of the Church of England but it was itself a symptom rather than a first cause of conflict.

We have already seen how the events of 1566 led to extremes of anti-episcopal feeling in London. In the tracts published in that year by the clerical leaders of the agitation there are some of the earliest full-flown presbyterian sentiments. 'Christ only and not godly magistrates must appoint what is necessary for his ministers,' wrote Robert Crowley, while to his colleague at St Giles Cripplegate, John Bartlett, belongs the credit for introducing the platform of high Calvinism in a series of ringing assertions included in his *Fortresse of fathers*: 'The lordship of bishops now exercised over both the rest of the clergy and over the lay people hath no ground in the word of God. Christ is only the head of His mystical body which is the Church as the prince or chief magistrate is the head of the politic body of his realm and country. The supreme magistrate is bound to obey the word of God, preached by Christ's messengers, and he is also subject to the discipline of the Church. Neither the prince nor any prelate hath any authority by the word of God to make any ecclesiastical law or rite, to bind men's consciences in pain of deadly sin to keep them.' It is significant that John Field was soon serving in this same parish where Crowley had been incumbent and Bartlett had preached.[13]

In the semi-separatist groups which soon developed there was great emphasis on discipline, the covenant of Fitz's congregation stating its necessity as a principal cause of the separation, 'for in the church of the traditioners there is none other discipline but that which hath been ordained by the Antichristian popes of Rome.' 'You preach Christ to be priest and prophet, but you preach Him not to be king', Grindal was told by the puritans taken in Plumbers' Hall. One member of this group demands particular mention. He was William White, a baker and an articulate lay divine who was twice imprisoned for his advanced opinions. Already in the late 'sixties White was given to quoting a dictum of Beza that 'where discipline lacketh, there is a licentious life and a school of wickedness.' White's writings in the puritan collection calendared as *The Seconde Parte of a Register* suggest that he may have exerted a telling influence over the young preachers, Field and Wilcox, and there is evidence that he worked in close harmony with them.[14]

But for some time – before Cartwright's Cambridge lectures – these views had no learned defenders. The acknowledged puritan leadership avoided provocation, still hoping that the authorities would concede a measure of freedom for tender consciences and some token that the process of reformation had not come to a full stop. All eyes were still fixed on Parliament. Sir John Neale believes that but for the absorption of all good protestants in the great matter of the queen's marriage and the succession, a major effort would have been made to revise the 1559 settlement in the Parliament of 1566. 'So long as the Parliament endured, we all had hope of amendment and kept silence,' wrote Gilby, probably with reference to this session. There was some attempt by the puritans to sponsor a whole series of unofficial bills, numbered alphabetically, which would have offered to reform the more familiar and pressing abuses of the ministry, such as non-residence and simoniacal presentations to livings. But the first of these bills, proposing statutory recognition for the Articles of Religion and strongly backed by the bishops, was the only measure to be given a run for its money, and even that was dashed through the queen's intervention.[15]

Little had been attempted and nothing achieved in 1566. But by the time Parliament reassembled five years later, in April 1571, the puritan ministers and their allies in the Commons were ready with a pre-arranged programme, and at once seized the initiative. Two members, William Strickland, representing Scarborough, and Thomas Norton, Cranmer's

116

son-in-law and the learned translator of the English edition of Calvin's *Institutes*, brought to the attention of the House of Commons the *Reformatio Legum*, Cranmer's programme of reformed church law, newly edited by John Foxe and printed especially for this purpose. With a committee appointed to sit on this document, Strickland and Norton led the House in renewed pursuit of the 'alphabetical' bills of 1566 (including a bill to impose general subscription to the Thirty-nine Articles), while Strickland, with great temerity, introduced a bill to purge the Prayer Book of all the objected ceremonies. These measures, taken together, would have completed the Reformation of 1559 in doctrine, worship and discipline. The Articles would have become a true *Confessio Anglicana*, a credal test for the whole Church and nation. And the effect of the *Reformatio Legum* would have been to give the Church of England discipline in the reformed sense without disturbing her episcopal constitution. For the godly bishop was still very much the hero of this programme. Evidently at this point the leaders still hoped to carry the bishops with them. In his first speech, Strickland proposed that a committee of the Commons should confer with the bishops about reform, and an attempt was made at bi-partisan discussion.

But 1571 marked a critical stage in the estrangement of the puritans and the bishops. Parker and his colleagues were evidently angered by the folly of Strickland and his friends in jeopardizing their more sensible proposals by an attack on the Prayer Book. The bishops were in any case unwilling to support the campaign for the enactment of the *Reformatio Legum*, while serious disagreement was revealed on the question of subscription to the Articles of Religion. The puritans desired – in the interests of their own sensitive consciences – to restrict subscription to the more strictly doctrinal of the Articles and with that limitation to use them as a searching test of lay as well as clerical orthodoxy. The bishops were unable to condone either of these proposals. A memorial to the failure to agree with the bishops in this Parliament is to be found in the words defiantly entered by the Commons in the final form of the statute that the clergy should be required to subscribe to those Articles 'which only concern the confession of the true Christian faith and the doctrine of the sacraments'; and the consistent refusal of the bishops to be bound by the sense in which the Commons intended these words to be taken.[16]

While Parliament was still in session, Jewel, Horne and Cox, three émigrés who had now lost all sympathy for radical protestantism, launched their own campaign against the puritans in sermons preached at Paul's Cross. Their theme was that those who enjoyed the grain of the wheat should not contend about the chaff, but White and Wilcox were quick to instruct the bishops on what was and was not essential for the Church.[17] After the dissolution of Parliament the bishops took steps to enforce subscription to the Articles in their entirety, which Convocation had made a condition for the renewal of all preaching licences. And the Ecclesiastical Commissioners summoned certain marked men – among them Goodman, Lever, Sampson, Wiburn, Field, and a brilliant young Cambridge graduate, Edward Dering – and demanded that they subscribe their acceptance of the Articles, the Prayer Book and the surplice. This, presumably, was the real crisis of conscience for these men, for Beza had earlier advised them to live with these things if need be, but on no account to give them their positive approval.[18]

Yet at this moment even Field had not entirely lost hope of the bishops. With Goodman, Wiburn and Dering he now offered 'a kind of agreement' to Sandys, Grindal's successor as bishop of London. This was a qualified subscription to the Articles according to the restricted parliamentary formula and to the Prayer Book 'for doctrine of faith and administration of the sacraments, so far as they make to edification.' Those associated with this démarche could not bring themselves to wear the surplice, but they would not condemn those who did. 'Neither would I break the unity of the Christian faith by withdrawing my duty from preaching the truth and faith in the Book of Articles contained. To the end that we might have occasion rather to go forward to perfection than backward.' But this gesture, such as it was, was spurned. By the early months of 1572, Field was silenced and reduced to earning his living as a frustrated schoolmaster. To Gilby he wrote with bitterness of spirit of 'the over-much tyranny of those that should be my encouragers' and of being 'unjustly put' from his people.[19]

In this mood the *Admonition to the Parliament* – public polemic in the guise of an address to Parliament – was as good as written. Wilcox and Field were perhaps at work on their joint manifesto as soon as it was known, in late March 1572, that a new Parliament would be called for May to consider the fate of Mary Stuart and the duke of Norfolk. Thomas Cartwright meanwhile responded to the insistent call of his supporters and returned from Geneva in April. According to Bancroft, writing twenty years after the event, the decision to issue the *Admonition* was taken by Gilby, Sampson, Lever, Field, Wilcox and others, meeting in conference in London before the Parliament. This one may doubt, for two of those named – Sampson and Lever – would not have endorsed the *Admonition*, and in Field's correspondence of this time there is evidence of his impatience with the conservatism of the puritan leadership, 'wiser men than I', as he wrote ironically, who hoped for 'amendment in some and for peace with all'.[20]

But we know from this correspondence that some such conference as Bancroft reports did take place, and we can hazard a reconstruction of the course of events. The assembled ministers would have dealt with a bill concerning rites and ceremonies which received its first reading in the Commons on May 17th, a measure which may have been seen by the extremists as the last resort before undertaking more desperate measures. In Parliament it was energetically recommended by 'those ardent irresponsibles', Robert Snagge and Tristram Pistor, who had supported Strickland's move for Prayer Book reform in 1571. The remarkable measure now before the Commons freely admitted in its preamble that 'a great number of learned pastors and zealous ministers' regularly set aside parts of the Prayer Book in favour of godly preaching exercises, and implied that this was with the approval of 'divers godly-minded prelates', though not of certain 'malicious adversaries of the truth'. It proposed that the penalties under the Act of Uniformity should remain in force only against popish irregularities and that these bishops should be empowered to license their clergy to omit parts of the legal service in order to devote themselves to other godly exercises, specifying the published orders of prayer of the French and Dutch congregations in London. This bill met its inevitable fate when it was first toned down by a Commons committee and then confiscated by the queen.[21] This was on May 23rd, and it is surely significant that it was after this, some time in June, rather than earlier in the session, that the *Admonition* appeared.[22] If our interpretation of events is correct, it was the failure of the attempt to secure a guaranteed toleration in the puritan bill of rites and ceremonies which finally persuaded Field and others who shared his exasperation to detach themselves from their more cautious leaders, a course which their friends in the religious underworld had perhaps long been urging.

The *Admonition* was more outspoken than anything that had yet been published by protestants against protestants in England. It was polemic of the highest order, measured and serious, but with shafts of infectious satire. There was no more of the talk of 'godly-minded prelates' which could still be found in the parliament bill of a month before. The names and offices of archbishops and bishops were now said to be 'drawn out of the pope's shop' and their government was 'Antichristian and devilish and contrary to the scriptures'.[23] The tract fell into two quite dissimilar halves: the *Admonition* proper, Wilcox's share, was a solemn and trenchant exposition of the outward marks of a true Church, with proof that they were sadly impaired if not wholly lacking in England. 'We in England are so far off from having a Church rightly reformed according to the pre-script of God's word, that as yet we are not[24] come to the outward face of the same.' Field added the vituperative and journalistic 'View of popish abuses yet remaining in the English Church', which was cast in the form of an answer to the 1571 demand for subscription. Field later admitted sole responsibility for the 'bitterness of the style', and it is this section which contains the really memorable phrases: 'an unperfect book, culled and picked out of that popish dunghill, the mass book, full of all abomina-tions' – 'reading is not feeding, but as evil as playing upon a stage, and worse too' – 'they toss the psalms in most places like tennis balls' – 'the commissary's court, that is, but a petty little stinking ditch that floweth out of that former great puddle.'[25]

While its authors proceeded somewhat triumphantly to Newgate, their little book ran into three editions by August. Other smaller pamphlets rode on the crest of the wave: notably *An exhortation to the bishops to deal brotherly with their brethren*, which compared the bishops to 'galled horses that cannot abide to be rubbed.'[26] In October, when Field and Wilcox were sentenced to a year's imprisonment by the lord mayor and aldermen of London, John Whitgift reported that the pamphlets were 'in every man's hand and mouth'.[27]

This literature has exercised an understandable fascination both then and since, which may explain why most historians of English religion have suggested that at this point presbyterianism became the central emphasis of the puritan cause. Yet most of the older leaders at once dissociated themselves from the new extremism, to such an extent that we are evidently witnessing the beginnings of a new movement rather than the conversion of the old. On the other hand, when the immediate pressures which prompted the *Admonition* relaxed three years later, a more moderate brand of puritanism would prove still to be the measure of most aspira-tions. Only in a limited sense did the puritan movement now 'enter its presbyterian phase.'

When we read the strictures of the older men, it is clear that they rejected both the matter and what they regarded as the disastrous manner of the *Admonition*. Laurence Humphrey visited Field and Wilcox in prison, but only to disagree with them. He deplored 'openly to publish such Admonitions as are abroad ... for that in some points and terms they are too broad and overshoot themselves.' In 1573 he was pressed to accept a bishopric, but though he refused he was careful to tell Francis Hastings that he thought it 'no sin to desire the good work of a true bishop. The name and the work are both commendable in Scripture.' He desired reformation but 'as a subject and orderly, without breach of peace'. Consider, he asked, 'whether a godly mind may not better help reformation having friends of voice and access than otherwise?' Four years later he yielded complete conformity and begged Burghley that 'as I have offended some by this my obedience, so I shall have such favour and countenance at her Majesty's hands that I shall now more freely and fruitfully proceed in my vocation.' 'The Lord be merciful to us, end all quarrels', was his prayer later in life. An unknown puritan hand has noted on a copy of one of his early letters: 'Written in time of his sincere affection towards discipline.'[28]

Thomas Sampson, now a preacher in Leicester, remained a radical spirit, but there is no evidence that he played an active part in the new movement. As he would later warn Gilby, 'I am not so forward in the matter as you do think.'[29] Humphrey's old college friend John Foxe, as one would expect of a persistent 'promoter of concord', washed his hands of the extremists. He later wrote: 'If I were a man to rage with them against bishops and archbishops, they would never have sharpened their arrows against me. They hate me because I prefer to follow moderation and public tranquillity.' Robert Crowley, the man of 1566, visited Field and Wilcox in Newgate, but he had probably already earned the scathing contempt which Field later expressed for his temporizing with 'popish dregs'. Whittingham had conformed in 1567; in the eyes of the godly he was a backslider and a lost leader. Other clerics of the older generation, Turner and Coverdale, were dead.[30]

No portent was more significant than the condemnation of the *Admonition* by Thomas Norton, the 'parliament man', sponsor of the *Reformatio Legum* in 1571 and the translator of Calvin's *Institutes*: 'Surely the book was fond, and with unreasonableness and unseasonableness hath hindered much good and done much hurt, and in nothing more than in increasing the papists' triumph against our Church ... I mislike much these men's course and fancies and matters contained in their book.' Even Theodore Beza, whom we have indicted as the inspiration of the presbyterians, deplored the manner of their protest. He told the minister of the French congregation in London that their impatient action had blocked his own more tactful approach to certain English 'seigneurs'. He wanted no part in it and although he asked for a copy of the *Admonition* to be sent to him he also demanded advice to enable him not 'to be involved more than I can help in such very indiscreet proceedings.'[31]

3 The Universities and the New Men

AT A TIME when the older nonconformists were repudiating the pretensions of the new upstart leadership, the universities, and especially Cambridge, were beginning to supply the rank and file of a new and larger puritan party, young men who were already accustomed to setting themselves against ecclesiastical and academic authority. Not all of this generation would necessarily emphasize what Cartwright emphasized, and comparatively few would follow John Field all the way in spirit and action. But they would have learned almost as a matter of course that the constitution of the Church in which they were to serve was popish rather than reformed, to be regretted if tolerated. 'I am no parson,' insisted a Shropshire minister, hot from Cambridge, 'no, I am no vicar. I abhor these names as Antichristian. I am *pastor* of the congregation there.'[1] What is more, these young graduates carried into the wider world of the parishes a sense of belonging to a fellowship and a cause, begun in the university and continued in the ministry. Here was the stuff of the organized conference movement of the 'eighties and of the more spontaneous 'spiritual brotherhood' of preachers which was the essence of the puritan 'church within the Church' in the early seventeenth century.

Cambridge, wrote John Strype, 'ran now much divided into two factions, whereof the younger sort, which were the majority, was much for innovations, and such were followers of Cartwright's principles; which the graver sort, especially the heads, laboured to restrain.' The 'graver sort' were not all old men. John Whitgift, Cartwright's formidable opponent, was his senior by perhaps three years, and vice-chancellor at the age of thirty-eight, at a time when most of Cartwright's supporters were in their late twenties. Yet such small differences in seniority separated one university generation from another, and they could cover the formative years of a man's development.[2]

Whitgift himself made the most crucial decision of his career in the years immediately before Cartwright's lectures thrust the university into turmoil. In 1565, as fellow of Peterhouse, he was one of the most promising of the young Cambridge protestants whose views on the ceremonies were about to be branded as 'puritan'. His first recorded utterance, a Paul's Cross sermon delivered on June 24th of that year, applied the parable of Dives and Lazarus to his own time, attacking luxury and covetousness, rack-renting and usury, but reserving its harshest strictures for the worldliness of the Roman Church. He told a seasoned tale of a friar who was preaching in St Peter's when the pope entered in full splendour. The friar began to throw himself about in the pulpit and to cry 'Fie on Peter, fie on Paul!' He could not, he explained, have praised the apostles at that moment without condemning their successor. 'By this the friar trimly and wisely reprehended the pomp of the pope.'[3] For the doctorate of divinity conferred on him in the same year, Whitgift defended the thesis that the pope is Antichrist. When the troubles over the surplice began in the later months of 1565, he was one of a group of seniors who sympathized with the younger, puritan dons and their pupils and tried to prevent the enforcement of Parker's Advertisements in the university. At this time Whitgift was Lady Margaret professor, with an enthusiastic following of the younger men, and this may partly explain his motivation. Dr Andrew Perne, the master of Peterhouse, warned Archbishop Parker that he had intrigued to keep the surplice out of the college, swearing 'that he had rather have spent forty pounds than for to have had surplices in Peterhouse.' But, added Perne, 'neither he nor any of his will lose indeed sixpence for the wearing of a surplice, as some of them reporteth, but will rather wear three surplices.'

Wily Dr Perne was the young Whitgift's friend and patron, and he knew his man. Before long the future archbishop had convinced himself that he should not sacrifice his chances of being usefully employed for the sake of things 'being of themselves indifferent.' At this time Cecil was surveying the university for reliable men of promise, and within a year of Whitgift's conformity it was arranged that he should preach before the queen and be advanced rapidly to the Regius professorship, a royal chaplaincy, and the mastership in quick succession of Pembroke Hall and Trinity. 'What or who am I,' he asked his patron, 'that you should be so careful for me?' 'Dr Whitgift is a man whom I have loved,' wrote Edward Dering, wistfully, 'but yet he is a man, and God hath suffered [him] to fall into great infirmities.'[4]

The new university statutes of 1570, which were promoted by Whitgift as vice-chancellor, served to correct what he recognized to be the inherent dangers of the old constitution. Power had hitherto rested with the regent masters, graduates of up to three years' standing, who were a majority of the teaching and governing body in a period of rapid university expansion. Perhaps no one knew better than the popular Lady Margaret professor of 1565 the temptation to defer to the opinions as well as to the voting power of the younger element. The new statutes transferred most of the powers of the regents to the heads of houses, an oligarchy of 'the graver sort'. But by the same token the change of constitution linked Cartwright's cause with the interests of all the younger fellows. It was resisted by half the total number of dons in Cambridge, and although not all these of 'the inferior sort' can have been convinced Cartwrightians, they were open to the appeal of a radically anti-authoritarian programme which the heads had condemned. The lists of names ranged in protest against the new statutes contain a large number who, in the wider world beyond the university, would win a reputation for preciseness and dissent. Rebellious attitudes contracted in this academic war of the generations would transfer themselves far beyond Cambridge, where some of the ruling heads were destined to be bishops and 'the inferior sort' their subordinate clergy. Whitgift's prophylactic may have prevented a university calamity – perhaps the election of Cartwright as vice-chancellor – but it positively promoted the growth of a movement of clerical revolt in the Church at large.[5]

Cartwright was expelled from his professorial chair and left for Geneva in December 1570. He returned in April 1572, and within a few months his last foothold in Cambridge was lost when Whitgift seized on a technicality to deprive him of his fellowship. But by 'buzzing these conceits into the heads of divers young preachers and scholars' Cartwright had not left his cause without a witness, and Cambridge puritanism was already independent of his inspiration. Edmund Chapman at Trinity, Robert Some at Queen's, William Chark at Peterhouse, John Millen at Christ's: all now showed their colours in sermons which maintained the Cartwrightian doctrines. If they were then expelled from the university (like Chark or Millen), or became respectable with increasing age and responsibility (like Some), there were always others to take their places. In 1570 Archbishop Parker was congratulating himself on having secured an able young fellow of Trinity, Thomas Aldrich, to serve as master of his own college of Corpus Christi. That Aldrich, at thirty, was the oldest member of the society he now headed sets these Cambridge ructions in their right perspective. But within three years Parker had cause to complain that the young master was 'an head precisian' and 'a great maintainer of Mr Cartwright'. His efforts to get rid of him aroused cheerful complaints from Aldrich's supporters about the 'pope of Lambeth and of Bene't College'.[6]

Of much more importance in the long run than the brief impact of a heated sermon and the passing glory of the academic martyr was the sustained influence over many years of puritan masters, tutors and college lecturers. We are here at the beginning of the great age of the tutors, 'guardians of finances, morals and manners' in their pupils and 'the most important influence on their education'. A tutor negotiated directly with his pupil's family to secure his fees as well as to fulfil his moral responsibilities. Puritan parents and dons sought each other out and together conspired for the godly advancement of their charges. Among what Thomas Fuller called the 'pupil-mongers', there were none greater in Cambridge than the celebrated succession at Christ's College of Edward Dering, William Perkins and Laurence Chaderton, which spanned the reign.[7]

Dering we already know. He was a star in the Cambridge firmament who burned himself out in a tactless letter to Cecil which assumed by its bitterness what was by no means certain: that the puritan cause in the university was all but lost. Perkins, the prince of puritan theologians and the most eagerly read, belonged to a later and more relaxed generation. He was Chaderton's pupil in the 'seventies, but hardly his successor, for Chaderton went on for ever: fellow of Christ's from 1568 to 1576, preacher at St Clement's, Cambridge, for fifty years, master of Emmanuel from its foundation by Sir Walter Mildmay (a fellow Christ's man!) in 1584 until 1622 and still alive in 1640 to see the Long Parliament, a patriarch of over a century. Chaderton was the pope of Cambridge puritanism. In the 'sixties and 'seventies he made Christ's a puritan seminary in all but name, and then in the 'eighties he carried the tradition over to Emmanuel. Much that was distinctive of English and American civilization in the seventeenth century was shaped in these two neighbouring colleges which bred John Cotton and John Milton. The tendency of Chaderton's influence over the years can be judged from an undergraduate's notes of his divinity lectures on St John's gospel, taken down in 1590. The Pharisees' opposition to Christ taught future preachers 'that the truth and ministers of the truth have many adversaries, yea, even amongst the learned and those that are of great authority in the Church ... This instructeth the ministers that they should not fear, but prepare their minds to suffer this particular cross of Christ.' If the Pharisees could err 'in making constitutions for the Church' then so could others; 'this teacheth us not to lie or trust upon the constitutions of men, and therefore that we ought so to be conversant in the Scriptures, that we may be the judge of what sort they be.' This was how nonconformists were made.[8]

After his great reputation was established, Chaderton accepted no pupils of his own but 'travailed what he could for the best placing of them.' Anthony Gilby's son Nathaniel, coming up to Christ's in 1578, could not therefore be placed under him, as Gilby had hoped, but was committed to a certain Mr Dickinson, 'a young man, very godly and learned' (but not, it would seem, a fellow of the college), and later passed on to a fellowship under Chaderton at Emmanuel.[9] Chaderton was by now preoccupied with the higher strategy of harnessing the university to the supply of learned preachers, conscious, with Walter Travers, that 'universities ought to be the seed and the fry of the holy ministry throughout the realm.' To this end he drew up a programme of studies to run over two years 'for the training up and exercising of students in divinity, whereby they may be made fit and meet to discharge the duties belonging to that profession.' The order consisted partly of 'mutual conference', partly of disputation. The traditional exercise of logical discourse needed no further explanation, except that the topics to be argued were to be taken from the principal questions in controversy with the papists 'and other heretics'.

'Conference', more of a novelty, was the method of biblical study first perfected by protestant humanists in Zürich and widely employed in the continental reformed churches. It was a method of searching out the true meaning of the text by bringing to bear the talents of a company variously schooled in the modern, humane studies: Greek and Hebrew philology, Greek and Roman history, comparative exegesis, as well as rhetoric and logic. Chaderton himself is said to have joined in weekly conference with the young Lancelot Andrewes and three famous puritan divines of the future, Ezekiel Culverwell, John Knewstub and John Carter. 'One was for the original languages; another's task was for the grammatical interpretation; another's for the logical analysis; another's for the true sense and meaning of the text; another gathered the doctrines; and thus they carried on their several employments, till at last they went out like

Apollos, eloquent men, and mighty in the scriptures.' Those famous meetings at the White Horse tavern of half a century earlier, in which the English protestant tradition began, have made a deeper impression on the books, but their impact on our history was hardly greater than these forgotten afternoons in Elizabethan Cambridge.[10]

In the Church beyond the university, the same method of conference was employed to equip the non-graduate clergy with the means to preach, and to maintain a general doctrinal agreement: these were the public conferences of preachers and aspirant preachers held in market-town churches and known as 'exercises of prophesying', a name derived from the archetypal Biblical conference in Zwingli's Zürich.[11] At first these 'prophesyings' had no necessary connection with the universities, and in many centres they were established long before Chaderton's Cambridge exercise. But as the puritan colleges began to supply a stream of preachers for parish churches and lectureships, these regular gatherings of clergy tended to perpetuate a godly familiarity first formed in the university. And when a higher opinion was needed, it was the usual practice – at least in the eastern counties – 'to crave the judgements of some godly men in Cambridge.'[12]

Clerical puritanism, as a cohesive, national movement, was created in the universities. It was here that the various regional and social origins of the Elizabethan preachers were submerged in a common brotherhood. John More from Westmorland and Thomas Roberts from Wales passed together through Christ's to become 'presidents or leaders of an army'[13] in the triumphant reformation of Norwich. They were contemporaries of Chaderton, who came from a staunchly catholic Lancashire family, and perhaps contracted his puritanism in the same college from the younger son of an ancient Kentish family, Edward Dering. William Perkins who continued the puritan tradition in Christ's was the son of a Warwickshire yeoman. John Knewstub from Westmorland and Oliver Pig from Lincolnshire were contemporaries at St John's and went on to lead the conference movement in Suffolk.

Of a rough-and-ready list of clergy and schoolmasters who have left some evidence of puritan convictions and who were active in the twenty years 1570–90, no less than two hundred and twenty-eight were in residence at Cambridge University at some time between 1565 and 1575, the ten years surrounding Cartwright's Lady Margaret lectures, and perhaps the most prosperous decade in the Elizabethan history of the university. At this time the three largest colleges (measured by the annual matriculations) were St John's, Trinity and Christ's. These were also the colleges with the strongest puritan element. Forty-eight of our puritans were at St John's, ten of them fellows; forty were at Trinity, sixteen of them fellows (including Cartwright, Travers, Edmund Chapman, William Whitaker, William Axton and Robert Johnson); thirty-one were at Christ's, seven of them fellows. These figures become more meaningful when we break them down by counties. Of some eighty-one puritan preachers who can be identified in Suffolk in the 'eighties, thirty were members of one college, St John's, and twenty-two of these were in residence at some point between 1565 and 1575; they included most of the ringleaders of the conference movement in the county. All but thirty of the Suffolk puritans were at Cambridge in the ten years around 1570.[14]

Not all of these hundreds of Cambridge preachers were to become militant presbyterians. As Professor Haller and Dr Porter have rightly emphasized,[15] the typical Cambridge puritan was no extremist: practical godliness concerned him more than platforms of church government. To know the situations in which most of these clergymen found themselves is to understand the dominant motif in most of their ministries. They were essentially pastors, faced with blank irreligion and ignorance in the souls under their care. They preached primary protestant doctrine, 'spiritual' and 'plain', rarely having occasion to touch on controversial matters, and the best of them became even more famous as physicians of the soul than as preachers. As Thomas Fuller wrote of Richard Greenham, the model puritan of Dry Drayton, 'his masterpiece was in comforting wounded consciences.'[16]

The more familiar traditions of pastoral puritan piety date from the last years of Elizabeth and largely from the first half of the seventeenth century, when the press satisfied a growing desire for godliness with works of 'practical divinity' and the exemplary biographies of puritan saints. Samuel Clarke's *Lives* trace the famous succession of Greenham, Rogers and Dod, Cotton, Gouge and Sibbes. But 'mere religion' was already the most urgent concern of many of the puritan preachers of the first generation: of Dering, godly counsellor of anxious Calvinist gentle-women, and of Wilcox, whose collected letters contained 'little but godly, plain and necessary exhortations and directions for the exercise of godli-ness'.[17] Wherein then lay their puritanism? These pastorally-minded puritans cared deeply about the failings of the established Church as they knew them at the parochial level: the lack of preachers, the shortcomings of the poorer clergy and the carelessness of the wealthy and the non-resident, the powerlessness of the pastor with no weapon of discipline in his hand. And although the label 'nonconformist' does not begin to describe what was distinctive about these men, nonconformists they were, and they could be stung into defiance by too peremptory a demand to conform. Presbyterians in an active, militant sense most of them were not, but they had little sense of loyalty to their ordinaries or to the Church conceived in an Anglican, hierarchical way; and by contrast a strong sense of belonging to their fellow preachers, gathered in conference.

So far nothing has been said of Oxford, a silence which may have seemed to confirm the familiar image of puritan Cambridge and churchy, conservative Oxford. It is time that the balance was redressed. The puritanism of Elizabethan Oxford has been persistently underestimated,[18] and only rarely has due recognition been accorded to the influence of what was perhaps the most remarkable puritan society in either university, Magdalen under Humphrey's presidency. Later in the reign the university had its own Chaderton in John Reynolds, president of Corpus Christi College. Admittedly the total of Oxford puritans is not impressive by Cambridge standards, although due allowance must be made for the weakness of Foster's biographical dictionary when compared with J. A. Venn's massive labours for the other place. Oxford's catchment area had not yet been so well watered by protestant influences as the eastern counties. Even so, I have traced forty-two puritan ministers who were in residence at Oxford in the decade 1565–75. And Oxford puritans were noticeably more extreme, brought up, it may be, in a harsher school. Field and Wilcox were both Oxford men, and so were many of the most radical preachers who were ringleaders of the definitely presbyterian *classis* movement of the 'eighties: for example John Oxenbridge of Warwickshire, Edward Fleetwood of Lancashire, Josias Nichols of Kent, Richard Crick of Norwich and the Dedham conference, Edward Gellibrand of Oxford itself. And almost all the leaders in Northamptonshire – the most presbyterian of counties – were bred in either Christ Church or Magdalen. At least seventeen Elizabethan fellows of Magdalen became puritan ministers, most of them of some prominence, and the college produced lay puritans of the calibre of Francis Hastings and Laurence Tomson.[19] (John Hampden and John Pym, one remembers, were Oxford men of a later generation.) Exeter College, too, was laying the foundations of West Country puritanism. In 1662, Devon would provide the largest number of ejected ministers of any county, sixty-four of them graduates of Exeter.[20]

If puritan conferences were a projection of university associations, the tendency of the Church to divide into puritan and anti-puritan factions equally had its beginnings in the universities. Every college with a group of puritan fellows strong enough to wield power or assert its distinctiveness was prone to factious disputes in which religion played a large part. It happened in St John's repeatedly and in Christ's; in Oxford it happened in Magdalen.[21] But the factions in Trinity were especially significant for the future, for the master was Whitgift and he passed on to Lincoln, Worcester and Canterbury without ever altering the headmasterly way in which he dealt with his inferiors, whether they were junior fellows or troublesome preachers. We possess an account of the troubled career of one of these, Giles Wigginton, which traces everything back to the friends and enemies made at Trinity in Whitgift's time. Making every allowance for the warped mind of this unbalanced and quarrelsome man, we see that the party lines were drawn in the university and not subsequently altered. From the beginning of his mastership, Whitgift made no secret of his dislike of 'such scholars and boys as durst be bold to reprove sin and to call for reformation', and already they were to him 'saucy boys, busybodies and meddlers with matters of estate'. Wigginton, 'as happy it was', was of their number. Whitgift had his kindred spirits – his 'complices' as his enemy saw them – and Wigginton won their hatred by his censure of their 'prelatical and Antichristian behaviour and proceedings on behalf of the pseudo-hierarchy or false holy government of the Church' and because he 'kept not company with them, but with the defenders of Christian reformation.' Whitgift took his friends with him to Worcester and thence to Lambeth as his officials and chaplains. Wigginton continued to meet with persecution because he regularly snubbed this coterie – on one occasion, in St Paul's, he shrank from Godfrey Goldsborough's outstretched hand 'as if he had been a serpent' – and because he 'refrained from the company and sermons of the prelatical in order to meet with the godly.'[22]

4 The Early Presbyterian Movement

'REVOLUTION' IS A WORD which comes readily and even glibly to the tongue of a twentieth-century historian. Yet it is not improper to describe John Field and his accomplices as revolutionaries, not merely because their demands were so extreme, but because they rested on traditional conceptions of the unity and comprehensiveness of the Church. Field almost certainly shared the company of the London separatists, and like them nourished a fervent hatred for the bishops and all their ways. For him, as for them, it was a matter of debate whether all the marks of a true Church of God were to be found in the Elizabethan establishment. Yet unlike so many 'simple gospellers', he dreaded the prospect of sectarian fission and saw no good in a separatist course. Field's quarrel with Elizabethan Anglicanism derived not from incorrigible dissent but from a Calvinist's zeal for unity. The pathetic confusion which divided the London godly was in his view the inevitable consequence of the episcopal insistence on a uniformity of a contrary and ungodly kind.

Sectarianism for Field was only a means to an end both more orthodox and more ambitious. There were other circles in which the young preacher enjoyed, or brazenly claimed, acceptance. He was an admirer and perhaps a pupil of Humphrey, a contributor of material to Foxe's *Acts and Monuments*, and a regular correspondent of 'Father Gilby'. No doubt he partly shared the mind of these mature reformers who never doubted that Elizabeth's Church, for all its faults, was a true evangelical Church, and he found it hard, if not impossible, to think of reformation in any other terms than as a public act to be imposed on the Commonwealth by law and discipline. 'For Sion's sake I will not hold my peace' was the motto of the *Admonition*; and of the *Second admonition* 'The Lord hath sent me to prophesy against this house and against this city.' So, after all, England was Jerusalem and not Babylon. Through the 'Christian acquaintance' of Wilcox, Thomas Wood and other partisans, the movement enjoyed the indulgence and even the active support of 'inferior magistrates', some of them men of great influence. With friends of this calibre it was no time to withdraw into a narrow and obscure separation. Yet there was need to convince these sometimes complacent allies of the desperate diagnosis of the Church's sickness which Field had learned in the religious under-world. From this source came the impatience which even Beza had deplored, and which now led Field and his friends to anticipate the legal enactment of the reforms for which their *Admonition* had clamoured. Already they were proceeding to practical measures which implied that they themselves and their congregations – 'our churches' – constituted the only true Church in England.

Their state of mind was later characterized in the Star Chamber by a London minister who was a member of Field's circle almost from the beginning. In 1591 Thomas Edmunds was to depose that 'some of the said brotherhood which have desired the said discipline' held that those congregations of the Church of England which had rejected it and which willingly submitted themselves to episcopal government were 'not to be accounted the churches of God so fully as those that had voluntarily subscribed themselves wholly or in some part unto the said discipline.' When they wrote of 'the church or churches of God here wish this or that', or 'the church in London hath done this or that', they meant especially the ministers of their own brotherhood or faction. With some justice Whitgift complained that the Admonitioners' 'whole intent was to make a separation and a schism, and to withdraw men from their ordinary churches and pastors.' Yet Cartwright was in good faith when he re-torted: 'We make no separation from the Church; we go about to separate all those things that offend in the Church, to the end that we, being all knit to the sincere truth of the gospel, might afterwards in the same bond of truth be more nearly and closely joined together.'[1]

The Elizabethan presbyterians were torn between an actual state of schism and their devotion to the Calvinist ideal of a Christian society in which the godly magistrate underwrote the discipline of the Church. They conducted themselves sometimes like separatists, sometimes like tenacious if aggrieved members of the establishment, and the discomfort of this ambiguous position was virtually chronic. Robert Browne, the separatist, has recorded his recollections of the inflamed puritan conscience as it afflicted him in his pre-separatist days at Cambridge in the 'seventies:

> While R.B. thought these things in himself, he moved the matter divers times unto others. Some did gainsay, and those of the forwardest, affirming that the bishops' authority is tolerable, and he might take licence and authority of them. Others of them said they would not counsel nor meddle for another man's conscience in that matter, but they themselves judged that the bishops preached the word of God and therefore ought not lightly to be rejected. Also they said that seeing they had the word and the sacraments, they must needs have withal the Church and people of God; and seeing this was under the government of the bishops and by means of them, they could not wholly condemn the bishops, but rather judge them faulty in some part. Then did R.B. again and again discuss these matters, as he had often before, as whether the bishops could be said to preach the word of God and minister the sacraments, or no.[2]

These contradictions would ultimately prove confusing and debilitating for the puritan movement, but for as long as the settlement of the Church appeared to be in a fluid state and there seemed to be a realistic prospect of further reformation, they were a potent stimulant. The rarefied and disciplined fervour of the sect was contained within the national Church, preserved from introspection by its devotion to a great public cause.

The ringleaders of the original presbyterian party were at first concentrated in London. The innermost circle contained several survivors of the Marian congregation in Geneva, one of whom, reproaching William Whittingham for his defection, could describe the stauncher puritans as 'a remnant of your old acquaintance'. They included Christopher Goodman, who was in London at the time of the 1571 Parliament and held a living in Bedfordshire from May of that year until the following March. Very active in the cause were two brothers-in-law, both sometime elders of the Geneva church, Thomas Wood and William Williams. Wood lived at Tottenham in the 'sixties, but before 1570 moved to Leicestershire where he served as an invaluable intermediary between London and the Midlands. He was a puritan of the puritans, fearless and contentious, always knowing the mind of the godly, never afraid to reveal it to high or low with caustic candour. Two other Genevan elders remained in

London and were still active in godly causes: John Bodley, financial sponsor of the Geneva Bible and father of the founder of the Bodleian, and William Fuller, whose place in 'the little flock of Hatfield' of the queen's youth gave him an easy entrée to the Court. Still living in Cheapside was a widow who might almost be described as a female elder or deaconess: Anne Locke, whom Knox had loved best of all his feminine acquaintance, and who in Mary's reign had deserted her husband and taken her babies to join him in 'the most perfect school of Christ that ever was in the earth since the days of the apostles.'[3]

Add to the Genevans the younger radicals among the London ministers, among them our informant, Thomas Edmunds, who came down from Magdalen to a London living in 1571. Later he would describe how almost at once he 'began to be acquainted with that sort of men here in the city of London that stand so much upon reformation', and of how he was 'drawn into that company' by Field and Wilcox 'especially'. The other 'ministers of the brotherhood' at that time were Nicholas Standon and Edward Saintloe (or Sinclair), two incumbents deprived in 1566, and William Bonham, Nicholas Crane and Seth Jackson. Edmunds describes how they met in their own houses 'by course' on Mondays and Thursdays, and conferred on some book of the Bible. Their meetings were private to themselves, although they might agree to admit a country minister coming to town who was already known to them or who wanted to make their acquaintance. Their conference already bore an embryonic relationship to the *classis* described in the handbooks of presbyterian polity. If it was a purely clerical body, then so for the most part were the early *classes* and synods of French and Dutch Calvinism. Edmunds's evidence confirms what there is otherwise no reason to doubt: that this body maintained an unbroken existence for the next twenty years and later served to co-ordinate the developing network of country conferences. Already Field was amassing his 'register' of petitions, accounts of trials and other 'troubles' from many counties, and the survival of this material from the early 'seventies onwards is in itself tangible evidence of the web of correspondence spun from the London conference.[4]

We should not lose sight of other London ministers of neo-Calvinist convictions who were not so closely dependent on Field. They included Robert Johnson, preacher at St Clement's without Temple Bar (not to be confused with his namesake, Sir Nicholas Bacon's chaplain); John Browne, the duchess of Suffolk's chaplain; and Dr Thomas Penny, one of Cartwright's Trinity contemporaries, a prebendary of St Paul's and a London physician described by Grindal as 'a chief doer in these matters'. Like

William Turner, Penny was a pioneer naturalist and a friend of the great Conrad Gesner.

All these were overshadowed by the young Cambridge prodigy, Edward Dering, who if not, as some thought, 'the greatest learned man in England', was for a time the most celebrated preacher in London. Dering combined a reputation for evangelical holiness with the sharpest of puritan tongues, to which the Kentish magnate Lord Abergavenny was mercilessly exposed in the very exordium of one of his 'godly and comfortable' letters:

> Though I know that our Saviour Christ hath given us a straight charge not to cast precious stones before swine, nor to give that which is holy to dogs; yet I see so many examples of His unspeakable mercies, that I know not any swine so wallowing in the mire, nor any dog so returning to his vomit, of whom I have not some hope that he may be a pure and clean creature in Israel. This maketh me bold with a good conscience to write unto your Honour ...

In 1570 the queen herself suffered Dering's righteous indignation in a reckless sermon on her responsibility towards God's Church which neither she nor the puritans ever forgot. When the failings of Cecil and Archbishop Parker were laid bare with equal candour, the way to preferment was blocked, to the sorrow of Dering's elder brother, a Kentish squire of ancient family. But this Elizabethan Savonarola went on to win a more than episcopal reputation as reader of the divinity lecture in St Paul's. In 1573 he defended some of the propositions of the Admonitionists and for a time drew the main fire of the bishops' counter-attack, but he was never so concerned with what he called 'the shadow of sin' – outward forms – as he was with its substance.[5]

Finally among these early presbyterians a place of special honour has to be reserved for Laurence Tomson, another Magdalen man and a lay scholar of rare distinction. With George Withers he entered the university of Heidelberg in 1568 (at the age of twenty-nine) and he lived for some time in Geneva, where he made a new translation of the New Testament, based on Beza, which was later included in the Geneva Bible. Tomson later served as Sir Francis Walsingham's secretary (one of those positions of the second rank which Calvinists in all the western European states exploited so effectively). He sat frequently in Parliament. Tomson was evidently a most important member of the presbyterian party. His letters to Gilby are written with authority, and when Wilcox was later in disgrace, it was enough for Field to quote the opinion of 'Master Cartwright and Master Tomson' that he should abandon his ministry.[6]

Such was 'the church in London'. In its name Field was now urging puritan ministers everywhere to draw together into a closer understanding through conference, and to agree on a Confession of Faith and a form of Discipline. This would be to erect a regularly reformed church on the neo-Calvinist pattern and in virtual separation from the establishment. At the same time every opportunity was seized to commend the drastic new programme to susceptible gentlemen, and perhaps even more to their wives. Two collections of the *Admonition* and the associated pamphlets have survived,[7] each inscribed with an address in doggerel, signed by Field and addressed to ladies of his acquaintance, 'my loving friend Mrs Wright' and 'Mrs Catesby, my very friend'. Two verses will suffice:

> Read and peruse this little book
> with prayer to the Lord
> That all may yield that therein look
> to truth with one accord;
>
> Which, though our troubles it hath wrought,
> it shall prevail at last,
> And utterly confound God His foes
> with His confounding blast.

Apparently Newgate prison was as good a base as any for these operations.

To justify the dangerous measures which were now in the air Field had to convince his correspondents that the bishops had put themselves beyond all brotherly regard. Gilby, whose support he coveted especially, was told that the quarrel was no longer confined to indifferent things: some bishops had already professed false doctrine 'in defence of their corruptions'. They had banished and imprisoned some brethren – these were the separatists of Fitz's church – and had made martyrs of others. Many had been driven to sectarian extremes 'as full of errors as opinions'. 'Again their own foreheads are made like brass, and those things which at first Christian religion withheld them from, now they command (as men fleshed in such wickedness) with all temerity and boldness; enclosed in their own fat, they speak proudly like men of the world, have set their face against the most Highest.' In vain Whitgift would protest that there was no question of violence being used. 'Thanks be unto God, there is no cause why you should fear.' The image of the bloody persecutor was an essential ingredient of Field's propaganda. Gilby was invited to compare 'our misery, their cruelty, our religion, their superstition, our duty, their negligence'. This was to deploy within the Elizabethan Church and within English protestantism the familiar dualistic theme of Christ and Antichrist.

With the older nonconformist leaders indifferent to Field's extreme diagnosis, the greatest danger facing the left wing was 'mutual dissension'; the remedy, conference. 'I write all this to this purpose, that as of late there was a conference, so it might again be renewed, everyone submitting their judgment to the mighty word of God, and simply for God's glory to take the matter in hand ... ' Behind these excited appeals was fear both of sectarian confusion itself, and of the polemical use which their enemies would certainly make of it. 'For we are charged to be heretics, Donatists, anabaptists and I cannot tell what.' True enough: Whitgift was soon assuring his correspondents that the *Admonition* contained 'the very steps and degrees to anabaptism', and in November 1572 his *Answere to the admonition* exploited this debating-point to the full. To refute these damaging charges, Field urged that a renewed conference should draft a puritan Confession of Faith. 'This thing, if it may take place and go forwards, I am persuaded that it will work much peace amongst us, otherwise I assure myself that there will follow horrible and grievous dissension, which shall break out into open persecution and destruction one of another.'[8]

To turn from these letters to the correspondence of the French reformed churches at a comparable stage of their development is to remain in the same rhetorical key and even to encounter the same phraseology. The fear of 'horrible and grievous dissension' is an echo of the exhortations which the French Calvinists were exchanging in 1559, in preparation for the first national synod in Paris which united them in a common Confession of Faith and Discipline. Field's letters had precisely the same significance. With Wilcox he was planning a general subscription to certain presbyterian principles, translating the *Admonition* into Latin for the purpose, with the intention of sending it out 'to the churches'. The projected Confession would presumably have been put to the same purpose. 'Let your churches understand our case,' Field wrote to Leicestershire, and added suggestively, 'the same that I write to you I write to others.' But in the event, Field and Wilcox were dissuaded from steps which would have made their schism formal, and they decided moreover that the puritan retort to Whitgift should not come from them, 'because our enemies seek by some second offence to condemn us to perpetual imprisonment, therefore by advice we stay our pens.' No doubt the visits of so many puritan ministers to Newgate in the winter of 1572–3 were not unconnected with this belated display of caution.[9]

Even so, some experiments in presbyterian practice were attempted, and with the encouragement of the London conference. The few surviving scraps of evidence for this enterprise are enigmatic, but they resemble the small part of an iceberg which projects above the surface, and it would obviously be perilous to proceed as if they were not there. Among Field's papers which later fell into the hands of Bancroft and were exploited in his exposure of the presbyterian movement was a 'bill' dated November 20th, 1572, and endorsed in Field's hand (though not necessarily contemporaneously) 'the order of Wandsworth'. According to Bancroft this document was evidence for the erection of a presbytery (in the sense of a congregational consistory) and of the election of eleven 'elders' with two 'approvers', Smith of Mitcham and Crane of Roehampton. It also contained a description of their office and certain general rules which 'were likewise agreed upon'. Bancroft tells us no more, although this evidence was as crucial for his purposes as it is for ours, and we must hesitate before joining the modern presbyterian denomination in celebrating November 20th as their anniversary. We cannot be sure that the word 'elder' appeared in the original document: the chances are strong that Bancroft introduced it, and in a loose and pejorative sense. Dr Scott Pearson suspected that this was an episode in separatist rather than presbyterian history (there is significantly no mention of the puritan vicar of Wandsworth, John Edwin) and, knowing how far Field leant in that direction, he may be right, although the distinction has little meaning at this remote date. But there is no reason, as Scott Pearson thought, to identify 'Crane of Roehampton' with Nicholas Crane, the separatist preacher. 'Mr and Mrs Crane of Roehampton' were among Thomas Wilcox's correspondents and one is inclined to identify them with Anthony Crane, master of the queen's household, and his wife Elizabeth who lived at East Molesey Priory, not far away. Elizabeth Crane would later marry the Northamptonshire puritan M.P. George Carleton, and at about the same time her Thames-side house was made available for the printing of the first of the Marprelate Tracts. Details like these arouse an appetite which is unlikely to be satisfied much further.[10]

Two other fragments provide some kind of setting for the Wandsworth evidence. Field's documentary 'register' includes an inquiry from a schoolmaster pressed by the congregation of a parish church to become its pastor, and the reply from the London conference overcoming his scruples and urging him to accept the charge. He is told that he must first be lawfully called to the congregation and then and only then ordained by the laying on of hands of the presbytery. The letter is undated, but the names of the signatories – Field, Wilcox, Crane, Standon, Sinclair – suggest that it was written early in the life of the conference, perhaps in 1571. The other evidence is the more startling in that it comes from the remoteness of rural Shropshire. In 1573 one of Cartwright's contemporaries at Trinity, William Axton, was brought from Cambridge to serve the cure of Moreton Corbet where the patron was Sir Andrew Corbet, a leading magnate of the Welsh Marches. If we are to believe Axton himself, no detail of reformed procedure was neglected in settling him in his cure. Having first preached 'divers times' in what he calls 'an ordinary assembly' of ten preachers, he was called to the ministry by a formal decision of this body. Episcopal ordination was later added, apparently as a mere civil appendage. Axton then entered his charge by the free election of the parishioners, to whom Corbet had delegated his rights as patron. After spending six weeks among his people, a neighbouring minister, 'one of my brethren', preached an induction sermon, after which he was 'chosen with one consent of them all to be their pastor.' Bishop Bentham appears to have been unmoved by these revelations, which would not have been made if Axton had not called in question the validity of the bishop's own calling![11]

In April 1573 Cartwright's *Replye* to Whitgift's *Answere to the admonition* appeared from a secret press and provided a new stimulus; a second edition followed in June. During Field's confinement Goodman seems to have acted as publisher, and he very possibly wrote the *Second admonition* (an obscure and diffuse essay which made little impact) which passed through the same press in November 1572. If so it explains why the authorship has remained a well-kept secret; Goodman's name was a lasting liability. A few details can be pieced together about the mechanical production of these and other minor tracts which continued during a year of fruitless search for the press by a pursuivant and other officers, acting for both the bishop and the Stationers' Company (actively represented according to the puritan press by 'Day the printer and Toy the bookbinder'). A puckish piece of doggerel on the title-page of one pamphlet is signed 'J.T.J.S.', while the second edition of Cartwright's *Replye* has an epistle with the signature 'J.S.'. Who J.T. was we do not know, but J.S. stands for John Strowd, a Somerset clergyman deprived of his living in 1568 and now something of a free-lance, a preacher and also a printer, though 'without long training up in this mystery'. The only clues to the whereabouts of the press are Strowd's statements in his preface to the *Replye* that he was not within easy reach of the author or of any 'that is made privy unto his book', and at his examination before the Ecclesiastical Commissioners that he was 'one hundred miles off'; that is from London, where the wife of Richard Martin, goldsmith and master of the Mint, acted as stationer for the book in Cheapside. This suggests that there may have been substance in the rumour on which the Privy Council acted in March that the *Replye* was being printed in Northamptonshire. This was already an important outpost of presbyterian activity, and the backers were some of the same gentlemen who would shelter the secret Marprelate press fifteen years later. However, in late August the bishop of London's pursuivant, acting on information supplied to Archbishop Parker and Bishop Horne by one Humphrey Needham (of whom more presently), caught up with the press at 'Hempsteade' – Hemel Hempstead? – and arrested a printer called Lacy 'with certain others of that confederacy', Strowd included. At the time of the arrest, one thousand copies of the second edition had been printed, of which only thirty-four fell into the bishop's hands. Many copies were already dispersed and the remainder were burned by Mrs Strowd.

This mishap was far from terminating Strowd's career. In 1574 he was preaching at Yalding in the diocese of Rochester. Driven from there and excommunicate he settled over the diocesan border at Cranbrook, a staunchly puritan district of the Kentish weald. There the vicar's son, Richard Fletcher (the future bishop of London and father of the dramatist), complained of the preaching of sufficiently inflammatory doctrine: 'that those which were not sent of the spirit should never do good in the ministry' and that the bishops 'would be called gracious lords, but you may call them ungracious knaves.' Fletcher junior retaliated by spreading rumours of the printing of seditious pamphlets 'within the compass of Cranbrook'. But by this time the puritans were relying on an overseas press, in Heidelberg, and Strowd was employed as a colporteur rather than as a printer, making good use of his busy Kentish perambulations to distribute Travers's presbyterian handbook, the *Explicatio*.[12]

The movements of the puritan press and of the printers are indicative of the widening influence of the presbyterian movement. During one of Strowd's periodic brushes with the ecclesiastical authorities in Kent, testimonials were signed in his favour in all parts of the county. Among the subscribers were several of the gentry, including Thomas Wootton, a friend and patron of Edward Dering, who would later do battle for the puritan ministers before Archbishop Whitgift, Martin Harlackinden of

Woodchurch, Wilcox's 'most intimate friend' and especial patron, and Dame Elizabeth Golding of East Peckham, an importunate friend of Dering.[13]

Cartwright's teaching was now being widely dispersed by his contemporaries and admirers from Cambridge: by William Axton as far away as Shropshire, by Richard Chambers as vicar of Hitchin, by Edmund Chapman as town preacher of Bedford: all were fellows of Trinity in Cartwright's time. Chambers was credited with preaching – probably in 1573 – that 'the godly are to sigh and mourn for discipline ecclesiastical and church discipline, and such as are used in churches not far hence.' Norfolk received new prophets: John More and Thomas Roberts from Christ's, Richard Crick from Humphrey's Magdalen and, presently, Chapman expelled from Bedford by the bishop of Lincoln. An impressive reformation was soon in progress in Norwich Cathedral and in many of the city's forty churches, with the warm approval of Bishop Parkhurst and the magistrates. 'Oh the heavenly harmony and sweet amity that then was amongst you from the highest to the lowest,' one of the Norwich preachers later remembered. 'No matters of weight were usually concluded in your common assemblies for the good of your city before ye had first consulted with your grave and godly preachers.' Leicestershire, where the Hastings family exerted a pervasive, moderate puritan influence, was at this time an important outpost of the presbyterian movement. Gilby at Ashby-de-la-Zouch and Sampson at Leicester were the most radical and outspoken of the older generation of puritan divines, and Gilby maintained sympathetic contact with the younger leaders. Laurence Tomson was living in Leicester in 1573, while Thomas Wood had established himself outside the town in Lady Jane Grey's old home at Groby.[14]

But the most remarkable conquests were made in Northamptonshire, a county not hitherto especially noted for its protestantism (it produced only one Marian martyr) and where there were a number of influential catholic recusant families, Tresham, Catesby and Vaux. Here the puritan preachers may have been the effective apostles of a more than merely formal protestantism, and Rome and Geneva were directly confronted. A literal model of Calvin's Geneva itself was devised for Northampton in 1571 by the first and most notable of the Northamptonshire preachers, Percival Wiburn. How far this project was ever fully realized may be doubted, for Wiburn's ministry in Northampton began in 1570 and was cut short early in 1572. Nevertheless 'the order of Northampton' – one might as well say the 'ecclesiastical ordinances' of Northampton –

sanctioned by the bishop of Peterborough, the mayor and other justices of the town and country, is a notable example of puritan enterprise. 'Will you not send Master Wyburn to Northampton,' asked Martin Marprelate in 1588, 'that he may see some fruits of the seed he sowed there sixteen or eighteen years ago?' Wiburn's order defined a weekly cycle of workaday sermons in the parish churches and the preparative services and main sermons and catechizings on a Sunday, as well as the four solemn communions of the year. Attendance was compulsory and regulated under discipline, which was exercised partly by the ministers and churchwardens playing the part of elders, and partly, as the equivalent of the Geneva consistory, by a weekly assembly of the mayor and bailiffs, assisted by the preachers and employing 'the bishop's authority and the mayor's joined together'. There was weekly 'prophesying' for the ministers of the town and neighbouring country, and a quarterly assembly of all the ministers of the shire, with the Calvinist practice of mutual 'censure'. The reaction from the local papists and 'neuters' was understandably vigorous. A printed ballad cast in the streets and inspired by the pope's excommunication of the queen was defiant:

> Maister Wyborne, alias tiburne tyke,
> Here dwelleth in this towne,
> Which sought by all the meanes he could,
> The Easter to pluck downe.
>
> But I of hym doe well pronounce
> And tyme the truth shall try,
> That he shall trust unto his heeles
> Or els in Smithfield fry.[15]

In 1572 Wiburn's enemies got the better of him, and in spite of urgent representations to the bishop from the earl of Leicester he was silenced. Leicester's letters are an indication of the backing which the reform of Northampton had enjoyed. Wiburn was called to the town 'from his book' at the instance of certain gentlemen of the county who no doubt procured his licence to preach as well as the bishop's approval for his 'order'. The identity of some of these gentlemen is not in doubt. They must have included George Carleton of Overston, Sir Richard Knightley of Fawsley and, in all probability, Roger Wigston of Wolston Priory, over the Warwickshire border, Antony Cope of Hanwell in neighbouring Oxfordshire and Peter Wentworth of Lillingstone-Lovell. Carleton and

Wentworth hunted together in the House of Commons where both sat for the first time in 1571; Carleton would later appoint Wentworth, his 'beloved in the Lord', overseer of his will; and Cope, sponsor of the presbyterian bill and book in the 1586 Parliament, was Carleton's stepson. In all probability it was Carleton who brought Wiburn to Northampton, for in October 1570 he was representing his interests in London.

Other preachers soon followed to occupy the ground which Wiburn had prospected. They included the Londoner Nicholas Standon, two unlicensed preachers dependent on Carleton, Andrew King and Edward Bulkeley, and two young Oxford puritans, both of Northamptonshire gentry stock, who were to be major figures in the puritan movement in the Midlands: Arthur Wake, rector of Great Billing, and Eusebius Paget, rector of Old. Wake married the sister of Roger Wigston of Wolston. Paget's militant protestantism perhaps dated from an injury done to his arm by the pax which he was handling in a religious ceremony at Oxford in his youth: 'Lame Eusebius Paget, the Lord's servant' was his normal subscription. On June 9th, 1572, perhaps in the very week that the *Admonition* appeared from the press, he had preached within a mile of Greenwich Palace that the Pharisees were 'as abbots and cardinals in the papacy, or (that I may speak more familiarly and plainly) like to our lord bishops amongst us.' There were soon some thirty godly converts 'going forward' in Wake's own parish and encouraging results elsewhere.[16]

The conservative state of Northamptonshire made these converts of the Calvinist preaching virtual separatists; and when they were deprived of a preaching ministry in their own parishes, their separation became open. In his visitation of March 1573, Bishop Scambler discovered that the puritans who had been deprived of Wiburn's preaching were flocking out of every parish in Northampton to the neighbouring village of Whiston to receive the communion 'with preachers and ministers to their own liking and contrary to form prescribed by public order of the realm.' It was at Whiston that Wiburn's son Nathaniel was born, which perhaps tells us all that we need to know about these Sunday excursions. At Carleton's own parish of Overston the Prayer Book was abandoned for psalm-singing and preaching by Standon and King, described by the bishop as 'men for their opinions not licensed by me to preach at this day.' Scambler complained to Burghley of these disorders, hinting that the stoutness of the puritans argued the support of 'great friends', meaning in all probability the earl of Leicester. That scurrilous libel *Leycesters Commonwealth* would later contrive to represent the puritan assemblies in gentlemen's houses as meetings of his political faction.[17]

The most eloquent memorial to this early Northamptonshire presbyterian movement exists in the will of an otherwise obscure person, a servant of Carleton, one Robert Smythe. The document was witnessed by the preachers, Standon and Bulkeley, Wiburn and Wake were executors, and Carleton added his own signature to that of the testator. Smythe began with a long homiletical preamble, remarkable in that it includes an affirmation of presbyterian faith: 'As I acknowledge all sovereignties to worldly and civil states allowed by God's word, so I profess that they have already drawn to their hands forth in the scripture, either by express words or general sentences, direct rules to govern God's Church, whereunto they ought only to keep themselves in such matters.' The remainder is redolent of the religious revolution which had swept over Northamptonshire in three years. Legacies of five pounds apiece are made to the preachers, Wiburn, Wake, King, Bulkeley and Standon, ten pounds to 'the faithful poor men of Northampton', including 'godly Grymston Potter', and ten pounds 'to the afflicted churches, either of the strangers or of our own'. There is some curious evidence of Smythe's own puritan conversion in directions to repay with interest sums as small as fourpence stolen years before as a boy in places as far away as Gloucester and Banbury.[18]

In Northamptonshire by this time the supposed uniformity of the community in a moderate Anglican protestantism was transparently a fiction. A political memorandum composed for Burghley's eyes by Carleton, perhaps in 1572,[19] assumes that the true protestants, here identified with the 'precisians', already form a distinct community, separated from the other two sorts of subjects, 'papists' and 'atheists'. 'This realm', he wrote, thinking no doubt of his own country especially:

hath a great people, daily increasing, which are professors of the gospel towards sincerity. And as they hate all heresies and popery, so they cannot be persuaded to bear liking of the queen's proceedings in religion, by reason that our Church here is not reformed. This people consist of all degrees, from the nobility to the lowest. And so hot is the desire of God's truth in them that they will not [re]frain themselves to favour any the laws or ordinances set forth by the queen in God's matters, but such as are void of all offence, and reformed according to sincerity. This people, as they do not like the course of our Church, so they do and will practise assemblies of brethren in all parts of this realm, and have their own churches in companies ...

Yet they are not to be punished, 'because they are the queen's own bowels, her dearest subjects.' Carleton proposes both that this godly party should be formed into a kind of military elite to be concentrated in the twenty counties nearest London, 'to be framed to the defence of the gospel and preservation of the state when the day of sorrow [Elizabeth's death?] shall come'; and that they should be permitted to withdraw from the rest of society, either by congregating 'in companies together, and to have their own churches' in England, or by resettlement in Ulster.

The first idea points to the Bond of Association to which loyal protestant gentlemen would subscribe for the queen's defence ten years later. But it also contains a premonition of the Cromwellian rule of the saints; for if the Crown were to fall into the lap of Mary Stuart, Carleton's militia would surely devote itself to the overthrow of the monarchy rather than to its preservation. The second, secessionist proposal was to have its ultimate and logical fulfilment in the puritan colonization of New England. But the immediate significance of this incisive yet curiously inconsistent document lies in its revelation of the confused mind of Elizabethan presbyterianism, torn between a genuine, if pragmatic devotion to the queen and an inclination to hang on to a privileged and dominant place in the Commonwealth as her very 'bowels'; and an actual state of schismatic withdrawal which in some places was already far advanced.

THE PAPER VICTORIES of their secret press brought the presbyterians to a state of temporary euphoria. In May 1573 Laurence Tomson reported that after the queen had read and re-read Cartwright's *Replye to an answere* she had forbidden 'the enemy of the truth' (Whitgift) to answer it. 'This is given forth in London; of the truth of it I am not certain.'[1] A few months earlier Edward Dering had found himself a fellow-guest at supper with one of the literary assistants employed by Archbishop Parker on his lives of the archbishops, the *De antiquitate ecclesiae Britannicae*. He told him to take his time over Parker's own life, 'for peradventure he should be the last that should sit in that place.'[2] This was table-talk, spoken 'merrily', but the same theme was to be pursued with venom as well as wit by an anonymous satirist, or perhaps a syndicate of young satirists,[3] in an annotated version of Parker's own official biography, *The life of the 70. archbishopp off Canterbury presentlye sitting Englished*, printed overseas in 1574. In case the reader should miss the point, it was announced on the title-page: *This numbre of seventy is so compleat a number as it is great pitie ther shold be one more: but that as Augustin was the first, so Mathew might be the last.*

To read Parker's correspondence without due allowance for his lugubrious nature (and, by now, ill-health) is to conclude that he had already morally surrendered himself and his order to these onslaughts. 'The comfort that these puritans have, and their continuance, is marvellous', he told Burghley in March 1573 ' ... and but that we have our whole trust in God, in her Majesty, and in two or three of her Council, I see it will be no dwelling for us in England.' That he should feel constrained to send the lord treasurer an account of his annual expenditure was a token of the defensive attitude which the bishops were now forced to adopt. So was his notorious offer to 'refer the standing or falling altogether to your own considerations, whether her Majesty and you will have any archbishops or bishops, or how you will have them ordered.'[4] In June he wrote: 'Before God, it is not the fear I am in of displacing,[5] but I would wish her Majesty's safety and estimation.' Sandys shared his despondency: 'Our estimation is little, our authority is less, so that we are become contemptible in the eyes of the basest sort of people.' Horne of Winchester agreed that the bishops were '*spectaculum mundo*', no, rather '*excrementa mundi*'.[6]

Parker and the bishops were angling for some acknowledgment from the Court and the Council of a common interest with the clergy in resisting the new subversion. But with few exceptions, privy councillors and courtiers took a complacent view of their embarrassment. Leicester's reaction to the *Admonition* had been to blame both sides for the divided state of the Church, but his actions argued as much contempt for the bishops as he showed sympathy for their opponents. He was Parker's enemy and a good friend of puritans of the calibre of Christopher Goodman and Percival Wiburn. Sandys was harassed at this time by 'sundry letters from noblemen' on behalf of Field and Wilcox, and was widely blamed for their continued confinement.[7]

The negative content of the presbyterian programme, which attracted the most attention, was deceptively anti-clerical in its tendency, and never perhaps were the anti-clerical and anti-ecclesiastical instincts of the age so much in evidence as in 1573. We are now in the aftermath of the St Bartholomew atrocities in France in the late summer of 1572, which seemed to confirm all that protestants had ever suspected about an international conspiracy against the gospel. It was no time for the bishops to convince the nobility and gentry that godly preachers were a threat to the state, or to erase the suspicion that as wealthy prelates their interest lay in preserving their own estates against just and patriotic criticism. As luck would have it, Parker chose this inauspicious moment to present some of the nobility with de luxe copies of his *De antiquitate*, decorated with the illuminated coats of arms of all the bishops, quartered with those of their sees, his own most prominent of all.[8] When he sent Burghley his copy, the archbishop already knew that his courteous little plot must backfire: 'Yet ye may relinquish the leaf and cast it in the fire, as I have joined it but loose in the book for that purpose, if you so think it meet; and as ye may if it so please you (without great grief to me) cast the whole book the same way.' In 1559 Laurence Humphrey had written that lordly prelates were unworthy of their calling even if they could vouch 'infinite descents and pedigrees of their race'.[9] Against this kind of prejudice Parker's only means of self-preservation was to warn the nobility that the puritans were bent on an anabaptist 'Münzer's commonwealth'.[10] 'Surely if this fond faction be applauded to, or borne with, it will fall out to a popularity, and as wise men think, it will be the overthrow of all the nobility.'[11]

The archbishop has left a revealing memorandum of an afternoon which he and the bishop of London spent in attendance on the Council in the Star Chamber in late May 1573, when Dering, Wiburn, Johnson and Browne were examined for their parts in dispersing the *Replye* or maintaining its doctrines. These ministers all had useful connections. Dering was an intimate friend of Mrs Catherine Killigrew, the sister-in-law of Burghley and Sir Nicholas Bacon, and Johnson was Bacon's own chaplain. Browne was chaplain to the duchess of Suffolk, and Wiburn had the backing of the earl of Leicester, as did Field and Wilcox who were examined separately on the same occasion. The two prelates sat through the afternoon without being asked to speak, until Parker at last broke in to say that unless something was done, the queen and the city would be disappointed. He was told: 'We see what they answer; we may not deal with them as in popish time.' The archbishop was then asked what he himself had to say against the ministers. When Parker replied that he had plenty of matter against each of them, but that he had not come to accuse them, he was asked what he and Sandys were doing there. They replied that they had been sent for, 'which was granted.' Burghley's version of the day's business was that after having asked for this judicial hearing, neither of the prelates had brought any specific charge against Dering, the principal defendant. In the strange atmosphere of this summer and autumn, Burghley on his side and the bishops on theirs were alternately demanding that Dering should be silenced and denying that the responsibility for his suspension was theirs. All knew the need for a stronger hand. None coveted the obloquy that would inevitably attach to those who showed it. The result was that Dering continued his popular St Paul's lectures until just before Christmas, when he was commanded to cease 'in her Majesty's name'.[12]

But Parker's afternoon in the Star Chamber was not entirely wasted. He seized the opportunity to ask Burghley for a royal proclamation against the puritan propaganda and Burghley saw that he got it. This was the first intimation of a reaction which was to gather force in the second half of the year. The proclamation, which appeared on June 11th, enjoined conformity to the ecclesiastical laws and required all copies of the *Admonition* and the *Replye* to be surrendered to the bishops or to the Council, unless a licence was obtained from a bishop to retain them. Yet when the twenty days of grace allowed by the proclamation were expired, Sandys had to tell Burghley that not one copy of the forbidden tracts had been brought to him, nor, as he supposed, to the Council, although without doubt there was 'great plenty' of them in London. A day or two later he wrote: 'Her Majesty's proclamation took none effect: not one book brought in.' In Norfolk several gentlemen and the dean of Norwich himself procured licences to keep the tracts. And more than two years later the Cornish diarist William Carnsewe noted receiving 'the Admonition of Cartwright for the new order of discipline, and the slipping of the Church of England', reading it, and passing it on to 'Ford the preacher'. When Lady Mary Grey – Lady Jane's sister – died in 1578, she left behind copies of the *Admonition* and Whitgift's *Answere*, and of Cartwright's first and second *Replies*.[13]

In the late summer Sandys found life in London no easier. The queen and most of the Council were absent on progress and the presbyterians still held the initiative. In July a so-called 'friendly caveat' which attacked the bishop in the most offensive terms circulated freely in the streets. In the same month a conforming clergyman put up to defend episcopacy at Paul's Cross was promptly answered from the same pulpit by Richard Crick, lately a fellow of Magdalen and soon to play a leading part in the East Anglian presbyterian movement. Crick's sermon included a defence of the proscribed *Admonition* and of its authors, 'saying that they sought a godly reformation, and a perfection in the government of the Church.' Sandys, who failed to apprehend Crick before he slipped back to Norwich, wrote of 'this tragedy'. Yet in August Paul's Cross again served as a presbyterian platform when Arthur Wake, on the eve of his potent ministry in Northamptonshire, broke a promise that he would avoid matters in controversy and proceeded to rail 'against the present state, and affirming to be good whatsoever Mr Cartwright in writing hath set down.' The seed sown in Oxford by Humphrey and Sampson was bearing unexpected fruit.[14]

In the same letter which reported these incidents, Sandys warned Burghley that the presbyterian movement had reached the point of formal organization from which Field had been dissuaded nine months before.

'There is a conventicle, or rather a conspiracy, breeding in London. Certain men of sundry callings are as it were in commission together to procure hands to Mr Cartwright's book, and promise to stand in the defence thereof unto death.' Cartwright himself was reported 'to lie hid in London, with great resort unto him.' Sandys urged that with Field and Wilcox he should be removed from the city, where 'the people resort unto them as in popery they were wont to run on pilgrimage.' Whereas a year before Field and Wilcox were needy prisoners, unable to pay for their keep at Newgate, they now held open court in Archdeacon Mullins's house and enjoyed the backing of aldermen and other wealthy citizens.[15]

Only in October 1573 did the reaction begin in earnest, when a second, more resolute proclamation censured bishops and magistrates for their negligence in suppressing nonconformity, and insisted on imprisonment for anyone who defamed the Prayer Book. If, as seems likely, this bears the mark of the queen's personal intervention, Elizabeth was probably provoked by two cases of criminal assault, both involving lunatics, but both associated with puritan fanaticism. On October 14th (six days before the proclamation was made) a young man of the Inner Temple, Peter Birchet, ran out into the Strand and stabbed the sea-dog John Hawkins, mistaking him for Christopher Hatton, the queen's latest favourite and already an unpopular figure with the godly. Later Birchet murdered his jailor, convinced that he too was Hatton. The most damaging aspect of this lurid affair was that Birchet had begun the day of his attack on Hawkins by accompanying another student to Thomas Sampson's regular lecture at Whittington College. The very day after Birchet's execution in the Strand, on November 12th, came news that one of the printers of the *Replye*, an ex-apprentice of John Day, had plotted to kill his old master and mistress, saying that 'the spirit moved him.' Parker spoke darkly of tyrannicide and suspected the reprinting of Goodman's *How superior powers oght to be obeyed*.

More than one writer has partially justified these fears by assuming that Birchet's attempt at assassination was a misguided act of zeal by a member of the lunatic fringe of the puritan movement. In fact Birchet seems to have been no more closely involved with the puritan ministers than any other student who was in the habit of attending Paul's Cross sermons and lectures, and there was a history of progressive mental derangement of a paranoiac nature, unconnected with religious mania, which two of his companions had had ample opportunity to observe during a Long Vacation jaunt into Wiltshire and Dorset. On this tour Birchet and his friends did fall in with the Genevan William Kethe, now a preacher in Dorset, but that was at a wedding feast at which his odd behaviour excited comment, and Kethe agreed with others present in taking him to be 'clean out of his wits'.[16]

Nevertheless, Elizabeth took the most serious view of the affair, probably because of her favourite's vicarious involvement, and she ordered a close examination of Birchet before his execution, to discover 'who moved him to it.' In early November the Council, at last stirred into action, set up special commissions to inquire into puritan disobedience and to enforce subscription from suspected persons to articles defining the law of the Church on the questions in controversy, a procedure of 'inquisition'. The assize judges who were about to depart on circuit were ordered by Burghley to pay particular attention to these matters, and in Essex the assize charge gave priority to the detection of nonconformity. In early December the Council issued a warrant for Cartwright's arrest.[17]

So began the second of the four major crises of Elizabethan puritanism. But like the earlier repression of 1563–6, Parker's inquisition was not carried out with equal thoroughness in every diocese. The puritans complained of the 'thrusting out' of 'the best, yea and all in manner that [were] wont to feed the people of God in Northamptonshire, in Warwick-shire, in Leicestershire, in Norfolk, in Suffolk and in many other places' and of the deprivation of 'twelve at a clap in some one diocese', but this was a great exaggeration. In the diocese of Norwich no one, least of all Bishop Parkhurst, was inclined to require subscription too strictly. In Norfolk it was supposed that the nonconformists would 'conform them-selves presently' so that the commissary thought 'there was no need to certify of them', and if there were some temporary suspensions in both Norfolk and Suffolk, those inhibited continued to preach in the public exercises of prophesying.

In Northamptonshire, on the other hand, the inquiry led to the prompt deprivation after only three weeks' suspension of five of the ringleaders of the presbyterian movement, including Wake and Paget. Two years later they still stood deprived and were petitioning Parliament for restitu-tion. The deprived ministers seem to have remained in the Midlands, encouraged by the gentry, officiating at puritan exercises in their houses and visiting as 'rangers and posting apostles' the prophesyings in which all had been moderators or speakers before their deprivation. From time to time they appeared in London, and in 1576 Wake and Wiburn spent a year in Guernsey where they took part in drafting the first Discipline of the reformed Church of the Channel Islands. The bishop of Peter-borough took advantage of Wake's absence to deprive him of a wealthy sinecure, the hospital of St John in Northampton, only to be shaken to his foundations by an irate earl of Leicester, with warnings to keep his hands off 'my loving friend' if he hoped for his friendship and good offices in the future. The wholesale deprivation of puritan ministers could not in itself pacify the Church; its effect normally was to intensify the schismatic tendencies in the presbyterian movement by diverting the preachers from the comparatively harmless pastoral preoccupations of their own parishes.[18]

It was in London that the episcopal repression of 1573 most closely resembled a persecution. In December the London clergy were summoned to St Laurence Jewry and ordered by the archdeacon and chancellor to subscribe and wear their surplices on the following Sunday, December 13th. Subscription was also pressed on the common lay people, 'such as they call puritans', and the non-subscribers, especially known members of the puritan underworld, were imprisoned. Dering had cause to be thankful that his wife, Anne Locke, kept clear of trouble. 'If any fall, God hath made her rich in grace and knowledge to give account of her doing.' But Wilcox reported that his protégé Thomas Edmunds, with William Fuller 'our dear friend and brother in the Lord' and 'divers others', were prisoners in the Counter; that William White with others was in Newgate; while Robert Johnson of St Clement's without Temple Bar, indicted by thirty of his parishioners at the Middlesex Assizes, was 'laid in the Gatehouse at Westminster' and 'others with him'. The prisoners were examined at leisure by the Commissioners, White on January 18th, Johnson on February 20th. Recommitted to the Gatehouse, Johnson spent his time writing polemics against Bishops Cooper and Sandys and Gabriel Goodman, dean of Westminster. To Sandys he complained of the danger to life itself of the prisons, 'filthy and unclean places, more unwholesome than dunghills, more stinking than swine sties'. Within a month or two he had succumbed to these infections, the fourth puritan victim of the London prisons. All this was grist to the mill of presbyterian propaganda. 'Very far are they gone,' Wilcox told Gilby, 'and as I suppose they will proceed further yet.'[19]

Cartwright spent some weeks in hiding and then escaped to the Continent at the end of the year. It was a hasty departure, but with a known destination: Heidelberg, the centre of a disciplined Calvinist state which at this time was swarming with French and Dutch refugees, the Palatinate. The university of Heidelberg was a thoroughly international body, and the professors were active in the politics and the diplomacy of the most active, not to say aggressive, protestant power in Europe.

In this congenial environment, Cartwright supervised the printing of his own *Second Replie* (Whitgift's *Defense of the aunswere* having appeared in February 1574) and other important manifestoes: Travers's *Ecclesiasticae disciplinae ... explicatio*, together with what may be Cartwright's own translation of this definitive handbook of presbyterian theory, *A full and plaine declaration of ecclesiastical discipline*, and a tendentiously edited collection of documents from the Marian exile, *A brieff discours off the troubles begonne at Franckford. The life of the 70. archbishopp off Canterbury* was another product of the same press.

Of these publications, Travers's *Explicatio* was the most significant, a lucid manifesto in excellent Latin, aimed at the learned European public. On August 9th, 1574, Sandys – who supposed Cartwright to be the author – wrote in alarm to Gualter of Zürich that the treatise was already printed and on its way to England, although he had not yet seen it. Gualter replied in the following March that the Zürich pastors had read 'your Cartwright's book', and that it contained nothing which had not already been confuted. They were astonished that Heidelberg should have thought fit to entertain such a guest as the author. Far from winning a wider support for their position, the presbyterians' manifesto merely served to draw fresh attention to the deep cleavage which now separated Zürich from Geneva and its satellites.[20]

A brieff discours off the troubles begonne at Franckford was an appeal to history which sought to correct the damaging impression that the conflict in the Church was of recent and factious origin. The materials were drawn from the archives of the English congregation at Geneva, which apparently included documents which the puritan group had taken with them in their secession from Frankfort in 1555. These had been in the possession of Thomas Wood, one of the elders, when the congregation dispersed after 1559, and it was perhaps Wood, with Field and others of the London puritan cell, who edited these papers to compose the *Brieff discours*. William Whittingham, traditionally supposed to have been the compiler, was asked to supply a transcript of an important letter of Calvin to the Frankfort congregation, but he probably played no other part in the enterprise.[21]

Wilcox and Field came out of confinement in the late autumn of 1573, although only a matter of weeks before they had been informed that their release would depend upon a special order of the Council. Evidently they still had powerful friends. Wilcox went off on a tour of puritan centres in the Midlands – we have letters from Ashby and Coventry – but was home again by early February, taking Field's place as Gilby's regular

London correspondent. Of Field himself there is no trace for eighteen months to come, and it is quite possible that he was no longer in England. Cartwright was not the only Englishman in the Palatinate at this time, and Field may have been among them, together with the John Fields of other repressed Calvinist churches: Hotman, Marnix van sint Aldegonde, Dathenus (van der Bergen) and many others. With Field out of action, Cartwright an exile, and the puritan press located overseas, the presbyterian movement was temporarily without firm leadership or direction. The repeated – and unlooked-for – prorogations of Parliament from July 1572 to February 1576 had deprived the puritans of their best chance of exploiting the public sympathy which they had enjoyed in 1573, and forestalled the great confrontation which both sides had expected. As late as April 1574 there was a conference in London and fresh talk of a puritan Confession of Faith and of commissioning Gilby to draw it up. But it is none the less clear that the momentum of the movement had been lost, and that a phase of puritan history had come to an end.[22]

This was not simply the result of effective 'castigation', as the bishops claimed. It is true that the inquisition had discovered the shaky cohesion of the puritan movement. Some had subscribed who had been expected to stand fast. There were angry recriminations against moderates like Dering and lost leaders like Whittingham. 'And will you for any worldly respects join hands with such bloody persecutors?' Some refusals to subscribe were based upon an uncompromising statement of the whole presbyterian programme; others on doubts about a few ceremonies. The unity in the face of adversity for which Field had striven was no nearer realization.[23]

But the relaxation of tension which now followed was due as much to the resumption by the authorities of a relatively tolerant attitude towards puritanism. Parker's momentary influence with the Council had owed much to Birchet's 'anabaptist' attempt at tyrannicide. Now Parker was deflated by a hoax so damaging to his case that it might have been perpetrated by a puritan *agent provocateur*.

In the spring of 1574 a confidence trickster called Humphrey Needham, who a year before had supplied the bishops with genuine information about the puritan press, procured the forgery of some letters purporting to be written by a certain John Undertree and a number of well-known puritan ministers, including Cartwright and John Browne. These he communicated to Bishop Horne and to Parker through his steward, Richard Wenslowe. The letters, full of code-names and elaborate secrecy, but, as Robert Beale later remembered, 'without any discretion or true orthography', suggested that Cartwright was back in England, that there were plans to print a new puritan manifesto in Bermondsey Street, Southwark, and that the enterprise was financed by the earl of Bedford and the duchess of Suffolk. Needham's motive seems to have been simple greed, together with an unexplained desire to injure Bedford. But he was soon entangled in his own fantasies and overstepped the mark with extravagant forgeries which suggested that the earl and his puritan accomplices – including Bishop Sandys! – were plotting the murder of Burghley, Hatton and the bishop of Winchester. Robert Beale, the puritan clerk of the Council, would later describe this as 'a lewd and malicious practice of Archbishop Parker of Canterbury and his brethren to entrap the earl of Bedford and others by slanderous and untrue surmises', but it was Parker himself who was trapped. 'The deep, devilish, traitorous dissimulation, this horrible conspiracy hath so astonied me', he wrote, believing it all, 'that my wit, my memory be quite gone.' Bonham and Standon, two of the ministers implicated, were imprisoned without trial on the sole evidence of these letters. Burghley, too, was deceived, carefully annotated the forged letters and personally ordered a raid on the supposed secret press in Southwark. Parker's steward was the first to smell a rat, and Needham was exposed, put on trial in the Star Chamber and sent to the Tower. Parker now wrote of 'this tragedy' and asked that the injured puritans be compensated. But he was never again in a position to urge the secret menace of puritan subversion on a Council naturally disposed to favour the godly party.

Within a year Parker was dead, and the arrival of Archbishop Grindal at Lambeth went far to restoring the confidence between bishops and puritan ministers which two years before had seemed lost beyond recovery.[24]

Part 4

Moderate Courses

'Any reformatory movement possessed of the least stability is bound to be a *via media* between extremes.'

(ROLAND H. BAINTON, *Studies on the Reformation*, 1964, p. 46)

1 Grindal

'And surely they were moderate *Divines* indeed, neither hot nor cold; and *Grindall* the best of them ... '

(JOHN MILTON, *Of reformation, touching church discipline in England*, 1641, p. 15)

In DECEMBER 1575 the queen consented to the translation of Edmund Grindal from York to Canterbury. Within little more than a year, the new archbishop fell into a disgrace from which he had still not been fully lifted when he died six years later. So brief was his effective tenure of the primacy that the high hopes with which it was greeted in certain influential quarters have been forgotten, its significance largely overlooked. We must now recover some of the atmosphere of that promising year, 1576.

Grindal was an archbishop for thoroughgoing protestants, one of the very few Elizabethan bishops who enjoyed the full approval of the protestant governing class and the equal confidence of all but a small embittered minority of the godly preaching ministers. He was conspicuously a gospeller: severe to papists, but in all his dealings with protestants an evangelical father in God, whose instinct was to proceed fraternally rather than judicially, let alone pontifically. His episcopal standards were those of the great Strasbourg reformer, Martin Bucer, and it was from Bucer himself, in all probability, that he learned them, when he was a fellow of Pembroke Hall and Bucer Regius professor of divinity in the same university. Grindal had repaid the debt by gathering many of Bucer's *Scripta Anglicana* and putting them in the hands of their German editor. They were published at Basle in 1577 with a dedication to the new archbishop, their appearance coinciding appropriately with the installation at Lambeth of the Bucerian ideal of a reformed church order. For Grindal, as for Bucer, it was inconceivable that the reformed bishop should rule as an autocrat, without consideration for his fellow-presbyters, and without their assistance. The protestant nobility and gentry were delighted with a bishop who was no prelate, and whose religious and political principles so nearly resembled their own. As for the puritan clergy, even Thomas Sampson, who deplored the high estate which an archbishop was obliged to maintain, and despised the 'policy' which had made Grindal a great lord, was prepared to believe that he would prove 'a Phoenix', uncontaminated and able to eschew lordliness and 'keep the humble and straight course of a loving brother and minister of Christ's gospel.'[1] More than that, Grindal contrived to preserve the public character of a transparently good man. Not self-seeking by nature, as a bachelor he was relatively immune from the economic pressures which gave many of his fellow-bishops a mercenary reputation.[2]

If Grindal was to the taste of the protestant laity, he was not merely their tool. His reputation – since the death of Jewel the only major international reputation in the English Church[3] – was much greater than modern, post-tractarian Anglican historians have allowed, and there was nothing incongruous about his elevation. Alexander Nowell, dean of St Paul's, subscribed to the common estimation of Grindal when he spoke of his friend as 'a man of the greatest wisdom and ability to govern, and unto whom the other bishops with best contentation would submit themselves', a view in which Burghley concurred. Yet Grindal's appointment implied the abandonment of much that Parker had meant by 'mediocrity' and the expectation of advance as the puritans understood it. Past contradictions between the conservatism of Lambeth and the aspirations of the émigré bishops were to be resolved in favour of progressive reform. As Knappen remarks, now at last was the time for the exiles to prove the wisdom of accepting episcopal office in 1559. 'If reform was to come from within the establishment, there would never be a more favourable opportunity, short of a change of sovereignty.'[4]

Grindal's constant patron, Burghley, had most to do with his promotion, which in itself is a point to be pondered.[5] As soon as Parker's life was known to be in danger, and even before Nowell prompted him, Burghley instructed Walsingham that Grindal was 'the meetest man to succeed him', instructing him 'to take my proxy for my poor voice.' What obstacles had still to be overcome can only be guessed at, but Parker died in May and it was not until Christmas Eve that the queen signed Grindal's congé d'élire. Cox of Ely, who was used to giving Elizabeth fatherly advice in these matters, urged her not to delay in choosing Parker's successor, but had nothing to say about Grindal's candidature, while remarking obliquely that evildoers would be more effectively coerced if Whitgift were given wider responsibilities. Cox was himself a logical successor to Parker, but had put himself out of the running by his second marriage (to William Turner's widow!) and his resistance to the designs on Ely House of Hatton, the queen's favourite. Whitgift, master of Trinity and dean of Lincoln, was hardly eligible as yet for the highest honour. Perhaps the queen was persuaded to see the unmarried Grindal as a tolerable *pis aller*.[6]

As soon as Grindal's appointment was confirmed, a privy councillor – possibly either Walsingham or Mildmay – wrote to tell him of the expectations it aroused. This anonymous letter is so revealing that it deserves to be quoted at length:

It is greatly hoped for by the godly and well-affected of this realm that your lordship will prove a profitable instrument in that calling; especially in removing the corruptions in the Court of the Faculties, which is one of the greatest abuses that remain in this Church of England. For that it is determined that Parliament should hold at the day prefixed, I could wish your lordship to repair hither with as convenient speed as ye may, to the end that there may be some consultation had with some of your brethren how some part of those Romish dregs remaining in [the Church?]* offensive to the godly, may be removed. I know it will be hard for you to do that good that you and your brethren desire. Yet (things discreetly ordered) somewhat there may be done. Herein I had rather declare unto your lordship at your repair hither frankly by mouth what I think than to commit the same to letters.

What a fascinating glimpse this affords of the politics of Elizabethan religion! Of dissatisfaction with Parker's regime now past; of the progressive bishops acting as catspaws for nervous courtiers in promoting moderate reform; of the extreme delicacy of the task, knowing the queen's jealously conservative attitude to ecclesiastical affairs.[7]

In the Parliament which coincided with Grindal's arrival in the south, 'somewhat' was at least attempted, and discreetly. Some of the M.P.s who were behind the puritan bill of rites and ceremonies in 1572, headed by Tristram Pistor, now sponsored a new programme of church reform. But this time, as Sir John Neale has shown, there was caution and propriety in both the manner and the content of the proposal. The motion was for

* There is a gap in the manuscript, which is a contemporary copy of the original.

a petition to the queen rather than for a bill, and the concern was with practical abuses rather than Prayer Book matters: 'the unlearnedness of the ministry, abuses of excommunication, want of discipline, dispensations and tolerations for non-residency and such like.'

The details of this programme are to be found in the fuller documentation of the 1581 Parliament, when it was resurrected and reduced to a schedule of 'articles' by puritan members, acting in collaboration with Walsingham and Mildmay, those same councillors – it is a safe guess – who were behind the 'discreet' proceedings of 1576. The 1581 articles represent a kind of blueprint for a reformed and episcopal Church of England. Some of the more material points were that none was to be admitted to the ministry except to a certain benefice with cure of souls vacant in the diocese of the officiating bishop; that the parish should be allowed the right to object to newly-appointed ministers within twenty days; that ordinations were to be public, on Sundays in the cathedral church, the bishop associating with himself for the examination of the candidates the dean and chapter or six learned preachers of the diocese. Excommunication was to undergo a most radical change: no longer the mere 'pain of contumacy', it was to be restricted to genuinely 'enormous crimes', and to be executed, not by lay officials, but by the bishops in person with the assistance of 'grave persons of calling in the Church' – no doubt the same six learned preachers. There was to be no commutation of penance except by order of the bishop with the assent of the dean and chapter or the six preachers. Stringent controls were to be placed upon the granting of faculties for non-residence, pluralities and marriage without banns.

In 1581 Whitgift opposed almost every one of these proposals with sound enough arguments, and Grindal himself added his critical comment to at least one of them, but there is reason to believe that much of this programme would have had the archbishop's blessing. It is reasonably certain that it was sponsored, not by the secret presbyterian organization (as Professor Neale is inclined to believe), but by the puritan councillors and courtiers who saw it as the completion of the protestant settlement, all the more necessary in view of the increasing pressure of resurgent popery. With good reason these distinguished promoters kept themselves in the background. But as that great puritan parliament man Thomas Norton makes quite clear in some of his letters, the burdens which he bore in the House of Commons were not all of his own shouldering.

To return to the Parliament of 1576: a committee, well-weighted with privy councillors, responded to Pistor's motion by drafting a moderate but earnest petition, complaining in no presbyterian sense of 'the lack of the true discipline of the Church'. The queen's response was not un-favourable, although she indicated that the bishops then assembled in Convocation were the proper source of redress. Within a fortnight there emerged from Convocation a collection of reforming canons which dealt with some of the Commons' grievances – as many, perhaps, as the queen was prepared to consider. (They received the royal sanction, unlike Parker's 'canons' of 1571.) This legislation dealt in some detail with the regulation of ordinations, admissions to benefices and licences to preach, and provided means to educate the inferior clergy. While if properly enforced these measures would have gone some way towards silencing the puritan opposition, their nature was administrative and non-controversial. This was much less than the puritans had intended, and in 1581 even Mildmay described them as 'little or nothing to the purpose'.[8]

But of his own accord Grindal now concerned himself with the more radical suggestion of his anonymous correspondent that the affairs of his own Court of Faculties should be put in order. Nothing, to a puritan mind, was quite so reminiscent of popery as this English version of the Roman *Penitenziaria*, with its licences to hold incompatible benefices in plurality, to receive orders at less than the canonical age and to marry in the forbidden seasons. In 1571 a bill had been introduced into Parliament which would have virtually abolished all these powers which, according to its puritan sponsor, made the archbishop of Canterbury 'as it were a pope', and there is no doubt that such a measure would have enjoyed wide popularity. When Parker's personal fortune was objected as a reason for denying the new archbishop full restitution of the temporalities of the see, Grindal replied significantly that 'the late archbishop had many occasions of wealth, the possibilities whereof are now taken away from his next successor', amongst them the making of 'more profit than hereafter is convenient by admitting children to cures.' He told the queen and the Council that he would offer no defence if they decided that the Court of Faculties should be dissolved altogether, and within a few months he had concluded an agreement with the Council whereby many of the more abused dispensations were to be 'utterly abolished, as not agreeable to Christian religion', including faculties to hold more than two benefices, for ordination or preferment at less than the canonical age, and for extra-parochial marriage without banns. Others were to be left to the con-sideration and control of the Council, and the fees – as much as sixteen pounds for a bishop to hold a benefice *in commendam* – were to be divided equally between the queen and the archbishop and his officers. A complete list of pluralists was prepared (it came to two hundred and sixteen) with the values of their combined livings (£20,064 3s. 6d.).[9] This, with much other information about the clergy, their quality, behaviour and capacity to preach, as well as about the value and patronage of their livings, might have been deduced from detailed surveys for which Grindal called in June 1576. These findings were apparently based upon the personal appearances of the clergy before their archdeacons.[10]

Grindal meanwhile had directed four leading civilians and ecclesiastical judges to report on the disorders in his three remaining courts – the Court of Audience, the Arches and the Prerogative Court of Canterbury – and to recommend reforms. He was told that 'in your Grace's Court of Audience as in all your courts, so things be out of order that few things be as they should be.' But all these projected reforms were forestalled – and perhaps it was no accident – by Grindal's fall from favour.[11]

At the same time the archbishop was conspicuously associated with a cause which all sincere protestants in public positions had at heart in the 'seventies: the provision of penalties for Roman Catholic recusancy stiffer than the shilling fine imposed under the 1559 Act of Uniformity. In 1571 both Houses of Parliament had passed a bill which would have imposed a quarterly attendance at church under pain of heavier fines, and compulsory annual participation in the communion, a real credal test for temporizing papists. The queen, consistent in her humane desire to distinguish between 'causes of conscience' and 'manifest disobedience', vetoed it. This measure undoubtedly had episcopal approval, and in the following Parliament the bishops appeared as the active but unsuccessful sponsors of a revived bill. Grindal, by now a seasoned veteran in the struggle against recusancy in the northern province, was probably the prime mover. In 1576 the bishops again took the initiative by introducing the measure into the House of Lords. Grindal was a member of the imposing committee of noblemen which sat on the bill and attempted unsuccessfully to disarm the queen's opposition by omitting the communion clause. During the five years which remained before the 1581 Parliament provided a more effective remedy for recusancy in statute law, the bishops were of all interested parties the most active in finding other means to enforce church attendance, especially the levying of fines for absence from the communion by virtue of their powers as Ecclesiastical Commissioners. This can hardly have failed to improve their image in the eyes of the godly.[12]

There was another, even more significant token of an officially-inspired move to the left in Grindal's first hundred days. The Geneva Bible, printed in a format suitable for domestic use and with its 'profitable annotations' in a Calvinist sense, had in effect been suppressed by Parker, who had little sympathy with either private Bible-reading or radical protestant propaganda. Now at last it had an English printing. Within two years of Parker's death, Christopher Barker printed in rapid succession two pocket and four folio editions as well as two impressions of Laurence Tomson's translation of Beza's New Testament. Tomson's New Testament was dedicated to his master, Walsingham, and Walsingham was also Barker's patron, lending his device of a tiger's head to the premises in St Paul's Churchyard where the bibles were printed.

There followed what appears to have been a bold attempt to force the pace of further reformation, prompted, it may be, at a high level. In 1578, a further edition of the Geneva Bible incorporated – with every appearance of official sanction – a travesty of the legally established Prayer Book which substituted the term 'minister' for 'priest' throughout, abandoned the popish names of 'mattins' and 'evensong', and omitted the orders for private baptism, confirmation and the churching of women. Variant versions of this puritan Prayer Book were to continue to appear with successive editions of the Geneva Bible for many years to come. While it is not easy to penetrate the motive lying behind this enterprise, it seems most reasonable to interpret it as an unauthorized attempt to revise the Prayer Book on moderate puritan lines. It was a prominent pointer to a reformed Anglicanism, certainly for the guidance of large private households, and probably for many parishes as well, where the ministers and churchwardens, disregarding the injunctions, purchased and set up the Geneva Bible for reading in church. And the whole volume was dedicated to the queen! Between 1578 and Whitgift's ascendancy in 1583, while Barker enjoyed a monopoly of bible-printing, there were sixteen further editions of the Geneva version and not a single reprint of the despised Bishops' Bible. As A. W. Pollard remarked, behind these ventures there was surely 'something more than ordinary trading'![13]

Meanwhile conformity to the standards of 1559 was not widely enforced, while preaching was warmly encouraged. In these altered circumstances doctrinaire attacks on episcopacy were of doubtful relevance and we hear less of them. The puritans were now directing most of their polemical effort into writing, preaching and disputing against the common Roman enemy. Even Field turned his talents in this direction, priming the pump with translations of continental theological works, prefaced with fervent appeals to likely noblemen to head the crusade against Rome. According to Thomas Norton, there was now a tacit agreement between the bishops and the 'preachers and other honourable and good men loving the peace of the Church' that all would 'join together against the papists, the enemies of God and of her Majesty, and not spend themselves in civil wars of the Church of God.' The bishops would not unduly burden the consciences of the preachers, and the preachers for their part would not disturb the peace of the Church. It was an understanding, as one minister put it, 'that they would preach to the circumcision and we to the gentiles.' Many preachers looked back on this as 'a golden time, full of godly fruit'. Josias Nichols of Kent remembered that non-preachers and absentee ministers had been forced to mend their ways, and that 'many thousands were converted from atheism and popery and became notable Christians.'[14]

We have now picked out some of the projecting features of a coherent, protestant approach to affairs at home and abroad, which was shared in varying degrees by Grindal and other like-minded bishops, together with the earnest protestant nobility and gentry and the greater part of the preaching ministry. This philosophy lies like bedrock under many of the policies and events of the high Elizabethan period: at home a desire to promote preaching, to reform the ministry and discipline of the Church, to deal roundly with papists; and abroad a protestant, ideological approach to problems of foreign relations, based on fear of a popish 'enterprise of England' and the conviction that religion and security would both be best served by a more positive intervention on the protestant side in France and the Netherlands. Elizabeth, in the last speech of her life, somewhat surprisingly defined 'foreign courses' as consisting chiefly in the maintenance of war;[15] her puritan servants would have been quick to agree, adding 'and of religion'.

If this doctrine had an author it was Walsingham; but Leicester with his brother Warwick was by now deeply committed to it and promised by the immense scope of his patronage to identify the ultra-protestant party with his own faction. The other great protestant magnates, Huntingdon in his government of the north, Bedford in the West Country, were of course aligned on the same side, as were Sir Walter Mildmay (allowing for the professional caution of a minister of finance) and Sir Francis Knollys. And as Professor Conyers Read has noticed, virtually all the government servants employed at a high level in French and Dutch and, one might add, Scottish diplomacy were puritans who looked to Leicester and Walsingham for support and preferment: Henry Killigrew, William Davison, Thomas Randolph, Robert Beale, Laurence Tomson – to name only the most notable. Opposed to this protestant world-view was the secular, disengaged mind of the queen, shared in part by Burghley and more fully by Christopher Hatton and the earl of Sussex; its ecclesiastical counterpart was the Anglicanism of Whitgift and of Hatton's bishop, Aylmer of London. This was how Court and country tended to divide on many of the issues of the time: on aid to the Dutch rebels, on the proposed Alençon marriage, on popish recusancy, on preaching and church reform. When the archbishop fell from grace in 1577 it was seen by contemporaries to have a bearing on all these issues, and Grindal's fortunes, for better or worse, were thought to indicate the future course of Elizabethan policy.[16]

The immediate occasion of Grindal's fall was the puritan practice known as 'prophesying' and the archbishop's refusal to be the queen's instrument in suppressing it. The prophesyings also represent for our purposes the most important single phenomenon of the protestant ascendancy over which Grindal presided, and we must now pay them our close attention. 'For surely,' wrote Thomas Wood, 'if they had continued they would in short time have overthrown a great part of [Satan's] kingdom, being one of the greatest blessings that ever came to England.'[17] That is to give the prophesyings a somewhat higher valuation than they have received in most histories of the period, where only Grindal's famous protest has won them a mention. But we shall see that Wood had no need to exaggerate the contribution of this institution to the further reformation of Elizabeth's reign.

2 The Prophesyings

'I know prophesyings was subject to great abuse, and would be more abused now; because heat of contentions is increased. But I say the only reason of the abuse was, because there was admitted to it a popular auditory, and it was not contained within a private conference of ministers.'

> (FRANCIS BACON, 'An advertisement touching the controversies of the Church of England', Spedding, *Letters and Life of Francis Bacon*, i. 88)

ELIZABETHAN MARKET TOWNS were natural centres of intercourse for the rural clergy as for any other social group, especially for such of them as were Calvinists with an instinct for brotherhood and mutual edification. Wherever the town and its dependent villages contained a good number of preaching ministers, there was likely to be a regular day when they could come together in the principal church of the place for 'exercise' – preaching, by one or more of their number – 'conference', and dinner at an inn. These comings-and-goings could have been observed in a score of towns like Bury St Edmunds, Colchester, Coventry or Aylesbury. At Burton-on-Trent, as at Bury, Monday was 'the day of the common exercise' in the last decade of the century, a 'famous exercise' as it was reckoned a few years later.[1]

It is not always possible to say when such a tradition was first established, or how long it continued. In some places the pattern is clear from very early in Elizabeth's reign; elsewhere, for example in the towns of the West Riding, the exercises were a novelty in the early seventeenth century.[2] In most districts, the exercises reached their heyday in the reign of James I.[3] Although widely acknowledged and sometimes actively encouraged by many of the bishops, they belong to the puritan church within the Church, rather than to official Anglican policy. They have left few traces in the formal ecclesiastical records, and the history of the reformed Church of England has normally been written with scarcely any recognition of their existence. Yet it was these regular gatherings, rather than diocesan synods or episcopal visitations and court-days, which gave the Elizabethan and Jacobean clergy – or at least an active, capable element of the clergy – a sense of responsibility to the Church beyond their own parishes.

In the early years such occasions were normally devoted to the practice of what was called 'prophesying', a kind of biblical conference derived from the example of many of the reformed churches overseas, and, ultimately, from a text of St Paul: 'Let the prophets speak two or three, and let the other judge ... For ye may all prophesy one by one, that all may learn, and all may be comforted.'[4] Sometimes, as at Zürich, where the term is first encountered, prophesying was an academic exercise in the spirit of biblical humanism, replacing logical discourse as the principal discipline for the schooling of future ministers. 'I thought myself during this disputation to have been in the divinity disputations at the Commencement time in Cambridge,' reminisced a Marian exile (John Scory, the Elizabethan bishop of Hereford) who had seen something of the practice at Emden. At Zürich, where prophesying supplanted the daily choir office of the unreformed Church, ministers and divinity students met early in the morning on five days in the week in the choir of the Grossmünster and shared in the systematic exegesis of the Old Testament, using the Hebrew and Latin texts. This exacting discipline was the basis of the systematic exposition of reformed theology in biblical commentaries, and even of the text of the Bible itself in the vernacular versions printed in Zürich and other reformation centres.[5]

But even when prophesying was primarily a part of higher education, it was often the practice, as it was at Zürich, to bring proceedings to a close with a vernacular sermon preached to a lay audience. In other churches, St Paul was understood to have meant something very much more democratic. In François Lambert's very early directions for the reorganization of the Church in Hesse, and later in John à Lasco's idiosyncratic orders for the stranger churches of Edwardine London, provision was made for weekly meetings of the congregation with its pastor, when the discussion of doctrine was open to all church members. This too was called 'prophesying'. The English exiles encountered something of the same sort at Geneva, and included it in their service-book, where it is variously called 'interpretation of the scriptures' and 'prophecy': 'Every week once, the congregation assemble to hear some place of the scriptures orderly expounded. At which time, it is lawful for every man to speak or inquire as God shall move his heart and the text minister occasion, so it be without pertinacity or disdain, as one that rather seeketh to profit than to contend.'[6]

At the one extreme, the prophesying was a learned expository labour, conducted in Latin among scholars and students; at the other, it could be a lively occasion for exercising the liberty of the children of God. In early Elizabethan London, prophesying of the congregational variety was known in at least one parish, but the practice is unlikely to have survived the reaction of 1566. It was subsequently a regular part of the worship of some English separatists.[7] Within the establishment, a similar function was served by the meetings of the godly with their pastor for 'repetition' of the sermon, which brought the Sabbath to an end in puritan parishes;[8] although this came closer to catechizing than to the free-for-all envisaged in Lambert's and à Lasco's orders, in which the pastor might have to struggle to hold his own against an opinionated and truculent people.

The Elizabethan prophesyings which concern us in this context were in the Zürich tradition, with some traces of the more popular variety. They grew partly out of official and semi-official projects for the improvement of the ignorant clergy, but more out of the spontaneous enterprise of the puritan preachers themselves. There was a tendency under a sympathetic bishop for exercises of the official variety to fall under puritan influence, and equally for puritan experiments to receive episcopal sanction, and so for the two institutions to merge into one.

In the reign of Edward VI, and again under Elizabeth, royal injunctions required the clergy with little or no academic qualifications to undertake biblical study, their progress to be regularly assessed by their ordinaries. Parker's Advertisements and the canons of 1571 delegated episcopal responsibilities in these respects to the archdeacons and their deputies in their visitations. While these royal and metropolitan orders imply some recognition of the need to instruct the great submerged mass of ignorant parsons, they made no provision for meetings to regulate the performance and examination of these 'tasks', and it was left to individuals to interpret them by convening regular conferences of their clergy. Under Edward VI, John Hooper, bishop of Gloucester – that Anglo-Züricher – had ordered quarterly gatherings of the clergy in their rural deaneries to determine doubtful matters in religion, 'and there to speak modestly, soberly and learnedly what they will.' In Elizabethan London, John Mullins as arch-deacon held half-yearly meetings lasting four or five days when he personally presided, asking 'of such places as seem to have any hardness', with the assembled ministers answering 'according to their skill'. Sandys as archbishop of York established meetings of the same kind in the Yorkshire archdeaconries in 1578 and Barnes of Durham and Chaderton of Chester took similar steps in their own dioceses.[9]

Elsewhere it was found more convenient to employ graduate preachers as supervisors and examiners of their unlearned neighbours. Very early in the reign, the archdeacon of St Albans, David Kemp, provided that 'every one of these meaner sort should have resorted once every week to some preacher that was next to every of them, within two or three miles, to be directed according to their discretion,' although this 'took none effect.' Cooper of Lincoln made a general provision to the same effect for his diocese in 1577, and in 1585 Archbishop Whitgift issued a similar order for the whole province. Finally, the Convocation of 1586–7 enacted detailed orders 'for the better increase of learning in the inferior ministers', which provided for the appointment of 'certain grave and learned preachers who shall privately examine the diligence and view the notes of the said ministers, assigning six or seven ministers as occasion shall require to every such preacher that shall be next adjoining to him.'[10]

From the 1560s there was a tendency for these schemes of extra-mural education to assume the shape of conferences organized for prophesying, something far from any intention of Queen Elizabeth. In the arch-deaconry of Essex by 1564 there were five centres of prophesying: Rochford, Maldon, Chelmsford, Horndon-on-the-Hill and Brentwood. At each of these, from two to five learned ministers moderated, and under their direction the remainder of the clergy were examined in their tasks before a public audience, so that all were 'for shame compelled to do something.' After the public proceedings, the ministers withdrew to continue their conference among themselves. In Sussex, where Bishop Curteys introduced the prophesyings in 1570 on a deanery basis, only the 'learned and discreet' spoke in public conference, while the unlearned were set tasks in which they were examined by four of the most learned ministers of the deanery after the people had departed. One can see that so long as the proceedings were in English, which, given the modest capabilities of most of the clergy, they were bound to be, it would be hard to find reasons to exclude the laity in rural districts starved of preaching.[11]

When the preachers entrusted with these responsibilities were puritans, there was a tendency both to encourage the popular audience still further, and for the members of the exercise to become conscious of their inter-dependence as a brotherhood. The whole process as it developed at St Albans was later described by David Kemp, the archdeacon. Kemp began monthly exercises in 1560 'privately among the ministers only', associating with himself as moderators Robert Johnson, Sir Nicholas Bacon's puritan chaplain from Gorhambury, and William Horne, vicar of Hemel

Hempstead. Kemp's method was to lead the clergy through some of the systematic theological compilations known as commonplaces, with three or four speakers on each occasion. In 1572 – a significant year – the proceedings were made public. This was at Johnson's request and the new orders reflect a novel emphasis on parity. Decisions were now taken 'by common consent'. There was to be no public disagreement: 'We suffer none to be reproved openly, nor one to impugn another, but if any happen to overshoot himself, it is talked of secretly and reformed among ourselves ere we pass the church.' Public prophesying was followed by private conference, when the learned ministers engaged in the reformed practice of mutual 'censure'. Then came dinner, when the unlearned who were not free to speak in the exercise were examined in the progress of their study.[12]

In other places the initiative lay wholly with the puritan ministers themselves. This was so in Norwich, where for all Bishop Parkhurst's sympathy, the preachers were in the main responsible for the prophesying established early in the reign, 'both for their better exercise and also for the education of the people'. In Coventry the fortnightly exercise, held 'almost since the beginning of the queen's majesty's reign' and attended by 'a great number of good and godly people', owed its institution to Thomas Lever, who was town preacher before he was archdeacon and who always moderated when he was present. Another Coventry moderator was John Oxenbridge, an extreme puritan, and in 1576 Bishop Bentham noted that the moderators, though learned, were 'as touching the apparel of ministers more obstinate than needeth' and the speakers 'too busy against the order of the communion book and apparel'. Oxenbridge established another exercise in his own town of Southam, and although this seems to have had the sanction of some of the local gentry in their capacity of ecclesiastical commissioners, the bishop was ignorant of its very existence. At Northampton, the weekly exercise for the ministers of the town and the quarterly gatherings for the whole shire were licensed by the bishop, but the real author of the scheme was the town preacher, Percival Wiburn. In both these meetings the preachers themselves, collectively, were in charge, censuring each other's doctrine, life and manners. Only when an erring brother ignored two admonitions was he referred to the bishop 'by complaint from all the brethren'. At Leicester, where the earl of Huntingdon's influence was paramount, the prophesying was set up by Jeffery Johnson, the town preacher, described by his bishop as 'somewhat a rash man, and so much as he dare inclined to novelties.' At Ashby-de-la-Zouch, again under Huntingdon's patronage, the exercise was presumably begun by Anthony Gilby. A disingenuous account of its history was later given to Bishop Cooper:

> First we the ministers, coming together ourselves by the law of them that were in office, the bishop your predecessor and his officers, and since your entry, by you and your officers, we would do nothing nor say any things in secret corners, lest we might have been misjudged; but, leaving open the church doors as was convenient, the people of themselves, knowing that it is always lawful to hear God's word, holy day and working day, by many or by few, did of themselves quietly come to pray with us and to learn some good lessons in God's schoolhouse.[13]

The early 'seventies were far from marking the first beginning of the prophesyings. But all the surviving orders with episcopal approval date from this time, which probably indicates a growing appreciation of the practice by some bishops and a deliberate attempt to harness its energies for the good of the whole Church. Three new bishops of these years – Cooper of Lincoln, Bradbridge of Exeter and Curteys of Chichester, 'Grindalians' all and all made bishops between April 1570 and March 1571 – were especially interested in encouraging the exercises. The ministers of Ashby spoke of prophesyings 'approved and allowed by divers godly bishops here in England, sometime by their hands and seals, sometime by their public charge and commandment given to their ministers to frequent the same.' This can be confirmed from stray references in the formal ecclesiastical records. Cooper bound recalcitrant clergy to 'frequent the exercise under pain of law' and Scambler of Peterborough appointed a popish priest 'to recant in the exercise at Oundle.' In Nottinghamshire, where exercises were set up in three or four centres after Grindal's arrival in the north as archbishop of York, offenders were regularly compelled by the archdeacon to perform their penance in the exercise. Bentham of Coventry and Lichfield licensed the Shrewsbury exercise in the very visitation of October 1573 in which he carried out Parker's 'inquisition'.[14]

But none of the written orders for prophesying seems to have originated with the bishops who sanctioned them. Parkhurst's orders for Bury St Edmunds were solicited 'by sundry godly and well learned persons as well of the clergy as otherwise, near adjoining to the town', presumably the puritan ministers and gentry. The Buckinghamshire 'rules and orders' were 'agreed unto' by the ministers, 'touching the exercise of themselves together.' And Bishop Cooper wrote on a draft of the Hertfordshire order: 'These orders of exercise, offered to me by the learned of the clergy of Hertfordshire, I think good and godly.' The fact that the Buckinghamshire and Hertfordshire, and for that matter, Bedfordshire orders are substantially identical argues for the collusion of the preachers of these counties, not for the bishop's authorship.[15] Nominally the bishop appointed the moderators, but to all intents and purposes they had chosen themselves. Cooper was supposed to keep a watchful eye on the conduct of the exercises, but in such a vast diocese his supervision could not have been effective. The replies to a questionnaire which Grindal sent to the bishops in 1576 suggest that none of them was in close touch with what was going on.[16] Even Bradbridge of Exeter, who claimed to moderate if 'nigh the place', could not supply the names of any of the moderators or leading preachers in his diocese.[17] Beyond doubt, the enterprise of the puritan ministers was what inspired and sustained the prophesyings.

In the years 1574–6, when the movement was at its height, there were exercises of this kind in at least four Nottinghamshire centres: Southwell, Mansfield, Nottingham and Retford; in several market towns of Lincolnshire, including Grantham; at Stamford, Leicester, Ashby-de-la-Zouch, Northampton, Oundle, Uppingham and Huntingdon; at Coventry and Southam; at Shrewsbury; at Aylesbury, Welwyn, St Albans and other centres in Hertfordshire and Buckinghamshire; at Norwich, Holt, Wiveton and Fakenham in Norfolk; at Bury St Edmunds in Suffolk; at Colchester, Chelmsford, Horndon-on-the-Hill, Maldon, Brentwood and Rochford in Essex; in Kent, Surrey, Sussex and Devon, and more precariously in Somerset, Gloucester and Hereford. The only districts where the bishops knew of no exercises were the city of London, the dioceses of Ely and Salisbury, and the whole of Wales. There is no information for the dioceses of Worcester, Bristol and Oxford; nor, at this date, for the greater part of England north of the Trent.[18]

Proceedings by this time followed a familiar pattern, with local variations in the roles assigned to moderators, learned preachers and ignorant clergy. Usually a moderator presided over a panel or 'table' of preachers, three or four of whom took it in turn to uncover their heads and preach on the text for the day, which they had reached in the course of the systematic exegesis of some book of the Bible. Each would take one of the formal 'divisions' of the text, the last speaker concluding with the practical 'uses' of the doctrine. A large public audience was present, hierarchically arranged, with two or three godly justices gracing the proceedings and perhaps sitting behind the preacher in the chancel seats.

After the appointed speakers had finished, the moderator would ask any learned man who might be present in the auditory to confirm or confute the doctrine delivered, although in the more discreetly ordered exercises this was not done in public. Left to themselves, the puritans would have allowed gifted laymen to take part. As in Scotland where all 'of pairts' were permitted to speak in the exercise, one use of prophesying was to encourage aspirants for the ministry. Meanwhile the godly would sit with their Geneva Bibles open on their laps, searching for the texts cited by the preachers. According to one observer, as soon as the public conference was over, the people would hotly discuss what they had heard amongst themselves, 'all of them, men and women, boys and girls, labourers, workmen and simpletons'. Meanwhile the ministers had withdrawn to another place to engage in fraternal 'censure' of the doctrine delivered and of their lives and morals. The day ended with a dinner which provided a more informal opportunity for the discussion of matters of common concern.[19]

The importance of this institution both for rehabilitating a debased clergy and for promoting a unity of belief based on instruction and assent rather than on ecclesiastical authority needs no emphasis. What may be less obvious without some sense of Tudor social values is the effect of the prophesyings on the 'credit' or prestige of the gospel and its adherents. Like the great open-air preaching conventions in the Netherlands and protestant funerals in France, the prophesyings were intended as a public show of strength. For this reason more than any other, the queen's attempt to suppress them was regarded by the godly as 'a great rejoicing to all God's enemies' and 'such a service to Satan as unless the whole religion should be overthrown a greater could not be done.' There is no disguising the popularity of the prophesyings, which held some of the fascination which televised 'confrontations' have for modern audiences. 'The diversity of translations conferred together, the interpretation of the tongues, and the several gifts that men have in their utterance,' explained the bishop of Exeter, 'doth more delight the auditory and pierceth deeplier the senses than the speech of one mouth at one time.' Cooper of Lincoln believed that gentlemen and gentlewomen would come six or seven miles to a conference who would hardly travel one to a learned man's sermon. David Kemp of St Albans was assured of the goodwill of the local dignitaries in that the masters of the town and the country gentlemen, 'severally, never missing', supplied them with free wine for their dinners. 'Our horsemeat cost us nothing, our dinner, faring honestly, but sixpence apiece. This is a sign that our doings is well like of. I cannot fare so at other times for my twelvepence.' Maldon in Essex went one better: the magistrates supplied both the dinner and the claret consumed by the moderator and principal speakers at their exercise.[20]

The greater the attendances of justices of the peace and other notables, the greater the credit an exercise would enjoy. At Northallerton, in the stony ground of the North Riding, it was said in 1595 that only the 'countenance' of the venerable earl of Huntingdon could ensure a respectable auditory for the regular Wednesday exercise. At Southam, three or four justices usually attended the prophesying which the Midland puritans rated 'undoubtedly without exception' the best in England. The earl of Leicester was present at the puritan exercises when he was in their vicinity. At Shrewsbury, the members of the Council in the Marches always attended when an exercise coincided with their presence in the town. And what a Norwich preacher so much admired in the religious and social life of his city was 'the continual resort that was every day through the year, and that for many years together, unto the holy exercises of religion, which were continually supported by worthy and sincere preachers, and graced by the presence of so many grave and religious magistrates.'[21]

3 Pastores Pastorum: The Promise of Grindal's Church

'Certainly, sir, this superintendence of eminent men, bishops over divers churches, is the most ancient, primitive, spreading, lasting government of the Church; wherefore, whilst we are earnest to take away innovations, let us beware we bring not in the greatest innovation ever was in England.'

'Let us not destroy bishops, but make them such as they were in primitive times. Do their large territories offend? Let them be restricted. Do their courts and subordinates? Let them be brought to govern as in the primitive times, by assemblies of their clergy. Doth their intermeddling in secular affairs? Exclude them from the capacity.'

(Speeches of SIR BENJAMIN RUDYARD and LORD GEORGE DIGBY in the House of Commons, Feb. 8th, 1641; quoted W. A. SHAW, *History of the English Church During the Civil Wars and under the Commonwealth*, i. 30, 32)

IF WE WERE TO ADD no more to this account of the prophesyings, then we should have failed to justify the prominence which they have already received in this narrative. Valuable though the exercises were for indoctrination and as a public vindication of the protestant gospel, their deeper significance for the Elizabethan Church was as an institution, an organ, in the corporate life of the clergy. By bringing the preaching ministry together in bodies which for some purposes were autonomous, the prophesyings necessarily had an influence on the Church's polity, and represented a small but important reform in ecclesiastical organization. When these potentialities have been recognized, it has usually been with the assumption that the exercises were presbyterian in their tendency, or at least subversive of episcopal government. As we shall see, the truth was less simple and more intriguing.

To appreciate how these preaching conferences had any bearing at all on administration and organization, we must again set the prophesyings in the wider context of Reformation Europe. In all the reformed churches where the ministers enjoyed any role in discipline, the organs of their government grew out of meetings which were at first restricted to 'conference'. In some Swiss cities the self-same bodies were styled 'colloquies' as they met for this purpose, and *classes* as they assembled for matters of discipline. In Strasbourg they went under the general name of *Kirchenconvent*, while in the French Reformed Church both functions were performed by *colloques*. Whatever their nationality, Calvinist pastors living within a few hours' ride of one another would always feel, and satisfy, the need to converse. It was easy for Thomas Nashe to laugh at the Devonshire minister who wrote in Latin to his neighbour 'and rapt it out lustily, "Si tu non vis venire mihi, ego volo venire tibi" '; but the instinctive craving of Calvinists for conference could not easily be denied. 'Though they dwell an hundred miles asunder,' complained Bancroft, 'and one never saw the other, yet they know of one another's doings, and their opinions that they hold. For the which cause, after their exercises, they have their private conferences for the better agreeing in their opinions; sometimes using subscription to them where they doubt of any man.'

At a later stage, when the construction of a national reformed church called for a unit of administration larger than the local congregation but smaller than the provincial synod, the conference was ready to be turned to this use. With the elaboration of the presbyterian polity in Scotland, the 'exercise' – counterpart of the English prophesying – proved serviceable as an administrative link between the congregational consistory and the twice-yearly synod. And with the establishment of *classes* (called 'presbyteries' in Scotland) the General Assembly even ruled that where an exercise was already in existence it was to be 'judged a presbytery'.[1]

In England a similar progression was envisaged in the *Second admonition to the Parliament*. The *classis* was here called the 'conference' and was defined as 'the meeting of some certain ministers, and other brethren, as it might be the ministers of London, at some certain place, as it was at Corinth, or of some certain deanery or deaneries in the country, as it might be at Ware.' The normal and regular occasion of their meeting was 'to confer and exercise themselves in prophesying, or in interpreting the scriptures', with the self-scrutiny and 'censure' which normally followed these proceedings. But when occasion arose, the conference was also to commission its members for various undertakings, to review the 'demeanours' of the ministers and to settle 'sundry causes within that circuit, being brought before them'. This was a blueprint for the English conference movement of the 'eighties, when Field's London conference would strive to impose on these meetings the formal character of Calvinist *classes*. In 1586 a parliamentary bill would propose the establishment of the discipline by assemblies of all the licensed preachers in every shire, meeting 'to keep the exercise by St Paul appointed, and called prophecy, or expounding the scriptures.' Having nominated elders in each parish, 'the conference' or 'the assembly' was to admit ministers to vacant cures and to act as a court of appeal for the churches of the shire. Evidently the prophesying was the *classis* in embryo.[2]

Yet there was nothing inherently presbyterian about the practice of prophesying itself. Where an exercise was established within the diocesan framework and with the consent of the bishop, the form of church organization which it foreshadowed was not presbyterian at all, but a modification of diocesan episcopacy. Not only was the bishop's superior authority acknowledged, so that the members of the Hertfordshire exercise could declare that their orders were 'ratified by our ordinary' and that 'the appointing of the ministers to our exercise belongeth unto our ordinary'; but imparity was built into the exercise itself by the appointment of a small number of perpetual moderators – sometimes only one – to take 'charge and order' of proceedings. A church assembly can only properly be called presbyterian where the parity of all the members is respected in the circulation of the office of president. Translated into terms of church polity, these arrangements spell out a system which is almost the reverse of presbyterianism: the principle of *episkopē* originates with the bishop (who receives his *jus jurisdictionis*, according to current notions, from the queen) and descends through permanent moderators, from the highest to the lowest in the Church. This was an hierarchical conception, even if its character was Erastian rather than catholic.

This is not to deny that there was an anti-hierarchical as well as a separatist tendency in much of the puritan enterprise which sustained the prophesyings, or that they could have functioned very happily without bishops. But as a matter of fact the bishops were there, and some of them took a positive interest in the exercises. When they harnessed the enterprise and directed it outwards towards the improvement of the unlearned clergy, they not only brought the practice of prophesying within the established scheme of things, but they also involved the moderators and speakers themselves in a kind of episcopal responsibility for their less favoured brethren, which took account of their superior learning and other qualities of leadership. Here was an indication of how episcopal government could be accommodated to protestant standards and made relevant to the actual state of the Elizabethan Church.

Even without a further reformation, the times were not wholly lacking in conscientious pastoral oversight. Not all bishops were utter strangers to the pulpit. And for all that the motivation of episcopal and archidiaconal visitation was highly suspect in the eyes of the laity, bishops and archdeacons could be found who undertook this responsibility with canonical regularity, and expected it to yield something more than their fees. In some jurisdictions chapters or synods were held of the ministers alone, meetings which the archdeacons were anciently required to keep by the canons, and in which, says Burn, the clergy were 'to consult and agree upon rules of discipline for themselves.' In the archdeaconry of St Albans these assemblies were held frequently and they transacted a variety of business from a grant of foreign aid for beleaguered Geneva to the election of proctors for the lower house of Convocation. There were always dinners on these occasions, to which all the ministers, absentees included, contributed wine. In the diocese of Ely there was a long-established tradition of annual synods of the whole clergy which met at Cambridge at Whitsuntide, and this was continued *'ex consuetudine antiqua et laudabile'* throughout the time of Bishop Cox. Yet while these assemblies correct an over-jaundiced view of late medieval ecclesiastical administration, they do not imply the deliberate adoption of Reformation standards. Bishop Cox's synods were normally held by his vicar-general in his absence, as they would have been before the Reformation; and at St Albans everything depended upon the energy of a certain Mr Rocket, official and registrar, rather than upon the archdeacon in person.[3]

Some of the earlier Elizabethan church leaders, like Hooper in the reign of Edward VI, introduced more exotic and definitely reformed pastoral devices. As we have seen, David Kemp, the first Elizabethan archdeacon of St Albans, took a direct interest in his charge and personally ran the St Albans prophesying. At least two bishops – Bradbridge of Exeter and Curteys of Chichester – knew what it was to moderate at a prophesying. Others made themselves responsible for the conferences in which the progress of the unlearned clergy in their extra-mural studies was tested. In these and other ways an energetic bishop could meet and know his clergy as father and brother rather than as lord and judge. There is no lack of evidence that the Elizabethans, puritan Elizabethans among them, were capable of responding warmly to such an example.

But what was feasible in a sparsely populated diocese of one or two counties was a flat impossibility in the diocese of Lincoln, which stretched from Hertfordshire to the Humber and from the borders of Derbyshire to the Wash, or even in a compact but closely settled diocese like Norwich. Observers were not slow to point out that if the godly bishop was to be more than an ideal figure, there must be a recasting of the units of pastoral care. John Aylmer, in the first months of the reign, had dreamed of a state in which 'every parish church may have his preacher, every city his superintendent, to live honestly and not pompously', and on this at least his adversary John Knox was agreed. He would have multiplied the number of English bishops by ten, 'so that in every city and great town there may be placed a godly learned man ... ' William Turner, for his part, had proposed an allocation of four bishops to each of the smaller shires, 'I mean no mitred nor lordly, no rochetted bishops ... ' This very simple idea was never ousted by the more sophisticated programme of the presbyterians, as anyone familiar with the views aired in the Long Parliament almost a century later will know. From the years in between, it would probably prove possible to recover a succession of moderate and pragmatic proposals of this kind: for example, a parliamentary 'plot for reformation' of Elizabeth's reign whose author thought that the size of a diocese should be determined by the distance that a bishop and the most remote of his clergy could be expected to cover in order to meet at least once a week for exercise, and so proposed a new pattern of one hundred and fifty dioceses; or the desire of the puritan civil lawyer, William Stoughton, to see fifteen bishops in each of the five shires of Lincoln diocese, 'to teach and to govern the same.' Such schemes were calculated to please the laity in that they normally involved the diversion of the bulk of episcopal endowments to 'other good uses' and the payment of modest stipends to the new-style bishops, a sure antidote for 'the pride of the clergy'.[4]

One needs no great subtlety to see that a similar pastoral end could be achieved with less disturbance to ancient institutions and endowments by retaining the existing dioceses while representing the bishop in the various divisions of his jurisdiction by lesser superintendents. These would differ from episcopal officials of the late medieval type in that they would themselves reside on parochial charges, and would represent the bishop pastorally rather than judicially. John Hooper wrote in 1552 of 'such as I have made superintendents in Gloucestershire'; these would be the 'deputies' who took charge of the quarterly conferences of the clergy in each deanery. Later, in their parting testament before their martyrdom, Hooper and John Rogers recorded their conviction that only by the use of superintendent ministers could the pastoral shortcomings of the Edwardine Church be remedied in any future protestant establishment. For every ten churches there should be 'one good and learned superintendent', supervising 'faithful readers' in the parishes and himself subject to the bishop's visitation.[5]

There was no necessity to break with tradition in defining the offices and units of administration of the bishops' coadjutors, for these lay ready to hand in the rural deans and deaneries. The rural dean in origin corresponded exactly to what these reformers meant when they spoke of a superintendent: he was in administrative matters an assistant bishop, a *chorepiscopus* appointed from among his fellow-clergy and charged with assembling them in monthly assemblies and quarterly rural chapters. Long before the Reformation, rural deans and chapters were moribund and in many places practically extinct; the growing sophistication of canon law and the tendency of late medieval ecclesiastical jurisdiction to become increasingly centralized and professional had led to an invasion of their sphere by the archdeacon, or rather by the officials who did the archdeacon's work. Yet rural deans were still technically on the establishment of many dioceses, and most of England was still divided into deaneries, often corresponding closely to the hundreds of medieval secular administration.[6]

Martin Bucer with his characteristic concern for discipline was perhaps the first reformer to suggest the resuscitation of *chorepiscopi* and their chapters. Perhaps it was under his influence that the abortive *Reformatio Legum* made detailed provision for the office. Rural deans were to be appointed annually from among the parish clergy to supervise both ministers and churchwardens. Though without coercive, punitive jurisdiction they were authorized to summon and examine offenders and to pass them on to the bishop or other ordinary. In addition they were to inform the bishop every six months of the number of sermons preached in their deaneries. In Elizabeth's reign the proposal to revive the rural dean continued to attract some interest, and at least one bishop – Bentham of Coventry and Lichfield – tried to breathe some new life into these old bones. In 1571, Convocation reflected the current interest by defining the procedure by which rural deans were to be chosen, while in the opening speech before Parliament in the following year, the lord keeper, Sir Nicholas Bacon, complained of the serious lack of ecclesiastical discipline and pointed to the remedy in 'the dividing every one of the dioceses according to their greatness into deaneries, as I know commonly they be; and the committing of the deaneries to men well chosen, as I think commonly they be not.' But although Bacon had hoped that something might be done in that very Parliament of 1572 to revive the office and to make it a credible instrument of discipline, the English rural dean was to continue his long slumber until a busier age of ecclesiastical improvement – the Victorian age – would again press him into service.[7]

It is here that the prophesyings become relevant. For what was the moderator of an exercise but a kind of rural dean, and what was the exercise itself but his rural chapter? Consider the powers conferred by Bishop Parkhurst of Norwich on three preachers appointed moderators of the exercise at Bury St Edmunds. They were to take 'charge and order' of proceedings, and each one of them had the power to convene the clergy at such times and places as he thought fit. They were to certify disobedient persons to the bishop's commissary in Bury, or if need be to the bishop himself. And they were allowed to use their discretion in making additional orders and decrees for the better conduct of proceedings.[8]

In 1578 the chancellor to the bishop of Norwich, Thomas Becon, devised an important scheme for the reform of the diocese which joined the modern innovation of the exercise to the 'ancient and commendable practice' of rural deans which he had encountered in thirteenth-century records at Norwich. As in the past, 'certain choice picked men', preachers resident in every deanery, should be made superintendents, to summon the ministers and churchwardens to a monthly prophesying 'if prophesying may continue', and if not, to a sermon. On these occasions they should inquire into disorders, deal summarily with minor offences and certify others to the bishop. They should also make reports on the popish recusants in their deaneries. A regular opportunity of conferring with the bishop and the chancellor could be provided by arranging that the superintendents should take it in turns to preach the Sunday sermon in the Green Yard at Norwich. They were to sit with the bishop and his chancellor in diocesan synods, when delinquent ministers and laymen were to be 'rebuked or suspended before all the clergy of the diocese and the whole congregation there assembled.' To reform procedure in the church courts, all processes should be directed to the superintendents who were also to have charge of probate matters. If these affairs were dealt with at the monthly prophesyings or sermons, those who were not inclined to attend 'of devotion' would frequent these exercises 'upon occasion of necessary business'. Lastly, the superintendents were to examine candidates for the ministry or for institution to benefices. By this means the bishop as 'pastor of his whole diocese' would acquire 'a special knowledge of every particular man', while he could dispense with the abused jurisdiction of commissaries and other officials, which Becon took to be the chief cause of the unpopularity of ecclesiastical government.[9]

The authors of other Elizabethan 'devices' showed a similar interest in the potentialities of the 'best learned preachers', and in 1581 the House of Commons proposed that they should be given a share in ordination and in the censure of erring ministers. Three years later the bishop of Coventry and Lichfield, William Overton, undertook a modest experiment on these lines, among other innovations calculated to please protestant opinion.

Four preachers of prominence, chosen for their local knowledge, were appointed to act as examiners of candidates for admission to benefices. This is an intriguing episode which raises many questions; Overton was no reformer himself, but he owed his bishopric partly to Thomas Becon, the author of the Norwich project, who now became his chancellor at Lichfield, and through Becon to the earl of Leicester who would certainly have approved of a scheme of this kind. Thomas Lever, archdeacon of Coventry until his death in 1577, had memorialized Overton's predecessor with 'notes for some reformation of the ministry and ministers' on closely parallel lines.[10]

Of the four examiners appointed by Overton, at least two were non-conformists and one of these, John Oxenbridge of Southam, was the most notorious puritan in the diocese. When Archbishop Whitgift, who knew this, vetoed his scheme, Overton suggested that 'this employing of their service may rather win them to conformity.'[11] That expresses the whole Grindalian policy in a nutshell. The use of the puritan preachers in these superintendent capacities directed their energies outwards to the Church at large, to its rustic dumb-dog parsons and uninstructed, undisciplined parishes. A puritan who was encouraged to take this wide and practical view of the real state of the Church of England was not likely to keep in the forefront of his mind the presbyterian proposition that all ministers were created equal. Nor could he evade the question by dismissing the ministry of the unlearned as no ministry at all. He was forced to proceed as though he believed that the parishes and the parish clergy of England, with all their faults, made up the Church of England, and he usually proved ready to use his superior gifts to instruct and discipline the ignorant, and to acknowledge that he held these powers from the bishop. Conversely, the narrow insistence on uniformity which was the mark of Whitgift's government would drive the puritans back into their own gathered brotherhoods from which the unlearned were excluded.

Whitgift chose to regard Overton's use of examiners as a dangerous innovation, 'a kind of seignory'. Yet there were many ways, short of a radical reform of the diocesan system, whereby the Church already made use of the 'learned preachers in each deanery'. In the diocese of Norwich an incontinent minister was ordered to make his purgation 'by eight ministers, being bachelors of divinity, masters of arts, or at the least public preachers'. A brief for the collection of funds to endow a grammar school at Kingston-on-Thames was committed to the 'careful endeavour of three or four preachers or other discreet ministers in every deanery'. And in the archdeaconry of Derby in 1586 the duty of assessing the ministers for a military subsidy was delegated to 'the preachers of Derby-shire', seven leading clergy of the county.[12]

Above all, the system of extra-mural education on which the Church depended in order to raise the standards of the ministry came to rest squarely on the co-operation of the graduate preachers as supervisors and examiners. In his first visitation after Whitgift had circulated his 'orders for the increase of learning in the unlearned sort of ministers', Bishop Aylmer's vicar-general, Dr Stanhope, appointed 'commissioners for examining the clergy', or 'commissioners for the assistance of the arch-deacon' in that function. In each deanery these comprised a small panel of about half a dozen examiners, with the unlearned ordered to resort to them on a certain set day, and 'such other times as you shall appoint.' (An order that the remaining graduate clergy should attend on the same occasions was rescinded.) In Essex, as we should expect, the commissioners included some of the more moderate puritan ministers, such as Edmund Chapman of Dedham and Laurence Newman of Coggeshall. Two years later, in 1587, Convocation made this practice general for the whole province. In the archdeaconry of Colchester, lists were regularly revised of preachers and those who were 'no preachers, but tied to the exercise'. In 1589, when Bishop Scambler prepared detailed orders for the exercise of the unlearned ministers in the diocese of Norwich, thirty-five preachers (many of them nonconformists) were appointed supervisors by formal commission. When puritans spoke of an exercise they meant a con-ference, not the mere performance and examination of written tasks, and this is evidently what the ecclesiastical authorities in Essex and East Anglia now provided, in what were called 'oppositions and exercises'. From all this it should be clear that in practice the form of government of the Elizabethan Church was not purely episcopal, in the sense of a simple monarchy, but constitutional, in the language of the time a 'mixed polity'.[13]

The moderate episcopacy prefigured in the prophesyings and to some extent in Elizabethan administrative practice, was fitted, as presbyterian-ism was not, to the actual condition of the Church, to the distribution within it of both learning and endowment. In a situation where both intellectual standards and livings were so unequal, it was surely absurd to speak of parity. The best of the puritan preachers inevitably enjoyed something of the quasi-episcopal standing to which reformers like Becon would have given formal recognition. Gilby at Ashby, Lever at Coventry, and Wiburn at Northampton were all episcopal men, fathers of the Church or 'presidents or leaders of an army', to borrow a phrase applied to the two leading Norwich preachers. Moreover, their position belonged naturally to the political and social geography of Elizabethan England. Norwich, Bury St Edmunds and Ipswich shared the same father in God in the bishop of Norwich, but each was a world of its own, and inclined to adopt its own spiritual leader. When John Aylmer recommended that every city should have its superintendent, he recognized that the market town, with its surrounding catchment area, was a natural social entity, which the diocese usually was not.

The remarkable position occupied by one of the Norwich 'presidents', John More, justifies these arguments. For upwards of twenty years, More exercised a kind of unofficial superintendency throughout much of Norfolk, and received a respect which was granted to none of the three bishops who occupied Ludham House in the same period. His titular status was sufficiently obscure: he was merely the senior of the two preachers normally attached to the church of St Andrew's, Norwich. But as the 'apostle of Norwich', More was influential far beyond his own small parish. The Suffolk minister Nicholas Bownd, who both married his widow and later occupied his pulpit, spoke two years after More's death of the 'many hundred sermons, or rather certain thousands' which he had delivered in Norfolk in the space of twenty years, preaching every day of the week and three or four times on Sundays, and of his great reputation with the godly knights and esquires of the shire. 'But alas, I cannot preach to the whole land', More protests in one of these sermons, addressed to the justices meeting in quarter session, and he exhorts them 'so many of you as have any voices in place and Parliament, where these things may be reformed, consecrate your tongues to the Lord in the behalf of your poor brethren ... ' 'Get you preachers into your parishes,' he goes on, ' ... bestow your labour, cost and travail to get them; ride for them, run for them, stretch your purses to maintain them; we shall begin to be rich in the Lord Jesus ... ' Puritan patrons found a less arduous way to follow More's advice: they relied upon him to find their ministers for them, an office which he seems to have performed as a matter of course. When the puritan ministers of Norwich were suspended by Bishop Freke, More's offer of limited subscription served for them all, and it came into the hands of the Privy Council as 'Mr More's conformity'. What was known in Norfolk as 'Mr More's catechism', more familiar elsewhere under the name of its co-author, Edward Dering, as *A short catechism for householders*, may well have served as the local standard of sound doctrine. A member of the bishop's household condemned himself out of his own mouth when he said that 'he had as lief hear a dog bark as Mr More to preach.' Without doubt More performed in Norfolk what protestants took to be the whole office of a godly bishop. If his position had been formalized by making him bishop of the diocese, say in 1575, in place of Freke, how many East Anglian puritans would have continued to insist on absolute parity in the ministry?[14]

The kind of ecclesiastical reform to which the prophesyings and exercises were a pointer was much to the liking of the protestant nobility and gentry. One cannot read Sir John Neale's account of the Parliaments of 1576, 1581 and 1584-5 without concluding that it was a church of this character – Grindal's Church – which these influential laymen hoped to see firmly established in England. Its attractions were thus summarized by Thomas Becon:

> I do not see but the minister thus sifted before his entrance into the ministry or taking any benefice, and by watchful oversight of superintendents urged to usual speaking at the exercises and restrained by admonition and other censures ecclesiastical from their loose loitering and greedy covetous life, the preaching of the gospel and other usual exercises of religion so frequented, the word of God would flourish, the enemy be daunted (who could not lurk in any corner) and her Majesty have an assured, safe, peaceable government.

No wonder that Becon's device was forwarded to the Privy Council by a group of puritan justices in Norfolk and Suffolk as proof of his 'desire of good proceedings'! The enthusiasm of the governing class will be all the easier to comprehend if we consider that the effect of these reforms would have been to reduce still further both the powers of the unpopular ecclesiastical courts and the social status of the higher clergy, while exposing spiritual government to lay interference. Becon recommended that such justices of the peace as were zealous in religion should always be present at the 'solemn assemblies and preachings' of his superintendents, while another scheme proposed that the six learned preachers who were to act as bishop's coadjutors should be appointed by the justices in each county. The tendency of such proposals was to make the shire rather than the diocese the working unit of church administration and to bring into close harmony, if not to unify, the spiritual discipline of the ecclesiastical courts and the government of the magistrates.[15]

In West Suffolk, Bishop Freke's commissary – that most despised of all ecclesiastical functionaries whose court had been described by John Field as 'a petty little stinking ditch' – had to fight hard for his rights against the natural leaders of society, puritan justices like Sir Robert Jermyn of Rushbrooke and Sir John Higham of Barrow, who exercised a severe moral discipline in their petty sessions at Bury St Edmunds. A marital offence was typically described in a formal report of these magistrates as 'quite contrary unto the word of God and the laws of this realm'. Both Jermyn and Higham possessed considerable ecclesiastical patronage and used it to promote a puritan, preaching ministry. Jermyn alone presented to ten parishes, besides strengthening the arm of the unbeneficed preachers in Bury. Richard Bancroft, who in his youth defended the unpopular cause of Anglican conformity in Bury, has left a brilliant caricature of the firm alliance between 'magistracy and ministry' in an Elizabethan market town. We hear the gentry approving with sonorous 'Amens' a sermon which is highly critical of the failings of the established Church but silent about the sins of the landlords. When the preacher descends from the pulpit we see the gentlemen 'rise full solemnly, and embrace him, with "God be thanked good brother", "The Lord bless you and continue his graces towards you", "We have had a worthy sermon, God make us thankful for it". "You shall go dine with me" saith one, "Nay I pray you let him be my guest today" saith another. I omit the like great kindness of the gentlewomen.' In Norwich the same godly conjunction was the anchor of society, 'magistrates and ministers embracing and seconding one to another, and the common people affording due reverence and obedience to them both.' One suspects that if the Elizabethan bishops were for all practical purposes commissioners for the queen, the lesser superintendents drawn from the ranks of preachers like these would have been the willing agents of government of the Church by the gentry; which is not to say that they would not themselves have influenced the quality of that government by their preaching, which was not always so subservient to the laity as Bancroft pretended.[16]

We are now in a position to present an image of the church which the protestant governing class seems to have desired and which the reforms associated with Grindal and other like-minded bishops were beginning to make an actuality. It was a typically Tudor conception of Church and Commonwealth indissolubly one (far removed from Andrew Melville's presbyterian concept of the 'two kingdoms') and anchored in godly and law-abiding order by the firm bond between gentry and preachers. The bishop was not denied a place in this scheme of things, but he was divested of every lingering shred of prelacy and regarded as a simple minister of the gospel whose first duty it was to preach the word of God, and who derived his power to govern from the queen, whose local representatives the justices were. He must never 'set himself against the gentry' as Whitgift was accused of doing in Kent a few years later, for it was the very mark of popery to subvert the authority of the governors in the eyes of the common people. But provided the bishop was prepared to conform himself to this pattern, there was no reason why he should not be respected throughout his diocese. But there was little room in a church of this kind for the ecclesiastical courts and their unreformed procedure, vexatious, covetous and lacking in moral earnestness; at least the powers of these courts must be curtailed. Church government was to be distributed among pastors in their own congregations, groups of preachers 'in their solemn assemblies', bishops acting in conjunction with other ministers and, of course, the justices of the peace themselves.

'Discipline' was provided for in the sense that immorality and irreligion were to be corrected in the lower orders and popery and papists detected. But there was no desire for 'discipline' as the strict presbyterians understood it. The character of this church was shaped by the emancipated temper of lay protestantism, and implicitly it was just as opposed to the neo-clerical pretensions of high Calvinism as to the prelatical ambitions of some bishops. The Dudley brothers, Leicester and Warwick, were good friends to the radical protestant preachers, but like their father Northumberland before them they were quick to complain of 'ingratitude' if a preacher was rash enough to point the finger at their own failings. As Warwick wrote on one occasion of his brother: 'I think it to be very hard dealing towards him who hath deserved so well at their hands as he hath done, to be so hardly rewarded.' Leicester himself betrays in his letters an aversion for the carping, curious Calvinist spirit which he obviously had difficulty in subordinating to the interests which required him to befriend the preachers of this persuasion. He told Thomas Wood that he had never in his life seen 'more envy stirring and less charity used' than in godly circles.[17]

These lay attitudes endured to be expressed with great eloquence by the generation which was represented in the Long Parliament. Sir Edward Dering, the grand-nephew of the Elizabethan divine, was to urge in his parliamentary speeches the pattern of a church which will by now be familiar: 'Every shire of England to be a several circuit or diocese'; the bishops to be chosen in the first instance by their fellow-clergy; the other ministers to share in government in the parish, and at the ruridecanal and diocesan levels. All this was seen to be a means to 'underprop the primitive, lawful and just episcopacy.' As an authority on the history of Dering's native county has remarked, 'the essence of that reform was clearly county-mindedness, not presbyterianism.'[18]

But we shall end with the sentiments of an Elizabethan, typical of his class if exceptional in his knowledge of ecclesiastical and constitutional procedure and precedent: Robert Beale, clerk of the Council. Beale could protest that he was 'none of them that would have archbishops or bishops pulled down, or the form of the Church altered. For I am not so foolish, but see that the estate cannot bear it without some harm, and therefore I meddle with no such matters.' But he could ask whether there was another reformed church 'under the cope of heaven' which tolerated 'two such notable absurdities and banes of God's Church' as the maintenance of a dumb, unpreaching ministry, and 'the whole exercise of the discipline of the Church and excommunication to be in one man.' Men in Beale's position found intolerable the clericalism implicit in Aylmer's boast that 'his consistory was wheresoever his person was. So I think', he added, 'that all law is locked up in the shrines of their venerable breasts, where it cannot be seen or known by lay fools, unworthy or uncapable of so high mysteries.' This lay temper would be equally repelled by presbyterian clericalism, whenever it turned from the negation of popery and prelacy to the positive advancement of its own high conception of a divinely ordained hierarchy of ecclesiastical tribunals.[19]

4 Reaction

'Thus yt is, moderate courses are subject to the callumniation of both extremes.'
> (WILLIAM BEDELL (later bishop of Kilmore) TO SAMUEL
> WARD, October 16th, 1604; Bodleian Library, MS. Tanner
> 75, fol. 127)

THE TENDENCIES DESCRIBED in the last chapter were checked and even in some respects reversed by the queen's peremptory order of 1576 that the prophesyings in the province of Canterbury should cease. Few episodes of Elizabethan church history are so suggestive of the gulf dividing the queen's church policy from the outlook of so many of her servants. According to the progressive protestant view now in the ascendant, the ministry of the Church should be an energetic force, converting the people to a godly obedience by proclamation of the word and discipline. There would be no security without subjection to the gospel, and no understanding of the gospel without preaching. But Elizabeth, who told Grindal that three or four preachers were sufficient for a shire, and who could express her content with a ministry of 'such as can read the scriptures and homilies well unto the people', took a thoroughly conservative view of the Church's function.[1] The guarantee of stability was the conformity of all her subjects, whatever their private opinions, in uniform religious observances, not protestant enthusiasm, which threatened the same wasteful conflicts which were ravaging France and the Netherlands, and which, given its head, would drag England into costly foreign adventures in the name of religion.

Before Grindal's defence of preaching and prophesying brought these differences into sharp focus, Elizabeth seems to have ordered the exercises to be put down whenever she was reminded of their existence. As early as 1574, before the death of Parker, the exercises in the diocese of Norwich came under suspicion when it was learned that four preachers suspended in the recent 'inquisition' were still using them as a platform. In March, Parker passed to Bishop Parkhurst an order 'to suppress those vain prophesyings', which he later claimed was general to the whole province. But Parkhurst, who dared not alienate the local puritan gentry, instructed his chancellor to put down only those exercises which were disorderly, and to do so on his own authority alone. William Heydon of Baconsthorpe, on whom the bishop was singularly dependent, at once rode up to London and procured a letter from Bishop Sandys and three councillors, Mildmay, Knollys and Smith, which assumed that the prophesyings had been threatened by 'some not well-minded towards true religion' and recommended their discreet continuance. Parker at once asked by what warrant his order had been countermanded, and rebuked Parkhurst for placing too much confidence in 'fantastical folk'. The poor bishop admitted that his letter from the councillors constituted only advice and not a warrant and asked Sandys for an explanation. But no sooner had he given his chancellor fresh instructions to suppress all the prophesyings in the diocese than Freke of Rochester (soon to succeed him) wrote with an assurance that no other bishop had received such an order and that he and others had merely taken steps to prevent abuse. On Parkhurst's death the Norwich ministers at once resumed their order of prophesying and in other places it seems to have suffered no interruption. Three years later, in contemplating his own predicament, Grindal wrote: 'The bishop of London, being commanded by the last archbishop of Canterbury to put down the exercise of ministers, continued it in his diocese.' This Sandys seems to have done on the Council's advice.[2]

A year later the queen heard of the exercise at Welwyn and through Sir Thomas Smith ordered Cooper of Lincoln to dissolve it. Cooper's only response was to ask the ministers and gentry of the district whether there had been any disorder and to return their favourable certificate. He was then told that he must dissolve the exercises 'in such sort' as he could 'conveniently'. Accordingly he allowed them in five or six places 'by little and little to be left', so that by the summer of 1576 the only exercise still surviving in the southern part of his diocese was at Aylesbury. Prophesying ended in the diocese of Hereford about the same time, Bishop Scory fearing what he understood to have happened in other parts, 'where some platform of Cartwright's Church under colour of such exercises hath been laid'; and Bishop Cheyney brought it to an end in the diocese of Gloucester, 'hearing what a do had been in Northamptonshire'.

Paradoxically, the threat to the prophesyings arose from the very strength of the backing they enjoyed. In a society so prone to faction as an Elizabethan English shire, the support of one party for the preachers and their exercises aroused the inevitable antagonism of their rivals. The enemies of preaching had a ready means of discrediting the godly by bearing incriminating reports to the Court, and for these there was fertile material in the hotter sermons of the puritan left wing. Cooper warned Grindal that the Aylesbury exercise was threatened by 'one or two of some countenance and easy access unto the prince', and in Lincolnshire, too, he feared 'some that seek to creep in favour, not only by their well-doing, but by the discrediting of other's welldoings, and so to suspect I have greater cause than I may conveniently put into writing.'[3]

The final crisis began in the summer of 1576 when, after fresh complaints from the judges of assize and some bishops, the queen was in particular 'most grievously informed' touching the conduct of both preachers and gentlemen at Southam in Warwickshire. The schismatic tendencies of the Southam exercise are clear. Its moderators were two extremists, John Oxenbridge, rector of the parish, and the deprived Northamptonshire minister Eusebius Paget, now moving around the Midland exercises as a 'posting apostle'; their backers included gentlemen like Sir Richard Knightley and (in all probability) Anthony Cope of Hanwell who would sponsor a presbyterian bill in Parliament in 1587 and whose home was only twelve miles from Southam. Puritans reckoned it 'undoubtedly without exception ... the best exercise in this realm' although Bishop Bentham knew neither 'when it began, nor how it was used.' The queen 'first of any' mentioned the reports of Southam to Leicester; Warwickshire was his country. But soon not only Leicester but Burghley and Walsingham were warning Grindal of the danger, and Grindal was ordering Bentham and Scambler to 'see reformation' and to send Oxenbridge and Paget up to London. While Bentham suppressed the Southam exercise, the Council did their best to save the remaining prophesyings from the queen's displeasure, and Leicester intervened to rescue the Warwickshire gentlemen from discredit.[4]

Behind this little crisis there may have been a deliberate effort to halt the progressive tendencies which Grindal's elevation six months before had encouraged. There is a suggestion of intrigue in a contemporary report that the queen was prompted to put down the exercises 'by Hatton and some other'.[5] Sir Christopher Hatton, the rising star in the Elizabethan firmament, was already viewed with suspicion in puritan circles. He was to assist the Anglican reaction of the next thirty years by his support of

Aylmer, Whitgift and Bancroft, and he may have chosen his church policy as a means of outpointing his principal rival, Leicester, whose alliance with the most radical protestant elements in the country was an embarrassment at Court.

Curiously enough it was Leicester himself who was at first blamed by the godly for the calamity at Southam. Coupled with rumours of what Camden called his 'straying loves', these reports persuaded the ringleaders of Midland puritanism that the earl had changed sides, and drew a torrent of angry words from Thomas Wood. Leicester's lengthy self-exculpation from these charges (eloquent of the value he placed on his reputation in these circles) was mingled with warnings of how delicately balanced the prospects were in that summer of 1576 and of the probability that the zeal-without-knowledge of hotheads like Wood would play into the hands of their enemies. 'I fear the over-busy dealing of some hath done so much hurt in striving to make better perforce that which is by permission good enough already as we shall neither have it in Southam nor any other where else, and do what we can all, and those all you think more zealous than I. And this have I feared long ago would prove the fruit of our dissension for trifles first, and since for other matters.' A couple of years later and in a different context, Walsingham would give an even more explicit warning to another zealot, the diplomatist William Davison: 'If you knew with what difficulty we retain that we have, and that the seeking of more might hazard (according to man's understanding) that which we already have, ye would then, Mr Davison, deal warily in this time when policy carrieth more sway than zeal.'[6]

Leicester's fears proved to be well founded. Within a few months Elizabeth summoned the archbishop into her presence to order the 'utter suppression' of all learned exercises and conferences and the 'abridging' of the number of preachers to three or four for each shire.[7] Grindal, like others before him, might have side-stepped the issue, taking advantage of the limitations of Tudor government and the protestant sympathies of so many of its local agents. Instead, being Grindal, he prepared to offer the queen a reasoned rejection of her commands. In the summer he had asked all his fellow-bishops for the fruit of their experience of the exercises. Had they improved the ministry and edified the people? Would their continuance be profitable? What orders did the bishops recommend for their regulation? And should a lay audience be admitted? Replies were received from all but six diocesans, and we have relied upon the information they contain in reconstructing the history of the movement.[8] Ten out of fifteen bishops expressed their qualified approval of the exercises, defending them on pragmatic grounds, although Bradbridge of Exeter thought their continuance 'right necessary, and for that it is a monument of the like practices holden in the primitive Church.' Grindal concluded from these letters that disorders had been generally reformed 'except at Southam'. But John Aylmer, archdeacon of Lincoln, warned him that in Leicestershire his inquiry had been committed to two known puritans and that he should treat their report with reserve. Aylmer knew the character of Midland puritanism – he had the occasional company of Whitgift as dean of Lincoln – and he would soon apply his experience to the painful diocese of London. But it is worth noting that of Grindal's episcopal colleagues, only one, Scory of Hereford, who had almost no personal experience of nonconformity, saw in the prophesyings what some Anglican historians have seen: presbyterianism in embryo.[9]

Meanwhile Grindal had extracted precedents for the practice of prophesying from a variety of biblical, patristic, medieval and modern sources. Many folios of his notes survive, some of them headed 'Quod prophetia sit retinenda'. This, together, with the file of bishops' reports, formed the basis of a projected reform of the prophesyings: 'Orders for reformation of abuses about the learned exercises and conferences among ministers of the Church.' Grindal proposed to subject prophesying to the more effective oversight of bishops and archdeacons, to prevent all participation by suspended or deprived ministers, and ante omnia to prohibit laymen from speaking. Nor were the exercises in future to be abused 'to make any invection against the laws, rites, policies and discipline of the Church of England established by public authority.'[10]

Finally, in early December,[11] Grindal sat down to write to the queen in terms which Elizabeth never expected to hear from a subject, and least of all from a bishop whom she had raised from nothing. Indeed, the precedents in Christian history for such a letter from a father of the Church to a prince were few and far between, and it cannot have helped his case that Grindal drew freely upon the Epistles of St Ambrose, whose resistance to the civil power was without parallel in the western Church before Hildebrand. His letter was both a spirited defence of the exercises and of the necessity of plentiful preaching, which the queen had denied, and a remarkable affirmation of the limits to royal authority in the spiritual sphere.

I am forced, with all humility, and yet plainly, to profess, that I cannot with safe conscience, and without the offence of the majesty of God, give my assent to the suppressing of the said exercises; much

less can I send out any injunction for the utter and universal subversion of the same ... If it be your Majesty's pleasure, for this or
any other cause, to remove me out of this place, I will with all
humility yield thereunto, and render again to your Majesty that I
received of the same ... Bear with me, I beseech you, Madam, if I
choose rather to offend your earthly majesty than to offend against
the heavenly majesty of God.

He ended with two requests, both quite inadmissible for a Tudor: that
Elizabeth should refer all ecclesiastical matters touching religion, or the
doctrine and discipline of the Church, to her bishops and other divines,
and that in these respects she should not 'use to pronounce so resolutely
and peremptorily, *quasi ex auctoritate*', as in civil affairs. 'Remember,
Madam, that you are a mortal creature.' Grindal deserved better than
to have this notable appeal for spiritual independence dismissed by Bishop
Frere in this century as 'a particular piece of characteristically puritan
crankiness'.[12]
  But for all its integrity and courage, Grindal's stand was certainly
tactless, and it proved fatal for himself and ultimately for the whole programme of moderate reform which had been discreetly advancing since
the death of Parker. In late February he proposed to come to Court to
speak with the queen, but was advised by Burghley to stay away and
make his excuse by the earl of Leicester whom he was to use as his
'intercessor'. Leicester saw the possibility of a compromise in the exclusion
of the laity from the exercises (Bishop Cox, Thomas Norton and Francis
Bacon all at various times made the same suggestion) but Grindal was not
prepared to yield even on this point. Later he refused to budge before the
'good persuasions' of the Council, adding, in the queen's view, 'a second
offence of disobedience greater than the first'. In April, royal letters were
drafted (apparently by Burghley) to all the bishops and a particular order
to Cooper of Lincoln, bypassing the archbishop and directly commanding
them to forbid 'a certain public exercise or (as they call it) prophesying',
and to permit only preaching by licensed preachers and the reading of
homilies. These letters went out on May 7th and must have taken effect
in most places in the course of the summer. Lever's exercise at Coventry
was suppressed by Bishop Bentham on June 18th.[13]
  The queen regarded Grindal's refusal to be the channel of these orders
as an extremely serious offence, and in late May she appointed certain
persons 'to consult for deprivation of the archbishop.' As Burghley wrote,
much perplexed, it would be difficult to find a precedent for the removal

of an archbishop, and the queen on advice had to content herself with suspending Grindal from the exercise of his office (without formal process) and confining him as a virtual prisoner to Lambeth. In mid-July, when he had been 'restrained of liberty now almost seven weeks', the archbishop wrote either to Burghley or Leicester, begging their continued mediation with the queen. In August, Leicester and Hatton assured his secretary that the case 'shall take end very shortly', and in November Grindal 'was put in assured hope of liberty.' But then, as he told his friend Matthew Hutton, dean of York, 'arose a sudden contrary tempest', and he was summoned to appear in the Star Chamber to make a public submission. Grindal prepared a form of apology which he entrusted to Sir Walter Mildmay, but instead of following Burghley's advice to 'cry pardon' without any self-justification, he persisted in defending the exercises and his own refusal to be the queen's instrument in their suppression.

If he had made his submission in no humbler terms than these, the archbishop might well have been deprived, but an attack of his old enemy, the stone, prevented him from making an appearance on two successive days (and those the last available dates of the term) and Lord Keeper Bacon had no choice but to adjourn the hearing. It is not hard to see in these moves the efforts of Grindal's friends to save him, and the queen bitterly complained of their dilatory proceedings and again demanded Grindal's deprivation. The legal difficulties were again pointed out to her, and Dr Thomas Wilson hoped she would be content with the more honourable course of the archbishop's resignation. Yet in late February it was reported that 'there is hope that the bishop of Canterbury shall do better and better daily.' In May, he was about to be delivered when reports from York and Durham of puritanism in the north again 'made a stay'. This was only the beginning of a long tale of indeterminate troubles from which final release only came with death, five years later. There is no doubt where the sympathies of almost everyone of influence were placed, the queen and a few personal enemies excepted. Bishop Barnes of Durham, no friend, felt bound to defend himself to Burghley against the charge of not having 'a good mind' towards the archbishop. But while the sympathetic interest of privy councillors (shared with almost all of the bishops) was a shield against actual deprivation, it was not sufficient to deflect the queen's displeasure.[14]

There was doubtless more to Grindal's problem than meets the eye in the documents. There were contemporary rumours, perpetuated in that unscrupulous libel *Leycesters Commonwealth* and repeated by Camden and

Harington, that the real cause of his troubles was Leicester, whom the archbishop had offended by preventing his Italian physician, 'Dr Julio' (Giulio Borgarucci), from obtaining a dispensation to make a bigamous marriage.[15] Knowing where Leicester stood, it would be easy to discount these tales if it were not for independent evidence of Borgarucci's interest in the archbishop's fate.[16] But 'Dr Julio' was physician to the queen as well as to Leicester, and no doubt had opportunities of his own to influence her mind against Grindal. Perhaps the proposed reform of the Faculty Office was now recoiling upon its author.

What is certain is that Grindal's troubles extended over the years when Elizabethan policy stood balanced on a knife-edge. It would be inappropriate in this context to trace even in outline the political fluctuations of the later 'seventies, in which domestic faction interacted with international issues, but one can hardly make sense of what was now on foot in the Church without at least a glance in that direction.[17] At Court there was a marked, if unequal, division between the alliance headed by Leicester and his 'spirit' Walsingham, committed to vigorous and even militant protestant policies, and a looser constellation of the restless, disaffected, and merely ornamental, including some scions of the older aristocratic houses, and some catholics and crypto-catholics. The connections here run from Burghley's unsatisfactory son-in-law, Edward de Vere, earl of Oxford, a secret convert, through his 'lewd' friends (Burghley's description) Lord Henry Howard and Charles Arundel, a likely candidate for the authorship of Leycesters Commonwealth, to Sir Edward Stafford, ambassador in France, and his powerful mother, and on to Howard's second cousin, the earl of Sussex; and more obscurely to Sir James Croft and Hatton, both suspected of catholic sympathies. A common interest in the destruction of Leicester was perhaps the strongest force holding these elements together. Leicester and his friends were in a commanding position, with a majority of the voices in the Council. Most of England's overseas envoys came from this group, especially those entrusted with missions in the Low Countries, and it was with Leicester and Walsingham that they normally consulted. Without a doubt we need look no further to explain the ascendancy of a moderate puritanism in England at this time. As for Burghley, whom one searches in vain for signs of a strong and consistent policy of his own, he reminded Conyers Read at this moment in his long career of 'a retired elder statesman'.[18]

The lines were occasionally drawn sharply and visibly, as in the famous tennis-court quarrel between Oxford and Leicester's nephew, Philip Sidney; an atmosphere of concealed and confused intrigue was more normal. The Leicestrians strove to maintain and enlarge their freedom of action, which they would have liked to employ in the pursuit of a forceful policy in the Netherlands, where in 1577 Don John of Austria presented a daunting challenge. They were equally committed to an initiative in Scotland, in support of Regent Morton, and to the harsher treatment of catholic recusants at home. Elizabeth shrank from the expense and the fanaticism of their doctrines. It was her estrangement and opposition, rather than the plots of their rivals, that the Leicestrians had to fear. The many puritans involved in their faction, or dependent upon it, saw religious retrogression as the only possible alternative to advance, especially when, late in 1578, the queen opened herself to the renewed advances of Francis of Valois, duke of Alençon and now duke of Anjou.

Anjou was an adventurer who was about to make a career for himself in the Netherlands – as a doubtful support to the rebel, protestant side. The French marriage negotiation was consequently an alternative in its devious way to direct English intervention in that area; but an unsatisfactory and even scandalous alternative in the view of the godly, and of those whose politics were founded upon godly principles. 'At bottom', wrote Conyers Read, ' ... the marriage issue was one aspect of a larger issue in which the old considerations dominant in European diplomacy, dynastic interest and balance of power, were set over against considerations primarily religious.'[19] Oxford, Arundel and their friends seized the French lever to lift themselves into a more favourable position, and even to angle for liberty of worship for their co-religionists, a cause in which the French showed only a mild and passing interest. The protestant ultras were in an agony of apprehension lest the queen should turn her ears from her true friends to those who echoed and flattered her own more cautious thoughts and, it may be, sentimental yearnings: Oxford, above all. In London in the late summer of 1579 there were noisy expressions of alarm from the pulpits and from the press, in the notable diatribe of Cartwright's brother-in-law, John Stubbs, *The discoverie of a gaping gulf wherinto England is like to be swallowed*, and other protests only a little less explicit. There is no mistaking the popular aversion, at least in London, from a foreign marriage to a papist of doubtful qualities, and yet this agitation was by no means spontaneous. *Leycesters Commonwealth* would later allege that the meetings of puritans at preachings and communions in great houses were secret gatherings of Leicester's faction; and it was at this time that extraordinary assemblies at Peter Wentworth's house at Lillingstone-Lovell, not far from Northampton, were brought to the Council's attention.[20] At this explosive moment, Leicester and his friends suffered a serious setback when the French disclosed to the queen the fact of the earl's secret marriage to Lettice Knollys, the widowed countess of Essex. Both Leicester and Walsingham were for a time banished from Court, and there was the chance of a real palace revolution, the infusion of new and hostile blood into the Council.

The events of this time seem to have strengthened the queen's resolve to be mistress of her own policy, free of all factions, and to avoid until all else had failed the extravagance of personal involvement in the Netherlands. Between this and her determination to maintain strict discipline on both the papist and puritan flanks, now to be more clearly manifested than ever before, there was a logical connection.

And so the brake was applied. Things might have been less favourable, if 'Monsieur' had succeeded in his suit, and with terms for the English catholics. But to have allowed what the French were not likely to have insisted upon would have been to offend in the opposite direction against the deliberate balance of Elizabeth's statecraft, and in spite of puritan fears it was never even a remote danger. 1581 was to see a swift response to papal intervention in Ireland and the arrival of the first Jesuit missionaries from Rome. The Parliament of that year enacted new penal laws, not as sharp as the Commons would have liked to have seen, but sharp enough. The Elizabethan state was now more clearly than ever at war with the Catholic Church. In November, the execution of Edmund Campion coincided with the presence of Anjou in England, and the last courtly motions of his disappointed suit. Nevertheless, for the puritans the check to their hopes was abrupt and sustained, and the endurance of Grindal's disgrace underlined their predicament. In January 1578, when it had been already clear that the queen was unlikely to be drawn in the desired direction, Sir Francis Knollys pointed to the archbishop's fate as a sure indication of the way that things were likely to go: 'But if the bishop of Canterbury shall be deprived, then up starts the pride and practice of the papists, and down declineth the comfort and strength of her Majesty's safety; and then King Richard the Second's men will flock into Court apace, and will show themselves in their colours ... '[21] Faced with a not dissimilar challenge in France in 1572, Catherine de Medicis had taken the desperate steps which culminated in the massacre of St Bartholomew. With her surer grip, Elizabeth merely kept an archbishop in limbo. It was left to Edmund Spenser, Leicester's servant and the poet of his party, to pronounce Grindal's epitaph in his *Shepheardes calender*, which is itself a veiled pastoral allegory of these events:

Ah, good Algrind! his hap was ill,
But shall be better in time.[22]

If the disaster of Grindal was one token of reaction, the changes that
now took place in the composition of the episcopal bench were another.
In the later 'seventies, the substance of power in the Church passed from
the progressive bishops of the *Zurich Letters* (Leicester's bishops?) and
into the hands of a new generation who were glad to adopt as their own
the queen's view that the status quo must be strictly and equally maintained against both papists and puritans. Parkhurst died in 1575, Pilkington
in 1576, Bentham in 1579, Horne in 1580, Cox in 1581. Scory might as
well have been dead, although he was to survive until 1585. Others who
remained trimmed their sails to the new wind: Sandys, now archbishop
of York, and without national influence, Cooper of Lincoln, translated to
Winchester in 1584, and Scambler who went from Peterborough to
Norwich in 1585. With few exceptions, the new occupants of their sees
were wholly unsympathetic to the puritan cause: Edmund Freke, translated from Rochester to Norwich in 1575; John Aylmer, bishop of London
from 1576; John Piers, bishop of Rochester in 1576 and of Salisbury in
1577; John Young who succeeded Piers at Rochester and whom Aylmer
described as 'fit to bridle innovators'; and, above all, John Whitgift,
bishop of Worcester from 1577. These appointments led to a rift between
the episcopate and the protestant nobility and gentry which was scarcely
more marked in the years of Archbishop Laud's ascendancy, and they
suggest a breakdown in the patronage of the puritan magnates who had
raised up many of the earlier Elizabethan bishops. The indications are that
the queen was now taking a more direct interest in bishop-making,
assisted by the rising man of these years, Sir Christopher Hatton, to whom
Aylmer owed his bishopric and who was to prove a friend in need to
Whitgift. The promotion of John Woolton to be bishop of Exeter in
1578, at the instance of the Russells, was merely the exception proving
the new rule.[23]

There is some evidence that the new bishops took office with explicit
instructions to tread the *via media*, and, as Aylmer was told through
Hatton, 'to cut off (even as her Majesty termed it) and to correct offenders
on both sides which swerve from the right path of obedience ... ' Able
administrator though he was, Aylmer lacked Whitgift's tough endurance
in the face of adversity, and in the early years, before help came from that
quarter, he tended to flag under the intolerable pressures to which a
bishop of London was subject. Within a year or two he was meekly

accepting a puritan ringleader, William Chark, for a preaching post at Lincoln's Inn, and positively recommending Walter Travers for his lectureship at the Temple.

But Aylmer had begun with bold and imaginative strokes which suggest a penetrating knowledge of puritan ways. He replaced the moderate John Hammond as vicar-general with Edward Stanhope, a firm disciplinarian with a distinguished career ahead of him. Early in his episcopate he took the extraordinary and unprecedented step of placing the puritan strongholds of Holy Trinity Minories and St Anne's Blackfriars under an interdict, thus recognizing that the militancy of these two parishes originated among the godly parishioners as much as from their pastors and preachers. And in January 1580 he struck at the unbeneficed preachers who never celebrated the sacraments nor read a Prayer Book service, the 'doctors', like John Field himself, who were the backbone of London's radical puritanism. All ministers, including salaried preachers and lecturers, were ordered to administer the sacraments in accordance with the Book of Common Prayer at least four times a year. As Field complained to Gilby, this was to invert 'a point of puritanism', the interdependence of the word and sacraments. 'Whereby he forestalleth many good men, either to throw them out, or else to gravel their consciences, that they may stick in the same filth that he doth of superstitious ceremonies.' Aylmer had a remedy for Field, who was preaching 'God knows what' in great houses. He and others like him should be deported from London to the 'barbarous countries' of the north Midlands to wear out their zeal on the papists. But Field's patron was now the earl of Leicester, and it was beyond Aylmer's capacity to dislodge him. In 1579 Leicester, Knollys and Lord Norris got him a preaching licence from Oxford University with which he embarked on a new career as parish lecturer at St Mary's Aldermary. Before Whitgift arrived at Lambeth to sustain him, these frustrations had reduced Aylmer to impotence and to vain hopes of a remove to some quieter diocese.[24]

Edmund Freke came to Norwich in 1575 with a similar mandate, and encountered the contempt of protestant East Anglia for a sometime moderate puritan who had turned his coat.[25] He faced a cathedral city with a large protestant immigrant community, saturated with Calvinist preaching and capable a few years later of producing one hundred and seventy-five substantial citizens willing to petition the queen for the establishment of presbyterianism; and two counties where there was perhaps less loyalty to the Anglican formularies than in any other part of England. It was a prospect to daunt a stronger man than Freke, who was ruled by a Mrs Proudie of a wife; 'this is *vox populi*, a principle well-known throughout all Norfolk, spread by his household, that whatsoever Mrs Freke will have done, the bishop must and will accomplish.' The essence of the problem was social – the bishop against the gentry – and Freke found the only course open to him in making common cause with conservative and crypto-catholic elements who for one reason or another opposed the ascendancy of puritan teachers and justices. With Aylmer pursuing a similar course in Essex, East Anglia was for several years flung into religious and factional turmoil. Some were saying in Norfolk that 'the state could not long stand thus, it would either to papistry or puritanism.'[26]

In Freke's primary visitation of 1576, there was a wholesale suspension of Norwich preachers, including the 'presidents', John More and Thomas Roberts. According to a puritan source, the effect of this was to silence nineteen or twenty exercises of preaching and catechizing in the city. The affair of the Norwich preachers dragged on for the next four years, and illustrates how remote were the policies of the greater part of the Council from those of the queen and the new bishops. After some unsuccessful petitioning by the ministers themselves, their cause was pressed in London by the most ardent puritan gentlemen of Norfolk, William Heydon and Nathaniel Bacon (the lord keeper's son by his first marriage). More and Roberts and perhaps other preachers made their personal appearance before the Council. The result of these efforts was that in August 1578, during the royal progress in East Anglia, the Council forced the bishop to accept a promise of limited conformity drawn up by More, to which seven of the other ministers put their names, and which he had already rejected; 'whereat', it was reported, 'I hear the bishop stormeth.' Sir Thomas Heneage, no friend of the puritans, wrote from Suffolk of 'the foolish bishop' who had picked a feud with 'divers most zealous and loyal gentlemen of Suffolk and Norfolk'. Two years later the preachers were again in danger, and on representations from the mayor and aldermen of Norwich, the Council sharply reminded the bishop of their earlier agreement, 'not doubting that he will use them as charitably as becometh a man of his profession.' The Council attached some importance to the Norwich compromise, hoping that it might form the basis for peace between the preachers and the authorities in other places.[27]

But while More and Roberts strove to remain in their pulpits by treading the path of the 'somewhat conformable' – they had promised to respect the bishop's authority and to pray for him publicly – others more extreme shook the dust of Norwich off their feet. Richard Gawton, a Norwich preacher with two small livings in the country, left for London and Field's clandestine conference after openly repudiating the bishop's authority before his consistory court. Three puritan canons and petty canons of the cathedral – Edmund Chapman, Richard Crick and Richard Dow – all left the county and later joined to form the nucleus of the important puritan conference which met in and around Dedham on the Suffolk–Essex border from 1582. A fourth preacher, Vincent Goodwin, left for Yarmouth.[28]

A direct result of this devastation of the pulpits was the outbreak of the most extensive and serious movement of separatism yet experienced in the Elizabethan Church, led by two hitherto obscure and even more extreme brethren, Robert Harrison, a schoolmaster at Aylsham, and Robert Browne, a Corpus man and a relation of Burghley, who had taken to preaching without a bishop's licence and whose experiences in and around Cambridge had gradually convinced him of the necessity of 'reformation without tarrying for any'. Browne has described in that fascinating account of the development of his radical thought, *A true and short declaration*, how 'he saw the parishes in such spiritual bondage, that whosoever would take charge of them must also come into that bondage with them. Therefore he finding the parishes too much addicted and pliable to that lamentable state, he judged that the kingdom of God was not to be begun by whole parishes but rather of the worthiest, were they never so few.' But much of the original motive force in Brownism, as in the London separation of ten years before, came from the frustration of 'simple gospellers', deprived of their accustomed preachers. 'Also, you are placed and displaced by the bishops; therefore, when we have most need of you, you are gone.'[29]

Meanwhile, as the Brownist schism assumed serious proportions in both Norfolk and Suffolk and carried some of its favourers into a voluntary exile in the Netherlands, Freke and his officers were engaged in an increasingly serious struggle with the dominant puritan faction in West Suffolk. The enemies of the preachers in Bury St Edmunds and the neighbouring villages were encouraged to bring charges of nonconformity and irregularity against them, whereupon they were dealt with by the bishop's officers or by the judges of assize, and either sent packing or clapped in Bury jail, which for a year or two nearly always housed three or four preachers of the gospel. The puritan justices – Sir Robert Jermyn and Sir John Higham in the van – sprang to the preachers' defence, retaliated in their own petty sessions against the non-preaching clergy, and in other ways trespassed on the preserve of the church courts. At last the bishop preferred formal complaints against the gentlemen to the queen, and the justices were called to answer. Once again, the consistent support which the Council afforded the puritan side is impressive. The assize judges, on the other hand, and especially the hot-tempered Sir Edmund Anderson, invariably took the bishop's part and could be trusted to deal unmercifully with any preacher brought before them. Eventually, through their means, Jermyn and Higham were suspended from the Commission of the Peace and Jermyn was subjected to the prize indignity of serving on a common jury, at a time when both gentlemen were deputy lieutenants of the shire, at the top of the county hierarchy! Leicester later secured their rehabilitation.[30]

With Grindal incapacitated, the standards which Aylmer and Freke were trying to enforce in their dioceses were already, in effect, the metropolitan policy of the Church of England. This was because Aylmer and Whitgift took Grindal's place in all but the routine administration of the southern province. Aylmer was president of the High Commission, which in these years was perfecting its procedure and exercising those powers, which implicitly it had always possessed, of an ecclesiastical court of first instance, able to intervene anywhere without respect to local immunities and political pressures. Henceforward puritan offenders would as often as not be dealt with, not in the bishop's consistory where their friends could help them, but by being 'horsed up to London' in what seemed an arbitrary and popish manner. This ran counter to the pastoral principles of the Reformation and against the tendency of those proposed reforms of diocesan government which were so much in the air at this very time.[31]

In 1580 Aylmer used his influence as president of the High Commission to procure a letter from the Privy Council, extending to the whole province his order that all preachers should regularly administer the sacraments. According to Robert Beale, clerk of the Council but not an impeccable witness because of a deep personal animus against Aylmer, the bishop used underhand methods to secure signatures to this letter, 'without any resolution or debating of the matter at the table', and afterwards sent it out under the seal of the High Commission, 'very much resembling that of the Council'. Aylmer presided in Grindal's place in the Convocation of 1581 and undertook other duties which normally belonged to the archbishop, such as appointing preachers for the Lenten sermons at Court.[32]

But at the Parliament of 1581 Whitgift was the commanding figure, riding up to Westminster with 'an orderly troop of tawny coats'. His natural assumption of the vacant leadership, which is apparent despite the formal deference made to Archbishop Sandys of York, suggests that he already knew himself to be heir presumptive to Augustine's chair. In 1576 the queen had promised an unusually restrained House of Commons that their petition for more effective ecclesiastical discipline would be referred to the bishops for action. The canons of 1576 had not satisfied the Commons nor the more radical privy councillors who sat in the House, and the matter was now reopened by means of an orderly negotiation with the bishops by four councillors acting for the Commons, Walsingham, Wilson, Hatton and Mildmay. But although some bishops were willing to join in a humble suit to the queen, Whitgift could not be persuaded to relax his relentless opposition to anything smelling even faintly of 'T.C. his platform'. Towards the end of the session the Commons distilled their requests in a series of articles which Mildmay and Walsingham brought to the queen's notice, the programme which we have discussed in an earlier chapter. Elizabeth referred the document to five bishops, headed by Sandys, but including Whitgift, and it is Whitgift's censorious comments, for the most part, which survive on the bishops' copy. If Beale is to be believed, Whitgift was quite unable on these occasions to restrain his heated, overbearing manner. He later reminded Hatton:

> No man can better remember what requests have been from time to time made by the Commons, which represent many millions of her Majesty's subjects. Her Majesty once promised her poor Commons that such abuses should be reformed, and commanded the bishops to see it done. But your lordships can I think remember what angry words the then bishop of Worcester used to your lordship and Sir Walter Mildmay. I have not forgotten what that honourable Councillor then reported.[33]

Even making allowance for Beale's prejudice, it seems certain that Whitgift made a deeply unfavourable impression on this Parliament. The effect of Mildmay's report to the Commons was that 'the whole House ... did impute the default to the bishops.' And Thomas Norton, who was normally a moderate critic of the Church's failings and certainly no presbyterian (he was a son-in-law of Cranmer), spoke freely and bitterly on the general theme of bishops at a supper-party at the end of the session. He was inclined to remember that some had been heretics, like Guest and Cheyney, both Lutherans and free-will men, or papists like Downham of Chester, and that all in general were prone to ordain unlearned and unfit ministers and to prove remiss in restraint of papists and the 'anabaptist' fanatics of the Family of Love.[34]

Both Mildmay and Norton, for tactical reasons which are obvious enough, were anxious to represent the bishops as the main obstacle to progress and to exonerate the queen's 'godly purpose'. In truth, of course, it was precisely because he shared his mistress's abhorrence for enthusiasm and innovation that Whitgift and his party were now to gain control of the Church. The modern Anglican, whose experience takes in the Oxford Movement and all its consequences, is inclined to praise Whitgift and Bancroft for their recovered sense of the Church's nature and dignity, and for the resistance they offered to secular interference in general and to the spoliation of its possessions in particular. Yet it was Grindal who had to plead with the queen for spiritual matters to be determined *in ecclesia, seu synodo*, not *in palatio*. If the independence and integrity of the Church experienced an apparent revival under his successor, this was because Whitgift's policies were invariably those of the palace. We are told that his dying words were '*Pro ecclesia Dei*'. But this archbishop was fortunate in that, unlike the High Church bishops of a century later, he never had to choose between his interpretation of spiritual truth and the Church's interests and obedience to the Crown. In this respect Whitgift was unlike Grindal too.

5 Exercises, Conferences and Fasts

'Conferences, disputacions, reasonings, prayers, singing of psalmes, preachings,
readings, prophes[y]ings, fastings and feastings and such like holy exercises.'

('Wiggenton's Visitation' (c. 1584), *Trans. Congreg. Hist.
Socy*, iii. 31)

THE MODERATE, PROGRESSIVE TENDENCIES of Grindal's archiepiscopate
withered under fire from both the opposed flanks of the Elizabethan
Church. The first check came from the queen and her party, but the blow
might never have fallen but for the provocations of the puritan left wing.
As Leicester warned his radical friends, their attempt 'to make better
perforce that which is by permission good enough already' threatened to
bring on the very reaction which they professed to fear.[1] Reaction in its
turn made extremists more extreme and revived the extravagant language
and action of the early 'seventies.

A significant sign of a return to 'civil wars of the Church of God' was
the reprinting of the *Admonition to the Parliament* in 1578, followed two
years later by the publication of Beza's anathema against diocesan episcopacy, *The judgement of a most reverend and learned man from beyond the
seas, concerning a threefold order of bishops*. In 1581 there were two new
editions of Gilby's bitter and journalistic *Pleasaunt dialogue betweene a
souldior of Barwicke and an English chaplaine*. And as if to convince the
queen that the spirit of Calvinism was irrepressible, the puritan press at
this point broadened its attack and began to assert the distinctive social
morality with which puritanism has been associated ever since. Besides
the celebrated 'anatomies' of the Elizabethan masters of this genre,
Gosson and Stubbs,[2] Thomas Wilcox jumped on the band wagon with
A glasse for gamesters (1581) and John Field took advantage of a fatal
accident on a Sabbath afternoon in the bearpit at Paris Garden to write

A godly exhortation to the people of London on the evils of Southwark (1583).

The downfall of the prophesyings had been greeted with cries of dismay from all the godly. 'The want of those godly exercises which were the universities of the poor ministries [*sic*] is greatly to be lamented,' wrote a Leicestershire minister from Cambridge to Gilby. 'With heavy hearts we will yield to your commandments, giving over this godly exercise until we by prayer and petition may again obtain it,' wrote Gilby and the other Ashby ministers to their bishop.[3] Whether the Ashby brethren really abandoned their meetings may be doubted. Elsewhere in the diocese of Lincoln, and in some other districts, there seems to have been no necessity to do so. Gatherings of preachers under the innocuous name of 'exercises' continued in many market towns, often with the connivance of the bishop, although a single preacher for each occasion now took the place of the panel of speakers who would have participated in a prophesying. Many sympathetic observers persuaded themselves that private conferences of the clergy, which normally followed an exercise, were not covered by the queen's ban. Thomas Norton, in certain 'Devices' of 1581, urged that such conferences should be set up in every deanery, 'in presence of ministers only, and not in assemblies of the people, for avoiding both of vainglory which may breed pertinacity in error, and so proceed to heresy, or of shame and contempt to their brethren.' Cartwright would later tell Whitgift that such conferences had been permitted in the dioceses of Coventry and Lichfield and Chichester, and the queen was assured that they were allowed by many bishops, 'and to our knowledge never disallowed or forbidden by any.'[4]

The pattern of the exercise was a sermon once, twice, or four times a month, preached in rotation by an association of 'the preachers of the country' and attended by the whole company as well as by the 'well-affected' of the town and the surrounding villages. The public sermon was followed by conference and a dinner. Cartwright reported that in the diocese of Lincoln, in particular, market-town sermons were the order of the day, and served as occasions for the ministers to meet and confer. In 1614 there were 'lectures' such as Cartwright had described in eleven centres of the diocese. Although from time to time 'put down' and 'sued for' or 'raised up' again, all the indications are that the exercise had been an established tradition in these towns for decades. When the bishop made 'a stay' of the Leicester exercise in 1611, the mayor and seventeen other leading townspeople testified of 'the great good that our whole town (and many also of the country) have received by their learned and godly sermons for the space of forty years and more.' Six years later the 'ordinary monthly lecture' was still in full swing.[5]

The picture is the same in East Anglia. Between 1606 and 1614, Bishop Jegon authorized market-day exercises in ten towns in Norfolk and Suffolk, each with a panel of up to thirteen speakers. In most cases this was a response to the joint initiative of the local ministers, 'knights and worthy gentlemen', supported by the well-affected townspeople, who would often offer some regular contribution towards the preacher's expenses. In some of these places we learn that there had been an earlier history of exercises, suppressed after 'busy-bodies' had sown 'the seeds of schism', but both the bishop and the learned preaching clergy hoped to avoid such 'inconveniences' in the future. At Bury St Edmunds, the exercise seems to have continued with little or no interruption throughout the later years of Elizabeth and into Bishop Jegon's time. In 1584 Bishop Freke sent instructions to his commissary to be communicated to 'such moderators of the exercise within every deanery by us lately appointed.' Six years later a minister who had fallen out with the puritan faction complained to his archdeacon of 'that shameful (as themselves call it) secluding me from the Bury exercise', and from the same year there is a reference to the agreement of certain ministers 'for the well-managing of their Monday exercise at Bury'. There are further references from the early years of James I in the correspondence of William Bedell, the future bishop of Kilmore and at this time a preacher in Bury, with Samuel Ward, master of Sidney Sussex College, Cambridge.[6]

In the northern province, where the queen's ban on prophesyings did not extend, and where the strength of popish recusancy put all other problems of church discipline beyond consideration, the exercises received the most open support of both secular and ecclesiastical authorities. Archbishop Sandys and Bishop Chaderton of Chester had arranged occasional conferences with their clergy, but three synods a year at Preston were inadequate for a sprawling, thinly-settled county, and they failed to satisfy the puritan clergy. In 1583 these 'preachers of the diocese of Chester', headed by the redoubtable Christopher Goodman, now arch-deacon of Richmond, agreed amongst themselves upon a programme of reforms which included the proposal to establish a monthly exercise in 'the middle town of every several deanery'. These were to resemble the prophesyings which were now prohibited in the south except that a single sermon was to replace prophesying before the people. This was to last from nine until ten, to be followed by private conference of the ministers until one o'clock. There were to be heavy fines for absence, and, as with the prophesyings, the intention of these proposals was to bring the unlearned and non-preaching clergy under the tutelage and discipline of the graduate ministers. The whole scheme was forwarded to the Privy Council, which responded by advising the bishop to confer with the best learned of his clergy and to provide for the exercises to be 'hereafter more frequently used, and in more places of the diocese.'

The result was a far more comprehensive order for exercise than anything yet seen in the south, drawn up by the bishop and eight preachers named by the Council. The exercises were to be held monthly, except in November, December and January, and in every deanery of the great diocese of Chester, which extended from Cheshire through the length of Lancashire to the fells of Furness and the wild region of Richmondshire on the Yorkshire side of the Pennines. Every exercise was supplied with four moderators (Goodman was named for Chester). Proceedings were to begin at six o'clock in summer, an hour later in winter, and all parsons, vicars, curates and schoolmasters were required to attend. The day was to begin with a roll-call and a sermon, preached by one of the moderators, in the presence of the ministers only. Exercise was to follow, 'the learned sort' speaking, 'the meaner sort' taking notes and undergoing examination. Last of all, a sermon was to be preached to the people, from eleven until midday. The orders went out on January 27th, 1585, and, as in other dioceses, the exercise still maintained itself in some places in the early years of James I. At this time the tradition began on the other side of the Pennines, in the great scattered parishes of the West Riding. In the mid-seventeenth century Oliver Heywood remembered the 'famous' monthly exercise at Halifax, and another Yorkshireman, recalling his youth in Wakefield before 1640, wrote: 'I went to many funeral sermons, lectures and monthly exercises.' Thanks to the earl of Huntingdon, as lord president of the Council in the North, weekly exercises were known in the North Riding, at Northallerton, at least as early as the 1590s, although the attendance was 'slender'. In Nottinghamshire the exercises may well have enjoyed a continuous existence from Grindal's days at York in the early 'seventies until the appearance and growth of Laudian influences in the diocese in the late 1620s.[7]

But in the south, after 1577, the propriety and even the legality of such proceedings were always open to doubt. In 1579 that quarrelsome cross-bench M.P., Arthur Hall of Grantham, was involved in a quarrel with Bishop Cooper, and declared that 'if Mr Bishop tromp at me in this wise ... I will tromp at him, and make his exercises known to the queen.' Some years later, when Bishop Chaderton, translated to Lincoln, licensed

an extraordinary exercise at Louth at the request of the lord lieutenant,
deputy lieutenants, and other justices of the shire, 'to spend the whole day
in the hearing of the word', Judge Edmund Anderson took violent
exception, 'urged thereupon the statute of conventicles' and threatened
prosecution and complaint to the queen if any, 'though never so great',
should resist him.[8]

The effect of this altered situation was not to put a stop to the meetings
of preaching ministers; these had never depended upon official inspiration,
and it was probably beyond the capacity of any ecclesiastical authority
to prevent them taking place. In some places the life of the puritan
preachers revolved around regular conferences with their brethren as
never before. The separatist Robert Harrison wrote contemptuously
enough of the habits of the unseparated ministers of Norfolk: 'There are
a company of preachers, as they call them, about you, and you use to go
two or three days a week, on foot or on horseback, as the weather makest
most for your ease, half a dozen miles perhaps, as it falleth out more or
less, and there you spend an hour in a pulpit, to get a little praise, to
commend or discommend one another, and all the day after feast and talk
of prophane things.' In 1584 a Kentish minister asked: 'Must the meeting
of ministers at a sermon, if they after dine together, giving thanks for
their meat, or haply asking a question for increase of knowledge, be
judged a conventicle?' And in Essex in the same year an innkeeper was
examined in the consistory court about certain preachers who met at his
inn on a market day, 'who they were and what they did?'[9]

But where the bishops were hostile, as they were in East Anglia and
Essex after 1576, these meetings were likely to be secretive, and correspondingly more divisive and factious. Instead of meeting openly in parish
churches and inns, the preachers tended to gather in their own homes. In
East Sussex the end of the prophesyings seems to have produced within a
few years a potentially schismatic situation. The prophesying at Lewes
had been broadly representative of the clergy of the county, and the
bishop's commissary had sat among them as moderator. But within a
few years of its suppression we find the puritan faction in command of the
exercise which had taken its place, and taking steps to eject six ministers
of the contrary party. One of the excluded preachers retaliated with
complaints that two laymen, one of them a survivor of the Geneva
congregation, were regularly participating in the exercise. At a sermon in
Lewes attended by at least a dozen preachers, he reproached 'the godly
ministers of that diocese' as 'the new brotherhood, the brotherhood of
separation, the separated brethren, private spirits, this new faction'. They

were further charged with repudiating the bishop's authority and with 'always craving for reformation.'[10]

Once such a faction had rid themselves of the company of the conforming clergy and of the unlearned, even the fiction of episcopal oversight was likely to be forgotten and the presbyterian principle of parity would determine procedure. So far as we know, the first occasion on which a society of puritan preachers gave themselves an explicitly presbyterian constitution was at Norwich in 1575. When Bishop Parkhurst died in February of that year, the Norwich preachers at once resumed their prophesying (put down a year earlier under Parker's orders), and drew up new orders of their own devising.[11] Parker died three months after Parkhurst, and for much of the remainder of the year there was neither a bishop of Norwich nor an archbishop of Canterbury. This did not mean that all ordinary ecclesiastical jurisdiction had come to an end, but the Norwich preachers acted as if this was the case. It was now 'judged meet by the brethren' that their exercise should be held every Monday in the cathedral; the table of speakers was to consist of 'such as shall be judged by the brethren meet to speak'; and the speakers were to submit to the orders which were and should be set down hereafter, 'by the consent of the brethren only, and not by one man's authority'. The provisions for the conduct of the exercise tell the same story: in place of the two or three moderators entrusted by the bishop with permanent charge of proceedings, the new order respected the parity of all the brethren, who were all qualified preachers; there was no reference to the unlearned, and no provision for their improvement by means of the exercise. Evidently the view had prevailed that they were no ministers at all. The private conference of ministers following the public prophesying was to sit under a moderator, but only a 'moderator or prolocutor for that present'. The office was to circulate, falling always on the first speaker from the previous week's exercise. Censures were to be delivered 'in the name of the rest of the brethren'. In the public proceedings the function of the moderator was artfully concealed. Theoretically it was open to any brother 'whom God should move' to speak to the text. In practice, the first speaker from the previous week or his deputy, sitting next to the principal preacher, conducted proceedings 'by some comely gesture, as by putting on their hat, and so referring it to him that sitteth next, from one to another, and that to be done by the same brother so oft as any new speaker shall rise up till it have passed through all in order as they sit, if there be so much time.' It was the office of the first speaker rather than of the moderator to make the final prayer.

This was a brief episode. In November Bishop Freke was confirmed bishop of Norwich, and we have already seen something of the devastation which struck the puritan pulpits of the city in his primary visitation. Yet we have not heard the last of the Norwich order of 1575. Seven years later three of its authors appeared in the clothing villages along the Suffolk–Essex border, and there they drew up a constitution for a conference which was the direct successor to that earlier experiment in Norwich. But before we reach the company of the Dedham conference, something must be said about a particular form of organized puritan activity which came into prominence in the intervening years: the practice of holding solemn 'fasts' as a kind of extraordinary elaboration of the regular round of lectures, exercises and conferences.

One of the commonest complaints of catholic controversialists was that protestants did not fast. The protestants retorted that on the contrary they alone fasted in the spirit of the New Testament by joining fasting to prayer and the preaching of the word in public assemblies, and by proclaiming a fast only for a particular purpose.[12] A handbook on the subject, The holie exercise of a true fast, possibly of Cartwright's authorship,[13] divided fasting into 'outward actions' of abstinence, which were shared with the papists; and 'inward virtues, helped forward by the bodily exercise', and these it was the virtue of the Reformation to have restored. The exercise consisted of a 'humbling and casting down' and 'a profession of our faith, that we shall be lifted up as high, through the grace of the Lord our God in Jesus Christ, as the conscience of our sins doth cast us down.' In other words, the fast was an occasion for instruction in the protestant doctrine of repentance, and this was to be 'fetched from the public preaching of the word.' It was to last for at least a whole day. 'And if the wrath of the Lord be hotter, then two days or else three.' It could be private, 'of a particular man, or household'. But 'upon some more general calamity of the Church' a public fast was to be appointed by 'them which (under Christ) have the government of the places where the fast is holden.'

Fasting in this sense was the practice in all the reformed churches, especially as the hardships of persecution and religious war multiplied in the 'seventies and 'eighties. England was no exception, and from the early years of Elizabeth occasional fasts were called for by episcopal injunction and even by royal command, on such occasions as unseasonable weather and the plague brought back from Le Havre by the English expeditionary force in 1563. Although these were comparatively decorous affairs, with the emphasis on prayer and private study and a sermon only 'if it can be', the form of prayer which Bishop Grindal drafted for use in 1563 borrowed extensively from the Geneva liturgy. Moreover, unless there was risk of infection, the publicly authorized fast was expected to bring the people together from more than one parish into some central meeting-place. As with the prophesyings, the pressure to hold such extraordinary assemblies seems to have come mainly from the puritans. Commenting on the impact of the massacre of St Bartholomew's night, Sandys as bishop of London reported that 'sundry have required a public fast and prayer to be had, for the confounding of these and other cruel enemies of God's gospel.' But in this matter of fasting the puritans were not over-disposed to 'tarry for the magistrate'. The Suffolk minister John Knewstub later taught that 'if it be holden out from the public assemblies, then the Lord casteth this charge of sanctifying a fast upon private and common houses. And if the private houses be sparred against it, through their careless masters, yet let every faithful person who trembleth and quaketh when the Lord roareth take him to his chamber for the humbling and submitting of himself before God.' A modern totalitarian regime would be hard put to suppress a movement which had these springs, let alone a Tudor government, many of whose local agents were themselves caught up in it.[14]

In the early 'seventies fasting was probably an occasional function of the association for prophesying, the ministers of Ashby-de-la-Zouch speaking of 'public praying, fasting and prophecy'. After 1577 the proclamation of a public fast offered a means of avoiding the queen's prohibition, for, like the prophesyings, these occasions brought the godly together from many parishes, and filled the morning and even the whole day with a succession of sermons, sometimes concluding with a celebration of the communion and a common meal. The town clerk of Barnstaple was reminded of the pilgrimages of pre-Reformation days by the 'trental of sermons' which drew numbers of men and women, on foot and on horseback, to nearby Pilton. Like pilgrims, those who took part in this 'holy fast' brought offerings. Collections of money always seem to have been made on these occasions, and the proceeds devoted either to the poor or for some special cause, such as the relief of the protestant strangers in London and elsewhere. In Norfolk, the preacher Samuel Greenaway was said to have 'himself ... appointed solemn fasts for reformation to be had, etc., and gathered money of such as came to the sermons of other towns, which he bestowed as pleased himself.'

For the fullest extant account of what else transpired at a puritan fast, we are dependent upon a curious Jesuit who witnessed the exercises which were held in full view of the distinguished catholic prisoners kept in Wisbech Castle. 'They used to come in crowds,' reported Father Weston:

> flocking from all quarters to be present at their exercises. These they used to begin with three or four sermons, preached one after the other. Then they went to communion, not receiving it either on their knees or standing, but moving by, so that it might be called a Passover in very truth. They had likewise a kind of tribunal of their own, and elders who had power to investigate and punish at will the misdemeanours of their brethren ... When the congregation was dismissed, after the long fast that had been imposed upon them all, and after the whole day had been consumed in these exercises, they ended the farce with a plentiful supper.[15]

By the early 'eighties, the fasting movement, if we may call it that, was near its peak. Percival Wiburn speaks in 1581 of fasts 'in divers places of this realm, and namely in the diocese of Lincoln, to give example.' In the previous year, an unprecedented spate of troubles called for this remedy, among them the growing dangers from both papists and sectaries, storms, bad harvests, and, to crown all, a mild earthquake. Wiburn wrote of 'the comets and strange sights that were seen in the heavens, the earthquakes here beneath among us', and eighteen years later a preacher could still attempt to arouse his drowsy hearers with reminders of this 'most lively resemblance of the resurrection'. The earthquake brought an order from the Council enjoining prayer and fasting on Wednesdays and Fridays, and in the summer of 1580 this afforded the puritans some protection. Yet if the fast held at Stamford in September was anything to go by, their response owed little to these modest recommendations.[16]

What happened at Stamford is known, both because this was Burghley's manorial town, so that correspondence connected with it survives in his papers, and because the Jesuit Robert Parsons made use of the incident to denigrate the puritans in the preface to that notable manifesto, *A brief discours contayning certayne reasons why catholiques refuse to goe to church*,[17] an attack which brought informed replies from both Field and Wiburn.[18] But there is no reason to suppose that the circumstances were otherwise unusual. In June 1580 the magistrates of Stamford, prompted by the puritan rector of Loughborough, Robert Johnson, decided on a public fast to be conducted by 'the godly learned preachers about them'. They would have proceeded without more ado and without higher authorization if 'some enemy, giving false information' had not reported to Burghley that Johnson, whose parish lay 'in the diocese of Peterborough, planned to bring 'six or seven other preachers, I know not whom' to Stamford, in Lincoln diocese, 'and there to erect a new innovation by decreeing to the people an universal fast, and to continue there I know not how long.' Burghley wrote to the aldermen and comburgesses applauding their zeal, but condemning the fast as a rank innovation if it went forward without the bishop's approval and with a preacher licensed in another diocese. The Stamford magistrates hastened to assure him of the godliness of their intentions and recruited a neighbouring nobleman, Lord Zouche, to remind the Lord Treasurer that 'he that denieth me amongst men, I will deny him before my Father which is in heaven.' Burghley submitted, applauding 'so holy an exercise', and merely insisting on the bishop's sanction. When Bishop Cooper was approached he replied cautiously – it is clear that other bishops had burned their fingers in similar cases – approving the project, but insisting that only the town preacher and one other Lincolnshire minister should be employed, 'without the confluence of other strangers that appertain not unto your town.'

No account was taken of his letter. As John Field reports, 'Mr Alderman and his brethren, very wisely considering that the exercise was now already appointed and warranted, ... kept their determination according to the order which was prescribed.' Robert Johnson preached in spite of the bishop's inhibition and the town preacher, John Hanson, took no part. Both clergy and laity came from near and far, among them 'those of calling, honourable and worshipful, magistrates and other in the town and abroad, beside divers godly and learned ministers and preachers'. Lord Zouche travelled from his seat at Harringworth, twelve miles away, and later signed a testimonial for the good conduct of the fast and the soundness of the doctrine preached. If Parsons's informant is to be believed (and the source is admittedly tainted) the preachers allowed themselves some inflammatory obiter dicta: 'What if neither the queen, Council, nor bishop have been present at the fast, nor allowed thereof? Yet we ought to undertake it. Percase it is not in the queen's chapel. What then?'[19]

The Stamford episode is a further reminder that we are not investigating the private enthusiasms of a small faction of clergymen, but rather a religious revolution which was continuing to make impressive inroads on the upper ranks of lay society. When Paul Wentworth proposed a public fast in the House of Commons as a preparation for the parliamentary business of 1581, no fewer than one hundred and fifteen members voted for the motion, as against only a hundred who voted that the fast should be merely private, 'everybody to himself'. The event was clearly remembered almost thirty years later by the then Speaker of the House of Commons, who recalled that Walter Travers, preaching at the Temple, had warned his auditory 'to forbear the next lecture day, it was appointed for the House of Commons for fasting and prayer.' This is some indication of the familiarity of the puritan fast for country gentlemen and burgesses, and of the favourable political conditions which must have obtained in many localities.[20]

The importance of the puritan fast in the story of the organized puritan movement was that it normally brought the godly together for some very good and explicit purpose. As Eusebius Paget defined it, a fast was an action 'by which the faithful prepare themselves to prayer when they take in hand some earnest matter', and Cartwright insisted that it was not to be proclaimed without good reason. On the other hand puritans seem to have faced no new situation without this preparation. The action of eight London preachers who 'having notice given that somewhat was to be done for God's glory, at one time joined in a fast' was typical. A fast might be held for a 'stirring up ... to greater godliness', or for relief from a variety of natural or human calamities, but often enough the motive was connected with the agitation for further reformation. According to Bancroft, who knew the ways of the puritans better than any, it was 'most notorious' that the puritans appointed public fasts especially 'when their fellows have been most busy to trouble the present estate of the Church.' Besides, they provided an occasion to talk about 'other matters' when the preaching and the prayer were done. 'There lurketh matter under that pretended piety,' Chaderton of Chester was warned by Archbishop Sandys, with his bitter experiences of the turbulent diocese of London.[21]

In the light of this discussion we may now approach an extraordinary meeting which seems to open a new and more active chapter in the Elizabethan puritan movement. In his exposure of the presbyterian movement, *Daungerous positions and proceedings*, Bancroft quoted from what was, with the exception of that scrap of paper called 'the order of Wandsworth', the earliest of John Field's papers to have fallen into his hands. This was a letter from the Suffolk preacher Oliver Pig, rector of Rougham, dated May 16th, 1582, and reporting an assembly of 'three-score ministers, appointed out of Essex, Cambridgeshire and Norfolk to meet the eighth of May' at Cockfield, a village not far from Bury St Edmunds where John Knewstub, the doyen of the Suffolk preachers, was rector, 'there to confer of the Common Book what might be tolerated, and what necessarily to be refused in every point of it; apparel, matter, form, days, fastings, injunctions etc.' 'Our meeting was appointed to be kept very secretly,' Pig told Field, 'and to be made known to none ... ' But he added: 'Concerning the meeting, I hope all things were so proceeded in as your self would like of, as well for reverence to other brethren, as for other matters. I suppose before this time some of the company have told you by word, for that was permitted unto you.'[22]

Ten years later this was all that Bancroft knew about the Cockfield meeting (although he himself had been brought to Bury to preach against the puritans less than a year after it took place) and as usual his information prompts more questions than it answers. We cannot tell whether it marked the beginning of a new advance in presbyterian action or whether there had been other conventions like this in the past. How were the ministers 'appointed', and did the initiative come from London or from a correspondence among the East Anglian ministers themselves? Something, perhaps, can be deduced from the fact that Pig visited London no more than six weeks before the Cockfield meeting was held.[23] It seems safest to conclude that the East Anglian puritans, loosely grouped in conferences and exercises according to their distribution and accessibility, and sometimes in larger groups for fasts, met in May 1582 in a much larger gathering, perhaps for a general fast as well as for conference, and that their action was prompted from London. That they used this occasion to hammer out a common policy towards the Prayer Book is not surprising. This was an urgent necessity throughout East Anglia where Bishops Aylmer and Freke, aided by the assize judges, were pressing the puritans very hard.

The Cockfield meeting was followed within a couple of months by another general conference held in Cambridge at the time of the 'Commencement' or graduation ceremonies in early July. In the same letter to Field Pig wrote: 'Concerning the Commencement I like well your motion, desiring it might so come to pass, and that it might be procured to be as general as might be; which may easily be brought to pass if you at London shall so think well of it, and we here may understand your mind, we will (I trust) as we can, further it. Mr Allen liketh well of the matter.'[24] (Walter Allen was rector of Rushbrooke, the home of Sir Robert Jermyn, the leading puritan gentleman of the county, so that his approval may have been tantamount to Jermyn's sanction.) Once again this is the first record we have of what was to become an annual institution. Yet since the majority of those concerned in the East Anglian puritan movement were Cambridge men of the same generation, such a conference may have been no novelty in 1582.

Two months after the Cambridge meeting there was yet another gathering, this time at Wethersfield, a village near Braintree in Essex, not more than a day's journey on horseback from Cockfield. Here the host was the lecturer of the place, Richard Rogers, whose instructive diary has come down to us to reveal something of the inner life and turmoils of conscience of the Elizabethan puritan divine.[25] The deprived Norwich prebendary Dr Edmund Chapman, since 1578 lecturer at Dedham, was the preacher on this occasion, 'and sundry other godly preachers and other persons were then and there assembled to hear him.' A farmer was indicted at the quarter sessions in the following spring, at the instigation of Lord Rich, the local magnate and a deeply-committed puritan, for railing in an alehouse against those who attended the exercise, saying: 'What make all these knaves here today? What, will they make a god of Rogers? There were forty of the knaves like rebels indicted at the last assizes and more had been if they had not made friends.' This seems to be a reference to the Bury Assizes of the previous July, when numbers of puritan preachers and laymen were prosecuted before Judge Wray and Judge Anderson and when Lord North and 'fourteen of the principal men out of Suffolk', seven of them knights, waited on the judges at their lodgings with an earnest request to 'handle trifling matters the more kindly for our sakes.' The background to these agitated meetings of the summer and autumn of 1582 was that at Bury there was now no preaching ministry at all. The preachers, wearied with 'the violent and continual practices' of their enemies, had taken their leave.[26]

The exercise at Wethersfield was 'a little before the feast of St Michael's', September 29th, 1582. A month later, on October 22nd, the ministers placed in a convenient circuit around Dedham – a town some twenty miles from both Wethersfield and Cockfield – met for conference and drew up and subscribed an order for regular meetings. This was, we can be sure, a new venture, in which Edmund Chapman, who had preached at Wethersfield, was the leading spirit. And now we begin to understand something at least of what had been brewing among the preachers all that summer of 1582. For the conference formed on that day in October was a permanent, regular body which kept minutes and filed its correspondence and other papers. More than twenty years later, in a Norfolk parish, the sometime vicar of Dedham who had acted as clerk to the conference was moved to make a transcript of all this material. What he recorded enjoyed the high survival-value which archives have so often possessed in the relative isolation of deepest East Anglia. At some time the Dedham papers passed into the possession of the Gurney family of Keswick Hall by whose permission most of the material was edited for the Royal Historical Society by the late Professor Roland Green Usher.[27] More recently they were purchased by the John Rylands Library in Manchester.[28] The Dedham conference maintained its existence for almost seven years, with regular monthly and occasional extraordinary meetings. Parker's record is complete and throws a continuous flood of light over the rise and fall of the so-called 'classical movement', the presbyterian plot to convert the Church of England whether by law or against the law. Without the Dedham papers, it would hardly be possible to write the history of this movement.

6 The Dedham Conference[1]

'Mr Farrar moved that his brother of Holbrook might be admitted one of our company, which was yielded unto by the brethren.'
'Mr Salmon moved whether Mr Farrer of Holbrook should know any more of our meeting, not having accepted of it hitherto. His brother answered that he found no readiness in him because he would not be tied to a place. The brethren required him to charge his brother to be silent.'

>   (Minutes of the Dedham Conference, December 5th, 1586;
>   March 6th, 1587)

A FEW MILES AFTER LEAVING COLCHESTER, the old road from London into East Anglia drops down a slope of surprising abruptness for this part of England and at the bottom crosses the placid river Stour. Beyond, over a landscape of water-meadows and willows which John Constable taught the world to admire, stands the perfectly-proportioned tower of Dedham church. Every village in this pleasant valley records its wealth and vitality in the fifteenth and sixteenth centuries, when this was the premier industrial district in England, and when its clothiers took pleasure in enriching and improving the communities from which they drew their livelihood. In the fifteenth century they made their parish churches one of the last glories of pre-Reformation England. Now their protestant descendants brought preaching and education into these same townships.

Their parish churches, with interiors designed to arouse the sentiment with which the later Middle Ages approached the mystery of the mass, provided an incongruous setting for Calvinist preaching and psalm-singing. One has to imagine the frescoes obliterated with whitewash, the windows clear-glazed, the ten commandments prominently displayed, the chancel filled with seats facing westwards, and, against all the logic of the building's conception, the attention of the congregation directed to the new wooden pulpit on the south wall with its sounding-board and hour-glass. A later generation has done its best to bring back the flavour of late medievalism into these churches and prefers to forget what they became in the sixteenth and seventeenth centuries. There are few tangible reminders of the vitality of that other tradition, now almost spent after four centuries: little but the bust of a seventeenth-century lecturer of Dedham and the pulpits, now flanking the chancel steps. The negative evidence of so much that cannot be restored looms larger and the positive virtues of these communities under Calvinism are not remembered.

One of the puritan clothiers with interests in the Stour valley was a certain William Cardinal of Great Bromley, a merchant and industrialist who was on the way to establishing himself as a landowning gentleman. In 1582 he purchased two of the four small manors which made up the village of East Bergholt, on the northern slopes above Dedham – Constable's birthplace. Cardinal's sister was married to Dr Edmund Chapman, a puritan fellow of Trinity College in Cartwright's time who had begun his career as a preacher in Bedford. Ejected by the bishop of Lincoln, Chapman migrated to Norwich where he preached and enjoyed a prebend in the cathedral. In 1577 the new regime of Bishop Freke sent Chapman on his travels again and in the following year Cardinal endowed a lectureship in the parish church of Dedham and installed his brother-in-law as the first lecturer. In 1581 the vicar of Dedham, one Timothy Fitzwilliam, fell foul of the bishop (reasons of conscience are not to be suspected) and Chapman acted temporarily in his place. A year later Fitzwilliam resigned and was replaced by Richard Parker, a preacher and a puritan, although without Chapman's learning and maturity. Meanwhile two more of that now scattered constellation of Norwich preachers had appeared in the district: Dr Richard Crick in Cardinal's own village of East Bergholt and Richard Dow in Stratford St Mary, a village a mile up the valley from Dedham. Neither Crick nor Dow seems to have found settled employment before 1582 but both were in the district by 1580 at the latest. One is bound to suspect some design in their migration from Norwich to this new and advantageous environment.[2]

Protestantism was an early tradition in these industrial villages, the successor to a strong lollard strain in the early sixteenth century. As early as 1556, in Mary's reign, we hear of conventicles and 'schismatic sermons and preachings' in Dedham, involving a clothier, a tailor, a husbandman and twenty other persons.[3] Moreover, the Stour valley formed the frontier between two dioceses, its parishes as far removed as possible from both London and Norwich. On the Essex side, the eye of the bishop was an archdeacon who fifteen years before had been among the first of the English presbyterians – none other than George Withers, who had opposed Erastus at Heidelberg, and who was now a steady, moderate puritan. On the Suffolk side the archdeacon of Sudbury, John Still, was in good odour with the godly.

The conference of ministers which met in and around Dedham must have grown from the desire of Chapman, Crick and Dow to reproduce in this new context the presbyterian experiment which they had pioneered in Norwich.[4] At their first meeting of October 22nd, 1582, when the formal order of conference was subscribed and thirteen subscribers 'chosen for the Assembly', these three headed the list of members, and Chapman and Crick were the first to sign. At the first conference under this constitution, Crick was the speaker and Chapman the moderator; at the second they exchanged places, while Dow was the speaker at the third. The 'note of such things as are agreed upon to be observed in our meetings' bore many affinities to the Norwich order of 1575. Like every previous order of prophesying, the proceedings were divided into two, the first half to be devoted to preaching, the rest of the time to be spent in conference. And as in the prophesyings, a book of the Bible was chosen 'to be continued in' progressively. As at Norwich, admission to the fellowship of the conference was by consent of 'the whole'. The speaker and moderator were chosen by the same general consent and all the brethren took their turns to fill the principal places. The censure which followed the sermon was of the same character: the speaker withdrew, the brethren gave their opinion of his doctrine, and the moderator acted as their mouthpiece. (In practice, the brethren preferred to avoid the embarrassment of confronting the speaker with their criticisms, and nothing was said when he returned to the company.) At first an attempt was made to adhere to the Norwich custom by which the moderator was always the first speaker of the previous exercise. Like the Norwich order and the Bury exercise (and so many fraternal gatherings of ministers to this very day) the conference was held on a Monday, although once a month rather than weekly.

At the same time, the Dedham order contained important innovations. The organization of the conference ignored the diocesan boundary. As at Cockfield five months before, its meetings were to be secret: 'Silence also to be kept as well of the meeting as of the matters there dealt in without it be first signified to the rest.' (Although within nine months 'it was said our meetings were known and threatened.') And whereas the Norwich preachers had met in the cathedral, and the prophesyings generally had been essentially public occasions, held in prominent churches, the Dedham conference, like John Field's secret cell in London, met in private houses and always in a different place. These perambulations both respected the equal status of the members and avoided the suspicion which would attach to repeated meetings in one centre. It was purely a clerical conference; so far as we know a sermon for the people formed no part of the proceedings. And whereas every order of prophesying had provided that two or three speakers at least should address themselves to the text, and the Norwich order had allowed as many to join in the public. speaking as time would allow, the Dedham order provided for one speaker only except when the conference met for prayer. and fasting. Another innovation which followed from the altered character of the meeting was the provision of definite time for conference about 'necessary matters' and for determining 'profitable questions', that is, for an adminis- trative function, and two-thirds of the available time was reserved for business of this kind. Decisions were minuted and preserved, together with the correspondence and other papers arising from the business. This was probably a new departure and a very significant one.

Much can be learnt from an analysis of the membership of the Dedham conference.[5] It had altogether in its history twenty members, and the membership never fell below thirteen. Of the twenty, one proved dis- loyal and dropped out at an early stage, and four left the district for employment elsewhere. There were seven members whom we should have no reason to connect with the puritan movement but for the survival of these records. In every other case the puritanism of the members is borne out by other evidence, either in ecclesiastical court records, or in the manuscript collections of the puritans themselves. The conference cast a wide net: as far as Colchester and Coggeshall in one direction and Ipswich in the other, while two of its members came from Boxford, a village several miles up the valley to the west, and divided their loyalties between Dedham and a conference in Suffolk. At a time when graduate clergy were still in a minority nationally, all but two of these twenty ministers were university men, seventeen of them graduates, and nearly all were from Cambridge. The only Oxford man (Richard Crick) had been a fellow of Magdalen. Three others had been fellows of their colleges: Chapman at Trinity; Laurence Newman, vicar of Coggeshall, and Thomas Stoughton, preacher at East Bergholt, at Queen's. Two were doctors of divinity (Chapman and Crick) and ten others held the master's degree. It is hard to see, on this showing, how the editor of the Dedham papers could justify the slighting remark that few of the puritans could be called learned or mentally vigorous and that 'the rank and file impress one as of a distinctly inferior grade.'

It is significant and highly typical of the more extreme wing of the puritan movement that in spite of this high standard of learning, only half of the members were in a beneficed ministry, and two of these left their parishes to become town preachers (at Yarmouth and Bury) within the life of the conference. The rest were placed in the lectureships endowed by local clothiers or in private households. William Cardinal's own village of East Bergholt contrived to support Richard Crick, a doctor of divinity, and two masters of arts, John Tilney and Thomas Stoughton, none of whom was incumbent of the parish. Four of the twenty seem not to have been episcopally ordained, although all exercised a ministry and presumably possessed some kind of a calling which satisfied the brethren.

The Dedham conference, especially in its governing orders, exhibited many distinctly presbyterian features, but we shall show that to call it a presbyterian *classis* would be to beg too many important questions. We have seen that in all the reformed churches there was a tendency for conferences or 'colloquies' of ministers to assume an administrative function and so to become the *'classes'* which are the hall-marks of the presbyterian system of church government. This stage had evidently been reached in the formation of the Dedham conference, and four years later a representative puritan assembly in London would rule that existing conferences of this type were to be known as *classes*.[6] True, there was no representation of lay elders at Dedham nor, so far as we know, in any other Elizabethan puritan conference. But in other reformed churches the lay representatives were often far outnumbered by the ministers in the early phases of presbyterian organization, so that these were often in the narrowest sense clerical bodies. In so far as the functions of the Dedham conference were administrative, the assumptions governing its conduct were those of presbyterianism. The members were 'chosen for the assembly', they were subject to its advice, if not direction, and they could not voluntarily leave its fellowship. When one member was irregular in his attendance it was decided that he should be 'earnestly dealt withal by some of the brethren and persuaded to join with us in our meetings ordinarily with diligence and cheerfulness.' In making decisions, the principle of parity was scrupulously respected, even the minority being invited to 'give their reasons.' But once made, a decision was supposed to be binding. Not merely the members but their congregations were expected to respect the advice of the conference in the agreements they made with their ministers and in any dispute which might arise between them. At the very first meeting it was debated whether Richard Dow should be 'placed' at East Bergholt or at Stratford St Mary, and at the second 'it was thought best to the brethren for divers reasons that Mr Dow should accept of his calling at Stratford.' At the sixth meeting it was decided that Dow should no longer 'read an ordinary lecture at Higham.' Later in the life of the conference it was 'thought good that men of fit gifts and good life should be found out to supply the churches' want if they can come in with favour.' Nearly every member of the conference at some time in its history asked for help in resolving the problems encountered in his ministry, especially the misunderstandings which seem to have arisen so often between pastor and people. The conference evidently assumed jurisdiction over the Church in its area in the widest sense. Those who objected that as yet there was no settled discipline in the English Church were told that those who desired it should voluntarily submit themselves to it.

Nominally, the conference only tendered advice and 'counsel' in all these cases, but there can be no doubt that its decisions had the nature of case-law. When a member was advised to baptize the child of offending parents only if 'some of the friends, or of the church that be godly, be procured to answer for it, and to bring the party to repentance if it may be', he was given an authoritative ruling, part of a growing corpus of tradition independent of the canons and formularies of the Church of England. The matters on which the conference was asked for resolution ranged from the interpretation of the biblical law of divorce and the lawfulness of baptizing bastards to the use of the Sabbath and the weighty problem of 'whether boys of sixteen years of age might put on their hats in the church.' The conference embarked on a methodical study of the Prayer Book, in no spirit of academic detachment, but in order to give a ruling on what should be tolerated and what left out. A catechism prepared by Dr Chapman was 'perused and allowed' by the conference as 'not inconvenient to be published for the use of the people of Dedham especially', and it was printed soon afterwards. Where the conference had no power to intervene directly, it used its influence with those who had. Pressure was put on a local worthy to suppress the famous morality plays which were staged on Whitsunday in the ruined chapel of Manningtree, at the head of the Stour estuary.[7] 'The magistrate' was spoken to about separatist conventicles in Colchester and Dedham, and the archdeacon of Sudbury was 'to be dealt with' about an 'ungodly sermon' preached by the vicar of Hadleigh, 'defacing the men of Antwerp.' (William Cardinal was a 'man of Antwerp' and so, no doubt, were other merchants and clothiers to be found among the more substantial members of the Dedham ministers' congregations.) Complaints against local clothiers who set their 'woadfats' (dyeworks) on the Sabbath day were to be referred individually to 'the godliest of that trade'. In some of these matters the brethren recognized that they had no formal right of interference. When someone asked what was to be done about the multitude of rogues who were troubling the country, it was not thought 'convenient' to deal in the matter except by exercising influence with the magistrates, and then only 'as a private man'. But from this it is clear that in matters 'of the Church' the Dedham ministers assumed a responsibility to act, not as 'private men' but as Christ's executors and vicars.

As these examples have suggested, the agenda of the conference was largely made up of parochial, day-to-day matters. The more learned brethren in Cambridge might be consulted from time to time about such a large and unresolved question as the interpretation of the fourth commandment. But there is little indication, certainly from the early years of its existence, that the conference was more than occasionally concerned with bringing its decisions and resolutions into line with those of other churches and so promoting the universal agreement and concord which was the authentic presbyterian ideal. Nor should one take it for granted that all the Dedham ministers were convinced that episcopacy was to be excluded from these wider aspects of church government. Certainly if we call this body 'presbyterian' we should not thereby endorse without qualification the charge of Richard Bancroft that the prime function of a puritan conference was to play its part in a coherent movement for the subversion of the episcopal polity of the Church of England. A few members were possessed by these wider ambitions and Dedham was soon to become involved in their schemes, but by no means all of the brethren were sure that such a violent upheaval was called for. It was the opinion of at least one member that although the place, calling and authority of bishops were not 'that which yet ought to be', their jurisdiction was confirmed by the laws of England and even derived from statute, so that it was by no means Antichristian.[8] True, the Dedham ministers managed their own affairs for the most part without reference to the bishops and often took a negative and hostile view of their courts and visitations. But the majority party in the conference seems to have adopted a pragmatic rather than a doctrinaire attitude towards the realities of life under the Elizabethan settlement. They were ready enough to invoke the powers of the archdeacons of Colchester and Sudbury against their opponents, and on one occasion they submitted to Archdeacon Withers a scheme for exercising his functions as the permanent moderator of a synod, 'where we may use our freedom in conference and determining of ecclesiastical matters with him as fellow labourers and brethren.'

Bishops and archdeacons were not to be ignored or entirely rejected. The position was not unlike that of the contemporary Scottish Church with its presbyteries and synods coexisting uneasily with an enervated episcopate.

If the 'presbyterianism' of the Dedham conference did not altogether exclude recognition of an Erastian episcopate, it was not inconsistent with a deeply ingrained tendency to what would later distinguish itself as the independent or congregationalist way. Both in their reluctance to be ruled as a body by higher assemblies meeting in London or elsewhere, and in their refusal to submit themselves and their congregations to the decisions of their own conference, these Elizabethan puritans displayed tendencies which would have scandalized the Scottish observers at the Westminster Assembly sixty years later. The Dedham conference weakened the general puritan strategy in Essex and Suffolk by drawing some of its members long distances from districts where smaller and less successful conferences badly needed their support. Yet Dedham could not be 'induced to part with any, who having joined themselves are willing still to cleave unto us.' Not even when a general assembly meeting in London decreed that the ministers should everywhere regroup themselves in meetings of a convenient size and distribution, and that no one conference should exceed a membership of ten. 'We reverence our faithful brethren at London with their gracious advices,' they wrote, 'and heartily praise God for that good which the Church receiveth from them,' yet they claimed to be 'best privy in our conference' of the 'inconveniences' which the loss of any of their members would entail.[9]

As collectively towards London and other conferences, so individually towards their own fellowship, the Dedham ministers found by hard experience that often the furthest extent of their loyalty was to reverence the 'gracious advices' of the brethren while remaining 'best privy' in their own affairs. In February 1585 Bartimaeus Andrewes, vicar of the Suffolk parish of Wenham, was admonished for being absent from his charge. Dissatisfied with his lot at Wenham, he was negotiating for a move to Yarmouth where he had been offered the post of town preacher at the comparatively princely salary of fifty pounds a year.[10] His parishioners opposed his departure, whereupon the conference assumed jurisdiction over the dispute, dealing both with the people of Wenham and with the magistrates of Yarmouth. At a special meeting held to determine the matter, the bailiffs of Yarmouth sent a messenger to wait on its decision. For a variety of reasons, most of the brethren spoke against Andrewes's proposal to leave, and Dr Crick said that if he were of Wenham he would as soon they should pluck out his eye as take away his pastor. 'Sir, if you cast out your eye you will give me leave to take it up,' was the retort of Mr Mayham of Yarmouth, but he went away 'unsatisfied'. Yet soon afterwards Andrewes left for Yarmouth in contempt of the will of the conference. The brethren sadly recorded that their responsibility in the matter was at an end, and they set about finding a new pastor for Wenham.

A rather different situation claimed the attention of the conference in East Bergholt. John Tilney, minister of the puritan congregation at 'Hog Lane' – either a semi-separatist congregation or a chapel of ease – was another preacher who quarrelled with his people, and especially with one man who counted him 'no minister, nor their church no church' and who later went off to be married by the separatist John Greenwood 'in a private house'. At length, Tilney's opponents succeeded in expelling him and invited in his place Dr Richard Crick who was already preaching in East Bergholt, perhaps as a lecturer in the parish church, perhaps in William Cardinal's family. Once again an attempt at intervention by the conference seems to have influenced the outcome of the dispute neither one way nor the other. But most of the members, as a protest against the 'people's course in rejecting and receiving their pastors without counsel of others', refused to preach at Crick's induction. One brother said flatly that 'though it were imposed upon him, yet he would not do it, seeing the church dealt as she did.' The months went by and Crick was still not received into his new charge. Eventually he was forced to approach the whole conference, 'craving to be let in, and that my face may not be turned away.' His letter constitutes one of the earliest statements of conscientious independency. The request was made in writing for fear of more 'boisterous words' for which Crick himself might have been responsible, 'being become now at the length as jealous for the honour of the church [his congregation] as any of you are for your own, or for his whom she hath most worthily thrown out.' If the conference again refused him, he would turn 'either to the right hand or to the left to see whether I may obtain so much favour of some good brother elsewhere.' But if his congregation learned of the attitude of the conference it would certainly assert its independence and, 'standing in need of counsel, they would profess themselves willing to fetch it from as far beyond London as London is hence, rather than from you, though ye would beg to be of counsel with them.' Crick wished that he had never heard the hard speeches which had been uttered against him in the conference. 'For then I should have been freed from my present fear, which maketh me, though with grief, willingly to absent myself at this time from your meeting, whose faces I have seen as if I had seen the face of God, whose backs I have beholden with far greater joy than ever I have done almost the eyes of any other company.'[11]

In these episodes the whole future course of puritan history seems to be contained in miniature. No one can doubt that the brethren of Dedham were making a serious effort to govern the affairs of their churches in the presbyterian fashion, to bring an element of 'discipline' and 'good order' into what they often called 'these confused days'. And those who think that they were motivated only by dry, intellectually conceived dogma should read Dr Crick's almost passionate plea for fellowship with his brethren. But their outlook was more congregational than ecumenical. When their own individual interests and those of their churches were touched, the instincts characteristic of independency invariably came to the surface and in the absence of any forceful sanctions, frustrated what was, after all, a purely voluntary discipline. If the puritans had been in power and had been able to put into general operation the principles to which most at this time paid at least lip service, no individual minister could have treated a *classis* or synod in such a casual fashion. But when that day at last came, sixty years later, independent habits had hardened into firm church principles and proved ineradicable.

How far was the case of Dedham representative of the general position in 1582, when the conference was first formed? Were the puritan ministers in other districts binding themselves by secret orders of meeting, and, if so, were they responding to a directive from the centre, from London? The Dedham papers provide only a very partial answer to these questions, but they can be supplemented by some fragmentary evidence from other sources. From the moment that Archbishop Whitgift set out to repress the puritan movement, that is, from 1584, it becomes clear that there was a capacity for organized action in every county where there were puritan ministers in any strength, and that their leaders could be brought into close touch with John Field and his friends in London. From this, something can be read back into the years before the crisis. We can assume that the puritans in every district were in the habit of meeting for conference and exercise and were in at least occasional contact with 'the church in London'. Yet this need not mean that they were all associated in formal, secret meetings of the Dedham pattern, or were attempting to exercise collective discipline with the confidence and determination which the Dedham conference acquired from an exceptional leadership and an unusually favourable ecclesiastical and social environment. On the contrary, the efforts of London in the coming years to encourage steps which had been taken long before at Dedham suggest that these developments in the Stour valley were precocious and unusual. Still less can it be assumed that there was already in existence a network of conferences pledged to the subversion of the state of the Church of England, as Richard Bancroft would have us believe. This point is crucial for the argument which this book attempts to sustain. We have said, and say again, that doctrinaire presbyterianism, and the more extreme and disruptive manifestations of puritanism generally, were aggravated, if not directly generated, by the repression of moderate puritan aspirations. Yet if a widespread presbyterian plot was under way as early as 1582, encouraged by the laxity of the Grindalian episode, and before Whitgift's general onslaught on the puritan conscience was launched, this analysis must be discarded in favour of Bancroft's conspiratorial view of puritan history.

The Dedham conference obviously owed much to the personal inspiration of Edmund Chapman and Richard Crick and through them to the unusual situation which obtained in Norwich as early as 1575. To this extent it was perhaps unique. Nevertheless its formation cannot have been unconnected with the extraordinary assemblies held at Cockfield, Cambridge and Wethersfield in the preceding months of 1582, which were described in the previous chapter. We are therefore entitled to suspect parallel developments elsewhere in East Anglia. There can be little doubt that the ministers led by John Knewstub in West Suffolk were similarly organized at about the same time, for they were linked in many ways to the ministers attached to Dedham. In April 1583 Thomas Cartwright wrote a common letter to 'his most loving and reverend brethren the ministers of Suffolk and Essex, to be directed unto them by the hands of Mr Dr Chapman and Mr Knewstub.' And later in the same year, after Whitgift's arrival at Lambeth, the Dedham conference decided what it should do and at once communicated its recommendations to London, Norwich, Cambridge 'and to the brethren in Suffolk'. Yet it could be argued that the puritans of Norfolk, Suffolk and Essex were already experiencing the pressures which became general throughout the province of Canterbury after 1583. Their conferences were their response to the repressive policies of Freke and Aylmer. Even so, the East Anglian ministers were imperfectly organized. There was no conference or exercise at such an important centre as Ipswich, nor, it appears, at Colchester, and Richard Rogers tells us that in his neighbourhood of Wethersfield the ministers made 'small use' of their meetings at this time.[12]

Beyond East Anglia, the position is much more obscure. John Field was kept informed of what was done at the Cockfield meeting of May 1582, and may even have prompted it, and it was he who proposed the conference held at Cambridge in the following July,[13] so it is reasonable to suppose that he was seeking to stimulate the same developments in other districts. The organization of the Midland counties may not have lagged far behind eastern England. Humphrey Fen of Coventry would confess in 1591 that it was 'about eight years now last past' that he and others began to 'treat and confer of the Discipline.'[14] That would place the beginning of formal conference in Warwickshire in 1583.

We are left with the detritus of fragmentary evidence, scattered awkwardly over the surface and only serving to show how little we really know. Between 1584 and December 1585, a Scottish preacher suffering a temporary, self-imposed exile in England found employment near Saltash, across the Tamar from Plymouth, as domestic chaplain to Sir Anthony Rous, father of the famous puritan writer and parliamentarian. When he returned to Scotland, John Cowper carried a testimonial signed by six Cornish justices and seven 'brethren of the exercise of Saltash' who testified that he had 'joined himself with our ministry of the exercise' and had 'taught in our presence at such times as were appointed to him.'[15] Was this how any exercise would normally conduct its affairs, drawing up formal 'letters fiduciary' for a member who was leaving its fellowship? Or was this an unusual favour extended to a Scottish minister whose Church would require a formal testimonial of this kind from an other than episcopal source? These questions cannot be answered with any degree of confidence.

But something at least can be learned of developments at the centre, in London. We have Thomas Edmunds's Star Chamber testimony that the cell formed by Field and Wilcox as early as 1571 continued its meetings uninterrupted throughout these years, and there are some independent traces of its activities. In 1577 the conference, enlarged by some representation from Norwich and Northamptonshire, was in correspondence with Cartwright in the Palatinate, and characteristically assumed the right to speak for all the English churches. From the following year there are some intriguing letters in the state papers which show that the London conference could perform the proper function of a presbyterian *classis* in finding and commending a minister for a vacant charge; the charge being the congregation of English merchants in Antwerp, a church which took advantage of its situation to abandon every vestige of Anglicanism for the liturgy and discipline of the continental churches. The London conference was enabled to act in this matter by the puritan government officials who made it their responsibility to find 'some honest, godly and learned man' for the Antwerp pulpit: these were Walsingham's secretary Laurence Tomson and Henry Killigrew on this side of the North Sea, and William Davison, the queen's agent in the Low Countries, on the other. William Chark, lecturer at Lincoln's Inn, was first mentioned, but after talking to Field, Killigrew had to report to Davison that he was not likely to be spared, and that his wife and children would prove an impediment. However, Field had 'promised to nominate shortly one or two that be unmarried.' A month later Killigrew reported that 'Mr Field looketh for an answer from a friend of his touching that matter which he is shortly to deliver to me and I the same over unto you.' The result of these negotiations was that Walter Travers was nominated and sent over to receive a presbyterian ordination from Killigrew's close friend, Pierre Loiseleur de Villiers, and other Antwerp ministers. He carried a letter of recommendation from Thomas Randolph to William Davison, from one puritan diplomat to another: 'Our hap is the harder that such men are forced to seek other places than to do their duties at home.' In 1580, when Travers returned to London, his place was taken by Cartwright. Throughout these years, the Antwerp congregation seems to have powerfully influenced the domestic puritan movement in a presbyterian direction.[16]

A rare insight into Field's place in the international Calvinist movement is provided by a letter which he received from a leading Scottish presbyterian, John Davidson, in January 1583. Davidson, who was already known to Field from one of his visits to England, began by acknowledging a letter of the previous July, which had encouraged the Scottish brethren at a low point in their fortunes. The very next day had brought a letter from La Rochelle 'tending to the same end, to wit, lamenting our troublous state and therewithal comforting us in our God. It is no small comfort brother (as ye and I have divers times spoken in conference), to brethren of one nation to understand the state of the brethren in other nations, and therefore let us practise it as occasion will serve.' The Scottish presbyterians now had the upper hand and proposed to use their new influence to approach King James VI and 'the whole state' as from the General Assembly and to ask them to appeal to Queen Elizabeth 'with her state and your church' for the reformation of the Anglican abuses, 'and especially that sincere men may have liberty to preach without deposing by the tyranny of the bishops.' An endorsement reads that Davidson's motion was 'liked by the brethren in England' while another note, perhaps

Field's, comments: 'Concerning this, to answer in general that the brethren shall think themselves beholding to them if they shall be so careful.' Accordingly, three ministers were appointed from the General Assembly of 1583 to ask the king to convey a motion to the queen to 'disburden their brethren of England of the yokes of ceremonies.' James undertook to do so, but failed to keep his promise.[17]

We catch a further glimpse of the puritan organization at work on a more than local scale in the spring of 1583, when Thomas Cartwright was urged to undertake a confutation of the Catholic version of the New Testament, recently published in Rheims.[18] This vast project was actively encouraged and financed by Walsingham and Leicester and to this extent it was of a semi-official character,[19] but the secret puritan conferences also made it their concern. The preface to the *Confutation*, when it was belatedly published in 1618, described how 'the reverend ministers also of Suffolk and of London did by their several letters earnestly exhort him in like manner unto this work.' We know from the Dedham papers that both the Dedham and West Suffolk conferences wrote in April 1583, and in his reply Cartwright spoke of having been 'diversely and earnestly dealt with' in the same suit. Moreover, a letter from some of the 'most learned men of the university of Cambridge', printed in the 1618 edition, was signed in a conference attended by most of the regular members of Field's presbyterian cell, and therefore almost certainly held in London, but also by three distinguished Cambridge divines, William Whitaker, master of St John's and the leading champion of Calvinist orthodoxy in the university, Roger Goad, provost of King's, and William Fulke, master of Pembroke Hall; and by John Ireton of Leicestershire and others. When the letter was printed, the names of those signatories who were still living were excluded and it is reasonably certain that Laurence Chaderton, who lived until 1640, would have been among them. The satirist Thomas Nashe drew an imaginative picture of the activity in Cambridge after Cartwright had begun the *Confutation*:

Were not all the elected in Cambridge assembled about the shaping of the confutation of the Rhemish Testament? Oh, so devoutly they met every Friday at Saint *Laurence* his monastery [Chaderton's college, Christ's], where the councils and fathers were distributed amongst several companies, and every one of the reformed society sent their combined quotations week by week in a capcase to my brother *Thomas*, yet wandering beyond sea; such a chaos of commonplaces no apophthegmatical *Lycosthenes* ever conceived.[20]

By this time the Calvinism of Chaderton and Whitaker no longer went unchallenged in Cambridge itself. Peter Baro, a theologian of French extraction who was Lady Margaret professor from 1574 and an aspirant for the Regius chair of divinity in 1580, had begun noticeably to diverge from the Calvinist doctrines of grace and predestination in his lectures on Jonah, delivered in the university in 1579. He soon found himself immersed in furious debate with the watchdogs of orthodoxy, Whitaker, Travers, Chark and Fulke, who accused him of teaching universalism and Arianism and sharing the delusions of the papists. Complaints were made to Sir Francis Walsingham and Laurence Tomson, who were persuaded to reverse their earlier favourable opinions of Baro. In the spring of 1583 Baro was warned by the minister of the French church in London of resolutions passed against his teaching in a 'clandestine synod' held in King's College House in London. Now because Dr Roger Goad, provost of King's, was involved both in this affair and in the conference which urged Cartwright to embark on the *Confutation*, I am inclined to think that they were one and the same meeting. Baro rode up to London to make inquiries, but Goad would reveal nothing, and Baro learned of the matter in detail only some eight or nine years later, when Richard Bancroft showed him the acts of this synod 'in a certain book'. This was possibly Bancroft's file of the letters and papers which were used in the Star Chamber case against the puritans, and in his polemical histories of the movement. Thomas Rogers, Bancroft's chaplain, may be presumed to have drawn upon the same source and probably referred to the same conference when he reported that some four months before Grindal's death (that is, in March 1583) 'the said brethren, at a certain assembly of their own appointing, among other things (as I find) decreed that if subscription unto the book of Articles of Religion ... should again be urged, the said brethren might subscribe thereunto according to the statute', that is, subscribe to those Articles 'which only concern doctrine.' This suggests that the puritans already envisaged the subscription crisis into which they would be plunged with the passing of Grindal, and that the most moderate and respected of the Cambridge leaders – men like Fulke and Whitaker – were already helping them to search for a formula of compromise.[21]

Bancroft himself, however, makes no reference to this conference (or conferences) in any of his writings, short as he was of material for these years, and the omission is not without significance. The whole episode is characteristic of the Church in Grindal's primacy: the co-operation of the extremists of Field's London group with learned Cambridge men and privy councillors in the defence of fundamental English protestantism against the false doctrine of Rheims and the heterodox theology of Baro. In their letter to Cartwright the Cambridge divines invited him to enter a battle 'not against a brother or fellow one of the same religion, but against inveterate enemies of the Church'. There was no material here for Bancroft's picture of the steady growth of a revolutionary 'Scottizing' conspiracy from its inception in 1572 until its frustration in 1591.

Nevertheless it seems probable that in the last two years of Grindal's primacy, the more extreme wing of the puritan party was planning some kind of presbyterian advance. Field's active encouragement of the East Anglian conferences in the summer of 1582 seems to connect with what a lapsed member of the London conference, Thomas Edmunds, later testified before the High Commissioners: that at first the London brethren had debated little but subscription, vestments and the Prayer Book, but that at a certain point 'things began to grow to greater ripeness', 'the name of discipline began to be in the mouths of many' and 'divers motions were made, and conclusions set down' amongst them, that the 'present government of the Church of England being concluded by them to be Antichristian, the only discipline and government of Jesus Christ (as they termed it) viz. by pastors, doctors, elders and deacons should be established in place of the other.' Regrettably, Edmunds gives no precise date for these potent developments. They happened, he says, with the arrival of various new members of the conference, including Walter Travers and William Chark. But those he names came to London at various dates between 1575 and 1580. Edmunds also says that when these things began to be debated he himself, 'misliking of these courses, departed out of their company', and that this was in 1583 or 1584.

Clearly this evidence cannot be taken as any sure indication that a deliberate presbyterian design was undertaken any earlier than 1584. However, Bancroft was also able to print a letter from Antwerp written to Field by a certain Mr Cholmeley (in Latin, which Bancroft translated), with the firm date of June 25th, 1583, two months, that is, after the London conference had corresponded with Cartwright about his *Confutation*. Acknowledging a letter from Field, Cholmeley told him:

I am glad with all my heart for the better success of your affairs, not only in that I hear of your assemblies, but most willingly of all in respect of your effectual practising of the Ecclesiastical Discipline. I will tell you that which is true, you have begun this course too too late. Whosoever shall now either refuse to begin or shall desist from so notable an enterprise, he shall bear his own sins. You ought to repent you for your former slowness.

Bancroft sets this evidence in the context of his argument that in 1583 the presbyterian Book of Discipline was already drawn up and that at an unspecified conference it was decided how far it might be put in practice without damaging the peace of the Church.[22] Although the possibility cannot be excluded that the author of the Book of Discipline – Walter Travers – had already completed an early draft (he had returned from Antwerp in 1580 and since 1581 had been lecturer at the Temple)[23] it must be denied, pending better evidence than Bancroft is able to supply, that there was at this time any attempt to promulgate it outside London, to have it allowed by country conferences or to put it into practice. Bancroft's case depends upon a document which belongs properly to a synod held in Warwickshire in 1588,[24] and which he chose to place five years earlier, on the flimsiest of internal evidence.

Unsatisfactory and partly conflicting as the evidence seems to be, the most distinct impression which emerges of the state of the puritan movement on the eve of Whitgift's appointment as archbishop of Canterbury is of the 'slowness' and the 'too too late' of which Field's Antwerp correspondent had complained. When Field wrote to Gilby in February 1581, some of his London news was almost two years old. And Field himself was ready to admit to his recent failings once the crisis of 1584 had developed. In February of that year he confessed to Chapman of Dedham that their 'intercourse of writing' had 'fainted of late' and that the reason lay in what he oddly calls 'this unhappy time of looseness and liberty' which had gained upon him and choked 'those good things which I thank God I was wont to feel in greater measure.' Whether or not Field had been lulled by Grindal's peace into an uncharacteristic complacency ('strongly drawn of late not to be so careful, diligent and zealous in God's causes as I was wont') it is certain that the innermost circle of the London presbyterians was in some disarray at this time. Thomas Wilcox had offended the Church by an undisclosed moral offence for which he was suspended from his ministry by the conference, Field leading the attack against him. He proved as reluctant as any of the Dedham ministers to recognize the disciplinary pretensions of his brethren when they touched his own interests, telling Field that 'he had been dealt disorderly withal, both for matter and manner' and that 'he had perhaps concealed as great infirmities of Field's and of some others, as his were.' Laurence Tomson thought him 'an unsound member, unfit to be continued in the body, unless he would be subject to the government of a body, especially the body of our saving God.' Field made the same point in his own more pungent and expressive English: 'If God hath made you an instrument to seek for the advancement of Christ's sceptre, kiss it yourself and be subject unto it.'

Left to itself, the puritan movement was chronically subject to ruptures and schisms of this kind. It was a necessary hazard of the attempt at corporate, democratically regulated leadership, which could easily degenerate in any particular situation into a practical dictatorship. Only one man had the power to close these sometimes wavering ranks, and in the autumn of 1583 he was on his way from Worcester to Lambeth House: John Whitgift, newly elected archbishop of Canterbury.[25]

Part 5

1584

1 Whitgift

LORD CHANCELLOR. What is that man? (pointing to Canterbury).

BARROW. The Lord gave me the spirit of boldness, so that I answered: He is a monster, a miserable compound, I know not what to make [call] him: he is neither ecclesiastical nor civil, even that second beast spoken of in the Revelation.

LORD TREASURER. Wher is that place, shew it.

(From the fourth examination of Henry Barrow before the High Commissioners, March 18th, 1589, printed, *The Writings of Henry Barrow, 1587–1590*, ed. Carlson, Elizabethan Nonconformist Texts, iii. 188)

IN THE YEARS OF GRINDAL'S IMPOTENCE there had been many warning sounds of what a puritan tract was soon to call *the strife of our Church*. Now, in July 1583, the death of the archbishop, blind and decrepit, forestalled an enforced resignation and enabled the queen to surrender the Church to a disciplinarian who shared her detestation of all faction and disobedience: Cartwright's old opponent, John Whitgift, who, if we are to believe his secretary and first biographer, Sir George Paule, had honourably refused the promotion *per resignationem*. The date of Whitgift's election – September 23rd, 1583 – was a decisive climacteric in the history of the reformed Church of England. As early as May 6th, Walsingham's secretary, Nicholas Faunt, had reported the likelihood that he would be Grindal's successor, but, as he thought, in little else except the title. Once Whitgift was in, he wrote gloomily: 'The choice of that man at this time to be archbishop maketh me to think that the Lord is even determined to scourge his Church for their unthankfulness.'[1]

Not all puritans shared Faunt's reaction to the first news of Whitgift's promotion. Paule noted the earl of Leicester as one of his master's especial friends before his elevation, and Robert Beale, the clerk of the Council, was comforted by both Leicester and Warwick, his brother, with assurances that, as bishop of Worcester, Whitgift had maintained a preaching ministry and had dealt 'charitably' with nonconformists who behaved themselves honestly; while it was generally rumoured that he had 'sundry times wished' that 'that unprofitable contention' between himself and Cartwright had never happened. In later years Beale would tell Whitgift: 'I would to God your Grace had at the first followed the advice which I know divers both honourable and others gave unto you.' The Dedham ministers were sanguine enough in early October to propose writing to Whitgift 'to be favourable to the Church and to discipline.' And there is something suggestive in Field's complaint that 'our new archbishop, now he is in, showeth himself as he was wont to be.'[2]

These illusions did not survive the inaugural sermon which the archbishop preached at Paul's Cross on the Queen's Day, November 17th, and which served to introduce his policy. Eighteen years had passed since Whitgift first preached from this famous pulpit, and for sixteen of those years the hot protestant of 1565 had grappled with the problems confronting Authority in the administration of Church and State. His theme now was not Dives and Lazarus, the pride of the rich and powerful and the affliction of the godly, but the necessity of obedience to the higher powers, prince, magistrate – and bishops. While he dealt with three kinds of disobedience, of papists, anabaptists and 'our wayward and conceited persons', Faunt noted that 'against these last was his whole bitterness and vehemency', meaning 'such as loved reformation.' Beale later told Whitgift that his sermon had 'dismayed both myself and sundry others, who supposed that your lordship would have run another course than it appeareth you have taken in hand.'[3]

A month before his appearance at Paul's Cross, Whitgift had already prepared, in co-operation with other bishops, a schedule of 'divers articles touching preachers and other orders for the Church'.[4] These were tendered to the queen by Whitgift and Piers of Salisbury in their own names and those of the bishops of London, Rochester, Lincoln, Peterborough and Gloucester. They received her approval and were promulgated to the dioceses on October 29th. Whitgift's articles were an instrument of wide-reaching reform as well as of discipline, but attention was drawn almost exclusively to the demand which they contained for subscription to three articles as the condition for exercising any ecclesiastical function. These ran:

1. That her Majesty, under God, hath, and ought to have, the sovereignty and rule over all manner of persons born within her realms and dominions and countries, of what estate ecclesiastical or temporal soever they be. And that none other foreign power, prelate, state or potentate hath, or ought to have, any jurisdiction, power, superiority, pre-eminence or authority ecclesiastical or

temporal, within her Majesty's said realms, dominions and countries.

2. That the Book of Common Prayer and of ordering bishops, priests
   and deacons containeth nothing in it contrary to the word of God.
   And that the same may be lawfully used; and that he himself will
   use the form of the said book prescribed in public prayer and
   administration of the sacraments and none other.

3. That he alloweth the book of Articles of Religion agreed upon by
   the archbishops and bishops in both provinces, and the whole
   clergy in the Convocation holden at London in the year of our
   Lord 1562, and set forth by her Majesty's authority. And that he
   believeth all the articles therein contained to be agreeable to the
   word of God.

For a puritan the first article was unexceptional, as was the third, if it were
limited by the statute of 1571 which had confined subscription to the more
strictly doctrinal of the Thirty-nine Articles. But the demand for subscription to the Prayer Book as containing nothing contrary to the word
of God, coupled with a promise to use that book and none other in their
administrations, touched the conscience of all precisians in the most tender
place, as Whitgift knew it must. The requirement was not new – Bishop
Bullingham had employed a similar formula in the diocese of Lincoln as
early as 1570, and subscription in only slightly different terms had been
required by Convocation in the canons of 1571 – but this was its first
general application. 'The causes of the same being either secret I cannot,
or not convenient to be published, I may not set down,' wrote Thomas
Rogers, a chaplain to Sir Christopher Hatton, two years later. There is
good reason to suppose that his master had more than a little to do with it,
but no cause to doubt Whitgift's frequent affirmations that it was the
queen herself who had given 'straight charge' for this policy to be
pursued.[5]

Those ministers of the Church of England who would be troubled by
Whitgift's demand for a total endorsement of the Prayer Book were
relatively numerous, and they were puritans in the broadest sense of the
term; of this generation of clergy, few with minds of their own would
subscribe to the Whitgiftian formula without a qualm. Hitherto it has
not been sufficiently appreciated that in selecting such a large and vaguely
defined target, Whitgift was plotting a course dangerous for himself,
full of encouraging possibilities for the revolutionary wing of the puritan

movement, and ultimately fatal for the unity and comprehensiveness of the Church of England. The alternative would have been to attack presbyterianism specifically in its chief protagonists, the unbeneficed preachers, and there is evidence that earlier in October such a policy was contemplated. George Northey, the popular town preacher of Colchester, was suspended by Bishop Aylmer primarily for saying in his presence 'that there was no ministry in England'. Strenuous efforts were made to restore him, but on October 10th the bailiffs of Colchester were informed that the case was governed by certain articles which the archbishop and his brethren had lately agreed upon by order from the queen – the earliest reference I know to the procedure then under preparation. These articles were 'many and diverse', but Northey was required to subscribe especially to these: that as a preacher he would also minister the sacraments and say service according to the Prayer Book, that he recognized 'the ministry of England and the lawful calling of bishops allowed by statute', and that he would put his name to the Thirty-nine Articles. This formula bears no relation to that presently adopted by Whitgift. Evidently at this stage the bishops were contemplating a flexible weapon which could be fitted to the particular case of a presbyterian town lecturer who confined himself to preaching. It would serve to isolate an extremist like Northey from other, more moderate ministers who would willingly subscribe such a formula; indeed, the bailiffs of Colchester complained of discrimination against their preacher since there were 'other preachers and ministers about us who continue their preaching and ministry in peace.'[6]

This bears the mark of Aylmer's government rather than Whitgift's. By the end of October, Whitgift had decided to attempt something more ambitious, or perhaps the queen had decreed it. The demand for unqualified approval of the entire contents of the Prayer Book was aimed not merely at the salaried lecturers with their tenuous connection with the establishment, but at the more numerous body of moderate nonconformists among the beneficed clergy; and no action was contemplated against the lay members of the extremist movement in London, such as had been attempted in 1573. Whitgift's aims, therefore, were different from those of Parker or Aylmer, and they were less realistic. His subscription formula was the product of a tidy, schoolmasterly mind which could tolerate no deviation from a rigidly conceived standard of clerical obedience. For the sake of what was surely an unattainable degree of uniformity, he made it more difficult to deal effectively with the hard core of extremists and placed his own episcopal order in grave danger. In the long run, the Whitgiftian policy, continued in their generations by Bancroft and the Laudians, was as much responsible as any puritan excess for destroying the comprehensiveness of the Church of England and its fully national character.

An immediate result of Whitgift's assault would be to reduce the differences between the majority with moderate puritan inclinations and the extremist minority. If large numbers of preaching ministers resisted subscription to the point of suspension or even deprivation, the archbishop's position would become exposed and precarious, and the radicals like Field would readily exploit the situation. The puritan press would advertise the folly of thrusting out so many godly preachers at a time 'when Jesuits, those of the Family of Love and others of all sorts swarm.' 'To go about to put out thirty or forty in a shire, and then to say, where shall we have preachers, is an odd kind of question.' So odd, in 1584, the year of William of Orange's assassination in Delft by a catholic fanatic, that Whitgift was certain to be opposed by powerful interests in both Court and country. Sir Francis Knollys, for one, was aghast to see 'the course of popish treason to be neglected' and zealous preachers, 'the most diligent barkers against the popish wolf', persecuted and put to silence, 'as though there were no enemies to her Majesty and to the state but they.' In early December, a Cambridge man used Paul's Cross for a forthright attack on 'the manner of proceeding against the ministers', and got away with it. On the other hand, courtiers and officials found in the Lenten sermons delivered at Court a few months later a sinister attempt to turn the mind of the queen against the preachers, one observer remarking on the 'travail bestowed to persuade her Majesty and the world that there was and is a great schism in the Church, when at no time in her Majesty's reign it hath been in greater peace, disturbance growing by the papists excepted.'[7]

The presbyterians would be quick to inform the indignant public that those who refused subscription did so not for 'trifles and things of no weight, as of variable ceremonies' but for 'matters of no small importance, even of the great and weighty cause of Christ's kingdom, by what laws and offices his heritage is to be governed and protected: that is, of the whole discipline of the Church of Christ.' A Leicestershire minister wrote that the archbishop's articles raised the question 'whether that form of discipline which in the primitive Church was established ought to be restored ... or that an abstract of popery will serve the turn.' The bishops were told to 'lay aside all pretence of the gospel, and of the peace of the Church, and say plainly, we fight for our own estate.' Whitgift enabled the extremists to represent all resistance to his articles as opposition to episcopal government, and furnished new ground for the claim that episcopacy was clean contrary to the gospel and to the safety of queen and Commonwealth. For this reason, while moderate opinion was shocked and grieved by the threat of subscription, the militant presbyterians accepted the challenge almost with relish. The one reaction is represented by Josias Nichols, a distinguished Kentish preacher who later remembered 'the woeful year of subscription' which had terminated the 'golden time' of Grindal's rule; the other by John Field for whom the golden time was 'this unhappy time of looseness and liberty', and who was stirred to new vitality by Whitgift's onslaught. 'The peace of the Church is at an end if he be not curbed. You are wise to consider by advice and by joining together now to strengthen your hands in this work. The Lord direct both you and us that we may fight a good fight and finish with joy. Amen.'[8]

Yet Field and his kind had as much to lose as the archbishop, if not more. To subscribe to the Prayer Book and the Articles was to acknowledge that the Church of England had no fundamental faults which could justify the pursuit of a divergent policy by any of its members, or the organization of a sectarian faction within the Church. Every puritan preacher would have to make a clear choice between the ideals of the nascent puritan movement and obedience to the society from which he derived his livelihood and in which he could alone hope to exercise a national prophetic ministry. If a majority of those who at first refused subscription later gave way, it would confirm Whitgift's jibe that the puritans were an insignificant coterie motivated by the natural rebelliousness of youth and far outnumbered by mature, conformable clergy. The pressure to conform would be felt especially by the beneficed family men who depended not on salaries, gifts and subscriptions such as sustained Field and the other 'doctors', but upon livings which would be sequestered or even, in the last resort, taken away. Past experience would tend to show that of any group of suspended nonconformists, only a few would resist beyond the point of deprivation, and this both Field and Whitgift must have known. The victory over the bishops, if it was to be a victory, would have to be won speedily, in not much more than six months. But such was the isolation of Whitgift in the first half of 1584 that his repudiation was a distinct possibility. A tense struggle now developed, triangular rather than two-sided: the moderate puritan parsons and vicars under contrary pressures from their ordinaries on the one hand and from the militant leadership of their own party on the other.

2 The First Round

PHILODOXOS [a Lawyer] Can yee exhort us unto concorde, and your selves at variance?

ORTHODOXOS [a Divine] You speak of that which was never seene in this world, nor never shall. For so long as God hath faithfull messengers, so long will also the Devill have his ungodly instrumentes ... Which part shall condescend unto the other? Which part shall yeeld? Shall those that holde the truthe give over? That is abhominable to bee spoken of and shall never be.

(*A dialogue concerning the strife of our Church*, 1584, p. 131)

THE FIRST DIOCESE to experience a general demand for subscription was Chichester, where Whitgift exercised his metropolitan jurisdiction during the vacancy of the see. Proceedings began in late November 1583 and revealed that, while the great majority of the clergy were prepared to comply 'without much ado', there were some twenty-four ministers who were willing to subscribe only with reservations. After canonical admonition, they were suspended. Early in December, eight of their number travelled to London and a delegation of three appeared at Lambeth. Whitgift was relieved to find that their scruples were not of a serious order and remarked: 'You seem to be sober and discreet men.' With these civilities, the battle was joined.

On the following day, all eight returned to find the archbishop 'in a fair chamber, matted', assisted by Aylmer, Piers of Salisbury, Young of Rochester, and Gabriel Goodman, dean of Westminster, his closest supporters among the higher clergy. In spite of 'a good fire of coals' their reception was less cordial, for Whitgift had been informed of a report 'all the city over' that upon the complaint of the Sussex ministers he should be sent for to the Court and ordered not to proceed with his articles. Although Aylmer assured him that he would soon learn to discount such rumours, Whitgift was determined to justify himself, informing the company that he had indeed been sent for to the Court five days before, but not for that matter, 'and I was used there of her Majesty and their honours better than I deserved, and to the end you may understand it the better, you shall hear Council's letter to me,' adding 'I mean to perform this that I have taken in hand to the uttermost.' The Sussex ministers were now allowed to subscribe conditionally, excepting from their subscription certain doubtful points. According to Whitgift, this was not to say that they had subscribed 'with protestation', which he had already told them he would not allow. Yet after their leader had been to the Court to meet 'a very honourable personage', this was how the archbishop heard their subscription described, and that it was 'very ill taken'. Small wonder that when the Sussex ministers called for their preaching licences two days later they found Whitgift angry, and that he hardened his heart against all subsequent nonconformist delegations.[1]

In interviewing the Sussex ministers, Whitgift remarked on the variety of their scruples, 'and some such indeed as I never heard of before. And if we call other out of Norfolk, they will as many doubts, and not these. And if we have as many out of Northamptonshire, they will other, and such as differ from both these.' As the archbishop rightly guessed, the various forms of answers to the articles with which the puritan ministers appeared before their ordinaries were drawn up county by county. A Leicestershire puritan addressing a former friend of the cause with connections in three Midland shires reminded him that 'among yourselves hath been consultation not a day or two ... neither are resolved of subscription.' No one was more aware than the puritan ministers themselves of the unfortunate impression which a variety of uncoordinated answers would convey. Chapman of Dedham complained that through 'too much strangeness' they were 'distracted into a miserable variety of answers to these articles, which I fear one day will be cast as dung upon our faces.' There was a busy circulation of arguments against subscription and of forms of limited subscription which could be offered with a clear conscience. The Dedham conference collected formulae of this kind from Cambridge, Sussex, Leicestershire, Devon, Norfolk and Suffolk, and Field's central 'register' contains over twenty such documents.[2]

But the crisis which Whitgift had engineered called for more than this: only a national conference could create the common front which would impress Authority and public opinion with the gravity of the puritan cause. 'Such a holy meeting is longed for of many,' Chapman told Field, and in the Dedham conference he moved that 'the bishops' proceeding did admonish the ministers to have a general meeting to confer what might be done.' 'It was thought good everyone should stir up his friend to consider of it.' But this was in April and it was not until the end of August – Bartholomew Fair time – that a general conference was held in

London. To this extent Whitgift's offensive had found the movement unprepared. In the absence of a conference, 'the church in London' assumed the privilege of dictating its own intransigent policy to the country conferences. Field was presumably in correspondence with the leaders in many counties. Besides, a stream of delegations was now converging on the capital from all parts of the province, ministers waiting upon the archbishop, the High Commission or the Privy Council. They would all make contact with the godly ministers in the city, with what effect the bishops suspected even as early as the interview with the Sussex delegation in December. 'It seemeth they have been with some in London since they went hence,' remarked Bishop Young, when the ministers hesitated to confirm their limited subscription; 'if I were as you, I would not care with how few such I were acquainted.'[3]

The battle for the souls of the moderate puritan ministry had now begun. The beneficed clergy were for the most part concerned to come to some sort of agreement with the bishops which would enable them to continue in their livings, unmolested and without injury to conscience. If they, like the Sussex ministers, were permitted to subscribe while noting their objections to details of the liturgy, nothing would please them better. But such an accommodation was the last thing desired by the London conference, and by a sprinkling of extremists elsewhere. Their view was that for the ministers to ask for terms by minimizing their objections to the formularies was to invite disaster. There could be no reconciliation between the godly defenders of the truth and their persecutors, no end to the struggle but the defeat of the Antichristian bishops. Reporting the subscription of the Sussex ministers, a correspondent of Nathaniel Bacon commented: 'This their manner of subscription is diversely judged of ... It may be there is sought to set some variance amongst them. But I hope they will be wary.'[4] A few days before this letter was written, John Field had seen the danger and had drawn up his own assessment of the expediency of subscription. Burghley filed a copy of his statement on the very day that the Sussex ministers had their last interview with Whitgift.

While Field drew up a list of specific errors in the Prayer Book, he based his case not so much on these as on 'the inconveniences which the use of it in general doth necessarily import', which he found 'intolerable'. The Prayer Book condoned a bare reading ministry; indeed its detailed rubrics seemed designed for 'a young babe or ignorant sot' rather than a man of learning. By its length alone the liturgy left neither time nor inclination for preaching, and on that subject Field professed to discover a 'deep silence' throughout the whole Book. He might have said that the ethos of the Prayer Book, the religion of the collects and responses, was foreign to the dynamism of reformed religion. Besides, subscription to the Prayer Book involved approbation of the Ordinal, 'wherein in a manner the whole discipline of the Church is perverted and overthrown.' Therefore those who considered 'only some particular faults in the Book' were advised of the perils of allowing it, 'though it were permitted of them to take exception against all the several faults and wants that be in it.' Might they not as well and better subscribe to Aesop's fables? 'Therefore we desire the bishops to take heed whereunto they urge us; the magistrates to resist them, that they do not urge us; the people to consider that we have cause to refuse, and admonish our fellow-ministers to beware of subscription.'[5]

Meanwhile, subscription was pressed in every diocese of Whitgift's province and provoked some bitter recriminations. On December 28th a Warwickshire minister told Burghley: 'Would to God your Honours knew the mutiny I hear of those articles tolerated by your lordships.' On the same day subscription was demanded in the diocese of Norwich. The ministers of Norfolk and Suffolk conferred separately and each sent to Bishop Freke their own schedules of those doubtful points which restrained them from subscribing. The bishop's replies failed to satisfy, and in January some sixty ministers in each county were suspended. In the same month, the ministers of Kent were called to subscribe, and were told that those who refused 'impugned the queen's laws.' Eventually, seventeen were suspended. In the diocese of Lincoln, the non-subscribers presented Bishop Cooper with a list of their doubts. Cooper described these as 'of no weight, but rather captious and uncharitable', but he replied with a 'satisfaction' for the sake of conformable men with genuine scruples. This document was not well received, at least by the more extreme spirits, for one surviving copy bears hostile annotations. In Lincolnshire some twenty-three ministers were suspended. In the archdeaconry of Buckingham there may have been as many as thirty who delayed subscription. In Leicestershire, something of a special case because of the great influence of the Hastings family, there was a general delay in subscribing with time granted for consideration; over three hundred were later recorded as making a limited subscription, which suggests a kind of moderate puritan front. In the archdeaconry of Huntingdon there were five non-subscribers, and these included Thomas Wilcox, who was now serving as a curate at Bovingdon in Hertfordshire.[6]

In the diocese of London things proceeded at an irregular pace: some

London ministers were offering limited subscription in mid-February, but Thomas Barber, preacher at St Mary le Bow, was not suspended until June, while Field, as lecturer at Aldermary, remained unmolested until March of the following year, 1585. In Essex, the Dedham ministers ruled in early March that 'if any of the brethren were called to subscribe, to require time to deliberate.' Elsewhere in the county suspensions took effect in the late spring. At least forty-three Essex ministers were eventually suspended. At first no non-subscribers were reported from the arch-deaconry of St Albans, but in October it was impossible to find a preacher in the Buckinghamshire parishes of the jurisdiction who was altogether free of suspension.[7] In the vacant diocese of Ely, eleven ministers were suspended. In the diocese of Peterborough (Northamptonshire), forty-five refused subscription. Evidence for the remaining areas is patchy, failing a search of the diocesan and archdeaconry records. Warwickshire probably had a considerable number of non-subscribers, other counties a sprinkling. There were four in Surrey. By June, when many had already yielded, the diocese of Oxford had two ministers who still resisted, Salisbury seven and Exeter three. In all there must have been between three and four hundred ministers who refused an immediate and unqualified subscription, the special case of Leicestershire aside. The bulk of these, as we should expect, were in East Anglia, the east Midlands, the Home Counties, London, and the Kent and Sussex Weald. In the northern province the puritans rejoiced that 'the bishop of Canterbury hath not as yet (God be thanked) stung us with his articles.'[8]

We should not underestimate the significance of the three or four hundred. The human tendency was to conform, and one gathers that many who subscribed had been expected to offer some resistance. In an analogous situation in Scotland shortly afterwards, an even smaller pro-portion of the ministry stood by the presbyterian system which had promised to become the established government of that Church. More-over, as the puritans never tired of pointing out, the only valid comparison was between the numbers of comparatively learned, preaching non-subscribers and conformable clergy of the same quality. As for the unlearned, one puritan told his conformist friend: 'my hat for your cap they will be on your side.'[9] Yet if an informed conscience impelled those who refused subscription, Whitgift was well aware that the opposition with which he was faced was not spontaneous dissent. Moral pressure was being applied by those who were just as intolerant of indiscipline and individualism as the archbishop himself.

As the ministers in county after county were suspended or threatened with suspension, they followed the trail of the Sussex ministers to London. In January, the Norfolk ministers appealed against their diocesan to the archbishop; the Suffolk group, with more realism, addressed themselves directly to the Privy Council and Burghley; while seventeen Kentish ministers, under threat of suspension, descended upon Whitgift without warning. 'They came to me unsent for, in a multitude,' the archbishop complained to the Council, 'which I reproved, because it imported a conspiracy and had the show of a tumult or unlawful assembly. This disordered flocking together of them at this time from divers places and gadding from one to another argueth a conspiracy amongst them and some hope of encouragement and of prevailing, which I am persuaded is not meant, nor shall by me willingly be consented unto.' He was angered by a report from Kent that the respectful humility which the ministers displayed in his presence was in contrast to their derision of his proceedings in their 'conventicles' at home. He now displayed the worst side of his character: a testy, schoolmasterly impatience which was always swift to dismiss his opponents as rebellious and captious youths who deserved the good hiding they would have got at Trinity. He told the Kentish delegation that 'none hath impugned the Book but boys, babes, princocks, unlearned sots' and he shouted down one of those who presumed to correct him with 'Thou boy, beardless boy, yesterday bird, new out of shell.' Other characteristic outbursts were carefully 'registered' by his victims: 'By my troth, Mr Fenner, you are as bad as the worst ... Can you tell me, I was a preacher before some of you were born ... If they enter into the ministry again and subscribe not, I will be hanged at Tyburn.' Robert Beale's sour comment on this kind of display was: 'It is an easy thing to govern and reduce babes in colleges and perhaps some in universities to their opinions. But it is an unfit and undiscreet thing either to have the same opinion, or to attempt the same in the whole realm, without better matter than I can hitherto see.'

It was by now clear that Whitgift intended to make no more concessions. To the Norfolk ministers he explained that as an oath in a court of law must be taken in the sense that it is proffered and not according to the private meaning of the party taking it, so subscription was required 'in that meaning which those that be in authority ... do set down, and not in that sense which everyone shall imagine.' The right which the Prayer Book allowed to seek resolution of doubts from their ecclesiastical superiors was equally a duty to have one's doubts resolved 'obediently'. Whitgift's system had little room for the liberty of the Christian man which Luther's pristine protestantism had asserted. No more, of course, had Field's.[10]

The Kentish ministers now appealed to the Privy Council, where their approach coincided with that of the Suffolk delegation. As early as December 1583 their lordships had implied where their sympathies lay when they commended to Whitgift's attention certain additional articles which dealt with recusancy and the kind of abuses in church government of which the puritans habitually complained; these were no doubt designed to redress the balance of the original schedule. Reluctant to act officially on the ministers' behalf as a body, individual councillors at that time advised the non-subscribers to 'sue particularly to them', so that Nathaniel Bacon in Norfolk was assured that Whitgift's cause would fail and his credit grow 'not one whit'. Now, in early February, the Council board was depleted by the illness of Burghley (gout) and Walsingham and Leicester (agues). Robert Beale, clerk of the Council, filled Walsingham's place as principal secretary, and under his influence the puritans were favourably received. Later Beale was forced to apologize for being 'overbold in speaking in Council' and for casting out heated words about 'papists, God's and her Majesty's mortal enemies'. The Council not only undertook to forward the petition of the Kentish ministers to the archbishop, but to 'require' that they should be handled with moderation and only suspended or deprived after due conviction, according to law and 'with conscionable favour'. Beale was appointed to carry both the Kent and Suffolk petitions to Lambeth on Sunday, February 2nd, and to require Whitgift's attendance before the Council on the following Sunday.

It was an acrimonious encounter. The archbishop 'entered his common and wonted place of boying' the ministers, while Beale insisted that weighty matters of learning and divinity were involved which he took to be insufficiently answered. The quarrel continued at a dinner-table at Court, in the presence of the earls of Sussex and Hertford, Lord Zouche and Bishop Aylmer. Aylmer, Beale's especial *bête noire*, reminded Whitgift that Beale was once his scholar and that he 'wished that he had as much power to beat him as ever he had.' Whitgift, with more restraint, accepted Beale's offer to memorialize him on the whole matter. The result, Beale's 'Book to the Archbishop', which reached him in early March, was the weightiest of all attempts to challenge the legality and propriety of his proceedings. Among its more ingenious if preposterous arguments was one already employed by catholic apologists: the Prayer Book to which subscription was urged was not in fact the book authorized by the Act of Uniformity, since it contained more than the three stipulated alterations to the Book of 1552. No answer was forthcoming from Whitgift, who in any case had never seen the second Edwardine Book.[11]

Two days after Beale's visit, Whitgift rebuked the Council for their encouragement of the ministers, especially since the queen 'in express words' had committed ecclesiastical causes to him. These were the words of resurgent clericalism, with which Whitgift would win a seat on the Council within three years; they were to reach their apogee with Laud, half a century later. 'It is not for me to sit in this place, if any curate in my diocese or province may be permitted so to use me.' The number of the non-subscribers was not great, and even in the diocese of Norwich they were far outnumbered by the obedient and quietly disposed. He begged their Honours not to call his doings in question and above all not to impair his credit by a summons to appear before them.[12]

But this was only the beginning of Whitgift's troubles. The Council was now bombarded with petitions: from twenty Norfolk ministers 'in danger of deprivation', from twenty-one Lincolnshire ministers, from seven Cambridgeshire ministers, from twenty-seven in the south and centre of Essex and from six in the north of that county (five of them members of the Dedham conference), and from 'the ministers of Oxfordshire'. Burghley received a supplication from two Midland ministers in the name of forty-five of their brethren in the diocese of Peterborough, and a perplexed letter from Archdeacon Withers of Colchester, the reformed radical of the 'sixties who had the Dedham ministers in his care, and who was forced to write in their favour: 'the importunity of some of my brethren suffering no repulse, nor taking any nay.'[13]

Nor did the petitions come only from clergy. There were perhaps many appeals of the type which arrived from 'the inhabitants within the town of Maldon and other places near-adjoining in Essex' which deplored the removal of 'good and faithful servants of God' for 'not subscribing to certain articles, neither confirmed by the law of God nor of this land.' There was nothing spontaneous about such petitions as we know from the Dedham minutes, where William Tay moved 'whether the churches should not join in supplication with others, being a duty to sue for their pastors being faithful and they deprived of them.' 'Means were made,' we read in the extremist account of the struggle, *The unlawful practises of prelates*, 'these things gentlemen of all sorts took to heart.' If the 'means' were even in a few cases comparable with the efforts made by the bailiffs of Colchester to regain their preacher, George Northey, the total effect must have been impressive. The agitation on Northey's behalf involved the town's patron, Sir Thomas Heneage; the town clerk and a prominent puritan lawyer, James Morice; their old preacher, William Cole, now head of an Oxford college; the earls of Leicester and Warwick; and Sir Francis Walsingham, 'pressing the hearing thereof at the Council table.' Sir Thomas Scot, one of the leading gentlemen of Kent, addressed Burghley on behalf of the Kentish ministers in the name of 'divers of my neighbours', and the Council received similar petitions from seven gentlemen of Cambridgeshire, and from five of the leading Norfolk justices, including Nathaniel Bacon and William Heydon. Nicholas Faunt had news to report to Nathaniel's half-brother Anthony of his formidable mother, Lady Ann Bacon, Burghley's sister-in-law. Lady Bacon was not often seen at Court, but recently she had displayed an 'earnest care and travail' for the preachers, 'resorting often unto this place to solicit those causes.' The tone of Lady Bacon's representations is perhaps reflected in Faunt's own bitter outburst to her son: 'And can there be any more evident token of the miserable calamity approaching, than to see the true teachers and pastors thus turmoiled by those especially that would seem to be the pillars of the Church, who, having the mark of the Beast, it is impossible that they should know the necessity of that sweet food of the gospel.'[14]

Whitgift's policies were undermined in quite a different way by the reasoned answers to his articles and other memorials which emerged from a number of the most respected of protestant scholars, lay and clerical, some of which seem to have become public property. Beale's 'Book' aside, the subscription campaign was scrutinized by Thomas Norton, the great 'parliament man' and translator of Calvin, by John Foxe, the martyrologist – in a letter of some five thousand words! – by Dr John Hammond, a distinguished civilian, and by a leading Cambridge divine, Dr Robert Some. While varying in their estimation of Whitgift's person and actions, all agreed that an unfortunate time had been chosen to attempt something unattainable and unnecessary. Foxe was the most benign of these critics, assuring Whitgift that no one else could safely occupy his seat, and betraying hardly an ounce of sympathy for what he called 'thoughtless youths' and 'restless innovators'. But even he saw grave danger and no profit in a rigorous inquiry by subscription. 'While we are disputing among ourselves, the Roman hawk is hovering around.' Norton thought it 'very hard' to make a public quarrel out of matters of conscience which many preachers were content to conceal. Whitgift should rather 'reward their peaceable silence with a gentle toleration.' Hammond's opinion was that 'such a uniformity ... as shall be void of difference of opinion never yet was, nor never shall be found, but only in ignorance.' It says much for Whitgift's obstinacy that for several months he shut his ears to this advice.[15]

There was a trace of unsteadiness, however. On April 24th he sent the queen a collection of the principal arguments deployed by the non-subscribers, with his answers, 'the rather because I understand that the said objections are given abroad into the hands of many, even of your Majesty's Court.' In a somewhat strident letter he assured Elizabeth that 'in this my endeavouring to reduce them to unity and obedience, I have not sought myself, but the peace and quietness of the Church, the maintenance of the laws and orders established by authority, and the satisfying of my own duty to God and to your Majesty.'[16]

A few days later Robert Beale called at Lambeth, ostensibly to recover his treatise with which he had visited the archbishop in March. An angry interview ensued. 'He fell into very great passion with me,' Whitgift complained to Burghley, 'which I think was the end of his coming.' Beale for his part protested that he had never heard such words as he received from Whitgift, although he had spoken with many at home and abroad 'far greater personages than his Lordship is.' (They included the Scottish queen, but this is revealing evidence of the social estimation of an Elizabethan primate.) Beale followed up this bitter exchange with an offensive letter and then left on a mission to Mary Stuart. In his absence Whitgift implored Burghley not to forget the letter, which touched his credit so close that he could not ignore it. 'The man also is so insolent that he glorieth in them even as he did in his intemperate speeches which he used to me in the Council chamber at the Court, and in my own house. Bearing with him doth puff him up.' On his return, on July 1st, Burghley asked for an explanation.[17]

The climax was reached on May 8th with the appearance at Lambeth of twenty-five Kentish gentlemen. All but four had subscribed a petition bearing no less than thirty-eight names which they had exhibited to the Privy Council on the previous day. The delegation was led by Sir Thomas Scot, who came closest to being the leading magnate in this shire which teemed with gentry but lacked any single head. It included prominent government servants and parliament men such as Thomas Randolph and Nicholas Saintleger and members of ancient Kentish families, Woottons, Derings and Finches. Among them were the two brothers of Edward Dering, the famous preacher who had died eight years before, Thomas Wootton, his patron, and Henry Killigrew, whose wife had leant so heavily on Dering's spiritual counsel. Here was the fruit of the puritan cultivation of the country gentlemen and their wives.

No episode more strikingly illustrates the contempt which the Elizabethan governing classes entertained for prelates. When in the course of
discussion Whitgift defended baptism by midwives, which was offensive
to puritans, 'divers of them muttered much', and Nicholas Saintleger
burst out with 'God forgive you.' Thomas Wootton told him that he had
seen six archbishops and that Whitgift was the first to set himself against
the gentry. A modern historian of Kent has written of the religious and
organic sense of community which characterized the society of the
county, and of how Archbishop Laud in a later generation offended these
values and appeared as 'an intruder into the family of Kent'. One senses
the same situation in this interview of May 1584. Yet the historian may be
as surprised as the archbishop seems to have been at the strength of the
gentlemen's feelings, for, as Whitgift pointed out, it was hard to credit
their claim that they lacked preaching when there were eighty or even a
hundred preachers in the diocese of Canterbury of whom only ten were
still silenced. One can only suppose that a mere handful of the licensed
preachers of the dioceses were acceptable to the puritan gentry, or that the
gentlemen were glad of any excuse to vent their anticlerical prejudice at
the archbishop's expense. All departed angry, promising to seek redress
from the queen and Council, except for Sir Thomas Scot, who was
impressed with the strength of the archbishop's case.[18]

The next day Whitgift confided in Sir Christopher Hatton, perhaps the
only courtier on whom he could depend. If these few preachers 'being of
none account either for years, learning or degree' were countenanced
against the law, against the conformable preachers and against himself, he
could do no more good in Canterbury or anywhere else. He assured
Hatton that 'unless such contentious persons were some way animated and
backed, they would not stand out as they do.' A few days earlier he had
frankly charged Beale with being one of those who were doing the
animating and the backing, by assuring the ministers that the articles
would be 'stopped'. This, he claimed, was 'spread abroad in every place
and is the only cause why many forbear to subscribe, which is true, neither
could he deny it.' But deny it, of course, Beale did, with righteous
vehemence.[19]

In early June, Whitgift was sent more tangible evidence of the pressures
which lay behind the agitation of the past three months. The archdeacon
of Lincoln reported that he had given the Lincolnshire ministers until the
end of May to subscribe, by which date he must certify their nonconformity to Whitgift. 'They answered that they would to London again
to renew their suit, and so departed.' On their return they recommenced

259

preaching and ministering in their own parishes and claimed the authority of their old bishop for so doing. (Bishop Cooper had departed for Winchester, and Lincoln, like so many dioceses in these troubled months, was now directly subject to its metropolitan.) The ministers were triumphant at the expense of the subscribers and were displaying to these lapsed brethren copies of a letter from Field. This exhorted them 'to stand stoutly to the cause, affirming the same not to be theirs but the Lord's' and asserted that those who had subscribed had 'made a breach (as I am informed he termeth it)', that they would never do good thereafter and that they were 'branded men'. The letter was closely guarded; although the puritans had numerous copies and showed them to their fellow-ministers, 'yet they will not part with any copy but to such as are of that side.' But Whitgift was told that if he were to tackle a certain John Huddlestone, vicar of Saxby, who was even then before the High Commissioners, he might track down the original letter, for he was supposed to have been the recipient. Field probably wrote in similar terms to every county where he had his correspondents. 'Weaklings, led by the masters of that faction' was a Lichfield prebendary's estimation of the remaining non-subscribers.[20]

Field's Lincolnshire letter can serve to lead us back into the organized puritan movement to view the subscription struggle from within.

If not weakening, the puritan conferences were perplexed and, if the Dedham papers are any guide, they felt the need to lean on others wiser than themselves. In April and again in May there were motions for 'a general meeting of learned brethren ... for better advice and consent about the cause of subscriptions.' London responded to this mood, if it did not inspire it, and on June 1st the Dedham brethren delegated Laurence Newman of Coggeshall (who lived closest to London) to 'understand the brethren's mind and certify us of it.' But London's mind seems to have been shared by only a few of the Dedham ministers and rejected by the majority. It can be deduced from London's proposal that they should communicate to the queen not only the reasons why subscription was refused but also 'a full draught of the discipline we desire'. On the other hand it seems to have been the Dedham brethren who wanted to discuss the more practical problem of what was to be done if the bishops gave them no relief: 'What charge they have from God of the Church, how far they may yield to cease for their preaching, and what duty is to be done by them in such a case.'[21]

The divergence of opinion which was possible even within one conference is strikingly illustrated from the Dedham papers. Among the moderates was Edmund Chapman, who wrote to Cartwright of the 'miserable distraction that is between the preachers and professors of our English Church for matter of ecclesiastical government' and confessed to 'some dislike of both parties for their hot and violent manner of proceeding, either seeking by all means to conquer and deface the other, not duly regarding the holy communion they have in their head, Christ Jesus, and among themselves, being fellow members of Him.' 'I know the truth is precious', he went on, 'and must be maintained and stood for, and put forward as far as any way is made open for it.' But might not 'a more mild and brotherly course' on their part better commend their good cause, so removing 'that huge block of our too open and bitter dissension' and with it not only hard feelings, speeches and actions but 'a great deal of sin?'[22] The appeasers were answered by fanatics like William Tay of Peldon[23] who spoke wildly of 'Antichrist tyrannizing the Church by our bishops, magnified and exalted above measure,' and demanded with a voice ripe for separatism, 'are these things yet to be tolerated?' Tay reminded his brethren of the Apostle Jude's condemnation of 'certain men crept in unawares ... filthy dreamers', who 'despise dominion and speak evil of dignities.' Their representatives in Elizabethan England were not, as one might suppose, the nonconformists, but the bishops, for 'dominion' signified the presbyterian church discipline and 'dignities' the presbytery. 'The truth of these points being searched and found out, the Lord give us courage and fortitude to stand in the truth and to quit ourselves like valiant men in the Lord His cause.'[24]

In August, Chapman proposed 'that a reconciliation should be offered to the bishops, that since we profess one God and preach one doctrine we may join together with better consent to build up the Church.' This was rejected by the majority, 'lest we should seem to yield in our cause, and sought to be of their company.' Meanwhile Tay had proposed that the silenced ministers should ignore the ban and continue preaching. The conference was doubtful and ruled that those who shared his opinion 'should bring in their reasons.' Tay's reasons included not only the condemnation of episcopacy ('the bishop's authority is Antichristian, *ergo* not to be obeyed') but the repudiation of all human government, a glimpse of the yawning, anabaptist gulf which their controversies occasionally uncovered: 'If it be lawful to keep silence at the bishop's inhibition, the strength and stability of the Church should depend upon a man. But that is intolerable, *ergo*, not lawful to be silent ... All authority over the Church either in placing or displacing ministers is given to Christ ... *ergo*, where Christ doth place, man ought not to displace.' A moderate opponent argued in reply that although the bishops' place, calling and authority were not all that they should be 'by the word', yet they were not wholly devoid of dignity and in the absence of any other established discipline 'ministers must take it as the voice of God and his authority.' Godly discipline was not an 'essential note' of the Church, for the true Church might exist without it, 'though indeed a maimed Church, sick and languishing'. Since the Church enjoyed only episcopal discipline, the ministers must labour on, 'bearing so much as with a good conscience we may.' The only alternative, and that, by implication, an impractical one, was to renounce the episcopally ordained ministry and 'erect discipline'.[25]

This was not courageous advice, but it was the philosophy by which puritan religion would survive within the Church of England for half a century to come. One sees what contrary tendencies were contained in tension within the Elizabethan puritan movement. The moderate spokesman is referred to in the minutes as 'another brother', but the spiritual grandchildren of these two contestants would find themselves in opposed armies and their great-grandchildren on either side of the great divide separating the established Church from Dissent.

3 The Second Round

Some puritan ministers were now ready for an honourable reconciliation with the bishops; others were on the point of repudiating their government altogether. The risk of a serious rift was acute in the summer of 1584, when in most dioceses terms were offered which enabled the moderates to resume their ministries with a quiet conscience. Such a settlement had been made at the beginning, with the Sussex delegation. Two months later fifteen of the more moderate London ministers offered a conditional subscription of the same kind, which Field had already declared to be 'naught'. A cynic would later characterize their kind as the 'demi-pure', who obeyed in part to please all, subscribed 'conditionally and agreeable to the word', and were protestant with the protestants 'to keep their livings', and with the puritans 'all peevish and precise'. We do not know whether their offer was accepted.[1]

On June 24th, Whitgift could still certify forty-nine 'recusants' in his province, without taking into account the puritan strongholds of East Anglia, Essex, Northamptonshire, Warwickshire and London.[2] But soon after this, the majority seem to have yielded to the various forms of accommodation now offered. This followed a deliberate change in Whitgift's policy. According to an extremist account of these events, *The unlawful practises of prelates*, it was after 'her Majestie's most honourable Council dealt very feelingly in the cause' that subscription began to be 'somewhat more tolerable'. Further time was granted in many counties, and eventually Whitgift 'suffered himself to be entreated' to require no more of many ministers than full subscription to the first and third articles, and a protestation to use the Book of Common Prayer and none other. 'To this many were drawn.' Whitgift's correspondence reveals that it was Walsingham and Burghley who commended this compromise to the archbishop. On a visit to Lambeth in early June, Walsingham promised Whitgift that from henceforth he would support his proceedings against the more turbulent nonconformists, while Whitgift in return promised not to deprive or suspend any minister 'for not subscribing only', provided that he undertook in writing to observe the Prayer Book and the orders of the Church. In future subscription would be required only of those who were about to be ordained or admitted to livings. 'Wherein I find myself something eased of my former troubles.' Burghley later reminded Whitgift of a similar promise, 'to deal only with such as violated order.'[3]

Some favoured preachers with patrons were restored unconditionally, among them the diarist Richard Rogers, lecturer of Wethersfield in Essex, who had heard Whitgift declare 'that none of us should preach without conformity and subscription; I thank God, I have seen him eat his words, as great and as peremptory as he was.' This was thanks to Sir Robert Wroth, who told him to preach 'and he would bear me out.' According to *The unlawful practises of prelates* 'some other special men' were relieved without any subscription at all: those whose authority would have discredited their 'too too severe proceedings'. More commonly the ministers made some kind of conditional or limited subscription, or a subscription with the protestation of 'a holy and godly resolution' in certain points by the archbishop or other bishops.[4]

The Leicestershire ministers signed such a formula, which included an undertaking to use the Prayer Book 'and none other'. They desired reform of certain ceremonies and had notified their objections to the bishop, who 'godly and mildly returned his answer therein.' 'Whereby we are more willingly moved to this subscription, and do promise still to receive the same book and none other, to administer the holy sacraments and to use the prayers therein contained, and to maintain peace in the Church of Christ.' There follows a remarkable protestation, defining the terms in which they were prepared to subscribe to the Ordinal and the corresponding thirty-sixth Article of Religion. The bishop had satisfied them that the Book 'alloweth not three distinct orders in the ministry, but that all are in the ministry of the word and sacraments *pares*, and that the distinction is in government political, to avoid division, and to maintain peace.' To this they were willing to put their names, and to promise 'so to deal as the peace of the Church by us shall not be troubled.' There could be no firmer repudiation of the principles and practices of extreme, presbyterian puritanism. This document is said to have been signed by more than three hundred, virtually the entire ministry of the shire, only Jeffery Johnson, the town preacher of Leicester, abstaining. If one wants a proof-text for the argument that Elizabethan puritanism is not to be equated with presbyterianism, this, surely, is it.[5]

Burghley communicated with the Kentish ministers through two of their gentlemen, Thomas Wootton Esq. and his son Edward, and instructed them to make their submission in similar terms, promising to use the Prayer Book and not to attack it in public, and to respect the peace of the Church. In Field's 'register' this formula is said to have been signed and tendered to Burghley not only by the Kentish ministers but by John Knewstub of Suffolk and John Oxenbridge of Warwickshire, perhaps in the name of other ministers in those counties. Rather less was conceded by fifteen ministers of north Essex, including four members of the Dedham conference. They asked that their subscription to the first article, of the royal supremacy, should be within the limits of the thirty-seventh Article of Religion, and to the third, of the Articles of Religion themselves, according to the letter and the spirit of the statute of 1571, that is, that it should be confined to matters of doctrine. As for subscription to the Prayer Book, this was politely refused. 'As we have been careful and still will be for the peace of the Church, both in ourselves and our people, so we humbly crave we may be tendered herein, not daring for conscience sake to subscribe thereto.' But by the end of the year most of the original non-subscribers could have said, with those who signed the Millenary Petition twenty years later, that they had 'in respect of the times, subscribed to the Book, some upon protestation, some upon exposition given them, some with condition, rather than the Church should have been deprived of their labour and ministry.'[6]

It is not easy to determine how many ministers were eventually deprived, but it seems probable that very few rejected the terms now offered. In Lincolnshire, none of the suspended ministers suffered deprivation; every member of the Dedham conference came to some sort of accommodation with authority, although many were in trouble two years later, in Aylmer's visitation of 1586. In Suffolk only the preacher whom Lord North had planted in Mildenhall, Thomas Settle, remained defiant. In June he was denouncing Whitgift as 'a very enemy to the Church and a tyrant and worse than ever Bonner was', and he was soon drifting into separatist company. At least one beneficed minister, George Gifford of Maldon, was deprived, but found it possible to stay on in the same town as a lecturer. It may be that a list in the puritan register of 'sufficient, diligent and godly preachers ... suspended from preaching, deprived of their livings and otherwise molested' represents a fairly complete record of those puritans who were never subsequently reconciled to a settled ministry within the establishment. Those whose troubles dated from 1584 included Dudley Fenner, a young Cambridge theologian of great promise, who as preacher at that Wealden stronghold of puritanism, Cranbrook, was 'suspended from preaching ever since the time of subscription.' Three other preachers, Lever Wood, Percival Wiburn and Edmund Rockeray, were deprived of benefices in the neighbouring diocese of Rochester, although in the case of Wiburn and Rockeray these livings were not parochial. The remaining names are those of Thomas Barber and John Field of London, a Mr Colset of Easton-on-the-Hill, Northamptonshire, and Thomas Settle of Mildenhall. There was no more long-term disturbance in the great subscription crisis than there had been in 1565–6 or 1573–4. But the intensified activity of individual diocesans and of the High Commissioners during the next six years ensured that the puritan ministry would rarely lack its local or individual crises which would provide constant fuel for reformist agitation.[7]

In allowing the release of the ministers on such easy terms, Whitgift was yielding unwillingly to pressure. He had no illusions about the value of the conditional subscription. He knew the legal casuistries in which the puritan was by now well schooled: how when he subscribed 'as far as the law requireth' he meant that the law required no such subscription; and that when he promised to use the Book of Common Prayer and none other he meant no more than that his services would consist of material selected from the Prayer Book. Yet by abandoning his general campaign against nonconformity, Whitgift was enabled to adopt a more flexible procedure which offered a real chance of breaking the power of puritanism as an organized force where that power lay, in the small minority of ultras.

The new weapon was an instrument of twenty-four articles, administered by the High Commissioners in virtue of the authority renewed to them in December 1583. The novelty of these articles has not always been appreciated; indeed they are often described as a reissue of Whitgift's earlier articles in the form of a questionnaire. In fact they are a largely original set of interrogatories, directed exclusively against puritanism. They were to be answered on the oath known as *ex officio mero*, which in effect required a man to incriminate himself, a civil law procedure already resisted by catholic recusants which was to arouse a storm of protest among the common lawyers. The first interrogatories obliged the examinate to confess the lawfulness of his ordination and to acknowledge the canonical obedience which he owed to his ordinary; to concede that by the Act of Uniformity all ministers were bound to use the Book of Common Prayer and no other; and that the queen, Lords and Commons had willed the archbishop, bishops and other ordinaries to enforce its observance. He was then charged with all the more usual nonconformist deviations from lawful procedure. Further interrogatories related to the activities of recent months. Thus in article twenty it was alleged that 'you at this present do continue all or some of your former opinions against the said Book,' and 'that you have used private conferences and assemblies or been present at conventicles for the maintenance of your doings herein, and for the animating and encouraging of others to continue in the like disposition in this behalf that you are of. Declare the like circumstances, and for what intent, cause and consideration.' Another article charged the examinate with having been required 'simply and absolutely to subscribe', which 'hitherto you have advisedly refused to perform and so do you persist.'[8]

The new procedure was employed selectively against those ministers now exposed as the most resolute nonconformists and the organizers of the resistance. On May 26th, Whitgift countered an approach from the Council in favour of seven Cambridgeshire ministers with the announcement that he proposed to dismiss them and proceed against them one by one in the High Commission 'in such manner and sort as I am well assured by the best learned in both the laws to be warrantable.' *Qui s'excuse, s'accuse.* This was as much as to admit that the *ex officio* procedure was already under fire. Three days later he replied to an appeal by Burghley on behalf of George Gifford of Maldon: 'It appeareth that the said Gifford is a ringleader of the rest, against whom also I have received certain complaints, to the answering whereof we mean to call him by virtue of the High Commission ... His deserts may be such as will deserve deprivation.' And deprived he was. Whitgift's commissary used the same word, 'ringleader', to describe Josias Nichols of Kent. In August, Robert Lewis of Colchester reported in the Dedham conference that the archbishop 'offered articles to some and an oath.' Colchester was the home of the puritan lawyer James Morice, who would later head the campaign in Parliament against this procedure, and it was perhaps from this source that the Dedham brethren were already informed that 'the judgment of the lawyers is that the oath offered by the bishops is not to be allowed.'[9]

Previously, the ringleaders had been dealt with in the same fashion as moderate and almost conformable men; not only had they benefited from the public outcry against this general onslaught on the whole godly ministry, but they had evaded inquiry into their own more subversive offences. Now the complaints of the Council and the country gentlemen were partly satisfied by allowing easy terms for the majority while the activities of the militant extremists were subjected to a more searching investigation. It is not difficult to imagine that Whitgift's new policy placed an intolerable strain on the solidarity of the puritan movement. The mass defection of the conditional subscribers enabled the apologists for the bishops to claim that the puritan ministry as a whole had 'allowed all' and retracted. Typical of this disturbing propaganda was the preface to a commentary on the Thirty-nine Articles published by Thomas Rogers, Hatton's chaplain. Rogers's book bore the splendid title of *The English Creede*, and its theme was the catholicity and harmony of the reformed English Church. Although he was forced to admit that some held back from subscribing the Prayer Book 'in every point', this apologist professed to believe that there were none 'that proudly contemn it, none that disdainfully despise it, none but in the fear of God and in public churches always and only do use it.' The offences for which some held back from subscription were 'for number but very few ... and remain for the most part in the directions and rubrics.' Yet Rogers lived in West Suffolk![10] This was what Field had feared from the beginning: the beneficed clergy had succumbed to the temptation to win their freedom by understating their case. The reformist cause was discredited because most of those supposed to maintain it had signed it away in their tortuous subscriptions.

Either Field or someone who writes in a similar style struck back at this kind of insinuation in the anonymous pamphlet, *The unlawful practises of prelates*,[11] a title which intentionally echoed the famous polemic of William Tyndale against Wolsey and the prelacy of his generation. Speaking darkly of a 'subtler hurt and privier sting' the tract claimed (as Whitgift might, with a different purpose) that subscriptions made with sundry exceptions were 'in a manner no subscriptions at all'. But by displaying the names of some celebrated preachers in one paper and concealing in another the protestations they had made, 'many were drawn also as unwary birds into the net, by the chirping of the birds first taken.' It was then put about that 'all things were well in the orders and liturgy of the Church of England, all things subscribed unto, that all had yielded, that whosoever mouths were open, they had subscribed.' On the contrary, the writer claimed, the popish corruptions of the Book were almost always excepted from the subscriptions. 'Alas, good men, how much their good desires and intents were abused ... Yet it is certain, many to this day hold out.' Four years later, another propagandist, John Udall, was confident that 'if it were to do again, hundreds of them would never do it, because they were subtly circumvented and deceived.' Since Whitgift knew that the subscriptions counted for very little, one wonders who was deceiving whom in 1584. But there is no doubt that the subscriptions gave the Church an appearance of specious solidarity in its imperfectly reformed state which could not have been more damaging to the cause of further reformation.[12]

The 'privy sting' was still further inflamed in December 1584, when the conference with their opponents which the puritans had repeatedly demanded[13] took place at Lambeth. It was a hasty affair, convened at the request of the earl of Leicester and held in his presence, assisted by Burghley, Walsingham and Lord Grey of Pirgo. For two days Walter Travers and Thomas Sparke (who would reappear nineteen years later at the Hampton Court conference) contended with Whitgift, Sandys and Cooper on certain controverted passages in the Prayer Book.[14] That a conference of this kind was held at all was a notable victory for the nonconformists and a tribute to the political support they commanded; as at Hampton Court in 1604, it gave recognition to their cause by the very fact that they could be effectively represented by delegates, and it appeared to put them on a level with the bishops. But the results were disappointing: the disputation was inconclusive for want of time, and in any case it avoided the larger issues. At the outset Travers and Sparke confined their *gravamina* to the readings from the Apocrypha prescribed in the lectionary and certain familiar abuses in the baptismal order. These two points were discussed for two days, and towards the end of the second day Travers deliberately evaded an attempt by Whitgift to lead him into the deeper waters of controversy surrounding the ministry and government of the Church. The radical objections of some puritans to the Prayer Book in its entirety were not discussed at all. This was not the last time that the reduction of puritanism to a number of specific grievances, each more or less trivial taken alone, would enable the opposition to claim that the puritan cause was frivolous. The same lamentable tactics, which owed nothing to the sure, revolutionary instincts of John Field, were to bring disaster at Hampton Court. After the Lambeth meeting, a rumour that the puritans had been utterly discredited was 'flown over the Thames' to Westminster, where Parliament was by then assembled. *The unlawful practises of prelates* was written to repair the damage.[15]

According to Whitgift, the 'honourable personages' who had presided at Lambeth were satisfied that he was in the right. His secretary and first biographer, Sir George Paule, confirms this, adding that they were surprised to find the puritan reasons 'so weak and trivial'. This, according to similar sources, was the reaction of James I at Hampton Court twenty years later, and it is probably not the whole truth. What is certain is that three months later Leicester launched a serious attack against Whitgift's policies in the House of Lords.[16] And the behaviour of the privy councillors and other courtiers in the months before the Lambeth conference makes it unlikely that they could have been so easily convinced. It is not easy to account for the energetic support which puritan preachers continued to receive in the later months of 1584, when only a tiny minority of extremists were still in trouble. Yet there is no denying the evidence of Whitgift's correspondence, which shows that in the second half of the year he was under almost as intense a bombardment as in the first.

The wide sympathy entertained for the remaining non-subscribers arose partly from the antipathy aroused by the *ex officio* procedure of the High Commissioners, especially among those whose education and experience were in the Common Law. Sir Francis Knollys in particular was conducting a private war against the judicial proceedings of the bishops which he believed placed them in danger of the large penalties of that vague and terrible offence, a *praemunire*, and he joined in formal disputation with Whitgift on this issue. On June 13th, 1584, Knollys told Burghley that he dared not continue his acrimonious correspondence with the archbishop without his encouragement. That he got it is suggested by his letter to Whitgift of a week later, which mounted a confident and fundamental assault against the alleged illegality of the bishops' and Commissioners' proceedings.[17]

On July 2nd Burghley himself sent Whitgift a letter which has become famous, in which he described coming 'by chance' upon the archbishop's new articles, which he described as 'of great length and curiosity, formed in a Romish style' and 'so curiously penned, so full of branches and circumstances, as I think the inquisitors of Spain use not so many questions to comprehend and trap their preys.' This much-quoted phrase was not entirely Burghley's own; it was lifted from a document which Robert Beale, the clerk of the Council, had submitted to him the day before: an answer 'concerning such things as have passed between the lord archbishop of Canterbury and him.' In this manifesto, Beale had complained to Burghley of the tendering of the *ex officio* oath which persuaded some 'through simplicity' to confess to things they had never done, 'which cunning dealing savoureth more of a Spanish inquisition than

Christian charity.' Burghley told Whitgift that he was constantly accused by privy councillors and other public persons of neglecting his duty in not restraining him. Hitherto he had been content to quote Whitgift's own statistical demonstration of the numerical insignificance of those ministers who still refused to subscribe. However, he again doubted the wisdom and even the justice of the archbishop's actions, after seeing a copy of the instrument of twenty-four articles as it had been administered to two ministers from Cambridgeshire. Evidently the twenty-four articles were no part of the archbishop's summer bargain with Burghley and Walsingham.[18]

The two ministers with whom Burghley was in touch, Thomas and Edward Braine, were now to provoke a serious disagreement between the archbishop and the lord treasurer. As the correspondence between them continued, Burghley told Whitgift that he thought his dealing with them was 'I will not say rigorous nor captious, but I think it is scarce charitable.' In reply Whitgift asked him if he preferred the friendship of two of the most disordered ministers in a whole diocese to his own. He had broken no promises. He had abandoned deprivation for not subscribing only, although it was fully justified in law, and this 'only to satisfy your lordship'. He had been forced to defend himself against such absurd charges as that he had taken this action in order to maintain his book against Cartwright, and that he had treated the two Braines with especial rigour merely because Burghley had spoken up for them. In September Burghley and Whitgift were contriving to co-operate in filling the vacant bishoprics, and the lord treasurer was expressing the hope that the Church would benefit from the new appointments; 'for sure your Grace must pardon me, I rather wish it than look or much hope for it.' He strongly advocated Walter Travers for the mastership of the Temple although he knew him to be the author of the presbyterian *Explicatio* and had been warned by Whitgift only three days before that he was an enemy of 'the present state and government'. And he continued to advocate 'the spirit of gentleness ... rather than severity', condemning the procedure by which 'certain simple men have been rather sought by inquisition to be found offenders than upon their facts condemned.'[19]

On September 20th, Burghley was joined by a majority of the Privy Council in complaining to Whitgift and Aylmer of irregularities committed against the godly ministers in Essex by the bishop's inferior officers, the chancellor, commissary and archdeacons, men 'whose offices are of more value and profit by such kind of proceedings.'[20] With their letter they forwarded the first of a series of surveys of the state of the ministry conducted by the puritans themselves, which were intended to give the lie to Whitgift's assertions of the strength of the conformable ministry and the insignificance of the non-subscribers.[21] The conclusion to be drawn from this Essex survey was that the puritans were the only learned and reliable clergy and that Whitgift's conformable preachers were for the most part idle or non-resident or immoral or unsound in religion. Besides being influenced by this survey, the Council seems to have studied a number of puritan documents detailing the 'disorders and corruptions' committed by the bishop of London and his officers in Essex, which are now filed among Beale's papers in the Yelverton collection of MSS. in the British Museum. All through the summer Sir Christopher Hatton had proved himself the archbishop's only constant friend at Court, but on this occasion even he added his signature. It was a foretaste of the onslaught which the bishops were to face two months later when Parliament met.[22]

But although only the most perceptive of observers could have known this, the great crisis was by now already over. If three or four hundred ministers had been still under suspension and threat of deprivation when Parliament assembled in November 1584, episcopacy might be unknown in the British Isles today. But by distinguishing, with belated statesmanship, between moderate and extreme puritanism and pressing his attack only against the second of these positions, Whitgift had ensured the ultimate confusion of his enemies. Six disturbed years lay ahead for the Church of England, but the eventual outcome was assured.

4 The Parliament of 1584-5

'Consider into what place youe ar advaunced, and what trust is reposed upon, what expectation of all men, what necessitye for the cause, what daunger for the tyme, howe you shall answere to God and his Church, howe you shall showe yourselves trewe subjectes to her Majestie or faithfull to your countreye ... And consider whether the lettinge passe of this occasione be not in some respecte to denye Christ, and to be ashamed of him before men.'

> ('A brotherly caveat to the godlye, zealous and wyse gentlemen of the Parlament House.' BM, MS. Add. 38492, fol. 38)

THE EXTREMISTS OF THE PURITAN MOVEMENT who – unless Field spoke only for himself – had found themselves disarmed and enervated by Grindal's tolerance had been stung into a renewed militancy by their first taste of Whitgift. None of them was safe from the High Commission, a punitive engine trained with some accuracy on those preachers now known to be subversive. But puritans of Field's quality responded positively to this challenge. 1584 saw an intensification of conference and propaganda, culminating at the end of the year in a counter-attack launched through the House of Commons, a political campaign without precedent in parliamentary history.

Later, 1584 was remembered as 'that fertile year of contentious writings'.[1] Ten years earlier the presbyterians had relied first on fugitive presses operated by amateurs and then on foreign printers. But now they mounted a new and open polemical attack from the London press of a highly skilled master of the Stationers' Company, Robert Waldegrave. Waldegrave, a Worcestershire man who had begun to publish under his own imprint in 1578, was more than a craftsman. He was a committed partisan, and one of the more reckless figures in Elizabethan puritan history, who was to print the early series of Marprelate Tracts and to end his career as king's printer in Edinburgh.[2] Before Whitgift's advent he had provided an outlet for the various writings of the more radical preachers, Field, Wilcox, Oliver Pig and others. Now, with the opening of the subscription struggle, his press was devoted to furthering the cause of the discipline. To list the books which Waldegrave printed during the next two or three years is to give an almost complete indication of the range and character of the publications which enjoyed the *imprimatur* of the presbyterian movement.

There was William Fulke's *Learned discourse of ecclesiastical government*, an early manifesto pirated by Field[3] as *A briefe and plaine declaration concerning the desires of all those faithfull ministers that have and do seeke for the discipline and reformation of the Church of England*. Both this and the anonymous *A dialogue concerning the strife of our Churche* have topical prefaces which may well be of Field's authorship, and which characteristically identify the cause of the 'faithful ministers' with presbyterianism, and call for a disputation to end the matter. The journalistic *The unlawful practises of prelates* has already engaged our attention. *An abstract of certain Acts of Parliament* conveyed a message of a different kind to a different audience. This was a compilation by a puritan lawyer of acts, injunctions and canons, so selected and arranged as to appear to prove the illegality of the bishops' and the Commissioners' proceedings. Waldegrave probably printed the *Abstract*, and he certainly produced the *Counter-poyson, modestly written for the time*, a reply by the puritan prodigy Dudley Fenner to the *Answer to the … abstract* of the dean of the Arches, Dr Richard Cosin. To complete the tally of puritan tracts printed by Waldegrave in or soon after 1584, one has to add *A fruitfull sermon* by Laurence Chaderton of Cambridge on the presbyterian proof-texts in Romans xii, a reprint of Beza's *Threefold order of bishops*, an engaging piece called *A lamentable complaint of the commonalty, by way of supplication to the high court of Parliament for a learned ministry*, and three collections of sermons by John Udall, preacher at Kingston-on-Thames, a distinguished and learned divine who was later to be closely involved in the Marprelate venture.[4] Also in 1584, Waldegrave seems to have printed the first English edition of the Geneva Prayer Book, of which more will be said in due course.

These were the products of the comparatively free years of puritan publishing. Even so, Waldegrave spent almost three months in prison in 1585 for his part in the production of some of these tracts. A year later, Whitgift secured the Star Chamber Decree on Printing which introduced the censorship of all published material – his own and that of the bishop of London – and in effect imposed penalties for the printing of what they deemed to be objectionable. These were the destruction of the press and the defacement of the type, the disablement of the printer and six months' imprisonment. Nothing deterred, the puritans reverted to reliance on foreign printers, and especially on Richard Schilders of Middelburg, printer to the States of Zeeland.[5]

The militant voice of the puritan press is a strong indication that the leadership of the puritan movement had now found a sense of purpose and direction for which it was merely groping before 1584. The correspondence of the country conferences with London now carried a stream of news and suggestions. 'We have as yet no new matters to prefer unto you,' wrote nine of the Dedham and Colchester ministers to Field, 'but as soon as we have concluded anything, we will forthwith send unto you.' Their correspondence revealed a common desire for a general meeting, and it was proposed that an assembly representing Norfolk, Suffolk, Essex, Kent and London should meet in London in late August, the time of the Bartholomew Fair, when a sprinkling of country clergy in the streets would arouse no suspicion. The Dedham papers show that London proposed the names of the delegates for this meeting from north, central and south Essex, and suggested that they should confront the queen with a 'general supplication', embodying 'a draught of the discipline we desire', as well as a statement of the reasons for which subscription was refused. The day on which the document was to be presented should be marked with fasting 'in as many places as may conveniently'. The Dedham ministers agreed to these suggestions but thought that the proposed fast should be confined to the ministers. Before the ministers met in London in late August the now customary assemblies of puritan clergy at both universities at the time of the annual graduation ceremonies provided additional occasions for formal and urgent conference. 'Here have been a good company of godly brethren this Act,' Field was told by Edward Gellibrand of Magdalen, the secretary of the movement in Oxford. 'Master Fen, Wilcox, Axton, the Scottish ministers and we have had some meeting and conference, to our great comfort that are here.'[6]

Gellibrand's reference to 'the Scottish ministers' is a reminder that the conflict between presbyterians and prelates was now one struggle on both sides of the border. In 1584 a palace revolution in Scotland brought to power the government of the earl of Arran and opened the way to an episcopalian reaction which sent some twenty of the more irreconcilable Scottish presbyterians into voluntary exile in England. They included Andrew Melville and James Melville his nephew, Patrick Galloway, John Davidson (Field's correspondent of 1583), Walter Balcanquhal, and other famous names, the hard core of Scottish presbyterianism.[7] In the weeks before the so-called 'Black Acts' were enforced, subjecting the Church to closer royal control through episcopal agents, Archbishop Adamson of St Andrews, on his way to Spa for a cure, had conferred with Whitgift on the best way to combat presbyterianism and had subsequently corresponded with the English archbishop. Although Whitgift made no secret of these transactions, his frankness did not save him from charges of collusion in the Black Acts. On the other hand Walsingham was open in his expressions of sympathy for 'the poor distressed ministers' of Scotland, and in his desire to unseat the regime of Arran and Adamson. So was William Davison, at this time English ambassador in Edinburgh. Rightly or wrongly, the task of restoring a presbyterian polity to the Scottish Church and of thwarting Whitgift's designs for the Church of England were identified in many minds as one and the same cause. This, and the very presence and influence of the Scottish exiles in England, must have strengthened the impression that 'the strife of our Church' was about the fundamentals of church government and the ministry.[8]

The Scottish ministers came south with an expectation of 'consultation with learned men, zealous brethren and whoever has defended the Lord's cause.'[9] Never was there a better illustration of a point made in a sermon by the Northamptonshire preacher, Eusebius Paget, now himself a kind of exile in north Cornwall: 'The curse of dividing and scattering the Lord applied as a means that his law might be taught in every corner of Israel.' The bishop of Exeter, Paget's unwilling ordinary, saw things in a different light and complained of 'the unquiet estate of this country by means of some seditious persons, expelled from other places, attempting to build their nest and to hatch their eggs here.'[10] One of the Scottish ministers who found his way to this diocese, John Cowper, was established at Saltash in the household of Sir Anthony Rous, who would later marry the mother of John Pym. Another Scot, David Black – a turbulent figure in an Edinburgh pulpit in years to come – had been employed for some time as schoolmaster at Kilkhampton, Sir Richard Grenville's parish on the northern borders of Devon and Cornwall, where Sir Francis Hastings of Leicestershire had procured the appointment of Eusebius Paget as rector. Between them, Black and Paget turned the remote peninsula of Hartland upside down. Black defamed the Prayer Book, preached and catechized though not in orders, and used the Geneva liturgy in the presence of Grenville himself and other Cornish notables. He was later charged by the High Commission with publicly declaring that 'there ought to be no bishops such as now are' and that 'the creation of bishops and ministers is neither godly nor according to the word of God.' He organized the 'gentlemen's sons' who attended his school, nicknamed 'the Reformed

College' by 'the adversary', and rode about the country with them, taking notes at sermons and abusing the conservative clergy.[11]

Meanwhile three of the most radical of the Scottish presbyterians, James Lawson, Walter Balcanquhal and Andrew Melville, settled in London, where they were joined in the autumn of 1584 by Field's friend, John Davidson. As early as July 4th, Lawson and Balcanquhal reported having 'talked with the godly and zealous brethren', and one has to imagine their disturbing and influential voice operating as a bias in all the counsels and conferences of the coming months. When Field was at last suspended from preaching in the following spring, part of his offence was said to be resorting 'to the Scottish ministers, being three of them, and sometimes they come to his house.' Denied the privilege of forming their own 'peculiar church', the Scots occupied some London pulpits during the autumn and winter of 1584-5; to what effect can be judged from the nickname given to Davidson by the bishops and others at Court: 'the Thunderer'. In October, one of the preachers, James Lawson, fell ill and, in spite of the pious ministrations of many 'careful mothers and sisters', died in the presence of eight of his fellow-ministers and other Scots, 'besides English men and women'. The burial was made an occasion for the kind of party demonstration which was common at huguenot funerals across the Channel. The preachers of the London conference competed with the Scots for the honour of carrying the bier, 'thickly, comely and courteously', and they were followed by other ministers, among them Field, Travers and Chark and the three ministers of the French Church 'with many Frenchmen', besides 'gentlemen, honest burgesses, famous and godly matrons', to the number of above five hundred.[12]

This convincing demonstration of international Calvinist solidarity was a token of what was to be expected throughout the winter months as it became clear that Parliament and Convocation would be summoned in November 1584. Once again, and in spite of past experience, it was hoped that Parliament would cure all ills. 'Oh tarry till there be a Parliament' was the cry during the months of subscription.[13] And now, even although the crisis of the summer was almost over, Parliament met at a propitious time for those who hoped to unseat the bishops, or at least to confound their policies. In June 1584, the government had made public its own alarming account of the web of conspiracy spun around Francis Throckmorton and the would-be assassin, John Somerville. A month later William of Orange was struck by the fatal bullet which is still to be seen embedded at the foot of a staircase in the Prinsenhof in Delft. These events had immediate repercussions. The gentlemen who assembled in Westminster in November, together with hundreds of their fellow-countrymen, were now committed by their hands and seals to a savage but realistic Bond of Association which promised death by lynch-law to the person who would profit from a similar act of assassination in England: by implication, Mary Stuart. The main business of this Parliament was to make provision for the queen's safety, a task which received lurid justification in mid-session when it appeared that one of their own number, the enigmatic Dr Parry, was plotting her destruction.[14]

Whether the organized puritan movement was a factor in the elections of 1584 is an open question. Two years later, on the eve of another Parliament, Chapman of Dedham expected the London church to conduct a national electoral campaign, and Field was urged to note all the parliamentary boroughs in the country and to use 'all the best means you can possibly' to secure the choice of gentlemen who might be expected to advance 'God's causes'.[15] Whether the composition of the House of Commons was influenced by canvassing of this kind or whether it merely reflected the mood of the hour, the puritans had never before been so strongly placed as they were in the Parliament of 1584–5. Gentlemen of proven godliness who had earlier sat for boroughs now represented shires: for example, Norfolk had Nathaniel Bacon and Suffolk Sir Robert Jermyn, while Sir Francis and George Hastings were the two members for Leicestershire. Only in Essex, of all their strongholds, did the political interest of the puritans fail: here the representatives were an unfriendly courtier (Sir Thomas Heneage) and a secret papist (Sir John Petre of Ingatestone). As for the borough seats, they were crowded with the most ardent supporters of the godly ministers: Robert Beale sat for Dorchester, Edward Lewkenor, Sir John Higham, Henry Blagge and Peter Wentworth's stepson, Geoffrey Gates, all Suffolk men and all puritans, sat respectively for Maldon, Ipswich, Sudbury and West Looe. James Morice represented his own Colchester, Laurence Tomson the earl of Bedford's boroughs of Weymouth and Melcombe Regis, and Walsingham's other secretary, Nicholas Faunt, Boroughbridge. Valentine Knightley, son of Sir Richard Knightley of Fawsley, was another Russell nominee at Tavistock. And this by no means exhausts the list. Yet this was also an inexperienced Parliament, lacking the tactical finesse of some of its predecessors: three hundred and twenty-two of the four hundred and sixty members were without previous parliamentary experience, and the radical leaders of the past, Norton, Pistor, Carleton, the two Wentworths, were all missing.[16]

The puritan conferences took steps to strengthen the hands of their protagonists. On November 2nd – three weeks before Parliament met – the Dedham conference was agreed 'that in every country some should be chosen, so far as we could procure it, that some of best credit and most forward for the gospel should go up to London to solicit the cause of the Church.' We can distinguish two special conferences of ministers in London which corresponded to two bursts of activity in Parliament, separated by the Christmas recess. There is a reference to the first meeting in a letter to Field from the secretary of the presbyterian movement in Oxford, Edward Gellibrand of Magdalen, dated November 29th, the first day of parliamentary business: 'Touching my departure from that holy assembly without leave etc., I crave pardon both of you and them.' From this alone it is clear that the conference was formal in character and subject to the normal rules of presbyterian assemblies. On February 1st, a fortnight before the puritan campaign in the Commons was reopened, Chapman invited the Dedham brethren 'to seek by what means the great cause of the Church that is now in hand might be dealt in and good done in it.' The conference concluded that John Knewstub for Suffolk and George Gifford and Robert Wright for Essex 'should be moved to deal for the Church, and letters to be written to them to that end.' On the following day, nine Essex ministers informed Field and Chark of their election, 'to join with you in that business.' Thomas Fuller, recording a tradition for which there seems to be no contemporary evidence, but which is plausible enough, says that the delegates spent 'all day at the doors of the Parliament house, and some part of the night in the chambers of Parliament men, effectually soliciting their business with them.'

Lobbying at Westminster was backed with prayer and fasting in the country. In early November, Dedham had agreed on the need for a fast 'against Parliament that was at hand', and directed each member 'to stir up his people to earnest prayer for the good of the Church.' The conference itself fasted at its regular meeting a month later, and on this occasion a member moved 'that everyone as he was acquainted with any gentlemen of worth and of godliness' should 'stir them up to be zealous for reformation.' In early January it was thought necessary to renew the fast and to know when 'the brethren of London' proposed to hold theirs, 'that we might join with them.' The Dedham and Colchester brethren accordingly wrote to Field for this information and any other instructions which he might have for them. A puritan pastor wrote out of Suffolk to his patron in the Commons: 'We cease not here in our small measure to lift up our unworthy eyes and hands toward the God of Heaven both in confessing of our sins and striving with his Majesty by humble requests for all necessary blessings upon you and the rest of your worthy yokefellows in the service of Jesus Christ.'[17]

With the ministerial delegates in London went an impressive accumulation of documents. Much of the material which survives in Field's 'register' and other similar collections, particularly the accounts of ministers' 'troubles', was probably gathered to influence M.P.s and other influential sympathizers at times like this. 'If it will then anything help the common cause, I pray you then use your discretion,' wrote a harassed Suffolk minister in sending Field an account of his misadventures which extended from 1581 to 1584.[18] We possess a file of the parliamentary and ecclesiastical papers of the member for Maldon, Edward Lewkenor, which illustrates the kind of material that he and his friends must have circulated in the House as they prepared to play their parts in the religious debates of this session. From this Parliament survive analyses of the state of the ministry in Essex, in Lewkenor's own hundred of Suffolk, and in part of his native Sussex. In addition there is a long account of the vexations of the godly in the Suffolk village of Lawshall, an exhortation from Lewkenor's curate at Denham and an anonymous 'brotherly caveat to the godly, zealous and wise gentlemen of the Parliament House', also, it seems, written out of Suffolk.[19]

The armament on which the puritan strategy chiefly depended was a survey of the condition of the ministry in a large number of parishes in some seventeen counties. This was in the course of compilation while Parliament was in session, and the work was completed only in time for the next Parliament, almost two years later.[20] These surveys listed the parishes, sometimes with the values of the benefices, and with the names of the incumbents, much in the style of the official returns which archdeacons and bishops were required from time to time to prepare, and stated whether they were non-resident, pluralists or non-preachers, or, by contrast, worthy, resident, preaching pastors. In commenting on the quality of the clergy the technical jargon of the clergy certificates – 'sufficient', 'unsufficient', 'honest of conversation', 'learned in the tongues' – was mingled with more detailed and idiosyncratic descriptions – 'an alehouse haunter, a companion with drunkards and a gross abuser of the scriptures', 'consumed by carding, dicing and gaming', 'a drunkard and whoremaster, and continuously weareth a pocket dag', 'a common gamester, the best wrastler in Cornwall'.

The most colourful of the surveys, those for Cornwall, Essex and Warwickshire, contain some striking vignettes of Elizabethan clerical life. These – if we are to trust the puritan surveyors – were some of the parsons of Elizabethan Warwickshire: 'an old priest and unsound in religion, he can neither preach nor read well, his chiefest trade is to cure hawks that are hurt or diseased, for which purpose many do usually repair to him' – 'he teacheth to play on instruments and draweth wrought works' – 'he bendeth himself wholly to the plough and cart, whence he is many times called to burial and churching' – 'he could not one day read the commandments for want of his spectacles' – 'learned, zealous and godly and fit for the ministry; a happy age if our Church were fraught with many such' – this last, Shakespeare's rector at Stratford-on-Avon. Archbishop Bancroft described these surveys as 'in manner of heathenish libels', and most writers have shared his low opinion of their value as evidence for the state of the Church. Admittedly one has to allow for the prejudice which colours such expressions as 'subject to the vice of good fellowship' and 'useth … to play after a sort the reconciler amongst the simple.' But when the surveys are compared with other sources of information it will probably be found that the ascertainable facts, especially of particular scandals, have not been invented or distorted. This was Canon Foster's impression of the Lincolnshire survey, and in Essex some of the scandalous cases reported can be traced in the records of quarter sessions and of the archdeaconry courts.[21]

What the surveys more certainly demonstrate is presbyterianism in action: the efforts of particular churches – in the case of Essex of 'the godly' in scores of parishes – co-ordinated in local and county conferences. The completed documents were finally sent up to London where they were transcribed (by copyists unfamiliar with the place-names) and, last of all, reduced to concise statistical digests which could be made a debating-point in Parliament itself.[22]

The motive for this prodigious and unrewarded labour is not hard to seek. It was to give the lie to Whitgift, who had never ceased to insist that the non-subscribing ministers represented an expendable minority of the total preaching ministry. 'I would to God a true survey were made,' the puritans retorted in the preface to one of the tracts of 1584. If those 'whom they term puritans' were put on one side, and the non-residents and pluralists on the other, it would 'need no arithmetician' to count the remainder. Evidently the laity were almost eager for the kind of exposures which Field and his friends now had in store for them. Burghley himself, whose jaundiced view of ecclesiastical administration was typical of his class and generation, could recommend that there should be 'a universal information had' of the sufficiency of the clergy, 'without any open visitation as the bishops and archdeacons continually do use only for gain.' In September 1584, the entire Privy Council was deeply impressed with an early version of the Essex survey, and Parliament was likely to be even more concerned at the total picture which emerged from so much of the survey as was eventually completed: 2537 parishes (roughly a quarter of the parishes of England) with only 472 preachers, as against 1773 'no preachers'; 467 references to pluralism and 353 to non-residence. The proper remedies for this situation were educational, administrative and, above all, financial. But the mood of 1584 did not encourage a Fabian, gradualist philosophy of reform.[23]

The intention of those who managed the campaign inside Parliament was to pick up the threads of 1576 and 1581: to press yet again for the moderate puritan plan for the renovation of the Church, together with the undoing of all that had happened in the past twelve months. As early as September 1584, Robert Beale hoped that Whitgift might be persuaded to forestall the inevitable onslaught. The archbishop had approached Beale through Walsingham to ask for his 'friendship and company', so that he felt free to offer advice in the form of a number of 'means how to settle a godly and charitable quietness in the Church.' These consisted largely of the Commons' proposals of 1581, pledged by the queen to be performed by the bishops (the legend still endured) 'and therefore the same is now looked for at their hands', together with a demand for the dismantling of every weapon in Whitgift's and Aylmer's armoury. No minister was to be pressed to subscribe, and proceedings *ex officio* were to be abandoned. Deprived and suspended ministers were to resume their ministries on bonds taken of the ministers and principal gentlemen of the shire that they would not preach erroneous, heretical or schismatical doctrine. None of the controverted points in the Prayer Book was in future to be insisted upon and only decency in apparel, not strict vestiarian uniformity, would be required. Readers of lectures and other preachers without cure of souls were not to be forced to minister the sacraments. Before Parliament met Whitgift should treat with 'some of the most modest and learned men on the other side' about the pacification of the Church. This token of good-will would 'satisfy' the Commons. Whitgift's reaction to these presumptuous directions was to tell Hatton through Bancroft that he was glad to find them 'so frivolous' and to prepare a new and detailed answer to the Commons' articles of 1581.[24]

And so the lines were drawn. Beale saw no answer to his memorandum, but within a few weeks he was one of the committee of the House of Commons which drafted a weighty petition of sixteen clauses for reference to the Lords, which took its pedigree from his own earlier proposals and from the programme of 1581.[25] This action had been prompted by the presentation of petitions from Lincolnshire and Warwickshire by the members for those shires, and for Essex by the member for West Looe, Geoffrey Gates. These documents were said to bear the signatures of 'very many ... of the gentlemen of the greatest worship in the same shires', and to complain of the state of the ministry and of the restraint of 'so many good preachers'. When a committee of the House of Lords had been assured that the petition of sixteen clauses reflected not merely the complaints of these three shires but 'the grief of the whole realm', they received it sympathetically and declared themselves willing to join in with the Commons 'in wishing the reformation thereof'. But at this point the Christmas recess suspended further activity.[26]

The Commons had shown a broad sympathy for the cause of the preaching ministers which is remarkable in view of the queen's express instructions at the outset of this session that they were not to concern themselves with matters of religion. However, the leadership had lacked brilliance; the occasion had not been seized as a Pistor or a Wentworth would have seized it. By the time Parliament resumed, on February 4th, the country constituencies were taking their representatives to task for their timidity. 'Is it ignorance?' wrote a Suffolk brother, troubled as to why God had not blessed the Church in setting up the discipline:

But those men have knowledge and be thoroughly persuaded in the cause. Is it lack of gifts? These men we know to be of great wisdom, knowledge and utterance. Then my heart melted with fear and I thought, O sin, sin, sin, that thou shouldst so take from us the favour of God, that in so fit a time and place, under so godly and Christian a queen, such godly and zealous and wise men should have their tongues cleave to the roof of their mouths, and be destitute of all power to promote so worthy, weighty, so needful a cause![27]

When the tale was taken up again in mid-February, these complaints were echoed in the House of Commons itself. 'We were very hot awhile,' complained one speaker, 'but now cold again. Our petitions are not looked to; we do nothing.' To stir up courage and passion, the news of the treason of that 'mercenary hellhound' Dr Parry had just broken. And by now further petitions, and probably surveys, were to hand for East Sussex and the Folkestone district of Kent. Evidently the larger surveys for whole counties were still not available, even by February 15th. Nevertheless, the Commons showed no hesitation in again turning themselves into a sounding-board for 'the grief of the whole realm'. With difficulty persuaded by Mildmay to wait for the Lords' answer to their earlier petition, they were utterly dissatisfied when at last the Lords' committee met the deputation from the Commons on February 22nd. Burghley, speaking first, reported that the queen had discussed their complaints with Whitgift and the other bishops and expected to see their legitimate grievances redressed by Convocation or by individual diocesans. But other matters, touching innovation, she thought 'not fit to be reformed'. Burghley's speech was without gratuitous offence, but he left it in no doubt that these matters lay outside the competence of the House of Commons. Whitgift, speaking next, confuted the Commons' petition clause by clause and refused to retract any of his disciplinary policies. In this his irritable, pedagogic nature was not suppressed, and members learned that some of the bishops had been preachers 'before some of us were born – at the least, when we were in our swaddling clothes.' However righteous the cause, such a posture argues a great lack of political judgment. One member spoke of 'the Cardinal and Metropolitical answer' and Beale later wrote that 'all that heard the answers made, charging the House to seek anarchies and breach of law, to follow Jesuits and anabaptists, may well think that in all the histories and records of times past, never any prince or subject gave such an insufficient or opprobrious answer.'[28]

Even at this point the puritans in Parliament, as in the country at large, were still nourishing the fond illusion that the queen was on their side, and that if she was once fully informed of their petitions she would 'with all speed cut off those abuses.' Elizabeth's real views were vigorously expressed five days later when the representatives of both houses of Convocation came to Court to offer the clerical subsidy. What would normally have been a formal audience became the occasion for a free-ranging discussion between the queen, Burghley and Whitgift on the topic of the moment: where to lay the blame for the shortcomings of the clergy. While Elizabeth's contempt for the prelates was equal to that of any of her advisers, she left it in no doubt that her bishops were to be the sole executants of her ecclesiastical supremacy and that she would not tolerate the parliamentary invasion of their domain. On the very same day, the committee of the Commons was preparing an answer to Whitgift which amounted to the contrary claim that church government in its entirety, including the power by which ministers were removed or deprived, was subject to the Common Law and therefore to statute and to Parliament, the maker of statutes. Before this statement, charged with constitutional significance, reached the whole House, the queen summoned the Speaker to Greenwich and returned him, on March 1st, with a renewed command not to meddle with matters of religion. 'She knows – and thinks you know – she is Supreme Governor of this Church, next under God ... Resolutely, she will receive no motion of innovation, not alter or change any law whereby the religion or Church of England standeth established at this day.' Abuses of the existing law were to be redressed by complaint first to the bishop, next to the metropolitan, thence to the Council and lastly to herself. Never had Elizabeth made it so clear that the settlement of 1559 was meant to endure. 'For as she found it [the state ecclesiastical] at her first coming in, and so hath maintained it these twenty-seven years, she meant in like state, by God's grace, to continue it and leave it behind her.'

Here, surely, was the moment of truth. Yet, 'so greatly moved and so deeply wounded' as the Commons were by this message, they were persuaded by the puritan leadership to assert their liberties 'underhand' by debating, of all things, a new bill of religion. They had already entertained two provocative bills, one imposing an oath of loyalty and equity on all archbishops and bishops, to be taken in the secular court of Chancery, the other regulating the fees in ecclesiastical courts and the conduct of visitations. The queen had expressly forbidden any further consideration of these measures in her message of March 1st. The new bill which was now launched in spite of the queen's command ingeniously professed to do no more than reinforce the statute of 1571 'for reformation of certain disorders touching ministers of the Church'. In fact it proposed to punish the ignorant and unfit clergy with imprisonment, fine and perpetual disablement, and to make a commission of laymen the arbiters of their fitness. There was no prospect of such a measure making much progress beyond the Commons' Chamber, but it was a vehicle of self-assertion and a renewed opportunity to debate what was by all appearance an obsessive theme for the gentlemen sitting in and represented in this Parliament: the state of the ministry. Who made the clergy? The patrons who presented them, the bishops who ordained them, or the inadequate stipends which attracted such poor material? Except for two or three dissidents, the House had no doubt where to lay the blame.

The queen, with the wisdom that distinguished her from her Stuart successors, gave Parliament its head for a time, and the bill passed rapidly through the Commons and was even debated in the Lords, where it provoked a clash between Whitgift and Leicester before passing into oblivion. This, according to the diarist Fitzwilliam, satisfied the Commons' purpose, although they went on in the course of March to debate two further ecclesiastical measures. Not until the queen ended this turbulent session on March 29th could Whitgift regard himself and the Church of England as safe. In her final speech Elizabeth made an explicit and classic statement of her church policy. She would neither 'animate Romanists' nor 'tolerate new-fangledness'. 'And of the latter, I must pronounce them dangerous to a kingly rule: to have every man, according to his own censure, to make a doom of the validity and privity of his prince's government, with a common veil and cover of God's word, whose followers must not be judged but by a private man's exposition.'

When the story of this Parliament has been told, a number of questions crucial for our understanding of the constitution of the puritan movement remains. To what extent was the direction and pace of the campaign inside Parliament influenced by the puritan ministers meeting in conference outside its doors, and by the godly, lay and clerical, whose gaze was fixed on Westminster? Or was it entirely controlled by laymen with public responsibilities like Robert Beale? How far was there a single design behind these parliamentary moves and what was the limit of its ambition? As we have described them, the aspirations of 1584 were those of 1576 and 1581. There was an almost obsessive interest in the improvement of the ministry and the relief of godly preachers, but no concern, so far as the main stream of agitation was concerned, for any fundamental alteration in the government or formularies of the Church. Was this merely the cunning of the extreme left, preparing covertly for the introduction of full-blown presbyterian measures, or do we have in this programme the frank expression of a practical, undogmatic puritanism which stopped far short of presbyterianism?

I have intentionally reserved until this point in our discussion an episode which throws some light at least on these problems. On Monday, December 14th, the very day that the first puritan petitions were brought into the House of Commons, Dr Peter Turner, a London physician and the son of the puritan naturalist William Turner, 'rose up and put the House in remembrance of a bill and book heretofore offered by him unto the said House.'[29] The book, which Turner must have committed to the Speaker or the Clerk at the beginning of the session, was the Geneva liturgy, the *Forme of prayers and administration of the sacraments* used by Knox's congregation in Mary's reign; and the bill would have established this as the only lawful prayer book of the English Church. Turner's bill further proposed to erect presbyterianism, committing the government of the Church to pastors and elders, acting through congregational consistories and assemblies of the ministers and elders of each shire. Nothing was said about the removal of archbishops and bishops and their offices, and by implication these were to remain as they had done in Scotland, their endowments undisturbed (for the time being), but without any ecclesiastical function.[30]

This was revolution, far beyond any innovation proposed in the petition of sixteen clauses which the Commons sent up to the Lords a week later. And whereas the whole trend of the Commons' proposals in this Parliament was towards a lay-dominated Church in a unitary commonwealth, subject to Parliament and the Common Law, Turner's bill raised visions of a dual system of government, with a discipline enforced by the ministers of God's word and the elders of the Church, in virtue of their divine calling. 'Full authority in all ecclesiastical causes under them' was to lie with the assemblies of preaching ministers in each shire, and the ministers so assembled were empowered to eject scandalous, heretical and popish ministers and to make choice of 'the worshipful and honest of the shire' to serve as elders. Nothing could be more instructive than the cold reception which the Commons gave to this measure. That bitter enemy of all forms of clericalism, Sir Francis Knollys, seems to have spoken against it, and Hatton's semi-official condemnation brought no rejoinder and persuaded the House 'that the said book and bill should not be read.' But later on the same day the House was all ears to hear the petitions from Lincolnshire, Warwickshire and Essex for the reform of the ministry! There seems little doubt that for reasons of principle as well as of tactics a House of Commons which was representative of the temper of the protestant gentry at large would have nothing to do with this nakedly presbyterian measure.[31]

And what of the puritan ministers in their conferences? Turner represented both bill and book as having been 'digested and framed by certain godly and learned ministers' – another token of the high Calvinism which inspired the bill, for the other reforming measures brought before this Parliament seem to have been drafted by parliament men and lawyers. Turner's 'book' was almost certainly a copy of the only English edition of the Geneva liturgy to survive from the reign of Elizabeth, especially revised for the occasion, and printed by Robert Waldegrave, no doubt under the direction of Field and other London preachers.[32] From this circumstance we can either conclude that there was a general agreement among the ministers to attempt to carry 'the discipline' in this Parliament, and that the petitions for reform of the ministry were intended by the preachers merely to prepare the way; a plan which foundered by finding insufficient support in the Commons. Or that Turner spoke only for the extreme wing of the puritan ministry, and perhaps for little more than the London conference, and the Scottish presbyterians then in London. By this stage in our story there is no need to labour the divergence of the unbeneficed London 'doctors', natural presbyterians, and the country clergy in their parishes with a vested interest in the Church as it was then constituted. We have a further hint of their differing interests from early in the life of the next Parliament, when Edmund Chapman would move in the Dedham conference that a letter should be sent to the godly brethren in London to indicate that whereas they seemed inclined 'to accept of none if they had not all', the judgment of Dedham was that 'some reformation might be accepted of if it were granted.'[33]

This is not to suggest that there were not some presbyterian revolutionaries hiding their true intentions under the comparatively moderate demands voiced in the 1584 Parliament. Turner himself played their game when he assured the Commons that his bill and book tended 'to no other end, as he conceived, than the glory of God, the safety of her Majesty, and the benefit of the Commonwealth' – and told them little else about it. But there were other ministers who wanted no more than the House of Commons was willing to ask for on their behalf. That this was the majority party would become sufficiently clear as the presbyterian extremists now turned their attention to the second part of their plan: the 'grand design' of establishing the discipline through secretly spreading its practice among themselves.

Part 6

The Grand Design

1 The Book of Discipline

'The grand design driven on in these decrees was, to set up a discipline in a discipline, presbytery in episcopacy.'

(THOMAS FULLER, *Church History*, v. 7)

AFTER CONFERRING WITH THE EXILED SCOTTISH MINISTERS in July 1584, John Field's Oxford correspondent, Edward Gellibrand of Magdalen, wrote to tell him of 'one point ... I would wish to be thoroughly debated among you and them.' This was 'concerning the proceeding of the minister in his duty without the assistance or tarrying for the magistrate.'[1] The Scots were in England for no other cause than their refusal 'to tarry for the magistrate': their unwillingness, that is, to recognize in the government of James VI the power to order the affairs of Christ's kingdom in Scotland. They were unlikely to have resisted the temptation to comment unfavourably on the conduct of their English brethren who, after so many years, were still content to suffer the Antichristian government of bishops, and for no other reason than that it was imposed upon them by the magistrate. This would have prompted Gellibrand's question: For how much longer was reformation to wait on the will of the state?

Tarrying was not a conspicuous habit of the English presbyterians. Long before this time they had seized every advantage offered by the loose institutional arrangements of the Elizabethan Church to behave as though the further reformation they desired was already an accomplished fact, arguing that 'every man that professeth himself desirous of discipline should exercise it himself in his own causes so far as he could.'[2] But these were not ecclesiastical anarchists: far from it. Their ideal was a disciplined uniformity more exacting than anything thought desirable under the Elizabethan dispensation. Turner's presbyterian bill of 1584 would have made it a penal offence to use even a form of private family prayer which was not conformable to the lengthy Calvinist confession of faith contained in the Geneva liturgy.[3] Within their own fellowships, the puritans were deeply disturbed by differences of doctrine and liturgical practice, and laboured to resolve them. But the assistance of the secular arm was needed to bind their own more turbulent members, let alone to carry this godly agreement beyond these restricted circles to the Church at large. There could be no general reformation without it. The voluntary and secret practice of the discipline was better than nothing, but it offered no lasting alternative to the public establishment of true religion. And such an establishment in England would not be without meaning: the magistrate for whom the English puritans tarried was not James VI but Elizabeth I, and many of the 'inferior magistrates' of England, privy councillors and local justices, already appeared to be on their side.

Yet by 1585 it was merely realistic to assume that there would be no legal establishment of the godly discipline in England so long as the queen remained the arbiter of the Church's destiny. The notion that Elizabeth was 'so constant a maintainer of the truth',[4] as the puritans understood the truth, was still a necessary fiction, if only because there was no acceptable alternative to her government within sight. The queen's Calvinist subjects, however dissatisfied they might be with her conduct of the Church, were as deeply involved as any of their contemporaries in the national *cultus* which had grown up around her person and which was stimulated by the unthinkable dangers which threatened the nation and the religion in her frail person. But, disillusioned as they were by the Parliament of 1584, they were now contriving to separate the myth from their practical strategy. 'Tush Mr Edmunds, hold your peace', Field was quoted as saying, probably after the demoralizing defeat of the puritan campaign in the Parliament of 1586–7; 'seeing we cannot compass these things by suit nor dispute, it is the multitude and people that must bring the discipline to pass which we desire.'[5] From the meetings of ministers in London in the winter of 1584–5 there dated a more serious intention than had yet found expression, even in the euphoric atmosphere of 1573, to set up the godly discipline outside the law, without the assistance of the magistrate.

It might be thought that such an intention was already implicit in the conferences of preaching ministers like that which had met in and around Dedham since 1582. But while these meetings already took many corporate decisions of an administrative nature, which affected in many ways the conduct of the churches and communities which fell within their view, they provided no formal alternative to the government of bishops and archdeacons. Their simple rules of procedure gave only a hazy definition to the mutual responsibilities of the conference and the congregations. And none of these meetings was as yet committed to any definite procedure in its dealings with other conferences or with higher, representative assemblies. This is not to say that the ministers were not already guided by the various published handbooks of presbyterian theory or by such knowledge as they might possess of the practice of other, non-episcopal churches. But the Dedham papers are sufficient to show that it was only as they attempted to put these by now familiar principles into operation that they discovered how variously they could be interpreted. What was needed was a 'Book of Discipline', a formal constitution to which the ministers could subscribe their names and by which they would thereafter be bound. If such a subscription were to involve an undertaking to put the Book of Discipline into practice, then the conferences would indeed become *classes* and synods and the exercise of the discipline would become as effective as it could ever be without the recognition of the state.

The French Calvinists had adopted such a form of discipline at their first national synod in 1559 and had revised it at La Rochelle in 1571.[6] The Scots had revised their first Book of Discipline in a presbyterian sense in 1578.[7] Two years earlier than that, the Northamptonshire puritans, Arthur Wake and Percival Wiburn, had acted as sponsors at the adoption of the first Form of Discipline of the Reformed Church of the Channel Islands.[8] Yet the English presbyterians had hitherto avoided committing themselves to a scheme which would virtually formalize their separation from the main body of the established Church and which would probably involve them in a conspiracy in the eyes of the law. In January 1585, Gellibrand of Oxford reported that he had sounded three or four men from various colleges about these things, but had found 'that men are very dangerous in this point.' They favoured reformation in general, 'but when it cometh to the particular point, some have not yet considered of these things, for which others in the Church are so much troubled; others are afraid to testify anything with their hands, lest it breed danger, before the time.'[9] That the more incautious spirits were convinced that 'the time' had now arrived is a token of the effect of Whitgift's policies on a movement which had for long exasperated its most extreme elements by its propensity to compromise and engraft itself into a partially reformed Anglicanism. This was also a response to the increasing pressure to conform to the practice of other reformed churches. It was at this very time that the French protestant refugees in England, who had met in annual colloquies since 1581, were adapting Nicolas des Gallars's *Forme de police* to serve as a constitution for all their scattered congregations.[10] And in June 1586 the reformed churches of the Netherlands drew up a Form of Discipline at a national synod held at the Hague, under the benevolent patronage of the English captain-general, the earl of Leicester.[11]

By the summer of 1585 the inner circle of committed presbyterians was already far advanced in the project of providing the English churches with a formal scheme of government of the same kind. 'Concerning our other business,' Field wrote to Walter Travers on July 3rd, 'I would wish that the Discipline were read over with as much speed as could be, and that some good directions were given for the brethren abroad,' who were 'very willing to join with the best, to put in practice that which shall be agreed upon by the brethren.' Field had probably already received more than one request of the kind which came from Suffolk 'for the several grounds and demonstrations for the holy Discipline, which we are sure you have in readiness,' and he told Travers that as soon as a 'perfect copy' of the Discipline was ready, he would 'wholly employ' himself in its distribution. Yet in November, Gellibrand wrote asking Field to 'hasten the form of Discipline and send it', and on January 30th, 1586, he wrote: 'I pray you remember the form of Discipline which Master Travers promised to make perfect, and send it me when it is finished. We will put it in practice and try men's minds therein as we may.' But the Book was not ready for dispatch to the conferences for at least another twelve-month.[12]

On the evidence of Field's correspondence, which later fell into the hands of Richard Bancroft, Travers was to be charged before the High Commissioners with being 'the author, or at least the finisher of the Book of Discipline'.[13] No other direct evidence of its authorship has ever come to light. Travers was without doubt one of the two principal ideologues of the English presbyterian movement. Twelve years earlier he had composed the most authoritative English account of the Calvinist scheme of church order, the *Ecclesiasticae disciplinae ... explicatio*, which is sometimes confused with the Book of Discipline of the 'eighties. Since 1581 he had filled the strategic post of afternoon lecturer at the Temple and had joined in the regular meetings of Field's London conference. After Richard Hooker's appointment to the mastership of the Temple in 1585, the difference between the puritans and their opponents was given some theological definition in the parallel courses of sermons which the two divines preached from the same pulpit, a confrontation which was a legend when Thomas Fuller published his *Church History of Britain* seventy years later. This famous debate was abruptly ended when Travers was silenced in March 1586. Nevertheless, he continued to reside in the Temple for some years to come. 'Allowing Mr Cartwright for the Head,' wrote Fuller, 'Mr Walter Travers might be termed the neck of the presbyterian party.'[14] It may well be that the Head himself had more to do with the Book of Discipline than there is now positive evidence to prove. When the Book was printed for the guidance of the Westminster Assembly in January 1645 as *A directory of church-goverament*,[15] the copy was said to have been 'found in the study of the most accomplished divine, Mr Thomas Cartwright, after his decease.' Cartwright had died more than forty years before that date, Travers only nine years before, at the great age of eighty-seven. But the copy would have been in the hands of Cartwright's literary executors, Arthur Hildersham and John Dod, and Dod was still alive in 1644.[16]

In April 1585, Cartwright returned to England after an absence of eleven years, spent latterly as pastor of the reformed congregation of English merchants at Antwerp and Middelburg, where one of his flock thought it no blasphemy to compare himself with the disciples and Cartwright with the Lord. Cartwright's return at this moment was a tonic for a somewhat lethargic invalid in the family of reformed churches. Bishop Aylmer at once took Cartwright into custody, presumably acting on the authority of the warrant issued in 1573, and there were repetitions of the scenes of that year, with multitudes visiting him in prison. If the bishop expected in this way to repair his tattered credit he was disappointed, for Burghley himself intervened to secure Cartwright's release. 'As soon as I knew of Master Cartwright's delivery,' wrote one brother, 'I sent for Master Travers and we had psalms of thanksgiving and prayers to the same purpose and a sermon.' The earl of Leicester – Field's patron – now took Cartwright under his wing and tried, without success, to persuade Whitgift to grant him a preaching licence. There was no rancour in Whitgift's refusal, but the archbishop knew that his old adversary had not altered his opinions. The early autumn took Cartwright back across the North Sea to take some part in the organization of Leicester's Netherlands campaign. By April of the following year the 'patron-general' of the puritan movement had rewarded him with the mastership of his hospital at Warwick, adding to a comfortable stipend of fifty pounds a further annuity of fifty pounds for life.[17]

It is tempting to associate the quickening of interest in the Book of Discipline with Cartwright's presence in England – and probably in London – from the spring to the autumn of 1585. But Travers seems to have been left with the delicate task of preparing a draft which could satisfy every shade of opinion in a movement which contained so many divergent tendencies. Presbyterian historians have blamed Travers's preaching obligations at the Temple and the demands of his famous contest with Hooker for the two years of delay before the Book of Discipline saw the light of day. But nothing could be less convincing. We are dealing with the history of a slight pamphlet of twenty-two pages, not a learned tome, and someone as conversant as Travers with the principles of reformed church order could have tossed it off in a week. François Lambert had taken no longer to reorganize the Church in the German principality of Hesse in 1525, and he had worked in a foreign language and with no precedents to guide him. Nor was the Discipline a marginal interest which Travers is likely to have neglected. But it was a public, not a personal document, and Travers was merely the draughtsman, not in any proper sense the author. Field writes to him about 'those or the like instructions which we had.'[18] The two years which he took to complete his task can only indicate the difficulty of finding a moral unanimity on the questions with which it dealt. 'You know there are certain things in it not agreed upon, and those of weight,' was Laurence Tomson's warning in 1573 about an earlier presbyterian manifesto,[19] and twelve years of undisciplined nonconformity had done little to clear these clouded issues. They were just as muddy in the 1640s when the Westminster Assembly found itself driven back to first principles in its search for a scriptural polity, to the exasperation of the closed mind of Scottish presbyterianism.

The documents which Dr Peter Turner deposited with the Speaker of the House of Commons in December 1584 represent, in effect, the earliest draft of the constitution of an English presbyterian Church. Besides Turner's bill, which proposed to create presbyterian assemblies in each shire, the copy of the Geneva *Booke of the forme of common prayers* which accompanied it was itself crudely adapted to serve the administrative needs of a national Calvinist Church. As it stood, this little book, even in Waldegrave's new edition, provided only for the worship and government of a single congregation: Knox's church at Geneva in Mary's days. But almost as an afterthought a final paragraph was added on a leaf which follows the printer's FINIS.[20] 'This may be sufficient for particular congregations,' runs this slight appendix, but for the purposes of visitation and the settling of appeals, 'meetings, conferences and synods of ministers and elders, chosen by particular churches and meetings, are to be held': the conference for every twelve churches, 'the great conference' of all such conferences in a shire, the provincial synod 'rising of the delegates of twelve great conferences', and finally the national synod. This scheme is not at all consistent with what seems to be the text of Turner's bill,[21] which provides only for an assembly of the preaching ministers of each shire (vested with a virtually episcopal authority over the parishes) and for annual general assemblies in the northern and southern provinces, with a general synod of the whole realm, to meet when occasion demanded and by leave of the queen. Here, it may be, is evidence of the divided counsels which delayed the promulgation of the Book of Discipline for so long.

The Book of Discipline was no doubt intended to replace these inadequate schemes, which bear the marks of having been hastily and carelessly prepared for the occasion. Of the various drafts which seem to have been discarded in the course of 1585 and 1586 no trace remains. The version printed for the eye of the Westminster Assembly in 1644 dates from the early months of 1587 and corresponds to most of the contemporary manuscript copies, although some of these embody proposed additions and amendments.[22] The Discipline was first composed in Latin, but was probably circulated to the country conferences in both Latin and English. The Latin text survives in five contemporary manuscripts but was not printed until modern times.[23] There are two independent and nearly contemporary translations, one of them corresponding exactly to the mid-seventeenth-century printed text.[24]

The Book of Discipline consists of two unequal parts, overlapping in a way which may possibly suggest a composite authorship. The first, 'The sacred discipline of the Church, described in the word of God', attempts to assemble all that can be gathered directly from Scripture of the ideal state of the Church, 'the discipline of Christ's Church that is necessary for all times.' Its incontestable authority is implied in the printed text of 1644 by the use of black-letter type. The second part, 'The synodical discipline', is a handbook of detailed regulations, 'applied to the use and times of the churches as their divers states may require.' These are said to be framed 'according to the analogy and general rules of the same Scripture' but their actual provenance is human, 'gathered out of the synods and use of the churches which have restored it according to the word of God, and out of sundry books that are written of the same.'[25] This explanation should save us from the labour of trying to derive the Book of Discipline from any single foreign source. By 1585 the English presbyterians could draw upon the accumulated experience of more than thirty years of improvisation in a dozen reformed churches. They were perhaps in closest sympathy with their neighbours north of the border and across the Channel, and traces of both the Scottish and French forms of discipline are probably to be found in the English directory. But the inner circle of the English presbyterians also possessed first-hand knowledge of the churches of Geneva, the Palatinate, the Netherlands and the Channel Islands, not to speak of the congregations of Calvinist refugees from four nations living in their midst. Besides, there had been more than twelve years of debate about these matters among the English Calvinists themselves, and this was reflected in the treatises of Field and Wilcox, Goodman, Travers, Cartwright, Fulke and Chaderton. The compilers of the Book of Discipline drew upon a wide and varied experience and doubtless added their own predilections and prejudices.[26]

The range of the Book of Discipline is wide. It provides for the conduct of public worship, according to the pattern of the Geneva Book, for preaching, catechizing and the administration of the sacraments, for marriage, the maintenance and training of divinity students and congregational discipline. Here our concern is with those parts relating to church government, and in particular with the treatment of two crucial problems: the distribution of authority within the congregation and the mutual rights and duties of the congregations and the higher presbyterian assemblies. In earlier English presbyterian handbooks the first problem had been variously handled, while the second had received inadequate attention. No doubt these were the weighty matters not agreed upon in 1573 and just as probably these were the things which delayed the completion of the Book of Discipline in 1585 and 1586. This should not surprise us. Stripped of their particulars, these are problems fundamental to the organization of communities, as old as the Greek *polis* or a medieval cathedral chapter, as contemporary as the modern industrial corporation or university department. The problems were connected, in that a polity which transferred power from the congregation into the hands of its officers might be expected to emphasize the authority over them of *classes* and synods, while a greater measure of democracy in the congregation was consistent with a looser confederation of local churches if not with pure congregationalism. Yet Travers himself, in the *Explicatio* of 1574, combined a marked preference for aristocracy at the local level[27] with apparent indifference to problems of church organization beyond the parish. And then there was the problem of the ruling elder: in the *Explicatio*, Travers was absorbed in the ideally potent figure and devoted much of his space to a definition of his qualities and powers. But the nearly contemporary *Second admonition to the Parliament* envisaged him as a mere 'assistant' to the pastor who was to use the advice of his minister 'chiefly'.[28]

And what was the elder?[29] A layman, an exalted churchwarden, annually appointed, partly as a safeguard against the clericalism of a dictatorial pastor? Or was he a non-preaching presbyter, an ordained and permanent minister of the Church who differed from the pastor only in that his business was government rather than edification? Generally, the tendency in Calvinist churches was to progess (or regress?) from a lay to a clerical idea of the eldership. Thus the earlier English manifestoes excluded the eldership from the ordained ministry of the Church and saw it as part of the diaconate.[30] But the Genevan *Forme of prayers* had always grouped the elders with 'the rest of the ministers', and Waldegrave's edition of 1584 specifies that their 'election and ordination is as the pastors': the prayer, trial and words of ordination respecting their special office.'[31] And now, according to the Book of Discipline, all the officers of the Church, pastors, doctors, elders and deacons are ministers, although the pastors and doctors alone are ministers of the word and sacraments. Pastors, doctors, elders together constitute 'a presbytery, which is a consistory, and as it were a senate of elders', although only the last are 'properly called elders.' The pastor presides over this body, even to the extent of 'directing of the eldership', but decisions are taken by a simple majority vote.

As in Travers's and Cartwright's earlier writings, the government of the congregation is oligarchical, and the role of the rank and file a largely passive one. 'By the common counsel of the eldership all things are directed that belong to the state of their Church.' But in all 'the greater affairs of the Church' such as the excommunication of a member, or the choosing or deposing of a minister, the consistory cannot act 'without the knowledge and consent of the church'.[32] Unlike the latest editions of the *Forme of prayers*, the Book of Discipline lays down no definite procedures for electing and ordaining a pastor, except that candidates are to be examined 'not only by one eldership, but also by some greater meeting and assembly'.[33] So this is a flexible constitution which might be variously interpreted by a dictatorial pastor, a determined eldership, a vigorous *classis* or a rebellious congregation.

There is more precision in the constitution of the higher presbyterian assemblies, the *classes*, rendered in the English translation as 'conferences', and the provincial, national and universal synods. In earlier manifestoes, the treatment of these bodies had left many questions unanswered. The account in the *Second admonition* was confused and very hypothetical, the writer evidently assuming that conferences would only occasionally intervene in the ordinary life of the churches. In the *Explicatio* Travers exhausted the subject in two of his one hundred and ninety-three pages,[34] and while Fulke's *Briefe and plaine declaration* had much to say on the general theme of synods, it made no attempt to define an hierarchy of assemblies adapted to English conditions.[35] So the Book of Discipline contains the first definitive treatment of synodical government in the English context.[36] It first explains that the 'communicating together' of churches is in order that 'all things in them may be so directed both in regard of doctrine and also of discipline, as by the word of God they ought to be.' The churches of a particular 'resort' instruct their representatives, equip them with letters of credence and send them to the assembly where matters are determined 'by the common opinion of those who meet so to communicate together.' Although no particular church has any authority over another, the assembly binds the whole. Every particular church 'ought to obey the opinion of more churches'; 'the less is alway to give place to the greater and all to the greatest.' An aggrieved party may appeal from assembly to assembly 'till he come to a general council.' 'But it is to be understood, that the sentence of the assemblies be holden firm until it be otherwise judged by an assembly of greater authority.' Only those who exercise public functions in the Church of ministry or eldership, and who have subscribed to its doctrine and discipline 'and have promised to behave themselves according to the word of God', are chosen for the assemblies, and only accredited representatives may vote, although other elders and ministers and deacons and students as well may attend and contribute to the discussion. In every assembly there must be a moderator, who is changed on every occasion. He provides for a record to be made of the acts of the meeting, delivers answers to questions, executes censures and generally conducts proceedings. Meetings open with a roll-call and the reading of the acts of the last assembly. After this the business belonging to the meeting is expedited: instructions from the churches and their letters of credence are read in order, the state of the churches is considered and matters of common concern determined. 'Lastly, if it seem meet, the delegates present may be censured.'

First among these assemblies comes the conference (or *classis*), a meeting of the representatives of 'a few churches, as for example, of twelve', composed of one minister and one elder from each congregation and meeting once every six weeks. This is both an administrative body and an exercise in which the ministers take turns to preach. But for the presence of elders, the practice is that of the Dedham conference. The members are

'specially to look into the state of the churches of that resort and conference', to see whether they observe the doctrine and discipline of the
gospel, to note that every church is supplied with a minister and other
officers, and that proper care is taken of the schools and of the poor.
The most important of these functions and the very hallmark of presbyterianism is the effective control which the conferences exercise over the
election of ministers, but on this the Discipline is strangely silent. To
learn about the procedure on these occasions one has to look at the
further edition of the *Forme of prayers* printed by Richard Schilders in the
Netherlands in 1586. When a vacancy occurs, the elders of the congregation are to seek the assistance of the pastors of the next conference to
them. Together they are to assemble the congregation and after exhorting
them to pray for a divinely inspired election retire to 'advise of one fit
for the place that is vacant' and to prove and examine him. Together
they ordain him with the laying on of hands.[37] In practice, as the records
of the Dedham conference would suggest, few congregations in need of
a new pastor were content prayerfully to accept the guidance of their
local conference. But practice, as we shall see, was somewhat far removed
from the theoretical arrangements of the Book of Discipline.

Twenty-four *classes* constitute a province and each sends two ministers
and two elders to the provincial synod, which meets every half year 'or
oftener, till the Discipline be settled', and three months before the holding
of any national synod. (Vanished, it will be noticed, is the 'great conference' of the shire proposed in Turner's bill and book of 1584.) The
ministers and elders – collectively the 'eldership' of a particular congregation – are charged with responsibility for appointing the time and place
of the next provincial synod and with all necessary preparations. To this
church are sent matters arising from the *classes* and matters of general
concern for the whole province, whereupon the eldership gives notice of
time and place and of the things to be debated. At the end of a provincial
synod, it is the further duty of the receiving eldership to supply copies of
the acts to the delegates and to forward them to the national synod. The
national synod, or convocation, is called in the same way, by a designated
eldership, but only on the advice of its provincial synod, and it is made up
of three ministers and three elders from each province. It deals with 'things
pertaining to the churches of the whole nation or kingdom, as the doctrine,
discipline, ceremonies, things not decided by inferior meetings, appeals
and such like'. Finally, at the summit of this graduated hierarchy of
assemblies, there is the ultimate projection of 'a general or ecumenical
Council'.

There is not the slightest suggestion that these assemblies are dependent upon the queen's consent for bringing them into being, arranging the time and place of their meetings, or for the authority of their decisions. The Book of Discipline serves the needs of a wholly autonomous kingdom of Christ and has no mention of Queen Elizabeth or of any other earthly sovereign. And if the magistrate has no place in the Church's government, why tarry for her?

2 The Bill and Book

'Specially you are commanded by her Majesty to take heed that none care be given or time afforded the wearysome solicitations of those that commonly be called puritans, wherewithal the late Parliaments have been exceedingly importuned.'

(SERJEANT JOHN PUCKERING, Speaker, addressing the House of Commons of 1586–7. Queen's College, Oxford, MS. 284, fol. 35)

PURITANS WHO SUBSCRIBED to the Discipline thereby promised to pray for its establishment, and 'as God shall offer opportunities and give us to discern it so expedient', to make humble suit to the queen, the Council and Parliament, 'and by all other lawful and convenient means to further and advance' it. In late October 1586 the opportunity was provided of a new Parliament. The puritans forgot their earlier disappointments and mounted yet another elaborate campaign. A presbyterian bill, more radical even than that of 1584, was presented to the House of Commons and with it a revised edition of the Geneva prayer book. What this Parliament was not permitted to see were the secrets of the Book of Discipline itself. These had another purpose which its subscribers had in mind when they undertook 'to be guided by it and according to it', so far as the laws of the land and the peace of the present state of the Church might suffer them.[1] From the conference of ministers gathered in London to take advantage of Parliament, and even before the presbyterian bill was brought on to the floor of the House, copies of the Discipline went out to the country, with a form of approbation and instructions for putting it into immediate practice. This was the double strategy to which Travers, Field and their closest confidants were now committed. The most magnificent of parliamentary failures was to be succeeded at once by the launching of the 'grand design' of a practical presbyterian movement.

The puritans had had time to prepare for this Parliament as they had not for the session of 1584–5. Although it was to be a new assembly, called especially to settle the great matter of Mary Stuart, the previous Parliament had stood prorogued until November 1586, so that there was always the expectation that it might be recalled.[2] The survey of the ministry was now as complete as it would ever be and its very incompleteness was made an argument for reform. For if this was how things were in the best furnished counties, where preachers could be found to conduct such an inquiry, 'it may be easy to gather how scant and how dear the preaching of the word of God is in other shires and countries.'[3] Four days after the opening of Parliament, statistical information digested from the surveys for eleven counties and London was summarized in a 'brief of divers countries and shires, gathered truly out of the surveys made the last Parliament, and partly this, 2 of November, 1586.' This was attached to a 'general supplication made to the Parliament', also dated November, an enormous and tendentious document of not much less than ten thousand words, containing a reasoned statement of the whole puritan case for the reform of the ministry and church government. The writer professes to look to the bishops as 'lights and examples to all the ministers of the Church', but his presbyterian convictions are only lightly concealed, and an indictment of the episcopal order is implied in almost every clause. Nevertheless, the ostensible theme is the ever-popular and relatively innocuous plea for a free, godly ministry: 'Command the golden candlesticks to be restored again, which have been taken away and removed from the midst of us, and let us not uncomfortably lead our life in the midst of this darkness.'[4]

This was the theme of a string of secondary petitions: one attached to the survey for Cornwall claiming to come from 'four score and ten thousand souls, which for want of the word are in extreme misery'; another from London which spoke of 'the woeful estate of many thousand souls'; and yet another from 'some of the students of the university of Cambridge', complaining that 'able men, furnished with sufficient gifts to teach the ignorant people' were deterred from entering the ministry while 'the very scum of the people' were preferred in their places, 'to the ruin of thousands of souls'. In the Cambridge petition the presbyterian motive again obtrudes: a grand disputation is demanded with twenty or thirty speakers on either side, to determine whether the Church is to be ruled by lord bishops and their chancellors, or by the eldership.[5]

Essex was a good source of combustible material, for Bishop Aylmer's visitation of the previous summer had left no less than forty ministers suspended or otherwise in trouble in that county alone, most of them for refusing the surplice. Among them were Chapman, Parker, Newman,

Tay and others of the Dedham conference and the entire membership of the Braintree conference.[6] This local crisis stimulated an outburst of organized activity throughout the county. In September the conferences were planning a grand petition to the Council 'for many towns', and 'Maldon to have one by itself'.[7] From Essex in November came a petition to the members for Maldon from the inhabitants of that part of the county; a supplication to the Council from ninety-eight inhabitants of the hundred of Rochford; a petition 'of certain hundreds in Essex to the Parliament'; 'the supplication of Dunmow' to Lord Rich, 'appointed to the Parliament', bearing two hundred and thirty-six names and dated November 1st; and a petition from twenty-nine parishioners of Leigh in favour of their suspended pastor, William Negus (lately a preacher in Ipswich and a member of the Dedham conference). Attached to this was Negus's personal account of his troubles and the statement that 'whatsoever the godly brethren shall agree upon concerning a supplication for the liberty of us, the ministers suspended, to be put up at this present Parliament, I willingly, as if I were present, do assent thereunto.'[8]

This by no means exhausts the tally of petitions inspired by this occasion, but these were the most significant, revealing as they do a well organized, quite unspontaneous agitation. In 1584 the petitions had been drawn up by gentlemen of worship, justices of the peace and others. These of 1586 professed to come from thousands of hungry souls, the poor Commons of England. But there is no doubt of their true source and inspiration, or that this was clerical rather than lay. And it is quite certain, more so than of the 1584 campaign, that this bombardment had no other purpose than to soften the ground for a direct presbyterian assault on the foundations of the Church of England. It seems that Field and his friends enjoyed an initiative which was not entirely theirs two years earlier. In June 1585, in anticipation of the customary meeting at Cambridge at Commencement time, the Dedham conference had proposed as topics for discussion the problems which were of perennial concern to its members: how far one might use the Prayer Book, the local dangers of separatism, whether the godly ministers should obey a summons to the ecclesiastical court. But one of the two extremists in the group, Henry Sandes of Boxford, moved on this occasion that 'some things might be considered of for the helping forward of discipline the next Parliament.' This the remainder of the brethren 'liked of, but deferred.' Nothing was done at Cambridge about the matters proposed by Dedham. Does this mean that the things which were exercising Sandes took up all the time? When Parliament opened in November, it was a cause of concern to the Dedham ministers that the brethren of London seemed to be interested in nothing less than a total presbyterian victory.[9]

Even in the parliamentary elections there is evidence of some concerted and not ineffective activity by the puritan conferences. When it became known that a new Parliament was summoned, requiring new elections, Chapman of Dedham warned Field – no doubt superfluously – to take note of all the parliamentary boroughs in the land and to use all good means to secure the return of religious gentlemen. 'Confer amongst yourselves how it may best be compassed.' The Council, on the other hand, had already directed that so far as possible the same members should be returned who had sat in 1584–5, so that this House of Commons was to contain a higher proportion of former members than any previous Elizabethan Parliament: more than half had sat two years earlier. It is all the more notable that among the new men who returned to this Parliament, or who came to Westminster for the first time, were a number of extreme puritans; among them Peter Wentworth and his good friend Anthony Cope, as members for Northampton and Banbury, and a young firebrand from a family of slightly unstable extremists, Job Throckmorton of Haseley, who was returned for Warwick.[10]

Did Field and his friends manipulate the mechanism which persuaded Cope and Wentworth to offer their candidature and these boroughs (later almost legendary for their puritanism) to return them? Job Throckmorton's election certainly contained some intriguing features. It was carried by the popular element in Warwick against the will of the bailiff and some of the principal burgesses of the town. Yet he afterwards claimed to have stood by persuasion of 'the best in the shire and, by your leave, by some of your own company'. The division suggested by these circumstances may well have had its religious aspects. They followed hard on Cartwright's arrival in Warwick as master of Leicester's hospital. Not long before the elections, the whole town had been shaken when a prosperous wool draper – and a hypocrite – had collapsed and died only hours after this latter-day Savonarola had taken him to task 'plainly and faithfully'. The association of political and social changes with the introduction of 'plain' reformed preaching is a familiar phenomenon in the history of some South German and Swiss cities in the sixteenth century. It would repay investigation in some English market towns as well.[11]

By whatever means they were elected, there was a group of members in this Parliament, most of whom had not sat in 1584, who were resolved to promote an all-or-nothing, presbyterian reformation: Wentworth, Cope and Throckmorton, Robert Bainbridge, Edward Lewkenor, the

Suffolk gentleman who sat for Maldon, and Ranulf Hurleston. In 1584 Peter Turner seems to have acted alone in sponsoring his bill and book; there were no prepared speeches from other members to support his motion when he had shot his bolt. But now there was a whole unofficial committee of members to handle the same cause in this Parliament, which met before and doubtless during the session 'for the preferring in Parliament a book touching the rites of the Church and a form of an Act for establishing of the same'. Above all there was Wentworth, a good parliamentary manager. It can be safely assumed that a general conference of ministers from the country was in session not far from Westminster at the same time. Indeed we have evidence of it. Part of its time was spent in a vain assault on Convocation with a Latin address 'tending to reconciliation', which contained Dudley Fenner's sharp invective. No doubt there was collusion between these clerical delegates and the secret committee of presbyterian M.P.s. When one of the conspirators – Throckmorton – had occasion to speak in the Commons of the 'lamentable outcries of the poor distressed souls of the land' he almost admitted as much: 'And it may be some of them stand now at your door, thirsting for relief.' The moderate puritan demands of 1581 and 1584 amounted to a lay programme conceived by laymen and tending to control of the Church by Parliament and the local commissions of the peace, and according to the English Common Law. But committed presbyterians like Wentworth or Throckmorton are hardly to be thought of as laymen in the same sense as Knollys, Norton or Beale. Beyond question they would have been ruling elders in a presbyterian establishment. When Sir Walter Mildmay later attacked the bill and book in Parliament, he defended the honesty of its sponsor, Anthony Cope, explaining that the documents had been 'put into his hands', presumably by the ministers.[12]

The bill which Cope and his friends had in hand was perhaps the most immoderate measure ever to come before the House of Commons. It was as deliberately revolutionary as the proposals of the moderate puritan parliament men were conservative. Of its two thousand five hundred words, the preamble occupied all but one hundred and fifty. This conveyed a tendentious account of the English Reformation from the reign of Henry VIII, representing it as a progressive process left woefully incomplete by the queen at her accession and since. Elizabeth had established 'a certain form of church government and common prayers, and caused certain penal statutes to be made for the strict observation of the same.' But Christ had committed the guidance of His Church to pastors, teachers and elders, and had ordained synods and councils, provincial and national.

307

These 'perpetual and necessary ordinances' were 'so perverted and corrupted in the order and discipline of this Church and in the said Book of Common Prayer and Administration of the Sacraments that scarce any part remaineth sound.' The remedy was prescribed in two terse enacting clauses. The first provided that 'the book hereunto annexed', the Geneva liturgy, should be 'authorized, put in use and practised.' The second clause proposed, with a startling economy of language, to make 'utterly void and of none effect' all such existing laws, customs, statutes, ordinances and constitutions as established and defined the worship, ceremonies and government of the Church. Not only the entire fabric of the Tudor ecclesiastical legislation, with the Prayer Book, but all that still survived from before the Reformation of canon law and of ecclesiastical institutions, offices and foundations: all came within the range of this engine of demolition. 'Tabula rasa,' exclaims Sir John Neale; 'stark revolution. Its like was never seen before in English Parliament.'[13]

Cope's book was a new edition of the *Forme of common prayers*, recently published by the Dutch printer, Richard Schilders,[14] and bearing the marks of the activity which had consumed the puritan movement in recent months. According to Bancroft, who referred to it in a famous sermon preached at Paul's Cross two years later, it contained 'not so few as 600 alterations' in the Waldegrave edition of 1584.[15] Certainly the revision was extensive. Some of the material was rearranged, and a number of changes made, some of them to accommodate the needs of the English congregations in the Low Countries. The procedures for the election and ordination of a pastor in a vacant congregation were emended in such a way as to emphasize the dependence of the congregation on the pastors of their nearest conference, and to reduce still further the element of congregational participation. In 1584 it had been assumed that the whole congregation would 'advise and consider' who might best fill the place, and the elders and neighbouring ministers were to act as examiners only if there was more than one nomination. Now they were 'to meet by themselves' and 'advise of one fit for the place.' And it was now directed for the first time that the pastors assisting in the election should share with the elders of the congregation in the laying on of hands in ordination. These changes may reflect a debate continuing within the movement. The clause, inserted as an appendix to the 1584 edition, which provided for the holding of conferences and synods, was now abbreviated and generalized, no longer defining a particular constitution of conferences. Finally, an entirely new declaration was added 'of the civil magistrate's authority in causes of the church'. This asserted that, 'besides this discipline of the church', God had placed 'the sovereign magistrate in the highest authority upon earth, next under him, within their dominions, over all persons and causes, as well ecclesiastical as civil, to see and command the ordering of them, as by his most holy word he hath appointed.' For all its echoes of Henrician language, this notable qualification of the Calvinist theory of government was probably inserted with a view to the susceptibilities of the Dutch authorities rather than out of any respect for the ecclesiastical supremacy claimed by Elizabeth.[16]

At this Parliament, as in 1584, the intensification of the Elizabethan crisis created an exceptionally favourable atmosphere in which to advocate a drastic reconstitution of the Church. For over a year a state of actual if undeclared war had existed with Spain, a conflict with overtones which our century would characterize as ideological. While English forces and an English captain-general campaigned in the Netherlands and the 'Enterprise of England' was under way in the Spanish Atlantic ports, the shadowy, disaffected, often simple-minded fanatics on the lunatic fringe of the English recusant community were again planning the assassination of Elizabeth to make way for Mary Stuart. In July 1586, Mary's incriminating correspondence with the principal plotter, Anthony Babington, was intercepted by Walsingham; in late September, Babington and thirteen of his accomplices were executed in St Giles Fields, an occasion exploited by the ballad-mongers and pamphleteers. In October, Mary was put on trial before a commission of peers, councillors and judges, the procedure for which Parliament had made provision two years before. She was found guilty. But the execution of the Scottish queen would be more a political than a judicial act, and the deed could not be accomplished without the participation of Parliament, the Grand Council of the Realm; as Burghley put it, 'to make the burden better borne and the world abroad better satisfied.'[17]

The Babington plot and Mary's proven complicity ensured a favourable hearing for any puritan measure which promised to make better provision for the safety of the queen and country. But if 'the great cause' excited religious passions, it also concentrated them on the single object of Mary's destruction, and until that was accomplished no other business could hope to make progress. For this was not so much a conventional parliamentary session as an extraordinary tribunal. Throughout November Parliament pressed for 'the speedy cutting off of the queen of Scots', while Elizabeth turned and twisted every way to escape the cruel dilemma 'that my surety cannot be established without a princess's head.' Some of the presbyterian members – Throckmorton, Bainbridge and Turner – were themselves prominent in this business. To destroy the Scottish queen, Throckmorton told the House, would be 'one of the fairest riddances that ever the Church of God had.' On December 2nd the House was adjourned until mid-February. The queen had been pushed a little closer to her dreadful decision, and Mary's fate was rather more certain, although it was not until the first week of February that the warrant for her execution was finally signed, sealed and dispatched. The execution was at Fotheringhay, on February 8th.[18] All this time the puritan campaign for further reformation hung fire. The great dossier of surveys and petitions, many of them dated early November, had not yet reached even the doors of Parliament.

The whole effort might have been wasted but for the urgent need of the government for a subsidy to finance the war in the Netherlands, for this brought about the resumption of Parliament on February 15th. In the event, the continued absence of many of the leading members of both Houses delayed serious business until the 22nd of the month. Thereafter, several days were fully occupied with a debate on the perils and necessities of the foreign scene, which led up to the grant of supply, and with much committee work on the same matters. This was another congenial theme for the extreme puritan members, and Job Throckmorton made another speech, as patriotic as it was godly. When Anthony Cope, the member for Banbury, rose to his feet on Monday, February 27th, to commend the presbyterian bill and book, he was probably seizing the first favourable opportunity that had presented itself since Parliament assembled three months before.[19]

What followed leaves us in no doubt that Cope had made the opening move in a carefully planned operation in which each of the presbyterian conspirators had his part to play. When the Speaker warned the House of the queen's command 'not to meddle with this matter', Cope's collaborators seem to have whipped up a cry for the book to be read, so that the Speaker was obliged to instruct the clerk to proceed. When someone then intervened to oppose the reading, Lewkenor, Throckmorton, Hurleston and Bainbridge rose one after the other with prepared speeches in support of the motion. They held the floor until the adjournment, and the House rose with the expectation of hearing the book read on the following day. But there was to be no reading. The next morning the Speaker had to inform the House that the queen had sent for the bill and book, together with Turner's bill and book of 1584, still in his possession since the last session; and that he had been obliged to comply. But this was not enough to bring an excited and indignant House to heel.

Instead of recollecting the queen's clear prohibition of any meddling with church matters, it fell into the kind of free-ranging and directionless discussion of ecclesiastical abuses which was so much to the taste of these religious, public-spirited and garrulous gentlemen. Among those who intervened was the member for the Carmarthen boroughs, Edward Downlee, the son of a Buckinghamshire landowner settled as a lonely Calvinist on his mother's estates in the fastness of west Wales. Downlee collaborated with Throckmorton in presenting a supplication for preachers to be sent to his adoptive country, in the form of a printed tract by that 'poor young man, born and bred in the mountains of Wales', John Penry. The occasion served for a sensational exposure of the idolatry of the Welsh, whose conservation of popish superstitions smacked of an underlying paganism. 'What ignorance they live in for lack of learned and honest ministers.' Other speakers followed to the same effect, well content to offer only minor variations on the eternal theme of the idle, blind, dumb ministry, the necessity for preaching, the dangers they all faced.[20]

It is probably significant that only one of our group of presbyterian conspirators is recorded as having taken part in this debate. Perhaps the others were elsewhere, considering what their next concerted action should be. When the House met on the following day, March 1st and Ash Wednesday, there seems to have been a new plan. Peter Wentworth took the floor, not to submit to the queen's intervention, nor merely to evade it as other gentlemen had done the day before, but characteristically to exploit it in a celebrated defence of the imagined liberties of the House of Commons. In the rhetoric of his ringing, prophetic questions, Parliament was entrenched in the fundamental constitution of the country with prerogatives of its own, a deadly threat to the Tudor conception of kingship. On this showing, Elizabeth was more than justified in regarding puritanism as a more insidious enemy than popery. Wentworth should have been supported by other speakers, for we learn that at this point John Butler, Lewkenor's fellow-burgess for Maldon in Essex, 'brake his faith in forsaking the matter.' The initiative temporarily lost, the Speaker responded to one of those messages which Wentworth found so objectionable, summoning him to Court, and the House was adjourned. Before evening Wentworth was in the Tower, where his collaborators – Cope, Lewkenor, Hurleston and Bainbridge – joined him the following day, their offence – the holding of extra-parliamentary conferences – not protected by privilege. Job Throckmorton was soon sent to the Tower as well, the penalty of some heated, undiplomatic remarks about James VI of Scotland.[21]

Meanwhile the book had not been read, and to those who were ignorant of its contents – the majority of the House – it must have seemed that the imprisoned members were in trouble for their devotion to the Commonwealth and their zeal for a godly preaching ministry. As for the accompanying bill, it was evidently no part of the conspirators' tactics to reveal its radical nature to the House, at least at this stage. In his speech, which we possess in full, Throckmorton spoke of the queen's safety, equated what was maliciously called puritanism with loyal, moral and religious conduct, argued the need for moral discipline, and diagnosed the bane of the Church and Commonwealth as ' "the dumb ministry, the dumb ministry", yea, if I were asked a thousand times, I must say, "the dumb ministry".'[22] Lewkenor – if the parliamentary diarist gives an adequate account of his speech – merely showed 'the necessity of preaching and of a learned ministry'. These speeches are no adequate indication of the aspirations of those who made them, but they are a good measure of the state of mind of the assembly which they were designed to convince, as was the undisciplined debate of the following day, when 'the dumb ministry' was the general complaint of the House.[23]

But for a revelation of what the enactment of Cope's bill and book would actually entail, the Commons had to wait until March 4th, and for three weighty government speeches delivered on that day by Sir Christopher Hatton (vice-chamberlain and soon to be lord chancellor), Sir Walter Mildmay (chancellor of the exchequer), and Sir Thomas Egerton (solicitor-general). By this time, with Wentworth and his friends in the Tower, the initiative had passed to more moderate puritan spokesmen. Hatton spoke in reply to a speech from Sir John Higham of Barrow in West Suffolk, member for the shire and deputy lieutenant, a representative of the more substantial country gentlemen who stood somewhat to the right of presbyterians like Wentworth, Cope or Throckmorton, in demanding nothing more than a free preaching ministry and a minimum of episcopal interference in the affairs of the Church in their own countries. Higham's purpose, indeed, was to speak in favour of the members committed to the Tower 'for speaking of their conscience', but the only reference he seems to have made to the cause for which they had been sent there was to complain about the lack of preachers in his own country. One might have supposed that there was nothing more at stake in all that had transpired than the condition of the ministry and the frustration of the Commons in their will to reform it. This was an impression which the government was bound to dispel by exposing the true contents of the bill and book, which would have been in the hands of the Council since the Speaker surrendered them five days before.

Mildmay's attack must have been particularly impressive. His godliness was not open to question, and he had associated himself with the moderate puritan aspirations of the two previous Parliaments. His speech left the House in no doubt of the unprecedented radicalism of the measures which they had been willing to entertain. 'He never saw the like to that – all to be repealed – the word so general that it may reach to Magna Carta.' Even the legislation against popish recusants stood to be repealed. Egerton, the ablest lawyer of his age, substantiated Mildmay's arguments in detail. The basis of his speech was an exhaustive list of 'alterations' which 'by this bill ... will follow.'[24]

But the most important of the three speeches was Hatton's: important both for its content, and because Hatton was only partly the author. In its drafting he was assisted – to say no more – by his chaplain, and that chaplain was none other than Richard Bancroft, the mind and the nose of anti-puritanism who long before this date had set himself to discover the dealings and devices of the precisians with such pertinacity that he now knew them almost better than they knew themselves.[25] Bancroft was an asset shared by Hatton and Archbishop Whitgift. 'He remained with the late lord chancellor twelve years at the least, for the most part in her Majesty's Court,' ran Whitgift's remarkable testimonial of 1597, 'and was in good reputation with him, and often employed in sundry matters of great importance, for her Highness's service. Since his said lordship's death, he hath remained with the like credit five years almost, with the lord archbishop of Canterbury.'[26] This constellation, combining Hatton's privileged position towards the queen, Bancroft's incomparable knowledge of the puritan movement, and Whitgift's unswerving determination to root out this schismatic conspiracy, was now in the ascendant, and there could be no worse portent for the puritans. One of the first fruits of the partnership was this speech, for what appears to be the original draft is in Bancroft's hand, and the speech was sometimes described as 'Doctor Bancroft's Discourse'.[27]

A manuscript volume in Lambeth Palace Library – MS. 178 – records the close collaboration in these matters of archbishop, lord chancellor and chaplain. It is in the hand of Whitgift's secretary, Michael Murgatroyd, and contains copies of Hatton's speeches and memoranda of important occasions in his career. Besides a copy of the speech against the bill and book,[28] the collection includes numerous other tracts, draft speeches and heads of arguments against the presbyterian platform, several of them evidently inspired by the events of this Parliament: for example, 'That the present form of our ecclesiastical government in England is both godly and necessary' and 'That the ordinances of our Church and the means appointed by law for their execution are good and commendable'. 'My divinity is not much,' says the writer of one of these pieces, with the voice of Hatton.[29] But the arrangement of these short treatises is reminiscent of Bancroft's earlier essays in the same vein; and some of them are clearly his work, such as a collection of 'Certain places of scripture which the precisians use'.[30]

There is no reason to suppose that Hatton was normally dependent on speech-writers. We have discarded the legend of the dancing chancellor and a proper estimate of his abilities now includes an appreciation of one of the great parliamentary orators of the age. But there can be little doubt that on this occasion Hatton leant heavily on the expert, and that his protestation that he spoke 'but like a politic man' and not as a divine was a mere pose. Much of his argument was typical of Bancroft's polemic, as he would perfect it in his famous Paul's Cross sermon and in his published exposures of the puritan conspiracy, *Daungerous positions* and the *Survay of the pretended holy discipline*. There was the same insinuation that puritanism inevitably tended to an anabaptist confusion, and the same shrewd appeal to the self-interest of the property-owning laity. The presbyterian revolution would be at their expense. It would deprive them of their ecclesiastical patronage, while the cost of maintaining the fourfold ministry in every parish would require the resumption of secularized church property, impropriate tithes and perhaps even abbey lands, besides the spoiling of bishoprics and cathedral churches. This part of Hatton's speech corresponds exactly to what Bancroft had written two or three years before in an unpublished fragment, 'The devises and practises of the precisians'. Every parish, he had then calculated, was to be burdened with the maintenance of ten or a dozen officers, with the consequence that 'noblemen and gentlemen must surrender out of their hands their impropriations, and such their possessions as did heretofore belong to the abbeys; cathedral churches must be overthrown; bishops' livings are to be altered.'[31] As Hatton told the Commons, 'it toucheth us all in our inheritances.' At the conclusion of this triad of official utterances, Hatton again intervened to tell the House that it was the queen's pleasure that they should take note of certain puritan tracts, and to dictate a short bibliography. This too smacks of Bancroft, who made it his business to go through every puritan pamphlet with a toothcomb. Hatton had spoken of Anthony Cope as having been 'slily led' into sponsoring the bill and book. But it looks as if there was some controversial divinity at work on his side of the House as well.

Indeed Cope's bill and book seems to have stirred up the learned clergy in the opposite camp into attempting a fresh refutation of presbyterianism. It was the beginning of an Anglican riposte which in the course of the next ten years was to produce much tedious and uninspired controversial writing and one work of genius, Hooker's *Of the laws of ecclesiastical polity*. When Convocation was dissolved late in March, it offered the queen an address containing an attack on the bill and book as 'absurd in divinity and dangerous in policy to this state, as it appeareth by the several writings of such as are favourers and devisers thereof, and by the bill and book itself.'[32]

In the last fortnight of this Parliament, the advocates of moderate reform made a last attempt to revive the programme of 1584, and once again it was proved how largely uncontroversial these proposals were within the House of Commons, and how in this moderate sense the main body of the House was solidly puritan in its sympathies. Sir John Higham, the spokesman for this interest, proposed a motion aimed at curbing Whitgift's *ex officio* processes against the puritan ministers, and 'that some good course might be taken to have a learned ministry.' The motion was popular. A large committee was appointed, with many of the same members who had prepared the petition of sixteen clauses which dealt with similar *gravamina* at the last Parliament: Robert Beale, Francis Hastings and zealous privy councillors like Mildmay. They were 'to confer upon some reasonable motion to be made unto her Majesty for redress in these things.' There is no record of what, if anything, was achieved, although such a 'motion' does seem to have been made. But Sir John Neale believes that at this point all religious debate was finally silenced by the arrival of a peremptory message from the queen, perhaps procured by Whitgift, 'why you ought not to deal with matters of religion'. This said nothing which had not been said before, but it made its points with rare acerbity. Her Majesty was fully resolved of the truth of what she had already established, 'and mindeth not now to begin to settle herself in causes of religion.' 'The platform which is desired' she found frivolous, and 'most prejudicial to the religion established, to her crown, to her government, and to her subjects.' If anything were amiss, it appertained to the clergy to see it redressed. 'Her Majesty taketh your petition herein to be against the prerogatives of her crown; for by your full consents, it hath been confirmed and enacted (as the truth therein requireth) that the full power, authority, jurisdiction and supremacy in church causes ... should be united and annexed to the imperial crown of this realm.' Those who had defied this principle remained in the Tower at least until the end of the session.[33]

The front door of the Church could not have been more firmly and finally closed against a further reformation, and, as we shall see in the next chapter, the presbyterian element in the puritan movement had already begun to concentrate its attention on other means of access. Yet the myth of the puritan queen somehow survived even this Parliament. Two years later an Oxford preacher assured his audience of Elizabeth's 'holy purpose to remove all the unlearned, as godly Nehemiah removed them that could not show their pedigree from Aaron.' Had not a bishop admitted openly at the visitation in Andover in September 1587 that at the late Parliament, if he and Archbishop Whitgift 'had not bowed before her Majesty, all the unlearned had been removed'?[34]

3 A Mixed Reception

SPERING   I will not stand to justifie the calling of the bishopps; I have a better calling than the calling of the bishopps.

BARROW   But what then thinke you of the calling of theis bishops?

SPERING   I confess it to be unlawfull.

BARROW   Set that downe under your hand.

SPERING   To what end; that were to bring my self into danger.

(Conference of Mr Thomas Spering, rector of St Mary Magdalene, Milk Street, and the separatist, Henry Barrow, March 14th, 1590. A Collection of Certain letters and Conferences in Writings of John Greenwood, 1587–90, ed. Carlson, Eliz. Nonconformist Texts, iv. 190)

THE PROGRAMME CONTAINED in the bill and book was so extreme, so manifestly unacceptable, not merely to the queen but to all responsible opinion, that one both marvels at the sanguinity of its sponsors, and speculates as to the precise place of these parliamentary manœuvres in their total strategy. There seems to be no doubt that two or three months before Cope's initiative in the Commons, the ministers meeting in London had already dispatched copies of the Book of Discipline to some at least of the country conferences, accompanied by 'articles of approbation' and other instructions. Since the safe way to distribute these documents would have been for the delegates themselves to carry them back to their homes, we may guess that the Book went out before Christmas, after the adjournment of Parliament on December 2nd, 1586.

The form of approbation[1] with which the conferences were now to be confronted begins with a confession that the Book of Discipline agrees with the word of God 'so far forth as we are able to judge and discern of it'; a general affirmation of desire to see it established, with the exception, as some copies allow, of 'some few points' referred 'for further resolution'; and a promise to advance it by supplication and suit, and to put it into immediate practice, so far as this is compatible with legality and the peace of the Church. More specifically, the subscribers declare that in their 'sermons' they will uniformly follow the orders of the Book in its provisions for preaching, the sacraments, baptism and the time of the Lord's supper. They also agree to follow the order of meetings set down, 'as far as it concerneth the ministers of the word', that is, excluding the participation of elders. They undertake to meet every six weeks in 'classical conferences' with their neighbours, and with such other brethren as they shall desire (or, as some copies significantly put it, 'shall be desired') to join with them. And according to the order of the Book, they will send their delegates to half-yearly 'provincial meetings'. In most versions the subscribers further agree to attend the general assembly every year and at all Parliaments, 'and as often as by order it shall be thought good to be assembled.' The Warwickshire ministers – the only ministers whose subscriptions the authorities could prove – later insisted in the Star Chamber that their undertaking to put the Book into immediate execution applied only to the order of their sermons and meetings, and that only in so far as 'the peace of the Church now established in England and the laws of the land' might allow, 'and no further'.[2]

With the form of subscription went other proposals, which survive as part of the Dedham copy of the articles of approbation.[3] It was decided that all the conferences represented in London when these proposals were made should for the time being constitute one province. Seven ministers were named to represent Essex at provincial conferences, 'and whomsoever else the brethren there shall think well of.' It was agreed that questions concerning the use of the Book of Common Prayer should be determined by the local conferences, 'seeing they already have had cause to discover the wants thereof, and to forbear them in many parts as they do.' (Dedham repeatedly failed to secure resolution from the higher assemblies on this perplexing problem.) The corrected Geneva liturgy was to be sent out to the conferences, 'preferred here at the Parliament', and used 'in the parts abroad' (the Netherlands?) if the brethren there thought good. Ministers were to provide for the future supply of the ministry by taking divinity students into their households and directing their studies. If they were unable to afford the expense, the charges were to be 'otherwise borne'. The oppression of the bishops and their officers and courts 'towards the people, but especially towards the ministers', was to be 'registered and gathered'. Collections were to be made to help the French protestant refugees. The next provincial conference was to be held at London 'about the midst of Michaelmas term'.[4]

So much for the proposals of the London assembly. How were they received in the country? In the past both nonconformist and Anglican historians have tended to agree in the assumption that the Book of Discipline expressed the common mind of virtually all the puritan ministry, and many have quoted the unsubstantiated figure of five hundred subscribers which cannot be traced behind Daniel Neal's eighteenth-century *History of the Puritans*.[5] But how many ministers in fact subscribed?

We learn from a letter received in Dedham in June 1587 that besides directing that ministers should 'sort themselves together' in classical conferences, the London assembly had advised that no meeting should count more than ten members, and that those which exceeded that number should 'sort themselves with others of their brethren next adjoining where defect was.' The five members of the barely viable Braintree conference, headed by Richard Rogers of Wethersfield, presently asked Dedham, with a membership of more than a dozen, to release Laurence Newman, who lived in their neighbourhood, at Coggeshall. Newman had known as early as January that such a request was likely to arise, and in February Dr Richard Crick of East Bergholt warned the Dedham conference that he too 'should be moved to be of another meeting.' Since neither Newman nor Crick had any desire to leave its fellowship, Dedham turned a deaf ear to these requests. The letter from Braintree was left unanswered for six months, and was then firmly rejected, together with a similar motion from Suffolk and the 'gracious advices' of the London brethren.[6]

Not only was the Dedham conference unmoved by the decision of a higher assembly regarding its own membership; it would have nothing to do with the Book of Discipline itself. Without the records of the conference, we should probably not have suspected this reaction from a body which already practised so much of the presbyterian discipline. But the minutes, short and cryptic though they are, are unmistakable. The Book had only two active sponsors: William Tay of Peldon, always the extremist of the group, and Henry Sandes of Boxford who was in regular correspondence with Field about the Book on behalf of his fellow Suffolk ministers, and who would later move that the bishops were 'not to be thought of as brethren.'[7]

In March 1587 Tay moved 'that the Book of Discipline set down by the brethren might be viewed, and their judgments given of it.' His motion was 'deferred', as it was at the next meeting on April 3rd. On May 8th, Tay was absent and in consequence the matter was again left on one side. But in another ruling on this occasion it was virtually admitted that there would be no subscription to the Discipline in this conference. In February, Sandes of Boxford had asked, with obvious reference to the Book, what his position would be if the same question were moved in both conferences of which he was a member, and contrary rulings given.

He was now told that he was free to give his opinion verbally in either meeting, but that so far as Dedham was concerned, 'to give our hands touching our judgment in matters was not thought safe in any respect.' In June, Tay was present, only to hear his renewed motion deferred yet again. On this occasion, Sandes brought a message from Suffolk asking for the help of Doctors Crick and Chapman 'for the concluding of the matter of discipline.' The request was an embarrassment. Nothing was done about it until August, when Crick confessed his reluctance to go to 'the conference at Mr Fowle's, 22 August', until 'at length it was laid upon him.' And this in spite of the fact that Thomas Fowle, rector of Hinderclay and Redgrave, was an old associate of both Chapman and Crick from the time when all three held office in Norwich Cathedral. At the same meeting, discussion of the Book of Discipline was postponed once more, since Tay was again missing. And on September 4th, 'the former matters', which must be taken to include the Discipline, were again deferred. And with that the subject seems to have been closed. Evidently the Dedham ministers were afraid to put their hands to such an incriminating document as the Book of Discipline, even if they were in general agreement with its contents; while in a more radical meeting like that in West Suffolk the brethren felt incompetent without outside help to decide on the large and controversial matters which it contained.[8]

But in the forward echelons of the party, the summer which slipped by so indecisively at Dedham was full of activity. A London minister, Thomas Barber, giving evidence in the Star Chamber in September 1591, dated two general conferences, in London and Oxford, to a time 'about four years now last past'. He remembered that in London the delegates assembled in the homes of various ministers, Walter Travers, Stephen Egerton of St Anne's Blackfriars, Richard Gardiner of Whitechapel and himself. The Oxford conference brought together the most famous divine of that university, Dr John Reynolds, with Travers and Chark from London 'and others', 'about the cause of discipline'.[9] In July two Essex ministers, Rogers of Wethersfield and his friend Ezekiel Culverwell, both from the Braintree conference, were in Cambridge at the time of the Commencement, when the puritans usually held a formal conference. A month later Rogers was off to London with his wife at Bartholomew Fair time, which may also tell a tale. Within a few days he set out for Cambridge again, or rather for the great Stourbridge Fair on the water-meadows by the Cam, when country parsons among other classes of people found it useful to stock up for the winter.[10] But on this occasion we need not doubt that his journey had a more than mundane motive.

Yet another general meeting coincided with those hectic days in Cambridge, and in early August Dedham had chosen its delegates: Robert Lewis of Colchester and Rogers's neighbour from Coggeshall, Laurence Newman.[11] As luck would have it, we possess what even Bancroft never saw: the formal Latin *Acta* of this assembly, headed 'September 8, 1587'.[12]

Among other things this document furnishes us with a list of names, arranged under counties, which probably indicates those who were normally to be written to in these districts, rather than the delegates attending this meeting. The correspondents for Suffolk were John Knewstub of Cockfield and Walter Allen, Sir Robert Jermyn's rector at Rushbrooke; for Essex, Rogers of Wethersfield and George Gifford of Maldon; for Kent, Josias Nichols of Eastwell and his neighbour, John Elvin of Westwell, two parishes deep in the puritan country of the Weald around Ashford; for Hertfordshire, two hot East Anglian brethren whose extremism was now taking them to fresh pastures, Oliver Pig and William Dyke; for Surrey, John Udall of Kingston, equally on the left wing of the movement; for Northamptonshire, John Barbon and William Fludd, of whom more presently; for Warwickshire, Cartwright and his close collaborator, Humphrey Fen of Coventry; for London, Field and Stephen Egerton of Blackfriars; for Cambridge itself, Laurence Chaderton, now beginning his long rule at Emmanuel.

As usual, what Chapman of Dedham had required of this assembly was some guidance on what the ministers should do if forced to choose between conformity and the loss of their livings: 'how far they might go with peace of conscience and the good of the Church.'[13] The problem of the more objectionable ceremonies and their 'indifference' – '*an simpliciter impia?*' – was certainly amongst the questions debated at Cambridge. And a ruling was given on whether ministers might take the oath at a bishop's visitation. But the Acts suggest that a greater share of the time was spent on the Book of Discipline, and especially in elaborating those provisions for their meetings which the subscribers had promised to put into immediate practice. The brethren devoted much attention to the extension of the conference movement and to means of persuading more ministers to join. They were to allay the suspicion of schism by continuing to share the communion of the Church in word and sacraments and in all other things, the corrupt ceremonies excepted; and by assuming no authority to bind outsiders by their decrees. It was agreed that letters between conferences should be written according to a common form, and such a form was set out for letters fiduciary; that the acts of higher assemblies should be forwarded to the next meeting following; and that secrecy should be employed in communicating the place and time and other necessary details of these higher assemblies from one person to another. By far the most intriguing proposals were a group of motions deferred for the further consideration of the brethren themselves and of the foreign reformed churches. (Whether this refers to the churches overseas or the protestant refugees in England is not clear. The operative word *exteris* could mean either.) These questions concerned the necessity of a worthy ministry, and the avoidance of communicating with the unworthy; refusing to acknowledge the authority of the hierarchy; and the utter repudiation of the unlawful discipline in order to take a stand upon 'our' lawful discipline. The drift of these proposals is clear. The puritan 'church within the Church' should definitely if not openly repudiate the established Church of the bishops as Antichristian and derive its validity from its practice of the true, reformed Discipline. The fact that these drastic motions were referred to further debate and the advice of other churches suggests that they did not pass unchallenged. Yet there can be no doubt that the Cambridge *Acta* in their totality represent the deliberations of a body which held itself to be the provincial assembly of a nascent English presbyterian Church, and that the inchoate body which it claimed to represent had moved under this direction one step nearer to separation.

Yet this same conference recorded a disappointing response from its constituencies to the Book of Discipline and its accompanying documents. Many conferences had returned no answers to the questions of whether the Book agreed with the word of God and how far it might be put into practice. The matter was postponed, and replies to those conferences which had registered their doubts were delayed 'until the rest of the conferences shall signify their opinion of the whole Discipline.' Meanwhile the Book was to be printed and in this form dispersed to the conferences. (There is no evidence that this was ever done.) And the order of holding conferences and meetings was to be summarized from the second part of the Discipline to encourage the more general use of prophesying and other exercises for the increase of knowledge. A sufficiently discouraging reward for all the endeavours of Cartwright, Travers and Field over a period of almost three years!

The Cambridge *Acta* suggest that as late as 1587 there were still districts supplied with a godly preaching ministry where the ministers were not enrolled in regularly convened conferences. In such places the machinery for receiving, debating and formally approving the Book of Discipline did not exist. Even in Oxford the arrival of the Discipline found the puritans ill-prepared to give it their consideration. Edward Gellibrand of

Magdalen, who had repeatedly urged the London brethren to speed up the distribution of the Book, now had to confess to Field that his friends were 'not resolved in all points of it, having had but small time to peruse it, nor the commodity of often meeting about it.' But they had done what one might have expected of them long before this time: they had organized a regular monthly conference under their own, local orders.[14]

Things were little more advanced in the Midlands, where only the news of the appearance of the Discipline seems to have brought the ministers together in classical meetings. This is surprising, in view of the early penetration of presbyterianism into parts of these counties, and into Northamptonshire especially. The vigorous action of Bishop Scambler in the mid-seventies seems to have blighted this early promise. Certainly most of the puritan ministers who were now to make Northamptonshire something of a presbyterian model were of a new and younger generation. Several of them came into their parishes only in the course of the 'eighties. These were Oxford men for the most part: Thomas Stone of Christ Church, rector of Warkton from 1583, Edmund Snape of Magdalen, curate of St Peter's, Northampton from 1586, Andrew King from the same college, rector of Culworth from 1583, John Barbon, a prominent Magdalen man and active in Northamptonshire from the late 'eighties. As a group these newcomers were more radical and whole-hearted in their presbyterianism than, for example, the Dedham ministers.

Almost all our knowledge of the movement in which these Midland puritans were now to be involved comes from the responses and depositions of Northamptonshire and Warwickshire ministers in the great Star Chamber trial of 1591, which will form the climax of our story, and much of it from the evidence of one John Johnson, vicar of All Saints, Northampton, from 1584, and by 1590 a renegade from the puritan cause who turned queen's evidence. There is a good deal of discrepancy between these different accounts, but a comparison of all the evidence points to a period between the winter of 1587 and the summer of 1588 when the Discipline was subscribed in Warwickshire and carried from there to Northamptonshire. According to Johnson, this event was awaited in Northampton with some impatience. During what he calls the 'interim', the ministers distributed themselves among three meetings which seem from the start to have been called without equivocation *classes*: the first 'of Northampton side', the second 'of Daventry side', and the third 'of Kettering side'. These seem to have shared between them some twenty-four members: Northampton nine, Daventry six and Kettering, the least successful in preserving its independent identity, nine. At the same time, a meeting for the whole county was set up in Northampton, 'the assembly of six' as Johnson calls it, consisting of two representatives from each of the *classes*. This was to follow the 1584 edition of the Geneva liturgy which (unlike the 1586 edition or the Book of Discipline) made provision for the 'great conference' of all the conferences in a shire.

In these months before their reception of the Discipline, the Northamptonshire ministers proceeded to draw up their own 'decrees and rules', a constitution comparable to the Dedham orders of 1582, and to keep a 'register book'. These rules (or so Johnson confessed) bound the ministers to conform to the word of God in their ministries, both of word and sacraments, and in all matters of doctrine and discipline to submit to the orders and decrees of the *classes* and to the censures of their brethren. When 'employed about the affairs of their church', members' expenses were to be reimbursed by the remainder of the *classis*.

Johnson's evidence includes an intimate description of the conduct of the Northamptonshire *classes*. The meetings were held in private houses 'but yet in their mother cities', Northampton, Daventry and Kettering. Proceedings began with the election of the moderator. One brother 'conceived a prayer' for God's guidance and then sat 'in scrutiny' while everyone secretly gave their voices. 'He that hath most voices is chosen.' Once elected, the moderator conceived another prayer that God would bless him in the course of his office, and placed himself 'at the table's end with his brethren by him'. A roll was then called and any who were absent at the first sitting down sat in order as they came, 'for avoiding of superiority'. According to another witness, Thomas Stone, the moderator propounded the questions, and invited discussion. It was also his duty to make a 'true summary' of the views expressed. His authority lasted until the next meeting, and the moderator of the assembly of six, who was chosen by the same procedure as the moderators of *classes*, was said to continue his authority 'over all the three *classes*'. The assembly had no set meetings, but met upon occasion signified by the *classes* to the moderator, which would happen commonly every six or eight weeks. The *classes*, on the other hand, always appointed the time of their next meeting, which was usually within a fortnight or three weeks at the most, although the moderator could call a meeting sooner if occasion warranted it. They met, said Thomas Stone, 'sometimes upon message, and sometimes by letters sent from the one to the other in that behalf.'[15]

The Northamptonshire ministers devised these arrangements at the prompting of a certain Mr William Fludd who, says Johnson, often came into their *classes* 'and gave instructions unto them for their proceedings.'

Fludd was not a member of any of the Northamptonshire *classes*, but freely and frequently offered his advice, 'like an apostle or patriarch or he knows not what, always taking upon him to be a chief director.' An 'apostle' meant a roving preacher without a fixed cure. Ten years earlier, the prophesyings in this same Midland country had been linked together by what Bishop Aylmer called 'a rank of rangers and posting apostles', who went 'from shire to shire, from exercise to exercise',[16] and Fludd was their successor. He was a man who 'did also ride much abroad to hear and see what was done in most places, so as whatsoever he directed was commonly concluded and followed.' It was his advice, for example, which led to the making of a survey of the ministry for the county and the sending of delegates to London at the time of the 1589 Parliament.

Not much is known about the mysterious Mr Fludd (or Floyde). Several clergymen of his names can be traced in the Midlands at this time, but our Mr Fludd was probably the deprived rector of Ashby St Leger. In 1587 and 1589 two of his children were baptized in Northampton. In the Cambridge *Acta* he is noted as a correspondent for Northamptonshire, and he represented the shire at a further provincial synod in Cambridge two years later. His name is linked with George Carleton, the forceful Northamptonshire M.P. and entrepreneur who comes into our story at several points. When Carleton was made superintendent of the distinguished recusant prisoners in Wisbech Castle, Fludd was one of four preachers whom Carleton thought most fit to convert them. (Another was the youthful Lancelot Andrewes.) Later, Carleton appointed Fludd an overseer of his will, together with Peter Wentworth, and it was perhaps knowledge of his 'posting' habits which prompted the reward of a gelding for his pains. Fludd's reputation was more than local, and in 1588 he was one of four presbyterian ministers to whom the London separatists addressed a challenge; the other three were Cartwright, Travers and Chark. In 1589 and 1590 he attended synods in London, and the probability is that he provided the main link between the Midland conferences and the capital. On one occasion he carried a letter to London from a Staffordshire minister, John Payne, a lapsed Brownist on the extreme leftward fringe of the conference movement, in order to confer with 'the learned preachers of London' about its contents. The letter advocated the erection of discipline without tarrying, 'because it is better to obey God than man.' Fludd himself was no separatist, but according to a later tradition, he remained a preacher in Northampton for twenty years with no other warrant than the approval of other 'godly and learned men'.[17]

So this was how the conference movement was carried to the Midlands.

Johnson's testimony provides further remarkable evidence of oligarchical and dictatorial tendencies in the Northamptonshire leadership. Membership of the county assembly at Northampton should have circulated among the members of the three *classes*. But in fact the representation never varied. Johnson himself normally represented Northampton together with Edmund Snape, a 'chief man'; Daventry was always represented by John Barbon and Andrew King; Kettering by Thomas Stone (another of the witnesses in the Star Chamber) and Robert Williamson. The local *classes* had nothing to do with the Book of Discipline or other great matters of the Church. These were handled exclusively by the assembly, which was responsible for all communication with Cambridge, Oxford and London. Snape, a committed partisan of Field's own quality, was the secretary who kept the register and took care of the correspondence. His letters went to Laurence Chaderton in Cambridge, Edward Gellibrand in Oxford and to Travers in London. (Johnson was speaking of the months after Field's death in March 1588.) Replies were usually addressed to Snape, 'in the name of the said brethren'. Meetings of the Northampton *classis*, as we learn from another witness, were held in either Snape's or Johnson's house. Evidently the nominally democratic structure of the conference movement in Northamptonshire was so managed that an inordinate share of power fell to a small oligarchy amongst whom Snape was paramount. Autocratic tendencies are inherent in the organization of most revolutionary parties, and the Elizabethan presbyterian movement was not the last radical cause which brought together the same few familiar names to general conferences, and in which the policies of the ruling cadres ran beyond what was thought safe and desirable by the rank and file.

When the Book of Discipline at last arrived in Northampton, probably in the early weeks of 1588, the brethren submitted to a mutual 'censure', which, as Johnson confessed to the High Commissioners, was partly a kind of penance for their past conformity to the orders of the Church and other failings, partly 'to prepare their minds for the devout accepting of the foresaid book.' Bancroft's gloss on this event was that there was 'such ripping up one of another's life, even from their youth', that, as Johnson reported, some did 'thereupon utterly forsake those kind of assemblies.'[18] This seems to have been the moment of Johnson's own departure. Those remaining appear to have subscribed with reservations, although Stone remembered that Snape received letters from ministers in London and Warwickshire, and from himself 'and others about Daventry', which contained 'a certain intelligence or advertisement of certain doubts or scruples whereof the said ministers wished to be resolved, and that good consideration might be had thereof.' And he recalled that there were 'many persons of the said assemblies' who never did subscribe.

At about the same time, the Discipline was subscribed in Warwickshire by twelve ministers, including Cartwright; Humfrey Fen, vicar of Holy Trinity, Coventry, and after Cartwright the leading Warwickshire figure; John Oxenbridge, rector of Southam whose church had been the scene of the most inflammatory of the prophesyings of the 'seventies; his son-in-law Edward Gellibrand,[19] whom we know as the corresponding secretary in Oxford; and two young Oxford men who were to stand with Cartwright and Fen in the Star Chamber: Edward Lord, a fellow of Magdalen, like Gellibrand, until 1586, and Daniel Wight, in whose hand the incriminating document was written. The subscribers seem to have met either in Coventry or in Lord's vicarage of Wolston, six miles away.[20] (Barely a year later the squire of Wolston, Roger Wigston, or rather his devout and determined wife, would provide shelter for the printers and the press which produced some of the Marprelate Tracts.[21]) The authorities later discovered the evidence of the ministers' subscription in the house of another subscriber, Edmund Littleton, together with the Book of Discipline itself and the acts of a provincial synod held in Warwickshire, headed *Acta conventus classium Warwic., die decimo quarti* [April 10th?] *1588*. It may have been on the occasion of this synod that the Warwickshire ministers made their subscription.

This provincial synod was held in accordance with the provision made at Cambridge in the previous autumn when the arrangements had been committed to the Warwick *classis* (in effect to Cartwright) on the advice of the other *classes* of the shire.[22] The questions referred from Cambridge were taken up in Warwickshire and, in particular, the perilous and burning problem of whether the brethren might repudiate the unlawful government of bishops and take their stand without further delay on the lawful discipline. Unfortunately the original Warwickshire *Acta* have not survived, and we are largely dependent upon Bancroft's rendering.[23] Bancroft told his readers that he would not trouble his paper with the original form of the document, and he was probably not above strengthening a phrase here and there in his translation. Nevertheless, there seems no doubt that the Warwickshire synod favoured a decisive, presbyterian advance. It recommended 'the faithful' not to communicate with unlearned ministers, although they might attend their services 'if they come of purpose to hear a sermon.' The calling of a bishop was held to be unlawful, for he was neither doctor, elder nor deacon. So far as the bishops dealt in ecclesiastical causes, there was 'no duty belonging unto them, nor any, publicly, to be given them.' It was not lawful to accept their ordination or to recognize their power to deprive 'except (upon consultation had with the neighbour ministers adjoining, and his flock) it seem so good unto them.' Otherwise the minister was to continue in his vocation until 'compelled to the contrary by civil force.' It was not lawful to appear in the bishop's court except under protest, nor was it permitted to pronounce suspensions or excommunications sent from the bishop. The Discipline was not to be put into general practice by the people until they were better instructed in it, but it was to be taught as occasion served[24] and 'men of better understanding' were to be 'allured, privately, to the present embracing of the Discipline and practice of it, so far as they shall be well able, with the peace of the Church.'

It would not be possible to come closer to separation from the Church of the bishops and yet avoid final, open rupture. The correspondence of the ministers whose common mind these Acts express confirms that by 1588 they were close indeed to schism. Humfrey Fen held it unlawful to receive the sacraments at the hands of a non-preacher and to 'come to the ordinary service read in the church except it be of purpose to hear a sermon.' Daniel Wight was glad to find himself at one with the Northamptonshire minister Arthur Wake, 'for he holdeth our bishops not for brethren, and I perceive they will prove it.' 'How say you,' Edmund Snape was quoted as saying, 'if we devise a way whereby to shake off all the Antichristian yoke and government of bishops and will jointly together erect the Discipline and government, and that in such sort as they that be against it shall never be able to prevail to the contrary?'[25]

How were these impatient presbyterians to avoid the path of the Brownists, losing sight of all wider aspirations in the exclusiveness of the gathered sect? How, in the parlance of puritan debate, were they to reconcile the demands of conscience with 'the peace of the Church',[26] understanding by the Church something wider than their own restricted fellowship? An answer was attempted in a further document in Daniel Wight's handwriting, seized by the pursuivants in Warwickshire and later printed by Bancroft as 'the Decrees', a paper headed, apparently, 'Things that do seem may well stand with the peace of the Church.' This may belong to a slightly earlier date than the Warwickshire *Acta*, but certainly not to 1583, where Bancroft placed it.

The 'Decrees' explains how ministers may conform to reformed practice both in entering and continuing in the ministry without openly disturbing the established, Anglican procedures. Candidates for the ministry are first to obtain a call from a particular congregation, which they are to communicate to their own *classis*, 'or else unto some greater church assembly'. After examination, this body is to commend them by letter to the bishop, 'that they may be ordained ministers by him.' Whenever a church falls vacant within its circuit, a *classis* is to 'deal earnestly with patrons to present fit men.' Once installed, the minister is to omit the more objectionable ceremonies of the Prayer Book, 'if it may be done without danger of being put from the ministry.' But the minister in danger of deprivation is to act according to the advice of his *classis*. Subscription to the Prayer Book or to the whole Book of Articles is never to be granted, 'no, though a man should be deprived of his ministry for it.' The congregational eldership is to be brought into existence by the simple expedient of turning churchwardens into elders and overseers of the poor into deacons. Provisions follow for the distribution of churches among *classes* and the more general meetings and for the conduct of these meetings. Among these arrangements, the county assembly figures prominently, a peculiarity, in all probability, of the Midland organization. Conferences on a national scale are defined as 'Commencements' and assemblies for the whole kingdom, which are to be held 'whensoever the Parliament for the kingdom shall be called, and at some certain set time every year.' This confirms the pattern with which we are now familiar of general meetings at the universities in the late summer and in London at Parliament time.

Thomas Fuller characterized the 'grand design' of the Decrees as 'to set up a discipline in a discipline, presbytery in episcopacy.'[27] No more apt definition of what the Elizabethan presbyterians were about has ever been offered. With the summer of 1588, and the little body of incriminating documents in Daniel Wight's hand, we have reached the climax of this audacious but sadly contradictory enterprise. Before we go on into the confusion, failure and defeat which lay ahead, it will be as well to take our bearings and to discover how far, at this apex of the Elizabethan age and of Elizabethan puritanism, presbytery within episcopacy was an accomplished fact.

Part 7

Presbytery in Episcopacy

'Mr Negus ... added this, that he thought every man that professeth himself desirous of discipline should exercise it himself in his owne causes soe farre as he coulde.'

(*The Presbyterian Movement in the Reign of Queen Elizabeth*, (*Dedham Minutes*), ed. R. G. Usher, Camden Socy, 3rd ser., viii. 45)

I The Congregation and its Ministers

In this section we shall try to establish how far a coherent presbyterian church existed within the larger fabric of the establishment, and we shall explore the institutions and nascent traditions of the puritan parishes. The ethos of the puritan 'church within the Church' will by now be familiar. We have sensed the situation of partial separation which John Johnson of Northampton conveyed when he reported that 'both ministers and people are called the godly brotherhood, denying in very deed the name of a brother to be proper unto any, but unto such as are of their own faction and opinion, and do join and labour with them for the said discipline.'[1] We know something about the distribution and organization of the conferences of preachers which provided the skeletal framework for a national presbyterian Church. We have found evidence of important divergences within the conference movement: of elements relatively tolerant of episcopal government, while others could no longer contemplate the bishops as brethren; of presbyterian convictions in some quarters and a firm resolve to impose the discipline, if not to submit to it; elsewhere, tokens of an incipient congregationalism, inspired by what can best be described as the free church spirit.

It remains to investigate the extent to which a single reformed church order – that of the Book of Discipline and the Genevan *Forme of prayers* – was being covertly realized at the local, congregational level in the election and ordination of the ministry and in the conduct of discipline and worship. In these respects, did every man do what was right in his own eyes? Or did Elizabethan puritan practice display any coherence? Was the tendency to presbyterianism, or to congregationalism? What signs are there of the abandonment of the formularies and procedures of the Church of England in favour of the forms of service and church government of the foreign reformed churches?

None of these questions can be answered with any degree of confidence. Yet the evidence will allow some tentative conclusions. In its congregational practice, the puritan church within the Church was a single if far from uniform entity. It contained an unresolved struggle between presbyterian and independent tendencies, although these were not yet identified by labels or recognized to be mutually incompatible. In this somewhat untidy institution, there were few clean breaks with Anglican practice, for it was characteristic of Elizabethan puritanism to work within the framework of established institutions and ways, rather than to reject the status quo too openly. The puritan liturgical standard was provided by the Genevan *Forme of prayers*; but the book which the puritan ministers actually employed and which provided the materials for their reformed order of service was the Book of Common Prayer. The puritans attempted to exercise discipline within the congregation; but they claimed the right to do so on the authority of the preface to the Anglican communion service. Their elders and deacons were disguised as the officers who were part of the normal establishment of a parish: churchwardens, sidesmen and collectors for the poor. They attempted to regulate admission to the ministry and to particular pastoral charges in an entirely novel way; yet the institutional arrangements of the English Church were so loose, so productive of anomalies, that means could often be found of attaining their ends without open violence to the existing system. As a London minister informed a separatist opponent, 'it followeth not because they are termed parsons, therefore they are not pastors.'[2] Yet this world of half-loaves and make-believe was a far cry from the monolithic, disciplined Christian community envisaged by the more rigid presbyterians. Whatever it was which was secretly growing within the puritan churches, it was not that.

The puritan church within the Church was only one of many diversities which subsisted and even flourished within the still disorderly amalgam of communities, jurisdictions and property rights which made up the Commonwealth. Elizabethan England was by modern standards an untidy society which might have been designed to frustrate the orderly aspirations and well-rounded theories of state of successive Tudor administrations. The legend lovingly created by the older nonconformist annalists of tyrannical prelates mercilessly harrowing innocent and helpless preachers is absurdly wide of the mark, as misleading as the once popular concept of a 'Tudor despotism'. A realistic assessment of the capacity of the Elizabethan ordinaries to enforce the ecclesiastical law must lead to the sober conclusion that nonconformity was ineradicable and that there was no means of entirely preventing a section of the clergy and their followers from conducting themselves as though the further reformation of the Church was already an accomplished fact.

In few respects were the principles of reformed church order and the traditions of the historic Church so apparently at variance as in the making and appointing of an ordained minister of the word and sacraments. According to Calvinist theory and practice, an aspirant for the ministry, having received the inward call of the Spirit, was to be outwardly called and elected, after due trial, by the congregation which he was to serve, using the assistance and advice of other neighbouring pastors. He was then (and only then) to be ordained to the ministry by the laying on of hands of the eldership of that congregation and of one or more of the ministers of the *classis*. The minister so chosen and ordained would have been set apart for one of two ministerial functions: either as a pastor, to 'have the oversight and charge of the whole parish, to instruct, to admonish, to exhort … and to minister the sacraments in the same parish'; or as a doctor, to teach and expound, 'so that he ought to be an exquisite and mighty man in the scriptures.'[3] The Anglican parson, on the other hand, proceeded in turn to the two dependent grades of the historic ministry, the diaconate and priesthood. And his ordination was by a bishop, who retained the 'oversight and charge' of the parishes in his diocese. The bishop ought not to ordain a candidate who lacked a title to a benefice, but this was a form of social insurance, as much for the ordinary as for the ordinand, and it was not equivalent to the priority of election to ordination in the reformed churches. The cure of souls in an Anglican parish was a function governed by rules and concepts of the Common Law, since it was normally associated with possession of the tithes of the church and other property which constituted a freehold right. The candidate for an appointment in the Church of England had to seek presentation to a benefice from the patron, followed by institution by the bishop (or collation if the bishop was also the patron), and last of all induction into the temporalities of the benefice by the archdeacon, acting under the bishop's mandate. In these processes the parish or congregation normally had no share.

To have introduced the reformed procedure into the Church of England by legislation would have meant a vast upheaval, involving the rights of patrons and the powers and very existence of bishops. The theological and legal implications of such a measure would have been almost without limit. Anglicanism and Calvinism here seem to have been nearly incompatible. Yet there were puritan ministers who believed that it was possible to enjoy the best of both worlds.

Amongst these trimmers were two London ministers, Mr Thomas Spering (or Sperin) and Mr Cooper, who were among several preachers appointed in 1590 to confer with the followers of Henry Barrow and John Greenwood, separatists who had renounced fellowship with the Church of England and were at that time confined in various London prisons. In early April Spering and Cooper were assigned to contend with Barrow and Greenwood themselves. Barrow was a fluent and resourceful controversialist, and much of his most devastating polemic was directed, with all the contempt of the extreme for the moderate left, against the puritan ministers who, as it seemed to him, evaded the logic of their own convictions. The puritans frequently declared the 'bishops and their train' to be Antichristian, yet they were not ashamed 'to receive their ministry from them and execute it under them, and that even when and since they laboured this Reformation.' Attacked in this tender spot, Cooper and Spering at first acknowledged the falsity of their position and fell back on the validity of the spiritual gift which they enjoyed, the inward calling. But under pressure, Cooper shifted his ground and claimed that the agreement which he had concluded with his auditory for his wages as a stipendiary preacher constituted a valid outward call. Told that they had received their ministry not from a congregation but from the bishops, both claimed that 'we had not our ministry of the bishops but by consent of a congregation', although they implied that by this they meant 'a congregation of ministers', that is, a *classis*. Spering moreover insisted that he had 'the approbation of the congregation also', which made him a minister before ever he went to the bishop. When Barrow suggested that in practice it was the patron and not the people who chose the parson, Spering contended that 'the patron's choice is the people's choice.' By this he meant that the patron's right had originally resided in the people, 'who have yielded their right unto him, as unto the wisest and worthiest amongst them'; an interesting and early example of a contractual theory of society, sustained by legendary history![4]

If we are to accept their own edited record of this encounter, the separatists had little difficulty in exposing the wishful and often confused thinking in Spering and Cooper's apologia. Yet parishes did exist, and in many parts of the country, where circumstances favoured the kind of quasi-presbyterian elections and ordinations which these two ministers claimed to have received. A substantial proportion of the patronage of parochial livings rested in the hands of landed gentlemen, and some of these lay patrons were ardent puritans who fully shared the aspirations of the preachers and were susceptible to their dogmatizing in matters of polity. In West Suffolk, Sir Robert Jermyn, one of the godliest as well as the most powerful of the gentry, presented to no less than ten livings, and his ally and equal in zeal and authority, Sir John Higham, to four. At least thirty more Suffolk parishes were at this time controlled by other puritan gentlemen and noblemen, who included Lord North and Sir Nicholas Bacon the younger.[5]

In these encouraging circumstances the patron's choice might indeed be the people's choice. We noticed in an earlier chapter the remarkable case of William Axton, a contemporary of Cartwright at Trinity College who was called from Cambridge to the Shropshire living of Moreton Corbet in 1573. As Axton himself told Bishop Bentham, he became pastor of Moreton Corbet by popular election, which Sir Andrew Corbet had conceded. After a period of probation, he was chosen 'with one consent of them all', after a neighbouring minister had preached on the mutual duties of pastor and people. Before this election Axton had preached 'divers times' on trial in 'an ordinary assembly of half a score preachers', and received 'their voices and free consent' for his entry into the ministry. Only after this did he receive ordination from a bishop, which he regarded as the least part of his calling. The substance, rather than the accident, of ordination lay in the approval of his brother ministers.[6]

There is no means of telling how common it may have been for a reasonable and godly patron to respect the views of the parish, but examples of this consideration can be found. In Norfolk, a number of justices including Nathaniel Bacon wrote on one occasion to the lord chancellor about the Crown living of Warham All Saints which, being worth less than ten pounds, was in his gift *ex officio*. The present incumbent was likely to be deprived for immoral behaviour and the principal parishioners had asked the justices to write on behalf of a certain Peter Stewardson, 'whom we know to be well affected in religion, of honest conversation and a preacher.' A few weeks later Bacon wrote again about another vacant living, recommending a Mr Robinson whose diligence as a schoolmaster and preacher 'I have witnessed unto me by divers good and the chief inhabitants of Burnham within seven miles of me.'[7]

In progressive East Anglia, at least, the weightier parishioners sometimes contrived to exercise the rights which would have been theirs as elected officers in a thoroughly reformed church. Of this the Dedham conference papers leave us in no doubt. William Negus was advised by the conference to remain in his Ipswich parish 'if the godly desired it and would maintain him.' Later he asked 'whether he might accept the calling of the church in Ipswich, or of the church in Lee.' When Bartimaeus Andrewes proposed to leave his parish of Wenham for the more prominent and lucrative post of town preacher of Yarmouth, it was said that 'the people of Wenham' would 'by no means consent' to his departure. And some members of the conference objected to the behaviour of the people of East Bergholt 'in rejecting and receiving their pastors without counsel of others.'[8]

'Counsel of others' meant the advice of the *classis*. A genuinely free election by the people was to become uncommon in established Calvinist churches, even where patronage was excluded, and the effective choice of a pastor would normally be made by the *classis*. In Elizabethan England the conferences of preaching ministers seem to have assumed advisory powers and often, in effect, the right to place a minister in a vacant charge which fell within their circuit. Puritan patrons, for their part, were probably more inclined to delegate the choice of a pastor to the other ministers of the shire or to one notable preacher than they were to allow a right of election to the parish. According to the Book of Discipline, a minister so chosen was to be considered duly elected if no one in the congregation raised a valid objection. In Norfolk, Nathaniel Bacon committed the choice of a new pastor for his own parish of Stiffkey to Walter Allen, a leader of the Suffolk puritans and rector of his friend Sir Robert Jermyn's parish of Rushbrooke. Allen made an unsuccessful effort to secure the famous Walter Travers, presumably through the proper channels.[9] John More, the 'apostle of Norwich', was employed in a similar capacity by Lady Knyvett and no doubt by other Norfolk worthies.[10] In Bury St Edmunds, where the townspeople claimed the right to elect the ministers of both their parish churches, 'their interest of nomination' was granted, by the advice of the gentry, to the popular archdeacon of Sudbury, Dr Still, and the leading Suffolk preacher, John Knewstub of Cockfield. The local justices explained that this was 'no more impeachment' to the bishop's jurisdiction 'than if a patron should take the advice of such like grave men whom they thought were fittest to name to present to a benefice.'[11]

The Dedham papers enable us to see these processes from the standpoint of the preachers. From its earliest days, the conference assumed the right to place its own members and to advise the neighbouring congregations on the choice of their pastors. In its first two meetings, the conference debated whether to place Richard Dow at East Bergholt or at Stratford St Mary, and decided that he should 'accept of his calling at Stratford.' Bartimaeus Andrewes was advised to stay at Wenham and William Negus at Ipswich, in both cases after members of the conference had conferred with their parishioners. When Andrewes nevertheless departed, the schoolmaster of Cockfield, Samuel Bird, was nominated to replace him, and 'it was thought good he should be heard preach, and so be allowed of by the brethren.' The minister so proved was to be a notable preacher in Ipswich at the turn of the century. Looking further afield, Chapman on one occasion asked the brethren 'to inquire and consider of some fit man for the pastor's place in Bedford', where he had once been town preacher himself, 'and to name him to him.'[12]

In the Midlands the *classes* aspired to the same powers. Bancroft had evidence of a Mr Hocknell who was presented to a Northamptonshire living by a patron who demanded 'some testimonial of the ministers of the shire, for his good conversation'. Hocknell applied to Edmund Snape, the 'chief man' of the Northampton *classis*, and was appointed a day, and a text on which to preach before the brethren. The *classis* met in Snape's church of St Peter's, heard Hocknell preach, and then set him aside for the censure. John Penry, the pamphleteer and separatist martyr, charged the company with the solemnity of their task, and after some debate Hocknell was called back, 'in some sort commended', but disallowed as a fit minister. But as in Essex, so in Northamptonshire, the decision of the brethren was not enforceable. Hocknell was an ordained man of six or seven years' standing with a valid presentation, and he proceeded to take possession of his benefice, 'contemning their censure.'[13]

Scattered in good numbers throughout the country was one kind of parish which was singularly open to presbyterian infiltration and scarcely supervised by the bishops. These were the churches where the tithes had in the past been appropriated to some religious house and conveyed at the dissolution of the monasteries to lay impropriators.[14] Where there had been no endowment of a vicarage, such churches were known as donative cures, since they were served by stipendiary curates who had no proprietary rights in the living and could be removed at the will of the impropriator and donor, who provided a modest and often beggarly stipend. These parishes blunted the disciplinary weapons of the Church, for their curates required neither institution nor induction from a bishop, but only a simple licence to serve the cure, and even this they may sometimes have dispensed with. Their presence was rarely recorded in episcopal registers and they were not subject to episcopal visitation. In

East Suffolk, an area profoundly affected by its monastic past, there were in the early seventeenth century at least fifty-six impropriate parishes, many of them lacking vicarages, and this figure does not include the seven impropriate churches of Ipswich, all donatives.[15] Town parishes in places like Ipswich, where more than one order of friars had been represented before the Reformation, were commonly in this condition.

Such poorly paid employment was unlikely to attract a learned man. Yet when the impropriator was a godly puritan, he might be prepared to pay the curate an adequate stipend out of his own pocket or to invite the contribution of the parishioners, and he would call in the assistance of the local ministers to find a competent preacher to fill the place. Robert Forth, a substantial Hadleigh clothier, owned the site of the once famous Suffolk priory of Butley together with the tithes of the parish, and he lived in the remains of the priory buildings. The preachers who served the cure and ministered at the priory were supplied from the Dedham conference. When Forth died in 1601 it was his desire that the curate then in charge should have a life tenure of his curacy, on the understanding that he would continue to give good counsel to his son from time to time.[16]

One further case will show how the donative cure could serve the presbyterian cause and frustrate ecclesiastical discipline. The Essex priory of Hatfield Peverel belonged to a London merchant, Edmund Allen, who claimed the right to appoint a curate to the church 'by reason it is a donative', and to pay him 'a certain pension' without presentation, institution, induction or licence, 'so as the person appointed were allowed by the laws of this realm to say service.' In about 1584 he appointed a certain Thomas Carew, whom Bishop Aylmer allowed to serve the cure at the request of one of the patrons of puritanism in Essex, Robert Wroth. After his appointment, Allen and the other parishioners agreed with Carew to make up his stipend to a reasonable living, an agreement which Aylmer represented as an illegal presbyterian election. Carew was soon suspended for nonconformity and the bishop attempted to replace him with a curate of his own choice. Allen and Carew put up a vigorous resistance, Carew declaring that 'the knot between pastor and people is not easily loosed.' Both were imprisoned for contempt and Carew was finally forced to leave the district. Undeterred, he made his way into the next diocese, and to another donative, the parish of St Margaret's, Ipswich. Here he preached for two years, still without licence, teaching, so it was alleged, that 'it was not lawful for princes nor magistrates to have any government in the discipline of the Church', but that 'he would have widows, elders and deacons and a brotherhood and a fellowship in the churches.' He was 'called' from St Margaret's to be curate in another Ipswich donative, St Nicholas's, but later returned to St Margaret's and finally disappeared from the scene in 1590 after Whitgift had ordered him either to appear before him or to abandon his unauthorized ministry.[17]

In some donative cures, the tithes were held in trust for the parish by feoffees, and in these circumstances the right of appointing the curate might be legally vested in the parishioners or their trustees. In five out of the seven Ipswich donatives the parishioners exercised these rights, and in 1637 it would be alleged by the magistrates of the town that 'time out of mind of any man living' the parishioners had 'elected and chosen such their stipendiary ministers, whom they have presented to the lord bishop of Norwich for his approbation and allowance.'[18] Some parishes of this type were notable puritan strongholds with a widespread influence. One of the most famous was St Andrew's, Norwich, where two ministers normally served, filling between them the roles of pastor and doctor. John More preached there from 1572 until his death in 1592 and he was assisted by a succession of less experienced preachers 'nominated by the feoffees in trust for the parish.'[19] Another congregation of the same quality was to be found in London at St Anne's Blackfriars, a parish at this time without church, churchyard or minister's house, yet where, in addition to the curate, one of the most popular preachers of the age, Stephen Egerton, was maintained by a 'great congregation', mostly of merchants' wives, and drawn from all parts of the city, meeting 'in a little church or chapel upstairs'. Of this parish it was said in later years that when any country ministers or godly Christians came to London about their affairs, 'they thought not their business fully ended unless they had been at Blackfriars Lecture.'[20] The strategic role of another London donative, Holy Trinity Minories, was noted in an earlier chapter.[21]

Several of the ministers who have appeared in this discussion claimed to be not pastors but doctors. These were the stipendiary preachers or lecturers, a growing class of clergy in the post-Reformation Church, many of whom were never rectors or vicars of a parish in their lives, and some of them content to remain in the deacon's orders which were sufficient for their limited function. Such was a correspondent of Field who preached every Sunday, 'having nothing to do at all with the form or Book of Common Prayer', and an Oxford man who set out for London, 'hoping here to have settled in a lecture of forty or fifty pounds.'[22] 'I am no pastor,' Mr Cooper told Barrow and Greenwood, 'I am a doctor', and when the separatists denied that there was any such creature in the Church of England he insisted: 'We have the doctor's office in our

Church.' Most puritans would have agreed with him. When Mr Andrewes of Wenham proposed to give up his rural parish to become town preacher of Yarmouth, one of his brethren in the Dedham conference objected that 'he might not go from being a pastor, which was the higher calling, to be a teacher, which was the inferior.' The London preachers who tended to dominate the conference movement, Field, Travers, Chark, Crook and the others, were all acknowledged for teachers. When Bishop Aylmer published an order requiring all such unbeneficed preachers to minister the sacrament at least four times a year, his action seemed to the puritans to be more than merely tactically offensive. There was a general complaint that he had taken away the office of doctor.[23]

Whether or not the town preachers and parish lecturers of Elizabethan England answered all the requirements of a reformed doctor, there is no doubt that it was even easier for ministers of this kind to be elected and placed with Calvinistic procedures than it was for beneficed parsons. Some lectureships were endowed, others were financed by a levy laid on the borough or parish, others depended more precariously on voluntary contributions. But all were stipendiary and the financial nexus between the doctor and his auditory was much closer to the primitive, apostolic ideal than the tithes which supported the parish clergy. This was especially noticeable wherever the godly inhabitants of a parish burdened with a non-preaching incumbent had hired a preacher to supply the want and had raised his wages amongst themselves. There were many advocates for such a policy. One anonymous writer gave any reader 'plagued with an evil minister' this counsel, 'which I see God hath put into the hearts of many people in the land: that, leaving the tithes and other emolument unto those upon whom the law doth cast them, men do otherwise provide for themselves at their further charge.'[24] So the parishioners of Lawshall in Suffolk found relief from a decrepit and immoral vicar, first in an 'extraordinary lecture' preached in their own church for three years, then in going out to hear sermons in other parishes, and lastly in raising ten pounds a year to support their own resident preacher. The choice of the preacher they proposed to commit to Mr Knewstub 'and other good men'. When Ipswich lacked a preacher in 1585, the town looked in the same direction, and accepted the recommendation of 'sundry doctors and godly learned preachers of the university of Cambridge': Mr Robert Wright. A year later Dr Fulke and Dr Still were asked to find an assistant for Mr Wright.[25]

In this, as no doubt in numerous other instances, the appointment of a preacher or 'doctor' was managed in something like the approved presbyterian fashion. All that a lecturer required from the bishop, or from some other competent authority, such as his university, was a licence to preach. Given an influential patron and the famine of preaching, licences were not hard to come by, and even so were often dispensed with. 'Silver-tongued' Henry Smith, a prince of Elizabethan preachers, was recommended to the parish of St Clement Danes 'by certain godly preachers' who had heard him preach elsewhere in London, 'and thereupon accepted of by the parish and entertained with a stipend raised by voluntary contribution, in which sort they had heretofore entertained other.' According to the bishop he was unlicensed. When John Udall was silenced at Kingston, he was 'called' north to Newcastle 'by some that feared God', who 'made mean' to the earl of Huntingdon. Licences were dispensed with, since, as luck would have it, there was neither a bishop of Durham nor an archbishop of York at the time.[26]

Private chaplaincies in puritan families lent themselves even more readily to presbyterian practice. Laurence Tomson, Walsingham's secretary, told Field that he had asked his mother 'to speak to you and our good brethren to provide me of some honest brother to catechize my family.' When the earl of Leicester set out as captain-general for the Netherlands in 1585, his choice of Humfrey Fen of Coventry as a chaplain was confirmed by both the Warwickshire and London *classes*. 'I am ready to run,' wrote Fen, 'if the Church command me, according to the holy decrees and orders of the Discipline.'[27]

The preaching and catechizing which went on in numerous substantial private households, serving a 'family' in the widest and loosest possible sense, in effect created so many private churches, presbyterian or congregational in form and in a state of virtual separation. Lord Rich's household at Rochford, in Thames-side Essex, was the spiritual domain of Robert Wright in the year before he settled as town preacher of Ipswich. Wright had received a presbyterian ordination from the ministers and elders of the Dutch, French and English churches in Antwerp. His great patron tried to bully Bishop Aylmer into granting this irregular preacher a licence, and though the bishop refused, he could hardly, as he said, 'send a power of men to fetch him out of a nobleman's house.' For his part, Wright denied that he needed a licence, since the election of ministers ought to be by the congregation, and he claimed to have been 'chosen in this sort in the house of Lord Rich.' By this token he claimed to be pastor of the household and to have the cure of souls. He never used the Prayer Book and boasted of his ignorance of its contents. There was nightly catechizing at the Hall, announced by the ringing of a bell, and many of the local inhabitants resorted there rather than to the parish church of Rochford. The local clergy, most of them Lord Rich's presentees, were censured in conferences at which Wright presided.[28]

Robert Wright was somewhat exceptional among the Elizabethan puritan clergy in that his only ordination was by a group of presbyterian ministers and elders in Antwerp, no bishop's hands having ever rested upon him. And according to presbyterian practice, he had first been elected to a regular preaching post in the Antwerp church. (As the London conference told an aspirant for the ministry on one occasion, 'that ordination should precede election, and not election ordination, we can in no wise grant thee.'[29]) Most would-be presbyterian ministers were in worse case: either they were episcopally ordained ministers of some years' standing, or they must 'pass through the bishop's hands' before securing a pastoral charge. How did they answer the separatist challenge that their callings were *ipso facto* defective? There were three ways, short of utter separation, by which the puritan could reconcile his conscience to the necessity of receiving orders or institution to a living from the bishop. He could, if his views were moderate, accept the bishop's orders as valid, while regarding him as the agent of the congregation and of the other ministers who had already given their approval. This was to make the bishop a 'bishop in presbytery', and it was the procedure envisaged in the Warwickshire 'Decrees', and actually followed fourteen years earlier by Axton in Shropshire.[30]

Alternatively, the puritan might respect the bishop as a civil magistrate only, and his ordination and institution as mere civil procedures. This was the view taken of the episcopal office in the *Acta* of the Warwickshire provincial synod. The clearest expression of this kind of puritan casuistry comes from the 'chief man' of Northamptonshire, Edmund Snape. 'Touching the substance of my calling to the ministry,' he wrote, 'I affirm that I had it of the Church of God, being approved by the learned and godly neighbour ministers, and chosen by the people of my charge to that function.' The allowance which he had from the bishop he took to be a thing 'merely civil, belonging to a civil magistrate; which authority he hath by Act of Parliament, and which therefore I might lawfully receive at his hands for the peaceable execution of my ministry.' But his obedience to the bishop was restricted to civil things, and if inhibited by the bishop he would continue in his office if he had the consent of his 'godly neighbour ministers'. All this was said in self-defence, to a Brownist. Yet to a parishioner Snape is reported as saying that he would rather have been hanged on the gallows than stand on the virtue of his letters of ordination, and that far from empowering him to be a minister, these were 'to be taken but as a civil ordination from a civil magistrate.' 'I attribute much to the civil magistrate,' Thomas Spering told Barrow, and therefore he received the bishop's licence and submitted himself to his obedience.[31]

The third possibility, barely one remove from open separation, was for a minister secretly to renounce his episcopal orders and accept re-ordination from his fellow-ministers. Things were coming to that pass in the Midlands by 1588, if we are to believe a deposition made by a Northamptonshire man before the High Commissioners in 1590. According to this witness, it was agreed by synods held within the previous eighteen months that ministers called according to the order of the Church of England had an unlawful calling, and 'should be induced to renounce their former calling by bishops, and to take a new approbation by them in their *classis* ... and that this is the Lord's ordinance, whereby only they must stand in their ministry.' After such a calling they could preach until called to some certain charge and then, and only then, were they 'to be holden full ministers' and to minister the sacraments. Yet even so they were 'to go to the bishop for writings', as to a civil magistrate. John Johnson deposed on hearsay that two of the Northamptonshire ministers, William Prowdlove and Nicholas Larke, renounced their calling by the bishop, 'and did take it again by the approbation of the brethren.'[32] They were far gone in Northamptonshire, but not so far as to join Barrow and Greenwood in forsaking altogether 'those disordered and ungodly and unholy synagogues'.[33] John Penry, who was in Northampton and London at this time, would later take the separatist course, but he carried no followers with him. As for Snape, he had many years of busy activity ahead of him as an acknowledged minister and preacher of the Church of England, even if his was a life spent on its uttermost frontier.

2 Discipline and the Eldership

No BLEMISH OF THE ELIZABETHAN CHURCH was more prominent or more wounding to the puritan conscience than the general absence of discipline, in the reformed sense of the term. This flaw was no mere superficial abuse; it ran deeper than the notorious failure of the church courts to provide credible checks on the moral and religious conduct of an emancipated laity. To the puritan mind, this incapacity was only incidental to the usurpation by bishops and archdeacons and their officials of powers of correction which were properly congregational and which in the first instance ought to be exercised by the officers of the local church, the pastor and elders. Rarely did the New Testament give such clear and inescapable directions as in Matthew xviii:

> Moreover if thy brother shall trespass against thee, go and tell him his fault between thee and him alone: if he shall hear thee, thou hast gained thy brother. But if he will not hear thee, then take with thee one or two more, that in the mouth of two or three witnesses every word may be established. And if he shall neglect to hear them, tell it unto the church: but if he neglect to hear the church, let him be unto thee as an heathen man and a publican.

This was an action wounding and severe, yet intimate and fraternal, and basically remedial in intention. Its relationship to the application of canon and civil law in the judicial processes of the ecclesiastical courts was so

346

remote that to the puritan eye it could appear that the English Church was wholly without discipline. Since it was commonly declared, in formal confessional statements, that discipline was an essential mark or token of the presence of the Church of God, its lack or serious perversion could well deprive a church of its very essence. Consequently, puritan ministers strove to make good the deficiency, if only to convince themselves and others that their parishes were indeed true churches, and that they themselves were pastors and not mere parsons.

'But now for your parish,' Henry Barrow told Mr Spering in their conference at the Fleet prison on March 14th, 1590, 'it consisteth of a confuse company of prophane, atheists, covetous, gluttons, vain, light, ignorant, and wicked people of all degrees and estates, of each sex and age, they being all generally without the knowledge, faith, or fear of God, without care of this life or of the life to come; to all which you in-differently administer and sell your sacraments, delivering them in a false manner, not according to Christ's Testament.' This was the very nub of the separatist case against the establishment, from which Barrow proceeded to dismiss Spering's 'whole ministry and ministration' as 'false and Anti-christian'. The allegation was so damaging that Spering was bound in mere self-defence to insist that on the contrary he administered the sacraments to 'none but unto such as he knoweth faithful, saying that he knoweth all the parishioners, both men and women, to be such, except one household.'[1]

Where there was common fame of scandalous conduct in a member of the congregation, the puritan minister who was worth his salt would attempt on his own authority to apply what he conceived to be the evangelical remedy. John Johnson of Northampton was to describe in the Star Chamber how his fellow-townsman Edmund Snape had dealt with a parishioner suspected of incontinence. First Snape made private attempts to bring the offender to public repentance before the congregation. When this failed, he preached 'a very bitter sermon' against him. This brought the man to church on the following Sunday. On this occasion Snape 'made a long prayer that God would give him grace to make a faithful acknowledgment of his sins', after which the penitent did what was required of him. Snape then 'after a sort absolved him, and withal entered into a great discourse how clear and free the offender was from that sin which he has committed, charging the congregation that no man should presume at any time afterwards to object his said offence unto him.' The next day the offending parties were married. The woman was either the daughter or sister of an elder or deacon of the church, and no public

347

example was made of her, which was why Johnson thought the story worth telling.[2]

The performance of public penance for sexual misdemeanours was a familiar part of Elizabethan parish life: the offender, arrayed in a white sheet, stood before the congregation and made his or her public confession at an appropriate point in the service, often spoiling the solemnity of the proceedings by some revelation of a far from penitent spirit. Snape had imposed no more than the church courts would have required in the same case. But only the bishop or the archdeacon had the legal power to apply this kind of discipline. The puritan minister who claimed, against all law and tradition, to be a pastor would have to enjoy a relationship with his congregation of exceptional confidence to carry through what Snape attempted at Northampton. Yet the more extreme course of excluding a parishioner from participation in the Lord's supper was allowed to any incumbent by the Prayer Book itself. The rubrics prefacing the communion office required, as they do to this day, that intending communicants should signify their names to the curate 'at least some time the day before'. If any so signifying were 'an open and notorious evil liver, or have done any wrong to his neighbours by word or deed, so that the congregation be thereby offended', the curate was empowered to 'call him and advertise him that in any wise he presume not to come to the Lord's Table' until he had shown evidence of repentance and of a serious intention to make amends. Barrow's protagonist Spering made full use of these rubrics. Parishioners of the servant class were admitted to communion on the production of metal tokens, and these were issued only to those who proffered themselves for examination. Barrow was convinced that this was the whole extent of the discipline which his opponent professed to employ. 'You have leave in your service-book to suspend from your sacrament, but not to excommunicate without the bishop.'[3]

Yet such evidence as we have suggests that to their own satisfaction the puritans equated suspension from the sacrament with excommunication. Dr Crick of East Bergholt was told by some of the Dedham brethren that the way to deal with 'some disordered persons in his church' was to use all means to win them, but, failing that, 'to excommunicate them after long patience, according to our Saviour's rule.' Another brother was advised that if 'some froward poor men that were every way disordered' continued to despise his admonition, then he should 'account them as none of his flock.'

It is also abundantly clear that the puritans repelled intending communicants as much on grounds of insufficient knowledge as of evil life, so exceeding the powers entrusted to them in the Prayer Book. At various times members of the Dedham conference withheld the communion from a 'froward' churchwarden, a perjurer, two men 'in hatred one against the other', 'a wicked man that did beat his wife' and a young man spied at the window of a serving-maid's bedchamber. All this was in the spirit of the preface to the communion service. But Dr Crick went further when he informed the ministers of a confession of faith made by a woman of his congregation and asked whether it qualified her for admission to the Lord's table. So did Richard Parker of Dedham when he asked for a ruling on 'what we might account to be a competent knowledge for a communicant.' Evidently the shorter forms of catechism, of which there was almost a glut by the end of the century, were employed not only as a medium of instruction but as a hurdle which aspiring communicants had to clear before enjoying the full privileges of the body of Christ. 'For I have been in a parish of four hundred communicants,' wrote Josias Nichols of Kent, 'and marvelling that my preaching was so little regarded, I took upon me to confer with every man and woman, before they received the communion ... In all the former questions, I scarce found ten in the hundred to have any knowledge.' Familiarity with the problems of a rustic Cambridgeshire parish led Richard Greenham of Dry Drayton, who was much consulted on matters of conscience and conduct, to recommend withholding the communion for some time after the commencement of a preaching ministry, until a period of 'continual public teaching' and 'some requisite trial' had ensured that the sacrament was not administered to 'most unworthy receivers'. This was to enforce the same lofty standards which prevailed in the Scottish Church at this time. Certainly the minister who adopted this practice was free from the charge of 'selling' the sacraments to a 'confuse company'.[4]

Some extreme situations may have existed in which the puritan minister used his discretionary power to exclude all but the truly godly, so in effect converting the parish into a sect and radically altering the basis of membership of that part of the national church. Such a parish was East Hanningfield in Essex, where the rector, William Seridge, repelled as many as nineteen parishioners at a time from a single communion and probably reserved the sacraments for the godly faction with whom he kept 'secret conventicles and meetings' on Sunday evenings. According to the puritans, those excluded were 'slanderers and railers against preachers and having greatly injured their neighbours and sowed discords.' Not surprisingly the contrary faction blamed the 'saints' and their conventicles for the discord. This deeply divided parish figures constantly in the records of the archdeacon's court. The godless parishioners were regularly cited for failing to receive, and invariably blamed the rector for refusing to admit them, while Seridge was as regularly cited for the offence of rejecting them. The sympathies of the archdeacon and his officials lay with the rector's adversaries. They licensed them to receive in a neighbouring parish and assured them that 'you did not call them saints and scripture men in contempt of their profession, but in respect of their abuse.'[5]

Yet none of this, not even Seridge's near-sectarianism, would have satisfied Henry Barrow. No one reading Matthew xviii could gather that the correction of faults belonged exclusively to one man, the pastor. It was the responsibility of every Christian and of the whole church. So Barrow complained with some justice: 'This your manner of suspending or separating is as popish as the rest ... ; where find you in all Christ's Testament that one man may separate any alone?'[6] Barrow understood 'tell it unto the church' to mean the whole company of the congregation. The exegesis was basic to the position of the gathered sect. Presbyterians, on the other hand, applied the text primarily to the elected and ordained officers of the congregation who included the elders as well as the pastor. The question remains: did the Elizabethan puritans elect and ordain elders in any of their parishes and so set up properly constituted consistories? Was discipline anywhere a reality in this full-blooded presbyterian sense? In 1591 Bancroft reported that 'it is not found as yet for any certainty whether they have hitherto made choice of any elders, but many vehement conjectures there are that they have.'[7] Four centuries later the historian is blessed with little more hard information, and is less free to indulge in vehement conjectures.

We must first beware of the loose employment in contemporary documents of the term 'elder'. A minister was, in one sense of the term, of the eldership, and some anti-puritan writers made a habit of speaking disparagingly of the preachers as 'elders'. It is quite possible that the 'elders' listed on that famous fragment of paper endorsed by Field in 1572 'The order of Wandsworth'[8] were not so described until Bancroft referred to the document in his *Daungerous positions*, twenty years after the event. We know that as a matter of policy only ministers were included in the membership of the Elizabethan conferences, *classes* or synods. We also know that at the provincial synod held in Warwickshire in 1588 it was decided that the people were not to be solicited publicly to the practice of the Discipline until they were better instructed, although 'men of better understanding' were to be 'allured privately to the present embracing of the Discipline and practice of it as far as they shall be well able, with the peace of the Church.'[9] This implied that as late as 1588 the leadership of the conference movement did not envisage the immediate conversion of any parishes into publicly organized presbyterian churches. But John Johnson of Northampton was to confess before the High Commissioners that the ministers in their *classes* had 'resolved to erect up their several presbyteries in their own parishes' and that he himself had been blamed for not taking this step. In the Star Chamber his evidence included – quite incidentally – the name of one John Nelson of Northampton who, as early as 1588, was 'an elder or a deacon of St Peter's, as this deponent thinketh.' Yet the opinion of a witness from this same parish (which was Snape's) was that the setting up of elders was 'only proposed and determined', and was thwarted by Snape's imprisonment in April 1590. In conference with Barrow in the Fleet in March of that same year, Stephen Egerton of Blackfriars, Field's close collaborator, asserted plainly that 'we abstain from excommunication, because we have no elders as yet.'[10]

The Church of England might have no elders, but every parish had its churchwardens and other lay officials, sidesmen and collectors for the poor, and its vestries, meetings of the parishioners to transact their common business. The document called by Bancroft 'The Decrees', probably drawn up in Warwickshire and carried into Northamptonshire, proposed that churchwardens and collectors for the poor might be 'turned into elders and deacons.' This metamorphosis would transform mere parish officers into holders of an ordained ministry, chosen by the church, after due warning 'of the ordinance of the realm, but especially of Christ's ordinance, touching appointing of watchmen and overseers in his Church.' At their election and ordination their duty to the church and the church's to them was to be declared. 'Then let them be received unto the ministry to which they are chosen, with the general prayers of the whole church.' Mr Spering assured Barrow that no pastor ruled alone, but had churchwardens and sidesmen joined with him. Challenged by the separatist, he set down this assertion: 'Some churchwardens and sidesmen may be elders', and this was defended with St Paul's teaching in 1 Timothy iv: 'For every creature of God is good, and nothing to be refused, if it be received with thanksgiving.' This was characteristic of both the mentality and the strategy of Elizabethan puritanism: as Thomas Edmunds of London put it in the Star Chamber, to conceal 'the names either of presbytery, elder or deacons, making little account of the names for the time, so as their offices might secretly be established.'[11]

At Northampton in Percival Wiburn's time, the quarterly communions were announced in the parish churches on four successive

Sundays, 'with exhortation to the people to prepare for that day.' A fortnight before the event, the churchwardens joined with the ministers in visiting every household, taking the names of those who proposed to communicate, examining 'the estate of their lives' and putting them from the communion if necessary.[12] The Prayer Book made no provision for churchwardens to be employed in this capacity. However, the Canons did lay on churchwardens the duty of presenting offenders to the bishop and archdeacon in their visitations. With some special pleading it was possible for the puritans to represent excommunication in the bishop's court as the confirmation of a censure already agreed upon in the congregation by the parson-pastor and the churchwarden-elders. Spering told Barrow: 'The bishop's excommunication is but an approbation of ours ... When any deserveth to be excommunicated, then I and the churchwardens present such to the bishop, and he excommunicateth them.'[13]

For the presbyterian discipline to be successfully intruded in this disguise, it would be necessary for the puritan incumbent to enjoy the confidence of his churchwardens and, probably, of other substantial elements in the congregation as well. Such favourable circumstances may have prevailed only rarely. The late Professor R. G. Usher believed that a majority of puritan ministers were opposed by their churchwardens, since few escaped presentment for nonconformity throughout their careers.[14] This is to forget that wardens were placed on oath at a visitation, or to ignore the solemnity of an oath for the sixteenth century. It was at least arguable, and a contemporary makes the point, that 'if by the bishops their officers and ministers they were not upon their oaths urged to present the not use of the ceremonies, they had forsaken them and forgotten them long since.'[15] But at any period of Anglican history there have been sufficient causes of tension between the incumbent and the lay officers of the parish to make it easy to believe that the puritan minister and his churchwardens were as often as not pitted against each other, and for reasons that need have had little direct connection with differences over ecclesiastical polity and ritual. There can have been few parishes where a puritan minister could not muster his faction of supporters, but equally few where the recommendations of the 'Decrees' were readily applicable. The Dedham papers show that in almost every parish represented in the conference the minister had to grapple with the opposition of unruly and unresponsive elements, and that this was not necessarily confined to the dregs of the community.

For this reason the puritan parishioners in many places formed a semi-separatist cell, an *ecclesiola in ecclesia*. As in East Hanningfield, they met with their pastor for 'repetitions' of sermons and other 'night conventicles', activities which will be described in the last chapter of this section. Some of these lay groups exercised a mutual discipline among themselves. In Richard Rogers's Essex village of Wethersfield in 1588 'certain well-minded persons' drew up a covenant 'for the continuance of love and for the edifying one of another.' It was no doubt in these cells that, according to the decision of the Warwickshire synod which met earlier in the same year, 'men of better understanding' were to be privately 'allured' to the practice of the Discipline. In the evidence given in the Star Chamber in 1591 we have a picture of Edmund Snape of Northampton embarking on this process of select indoctrination with four parishioners, sitting 'in the great seat' of St Peter's church, apparently in the summer of 1589. An artisan of Kingston-on-Thames, well instructed by his preacher, John Udall, told Bancroft 'without any staggering' that to pray 'Thy kingdom come' was to utter a plea 'that we might have pastors, doctors, elders and deacons in every parish, and so be governed by such elderships as Christ's holy discipline doth require.' According to one of Snape's parishioners, and the testimony has a ring of authenticity, it was 'Mr Snape and those of his friends in his congregation' who proposed to elect elders and deacons 'amongst themselves', and John Johnson reported that elders had been chosen and consistorial discipline practised 'so far as they may amongst themselves, without any apparent show thereof, to the overthrow of their safe standing.'[16]

Johnson's evidence contains a unique account of the way in which a concealed eldership could secretly administer evangelical discipline within such a group of godly initiates. In the 'interim', while the Northamptonshire puritans waited for the Book of Discipline, 'there was a general consent and purpose had amongst the brethren touching a secret kind of excommunication, for example sake. If a layman committeth any sin, one of the elders was to admonish him. And if the party were obstinate, the said elder might take two or three with him the second time. And if that served not, the said sinner or party offending was to be debarred from the communion.' Only if the offender still persisted in presenting himself at the communion was he openly repelled, 'upon pretence of certain words in the Communion Book, so as thereby they might keep their own course for their discipline and yet have a cloak to cover them withal out of the said Book of Common Prayer.'[17] Yet an elder appointed and functioning in these circumstances could be no more than a pale shadow of the authentic presbyterian ruling elder, guardian of the behaviour and the conscience of all the inhabitants of the parish. Those not of the faction

353

would resist these assumed powers of discipline, and resist them with impunity.

But where a puritan minister met with no serious challenge and was upheld by men of substance, presbyterian elders or some select parishioners with comparable powers may have exercised a wider authority over the whole community. At Kilsby in Northamptonshire in 1588 the pastor nominated six parishioners whom he 'thought sufficient to determine and end all matters of controversy in the said town.' These officers were called elders, but neither their office nor the mode of their appointment corresponded very closely to the eldership in the 'best reformed churches'. At Dedham, the puritan ministers seem to have followed a similar course, associating nine of the more substantial and reliable townsmen with themselves for causes of discipline, who were variously styled 'ancients of the congregation' and 'ancients of the town'. Together with Dr Chapman and the vicar, Mr Parker, they agreed on a schedule of orders which might be called 'the ecclesiastical ordinances of Dedham'. Like the more famous Geneva ordinances of 1541 they provided for the regular attendance of representatives from every household at all services and sermons, and for a monthly celebration of the Lord's supper. On the Tuesday after the communion day, the ministers and ancients were to sit, in effect as a consistory, 'to confer of matters concerning the good government of the town.' And accompanied by the constable, they were to make quarterly visitation of the poorest and least savoury quarters. Perhaps other clothing towns in the Stour valley attended to their spiritual and moral government by the same means. When Henry Sandes of Boxford complained of persons who stayed away from the communion, he was advised that 'the ancients in the town should deal with them.' These 'ancients' are to be identified with the 'headboroughs' of the town, rather than with the churchwardens. They corresponded to what in another of these Stour valley communities were called 'the chief and forwardest in the congregation'.[18]

In larger, corporate towns where there was any puritan presence and influence, it was usually left to the governing body to compose and enforce orders for the frequenting of sermons, and to punish various manifestations of irreligious and immoral behaviour.[19] Where the magistrates were zealous, the preachers were unlikely to make much of the Calvinist distinction between secular and spiritual authority, although they would not neglect the equal Calvinist insistence on the mutual interdependence of 'ministry and magistracy'. It was, so to say, Zürich or Strasbourg rather than Geneva. Equally, in the countryside, a religious justice of the peace was more effective as an instrument of moral discipline than an elder with no public standing. Even in the Dedham conference the reaction to a report of some fresh offence or scandal was more often than not 'to complain to the magistrates.' In an established Calvinist Church, the *jus reformandi* of the Christian magistrate and the spiritual calling of the lay elder would often find themselves in competition if not in conflict. So it would be in the days of the Long Parliament and the Westminster Assembly, in the 1640s. But in the confusion and pragmatism of the Elizabethan age, the puritans were content to provide for discipline by whatever means lay to hand, whether by a Prayer Book rubric, a godly churchwarden, a religious magistrate or even the bishop or archdeacon. But only in exceptionally favourable circumstances were they able to conjure up the eldership, and their enterprise has left very little trace behind it.

3 Worship

THE LIFE OF THE PURITAN was in one sense a continuous act of worship, pursued under an unremitting and lively sense of God's providential purposes and constantly refreshed by religious activity, personal, domestic and public. 'He was much in prayer; with it he began and closed the day. In it he was exercised in his closet, family, and public assembly.'[1] Some of these characteristically puritan 'exercises' have been described earlier in this book; others will be discussed in the chapter which follows. Here we are concerned only with puritan participation in the sacraments and in what took place in the parish church on Sundays, that is, with the principal occasions on which the congregation met for the service of God and to hear his word expounded. A definitive account of the worship of the puritan parish would require a book of its own and can hardly be attempted in these few pages. Our investigation will be restricted to two questions only: to what extent was there a uniformity of liturgical practice among the Elizabethan puritans, serving in itself to define the puritan church within the Church, rather than the state of anarchy represented by their opponents, the Prayer Book 'commonly broken by every minister at his pleasure'?[2] And how far was the spirit and form of that practice still governed by the Book of Common Prayer, how far, on the other hand, determined by the Genevan *Book of the forme of common prayers*?

It is perhaps necessary to establish at the outset the primary fact that the Elizabethan puritans were willing to enclose their worship in a fixed and

356

invariable order, for Bancroft reported that 'the most of them think there ought to be no prescribed form at all.' Admittedly, Field and Wilcox in the *Admonition to the Parliament* had rejected outright any 'prescript form of service'. The model which their manifesto extolled was the supposed practice of 'the old Church', when 'ministers were not tied to any form of prayers invented by man, but as the Spirit moved them, so they poured forth hearty supplications to the Lord.' Dr Horton Davies, who is perhaps over-inclined to regard the early puritans as ancestral to the free church tradition in which he himself stands, has implied in his study of *The Worship of the English Puritans* that such a marked prejudice against set forms of prayer was representative. 'Generally,' he writes, ' ... the puritans felt that the restraint of a liturgy and its unsuitability for varying needs of varying congregations and times, made it undesirable. In this they departed from the Reformed tradition.' This may have been true of the Elizabethan separatists, who regarded all 'stinted prayers and read service' as 'but babbling in the Lord's sight', and who would not even consent to repeat the Lord's Prayer, but it does not convey the attitude and practice of the puritans properly so-called who remained within the establishment and who are the object of our study. George Gifford, the deprived vicar of Maldon and no moderate, undertook to defend 'read prayers and devised liturgies' against the separatist John Greenwood, and he was not afraid to affirm: 'About the commanding a prescript form of prayer to be used, our Church doth agree with all godly churches, yea the reformed churches have and do practise the same ... There would sundry inconveniences grow for want of a liturgy, or prescript form of public prayers.'[3]

The *Admonition* indirectly reflected the radical notions of the early London separatists who seem to have made at least a passing impression upon the youthful Field and Wilcox, and it must not be taken to speak for the puritan ministry at large, or even for its authors in their maturity. Hooker knew that they 'retracted' their first opinion 'upon better advice', to the extent that Cartwright and his associates later 'proposed to the world a form such as themselves like.'[4] This, of course, was the *Forme of prayers* as reprinted by Waldegrave and later by Schilders. It is now no longer in serious dispute that the Scottish Calvinists who were the contemporaries of the English puritans intended their Book of Common Order, the Scottish recension of the Geneva Book, to be, in Dr Maxwell's words, 'much more than a directory', although rather less than a liturgy in the strict sense. Thanks primarily to the work of Dr William McMillan, the notion of M'Crie that the Book was intended only as a 'help to the ignorant, not as a restraint upon those who could pray without a set form' has been shown to lack historical foundation.[5] So closely allied were the Scottish and English Calvinist movements that it would be surprising indeed if English puritans generally maintained a prejudice against set forms and orders of service from which their Scottish brethren were immune. We have Thomas Cartwright's assurance that in the years when he was most at liberty to do as he pleased, 'in the space of five years I preached at Antwerp and Middelburg, I did every Sunday read the prayer out of the Book.'[6] Therefore one can only give a qualified assent to the suggestion of Horton Davies that the practical difference between puritan and Anglican worship was one of 'the puritan emphasis on free prayer over against the "stinted forms" of the Establishment'.[7]

Yet the worship of sixteenth-century Calvinists is liable to an equal distortion if viewed through the spectacles of the modern liturgical movement. For the Elizabethan puritans, the liturgical part of the service was always subordinate to the ministry of the word. One of their more serious objections to the Prayer Book was that it reversed these priorities, 'so that they make the chiefest part, which is preaching, but an accessory, that is as a thing without which their office may and doth consist.' If the puritans attached equal importance to the due handling of word and sacraments as marks of a true Church, it remains true that they held the sacraments to be of no value without the word, so that a sermon was obligatory at all ministrations of the Lord's supper or of baptism. Richard Chambers, vicar of Hitchin and a fellow of Trinity in Cartwright's time, could even assert that 'the sacraments of baptism and the Lord's supper are polluted without a sermon,' while an Essex villager stoutly refused to go to church if there was no sermon, 'for he sayeth that public service read in the church is no service unless there be a sermon.'[8] On the other hand, the puritans frequently indulged in exposition apart from any sacramental or liturgical action. While we confine our discussion to the ordinary Sunday worship, derived from the liturgy of the Lord's supper, we must not forget the parallel development of lectures, catechizings and other 'exercises' in which the sermon occupied the whole time and attention of the company, with one or two prayers and psalms as mere accessories.

'Simplicity', 'sincerity' and purity were the touchstones of puritan worship, and to these qualities we might add directness and brevity, for although individual puritan prayers might be diffuse and totally lacking in the lapidary quality of the collects, the whole action was directed towards a definite end and differed radically from medieval and Anglican worship, which dwelt richly upon devotion for its own sake, and delighted in antiphon and repetition. So Field had complained in the face of Whitgift's demand for subscription of 'the quantity of the things appointed to be read, said, sung, or gone over' in the Prayer Book, 'which is so great that through the tediousness thereof it maketh the minister unable to speak and the people unapt to hear.' Granted the need for a sermon of heroic proportions, the difficulty of matching reformed with traditional values was a real one. Generations of Anglicans still to come would cheerfully endure the combination of an hour's preaching with devotions compounded of mattins, the Litany, and the first part of the communion service; but the puritans were perhaps entitled to cavil. As Professor Ratcliff has remarked, it was the 'shape' and the 'letter' of Anglican worship, much more than the doctrine it sustained, which was a perpetual source of stumbling for the puritan conscience. By eastern standards, the Latin liturgical tradition is noted for its restraint, but as the puritans viewed the function of public prayer it lacked economy and proportion, even in Cranmer's adaptation.[9]

Secondly, it has to be conceded that the Elizabethan puritans, like their Scottish counterparts, found room for elements of freedom – though not of spontaneity – within the invariable order of their worship. Such an approach to the regulation of public prayer was of the essence of a Book of Common Order rather than of Common Prayer. For one thing, metrical settings of the psalms, 'Geneva psalms', were introduced with some of the freedom with which hymns are employed in modern church services. In the reformed tradition, utterance in prayer was reserved almost exclusively to the minister, popular participation in responses and the Litany was virtually excluded, and psalm-singing was the only element of the service in which the people actively joined, and it was one to which the puritans attached great value. Singing could be used to fill an awkward gap in proceedings,[10] and it was normal to begin and end proceedings with a psalm, and to sing another psalm immediately before the sermon. We hear of the people of the Suffolk village of Palgrave 'being assembled together by the ringing of a bell, they sitting quietly in their seats in the church, and being ready to sing a psalm.' At Maldon, where George Gifford preached a regular lecture on market day, we hear that 'the psalm was in singing before the sermon (and the same more than half sung) and Mr Gifford was gone out of his seat to the pulpit.' As for the final psalm, an anonymous London writer complained in 1589 that too many worshippers 'abide not the prayer after the sermon, much less the psalm and blessing in the end.'[11]

Turner's bill, which accompanied the Waldegrave edition of the *Forme of prayers* into Parliament, as well as permitting congregations to sing psalms in metre according to the order taken by their ministers and elders, would have allowed ministers to 'make prayer or give thanks in the public assembly' in addition to the prayers of the Book, provided they always conformed to the Confession of Faith contained in the Book. In fact it was common, especially immediately before the sermon, for the minister to 'conceive' a prayer not to be found in any printed service book, and to insert other invocations and thanksgivings to fit particular and exceptional occasions. Of William Bedell, the future bishop of Kilmore and a very moderate and learned puritan, it was said that as preacher of Bury St Edmunds 'his prayer before sermon was not set, nor fixed always to the same form of words, but various in expressions, as the time and present occasions most required.' In the opinion of the mature John Field, the infinity of such occasions was one good reason for God's appointment of a public ministry in the Church, for 'it is an impossible thing to set down all prayers that are needful.' Hence what may seem to a modern observer paradoxical: the puritans were more ready to provide collections of written prayers for use in private households, churches in miniature which lacked an ordained ministry, than to limit 'the public calling upon the name of God' to prescript forms. One such successor to the 'primers' of earlier years, Edward Dering's generous collection of *Godly private praiers for householders*, was kept in constant supply by the book-trade for more than fifty years.[12] And Field himself was the author of a collection of *Godly prayers and meditations ... for the use of private families* which went through as many as three impressions, although this, as we should expect of its author, was little more than a vehicle of propaganda in favour of a further, presbyterian reformation of the Church.[13]

Most such collections of devotional material will be found to contain examples of the prayers used by celebrated divines before or after their sermons, and from this alone one is bound to conclude that, in spite of the variable nature of these prayers, truly extempore invocation was the exception rather than the rule. Cartwright recalled that all the time he preached in Warwick he used before the sermon 'a set and accustomed form of prayer, howsoever I read it not out of the Book.' William Bradshaw later adopted 'Master Cartwright's practice', which was to use a constant form of prayer, only varied to fit special circumstances. Whether other ministers, especially in Warwickshire, chose to use Mr Cartwright's very words we do not know, although it is very probable. But the prayer used by Thomas Sampson on such occasions circulated in print, and in 1572 the churchwardens of Wandsworth laid out a penny on its purchase. Dering's *Godly private praiers* include the prayer which he used before each of his famous lectures in St Paul's, and this occurs in a manuscript collection of prayers, together with a number of alternative forms for use at this point in the service, 'a thanksgiving by the preacher after the sermon', prayers and thanksgivings for the communion service, and 'a prayer used by Mr John Calvin ordinarily at the end of his sermons.' Field's *Godly prayers* as first printed were a mere appendix to a collection of Calvin's prayers. In short, the evidence confirms the balanced view of the mid-seventeenth-century author of *The character of an old English puritane*: 'He esteemed that manner of prayer best where, by the gift of God, expressions were varied according to the present wants and occasions; yet he did not account set forms unlawful. Therefore in that circumstance of the Church he did not wholly reject the Liturgy, but the corruption of it.'[14]

Although they were far from sharing the excessive respect for liturgical uniformity which we find reflected in the English Prayer Books and the accompanying Tudor legislation, the puritans never doubted that the interests of good order and of religion itself demanded that they should conform among themselves even in their nonconformity. It may have been, as Bancroft alleged, that 'within four mile compass of Bury' there were 'six or seven kinds or forms of baptism'. But the historian is in a position to recognize, as the controversialist was not, that this was a situation which the puritans themselves deplored. Moreover, there is no reconciling Bancroft's allegation of variety with his claim that 'there be no precisians in England, though by great distance of place they be severed, but they know by reports one another.' Nothing exercised the Dedham ministers more than that their conference and correspondence should lead them to agreement in their use of the Prayer Book and in their qualified subscriptions to its contents. They agreed to adopt a common practice with respect to the prayer before the sermon, and that they should minister the communion in their parishes 'all upon one day'. Edmund Chapman commended these motions, and suggested that 'the orders of our churches for government might be imparted one to another, and the best to be taken and used, that there might be as much con- formity as might be outwardly.' The subscription to the Book of Discipline of the Warwickshire ministers implied a promise 'uniformly to follow' the order of the Book in the chapters relating to sermons and the sacra- ments of baptism and the Lord's supper.[15]

There is no need to search far for what the more committed presby- terians, at least, would have made the norm of English reformed worship

We have it in the Genevan *Forme of prayers*. The successive revisions of the Book which can be traced through Waldegrave's edition of 1584 and Schilders's of 1586 are evidence of the importance which was attached to a wide and indeed general acceptance of this reformed formulary. If either Turner's or Cope's bill had been enacted by Parliament, this form of prayers 'and none other' would have been invested with no less authority than the Act of Uniformity of 1559 had conferred on the Book of Common Prayer. We must therefore pay some attention to the contents of this Book, and to the liturgical standard which it represents.

According to the earliest Calvinist ideal, the normal meeting-place of Christ with His Church was around His table on the Lord's Day. Calvin himself had insisted that the Lord's supper should be celebrated 'frequently and at least every week'.[16] In practice neither in the original home of Calvinism nor in any other Calvinist church did it prove possible to break the long habit of communicating only once or twice or at most four times in the year. On this issue, some of the English puritans shared both the vision of a Calvin or a Knox and its frustration. In Dedham, Dr Chapman attempted to establish a celebration of the Lord's supper on the first Sunday of every month, but the other ministers of the conference could not be persuaded to adopt the same practice. And in Dedham itself even the 'ancients' of the congregation who had agreed to the order could not be kept to a regular attendance.[17]

Nevertheless, the original conception of the normality and centrality of the communion service shaped the liturgical practice of the Calvinist congregation.[18] As in Anglican worship, the ordinary Sunday morning service provided by the Geneva Book was a form of ante-communion, the first part of the service of the Lord's supper, constructed around the ministry of the word. There was at first a short 'reader's service', consisting of chapters of scripture and scripture sentences roughly corresponding to the service of mattins which the Prayer Book intended to precede the main act of worship. The public proceedings followed, with confession of sins, the singing of a metrical psalm, a prayer for illumination concluding with the Lord's prayer, the reading of the text from the canonical scriptures (the Apocrypha was excluded) and the sermon, which of course occupied most of the available time. The sermon was followed by the main intercessory prayer for the whole state of Christ's Church, concluding with the creed, the ten commandments and the Lord's prayer (these last items omitted in the Middelburg recension of 1586). The service ended with another psalm and the blessing. On the infrequent occasions when the Lord's supper was celebrated, according to the *Forme of prayers* 'once a month, or so often as the congregation shall think expedient', the elements would be brought up to the table after the intercessions and during the singing of a further psalm. The minister would then pronounce the words of institution and an exhortation which included the 'fencing of the table'. He would then proceed with the eucharistic prayer of consecration derived from the ancient canon of the mass, but consisting almost entirely of adoration, thanksgiving and commemoration, long and didactic. There followed the fraction of the bread and the delivery of the elements, the focal point of a service which emphasized action rather more effectively than the contemporary order of the Anglican Prayer Book. The communicants then assembled round the table, set lengthwise in the most convenient part of the church, and seated themselves as guests at a meal over which Christ Himself presided. While the communion proceeded, the narrative of the passion or other suitable places of scripture might be read from the pulpit. The service ended with a short thanksgiving, a psalm and the blessing.

Such was the form of worship which Dr Turner and Anthony Cope commended to the House of Commons in 1584 and 1587. Was something of this kind already practised by the puritans and did they go so far as to make unauthorized use of the Geneva Book itself? In 1586 the general conference which met in London at Parliament time resolved that the corrected Geneva Liturgy, besides being preferred in Parliament, should be 'communicated with the conferences' and 'used in the parts abroad, if the brethren there shall think good.' 'Abroad' in Elizabethan parlance need not necessarily mean 'overseas', but there seems no doubt that this was what was meant in this context. The Book was to be used by the congregations of English merchants and others domiciled in the Netherlands, and this use is reflected in the recension of the Book recently printed by Schilders at Middelburg. This distinction must imply, to say no more, that the Book was not recommended for use in public worship in England. In defending their position against the separatists, the puritans could never pretend that they had abandoned the use of the Prayer Book in favour of a more perfect form. George Gifford of Maldon could only assure Henry Barrow that 'many ministers there be in England which have not approved the Book of Common Prayer further than they are persuaded it is consonant to God's word, nor used anything therein which they judge corrupt.' Barrow's immediate retort to this was: 'But you know none that use not the Book.' There is today no means of giving him the lie. What are somewhat ambiguously described as 'Geneva books' and 'psalm books of Geneva tome' were purchased by some London parishes in the very early years of the reign, before the vestiarian troubles of 1566. But from all the reign of Elizabeth there is but one authenticated case of a puritan congregation making use of the Geneva Book, and that was the congregation of semi-separatists who met in Plumbers' Hall and elsewhere in the aftermath of the vestments crisis in London in 1566.[19]

On the other hand it would be rash to state emphatically that the order of the Geneva Book was never followed in Elizabethan parish churches. What are we to say of the 'new order of service, contrary to her Majesty's order and book' introduced by one 'busy fellow' into Norwich Cathedral in January 1575? of the two Suffolk ministers who in 1574 'refused to use and observe' the Prayer Book order? of the parish of St James's, Bury St Edmunds, where there was 'little service' but 'Geneva psalms and sermons'? or of the parish of Tydd St Giles, near Wisbech, where the parson was said to have boasted in 1583 'that he never proceeded according to the Book of Common Prayer, nor never will'? What was happening at Dedham in 1590 where there was no service according to the Book of Common Prayer, 'but preaching and baptizing by strange ministers'?[20] Yet we are probably justified in supposing that only in very exceptional circumstances would a puritan minister read the services in the parish church from the Genevan Book. (What he might do in private households was another matter.) The Book must have been a rarity in England before it was reprinted by Waldegrave in 1584 and after that its circulation was probably restricted. Moreover, it could only have been in unusually 'godly' parishes like St Andrew's, Norwich, and St Anne's Blackfriars that a minister would have been able to introduce an entirely alien liturgy without risk of immediate complaint to the authorities. If it had been otherwise the puritans would not have discussed so endlessly 'how far a pastor might go in reading the Book of Common Prayer.'

Once again the evidence requires us to imagine not a clean break with Anglicanism but the kind of pragmatic compromise which was so characteristic of Elizabethan puritanism. The puritan bill of rites and ceremonies which ran its course in the Parliament of 1572 spoke suggestively of 'a great number of learned pastors and zealous ministers' who with episcopal permission, or so it was alleged, 'omitted the precise rule and straight observation of the form and order prescribed' in the Prayer Book 'with some part of rites and ceremonies therein appointed', and had 'conformed themselves more nearly to the imitation of the ancient apostolical Church and the best reformed churches in Europe ... '[21] This, it seems safe to say, was the puritan way: to employ the Prayer Book 'and none other', but in their use of it to conform 'more nearly' to the liturgical standards of the best reformed churches, even to the extent of constructing from Anglican forms of service a worship which approximated to that of the Genevan Book. As we have seen, there was at least a skeletal relationship between the two liturgies, and by reducing 'the quantity of things appointed to be read, said, sung, or gone over' in the Prayer Book, something not unlike the austere Calvinist form was left. To be sure this was no mere revision of the Prayer Book by the omission of a ceremony here and there, but a wholesale mutilation. But the legal fiction of its use was retained. As Whitgift and Bancroft well knew, a puritan might solemnly promise to use the Prayer Book in all his ministrations without binding himself to use it according to the statute, injunctions and rubrics.

That the puritans were prepared to 'doctor' the Prayer Book to accommodate their grievances is attested by the series of what Procter and Frere called 'emasculated' Prayer Books which appeared from 1578 onwards, bound up with the Geneva Bible. These versions, some of which omit altogether such objectionable services as private baptism and 'churching', have recently been the object of fresh scrutiny by Mr A. E. Peaston, who is sure that they do represent an unauthorized enterprise of revision and not, as has been suggested, an innocent publisher's response to the need of an abridged Prayer Book for everyday use, part of the 'portable library of Divinity' which the Geneva Bible in effect supplied. Be that as it may, they are probably to be seen as successors to the mid-Tudor 'primers', intended for domestic rather than congregational use. In any case the publishers were not so audacious as to tamper in print with the structure and content of the main services, and, apart from the alteration of 'mattins' and 'evensong' to 'for morning' and 'for evening', the general substitution of 'minister' for 'priest', and the omission and alteration of some of the rubrics in the communion service, the major elements of the Prayer Book remain undisturbed in these editions.[22] For our knowledge of what the more extreme puritan clergy actually practised in their parishes we have to look beyond the printed evidence to manuscript sources.

Here there is no lack of evidence that, besides discarding the surplice, vestments, and other 'nocent' ceremonies, the puritans often truncated the service so as to alter radically the proportion and balance of the services compiled by the English liturgical reformers. If the Prayer Book was, as they complained, a mingle-mangle, they mangled it still further. It was said of Richard Bowler, rector of the parish of Leverington in the Isle of Ely, that in his use of the Prayer Book he 'addeth and diminisheth at his pleasure.' Like his neighbour, Clement Martin, rector of Tydd St Giles, he often omitted the Litany 'by reason of the sermon'. In the ministrations of Josias Nichols, the leading Kentish puritan minister, 'divers things were pretermitted', as the *Venite, Te Deum*, creed, collects and Litany. Nichols began 'sometimes with the general confession or the Lord's prayer and the psalms and lessons; and the sermon, continuing for one hour and a half, and singing a psalm before and after the sermon, ended their prayer.' William Jenkynson, vicar of Croxton near Thetford, was said by one of his parishioners to omit the commandments, the Litany, 'and, as he verily believeth, the epistle and gospel, but certainly cannot depose, because he useth to read then a portion of scripture.' At St Margaret's, Ipswich, a local blacksmith declared that his curate, Thomas Carew, had 'divers times read part of the service, and part he have omitted.' Another member of the congregation, a weaver, told how Carew used to read the first and second lessons with a few prayers, 'and then do go to his sermon, and so do leave most commonly all the rest unread, as the Litany, the ten commandments, and the epistle and gospel.' As a local vintner represented Carew's order, 'at some time he would say one piece of Common Prayer, and at another time another piece.' Gilbert Baker of the Suffolk village of Flixton had never known his minister, Thomas Deynes, to read the psalms, the first and second lessons, the Litany, or the epistle and gospel, but testified that 'he have used to begin with prayer, and then read a psalm, and so proceeded to expounding without reading any more.'

Such examples could be multiplied without materially altering the general picture which has now been established. These ministers might have been consciously following the advice imparted by Bishop Grindal to William Cole, preacher to the Merchant Adventurers in Antwerp, in 1564, which was to use the Prayer Book and only the Prayer Book, but to take 'as much and as little thereof as to your discretion by the advice of the seniors shall be thought good', so that, unless there was a communion, no assembly would exceed an hour and a quarter in length, 'with sermon and all'. With good reason the new Canons of 1604 would enjoin the clergy to observe the orders, rites and ceremonies of the Church, 'without either diminishing in regard of preaching, or in any other respect, or adding anything in the matter or form thereof.'[23]

It would be foolish to deny that here was liturgical variety, not to say anarchy, or that there may have been almost as many versions of a Prayer Book service as there were puritan incumbents. But it would be no less shortsighted to overlook that all these do-it-yourself reformers were at pains to construct from Prayer Book materials a service of the same general character, subordinated to the sermon, and consisting of prayer, scripture-reading and psalms. Without much doubt, the *Forme of prayers* would have met the requirements of all but a few of them, and it is possible that knowledge of at least the main outline of the Geneva liturgy may have influenced their highly selective use of the Book of Common Prayer. It was doubtless only the failure to obtain legal establishment of this form which was to lead to a situation in which a lack of form would be regarded as a good in itself.

Only in the field of ceremonies, and especially in those incidental to the ministration of the sacraments, is there evidence of notable divergence in the practice of the Elizabethan puritan clergy. We have already quoted Bancroft's report of six or seven forms of baptism in the immediate neighbourhood of Bury St Edmunds. Twenty years earlier, Archbishop Parker's account of 'Varieties in the service and the administration used' had mainly related to ceremonial differences such as Bancroft probably had in mind. Parker's catalogue is the more informative in that it may well have been compiled from certificates submitted by the bishops and other ordinaries. Some baptized in the font, others used a basin. Some used the sign of the cross, others not. Some set the communion table in the body of the church or in the chancel, tablewise; others put it a yard from the east wall or in the midst of the chancel, altarwise. Some wore surplice and cope, some ministered in a surplice only, while others wore neither. Some used a chalice, or a special communion cup, others a common cup. Some used wafers, others common bread. The communion might be received kneeling, sitting or standing.[24]

There were certain observances required by the rubrics and by royal and episcopal injunctions which we can assume that no puritan willingly used. By definition, so to speak, the puritan ministered the communion in his black gown from a table which in no way resembled an altar, probably avoiding the north side indicated in the rubric on account of its Old Testament priestly associations.[25] He used common bread (here following the Prayer Book and disregarding the contradictory requirement of the Royal Injunctions of 1559) and probably a common cup. At baptism he omitted the sign of the cross, and perhaps, like one Essex incumbent, laid his hand on the child's forehead instead.[26] In eliciting the baptismal vows, he converted the 'dost thou' of the Prayer Book into a 'do you'. For fear of any ambiguity in this respect in the order of the 1559 Book, the puritan wished to leave it in no doubt that the godparents acted on behalf of the child and not merely as its voice. Standing for the gospel and bowing and genuflexion at the name of Jesus were discouraged.[27] The accepted attitude for worship was to remain seated and covered.[28] The ring was not used in marriage. But apart from what might be called these negative observances, there was much variety, which can be partly explained by the varying architectural and other physical conditions imposed by different churches and congregations, but also by theological differences of potential magnitude. There was a 'high' and a 'low' Calvinism in the later sixteenth century, and indeed it is possible to doubt whether many of the English puritans in their sacramental doctrine, or in their underlying concepts of the mediation of grace, followed Calvin at all.

As we have already noted, some puritans desired what for the sixteenth century was a frequent celebration of the communion, once a month. A quarterly ministration was more often thought to be desirable, especially in urban parishes, and in Barnstaple Eusebius Paget strenuously resisted a move to increase the number above the annual 'four grand communions', which was the Northampton, and for that matter the Geneva model. These were more than procedural variations, for they probably concealed the difference between a relatively high and low doctrine of the eucharist and of the real presence. One of Paget's supporters asked: 'Do they make so much ado for chewing a piece of bread and drinking a cup of wine?' Josias Nichols of Eastwell seems to have abbreviated the words of administration so as to weaken the emphasis on the eucharistic presence, but how general this practice may have been we have no means of telling.[29]

There was as much variety in the means of distributing and receiving the elements as there evidently was in the doctrine of what they represented or conveyed. The puritans abhorred kneeling, either as implying popish adoration of the real presence, or, as one Essex parishioner explained, 'for that he thought it was not according to the word of God, for that Christ ministered it sitting.' This was William Axton's doctrine at Moreton Corbet in Shropshire, where the elements were received – and probably administered – seated. Some observed the custom of bringing the elements down to the people sitting in their seats in the body of the church, as at Nichols's Wealden parish, where the minister first delivered the bread to the communicants 'sitting in the pews', and then passed the cup to the clerk, who 'delivereth the cup to the first communicant and one taking the cup of another they drink all of it.' The same order was observed at Brentwood in Essex, where the minister, Mark Wyersdale, 'gave the cup to [one] and that one delivered it from one to another.' Elsewhere the custom was to sit round the table on forms, as at the last supper. In one Yorkshire parish we hear of the communicants sitting 'in order, at the table'. Unless, as in Scotland, a stock of long tables was kept in the church or imported for the occasion, such a rule could hardly have obtained in large churches, especially when the communions were infrequent 'grand communions' for which minister and churchwardens laboured to procure the maximum attendance. In such circumstances standing was the accepted posture, as to this day in the French Reformed Church. What Bancroft at the Hampton Court conference called the 'ambling communion', in which the people received the elements as they walked past the table, was practised by Walter Travers at the Temple church in London. The fullest description of the standing communion as practised in England comes from the 'order of Northampton', sanctioned by Bishop Scambler of Peterborough but probably the work of Percival Wiburn:

> The manner of this communion is, besides the sermon, according to the order of the queen's Book; saving the people, being in their confession upon their knees, for the dispatch of many do orderly arise from their pews and so pass to the communion table, where they receive the sacrament, and from thence in like order to their place, having all this time a minister in the pulpit, reading unto them comfortable scriptures of the passion or other like, pertaining to the matter in hand.

At Watford, the late Elizabethan vicar, Anthony Watson, was said to have received the communion standing, and to have ministered it to the people standing and sitting.[30]

Little needs to be added to what has already been said about the conduct of baptism. The puritans were far from denying baptismal regeneration outright (although they would perhaps have disagreed among themselves as to what was to be understood by that doctrine). But they sought to avoid a superstitious use of the sacrament by their insistence that it be used only in public assemblies, 'annexed to the preaching of the word', and not administered privately, or by midwives. They also eschewed any fiction of the infant taking the baptismal vows in person, and were careful that the godparents should be properly approved members of the congregation, many, though not all, insisting that the sponsors should be the natural parents. (When Richard Greenham of Dry Drayton was asked to baptize the child of a man too ill to come to church, he consented only after a message had been brought from the father consenting to the baptism, and on condition that he would personally answer for the child as soon as he was able.[31]) Normally a puritan pastor would require the use of names that were biblical or otherwise authentically Christian: More Fruit, Faint Not, Perseverance, Sufficient, Deliverance.[32] Most puritans probably baptized in a basin or a dish rather than in the font, an implicit denial that their church was in any way the successor of the popish congregation which had earlier made use of the same building.

Finally a word or two must be said about puritan burials. The most radical puritan view – represented in the Admonition literature – was that burial was an office of simple piety which belonged to every man, and not merely to an ordained minister. Moreover, 'it is never read or found either in the Old Testament or the New, that God either appointed, or that there was used any service for, or at, and in the burial of the dead.' Funeral sermons were attacked by the *Admonition* as a surviving relic of the 'trental' of masses observed at popish funerals, although many puritans were later to be assiduous preachers and hearers of funeral sermons. Others less extreme contented themselves with objections to the unnecessary pomp of Tudor funerals, the popish 'ringing and jangling' of bells, or to the Prayer Book's charitable assumption of a 'sure and certain hope of the resurrection to eternal life'. The Genevan Liturgy in the English versions of the 'eighties made provision for an austere and simple order of burial which would probably have been to the taste of most Elizabethan puritan ministers: 'The corpse is reverently to be brought to the grave, accompanied with the neighbours in comely manner, without any further ceremony.' Other recensions provide for 'comfortable exhortation' in the church 'if it be not far off.'[33]

There is evidence to suggest that some puritan burials were performed in the spirit of the Genevan book, if not according to its precise directions. Eusebius Paget had as his chief supporter and accomplice in North Cornwall a Scotsman, David Black, who was later to cut a notorious figure in an Edinburgh pulpit. When one of Paget's children died in the absence of the father, Black took it upon himself to bury the infant in Kilkhampton churchyard. It was 'laid in the grave and a psalm only sung, and no service at all said.' In London, which killed off so many of the people who constantly flooded into it from all parts of the country, it cannot have been an easy task for the ecclesiastical authorities to be sure that every funeral was conducted with the full Prayer Book rite, especially if it took place in one of the new burial grounds which were not attached to any one parish. In May 1590 the High Commissioners made an order regarding the new Bedlam churchyard from which we deduce that this had been used for burials outside the order of the

Church by 'divers fantastical persons', who carried their dead thither 'out of sundry places of the City of London'. It was to this burial ground that a great international procession of Calvinists, English, Scottish and French, had carried the body of the Scottish minister James Lawson, when he died in London in 1584. And Bancroft was to confirm in *Daungerous positions* that the things done in 'the new churchyard in London' were evidence that in this respect at least the puritans had put their Book of Discipline into practice. The famous puritan divine Edward Dering was buried in this place, and one of his disciples later arranged through his will to be interred 'as near as may be' to his body. In life and even in death, solidarity was the mark of the early puritan tradition, and in nothing so much as in the worship and service of God.[34]

4 The Meetings of the Godly

'For the meetings of the godlie is like a great many firebrands layde together, in which though there be some heate when they are apart by themselves, yet being laid together it is doubled, and otherwise every one would dye of it selfe: so though every man hath some grace of God's spirit in himselfe, yet it is *greatly increased by conference.*'

(NICHOLAS BOWND, *The doctrine of the Sabbath,* 1595, p. 219)

THE EARLY YEARS OF THE SEVENTEENTH CENTURY saw the emergence of a group of puritan publicists whose oddly contradictory posture sometimes perplexes those who prefer to keep the religious factions of that time in neat categories, corresponding to the denominations and parties of more recent church history. These were non-separating congregationalists, so-called because they shared all the convictions of congregationalism without acknowledging that these demanded a deliberate act of secession from the established Church. They held that the Church of God was composed of gathered, convenanting companies of the godly, 'be they never so few', and that it existed in no higher form than in the independent and autonomous local congregation. Yet they were satisfied that these principles were not inconsistent with a public establishment of religion by the magistrate and need not be compromised in the Church of England as they found it in the reign of James I.[1]

Our direct concern is not with these ideas of church order (which were to have a great future in Massachusetts) but merely with an argument which was employed to justify this apparently almost untenable position. It was acknowledged by those who took this stand – most notably by William Ames, a theologian of European stature[2] – both that the services of the Church established under the Act of Uniformity were corrupt and that the principle of compulsion which the same statute embodied was unlawful. Yet they pointed to the many other exercises of religion which flourished within the national Church, 'wherein none are present

by constraint, and where the service book doth not so much as appear.'[3]
So long as these benefits were freely enjoyed they saw no need of separation. In the last chapter we found what the more extreme puritan clergy
made of the legally established services of the Church, and of the 'corrupt'
Prayer Book which they were bound to use for all these occasions. We
now pass on to other fields of puritan activity which were free of these
restraints. These were those other, voluntary religious exercises which
mingled prayer, exposition of the word and psalm-singing in varying
proportions, and in which the Prayer Book had no place.

Some of the larger assemblies which drew the godly together from a
wide catchment area have been described earlier in this book: the
prophesyings and the regular market-town exercises and occasional
preaching fasts and communions which succeeded the prophesyings. But
besides these notable attractions, many districts in the Midlands, South
and East of England were furnished with a regular programme of sermons
and catechizings on Sundays, and of lectures on one or more weekdays.
'I could like the better if the preaching might be only upon the Sabbath
day,' complained an Essex 'atheist' in George Gifford's homely dialogue,
The countrie divinitie; 'but now they run in the week days and leave their
business and beggar themselves. They go to other towns also, which is a
pity that it is suffered; it is a great disorder.' A group of Essex villagers was
told in the archdeacon's court: 'If you can trot to sermons, we will make
you trot to the courts.'[4]

'Gadding to sermons' was a phenomenon widely noted by curious and
often hostile observers. William Glibery, a comedian *manqué* though vicar
of Halstead in north Essex, saw his own domain invaded for a Sabbath-day
exercise by Richard Rogers and his train and delivered from the pulpit
his own salty opinion of sermon-tasters: 'It is no matter. Every man as
he loves quoth the good wife when she kissed you wot what.'[*] The
scandalized puritans reported that in another sermon Glibery had offered
to lay twenty pounds that 'if I were let alone with these same gadding
heads that run about thus to sermons, I would, saith he, in a month
bring them to what religion I list.' When William Dyke, one of the
hottest of the puritan preachers, occupied the pulpit at St Michael's, St
Albans, it was said that 'many absent themselves from their own parish
churches on the Sabbath day, yea refuse to hear their own ministers being
preachers, and repair to Dyke to hear him, and many of this gadding
people came from far and went home late, both young men and young

* The modern version runs: 'Everyone to his taste as the old lady said when she kissed
the cow.'

women together.' That this was the pattern of the puritan Sunday in rural Essex the act-books of the archdeacons' courts show in profuse detail. The preaching of Gifford at Maldon and of a score of other preachers attracted followers from surrounding parishes not supplied with an acceptable ministry. So ineradicable had the habit become that in 1587 the official to the archdeacon of Essex licensed a group of eight from the parish of Shopland to go elsewhere when there was no sermon in their own church, provided that only two of them were absent on any one occasion. In the following year, six parishioners of Canewdon asked for a similar licence to release them from their own parish on all but one Sunday in the month.[5]

One East Anglian preacher extols the example of the gospeller who says to his friend: 'I pray you, neighbour, let us go together to such a sermon, or such a godly exercise, and *I will go with you.*' The puritans were outward-looking and eager to convert their neighbours, but the new initiate found himself in a partly enclosed society, subject to its own laws and discipline. When the godly of Nayland (in the Dedham area) accompanied one of their preachers to neighbouring Boxted, where he was to take the service, the vicar prudently left off his surplice, knowing, as one Boxted clothier later reported, that 'some that came out of Suffolk side would have liked him the worse if he had worn it.'

The godly would not willingly receive communion from their parish priest if he were a non-preacher or otherwise objectionable. William Dyke was said to have received many from the parishes around St Albans to his communions, 'for that their ministers were no preachers.' While still a schoolmaster at Brentwood, George Gifford went with his wife to Lord Rich's parish of Little Leighs to receive communion. Years later, as vicar of Maldon, he himself welcomed communicants from other parishes, who spoke of receiving 'with Mr Gifford, vicar of Maldon'. Parents would fetch a preacher from outside to baptize their children, rather than submit them to the sign of the cross. In all this we can see the pattern of the puritan church within the Church. It was a pattern which undermined the national Church and its local expression, the parish, institutions which were at least as important to orthodox puritan thinking as to institutional Anglicanism. These aspects of 'the meetings of the godly' we shall discuss presently.[6]

But first we have to take stock of something even more corrosive of the traditional structures of Christian society than the habit of 'gadding abroad': the existence of gathered groups of puritans within the parish, constituting a church within the Church in minuscule. The history of *ecclesiola in Ecclesia* provides a strand of its own in the wider history of the post-Reformation Church, from the *Christliche Gemeinschaften* of Martin Bucer's Strasbourg to the Methodist class meetings of the eighteenth century and beyond. Yet the Elizabethan chapter in this story has been almost totally overlooked, even in the remarkably comprehensive survey of these movements recently published by Dr F. W. B. Bullock, which explicitly acquits the English puritans of any tendency to nourish a church within the Church.[7] But, as we discovered in the opening pages of this study, a leaning to separation was implicit in the inevitable isolation of real and fervent protestants in a nominally protestant and largely indifferent environment. The pastor, as a member of the Dedham conference saw him, must 'always be catechizing his people, inquiring what Christ is, what cause they have to love and make much of Him.' The godly, for their part, were 'to be ever inquiring after Him, comforting one another, conferring, meditating, praying, stirring up one another, so that by these means ... we may grow on in knowledge and obedience.' Those who followed this way of life could hardly escape the charge of 'singularity' when, like Richard Baxter's family in Jacobean Worcestershire, who were called 'puritans, precisians and hypocrites' by the common sort of people, they 'rather chose to read the scriptures than to do as they did.' The primitive Christian desire for mutual edification and encouragement was satisfied in house-meetings, sometimes of the pastor with the more initiated of his flock, sometimes of the godly alone, without clerical guidance. In these gatherings the puritan church within the Church had its tangible local expression.[8]

Those who met in each other's homes were the same godly persons who followed the preachers from church to church. Sermons, lectures and other exercises took place in the hours of daylight. These more intimate and local meetings were held after supper. 'Night conventicles', as Bishop Aylmer called them,[9] were not easily distinguishable from the ordinary religious exercises of a private household. When one considers the size and composition of even a modest middle-class or yeoman 'family' at this time, it is apparent that the Elizabethan community contained within itself a number of smaller communities, a point often observed at the time. The head of a household, in contemporary thought, was a kind of magistrate, ruling over a small commonwealth composed of wife, children, apprentices and servants. Moreover, as Geree tells us in his *Character of an old English puritane*, 'his family he endeavoured to make a church.' It had the discipline of a church (no immoral servant would be suffered to remain under the roof) and it received the instruction of a church, for the godly householder catechized his children and retainers morning and evening, and presided over exercises of 'repetition' of the doctrine heard in sermons.[10] If the household were sufficiently large and prosperous he might employ a learned man to do this for him. These private domestic devotions were outside the provisions of the law and beyond the competence of the state to control. They imposed a severe restriction on the capacity of Tudor ecclesiastical legislation to promote uniformity in religious practice and opinion, a factor as relevant for recusant as for puritan history. As Elizabeth herself knew, every London merchant had to have his schoolmaster and 'nightly conventicles', where even maid-servants learned to control learned preachers.[11]

Domestic religious exercises became public rather than private, and disorderly if not illegal, when persons not of that household were present. In the 1580s, bishops' visitation articles begin to echo a familiar refrain: 'Doth he or any other preachers remaining in your parishes ... keep any exercise of expounding, or read any lecture in private houses whereunto other besides those of that family do resort?'[12] But given the openness and diversity of the Elizabethan household, it could not be easily proved or disproved that those present at such a 'reading' or 'expounding' were all of one family. As preacher of Maldon, George Gifford went from house to house in the evenings, sharing the family meal and joining in the family prayers, which seem to have followed supper in all the godly households of the town. Sometimes others who were not of that household would drop in on 'necessary business', and would stop to pray. Quite possibly this innocent explanation conceals the existence of an organized conventicle which met in various houses to avoid suspicion. But it would be a hard thing to establish even in the church courts where the prosecutor was judge in his own case. When one William Walker of Cold Norton, near Maldon, was cited in the archdeacon's court for 'using unlawful reading and catechizing in his house by one Faunce of Maldon and John Gardiner of Heybridge', he could offer the defence that he used catechizing and reading 'in his own house and with his own family only' and that Faunce was a member of his family.[13]

Even if more than one household were represented at a prayer meeting or catechizing it was far from certain that the proceedings were illegal. The Elizabethan Commonwealth was no police state, and it was not thought acceptable that the law should interfere with the social gatherings of friends and neighbours. It would be necessary to prove that the motive of their gatherings constituted a conspiracy, and respectable Elizabethans were reluctant to believe that devotional meetings and the imparting of sound religious instruction could be anything but 'good proceedings'. Puritans were inclined to complain with some justice that while their godly meetings might be castigated as a conventicle, twenty men could meet together in an alehouse to misspend their time, and 'all this is no harm, it is but good neighbourhood, it is no conventicle.'[14] It was an appealing argument, especially in the Elizabethan context of ideological warfare. While Gifford of Maldon was holding his nightly prayer meetings, Robert Palmer, who had displaced him as vicar, was to be discovered in his bowling-alley in the orchard, 'daily and weekly', and that with 'a great sort or swarm of men'. According to the local report, he spent so much time there 'that he cannot set down.' Nevertheless, the evenings found him playing at tables in the New Inn.[15] Which of these assemblies, the puritan was inclined to ask, was a threat to the good ordering of society? Those who frequented these 'conventicles' were no separatists, but for the most part 'diligent and ordinary frequenters of public assemblies with the people of God'.[16] To our eyes there is little doubt that the threat to the security of Church and Commonwealth lay in the catechizings and expoundings, not at the ale-house and bowling-green. It did not seem so to many religious persons at the time. In any case it was a danger which the machinery of state and of ecclesiastical government could only partially prevent. The 'meeting of the godly' was liable to become a conventicle, if not the nucleus of a sect, wherever the godly were deprived of a preaching minister or for any other reason alienated from their parish church. Where the zeal for precise uniformity of a Whitgift or a Bancroft, or of the queen herself, was the cause of such a condition, the authorities could be said to have promoted a situation which they could not subsequently control.

A familiar form of domestic 'exercise' which might bring together more than one family, was the meeting on Sunday evenings for 'repetition' of the doctrine delivered and gathered in the course of the day's ministry. 'What he heard in public' the puritan 'repeated in private, to whet it upon himself and family.' The Suffolk minister Nicholas Bownd, in his influential book The doctrine of the Sabbath, first published in 1595, regarded such meetings as a regular and necessary part of the Sabbath proceedings. The people of God were to confer together, and especially with the minister, on the word of God as they had heard it preached, and they were to sing psalms. John Udall, while preacher at Kingston-on-Thames, recommended this as 'a very profitable way'. 'After that the sermon is done, we ought at our coming home to meet together, and say one to another: "Come, we have all been where we have heard God's word taught. Let us confer about it, that we may not only call to remembrance those things that every one of us have carried away, but also that one may have the benefit of the labours of others." ' Masters of households and heads of families were to use the occasion for a kind of catechizing, 'that forsomuch as children and servants be often careless in attending unto the word of God, the very fear of rebuke or correction at their father's or master's hands will make them learn somewhat.'[17]

But house meetings were not restricted to these Sunday evening 'repetitions'. Gifford of Maldon seems to have spent most evenings of the week in ministering to small groups of his devotees. Thomas Redrich, vicar of Hutton, 'read a lesson and answered to a question' in a conventicle at Laindon Hills on a Monday and a Tuesday evening. From time to time puritans gathered in each other's houses for a fast, with prayer and preaching, a corporate act of humiliation. Such occasions were private fasts, distinguished from the public fasts held in churches and yet, as Nicholas Bownd insists in his treatise on fasting, they were to be open to godly neighbours and friends out of 'divers households', 'gathered together upon their own private motion; and yet orderly and in the fear of God.'[18]

Occasionally something very like what the nineteenth century would learn to call a religious revival would grow out of these gatherings. In 1584 the preacher Thomas Settle was placed, with the encouragement of the locally powerful Lord North, as curate in place of the absentee vicar of the fenland town of Mildenhall. Settle was a radical, impulsive preacher who that summer publicly compared Whitgift to Bonner as 'an enemy to the Church and a tyrant'. He found little response from the people of Mildenhall, 'altogether worldly minded, being frozen in their dregs, which seem to have made their large fen their God.' But even Mildenhall had its few godly, and to them were added others from neighbouring parts of East Anglia. In the winter of 1584-5, Settle and his followers held frequent meetings 'at midnight and at other unlawful seasons of the night' in the Barrow Inn where the preacher had his lodgings. To these conventicles came two Mildenhall butchers and a number of other tradesmen and gentlemen from Bury, Thetford and Barton Mills, 'persons thought and commonly reputed precise, and such as observe not order.' Their practice was to shut themselves up privately in a chamber after supper, and there to use prayers, 'whereof', according to the landlord, 'the noise might be heard to the furtherside of the street, so as the other guests of the house complained of the disquiet they received thereby.' Settle also went over to Bury to hold similar meetings in the house of Mr Johnson, a glover. It comes as no surprise to learn that he later adopted a separatist position. In 1586 he told Whitgift to his face that even if he suspended him from preaching, 'I am called to preach the gospel and I will not cease to preach the gospel.' He spent the next four years in Westminster Gate-house.[19]

'Night conventicles' are particularly well documented for the county of Essex. They occurred at Strethall, on the Cambridgeshire border, as early as 1574. Ten years later, the examination of some parishioners of Aythorp Roding for holding unlawful and seditious assemblies revealed that about ten persons 'of his kindred and neighbours' had met in the house of one Davies, 'being invited thither to supper.' There they 'conferred together of such profitable lessons as they had learned that day at a public catechizing.' After supper some listened to a reading from Foxe's Book of Martyrs while others attended to the vicar, John Huckle, at that time suspended for not subscribing, 'who was then in company with them, and was reading by the fireside a piece of a catechism ... which he had then in his hand.' Finally all sang a psalm and prayed 'according to the Form of Prayer, and so departed about ten o' clock at night.'

At East Hanningfield, near Maldon, William Seridge, the rector, used to meet regularly 'for the better sanctifying of the Sabbath day' with some fourteen persons and their wives, including one of the churchwardens and the schoolmaster with their wives, and six persons from other neighbouring parishes. Together they engaged in prayer and psalm-singing, 'which order of exercise he useth to use sometimes more, sometimes less.' At Great Wakering, on the Thames estuary, where the parson was no preacher, the godly met among themselves on Sunday evenings to confer on 'the parcel of scripture that they heard that day', presumably at sermons in other parishes. Sometimes they met 'at one neighbour's house, sometimes at another's, that are well given.' As at Aythorp Roding, they sang a psalm before dispersing.[20]

Since these meetings were an extension of normal family worship, there is every reason to suppose that laymen took a lead in prayer and even in expounding doctrine. At Great Wakering there is no suggestion of the presence of a minister. In the Dedham minutes we even find a brother inquiring 'whether it were convenient a woman should pray, having a better gift than her husband?' The sects of the mid-seventeenth century would provide scope for female prophecy, and even for female government. Elizabethan puritanism already had its gifted women, even its prophetesses, like Ursula Grey, daughter of the jailer who kept the distinguished recusant prisoners at Wisbech Castle. Before the Jesuits achieved the notable coup of her conversion, Ursula was, we are told, 'entirely given up and devoted to the sect of the puritans', and a teacher among them.

Whereas the familiar complaint of the preacher was that with the generality of his hearers the doctrine 'went in at the one ear and out at the other', the godly had always to confirm or dispute what they had heard. This they probably did not only in formal 'repetitions' but on the spot, as soon as the sermon was over. According to the Jesuit William Weston, who witnessed the extraordinary preaching exercises and open-air communions held at Wisbech within sight of the prisoners, the people who attended had their Bibles open on their laps and looked up the texts cited by the preachers. After the exercise 'they held arguments also, among themselves, about the meaning of various Scripture texts, all of them, men and women, boys and girls, labourers, workmen and simpletons; and these discussions were often wont, as it was said, to produce quarrels and fights.' Of the conventicles around Cranbrook, in the weald of Kent, Richard Fletcher, later bishop of London, wrote: 'It is a common thing now for every pragmatical prentice to have in his head and mouth the government and reformation of the Church. And he that in exercise can speak thereof, that is the man.'[21]

If as much attention had been paid by historians to the busy life of the puritan laity in sermons, catechizings and house meetings as has been given to certain acts of ceremonial nonconformity by the puritan clergy, the rationale of the non-separating congregationalists would not now seem a mere casuistical curiosity. There was an extensive area of corporate religious experience within the establishment over which the official Church had little control, and which is still for the most part unexplored and unmapped. Whether these godly doings were private or public in character was a point of dispute between the non-separating congregationalists and their separatist opponents, but for all practical purposes the distinction had little meaning. In so far as those who lived in this territory thought much of the Church, they probably understood it in something like the way that the non-separators, Jacob, Bradshaw and Ames were later to make public. Theirs was the leaven that leavened the whole lump. So long as their meetings were not called in question, the Church of England had within it the essential ingredients of the true churches of God.

As for those separatist movements which did from time to time erupt, some at least are probably to be understood as the response of such a group to persecution or to the deprivation of its leadership. To take three examples from three isolated periods and areas: the beginnings of separatism in London in 1566, the Brownist movement in Norfolk around 1580 and the separation of the Nottinghamshire and Lincolnshire 'pilgrims' in the early seventeenth century. All concerned voluntarist groups which already, before their separation, seem to have possessed some identity as gathered companies within the establishment. Each of these separations followed hard on periods of energetic episcopal activity when preachers had been suspended and displaced, and when what Ames called the 'connivance of those that are in authority' was temporarily withdrawn. But many more such groups remained within the fellowship of the parish, their separatism only potential. Ames wrote with reason of the 'thousands in England' of essentially congregationalist opinions, 'which remain members of the ordinary parishes there.'[22]

'The meetings of the godly' therefore deserve close scrutiny, for they may prove to contain the pattern of future developments which were to be as distasteful to presbyterians as to conforming Anglicans. The presbyterians and the puritan ministry in general went forward on the assumption that religious experience would normally be found and contained within the local church, directed and controlled by the teaching of the church and its magistracy, by pastor, doctor and elders. And they assumed that the membership and character of that church would be parochial and in practice involuntary, as it always had been. But partly as a consequence of the frustration of puritan hopes of a further reformation of the parish churches, the godly were gathering in increasing numbers in non-parochial meetings, whether of people from more than one community drawn out of their parishes to various preaching occasions, or of semi-separatist cells within the community. As Bancroft pointed out with some precision, although the puritan ministers preached 'in our material churches', the parish in which they preached was not the Church 'properly in their sense, but as many thereof only as are joined unto them' as a godly company, 'and those furthermore, who, leaving their own parish churches, do come unto them.'[23]

Such a situation pointed unmistakably to voluntarism and independency. In defending his non-separating position to separatists, William Ames proposed that the covenant by which an independent church is constituted had been made in effect by any group of Christians meeting together voluntarily.[24] He might have added that some such groups had gone so far as to formalize their meetings with a written covenant, subscribed by all the participants. In 1588, in Richard Rogers's Essex township of Wethersfield, a covenant was agreed upon by 'certain well-minded persons' who were meeting according to their custom 'in a

Christian man's house', in company with Rogers himself. 'Their meeting', Rogers informs us, 'was for the continuance of love and for the edifying one of another, after some bodily repast and refreshing.' By the terms of their covenant the company – 'well nigh twenty persons' – confessed to the unprofitableness of their Christian profession and agreed to forsake worldly things and to 'turn to the Lord in all sincerity.' They went on to bind themselves to a common rule of devotions and to make a habit of conferring with one another of their spiritual estate. It is true that their covenant was concerned not with church order but with the cultivation of personal spiritual experience ancillary to the benefits derived from public worship in the parish church. Yet there is significance even in this inward-looking pietistic preoccupation. Rogers preserves the covenant in the context of his *Seaven treatises*, itself a manual of personal devotion and symptomatic of a new departure in puritan religion.[25]

The more thoughtful of the puritan clergy were aware of the dangerous trends which we have indicated in this chapter, especially if they were losing their own parishioners to a more popular preacher. This was the fate of poor Robert Lewis of Colchester, a member of the Dedham conference whose auditory was drawn away by the town preacher, George Northey, and who bravely competed to the extent of preaching on the same texts, strengthened by a ruling that 'the people of every congregation should join with their own pastors in the use of the word and sacraments.'[26] In 1589 an anonymous treatise appeared from the press to the same effect, entirely devoted to *perswading the people to reverence and attend the ordinance of God in the ministerie of their owne pastors*.[27] Yet most Elizabethan preachers were pragmatists to whom mere godliness seemed an overriding consideration, and few cared how that priceless commodity was acquired and cultivated. Their indifference, coupled with the indefinite postponement of any further reformation, prepared the way for the seventeenth century, when separating and non-separating variations of congregationalism would more than hold their own with the 'old English puritanism' of Elizabethan days.

Part 8

Discovery, Prosecution and Dissolution

1 Partly Fearing, Partly Hoping

'There is little hope of any better state to the Church. Sudden dangers are greatly to be feared. We are generally so secure and so little dreaming of them.'

> (Entry of RICHARD ROGERS of Wethersfield in his diary for July 1589; *Two Elizabethan Puritan Diaries*, ed. Knappen, p. 84)

1588! THE 'YEAR OF WONDERS' for which apocalyptic calamities had been anciently prophesied proved, as even modern schoolboys know, a wonderful year in a better sense for the protestant England of Elizabeth. The defeat of the Spanish Armada could not yet be seen in perspective as an historic watershed, but it was at once hailed as a providential if not miraculous deliverance. The atmosphere was still one in which 'sudden dangers' were to be feared, but with this went a heady confidence that 'the Lord no doubt is on our side, which soon will work their fall.'[1] It was the climax of that movement of national self-assertion which was one facet of the English Reformation. Yet this year which saw the vindication of English protestantism marked the beginning of a definite decline in the fortunes of the puritan movement. Not of puritan religion: that was something now widely dispersed and year by year growing roots which were not to be easily torn out. But puritanism as an organized force devoted to the achievement of a presbyterian revision of the 'outward face' of the Church was now under sentence. Josias Nichols of Kent, speaking of this time, recalled a mood of 'partly fearing and partly hoping', while 'the time slipped away, and men's minds wavered this way and that way.'[2] The hopes were extravagant, even apocalyptic, and themselves symptomatic of a lack of stability. The fears were the reflection partly of an increasingly menacing ecclesiastical and political situation, partly of an inner uncertainty of direction and purpose.

The precise causes of this failure of morale remain a matter for discussion. Historians have often pointed to the defeat of the Armada as a reason in itself for the collapse of the puritan movement. The suggestion is that puritanism had for long sheltered behind the excessive fear of international papal aggression which was alleviated by the events of August 1588. Yet it was to take many years, not a few months, to remove the real danger of Spain and the scarcely rational dread of Jesuitical subversion. It is true that in a highly patriotic speech to the Parliament which met in the aftermath of the Armada, Sir Christopher Hatton as lord chancellor lumped papists and puritans together as equally dangerous subjects. Yet while such an opinion would continue to shock an old-fashioned protestant like Sir Francis Knollys,[3] it was one which Hatton had long shared with the queen herself. The essence of the alteration in the political scene was that those who took this intransigently Anglican stand now enjoyed much greater freedom of action. The reason for that may be found not so much in the naval victories of August as in the death on September 4th of the man whom Izaak Walton was to call 'the reputed cherisher and patron-general' of the puritan party: Robert Dudley, earl of Leicester.

Leicester's death had been preceded by the slow attrition of his political influence, to the advantage of enemies who were diametrically opposed to Elizabeth's old favourite in their religious policy. The evidence of his church patronage suggests that in his prime Leicester lent his support with some consistency to those best described as Grindalians: zealous preaching protestants who were moderate puritans in their attitude to current controversies and not disposed to stand on their ecclesiastical dignity. But in his later years he moved closer to the more extreme, presbyterian fringe. He was friendly to John Field, installed Cartwright as master of his hospital at Warwick, and took Humfrey Fen and John Knewstub as chaplains to the Netherlands during his captaincy-general. A young Oxford puritan left his preaching to become his secretary and both he and Fen sought the approval of the London *classis* for their appointments. That Leicester now made friends of this kind is itself a token that he had lost the effective patronage of major ecclesiastical appointments of which he had once boasted. This was a direct consequence of the rise of Whitgift, which he had not opposed but which he must have lived to regret. The earl and the archbishop confronted each other over church policy in the House of Lords and, if we are to believe a story told by Izaak Walton, in the presence of the queen herself. During Leicester's absence in the Netherlands, Whitgift was made a privy councillor, apparently by Burghley's means. He was the first prelate to sit on the Council since the death of Cardinal Pole, 'whereat', the archbishop's secretary and biographer tells us, 'the earl was not a little displeased.' Lords Buckhurst and Cobham, both adversaries of Leicester and 'joined in like affection to the archbishop', were preferred at the same time. Thereafter, according to Sir George Paule, 'the archbishop's courses ... were not so much crossed nor impeded as heretofore; but by reason of his daily attendance and access, he thus oftentimes gave impediment to the earl's designments in clergy causes.'[4]

With the death of Leicester, the political foundations of Elizabethan puritanism began to crumble away. Other powerful friends were soon to follow him: Sir Walter Mildmay in 1589, Leicester's brother Warwick and Sir Francis Walsingham in 1590. The earl of Bedford had gone in 1585. Of the old guard, Sir Francis Knollys was now left virtually alone, a political dinosaur, and more than ever torn between his private conscience and his public duty as a senior privy councillor. The earl of Huntingdon would survive until 1595, but he was without much influence at Court. In the wake of the high Elizabethans and in the few years that were to elapse before the young earl of Essex began to build the great following that dominated the 'nineties, there arose what the seventeenth-century annalist of nonconformity, Roger Morrice, called 'the little faction'.[5] The 'father' and 'common head' of this alliance was Hatton, who was himself to die in 1591, but who reached the summit of his career in 1587 with his appointment as lord chancellor. Whitgift, who, as Paule tells us, had 'linked himself in a firm league of friendship' with Hatton, was the other principal member of this axis. Almost its raison d'être was to oppose the puritans and defend the integrity of the Church and its possessions.

This cause was served by a group of able divines and civil lawyers who can fairly be described as anti-puritans and who were now approaching the height of their powers: notably Richard Bancroft, who served Hatton and Whitgift in turn as chaplain and made an additional human bond between them, Dr Richard Cosin, dean of the Court of Arches and a most active high commissioner, Matthew Sutcliffe, Richard Lewyn and others.[6] It would be misleading to say that these men had all their own way in church matters in the late 'eighties. But they alone pursued a considered, forceful policy, and even Burghley, for all his abiding suspicion of Whitgift's conduct of religious affairs, was little more disposed to offer resistance than he had been to oppose Leicester and Walsingham in their heyday. The strength of the 'little faction' lay in their close interpretation of the queen's own mind and wishes in matters of religion, whereas Leicester and his friends had favoured a party and a policy to which the queen herself was utterly averse. John Udall of Kingston put a prophecy into the mouth of an adversary in his dialogue *Diotrephes*, printed in this year of Leicester's death, that 'if their lordships were taken away, the credit of the gospel would fall to the ground, and men would not regard it.' The accuracy of this analysis (which Udall had meant to refute) was now to be seen. Thomas Digges would later sorrowfully recall that in the earl's time 'it went for current that all papists were traitors in action or affection. He was no sooner dead, but Sir Christopher Hatton ... bearing sway, puritans were trounced and traduced as troublers of the state.'[7]

There was another death in 1588, as disturbing to the cause in its own way as that of any of the great puritan courtiers. On March 26th John Field was buried in St Giles Cripplegate, where he had once preached. Another London minister, noting his death some years later when other puritan zealots had gone to the gallows and when Field's activities were known from Bancroft's disclosures, thought it remarkable that he had died in his bed. No substitute was ever found for Field's unusual talents as an organizer. Walter Travers took over the function of corresponding secretary in London, but with none of his predecessor's dynamic opportunism. Very few further papers were now to be added to the 'register' which Field had made it his business to gather. For this reason alone the puritan movement becomes harder to see as a coherent whole with his passing.[8]

The loss of Field must have increased the confusion and uncertainty which were now besetting many members of the movement. For how long could they willingly prolong 'this disorderly time' in which an anomalous situation was tolerated in expectation of a further reformation which never came? Josias Nichols of Kent later remembered that he and others still partly hoped 'as though the reverend fathers themselves ... would at the length have joined with us, to the ending of these unwholesome strifes', or that God, 'pitying his Church, would have raised up some means to further his own cause.' But even those whose lives were founded on belief in divine providence must by now have doubted that their help lay in any such direction. How often had they knocked at these doors? A strong influence was being exercised from the left, by those who had cut this Gordian knot with the clear, sharp arguments of separatism, a way now more strongly supported than ever before and ably led (from the Fleet prison!) by a renegade Essex minister, John Greenwood, and a well-connected gentleman with university and legal training, Henry Barrow. Barrow and Greenwood condemned the Church of England out of hand with a resounding fourfold formula which attacked 'the unworthiness and confusion of the people', together with the unlawfulness of its ministry, worship and government. Those who accepted and acted upon this indictment experienced the sense of release and of strength that must come to anyone who is able to base his actions on an apparently watertight dialectic. Greenwood had no doubt that his ministry as an Anglican parson had been 'wholly evil, both in office, entrance and administration', and that he had left it in obedience to God's clear commandment. His opponents could only protest, with evident lack of assurance, that though there were 'some defaults' in their outward calling, they were true ministers 'in an extra-ordinary time'.[9]

Nichols regarded the new separatist wave as one of three 'most grievous accidents' which overtook the godly ministers at this time and did 'very much darken the righteousness of our cause.' But was the cause righteous? There was the rub. Perhaps the separatists were right and the error that they had made was to hold fellowship with unlearned, non-preaching ministers and oppressive bishops. In the Midlands the members of the *classes* were writing to one another in almost hysterical terms which suggest that in their minds at least they did not live in the same church as their opponents and looked for no peace from that quarter. Edward Lord of Wolston wrote that the painful preaching ministers were now 'in worse sort suppressed' than by the papists under Mary, for they had acted according to law, 'which is otherwise now with us.' 'Buckle with the bishops, massacre the malkin ministers,' was his advice to his fellow *classis* member, Daniel Wight of Stretton. 'I trust in God to see the day that in all England a man shall not find a [square] cap to cover a close stool.' Wight echoed this refrain:

Let my tongue cleave to the roof of my mouth, let all God's graces forsake me if I cease to pray and preach against the corruption of bishops – I mean the [e]state itself, and all their confederates, especially their new creatures, that is our vile servile dunghill ministers of damnation, that viperous generation, those scorpions. We build up the battered and scattered walls of Jerusalem, howsoever for a while Babel build itself, which I trust shortly shall prove Babel, even miserable confusion.[10]

But in these circles there was no talk of building in another place, no thought of separation. Rather the policy was, as Wight wrote, to 'take our pennyworths' of the bishops 'and not die in their debt.' Like a certain puritan burgess of Kingston, it was the non-preachers that they hoped to see 'pulled out of the Church by the ears.' There was a vague expectation of some kind of apocalyptic victory which would bring in the discipline 'all in one day'; in more sober terms, a movement from within the establishment so irresistible that it would leave the bishops and their dupes high and dry. Edmund Snape was supposed to have said to some trusted parishioners in the great seat of his Northampton church on a summer day in 1589: 'How say you if we devise a way whereby to shake off all the Antichristian yoke and government of bishops and will jointly together erect the Discipline and government, and that in such sort as they that be against it shall never be able to prevail to the contrary? But peradventure it will not be this year and half or more.' When his confidants asked how these things might be, Snape went on to tell them of the existence of three or four small *classes* of ministers in every shire, of their debates about the Discipline, of the deliberations of weightier assemblies at Cambridge and London, and 'that they should practise the same in their several churches and congregations, and then that the same Discipline should be put in practice by the said ministers, together with the people.' Edward Lord of Wolston may have had the same day of triumph in mind when he asked his brethren to consider how bishops, deans, archdeacons and their officers were to be provided for under 'the reformation', 'that the Commonwealth be not thereby pestered with beggars.' Field himself, if we are to believe Thomas Edmunds's Star Chamber evidence, was convinced towards the end that 'seeing we cannot compass these things by suit nor dispute, it is the multitude and people that must bring the Discipline to pass which we desire.'[11]

But Field was now dead, and alive could even he have said when the day of which Snape had spoken was to be? or where the multitude of initiated presbyterians was to be found who were to 'bring it to pass'? In the meantime, relations with the non-puritan clergy remained a perplexing problem and one on which the separatists pressed the preachers hard. In Northamptonshire it was reckoned 'that the dumb ministry was no ministry', but if so, on what grounds could the puritans remain in even nominal fellowship with it? In July 1588 the diary of Richard Rogers of Wethersfield reveals that it had now 'come in question' in Essex whether 'there may be any receiving with an unpreaching minister', and two years later Rogers noted that this problem 'doth still spread further undissolved.' All this time there was no more than general agreement on the form of church government which the puritans professed to desire. After a visit to London which brought him into contact with the separatists as well as with the ministers of his own party, Rogers confessed his grief 'for the variety of opinions about governing Church in the learned. It troubled me sore to see my unsettledness therein.'[12]

The later months of 1588 saw the second of the 'grievous accidents' which, as Josias Nichols remembered, damaged the failing cause at this critical moment. The mood of angry frustration on the extremist fringe of the movement found an outlet in the voluble, satirical diatribes of 'Martin Marprelate'.[13] Who Martin was we may never know, but his publishers were familiar figures in the puritan movement: Robert Waldegrave, the devoted presbyterian printer, the fervent young Welshman, John Penry, and Job Throckmorton of Haseley, a Warwickshire squire who had been one of Wentworth's most useful allies in the last Parliament. Waldegrave had recently printed a number of provocative pamphlets by Penry and John Udall, preacher of Kingston and one of the most fluent and learned of puritan controversialists. He had printed sermons for Udall as early as 1584. He now published a clever and mildly offensive dialogue, *The state of the Church of England laid open in a conference*, usually known as *Diotrephes* from the name of one of the protagonists, and, for the learned public, a trenchant presbyterian manifesto, *A demonstration of the truth of that discipline*. For the restless Penry he printed a further essay on the scandalous religious condition of his native land, *An exhortation unto the governors and people of Wales*, and later in the year an apology for the presbyterian discipline, *A defence of that which hath bin written*. Penry's most recent experience had been in the *classis* at Northampton, where he was about to marry a local girl, and these writings brought into print for the first time the current Northamptonshire opinion that 'unpreaching ministers' were 'no ministers, because the Lord sent them not', and that it was a sin to communicate with them.[14] Udall's *Diotrephes* was printed in April 1588, on Waldegrave's own premises in London. Later the same month the house was raided and a press, some type and copies of the dialogue seized. In May, the Stationers' Company ordered the destruction of the press and the defacing of the type, in accordance with the Star Chamber decree of 1586. Thereafter Waldegrave was a fugitive printer, dependent at first on the friendly offices of the widow of a prosperous government official, Mistress Elizabeth Crane. It was at Mrs Crane's country house at East Molesey that the remaining Udall and Penry tracts were printed.[15] And then, in mid-October, appeared the first of the Martinist libels, *The epistle to the terrible priests*, which announced itself as 'printed overseas, in Europe, within two furlongs of a bouncing priest, at the cost and charges of Martin Marprelate, gentleman.' 'Europe' was Mrs Crane's establishment at Molesey, and little more than two furlongs away, over the Thames, was Hampton Court Palace. The printer was Waldegrave, using a new and distinctive fount of continental black-letter type.

From Molesey the press was soon withdrawn into the comparative security of the puritan country estates of Northamptonshire and east Warwickshire. There, with Penry's active assistance, Waldegrave printed two further tracts and a broadside before giving up his part in the enterprise and making himself scarce with his 'Dutch letters'. Waldegrave's departure was in April 1589. After an interval new printers were found, an inferior practitioner called Hodgkins with his assistants, and new copy, probably not from the original Martin's pen. It is at this point that Job Throckmorton's guiding hand becomes visible as author and manager. After a further journey, the printers, with one of their presses, were finally detected and seized in August, a mile out of Manchester. Six of Martin's fireworks[16] had by then exploded, and a seventh, *The protestatyon of Martin Marprelate*, appeared with superb impudence, a month after the arrest of Hodgkins and his men in Lancashire.

The first two of Martin's 'pistles' retain a remote connection with the literary skirmishing which had begun with Field's publication four years before of the presbyterian manifesto, *A briefe and plaine declaration*. They were inspired by Dr John Bridges, dean of Salisbury, who had threatened to smother further discussion under the weight of his fourteen-hundred-page *Defence of the government established*. The Marprelate Tracts were the most devastating retort to this kind of polemic that could possibly have been devised. 'Oh read over D. John Bridges, for it is a worthy worke' was the running headline of both the *Epistle* and the second tract, which announced itself as the first part of a convenient *Epitome* of the dean's argument, which he had 'very briefly comprehended in a portable book, if your horse be not too weak, of an hundred, threescore and twelve sheets of good demy paper.'[17] The third, and perhaps the last of the 'primary' tracts, was directed at Bishop Cooper of Winchester, who had hastened into print to admonish England on this latest threat to its security, and the title alone was a triumph, borrowed from a familiar London street-cry: *Hay* [ha' ye] *any worke for* [the] *Cooper*. It was the genius of Marprelate to see that the Achilles heel of the establishment was the vulnerability to ridicule which high ecclesiastical dignitaries have seldom lacked, and to recognize that this comic aspect of the bishops' enormities could be exploited to give them the widest currency. This was great satire, better than that of the professional wits of the day, Nashe and Lyly, who were hired to reply, and rescued from triviality as much by the rare quality of the prose as by the underlying seriousness of the satirist's intention. The chief victims – Whitgift, Aylmer and Cooper – were not the most ridiculous or vulnerable of the bishops, but they were the most prominent and dangerous, and Martin's mud sticks to these three unfortunate prelates to this day.

Most Elizabethans who got their hands on the tracts must have been entertained by Martin's scandalous humour. If it had been otherwise the serious point of the exercise would have been lost. Martin knew what we are not surprised to hear: that 'the most part of men could not be gotten to read anything' that had been written either in defence of the discipline or against the bishops. 'I bethought me, therefore, of a way whereby men might be drawn to do both.' Here, at last, was the appeal to 'the people'. One measure of Martin's success was that humorists and stage-players rather than learned divines were now commissioned to defend the opposite side. But according to all respectable, responsible opinion, the tracts were lewd, seditious libels, 'against all Christianity' as Whitgift put it. Francis Bacon was in good company in calling the fashion which Martin had begun 'this immodest and deformed manner of writing ... whereby matter of religion is handled in the style of the stage.'

In spite of the common ground they shared with the satirist, all but a few of the puritan divines had their own reasons for joining in the censure of Martin. He made fun of a solemn matter and defiled the cause with unprecedented scurrility. What was worse, he brought his supposed friends into danger. This Martin himself acknowledged: 'Those whom foolishly men call puritans like of the matter I have handled, but the form they cannot brook.' The printer, Waldegrave, soon found that all the preachers with whom he conferred 'do mislike it', and this was one of the reasons why this very courageous man abandoned Martin in mid-course. Cartwright was able to assure Burghley that 'from the first beginning of Martin unto this day, I have continually upon any occasion testified both my mislike and sorrow for such kind of disordered proceeding.' Josias Nichols deplored this 'foolish jester' from whom the preachers had earned the new name of 'Martinists'; 'how justly God knoweth.' 'Then did our troubles increase, and the pursuit was hardly followed against us.' And Thomas Brightman was to give his opinion in an influential commentary on the Apocalypse that if 'the angel of the Church of England' had been in any estimation, men 'would rather have cast those writings into the fire, than have worn them out with continual reading and handling of them.'[18]

Yet in the web spun by Martin and his collaborators, most of the threads lead to the puritan preachers and their lay patrons. Mrs Crane, who sheltered the press at the beginning, kept what was virtually a puritan salon in her London house. Was this the London 'haunt' of Waldegrave and Humfrey Newman, the cobbler who distributed the tracts? Some time in 1589 Mrs Crane married George Carleton, the Northamptonshire M.P.

who had always been a strong supporter of the cause, and who at his death a year later would appoint as the overseers of his will Peter Wentworth and William Fludd, the Northampton preacher.[19] From East Molesey the press travelled to Fawsley, the Northamptonshire home of another godly patron of the movement, Sir Richard Knightley, whose affairs at this time were partly in Carleton's hands.[20] From there the operations shifted to the White Friars at Coventry, the house of John Hales, Knightley's nephew by marriage, and so to Wolston Priory, six miles across Dunsmore Heath, and to the hospitality of Roger Wigston and his wife. If Mr Wigston was not entirely happy about the arrangement, his wife, who was absent at a fast in Coventry when the printers arrived, would later tell her judges that what she had done she did out of 'zeal of reformation in the Church'.[21] Then there was the involvement of Udall, Penry and Throckmorton, and of other puritan publicists who in method and even in whimsicality anticipated Martin himself: the eccentric Giles Wigginton of Sedbergh, Whitgift's sworn enemy, whose name at once occurred to the archbishop on the appearance of the first tract; and John Field himself, whom Professor Dover Wilson has called Martin's 'spiritual father'.[22]

Field, though dead six months before the printing of the *Epistle*, may well have had more to do with the paternity of the tracts than we now have any means of knowing. Martin's distinctive polemical method, the raking up of past episodes and discreditable anecdotes, grew out of the martyrological technique of 'gathering' and 'registering' the troubles of the godly, learned by Field from John Foxe and employed to good effect in the amassing of the puritans' own documentary files. A comparison of the tracts with the puritan register suggests that Martin must have been directly dependent on this very collection for some of his material. Henry Sharpe, the garrulous Northampton bookbinder, would later reveal what Penry had told him: that the *Epistle* was made from 'some such notes' as were found in Field's study, and 'that Master Field upon his deathbed willed they should be burnt, and repented for collecting them', from which Sharpe concluded that it was 'of Master Field's doing'. Were not the bishops threatened in the tracts with the very weapons that Field had forged? 'You shall not call one honest man before you, but I will get his examination ... and publish it, if you deal not according to the former conditions ... Secondly, all the books that I have in store already of your doings shall be published ... I mean to make a survey into all the dioceses in this land, that I may keep a visitation among my clergymen.'[23]

This is not the place to embark on an extended discussion of Martin Marprelate's identity, which may have been a secret kept even from his closest collaborators. 'I am alone. No man under heaven is privy, or hath been privy, unto my writings against you. I use the advice of none therein.'[24] Penry was almost his *alter ego*, but his voice and style were not Martin's. Job Throckmorton – whom Pierce came close to identifying with Martin and whose candidature is favoured by Sir John Neale – contributed to the secondary series of tracts, when Martin's 'sons' had supposedly assumed their father's mantle, and with Penry he clearly managed the whole enterprise at this stage, probably as the senior partner. His sallies into what can best be called para-Martinist literature, especially in the tract called *M. Some laid open in his coulers*, printed by Waldegrave in La Rochelle later in 1589, expose a genius with a richly comic imagination. And now Neale's discovery of the parliamentary speeches of 1586–7, hitherto unknown, are a further revelation of his potentialities, and of a style close to that of Martin.[25] But Penry's repeated denials that either he or Throckmorton was the original Martin, coupled with Throckmorton's own offer to take an oath 'that I am not Martin, I knew not Martin' must carry some weight.[26] And the fact that Penry and Throckmorton were under the necessity of completing the 'unperfect papers' of the fifth and uncharacteristic tract, *Theses Martinianae*, and made a poor job of it, carries more. This was nothing but a draft of the arguments which had been used in *Hay any worke* or were intended for use in the still incomplete 'More worke for Cooper', and it is very likely that Martin, whoever he was, never intended it for publication. 'Martin Junior's' affirmation that 'he keepeth himself secret from all his sons' and that 'we can neither know where our father is, not yet hear from him' may then have been no ruse but the simple truth.[27]

Positive evidence of the authorship of the first three tracts – stylistically distinct, Dover Wilson believes, from the secondary series – we have none, partly because Waldegrave was never taken and examined. If they contain a still unresolved problem, which is probable, it is most likely to yield to a minute investigation of the personnel and organization of the puritan movement in the Midlands, where the mood of the hour ('buckle with the bishops, massacre the malkin ministers') was attuned to the Marprelate adventure. Martin, the author of the first three tracts, may conceivably prove to have been a gentleman from this part of the country. If not Throckmorton, why not George Carleton, Mistress Crane's husband of 1589, perhaps abetted by that shadowy 'chief director' of puritan strategy in Northamptonshire, William Fludd? Miss Katherine Longley, late of the Surrey County Record Office and now at the Minster Library, York, has collected a quantity of circumstantial evidence which can serve to link Carleton with many local and biographical references in the tracts. And she has offered a new solution to one of the more baffling of Martin's ciphers. The *Epistle* was 'given at my Castle between two wales' (not 'whales' as Pierce renders it). Carleton was superintendent of the prisoners in Wisbech Castle, a place positively surrounded by place-names which enjoy the prefix 'wal' in reference to a Roman wall or bank: the Walpoles, West Walton, Walsoken, even Wales Field. And he whimsically christened his son 'Castle Carleton'.[28] Admittedly in hunting Martin we are looking for a genius whose use of language was highly idiosyncratic. But Carleton was a man of sharp wit and supreme self-confidence, by no means uncritical of 'our grave reformers'. 'I like them so well', he could write, 'that I will not trust them in so good a service.'[29]

What is certain is that the presence of the Marprelate press in the Midlands drew·the attention of the pursuivants into that area. The studies of the puritan ministers were visited, among other likely sources of information, and yielded, if not evidence of Martin, papers which exposed the network of presbyterian *classes* and the text of the Book of Discipline itself. The activities of Martin and his sons thus led directly to the uncovering of what had hitherto been a well-kept secret, an exemplary prosecution of some of the leading ministers before the High Commissioners and in the Star Chamber, and the subsidence of the organized puritan movement.

These discoveries were probably made in the late autumn of 1589, as the movements of Martin were reconstructed through the examinations of his principal collaborators. The Northamptonshire and Warwickshire ministers were to be summoned before the High Commissioners in the course of the following winter and spring. But right up to this moment the 'grand design' of the *classis* movement continued. 1589 was another year of conferences and political agitation. Evidently the ministers, in Richard Rogers's phrase, were 'so secure and so little dreaming' of the sudden dangers that now faced them.

In February 1589 another Parliament met, from which the puritans could surely hope to gain nothing. In his opening oration, Lord Chancellor Hatton mingled a patriotic attack on England's external enemies with the most explicit warning yet given in that place of the queen's inflexible opposition to all would-be promoters of a further reformation. Parliament was told that these men 'of a very intemperate humour' grieved her Majesty more even than the papists, whose hostility was at least open and known; that she found their platform and devices absurd, dangerous, and tending to innovation and tyranny; and that she was convinced that the

Church of England 'as now it standeth in this reformation' would bear comparison with any Christian church in history. They were not to 'so much as once meddle' with matters of religion, except to bridle the discontented, 'whether papists or puritans'. The parliament sermon, preached by Dr John Still, seems to have contained matter to the same effect.[30]

On the following Sunday, February 9th, Richard Bancroft preached at Paul's Cross a sermon which is rightly regarded as a minor landmark in English church history. If we are to believe what Whitgift later testified, the preacher was even at this time engaged in hunting Marprelate and his press, and he was to devote much of the next four years first to the prosecution and then to the literary exposure of the presbyterian movement. This sermon was a foretaste of his disclosures and of the forensic ruthlessness of his use of them, which may recall for the modern reader the methods of Senator Joseph McCarthy in our own time. The puritans were 'false prophets', seeking after singularity, all one with Arians, Donatists, anabaptists and other sectaries. What made them dangerous was their sinister alliance with 'the lay factious' whose identity was hinted at with a characteristic and menacing vagueness: 'Some, whether bishops or men of as great or greater authority'. The Church of England, with its episcopal government, was sharply distinguished from the foreign Calvinist churches, and especially the Church of Scotland, which suffered the same rough treatment as the English puritans.[31] Never had Paul's Cross heard such a confident defence of the established Anglican polity. Bancroft did not go so far as to assert directly the *jus divinum* of episcopal government, but it is significant that some at the time and many since have read the highest doctrine of episcopacy into his words.[32] Such a diatribe would hardly have been uttered in the earl of Leicester's time, yet now it was published within the month, according to Whitgift, 'by direction' from Hatton and Burghley. In thanking the English ambassador in Edinburgh for his prompt reaction to the protests which the sermon had aroused in Scotland, Bancroft implied that the archbishop and the lord chancellor, 'who are acquainted therewithal', had as much cause as himself to be grateful. Surely this sermon was, as Whitgift later wrote, 'to special purpose', and no wonder that Stephen Egerton of Blackfriars wrote to Humfrey Fen of Coventry: 'We expect no good in the cause of religion, we rather fear some evil.'[33]

Nevertheless, the Midland *classes* prepared to mount yet another parliamentary campaign in the style of 1584–5 and 1586–7. By the 'advice' of the roving agent, William Fludd, the Northamptonshire ministers carried out a complete survey of the churches and clergy of the county, hoping, as John Johnson later deposed, that their example would be followed by the brethren in other districts. Moreover, the assembly of six in Northampton resolved to send up to London one or two duly accredited representatives from each of the Northamptonshire *classes* 'to attend at the Parliament, and to join themselves with the brethren of other countries, and to offer disputation if it should be thought meet, or otherwise to undertake any other matter which should then and there be determined of amongst them.' These decisions were circulated by Edmund Snape to London, Oxford and Cambridge, and Johnson implies that in the circumstances which now prevailed they were something of an embarrassment. For once it was not London which was leading the country ministers into a radical course of action. Walter Travers sent Snape a letter 'of much cunning' in which he 'seemed nothing to mislike' of the proposed survey of the ministry, but suggested that there was too little time to prepare it before Parliament was due to meet. But Travers welcomed the proposal to send up delegates as a matter 'meet to be followed'. Although we cannot be certain that Johnson was not confusing the events of 1589 with those of 1586–7, it seems that a general conference was held to coincide with the Parliament, attended, as Johnson thought, 'from the most parts in England'. Northamptonshire sent up three or four ministers, 'as Mr Settle for Northampton and Rogers for Daventry', with the understanding that substitutes would be sent if any of these were imprisoned. Johnson adds that one resolution was that 'some twenty or thirty of them should have come in their gowns with all gravity to the door of the Parliament house and there by petition to have desired a disputation.' This was proposed by Mr Fludd, resolved by the Northampton assembly of six, 'and not mis-liked' by Mr Travers. Again that tell-tale phrase![34]

In spite of the queen's absolute prohibition, a kind of religious disputation was proposed in this Parliament, which tends to confirm Johnson's testimony, although what the puritan members had in mind was not a clerical debate but a conference 'before the Lords of the Higher House and a committee of the Lower House, in the presence of the bishops and all the judges of the land'.[35] Nor was there any question of the presbyterian discipline forming the subject of this conference, as Snape and Fludd and their friends would no doubt have desired. The proposal seems to have been made in the Commons by one of the youngest and least experienced members, a student at the Inns of Court called Humphrey Davenport. But behind Davenport were concealed some of the acute legal minds which were now to prove the most valuable of all the resources which the puritan movement still possessed, notably those of Robert Beale, clerk of the Council, and James Morice of Colchester, who both sat in this Parliament.

The puritan lawyers must by now have known that there was scant hope of obtaining even a moderate revision of the religious settlement in this or any other Parliament. But they were equally aware that if the existing laws were favourably interpreted and the bishops entangled in the many constitutional difficulties that only waited to be uncovered, the position of the puritan ministers might yet prove to be impregnable. So the nineteen 'motions' on which a conference was proposed were almost entirely defensive and concerned with supposed innovations and breaches of the law by the bishops and their officers: these included the *ex officio* procedure of the church courts which made the prosecutor judge in his own case and the defendant his own accuser; and the silencing, imprisonment and deprivation of ministers for failing to subscribe and for other 'causes not expressly appointed by law'. By now the lawyers were able to parade a useful array of legal quibbles to confuse the processes of ecclesiastical discipline, and to threaten the bishops with the dire and vague threat of a *praemunire*. For example, it was suggested that the Prayer Book which the church courts wielded as a penal instrument had no legal standing, since it contained more than the three alterations stipulated in the Book of 1552 by the Elizabethan Act of Uniformity.

These 'certain motions' are a portent of the future growth of legal and constitutional puritanism, as was a bill deposited with the Speaker towards the end of the session which cited Magna Carta against the arrest and imprisonment of the queen's subjects without due process of common law. But no progress was made in this direction by this Parliament. A privy councillor, Mr Secretary Wolley, intervened to prevent a debate in the Commons, and the 'motions' remained with the Speaker, unread, until the dissolution. An approach was subsequently made directly to the archbishop, but Whitgift covered the margins of the document with characteristically thorough and caustic comments.[36]

Blocked in this direction, the puritans in the Commons launched a bill to abolish, virtually without dispensation, all pluralities and non-residence. Ever since 1529 and long before that, there had been no more popular subject of indignant discussion among the laity than these familiar and odious twins, and the measure had an extraordinarily good run. At the second reading Beale led the attack in a debate which was mostly in favour of the bill. The Committee which sat on it included such notable puritans as Sir Francis Knollys, Francis Hastings, Sir Robert Jermyn, James Morice and Beale himself, and their revised bill was given the easiest possible passage through the House. In the Lords, Burghley could not resist making a speech which was mostly for the bill and thoroughly unflattering to the bishops, some of whom must have been present. With other lay peers he seems to have objected strongly to the officially inspired proposal that the queen should be left to confer privately about the alleged abuses with the lords spiritual. But after a first reading in the Lords the bill was suppressed, no doubt on the queen's instructions. There were almost unanswerable objections to it, granted the depressed economic state of the Church and the inequality of benefices, if learning was to be rewarded and Church and State adequately served. Probably many of those who spoke for the bill were aware of the strength of these arguments and knew that the measure had no chance of becoming law, but were determined to take full advantage of an opportunity to vent their anticlerical feelings. In this way Elizabeth's refusal to allow Parliament to have any say in church reform could be an incitement to irresponsibility. Robert Beale's papers show that once again this campaign was nourished by the circulation among members of 'registered' grievances against the higher clergy. Sir William More of Loseley brought up a petition from the inhabitants of South Farnham (Bishop Cooper's neighbours!) with a long and tendentious account of the failings of the ministry in that part of Surrey. And someone else sent on its travels a document which seemed to prove that the unpopular Bishop Overton of Coventry and Lichfield had paid a lump-sum of a thousand marks to one individual and an annuity of twenty pounds to another for services rendered in helping him to his bishopric.[37]

Sir John Neale believes that before this short and poorly documented Parliament ended, on March 29th, the puritan members made a further attempt to gain 'a Christian and peaceable toleration, not contrary to the law' for the godly ministers. Two petitions survive – one of them in the name of the doughty John Stubbs – which are studied in their moderation and designed to counteract Bancroft's disturbing propaganda. 'We are no schismatics, no libellers, rebellious or disordered persons ... We desire that by a preaching ministry all the people of your kingdom may be taught to obey and serve your Highness.' All to no avail. In Lord Chancellor Hatton's final oration – unfortunately lost – the door was yet again firmly closed. We are told that 'the fanatical humour' of the precisians and puritans was zealously reprehended, and notice given of the queen's 'benign inclination' if not to prosecute yet to suppress them.

Six months later, in early September, puritan delegates from London, the Midlands and East Anglia met in Cambridge for a provincial conference. It was Stourbridge Fair time, by now a regular occasion for a general meeting at the university. Yet it is safe to say that no such meeting took place a year later, in September 1590, or perhaps ever again. This is in fact the last general conference of which we have any knowledge, if we except the emergency meetings held in London a year later at the time of Cartwright's imprisonment. As luck would have it, it is one of the best documented of all Elizabethan presbyterian assemblies, even though we have no *Acta* or other primary records. The conference took place in St John's College, a community still, as ever, deeply divided in religion, and it was perhaps inevitable that rumours of this 'presbytery' should spread beyond Cambridge. In the autumn of 1590 they were investigated by Burghley, as chancellor, and before the whole Privy Council.[38] A year later, some details of the meeting emerged from the Star Chamber proceedings against a representative group of puritan ministers.[39] Others came to light in 1595 when the election of a new master and the jostling of the two factions in the college revived memories of the episode.[40]

The meeting-place was the Master's Lodge, at that time occupied by a senior fellow and the leading puritan at St John's, Henry Alvey. The master, the famous divine William Whitaker who was Laurence Chaderton's brother-in-law, was absent in his native Lancashire, and later claimed ignorance of the whole affair. After his death the rival faction would explain that Whitaker was an ineffective head, over-studious and overindulgent to the precise sort. The list of delegates to the conference consists for the most part of hardened, professional presbyterian leaders: Cartwright himself for Warwick, Snape, Fludd and Stone from Northamptonshire, Gifford for Essex, Walter Allen for Suffolk, Thomas Barber for London and Chaderton of Cambridge. A more surprising name was that of William Perkins of Christ's College, then on the threshold of his great theological reputation, for Perkins, so far as we know, played little other part in the presbyterian movement. The moderator was a local Cambridgeshire minister, John Harrison, vicar of Histon.

Stone, Perkins and Barber all admitted in the Star Chamber that their conference had to do with the Book of Discipline. According to Barber 'they did correct, alter and amend divers imperfections' in the Book (perhaps at the prompting of Perkins, the theological expert) but Stone implies that this was meant to be a final revision, for having 'perfected' it, they 'did then and there ... voluntarily agree amongst themselves that so many as would should subscribe to the said Book of Discipline after that time.' But how much did it now matter whether or not the long process of revision was at last complete? The Discipline had been under consideration for at least four years, and by now these constitutional debates were more than ever detached from reality. Hope of securing its legal establishment there was none; most puritan ministers, even members of conferences, found it an embarrassment; its covert and voluntary practice was full of irregularities and posed with increasing urgency the problem of relations with the Church at large.

Consequently we find the delegates discussing 'in scholastic manner', that is with dialectical formality, whether 'the unpreaching ministers in the Church of England were ministers or not, and whether the sacraments ought to be received at their hands or not.' This was the crucial question which had faced 'precise' protestants ever since 1559. With its 'confusion' and generous hospitality to thousands who were no true gospellers, was the Church of England a true school of Christ, and were the ministers on whom it bestowed its outward calling called by God? At Cambridge 'some were of one opinion [Snape and Fludd?] and some of another [Cartwright, Gifford, Chaderton?]' and it proved impossible to come to any conclusion which could be stated in writing and subscribed. Bancroft would later give it out that at the moment of discovery, the presbyterian leaders were dangerous conspirators who had it in their capacity to seize control of Church and State, whether by propaganda, practice or force. The truth seems to have been that after years of frustration these were disappointed and confused men whose movement could hardly have been held together even if the High Commission and its pursuivants had not chosen this moment to strike.

2 On Trial

'Master Cartwright is in the Fleete for refusall of the oath (as I heare) and Master Knewstubs is sent for, and sundry worthy Ministers are disquieted, who have beene spared long. So that we look for some bickering ere long, and then a battell, which cannot long endure.'

(GILES WIGGINTON 'to Porter at Lancaster', November 6th, 1590; Daungerous positions, p. 143)

IN ONE OF HIS MORE FOOLHARDY JESTS, Martin Marprelate pretends to publish Archbishop Whitgift's instructions to the pursuivants who were sent out to hunt for him, scattering a handful of clues as to where he may be found: 'As for you that go into the country, I would have ye especially go into Northampton and Warwick shires, and command the mayor and constables of Northampton to keep watch and ward for Sharpe and Penry, and if they can take them, let them bring them up ... ' These words were printed in Wolston, six miles from Coventry, in late July 1589, when so far as we know the authorities had no certain knowledge of the whereabouts of the Marprelate press. Perhaps to confuse the scent, Martin urges other pursuivants to 'go into Essex, Suffolk and Norfolk', and here he drops the names of some leading puritan preachers: John More of Norwich, Walter Allen and John Knewstub of Suffolk and Robert Wright of Essex; these 'with many others, all very seditious men'.[1]

Were these districts and these individuals already suspect and already visited by the pursuivants when this challenge was delivered? It would account for an otherwise almost inexplicable lack of caution and fidelity on the part of 'Martin', at this time probably Throckmorton. What is sure is that as soon as it was known – in the autumn of 1589 – that the Marprelate press had been trundled about the Midlands, the attention of the pursuivants was drawn to the home of every notorious puritan preacher in Northamptonshire and Warwickshire. We hear of Edmund Snape of Northampton fearing 'a search to have been intended for books not authorized', and hiding his stocks of *A defence of the ecclesiastical discipline* and other illicit publications in the back-house of a tanner.[2] But he must have been less careful with his personal papers, for the authorities soon had possession of some embarrassing documents, including a declaration that he did not derive his ministry from the mere 'civil ordinance' of a bishop's ordination. The studies of at least five other ministers yielded potentially incriminating papers, which together exposed the whole 'grand design' of the presbyterian movement. They included a copy of the *Acta* of the Warwickshire synod of 1588, with its further evidence of the Cambridge synod of 1587, and the 'Decrees', both in the hand of Daniel Wight of Stretton and from his study; and a copy of the Book of Discipline itself, with the articles of approbation, bearing the names of the Warwickshire subscribers, all in Wight's hand, but 'found in the house of Edmund Littleton'.[3]

And so the quest for Martin Marprelate merged into a hunt for further traces of the clandestine presbyterian movement of which even an absorbed observer like Bancroft had hitherto enjoyed only a blurred impression. That the two investigations were closely connected is suggested in the testimonial which Whitgift composed for Bancroft in 1597 when he was a candidate for the bishopric of London.[4] Bancroft was 'by his diligent search the first detector of Martin Marprelate's press and books, where and by whom they were printed'; he instructed the queen's counsel when Martin's agents were brought into the Star Chamber, and it was on his advice that the anti-Martinist satires were commissioned. It was also 'by his diligence to find out certain letters and writings' that Cartwright and his accomplices, 'their setting up their discipline secretly in most shires of the realm, their *classes*, their decrees, and Book of Discipline were first detected.' And it was Bancroft who gave 'the chief instructions' which guided the framing of the bill and articles against the ministers in the Star Chamber. Professor Owen Chadwick, doubting whether Bancroft played such a prominent judicial role in the hunt for Martin, has suggested that this extraordinary document should be handled with caution.[5] Admittedly the writer had a motive for exaggerating the services of his candidate, and there is good reason to suppose that Bancroft's fellow commissioner, Richard Cosin, who was dead by 1597, was no less active in these investigations. Yet there is independent evidence to link Bancroft with the prosecution of Martin's 'agents',[6] and Chadwick's main argument–an argument from silence – that as late as October 1590 the name of Waldegrave meant nothing to the author of *Daungerous positions* is not convincing.

On the evidence discovered in the Midlands, a case was to be constructed against Cartwright and eight other ministers and pressed home, first before the High Commissioners, and then in the Star Chamber. This was to be an exemplary prosecution in which, in effect, the whole presbyterian movement was placed on trial. But the great case against the nine ministers was only a part of the most intelligent and professional assault yet mounted against puritan dissent. This vigorous repressive operation aroused less public resentment than Whitgift's subscription campaign of 1584, partly because of the altered political circumstances, but also because its target was selected with more discrimination, and conducted almost exclusively by the High Commission, rather than in a variety of ecclesiastical courts.

The days were now past when London was an open city for puritan extremists. *Agents provocateurs* haunted the booksellers' stalls in St Paul's churchyard, engaging the clergy who came to buy books in conversation, and pretending a sympathy for the cause.[7] In March 1589 the High Commissioners directed an injunction to every parish in the diocese of London, forbidding the entertainment of irregular preachers. This was to be read publicly in church and a copy entered in the churchwardens' book of accounts, extending an earlier order which had banned certain preachers by name from all pulpits in the city: among them Thomas Barber, George Gifford and Thomas Carew, and 'especially' the Yorkshire preachers Giles Wigginton and John Wilson and the Scotsman, John Davidson.[8] At Cambridge, the Commissioners ejected two puritans from the university for preaching objectionable sermons, after the two young men, Cuthbert Bainbrigg and Francis Johnson, had offered a notable resistance to the procedure of the court in tendering the oath *ex officio mero*. (Johnson would later succeed Barrow and Greenwood as leader of the separatists and would minister to their congregation in Amsterdam.) The preacher of an offensive sermon at Oxford, William Hubbock, a Magdalen man, was dealt the same penalty, and all three were in prison in the early months of 1590.[9] Many famous preachers, among them George Gifford, Robert Cawdry, Eusebius Paget and Richard Rogers were continually harried throughout 1590 and 1591.[10] William Dyke's disturbing ministry at St Albans was silenced in the autumn of 1589.[11] A chaplain of the earl of Essex was deprived of his living.[12] And in June 1590 the young Arthur Hildersham, a protégé of the earl of Huntingdon at Ashby-de-la-Zouch and a famous name of the future, was obliged to give his bond to the Commissioners not to use his ministry in any place, although this prohibition was later mitigated to allow him to preach north of the Trent.[13]

Puritans had normally been left to their own devices in 'the north parts'. Thanks to the great strength of popish recusancy, especially in much of Lancashire, protestant preachers were at a premium and were almost never required to conform to the standards of 1559.[14] The Lancashire preachers – a compact, well-organized, not to say presbyterian body – were encouraged by the Privy Council to set up a network of exercises throughout the diocese of Chester at a time when the queen's ban lay against the prophesyings in the south. These preachers – heavily concentrated in the relatively protestant, south-east corner of the county – were the government's watch-dogs in a country which was full of disaffection and potential danger. There was no subscription in Lancashire, or anywhere else in the northern province, in 1584. And twenty years later, at the Hampton Court conference, James I listened sympathetically to a special plea from Laurence Chaderton that the ceremonies should not be imposed in 'some parts' of his native country, for fear that many won to the gospel would thereupon backslide 'and revolt unto popery again.'[15] So it is some indication of the strength of the anti-puritan reaction at this time that Whitgift and his allies were prepared to sweep all such considerations aside. The new broom was Archbishop John Piers, translated from Salisbury to York in 1589. In his metropolitan visitation of the collegiate church of Manchester and of the Lancashire deaneries in the summer of 1590, at least fifteen clergy from Manchester deanery and several from elsewhere were presented for failing to wear the surplice and for some other nonconformist practices; while it was discovered that none of the fellows, ministers or choristers of Manchester College ever conformed in this respect. Piers issued an ultimatum that the offenders must minister in surplices, and on this he took his stand, although he was warned by the leading protestant gentleman of the district, Edmund Hopwood, and even by Bishop William Chaderton of Chester, that in a county deeply divided between 'obstinate papists' and 'zealous professors of religion' the effect of his order would be to confirm the one in their recusancy and drive the other into schism. In any case the decision does not seem to have been in Piers's hands, and the whole episode should probably be understood as an effort by Whitgift to bring the administration of the northern province into line with his own.[16]

The preachers on their side were equally inflexible, no doubt relying on the government in the south to come to the rescue. Their spokesman, Edward Fleetwood, rector of Wigan, warned Burghley of the political consequences of these policies. The judge riding the assize circuit, Thomas Walmesley, was a Lancashire man, a suspected papist with a known recusant for a wife, who dealt gently with the disaffected but punished even trivial acts of nonconformity as 'high points of Martinism'. The churches were emptying of people and the enemy was greatly encouraged. The sequel seems to demand some such intervention at the highest level as Fleetwood evidently expected, probably by Burghley himself. A year after the original ultimatum, the ministers showed no sign of conformity, and a year later still the surplice was not worn in Bolton. Yet no one was suspended, let alone deprived, and ten years later the preachers were able to refer to letters from Walsingham, Heneage and Burghley which had hitherto preserved their freedom to 'live according to their preaching', 'being in a place so full of papists.' But this was Lancashire, and the remarkable aspect of this case is that the preachers were even required to conform. In the south, as a letter-writer noted in 1590, 'these sharp proceedings make that sect greatly diminish.'[17]

Some of the sharpest proceedings were to be witnessed in the prosecution of John Udall and this, like the trial of the nine ministers, had a partly exemplary function. Thanks to the earl of Huntingdon's helpful intervention, Udall had enjoyed a year as preacher of Newcastle-on-Tyne, far away from his earlier activities at Kingston. But not even the friendship of the lord president of the Council in the North could protect the author of the *Demonstration of discipline*, the writing of which the judges had already deemed a felony. Arrested at Newcastle in mid-winter and brought south in bitter weather, Udall was examined by the High Commissioners on January 31st, 1590, imprisoned and brought to trial for his life at Surrey Assizes in July.[18] That the assize was held at the archbishop's manor of Croydon may be some indication of the forces which were at work. On both days of the trial, prepared speeches were delivered, directed not so much against Udall as in public censure of the movement which he represented. The second of these, from one of the judges, Serjeant John Puckering, professed to be no more than an interjection prompted by Udall's assertion that his cause was 'the undoubted truth of God', so that he should not be allowed to 'go away with that speech unanswered to buzz into the people's ears such a conceit.' But what followed was a 'large set speech', substantially to the same effect as Hatton's parliamentary attack on Cope's bill and book of 1587 and, it appears, equally indebted to Bancroft.[19] At a further trial in Southwark in February 1591, Udall was sentenced to death. There followed a year of submissions and appeals, including a personal intervention by James VI of Scotland. He was finally pardoned on the condition that he would leave the country to preach to the Turkey Merchants in 'Guinea', but his death either frustrated or immediately followed his release.[20]

The Lambeth circle would have liked to deal as roundly with those whom Bancroft at Paul's Cross had called the factious laity. According to Robert Beale, Hatton and others 'earnestly went about' to enforce subscription to certain articles 'throughout the whole realm'. The articles in question were designed as a kind of appendix to the Articles of Religion. They affirmed that all ecclesiastical authority and jurisdiction were indissolubly linked to the Crown; that there ought not to be any synods, conventicles or assemblies with power to make ecclesiastical laws without the queen's assent and by her authority; that episcopal government was lawful by the word of God and presbyterian government both unlawful and dangerous; that it was both seditious and ungodly to teach or maintain that there ought to be a presbytery or consistory with power to excommunicate or depose the queen for any cause; and that the Church of England was a true member of the Church of Christ, its sacraments and order of public prayer such that no one should make a schism, division or contention in the Church or withdraw himself from it. Although this new standard of conformity and obedience may have been primarily intended as a clerical test, Beale reports that Whitgift meant to make all lawyers and justices of the peace subscribe to it, a procedure which Bancroft had hinted at in his sermon. For what his testimony may be worth, Beale claims that it was his own prompt action in pointing out that the third article appeared to advance a *jus divinum* claim for the authority of bishops which moved the queen 'to stay that perilous device.'[21]

In the course of the winter of 1589–90, the High Commissioners probably interrogated scores of preachers in an attempt to build up a fuller picture of the clandestine presbyterian organization of which they now had some knowledge. Most of the ministers seem to have been hostile witnesses, but there were two exceptions. Richard Parker, the young vicar of Dedham, betrayed the names of several of his own associates, including Chapman, Crick, Dow and Tay, and he revealed the existence of the Braintree conference, naming Culverwell, Rogers and Gifford. But Parker had intimate personal reasons for instability at this time which we shall have to take account of later, and none of those he named seems to have divulged any further information. Bancroft must have concealed a large number of unrewarding examinations under the phrase 'and so likewise the depositions of others', which are ostensibly omitted from the account in *Daungerous positions* for fear of being 'too tedious'. But the Commissioners discovered one prize witness in John Johnson, vicar of All Saints, Northampton, on whose testimony we have depended as heavily as ever Bancroft did. Johnson seems to have presented himself as an informer, in resentment at his censure by the Northampton *classis*. By April 11th, 1590, part at least of his evidence had been given, for on that day Edmund Snape wrote to his friends in Northamptonshire: 'I would judge John Johnson to have been the man, because (to my remembrance) persons and things of his time being mentioned, he only is not named.'[22]

It was presumably by means of these examinations and on the basis of the documentary evidence already accumulated that the choice was made of the ministers who were later to appear together in the Star Chamber. They were Edmund Snape, Andrew King and William Prowdlove of Northamptonshire; Thomas Cartwright, Humfrey Fen, Daniel Wight and Edward Lord of Warwickshire; John Payne of Hanbury in Staffordshire and late of the same county, an obscure lapsed Brownist who seems to have been included solely because of the usefulness to the prosecution of his inflammatory correspondence; and with them a roving preacher from Devonshire, Melanchthon Jewel. The inclusion of Jewel is hard to explain except by reference to the close association between this prosecution and the Marprelate affair, for it would be alleged in the Star Chamber that Jewel had 'penned, received or delivered forth' illicit books and pamphlets and had publicly commended them. Snape had been examined on two occasions before April 11th and, with the exception of Cartwright, the other defendants had probably made their appearance before that date. On each occasion the judge tendered a general oath, *ex officio mero*, after which he would have assumed the role of prosecutor, presenting the examinee with a schedule of articles which assumed his guilt and which his oath would require him to answer. But all the ministers refused to take the oath, so automatically blocking any further proceedings, although the High Commission could punish the contempt with imprisonment. On the first occasion 'the issue was prison, the second close prison', or so for Snape.[23]

The ministers were prepared to take this stand both by earlier precedents, such as the Bainbrigg and Johnson case, and by the advice of the puritan lawyers who hovered behind them throughout the judicial ordeal which lay ahead. The campaign of the common lawyers against the oath – in which they had a certain professional interest – was reaching its climax at about this time. In East Anglia the justices, and even the assize judges, publicly criticized the procedure, and in December 1590 Hatton had to deliver a prohibition from the queen to the outgoing judges, forbidding any further reference in their charges to oaths in ecclesiastical courts.[24]

In a common statement of their objections, the ministers repeated the opinion of their 'learned counsel in law' that the procedure was against both the common and the ecclesiastical laws of England. There were many proofs of its irregularity in common law, and all canons and ecclesiastical constitutions which were contrary to that law had been abrogated by the Henrician legislation. In stating his personal reasons for refusing the oath, Humfrey Fen appealed beyond these authorities to 'the law of love and fellowship' which would not allow him to betray the names and secrets of others. Moreover, he added realistically, 'the most of us being already known unto you', the only effect of betraying names would be to destroy the trust of brethren.[25] The High Commission recognized an organized resistance, betraying 'some confederacy together', rather than a display of individual conscience. The prisoners were later asked in the Star Chamber to acknowledge not only that they had refused the oath but that they and others of their acquaintance had persuaded their friends to refuse it. It then emerged that Snape had formally referred the question to the Northamptonshire *classes* at the request of his fellow-ministers still in the country.[26]

According to Bancroft, the most substantial of the reasons advanced by the ministers for refusing the oath was that they would not swear to answer articles which they had not yet seen. Accordingly they were shown 'the general sum of them' and, when this failed to suffice, the interrogatories themselves. Snape still refused the oath, but at once wrote to the Northampton and Kettering *classes* and, it seems, to other ministers elsewhere, with news of what the articles contained, 'that in both places you might be forewarned and forearmed.' Particular places, occasions and persons were named, and Snape's Northampton friends were 'yet more particularly discovered.' The conclusion was that their meetings 'will not, they cannot be any longer concealed.' The shock was so great that Snape was at first disposed to make a clean breast of the whole business. 'It must come to trial. In the cause of murder etc. it is wont to be inquired whether the party fled upon it. Consider and apply this matter, and the Lord give us wisdom in all things.' His letters were written in Bancroft's view, 'not without the great providence of God', for they were promptly intercepted and served to confirm the value of the evidence already collected. 'For thereby their whole plot, and all in effect that was laid to their charges was discovered.' Those named by Snape were now examined, including Henry Sharpe, Sir Richard Knightley's vicar at Fawsley, some of his own parishioners, and Johnson, for the second time, on May 16th. And another minister with a grudge against his brethren now appeared: Thomas

Edmunds, who was to talk freely in the Star Chamber about John Field and the London *classis*.[27]

Finally, Cartwright himself was selected for interrogation and added to the number of those imprisoned for their refusal to take the oath. As early as May 20th the head of the party had been sent for by a pursuivant and had already determined to refuse the oath. Still in Warwick at the end of August, he could write of 'the day of my trouble approaching'. But although his hearing was originally arranged for September 1st it was not until October that he was brought to London and examined in the consistory at St Paul's. The articles against him – thirty-one in number – have survived. They relate partly to his activities in the Netherlands, including his supposed presbyterian ordination, his ministry in Warwick, and his alleged connection with the Marprelate Tracts and Udall's writings. Only the last seven concern his part in the Book of Discipline and the conference movement.[28]

That Cartwright had remained immune for so long can only be explained by the influence of powerful friends. These included Serjeant Puckering, who in his public capacity would prepare the Star Chamber case against the ministers, Burghley's secretaries, and the lord treasurer himself, who were all among his correspondents at this time. Burghley was now, as always, a reluctant spectator of the proceedings against the puritans. In mid-July Whitgift sent him a copy of the articles against the ministers with the comment (in which a note of special pleading can be heard) that 'it be manifest by certain letters and other writings which were found in their houses that they are culpable in the most of them.' In October Burghley advised the archbishop not to incur the suspicion of personal rancour by taking his place among the other commissioners who were to examine Cartwright. He defended the puritan leader's recent career and reputation much as they were represented to him in Cartwright's frequent letters, and complained: 'I see not that diligence or care taken to win these kind of men that are precise, either by learning or courtesy, as I imagine might reclaim them.' So isolated was the lord treasurer from those now effectively in power in the Church that it was on Cartwright that he relied for an account of how the Commissioners had dealt with him. Cartwright's imprisonment in the Fleet in late October was a staggering blow for the puritan cause and, coupled with the queen's 'heavy displeasure' against him, it indicates an intensification of the reaction which Burghley, for one, was powerless to prevent.[29]

About a week or a fortnight before Cartwright's committal the last general conference of which we have any knowledge met at Richard

Gardiner's rectory in Whitechapel. It was an extraordinary meeting, called to decide whether or not it was 'fit or convenient' that Cartwright, as the acknowledged doyen of the movement, should make a full or partial confession of what the ministers had done in their assemblies. The deposition later made in the Star Chamber by the Northamptonshire minister, Thomas Stone, which is our only source for this episode, shows that he, for one, was in favour of a frank confession. But as Bancroft points out, Cartwright's own bearing in the Star Chamber is sufficient indication of the majority opinion that he should resist interrogation. The conference also debated whether to present a petition to the queen on behalf of those already in prison or about to go there, 'for or concerning the said cause of discipline'. The delegates, besides Stone, included Cartwright himself, Chark, Travers, Egerton, Barber and Gardiner of London, Barbon and Fludd from Northamptonshire, Oxenbridge from Warwickshire, Gellibrand from Oxford, Culverwell for Essex, and others whose names Stone had forgotten. He implies that this was one of a series of such meetings held in London at the houses of Barber, Gardiner, Travers and Egerton throughout the emergency which had prevailed since the parliament of 1589, and attended from time to time by Chaderton of Cambridge, Brown of Oxford, Gifford of Essex, Allen of Suffolk and Sommerscales of Lincolnshire, as well as by those who were present in October 1590.[30]

The imprisoned ministers were by no means excluded from the urgent conference and correspondence with which the puritans were responding to the crisis, and Snape's claim that he had been placed in 'close prison' should not be understood too literally. Cartwright was in the Fleet, King, Wight, Fen and Payne in the Clink, Snape, Jewel and Prowdlove in the Bailiff's house of St Catherine's, and Lord over the river in the White Lion in Southwark. Yet the united front which all nine ministers maintained in the face of interrogation both before the High Commissioners and in the Star Chamber does not suggest isolation. The ingenuity of Barrow and Greenwood turned the Fleet into a clandestine publishing-house at this very time, and the puritan ministers enjoyed the same latitude, which was no more than characteristic of Elizabethan prison life. Fen had 'the liberty of the house and garden and access of friends', and he was allowed to go with his keeper to hear Lancelot Andrewes's sermons in St Paul's. Closer confinement followed his last appearance before the Commissioners in December. Yet as late as August 1591 all the prisoners, Cartwright excepted, had 'access unto them from all their friends', and even Cartwright, who could not be safely allowed this privilege, was permitted visits from his wife and those who had 'necessary business' with him. Letters and forms of petition inevitably passed to and fro with the visitors.[31]

The chance survival of one such letter, from Fen to Edward Fleetwood, rector of Wigan and leader of the Lancashire preachers, preserves almost the only evidence we possess from the Elizabethan period of consultation between the puritan ministers north and south of the Trent. The crisis which confronted the Lancashire ministers in the later months of 1590 has been described earlier in this chapter. To wear or not to wear the surplice was a question never before faced in Lancashire but familiar enough in the south, and Fleetwood had written for advice to two of his old Oxford friends, the famous divine Dr John Reynolds and Humfrey Fen. Their replies illustrate that fundamental divergence between moderate and intransigent puritanism which runs through the whole history of the movement. Reynolds, while deploring the troubles which had descended upon the Lancashire ministers, advised conformity, and quoted in his support that passage in Cartwright's *Rest of the second replie* which had caused so much heart-searching in extreme puritan circles almost fourteen years before. He added this shrewd and revealing comment: 'The godly would mislike thereof and would depart (divers of them) from their public ministration. But they should do amiss then.' For the ministers to abandon their ministry for a thing merely indifferent would be a much greater evil and a triumph for the papists.

Fen saluted his 'reverend brethren and the rest, much beloved in the Lord' and sent 'the judgments of those whom you reverence in the Lord', which, in spite of his confinement, he had 'laboured to understand.' All were agreed that 'teaching ceremonies' such as the sign of the cross in baptism were to be refused at all costs. There were those who excluded the surplice from this category and offered the same advice as Reynolds, but some of this group referred all decision to the Lancashire ministers 'which know the country better', and thought that the surplice should not be worn if this would lead to the intrusion of other, more objectionable ceremonies. 'The greater part', however, held the surplice to be a teaching ceremony and therefore to be rejected. But it was everyone's conviction that the ministry of those who yielded to the surplice was not to be refused. For practical advice, Fen recommended the standard puritan tactic. The ministers were to seek postponement of the evil day and use the time gained to make representations to the Privy Council, 'declaring the extremity of the Church by so untimely an urging of these ceremonies.' Of southern news, Fen had nothing to write except 'that we remain as uncertain from men of our issue as before, though we doubt not but our God, always like himself, hath an issue full of refreshing and comfort for us after the days of our trouble.' He asked 'our beloved in the Lord' to continue their prayers.[32]

It was evidently in December or January 1590–91 that the prisoners began to ask their godly friends for more than prayers. The five ministers with parochial charges – Snape, Lord, Fen, Wight and Prowdlove – wrote to their congregations suggesting that they should petition the queen for their deliverance; while Snape wrote other letters to the mayor of Northampton, in the hope of procuring a concerted petition from several towns, and to the godly of Northampton in general, persuading them to meet together with Weedon and Wolston', that 'some pity may be had of us and our people.' This was done only after the ministers themselves had sent two unsuccessful petitions of their own to the High Commissioners. But the action which followed was regarded by the authorities as a 'tumultuous course', constituting in itself a seditious conspiracy, and it would later form the basis for one of the major groups of charges in the bill exhibited against the ministers in the Star Chamber. The petitions were yet another disturbing revelation of the capacity of the puritans to work through a whole network of secret conventicles within the national Church itself. The leading petitioners – prominent townsmen of Coventry, Stretton, Wolston and Northampton – were sent for by the Privy Council and made to sign a form of submission. In April a Mr Clarke of Warwick was warning John Rogerson, a future mayor of Coventry, that if anyone should ask him what news he had of 'Mr Brynkell and his neighbours' (Robert Bricknell had signed the Stretton petition), 'say no more to them but this, it is best for them to keep themselves out of the way in some unknown place till I send them word. I will send word to you when you may go abroad in safety.' Like the lollards before them, these lay puritans were 'known men', and it alarmed the government to find evidence of their secret confederacy.[33]

A further indication of the lack of spontaneity of the petitions was that they were redrafted in London before being presented. Fen described a conversation with those who brought the petition from Coventry in which it was agreed that this should be done. The probability is strong that the puritan lawyers were responsible for these alterations, as they may have been for the whole plan of concerted action. Robert Beale wrote to Whitgift on Fen's behalf, capitalizing his own connections with Coventry and referring to the appeals of his 'kinsfolk, allies and friends in those parts' and requesting Fen's release on bail until the following term.

Moreover, Beale's papers contain the drafts of two broadsheet petitions to the queen, both amended in his own hand. One which purports to come from the ministers' congregations refers to efforts made by 'our magistrates and justices in the country', which had done the ministers 'little good'. The other petition is supposed to be from the prisoners themselves, although even the style by which they sign themselves is scrawled in on this copy by Beale. Another, more elaborate petition to the queen survives in which the ministers embark on a lengthy self-exculpation. An accompanying appeal to Burghley explains that they have 'at last advised to present our lamentable distress unto the gracious consideration of our dread sovereign.'[34]

By this time the High Commission had dealt with the nine ministers to the limit of its powers. Snape's sentence survives, dated July 11th, 1590, and signed by an exceptionally large body of commissioners, including the archbishop, the lord chief justices, the principal legal officers of the Crown, Mr Recorder Fleetwood, and Drs Cosin, Stanhope and Bancroft. Snape was convicted of offences against the Act of Uniformity and of contemptuously refusing the oath. He was removed from his ecclesiastical offices, degraded from the clerical order, and declared incapable of holding any future title, order or dignity in the Church, although this was later mitigated to a suspension of ten years.[35] No doubt the other defendants were similarly dealt with on the same occasion. Whitgift was later to remind the queen that 'Cartwright and his followers' had all been censured by himself and other ecclesiastical commissioners in the presence of some of the judges and legal counsellors.[36] By the spring of 1591 the ministers could say that with one exception – Cartwright, who retained his hospital at Warwick – they had all been deprived of their livings, degraded from the ministry 'and yet are restrained of our liberty, without any limitation.' These sentences were no doubt heavy, even extreme, but they contributed nothing to the proof of the seditious conspiracies which preoccupied Bancroft and his colleagues. 'The thing they aim at is a conventicle,' Snape had written a year before. So it was, but they were no nearer to it. Because the ministers had, so to say, pleaded the fifth amendment, nothing had been judicially established, and in Snape's sentence there was no mention of *classes*, synods or Book of Discipline.[37]

In the winter and spring of 1590–91, the High Commissioners worked industriously to obtain some kind of confession of these matters. Fen made a further appearance before Christmas, which was again characterized by 'obstinate contempt'. Some weeks later Stanhope and Bancroft came to the Fleet to confer with Cartwright, and in March Whitgift invited him to answer in writing, but informally, a new set of twelve articles relating exclusively to the Book of Discipline and the classical meetings. Was Cartwright the author of the Book, or if not who was, 'as it is commonly reported, received or believed amongst you [sic] brethren?' Where and when had the Book first been offered for consideration and approval and by whom, and by what assembly allowed and approved? And so on. But Cartwright was not to be so easily drawn. He returned an evasive reply, no doubt based on legal advice. The general fact of the meetings was acknowledged, but only in the course of an intricate defence which represented them as harmless professional associations of clergymen. The central charge, that of a seditious intention to practise the discipline without due authorization, was emphatically denied.[38]

On a Saturday afternoon in May, Cartwright was yet again before the Commissioners: among them Aylmer, Popham, Lewyn, Bancroft and Stanhope. The hearing was arranged without warning and with some secrecy, in Aylmer's house by St Paul's. Obviously the Commissioners still hoped that the older, more responsible Cartwright might be detached from the other prisoners and persuaded to make a frank confession. But all that emerged from a hard afternoon's wrangling was an act recording yet another refusal of the *ex officio* oath.[39] This was the last intervention by the High Commissioners in the matter, for in the same month the attorney general exhibited a Bill against the ministers in the Star Chamber, and on May 13th they made their first appearance before that court.

3 The Star Chamber

WHEN CARTWRIGHT APPEARED before the High Commissioners for the last time, in May 1591, it had already been decided to transfer the trial of the nine ministers to the Star Chamber. According to one account, the decision was made by Whitgift and Hatton.[1] If so, it was also the recommendation of the leading lawyers of the day.

A brief of the case had been prepared – one suspects by Cosin and Bancroft – and headed: 'The proceedings of certain undutiful ministers tending to innovation, so far as is hitherto disclosed by certain papers and letters found amongst them.' Burghley's copy is dated February 3rd. This sets out to establish a clear intention on the ministers' part to put their Book of Discipline into practice, and the case is argued mainly from the documents discovered in the Midlands, the 1588 *Acta*, the 'Decrees', the evidence of the election of elders at Kilsby, besides the Book itself, with the articles of approbation and the names of the subscribers. Extensive quotation of the ministers' correspondence is used to demonstrate their involvement in the spirit, if not the fact, of the Martinist libels.[2] A further paper relies mainly on the evidence of printed pamphlets, including the tracts themselves, to suggest that the whole tendency of the puritan movement was towards forceful and even violent revolution. These documents were shown to the judges and principal law officers of the Crown and, it seems, to Whitgift's own legal adviser, Sir John Boys, and with them these questions: was it not expedient that these dealings should be 'more particularly yet discovered' and, if it could be, suppressed? And, faced with the stubborn refusal of the ministers to make a confession, what course was best to be taken 'for the terror of others'? Had the prisoners already incurred that vague and terrible thing, a *praemunire*? Or should 'some exemplary corporal punishment' be meted out in the Star Chamber?[3]

'After long consultation and deliberation', the lord chief justices, the chief baron of the Exchequer, the attorney general and solicitor general and Serjeant John Puckering gave their opinion. This was that the High Commissioners had dealt with the ministers to the full extent of their powers; but that 'these enormities', aggravated by 'so intolerable disobedience' in rejecting the oath, constituted a matter 'of as great and dangerous consequence to the Commonwealth as any that of long time hath happened'; so that the best remedy was a speedy, public hearing in the Star Chamber and 'an exemplary punishment to the terror of others'. This should be as severe as any sentence which that court could inflict. 'The most fit punishment', in their lordships' opinion, would be perpetual banishment to some remote place from where there would be no danger of return or of causing any further disturbances. On a scrap of paper, Serjeant Puckering, queen's counsel in the action now to be mounted, noted some useful precedents: eleven cases in which the offence had been the slander or disturbance of magistrates. In ten of them the penalty had been banishment; in the eleventh the pillory.[4] Only a year before, Puckering had prepared the brief for the Star Chamber case against the gentlemen and ladies who had sheltered the Marprelate press, and in spite of their good social standing and, in most cases, fairly remote connection with Martin, he had secured crushing fines and sentences of imprisonment at her Majesty's pleasure.[5] As for Mrs Crane, *alias* Carleton, hostess to the press at East Molesey, her case was even more to the point. For her contempt in refusing the *ex officio* oath before the High Commissioners she had been fined a thousand marks, and to this was added a further fine of five hundred pounds and imprisonment in the Fleet in respect of the original offence.[6] So the outlook for Cartwright and his friends was not bright. Yet, as we shall see, the hearing in the Star Chamber was to be anything but speedy, and in this case there would be no sharp, exemplary punishment.

We are fortunate in possessing an account of the first appearance of the nine ministers in the Star Chamber on May 13th, even if our source is the biassed pen of Sir Francis Knollys.[7] As a privy councillor, Knollys formed part of the honourable presence in a court which was nothing but the Council sitting in a judicial capacity, assisted by the judges. But on this occasion he was an isolated figure who was not invited to preliminary consultations held in the dining-chamber to decide the course of action. This caucus consisted of Whitgift, Hatton, Buckhurst, the chancellor of the Exchequer, Sir John Fortescue, the two lord chief justices and Sir John Popham. Popham, as attorney general, was technically the plaintiff, on the queen's behalf, and if, as Harington remembered him, he habitually referred to puritans as 'seditious sectaries',[8] he cannot have found his position uncongenial. One notes that Burghley was an absentee; indeed, Knollys's account was written for his benefit. The ministers appeared, accompanied by their counsel, Nicholas Fuller. He was a counsellor at law much employed by the Privy Council, and one of the most diligent of puritan lawyers. Fuller had already made an irregular intervention at Udall's trial, after Udall had been denied counsel. And in the next reign he would end his days in prison for his intrepid advocacy of the cause.[9] Popham now opened proceedings with a vehement attack on the ministers for refusing the oath. Fuller began to reply, only to be interrupted by Hatton with a direction that the archbishop should appoint a doctor of divinity and a doctor of civil law to assist the attorney general.[10] According to a later representation of the proceedings, this barely concealed the fact that Popham, for all that he had 'informed very straightly against the ministers', had failed to have his witnesses ready and briefed to prove the matter.[11] Knollys says that Hatton asked him then and there what he thought of the procedure, to which the veteran courtier had somewhat stiffly replied that he was 'not made privy to the true causes' alleged against the prisoners. There can be little doubt that the two doctors appointed to assist Popham were Bancroft and Cosin. Cosin was to act as examiner of the ministers when the case reached the stage of interrogatory and deposition, and the handwriting of both men is liberally distributed throughout the papers collected by the queen's counsel, Puckering, in his conduct of the case.

The bill and answer are not extant, but several abstracts of their contents survive, such as that later sent by Cartwright to Burghley, with a reference to 'the long books of both sides'.[12] The whole effect of the answer, in the eyes of counsel, was that the ministers had 'confessed their denial to take the oath before the commissioners, and for the rest of the most material matters have made an uncertain and insufficient answer.' The judges thereupon made a direction, indicating where the answer was insufficient and should be amplified. The prisoners accordingly made a second appearance on May 17th, the last day of the Easter Term. The fanatic Edmund Copinger, who will come into our story presently, reported the news to his protégé Hacket and declared his intention to be present: 'And I fear if sentence with severity shall be given, I shall be forced in the name of the great and fearful God of heaven and earth to protest against it.' But in so saying, Copinger betrayed a woeful ignorance of the rules of combat in the Star Chamber. There was as yet no question of a sentence, and the defendants, ably advised by Fuller, exhibited a second answer, 'in many points as imperfect as before'.[13]

Star Chamber procedure now followed its inevitable course, and interrogatories were drawn from the bill on which the defendants were examined. The record of this interrogation and that of the witnesses for either side survives in the Public Record Office and represents the most valuable of all sources for the history of the Elizabethan puritan movement.[14] The initial examination of the defendants was conducted by Cosin and lasted for more than a week, beginning four days after the commencement of Trinity Term. The work was complete by June 16th. The result was again unsatisfactory, the ministers in the opinion of counsel answering 'not at all the most part and the principallest interrogatories'. The judges were again consulted and gave direction as to which interrogatories were to be 'better answered'.[15] But the re-examination which took place on June 19th was just as unproductive, the defendants persisting in their reluctance to answer those questions on which, in effect, the case hung. According to Bancroft, it had been 'commonly expected' that the case would have been wound up before the end of Trinity Term. On June 14th Copinger, now a little madder still, wrote to a friend that if the preachers were to appear the next day, and if 'our great men' were to deal with them as it was thought they would, 'if God do not throw some fearful judgment amongst them, so as some of the chief of them go not alive out of the place, then never give credit to me in anything whilst you live.' But the lawyers prevented any such bloody apotheosis, and when term ended on June 23rd the prisoners had still not made their appearance.[16]

The reason for this unexpected delay in bringing things to a conclusion was the lack of sufficient evidence to convict of the most serious charges, given the highly professional resistance of the puritan lawyers. What those charges were and how the puritans answered them will be apparent from much of what has gone before, but it will be as well at this point to pause and consider the central *gravamen* of the case against the ministers. The contention of the bill and the suggestion of the interrogatories was that the Book of Discipline and the *classes*, synods and assemblies in which it had been discussed and allegedly practised represented a seditious attempt to supersede the queen's supreme authority in ecclesiastical matters. Those who were parties to this conspiracy had believed and taught that the queen had no lawful ecclesiastical authority, and that even in civil matters she was subject to correction and control. And they had looked upon their own brotherhood as the Church in a sense which excluded those members of the national Church who had not subjected themselves to their Discipline. This is the trend of a score of papers bearing the rapid and barely legible notes of Serjeant Puckering, many of them passed to him by Cosin or Bancroft, or by others in the Lambeth circle.[17]

Against this charge it was the unvarying plea of the prisoners, reiterated often word for word in their answers and in successive petitions and other representations, that they had entertained no intention of separating from the established Church; that their meetings, which they acknowledged, had been innocent of any such motive; and that both their associations and the Book of Discipline represented nothing more sinister than a means of submitting to authority a system on which they had themselves agreed and which they hoped to see legally established. Their subscriptions to the Book implied, not a resolve to put it into immediate execution, but a desire 'to show their consent in that desired reformation wherein they are charged to disagree', and this they did because the state of the ecclesiastical discipline was defective, by almost universal admission: witness 'sundry statutes', the Book of Common Prayer itself, and that abortive programme of canon law revision, the *Reformatio Legum Ecclesiasticarum*.[18]

This defence, no doubt, was the work of the lawyers, and perhaps owed much to Nicholas Fuller. Therefore especial interest attaches to Robert Beale's analysis of how the case lay, sent in a characteristic manifesto to Whitgift. Beale argued 'by the laws of the realm' that since Henry VIII (in the Act for the Submission of the Clergy) had abrogated all ecclesiastical law which conflicted with the common laws of England, and since the work of the commission for canon law revision had never come to fruition in statute, 'there is as yet no certain ecclesiastical law for the government of the Church of this realm.' Whatever the ministers had done they had done in a legal and constitutional vacuum which placed a certain responsibility on all members of the Commonwealth. It was therefore proper for them to 'meet to think upon some plot of reformation, to be afterwards propounded and established by authority. I do not think that can be matter offensive to law, as it is taken.' But if the ministers had given orders, assembled *classes*, colloquies and synods for erecting presbyteries or elderships, or prescribing canons and rules to be followed by themselves or others in their charges, and if they had used any censures: 'this is offensive to law and, being proved, will touch them indeed.' The fact of 'execution' of such 'private draughts and conceits' might constitute high treason, and at the very least came within the compass of a *praemunire*, with fine and imprisonment at pleasure, 'if the penalty be not more.' But there had been no such 'execution'. The action of the ministers was only to 'think themselves of such a plot of reformation as they desire to be further established by her Majesty and Parliament.' That they had kept their affairs secret was no more offensive than if a man should secretly pen a statute, not intending to put it in use of his own private authority but to offer it to Parliament. If the preparation of the Book of Discipline was deemed offensive and heinous, then so must have been the writing and printing of the *Reformatio Legum*.[19]

The same tale was told by some of the *classis* members still at liberty, who offered 'in all singleness and sincerity' to explain the reasons which had moved them and the ministers in prison to subscribe to the Book. Contemplating the diversity of dangerous sects which opposed the established religion, they had thought it desirable to distinguish themselves by a written statement of 'that which we desired to have reformed in the Church of England.' The contents of the Discipline were drawn partly from the *Reformatio Legum*, partly from other books of learned men, partly from the example of the churches of Zürich, Geneva and other places overseas. Their subscription was voluntary. They had hoped 'when time and opportunity should serve' to offer the Book to the queen, Council and Parliament. 'For we were not ignorant into what offence and penalty of law we should have incurred if we had done otherwise.' They had made no ministers, used no censures, and had not abrogated or in any way meddled with the exercise of the bishops' jurisdiction. Their meetings had been opened with prayer for those in authority and were devoted to matters of practical urgency encountered in their daily ministries. They had followed the practice of the prophesyings, 'for a good time tolerated', and of the meetings restricted to clergy which had succeeded them, and which the queen in her letters to the bishops had implicitly allowed.[20]

There are some obvious flaws in this argument. The *Reformatio Legum* had been drafted by a royal commission, appointed by statute and warrant. The analogy with the drafting of a private parliamentary bill was equally false, for the matter in question was public, touching the queen's prerogative, in which private subjects were forbidden to meddle. Beale was claiming for an entirely unprivileged group of private individuals powers which Elizabeth would not even concede to her own Parliament.

Moreover, like Bancroft, we will be moved by many 'vehement conjectures', if not by plain evidence, to believe that the presbyterian movement was much less innocent and law-abiding than these plausible explanations would pretend. Yet this defence, if not unassailable, was to prove adequate. In the last resort the structure of evidence which Bancroft and Cosin had so laboriously erected was to prove incapable of sustaining the serious charges they based upon it.

In their interrogation, the ministers were frequently confronted with a volume of at least one hundred and thirty folios or pages which contained, amongst many other documents now unknown, the prize exhibits for the prosecution: the Book of Discipline itself and the documents uncovered in the Midlands.[21] The reader of this study might suppose that the Crown had no need of further witnesses, but this would be to assume knowledge of papers which were not at this time in its possession. There is no evidence that John Field's personal correspondence had yet come to light, although when Bancroft came to write his *Daungerous positions* and *Survay of the pretended holy discipline* two years later, he was able to refer to some fifty letters from various correspondents to Field, besides some of Field's own writing and the 'order of Wandsworth' of 1572. If these papers had been seen in 1591, Walter Travers would have been known as the author, or at least the reviser, of the Book of Discipline, and he too would surely have been found in the Star Chamber.[22]

As for Field's great 'register' of documents, which existed, somewhere, at this time, in bundles of loose papers, these were never discovered.[23] Bancroft would later see what the puritans chose to publish in *A parte of a register*, but never the much larger body of evidence to which we have easy access through Peel's calendar, *The Seconde Parte of a Register*. And Richard Parker, in spite of his indiscretions before the High Commissioners, had not divulged the Dedham conference papers which he was much later to set in order in the seclusion of a Norfolk vicarage. In Beale's far from impartial opinion, the evidence actually in the hands of the prosecution was unimpressive, so that 'when they had incensed her Majesty with many great and intolerable things (if they had been true) *ita ut montes viderentur parturire*, a silly and ridiculous mouse would come forth; that is, there would be no lawful and sufficient proof found of such unlawful and heinous matters as were pretended.' Bancroft and Cosin were aware of subjecting the evidence to a certain amount of strain. Reference was made again and again to a letter from the insignificant John Payne to William Fludd, where almost alone in all the confiscated documentation it was stated unequivocally that if the magistrate could not be induced to establish the Discipline, 'then they ought to erect it themselves, because it is better to obey God than man.' Since Payne was a former Brownist, all too obviously of the lunatic fringe, Bancroft and Cosin were reduced to the lame argument that 'because that Payne's writing will be excepted against' it was to be observed that none of the others would condemn his opinion; they would only blame his lack of discretion.[24]

Everything now depended upon the testimony of the witnesses who were to appear on the attorney general's behalf. The examinations were conducted against a background of events more discouraging for the defendants than ever. On July 16th, two confused puritan gentlemen, Edmund Copinger and Henry Arthington, mounted an empty cart by the cross in Cheapside and proceeded to proclaim to the astonished bystanders 'news from Heaven': an illiterate but 'gifted' simpleton called William Hacket was the new Messiah and king of Europe. The queen had forfeited her crown. They themselves were prophets of mercy and judgment, 'witnesses of these things'. Hacket's rule ended twelve days later on a scaffold erected at the scene of their demonstration, with a screaming tirade against God and the queen which horrified a crowd knowing nothing of psychopathic disturbance, but able to recognize blasphemy and treason. As for Copinger, he starved himself to death in prison.

Nothing more convenient to Whitgift's party could possibly have happened than this lurid echo of the anabaptist excesses of sixty years before. It was Strasbourg, Amsterdam and Münster all over again, a fresh visitation of Melchior Hoffmann and John of Leyden; did not Copinger and Arthington repeat the classic claim of these arch-enthusiasts to be the two 'witnesses', Enoch and Elijah? Bancroft would make this affair the logical climax of his literary exposure of the puritan movement: 'English Scottizing for Discipline by Force'. Cosin devoted a whole book to it: *Conspiracie for pretended reformation*. Among the confused aims of these poor creatures had been the deliverance of the imprisoned ministers, and for months Copinger had hung about the prisoners and their friends, especially Wigginton and Throckmorton, eager to prove that he and his protégé 'had a gift'. The puritans experienced the embarrassment of all sincere Christians when confronted with enthusiasts who thrust themselves into their company and talk their language. Some of them wrote noncommittal but compromising letters in which they took care not to quench the Spirit. Much of this correspondence came into the hands of Whitgift's party who were perhaps hopefully waiting for something like the climax which eventually came. It was all grist to Bancroft's mill, and with the ingenuity of the natural investigator he was to claim that if Cartwright did not actively encourage Copinger's attempt, neither did he discourage it. So the absence of any writing from Cartwright to the fanatic became itself a suspicious and significant fact.[25]

Josias Nichols remembered this as the third 'most grievous accident', which did 'very much darken the righteousness of our cause.' Tom Fuller preserves the plausible tradition that for many months to come no courtier dared to present a petition on the ministers' behalf, 'being loath to lose himself to save others, so offended was her Majesty against them.' In June no less a personage than the king of Scots had written personally to Elizabeth in favour of the nine ministers and Udall. Now any good done by that and other appeals was undone. Udall himself now thought it 'bootless to sue.' Worst of all: four days after the incident, Nicholas Fuller was committed a close prisoner to the Fleet by the same warrant which ordered Hacket's execution, and Popham and Puckering were sent to examine him. The nature of Fuller's offence is unknown; perhaps he had offered to represent the conspirators at their trial. What is certain is that as a by-product of the Copinger-Hacket affair the ministers' legal representative was now himself in limbo.[26]

The first of the Crown witnesses to be examined, 'from six of the clock in the morning till seven at night', was Thomas Stone, rector of Warkton, and a leading member of the Kettering *classis*. The long day was for once productive, for Stone had decided to reveal, in superfluous detail, everything about his association with the meetings in Northampton and elsewhere, the names of those present, the matters discussed, the procedures followed. For the first time the examiners learned of the general conferences at Cambridge and London in 1589 and 1590. Not surprisingly, Stone was attacked from all sides for betraying his friends and casting aspersion on those whose depositions had been less informative. In self-defence he explained that having taken an oath tendered by a lawful magistrate, 'in a plea for the prince, to a lawful end', he had no choice but to tell the truth. The ministers should 'stand so upon the integrity of their own actions, as that they should not be doubted of, suspected, examined, censured, etc.' Besides, he saw no possibility of concealing the circumstances any longer. Letters and writings had been intercepted, the magistrate was 'resolutely set to search them out', and others were to appear as witnesses who shared his view of the matter. To pretend to be clear of these things was to leave 'the burden upon eight or nine men's shoulders which ought to be eased by many.' If Stone thought that the case was as good as proven, he was ill-advised. But the prosecution was not helped by the conflict of his evidence at many points with that of John Johnson.[27]

In August attempts were made to discover more about the St John's conference of 1589 from Henry Alvey and William Perkins. In early September Thomas Barber, the suspended preacher of Bow and a leading London *classis* member, made a full and valuable deposition. Later in the month Edmund Littleton, Anthony Nutter and Hercules Clevely added a few details to what was known of the movement in the Midlands. In October Snape's parishioners were asked to repeat that conversation in the great seat of St Peter's church which suggested that their pastor was expecting and preparing for a presbyterian revolution, although none of them was able to confirm that Snape had used the crucial phase, 'all in one day'. It was not until October 13th and 30th respectively that the prize witnesses and the only really disloyal brethren, Thomas Edmunds and John Johnson, were examined. Edmunds was garrulous, but his recollections were neither precise nor recent. Even Johnson's story fell short of proving the full substance of the alleged conspiracy, and nothing in the other depositions had substantiated this central charge. Crucial questions about the attitude of the puritans to the royal supremacy and the Church of England as established by law were invariably bypassed, and none of the witnesses could be said to have established beyond question that the Book of Discipline had been put in practice. As for Johnson's and Edmunds's evidence, it was invalidated by palpable malice.

The pressing into service at this late date of such biassed witnesses as Johnson and Edmunds is evidence of the effectiveness of the counter-questioning which had now begun on behalf of the defendants. The interrogatories prepared by the defence were more confident and decisive than those of the prosecution. Their theme was one with which we are now familiar. The meetings had been voluntary and unexceptional; it had not been concluded or so much as debated that the Discipline should be brought in 'by force or by any other means than dutiful and peaceable'; none of the defendants had ever taken part in any capacity in the election, ordination or confirmation of any minister, elder or deacon. And so on. Nutter, Clevely and Barber confirmed almost every point. Even Stone made admissions which blunted the edge of his earlier deposition. He could not say that the defendants had ever allured or persuaded any of the people to practise the Discipline without the consent of the magistrate; he could not think of anything done by the defendants which would suggest that they intended their decisions to have the force of law without authority from queen and Parliament; he was sure that no one had been persuaded by the defendants to forsake his calling, or to despise the authority of the ecclesiastical courts.

Johnson's examination brought to an end the process of interrogation and counter-interrogation. From this point on the progress of the case is obscure, and there is no formal record of later proceedings. In February 1592 Cartwright sent Burghley a summary of the case which contained abstracts of the bill and answers and the depositions of the witnesses for both sides, with a further informal answer 'to the things of moment deposed against the defendants'. This was a conflation of the evidence, designed to demonstrate the confusion that lay over the whole case, and the many contradictions between the evidence of one witness and another, and even between what the same witness deposed on two separate occasions.[28] Yet Puckering's papers contain ample evidence of the preparations for the final proceedings in which it was to be argued that the allegations of seditious practice had been made good. Sheets of rough notes record his own effort to establish from answers and depositions and from the very semantics of the Book of Discipline itself the crucial fact of what Beale called 'execution'.[29] On December 12th, 1591, the attorney general sent Burghley a moderately confident opinion of how the case stood, no doubt in response to a request from the lord treasurer to whom the prisoners had now applied for release on bail. 'The books are very long,' Popham wrote, 'and yet I have read them through almost all.' He was satisfied that the ministers 'had a full resolution' to exercise their Book of Discipline in so far as this might be done with the peace of the Church and the law of the land; and that in some of their assemblies they were prepared to win as many other ministers to embrace it as they could, to urge the people to accept it, and then to repudiate the government of archbishops and bishops. This was what they meant by 'peaceable means', since the Discipline could not be established by the queen and Parliament.[30]

It was a nice point, and Popham was too sanguine. In fact the case had already drifted into stalemate. According to an anonymous correspondent of Burghley – probably Knollys – the upshot was that the lord chief justices persuaded Hatton 'and the rest', after dinner in the Star Chamber, that they should proceed no further 'until they should have matter to prove some seditious act de facto.' By January 1592 Knollys could say with confidence that if the bishops and the lord chancellor 'or any for them' could have proved that one point, 'then Cartwright and his fellows had been hanged before this time.' The Star Chamber could not inflict the ultimate penalty, but Knollys's main contention stands. There was no sentence, and early in 1592 the position of the ministers was much as it had been twelve months before.[31]

That the judges intervened to stop the case while the lord chancellor was still alive rests only on hearsay. Hatton died on November 20th, 1591, and his death led to an immediate change of climate. Arthur Hildersham, banned from exercising his ministry anywhere south of the Trent, was relieved by the High Commission in January 1592, thus enabling Huntingdon to present him to the vicarage of Ashby-de-la-Zouch.[32] 'Great comfort is to the Church by the death of the lord chancellor,' wrote one puritan to another, 'and appearance of deliverance to the ministers that have until now had none.' There were rumours that Burghley had spoken 'some good words' in their favour, and that the earl of Essex was to succeed Hatton as chancellor of Oxford University 'for which office the archbishop (as I heard) laboured to have Lord Buckhurst.'[33]

The reaction in the puritans' favour was by no means so complete as this. Whitgift was in fact successful in making Buckhurst chancellor of Oxford, and his influence seems to have helped Puckering, who had worked so hard in the prosecution of the nine ministers, to step into Hatton's great office of state. When Parliament met again a year later, in February 1593, Whitgift would be instrumental in procuring against puritan sectaries a savage piece of legislation which had begun life as a House of Commons bill against recusants; and when the archbishop seemed to be suffering a parliamentary defeat on this issue, he would hasten the execution of Barrow and Greenwood – out of malice for the Commons, or so it was said at the time. A few weeks later John Penry was sent to the scaffold. All this was to Burghley's impotent sorrow.[34] Yet Cartwright, to whom the archbishop 'in my lord chancellor's life' had denied the favours enjoyed by the other prisoners, now thought it worth while to renew his appeals. Similarly Udall knew there was no point in suing for reprieve 'till the lord chancellor was dead', and it was now that he was reprieved. Four Cambridge heads of the moderate puritan party, including Whitaker of St John's and Chaderton of Emmanuel, thought the moment propitious to point out to Burghley that 'divers of the true friends and lovers of the gospel' had of late years suffered more severely than 'many known papists'.[35]

But the way out of prison was still tortuous. In December all nine ministers petitioned Burghley unsuccessfully for release on bail. A further approach through Knollys opened the way for an appearance before the Privy Council, when the cold of January increased their chance of a merciful reception. As a result of this interview the prisoners signed a submission which contained a most important statement on their classical meetings. They still insisted that these assemblies had been innocent and profitable, but understanding that 'such prescript and set meetings' were offensive to her Majesty and their lordships, they regretted that they had provoked this displeasure and promised thereafter to 'avoid the occasion of offence.' They added that their submission would have been made earlier if the archbishop had not confronted them with yet another lengthy collection of interrogatories. By this time, thanks to the queen's 'princely compassion', the prisoners in the Clink and the White Lion – Wight, Fen, King, Payne and Lord – were allowed on a bail of forty pounds to go to church on Sundays, and Fen and King were permitted to leave their prisons on one other day in the week to conduct their necessary business. Snape hopefully asked Whitgift for similar privileges, to go once a week into the fields or gardens for the sake of his health, and to go into the city to look after the affairs of his brother and of his invalid wife.[36]

Everything now rested with Whitgift. Burghley was already on the ministers' side, and moved the archbishop to the extent of obtaining the same concessions for Cartwright as the others already enjoyed, and even some talk of 'a quite discharge'. But late in February little progress had been made, and Whitgift alarmed the prisoners by letting it be known that they must sign a further submission as the condition of their release, containing admissions which for two years they had refused to make. The health of four or five of them was by now broken. One of the prisoners[37] had 'continually voided blood by urine' since October, and he bore the additional burden of a 'poor lame wife and seven small children'.[38]

The document to which subscription was now required was none other than that new set of articles which, according to Beale, might have been used as a test for secular magistrates. In effect it was a form of public humiliation for any sincere presbyterian. The ministers refused to sign. Then in April the Council sent seven of the prisoners yet another schedule of interrogatories, closely resembling those they had answered in the Star Chamber in the previous June. Their replies on this occasion (all of which are extant) are of some interest, since in these more informal circumstances they were prepared to answer general articles which they had bypassed before as impertinent. Cartwright, for example, offered a major theoretical statement on the place in the Church of the Christian magistrate. All were required to acknowledge their fault in subscribing to the Discipline and putting it in practice. Most of the ministers merely referred to their previous submission to the Council, so implicitly repeating their promise to forswear their meetings in the future. But Snape and Prowdlove persisted in their denial that they had ever subscribed the Book, and Prowdlove insisted that the meetings in which he participated were voluntary and informal and not according to the Book. Nevertheless even he promised that he would not 'hereafter in such sort meet in conference.'[39]

Partial relief followed. By May 21st Cartwright was in Hackney, under house arrest. Wight, permitted to walk abroad with his keeper, found himself too weak to profit from the privilege and asked to be treated like the other prisoners and removed 'in or about the city'. Once established in these easier circumstances the prisoners would try to get back to the country. By the autumn the Warwickshire ministers had succeeded, and they now asked Whitgift for relief from their own and their sureties' bonds and even for liberty to preach. They were due to appear before him on October 3rd, but asked to be excused in view of the plague then raging in London.[40] The Northamptonshire ministers seem to have lingered in London, even teaching in secret.[41] Melanchthon Jewel eventually got back to Devon and unrepentantly resumed his old way of life as hedge-priest and book-peddler. Within a year or two he would be arraigned before Judge Anderson for dispersing seditious books.[42] But the ministers were not fully cleared for years, if at all. In 1596 Matthew Sutcliffe wrote that the Council had shown Cartwright 'great favour' and had accepted 'a certain submission'. 'But that he should be quite discharged, I cannot believe.' He was still bound to appear at any time within twenty days warning. And just as well, in case 'he run on his old courses.' In 1595 Cartwright left England for Guernsey.

It is a curious, Kafka-esque story, typically Elizabethan, with no tidy conclusion. Of sharp exemplary punishment there had been none, and Bancroft, Cosin and Sutcliffe were obliged to write their sensational books, full of 'vehement conjectures', to establish in print what the lords in the Star Chamber had failed to censure. 'If he be not dealt withall judicially by law,' wrote Sutcliffe of Cartwright, 'yet may it please him to give us leave to talk of his misdemeanours extra-judicially.'[43] Among a mass of ephemeral polemic, valuable only for the evidence of the puritan organization which it preserves, there was one extra-judicial indictment of permanent and magisterial quality. The first four books of Hooker's *Treatise of the lawes of ecclesiasticall politie* appeared in 1593 and, by defining in generous philosophical terms the distinctive position of the Church of England, served to throw into sharp relief the 'singularity' of the puritans. Many of Hooker's arguments have seemed to posterity almost unanswerable. But his intervention was very far from decisive at this time, and the fact that there was no weighty retort from the other side does not indicate, as some have suggested, that the puritans acknowledged defeat. Not only was the puritan cause generally depressed at this time, but the public and the booksellers were less than enthusiastic about these well-worn controversies, and it was not yet generally recognized that Hooker's work was in a class of its own.[44]

Nevertheless, the long imprisonment and trial had worn down and all but defeated the nine ministers and the movement for which they stood as representative figures. They had promised to end their formal meetings. It was all over, at least for the moment. When a new Parliament was called, early in 1593, the puritan lawyers were conspicuously present, Beale, Morice and Fuller, but their prearranged campaign, for all its enterprise and courage, was purely defensive in its aim, directed against the *ex officio* oath and kindred abuses of the ecclesiastical courts. And of course it failed. This Parliament saw Whitgift and his party so much masters of the situation that, as Sir John Neale has shown, it was a Commons bill against recusants which was transformed into the first and only act of an Elizabethan parliament which dealt exclusively, and severely, with protestant sectaries. For the remainder of the reign, puritanism was effectively outlawed by a government vigilant against the least overt demonstration of the old radical spirit. In Norwich in 1596, the bishop and his fellow ecclesiastical commissioners suspended a minister *durante beneplacito* and imposed on him a public penance for the offence of merely possessing a 'seditious' presbyterian sermon printed by Waldegrave. And in the following year, Whitgift saw fit to rebuke his brother of York for the dangerous 'novelty' of writing 'Christ's tide' rather than 'Christmas' in an official letter.[45]

4 Underground and Diverted

'And what know yow or me whether all the fruites of your labers be yet risen and sprunge up, or lie still closse and hidden under the grounde, bicause of the stormy and sharpe seasons and winterlike wether ... You have no cause to repente that ever you tooke yt in hande.'

(EDMUND CHAPMAN TO THOMAS CARTWRIGHT, *c.* 1591?,
Dedham Minute Book, pp. 77–8)

AT THE EARLIER STAGES OF OUR STORY we had occasion, repeatedly, to notice that Elizabethan puritanism was a phenomenon both wider and more elusive than presbyterianism. In recent chapters the presbyterians have stolen the show, since they played the most conspicuous role in the puritan drama of the 1580s. That is the measure of their success, John Field's achievement primarily. The result has been that, faced with the collapse of their campaign to remould the national Church, historians have found themselves asking what became of puritanism in the aftermath. If this had been the end of the story there would be no problem. But as everyone knows, puritanism was to re-emerge under James I as a powerful and increasingly formative influence in English life.

If there is an apparent difficulty here it arises from a misconception of the relation of puritanism to what can properly be called the puritan movement. After 1590 the attempt to carry through a further reformation of the Church was temporarily abandoned, by tacit and, it would seem, almost universal consent. The imprisoned ministers promised to give up their 'prescript and set meetings', and in so doing they morally bound the movement they represented. Chapman of Dedham, writing to comfort Cartwright in the moment of defeat, conducts what is virtually a post mortem into 'this great cause of church government'. True, his letter implies a tactical withdrawal rather than utter defeat. As Fuller puts it, the brethren 'did not so much practise for the present as project for the future, to procure hereafter an establishment of their ecclesiastical government.'[1]

But when the day of opportunity at last returned, in 1603, the discipline had lost much of the commanding appeal which it possessed in John Field's day, and English presbyterianism had begun a long decline from which it would be rescued only by the political crisis of the mid-seventeenth century and Scottish intervention. Some had been impelled, often by the teaching of the presbyterians themselves,[2] into a separatism which was at least a rational adjustment to things as they were. Both they and the many of not greatly dissimilar views who made no overt gesture of separation now added to their dislike of bishops the distaste for the 'rabbinical' tyranny of the presbytery which William Bradshaw disclosed in the treatise *English puritanisme*; 'wherein,' as John Paget complained in 1641, 'there is such a peremptory restraint of all ecclesiastical authority unto particular congregations.' In 1604 Bradshaw could already claim, perhaps with a view to warning off Scottish presbyterian intruders, that this manifesto embodied 'the main opinions of the rigidest sort called puritans.'[3] By this time the official voice of a less rigid English puritanism, as heard in the millenary petition and at Hampton Court, called for reasonable changes in the national Church which would fall short of any essential alteration of its ministry and government. So long as there was any chance of that voice being heard, moderate puritanism seemed to embody an equally sensible accommodation to political realities. But presbyterianism, if it remained for many a remote ideal, was practically an untenable position.

Meanwhile, puritan religion was working its own quiet and often unobserved revolution which would in time effect changes in English society quite as profound as those ever dreamed of by the presbyterians. If a further reformation of the Church of England was, for the moment, out of the question, it was time to turn with vigour to the reformation of towns, parishes, families and individuals, to be lost in the warfare of the spirit. Hence the paradox that the miscarriage of the further reformation coincided with the birth of the great age of puritan religious experience.[4] Francis Marbury, once a Northampton hothead and even suspected of being Martin Marprelate, was now preaching peacefully enough in Lincolnshire. In 1596 he would declare that he knew of no minister or of anyone else 'in all this country' who so much as favoured the erection of a presbytery. 'Neither are the people made acquainted with the controversy of discipline in all Lindsey coast that I can perceive. For men have enough to do to stand by that religion which her blessed Majesty hath approved unto us by her express laws.'[5] (That his daughter, the future Anne Hutchinson, was at this time in the formative years of her childhood may

P

belie these soft words. She was to be a sufficiently disturbing influence in the infant colony of Massachusetts.) Richard Baxter would describe in similar categories the churchmanship of the Worcestershire ministers, half a century later. Nor was it entirely novel in the 1590s to retain this sense of the proper priorities. Some of the most acceptable of the early puritan preachers, such as those twin fellows of Christ's, John More of Norwich and Edward Dering, had never identified themselves closely with the protest against ceremonies and episcopal government. Their consuming desire had been to preach and to live the gospel, and it was only the apparent indifference of their superiors to this ideal that had made them rebels.

But now the temporary exhaustion of old controversies by the puritans and their opponents – not to speak of the exhaustion of the literate religious public – brought the essential matter of salvation to the forefront. William Perkins was to treat it as an exact science, and his books, for all their theological technicality, enjoyed a ready sale. So did those generous medicines for a distressed conscience, the *Seaven treatises* of Richard Rogers, a preacher who now seems to have been wholly diverted from the vexed problems of church government. At the same time the Calvinist assumptions of these divines were challenged, as they would not have been ten years before, by the reaction against Geneva which was gathering force amongst a party of avant-garde divines in Cambridge, and this nascent English 'Arminianism' would lend to orthodox, Calvinist puritanism a new theological distinction. In an age in which all churches and confessions were obsessed with rival doctrines of grace, Perkins was the first English Calvinist to win a major European reputation, virtually the first puritan theologian in the systematic sense, if we exclude the young prodigy Dudley Fenner, who died in his twenties in 1587.[6]

For Perkins, as for his readers, the crucial question of religion was how a man might be sure of his salvation, which for a Calvinist was to have assurance of his election. Although Calvin himself had not encouraged introspection, it was an axiom of his doctrine that the ungodly and the backslider had never received a true calling. So conversely the godly Calvinist tended to find a source of hope in his own fruitful life. By the early years of the new century, the reader of English puritan theology might be forgiven for supposing that his salvation depended in some degree on the quality of repentance and obedience in his own life. Perkins and his successors had much to say about a covenant or contract which God had made with his people, and about the moral obligations which it imposed. As Perkins insisted, 'God's promise to man is that whereby he bindeth himself to man to be his God, if he perform the condition. Man's promise to God is that whereby he voweth his allegiance to the Lord, and to perform the condition between them.'[7] The notion of a covenant between God and man was not new to protestant theology. That man can choose as well as be chosen is an idea so prominent in the Old Testament that it was bound to obtrude, and it coloured the teaching of the Zürich reformers and, in England, of Tyndale. Nor did 'covenant theology' as it was taught early in the seventeenth century necessarily distort Calvin's doctrine of the sheer gratuitousness of salvation, as some writers have supposed. Perkins does not anywhere say that man can voluntarily choose to enter into a covenant with God. Nevertheless, some puritans wrote and behaved as if they believed that grace was granted as the reward of obedience. It was a somewhat natural though not a legitimate deduction from orthodox teaching, and to some extent the wheel had come full circle.[8]

Thus Calvinist and covenanting neo-Calvinist alike were prone to train the sensitive organ of conscience on their daily lives for signs of encouragement or warning: witness the introspective diaries of Richard Rogers and Samuel Ward.[9] Whatever he professed to believe about the bondage of the will, for all practical purposes the puritan co-operated strenuously in his own sanctification and took pains to hold himself upright in all his dealings. Consequently the preachers were required to be guides of conduct as well as proclaimers of good news. The laity were eager to receive expert clinical help in these matters, where they would not easily submit to the overruling of a clerical discipline. So Perkins and his contemporaries, like the second generation of Calvinist teachers elsewhere in Europe, began to apply their attention to the Law as much as to the Gospel and to provide through their preaching and writing a means of self-discipline. By the turn of the century, few passages of Scripture can have been more frequently or systematically expounded than the ten commandments.

Wherever the Bible failed to offer specific moral guidance, the fully accomplished divine offered to try 'cases of conscience'. So began the construction of a protestant casuistry which was to grow up alongside the rival systems of the catholic moral theologians.[10] Puritan casuistry was no more a new invention than puritan gospel preaching; witness the 'comfortable' letters written by Knox, Dering and Wilcox, especially to their female correspondents. But Perkins, with the orderly approach of a new schoolman, was the first protestant anywhere to attempt to encase the subject in a formal system. A by-product of puritan casuistry was the exemplary biography, and the 'lives of eminent divines', gathered into Samuel Clarke's garner, would in themselves serve to fix the pattern of puritan piety as they set in conventionalized relief the profiles of scores of puritan saints whose Elizabethan forerunners are little more than names. These literary productions, theological, 'practical' and biographical, gave the new puritan age its distinctive historical flavour, as William Haller captures it in his *Rise of Puritanism*.

Elizabethan society being what it was, industrious and accumulating, puritan moralists were obliged to occupy the field of what we should call social ethics.[11] In 1594, for example, the Suffolk preacher Miles Mosse delivered a course of sermons on the subject of usury, an 'arraignment' and 'conviction' of that practice which illustrates the superficiality of representing Calvinism as in any simple sense the progenitor of capitalism.[12] Another burning topic was the nature and use of Sunday, a subject which also had a direct bearing on work and profit, but which was handled theologically by the divines. Was the fourth commandment in its entirety a moral law, binding on Christians, or were its detailed provisions a discarded Jewish ceremony? How was each part of the day to be spent, and which occupations, which recreations were lawful?

The Elizabethan Church followed the medieval tradition in forbidding Sunday work, but this was regarded by the first protestant generation as a merely political restriction of the unfettered spiritual liberty of a Christian man. The novelty of the new Sabbatarianism lay in the insistence that the strict observance of the Sabbath was a perpetual necessity, part of man's moral obligation. Not only did this provide the hallowing of the Lord's Day with a theological rationale which puritans could accept; the obverse of the doctrine was that the Church could not make any other days holy which were not so appointed in God's word. As the Book of Discipline tersely remarked, 'holidays are conveniently to be abolished', and that, as Mr Christopher Hill points out, was a doctrine which had its uses. In the 'eighties the Dedham ministers differed on the problems of the Sabbath in formal disputation. Ten years later it had become virtually an official – and prominent – doctrine of puritanism, asserted in several systematic treatments of the ten commandments and in separate treatises, most notably by Richard Greenham of Dry Drayton – a leading puritan casuist – and by his friend Nicholas Bownd, rector of Norton, Suffolk. Bownd's *True doctrine of the Sabbath*, like Mosse's *Arraignment and conviction of usury*, seems to have grown out of a course of sermons preached in the Bury exercise. And it was in a Bury pulpit, in 1599, that the word 'Sabbatarian' seems to have been first used polemically, by Thomas Rogers, rector of Horringer and one of Bancroft's chaplains. Rogers later claimed the credit for exposing to the government a sinister new device of the disciplinarians to assault the Church 'from an odd corner and after a new fashion' with 'Sabbath speculations' which were presbyterian in inspiration. If this was to attribute to these preachers a guile of which they were probably innocent, there can be no doubt that moral problems, the Sabbath above all, had now replaced the reorganization of the Church as the leading concern of the East Anglian puritans.[13]

These few pages may have served to explain how Dr Haller could begin to discuss 'The Rise of Puritanism' at a point which we have reached only in our penultimate chapter. But our concern is not to pursue these wider aspects of the puritan ethos, determinative as they were for much of modern English civilization, but merely to trace the hidden history of puritanism as an organized movement from the collapse of 1590 to the revival of 1603. The fact that a new campaign for further reformation was launched on the accession of James I, and launched very largely with the methods of 1584-9, from the same parts of the country and under some of the same leadership, should be proof enough that the roots of the puritan movement had not been seriously disturbed by the late Elizabethan reaction. Formal conferences approximating to *classes* and synods may have ceased in almost all districts, and there was probably no longer any central direction. But it would have been beyond the power of a far more resourceful government than that of Elizabeth I to have carried the process of repression much further. The superstructure of the presbyterian movement had been erected on a foundation of market-town exercises, fasts and informal conferences which were a permanent part of English religious life, at least in some dioceses, from the earlier years of Elizabeth to the Laudian repression of the 1630s. The Bury exercise, for example, went on undisturbed through these years, and from a ministry held together in these informal ways would later come the concerted opposition to Archbishop Bancroft of the 'seventy-one brethren of Suffolk'.[14]

For the persistence of similar associations at various places in the Midlands a certain amount of incidental evidence can be gleaned from the strange adventures of the Nottinghamshire preacher John Darrell, who established a mushroom reputation in the late 'nineties as a professional exorcist. Darrell's 'instrument' for casting out devils was the puritan exercise of prayer and fasting, and it was this which especially aroused the alarm and distaste of the ecclesiastical authorities.[15] Darrell encountered his first subject, Thomas Darling of Burton-on-Trent, when with Arthur Hildersham of Ashby-de-la-Zouch and 'divers other preachers' he visited the house in which the boy was lodged. This was in May 1596, on a Monday, 'the day of the common exercise at Burton'. Darling subsequently accompanied the exorcist to 'several exercises' at Burton, Appleby and Packington. When Darrell received a call to carry his strange ministry to Lancashire, he first sought the advice of his brother ministers 'met together at an exercise.' In Lancashire, where seven deranged children were exposed to his gifts, he had the co-operation of the local preachers in organizing public fasts. When he was later invited to deal with the Nottingham boy William Sommers, whose self-induced 'possession' eventually led to his downfall, Darrell first advised the town to seek the 'help and assistance of some godly learned in the ministry next adjoining unto them', and when he consented to come to Nottingham in person it was to meet Sommers 'at supper with divers preachers at the sign of the Castle'.[16]

The impression of some authorities that there were no more puritan conferences after about 1590 may well rest on the evidence of the Dedham minutes which end abruptly at midsummer 1589. On June 2nd the conference according to its usual custom arranged the place, speaker and moderator for the next occasion, but no further meeting is recorded. 'Thus long continued through God's mercy this blessed meeting,' wrote Richard Parker, the vicar of Dedham, 'and now it ended by the malice of Satan.'[17] But the case of Dedham has some unusual features which make it a dangerous basis for generalization. Parker says that 'some cause' of the end of their meetings was 'complaints against us preferred to the bishop of London, for which cause I was called up to London and examined of it.' This is plausible enough, for Parker's examination is independently recorded in Bancroft's *Daungerous positions*. But Parker goes on to say somewhat vaguely that 'the chiefest cause was the death of some of our brethren and their departure from us to other places', which could not be less convincing. In June 1589 Dedham could still draw upon thirteen of its members, which makes it the largest conference in the country of which we have any knowledge, and the younger men who continued to come into the district would maintain the puritan tradition of the Stour valley far into the seventeenth century. But it is true that Parker himself left Dedham in October 1590, and in circumstances which cast some doubt on the value of his testimony.

Since the early months of 1588, the vicar of Dedham had been in trouble.[18] First there were reports of an immoral association with the miller's wife of the next village, Stratford St Mary, and these were examined by the bishop's commissary. Although Parker cleared himself of this charge, with the help of a deathbed confession made by the miller's wife, a year later the whole town suspected an attempt on the chastity of two married women of Dedham: the wife of Robert Thorne, a sidesman, and the wife of one John Martin, a poor man who rented a shop and the rooms above it in part of Parker's bachelor vicarage. For his misbehaviour with Mrs Thorne and certain 'filthy speeches' overheard by a maid, Parker had been presented to the archdeacon and enjoined penance. Questioned by the more substantial townsmen about his dealings with Mrs Martin, he admitted that he had 'asked her the question, "but", quoth he, "I protest before God that I never did the deed with her."' This was at midsummer 1589, the very time of the last recorded conference. In November, Martin brought proceedings, and by the end of the year the vicar 'with weeping eyes' was begging one of the churchwardens to 'stand his friend and consider his estate, being a young man, and that his credit once taken away, he was utterly undone.' The case was heard in the consistory court in May and July 1590, and by October Parker had resigned the living.[19] Twelve years later he became vicar of Ketringham in Norfolk – one would like to believe, as a happily married man – and it was there, in 1604, that he recollected what happened in June 1589 to the 'blessed meeting' of the Dedham ministers.

Formal monthly conferences may well have been suspended at Dedham. But the puritan clergy who remained in the district were still a close and fervent brotherhood. In October 1593 Nicholas Faunt, once one of Walsingham's puritan secretaries, stayed with the Cardinal family at East Bergholt, a mile from Dedham, and from there reported to his friend Anthony Bacon that 'the ministers here, so far as they dare, are not unmindful in their solemn fasts and other exercises of our state and the danger so imminent thereunto.'[20]

The Stour valley was only one of several pockets where radical puritanism maintained itself with the utmost secrecy and even extended its influence during this unfavourable decade. Another such enclave lay around St Albans, where the mother of Anthony and Francis Bacon, the increasingly eccentric Lady Ann, at Gorhambury provided shelter from the storm. This was where Percival Wiburn spent his declining years, in company with a younger preacher, Humphrey Wilblud, who was employed to catechize Lady Bacon's household. Thomas Wilcox, who may still have been curate at nearby Bovingdon, spoke warmly of the old lady's kindness to 'God's saints and faithful servants here', who included not only 'common professors', but 'many worthy ministers' and himself in particular.[21] It may be that Field's manuscript 'register' came to Gorhambury at this time, perhaps via Wilcox, and that the selection printed overseas in 1593, *A parte of a register*, was prepared for publication under the same roof.[22] Another of Lady Bacon's visitors was William Dyke, ejected from his preaching curacy in her parish of St Michael's. In 1591 he became preacher over the boundary of Lincoln diocese at Hemel Hempstead, where Richard Gawton, a veteran of the Norwich ejection of 1576, was vicar. Later Lady Bacon used the influence of her son Anthony and the earl of Essex to transfer the vicarage to Dyke and to obtain a licence to allow him to minister the sacraments, although he was only in deacon's orders. Meanwhile at St Michael's the tradition established by Dyke was continued by a new and fanatical vicar, Erasmus Cooke.[23]

Some time in the early 'nineties this Hertfordshire circle played host to an assembly of ministers from other dioceses, and as a result Cooke and other ministers were convented before Bishop Aylmer and censured. It emerges from Cooke's defence that their conference took place during an outbreak of plague, and the probability is strong that the occasion was the autumn of 1593 when the danger of infection in London drove the whole business and following of the Michaelmas term to St Albans. The unusual throng would have provided the kind of cover which the presbyterians had earlier found in London during the days of the Bartholomew Fair. And there was no Bartholomew Fair in 1593, because of the infection.[24] John Clark, who was mayor at the time of the St Albans term, was a fervent puritan who had sheltered the fugitive Penry and had 'much conference' with him, one of the 'gadders' who had left their own parishes to hear Dyke at St Michael's and, of course, a good friend of Lady Bacon. As mayor he was charged before the High Commissioners with allowing unlicensed ministers to preach in his house, 'and some such as have been especially disliked and disallowed by authority.'[25] At his visitation on April 30th, 1596, the archdeacon delivered a special charge from Aylmer's successor, Bishop Fletcher, against the holding of unauthorized public fasts. Yet on the following Whitsunday Erasmus Cooke presided over an extraordinary fast at St Michael's which drew ministers from outside the archdeaconry and people from 'other and foreign parishes'. Only Cooke preached, delivering in all three sermons which, interspersed with prayer and psalm-singing, occupied six and a half hours. Obviously St Albans was a place where radical puritans could still cock a snook at authority. Yet even Lady Bacon, in writing to Anthony in favour of her protégés and against their enemies, 'biting vipers the whole part of them' with 'their backgone bishop', told him: 'Burn this, I write so true. Beware liberal speeches these suspicious days.'[26]

From Northamptonshire there is one scrap of evidence to suggest that there at least the presbyterian *classes* continued to maintain a secret existence. In 1595 Edmund Snape arrived as chaplain at Mont Orgueil, Jersey. His counterpart at Castle Cornet, Guernsey, also newly appointed, was none other than Thomas Cartwright, and together the two English chaplains were to reconcile the divided presbyterian churches of the Channel Islands and to share in the revision of their Discipline. Snape carried to his new appointment letters fiduciary 'des Eglises de la province de Northampton', which were duly registered in the minute book of the colloquy of Jersey. Apparently even at this time the unrepentant presbyterians of Northamptonshire constituted in their own eyes the formal *classis* of a concealed presbyterian Church. There does not seem to have been any radical change in puritan Warwickshire either. In 1596 Bishop Bilson could complain of Warwick 'and the parts thereabout' as 'freighted with a number of men precisely conceited against her Majesty's government ecclesiastical', who were as much a vexation with their 'curiosity' as the papists of the western parts of his diocese in their obstinacy. Ten years later no less than twenty-seven Warwickshire ministers would refuse the subscription imposed under Archbishop Bancroft's new Canons, a figure which suggests a steady growth in the movement since the 'eighties.[27]

In Devon and Cornwall, too, puritanism was to prove stronger and more vociferous by the early years of James I than ever it had been in Whitgift's time, and, though evidence is scanty, these seem to have been anything but idle years for the West Country puritans. There is a story that Bishop Woolton of Exeter was found dead in his privy at the very hour when several ministers were waiting in his consistory, expecting to be deprived. This was in March 1594. Bishop Cotton complained six years later that his diocese was full of puritans who followed 'rattle-headed preachers' from town to town. We hear highly coloured complaints of 'twenty factions in one city or town corporate', of conventicles in gardens and fields, of 'sermons preached at midnight', and of an intended 'passover' 'by a sudden search prevented.' Among these rattle-headed preachers was our friend Melanchthon Jewel, one of the Star Chamber defendants of 1591, who still lived as 'a vagrant minister, without any maintenance', preaching up and down the country in private houses. Another was John Travers, brother of the more famous Walter and brother-in-law to his adversary Richard Hooker, who had been suspended and imprisoned in 1585 for proclaiming unauthorized public fasts. Almost twenty years later he was still reckoned by his fellow puritans to be 'resolute'. He was one of thirty-five ministers of the diocese of Exeter who at first withstood Bancroft's new onslaught in 1604, of whom twenty-three suffered at least a temporary suspension.[28]

From 1600, the expanding puritan movement in the West Country was stiffened by the presence of Edmund Snape. His ten-year suspension ended on July 11th of that year, by which time he had become a controversial figure in Jersey for his unorthodox teaching on marriage. Only a matter of days before he would again be free to minister in England, the magistrates of Exeter received letters in his favour from two godly old ladies, the countess of Warwick and the widow of Sir Amyas Paulet, which prompted them to elect him to the post of city preacher. Other letters from the court persuaded the bishop, against his better judgment, to grant a preaching licence. It was decided that Snape should preach twice on Sundays in the only building large enough to contain a good proportion of the inhabitants, the cathedral.

It was an improbable arrangement, and the city fathers were well advised to provide for the suspension of Snape's salary in the event of his being silenced. According to Bishop Cotton, the preaching was all of divine judgment and predestination, and bred contention, tumults, conventicles and factions. After private admonitions and an interview with the canons of the cathedral, he personally and privately inhibited him. For a hardened veteran like Snape this scarcely regular procedure was open to exploitation. He at once preached to a group of his followers at the unprecedented hour of six in the evening, which led to his suspension from preaching anywhere in the diocese, but above all in the cathedral. He responded by preaching at Crediton and Budleigh and catechizing in private houses in Exeter itself. Snape's standing in the city was good, and for a long time the chancellor of the diocese hesitated to make his suspension formal and official. When at last the inhibition was published, in May 1603, the preacher appealed to the archbishop's Court of Audience, to the Privy Council and to Parliament itself, with strident complaints of the irregularity of his suspension and the hardship suffered by a wife, 'six little children' and four orphans who were dependent upon him. The Council was sufficiently sympathetic to require the bishop to allow Snape to preach anywhere outside the city of Exeter itself.[29]

We have now crossed over into the new reign almost without noticing it, for Snape's tempestuous career illustrates the artificiality of making any separation between the organized puritan movements of Elizabeth's

reign and of the early years of James I. In December 1603 Snape sent
an account of his adventures to his friends in Northamptonshire, and
told them that 'being set free from Exeter' he hoped to be able to return
to them. Ten days later he found employment, not in his old county
but as preacher in another church of cathedral-like proportions, St
Saviour's, Southwark. Here he succeeded another old Northampton
preacher, Francis Marbury, and he seems to have owed this appointment
to Sir Christopher Yelverton, a good friend of the Northamptonshire
puritans and a patron of an earlier preacher of St Saviour's. In the winter
of 1604 we find him conferring with two of his militant brethren from
the West, Melanchthon Jewel and John Travers, and with Arthur
Hildersham. By this time he was again suspended and out of a job. Snape
was a true successor of Field, and if he could have maintained a permanent
footing in London he might have made a deeper impression on the history
of the English Church. Latterly we catch a suggestive glimpse of him,
swaying opinion in the House of Commons of 1606 against a bishops'
bill 'for conformity'.[30]

Not only did the puritan movement continue to hold its ground in
some localities throughout the late Elizabethan reaction, but at the local
level its patronage could not have been seriously damaged. In Norfolk
and Suffolk there were still the Bacons, Jermyns and Highams, and Sir
Edward Lewkenor; around Banbury, Sir Anthony Cope; in Northamptonshire the Knightleys and Yelvertons and the many other families
which would stand by the preachers in the crisis of 1604; in Leicestershire
and now also in Somerset, Sir Francis Hastings. It was at the centre, in
the Court, that things had changed. Here there was a rather desperate
reliance on ageing widows like Lady Bacon and the countess of Warwick.
One of these dowagers, Ann Bacon's sister, Lady Elizabeth Russell,
hoped to prop up the failing cause by securing the promotion of James
Morice to the Council Board. Her letter of recommendation to Robert
Cecil betrays in every line her distaste for the new men:

Oh, good nephew! the gravity, wisdom, care of maintaining law
of the land, learning and piety of the man I find such as in my very
heart I could be content to live with bread and water as long as I
might with life, on condition, *in publicum bonum* in respect of God's
Church and maintenance of the state by the laws of the realm and
not by rigour, as well for private good of your good father, that
lacketh such a one to back him, and in his absence to supply, this
man were a councillor and master of the rolls.

Morice had spent eight weeks in confinement as a consequence of his spirited attack in the 1593 Parliament on the abuses of the church courts, which gives the point to some of these sentiments. The puritan political interest was without a head. In the last two parliaments of the reign the puritan gentlemen were uncharacteristically docile, when they were not missing altogether. In 1597 Robert Beale, Morice's fellow-campaigner against the *ex officio* oath, was absent from the Commons for the first time since he took his seat in 1576; and by then Morice himself was dead, and with him Peter Wentworth, whose last four years had been spent in the Tower, the penalty of his initiative on the dangerous matter of the succession. With their passing, political puritanism was bankrupt. The decline of puritan influence at Court and its steady progress in the country were developments full of portent for the political as well as the religious history of the coming half-century.[31]

It might just conceivably have been otherwise. As the turn of the century and the end of the reign approached, one man shone out from his contemporaries and aspired to a monopoly of power without precedent in Elizabethan politics: Robert Devereux, earl of Essex. It was perhaps inevitable that the puritans should place their hopes on this meteoric career. They were in good company. But they at least had cause to expect some relief from Essex. He was Walsingham's son-in-law, Warwick's nephew, and, above all, Leicester's stepson and, as it seemed, his natural successor. Only five days after the old favourite's death in 1588, Francis Hastings sent Essex a pious harangue, the effect of which was to encourage him to follow closely in the same paths. Leicester was 'that honourable, worthy gentleman whom God used many times as a notable instrument for the good both of the Church and Commonwealth.' Essex was to strive 'not only to succeed him but to overgo him in his care in this behalf', and most particularly that 'the whole strength of your credit ought to be bent to comfort and countenance the well-affected in religion and watchfully to forsee that the contrary sort be kept back.'[32]

There is no doubt that for a year or two Essex went out of his way to please some of the most extreme puritan elements. At his trial he was to protest that he 'never was sectary', but to admit having 'dealt against the bishops, having been in his young time led thereunto by some hot spirits which since were grown to a better temper.'[33] Was this in reference to his rumoured connection with the Marprelate affair, to which Martin himself had drawn public attention? In March 1590 a newsletter reported that the puritans 'hoped well' of Essex, and that he was to join with Sir Walter Raleigh 'as an instrument for them to the queen', and there is no doubt that in the same year both Raleigh and Essex spoke up for the imprisoned John Udall. John Penry later thought it worth his while to address the earl from prison with a frankly pragmatic invitation to assume the vacant leadership of the radical puritan party. 'And bear with me, good my Lord, if I be overseen in taking you for the meetest man of all the nobility and Council of England for this work. The fault shall be yours and not mine if I have taken my mark amiss.' The programme which was offered to Essex was that of a second dissolution of ecclesiastical foundations, the suppression of the hierarchy and the disposal of glebes, tithes and endowments for secular purposes. 'Why should not Queen Elizabeth, and that by means of a second earl of Essex, accomplish this work? ... Is not a Devereux as meet to effect the action by her authority as a Cromwell was under her father's now to do the like?'[34]

Whitgift's biographer, Paule, confirms Essex's protestation that this was nothing but a youthful dalliance. Later, and especially after Walsingham's death, the earl 'grew very calm', held a neutral course, and finally, impressed with the queen's high opinion of Whitgift, threw in his lot with the archbishop, 'cast off those novelists', and offered 'to run a course for clergy causes.' This was why Whitgift was faithful to the earl in his disgrace and fall. This certainly exaggerates the depth of Essex's conversion, and Sir Henry Wotton's recollection is to be preferred when he tells us that the earl continued to divide 'his affection between two extremes', bearing 'a kind of filial reverence towards Dr Whitgift', but also esteeming Cartwright, even if he made a 'distinction between the persons and the causes.' Cartwright was certainly a regular correspondent, and to all appearances one of the earl's most sedulous flatterers. Was it apt to call the young Essex 'a father of his people', or altogether wise to compare him to Saul? Similar sentiments were echoed from all sides. The preacher to the Merchant Adventurers in Middelburg told him: 'All men's eyes are upon you now, at home and abroad,' while Josias Nichols of Kent was eager to express 'what hope and expectation there is among her Majesty's most faithful subjects concerning you.'[35]

What did Essex do to deserve or repay such fulsome expressions? Like Leicester he had a taste for moderate puritan chaplains, but not all his chaplains were puritans. One indeed became a papist on the Cadiz voyage (William Alabaster) and another (John Buckeridge) was an early 'Arminian' and tutor to the future Archbishop Laud. Like Leicester again he received the dedications of many puritan books, and Nicholas Bownd's

True doctrine of the Sabbath appeared in 1595 with a full-page engraving of the Devereux arms. It is true that all kinds of books were dedicated to Essex (including Robert Parsons's *Conference about the next succession*!) but some of these puritan authors acknowledge tangible favours received.[36] Essex used his influence from time to time on behalf of individual puritan preachers. For example, he was a patron of William Hubbock, the Magdalen man whom the High Commissioners expelled from Oxford in 1590. And in 1598 he was 'ernest' on behalf of Stephen Egerton of Blackfriars who had been exposed by Bishop Bancroft's primary visitation as the only persistent nonconformist in London.[37]

Some of these good turns were doubtless performed to oblige one or another of his friends and kinsmen, or others in the extensive Essex faction. If William Dyke was helped into a settled ministry at Hemel Hempstead, this was a token of his desire to please Francis and Anthony Bacon and of theirs to satisfy their mother, not an indication that Essex sympathized with Dyke or even knew anything about him. But the connection with Egerton may have been much more significant, for in the first years of the new reign the preacher of Blackfriars would emerge wearing John Field's mantle as London leader of the militant puritan ministry. Essex's patronage therefore carries suggestive echoes of the protection which Leicester and Warwick extended to Field twenty years before.

Egerton, with other London preachers, not all of his party, was to be caught up in the final events of the Essex tragedy. At the time of his first disgrace and illness, after the return from Ireland in the autumn of 1599, special prayers were uttered for Essex as 'that noble Barak' by ministers 'not respecting the earl of Essex his restraint as they ought to have done', Egerton amongst them. And preachers at Paul's Cross touched dangerously on the earl in their sermons. Later there were preachers in the very mixed entourage which hung upon Essex shortly before the debacle of February 1601. Robert Cecil contrived to put a sinister interpretation on their presence, and it was even said that there had been mention of the Calvinist doctrine that the lesser magistrates had a right to restrain princes. Whether the preachers really had some curious place in the plot, like Shakespeare's players, or whether as Essex insisted, they were engaged in innocent 'spiritual conferences' for his 'consolation' is an open question. But that they were there, in Essex House, preaching to crowds of godly citizens, there is apparently no doubt.[38] Bancroft took early advantage of Essex's confusion to suspend Egerton's popular weekday lectures, on the grounds partly of some suspicious content in a sermon preached on the day of the rebellion. And on the Sunday following, February 15th, not only Egerton but two other leading puritans, Anthony Wotton of Tower Hill, Essex's chaplain, and Edward Phillips, preacher at St Saviour's, Southwark, failed to deliver from their pulpits the official account and condemnation of the rebellion. They were prepared to condemn the fact, but not to publish Essex's treason as of their own knowledge, or, apparently, to blacken his whole reputation.[39]

But for the events of that February all this might have made sense for the cause of puritanism, and for us. Late Elizabethan politics cannot be understood apart from the discreetly muffled struggle for the succession. It was the expectation that 'the Scottish mist' would 'turn into a parching sun'[40] which kept the puritans relatively quiet through the 'nineties, and which may also suggest what kind of hopes they placed in the earl of Essex. All the authorities on the tortuous history of James VI's progress to the English throne are agreed that he enjoyed some kind of understanding with Essex at a time when his relations with Robert Cecil were cool and distant. He also deliberately led the puritans – as he did both the other major religious parties – to expect some benefit from his accession. Can we link together Essex's negotiations with Scotland, his interest in such an important representative of puritan opinion as Stephen Egerton, and James's own profession of affection for the gospellers in both Scotland and England? 'That Presbyterians in both kingdoms were working for James's accession is', says David Harris Willson, 'highly probable.'[41] There can be little doubt that if Essex rather than Cecil had conducted the king into his English inheritance, the outlook for the puritans would have been somewhat brighter.

Not that they were greatly discouraged by the downfall of their idol. In these last Elizabethan years the puritans were not closely in touch with political realities, and they were willing to listen to any encouraging sounds projected in their direction. Once Essex was out of the way, Cecil himself was invited to make overtures of his own by Egerton, Sir Francis Hastings and Sir William Fitzwilliam.[42] The culmination of this mood would come in the sublime confidence of the Millenary Petition, which Egerton, in all probability, had a hand in drafting: 'God, we trust, has appointed your highness our physician to heal these diseases; and we say with Mordecai to Esther, "Who knoweth whether you are come to the kingdom for such a time?"'[43] The dashing of these hopes at Hampton Court is the last chapter in the history of the Elizabethan puritans and of their largely abortive movement for the further reformation of the Church of England.

5 The End of a Movement

As ELIZABETH'S REIGN at last approached its conclusion, Josias Nichols described how the godly ministers, finding 'the mighty winds and strong stream' against them, had reserved themselves 'to a better time, when it should please his gracious wisdom to make his own truth to appear, and to move the minds of our superiors to be more favourable.' Although it was dangerous to say so in as many words, even in 1602, the 'better time' could scarcely be looked for so long as the old queen survived. The magistrate for whom the puritans had tarried so long was the king of Scots. Peter Wentworth – their self-appointed vocal conscience on the delicate subject of the succession – had come out in favour of James VI by 1594 at the latest, and it was the puritan printer, Robert Waldegrave, now in James's service, who made this preference public in the second edition of Wentworth's *Pithie exhortation to her Majestie* which appeared in Edinburgh four years later. As early as 1593, that learned if pugnacious divine, Hugh Broughton, had threatened the bishops with a 'Scottish mist', and six years later he addressed the Scottish king as 'next defender of the faith, by the title and right of England', adding as an afterthought, 'if it so please God and R.E.' Later he was one of several preachers who would have some claim on James I, as he put it, 'for publishing of your right and God's truth.' Was it mere chance that two of the four puritan spokesmen at the Hampton Court conference, Thomas Sparke and John Reynolds, were among those ministers who had earlier canvassed the Scottish claim?[1]

James, for his part, took pains to cultivate his admirers. As Calderwood

448

tells us, 'the formalists, the papists, the sincere professors had all their hopes', and he neglected none of them. In the preface added to the 1603, English edition of *Basilikon Doron*, which by a lucky chance was on sale in London within days of Elizabeth's death, James professed respect for 'the learned and grave men' of both sides in the divided English Church. Anabaptists, familists, and other 'brainsick and heady preachers' of the quality of Browne and Penry, were distinguished from those honest and moderate men for whom bishops smelt of a papal supremacy, and the surplice, square cap and other ceremonies were 'outward badges of popish errors'. This was in qualification of the attack which the treatise itself contained on the 'conceited parity' of the presbyterians, 'our vain, proud puritans'. Again, as he left Edinburgh for the south, James told a deputation of Scottish ministers that he would 'show favour to honest men, but not to anabaptists.' These calculated remarks had a profound effect on the puritan response to the new regime. Even after James's true intentions were apparent, the puritans remembered among his 'bypast actions' the profession of sympathy for those who preferred 'the single form of policy' of the Scottish Church to the 'many ceremonies in the Church of England'. Hence the sanguine rhetoric of the millenary petition, and the euphoric tone of the puritan correspondence of 1603. 'We do now with patience expect the consummation of our gracious king's coronation,' wrote Stephen Egerton to Northamptonshire in July, 'after which we hope he will hearken to our motions in the behalf of the Church.' At Norwich in early August one John Robinson of Emmanuel College – who may well have been the future pastor to the Pilgrim Fathers – addressed himself to the text 'This is the day which the Lord hath made', and was encouraged to launch into a confident and explicit attack on the unlearned ministry and the sundry abuses of Church and Commonwealth. Not an unusual theme, but it was thought appropriate to a sermon preached before the mayor and aldermen on James's special day, the anniversary of his deliverance from the Gowrie Plot, three years before.[2]

Dr Mark Curtis has recently suggested that there may have been more substance in these hopes and less of either naivety or guile in James's promises than most historians have been prepared to allow. In 1603 a new reign could still seem to demand a fresh settlement of religion, and the proposed conference, called for in the Millenary Petition and offered at Hampton Court, aroused echoes at least of those formal dialectical exercises which in the recent past had served to introduce religious change in many parts of Europe, as in England in 1559. Like any puritan, James understood by the ministry a ministry of the word, and he had been reared in a Church with few ceremonies, poised between the presbytery and an effete form of diocesan episcopacy.[3] In 1603 it might still have been expected that relations between that church and the Church of England, and between the two kingdoms, would become most intimate, or even, as James himself hoped, that both might be subsumed under some greater political entity, 'as two twins bred in one belly, to love one another as no more two but one estate.'[4] So far as we know, James knew little of the English bishops before his accession, and they are known to have been nervous of his intentions. On the other hand, his immediate entourage now included those men who could interpret the mind of the puritans to the king and his to them: in particular Patrick Galloway, one of his Scottish chaplains, and a puritan gentleman from Northamptonshire, one Lewis Pickering, who had gained a foothold in Court by riding hard to Edinburgh after the death of the queen.[5]

In the summer of 1603 there was more than one sign that a vigorous wind of reform was about to stir the Church. In July the king wrote to the vice-chancellors of Oxford and Cambridge to announce his acceptance of a puritan remedy for the lack of a learned ministry. As the leases of the impropriate parsonages in royal possession fell in, he would let them only to 'learned and painful preachers' without increasing the rents. The point of the letter was to invite the universities to beggar themselves by following the royal example.[6] Meanwhile Whitgift was sufficiently disturbed by the puritan propaganda first to institute a thorough survey of preaching ministers, and later to require of his suffragans an extensive statistical account, parish by parish, of communicants, recusants, pluralists, non-residents and impropriations.[7] Moreover, the archbishop was inclined to take the most serious view of the complaints of corruption in the ecclesiastical courts which had been freely expressed in the last years of Elizabeth and were now, on his own admission, 'more earnestly renewed than at any time heretofore.' On July 4th, the High Commissioners called for an inquiry into the alleged venality and petty tyranny of bishops' chancellors, archdeacons, commissaries and other officials. The bishops were to look into the excessive frequency of court days, the abuse of the *ex officio* procedure, the uncanonical commutation of penance without the bishop's warrant, 'the hard and imperious using of the clergy when they appear before them', and the irregular grant of marriage licences.

This led to a major upheaval in the establishment of at least one diocese. Bishop Jegon of Norwich (himself a new broom, appointed to the see in February) undertook a searching interrogation, summoning his chancellor and the commissaries with their registrars from the four archdeaconries of the diocese. While this process was successfully deflected by the leading officials, it seems to have exposed as offenders – or perhaps scapegoats – the apparitors and proctors of the courts, a class detested since the days of Chaucer's repulsive 'summoner'. In mid-August, Jegon signed orders for the 'present suppressing of the multitude and iniquity of apparitors in my several jurisdictions, against whom I have received many foul complaints.' All were summarily suspended, and those readmitted were made to forswear bribery and extortion as a condition of their appointments. [8]

The danger is that we may be misled into exaggerating the strength of James's reforming intentions by failing to take account of the passing influence over this impressionable monarch of his Scottish chaplain, Patrick Galloway. This man was an accomplished courtier and an old friend of the English puritans of some twenty years' standing. 'We are much bound to Mr Patrick Galloway,' one of them wrote to a Scottish correspondent, 'for his constancy in the behalf of the cause.' According to Whitgift, James's letters to the universities about the better use of impropriations were procured by Galloway and 'some others, altogether ignorant of this our state'. The 'others', Scotsmen evidently, may have included the earl of Mar, an old friend of the preachers on both sides of the border. It was on Galloway that the puritans relied for court news in the months before the conference, and Galloway who in this hopeful season was reported as swaying James against the bishops and in favour of the puritan cause. In December it was said that he had propped up the king's failing resolve to hold the conference, after this had been undermined by Bishop Bilson of Winchester. And when the puritan spokesmen appeared at Hampton Court, Dudley Carleton would refer to them as 'Patrick Galloway and his crew'. So dependent was the whole puritan strategy on this Scottish manipulator that when his schemes collapsed in the reaction which followed the conference, there were those who arrived at the desperate conclusion that he had served as the 'instrument' of the bishops. [9]

From what Galloway and James himself had led them to believe, the puritans were convinced that they could hope for substantial concessions if only they were careful to moderate their demands. The king, it was said, was resolved to have a preaching ministry, to mitigate subscription, and to reform the abuses in church discipline. But there must be no suggestion that the ministers sought an upheaval of the political and ecclesiastical order, or that they claimed a private authority to reform the Church. Hence the title of Nichols's tract, published before the queen's death, *The plea of the innocent*, with its fulsome assurance that the godly ministers waited upon the favour of their superiors and asked no more than that the 'lordly dignities and power of our bishops' might be examined by scripture and brought back 'a degree or twain nearer to Apostolic practice and Christ's institution'. The millenary petitioners spoke (in obvious reference to James's declared sympathies) 'neither as factious men, affecting a popular parity in the Church, nor as schismatics, aiming at the dissolution of the state ecclesiastical.' The assumption of some commentators that the full programme of presbyterianism was at least implicit in their petition will not survive a careful reading of the text. Its general moderation is conveyed by the modest request that the *ex officio* oath might be used 'more sparingly'.'[10]

In the summer of 1603, as they waited for James's first Parliament and the promised conference, the puritan leaders mounted a highly professional campaign, designed to disprove what James was being told from the other side: that the puritans were very few, the Church basically sound, and that if he pleased the bishops 'he shall please all England.' The principal organizers were Galloway and Pickering, referred to in more than one of these documents as 'some of credit and near to his Majesty'. Other key figures included Stephen Egerton of Blackfriars, Field's lieutenant in the campaigns of the 'eighties and a witness of his will;[11] Arthur Hildersham of Ashby-de-la-Zouch, 'chosen', as his *Life* tells us, 'with some few others of his brethren', and 'chiefly entrusted to manage that important business';[12] Edmund Snape; and Henry Jacob, a disturbing ally whose views were very close to separatism. Their task was one of some delicacy. It was to impress the king with the strength of the puritan party in the country and with the seriousness of its intentions, without at the same time arousing his suspicion of a factious and 'Scottizing' conspiracy.

One might suppose that these almost incompatible objectives had been as well balanced as could be in the Millenary Petition, which spoke vaguely of 'more than a thousand' supporters but bore no signatures. However, the counter-attack of their opponents, which included a public censure of the petition by the University of Cambridge and in July a semi-official *Answere* from the vice-chancellor and doctors of Oxford, seemed to call for a show of names. Directions were issued from the high command, 'advices tending to reformation', which were to pass 'from one faithful brother to another with all speed and heed'. Numerous petitions were asked for of three kinds, from noblemen, gentlemen and ministers, 'signed with as many hands of every sort as may be procured,' and directed to Cecil, the Scottish sympathizers at Court, the earl of Mar and Sir George Hume, but more especially to the Council. No petition was to carry more than a few names, 'to avoid the suspicion of conspiracy', and their wording was to vary, presumably for the same reason. They were to desire reformation according to the word of God and the example of the reformed churches, 'provided that they do not expressly desire the removing of bishops.' The emphasis was to be upon the alleged abuses of the existing laws and polity, the *ex officio* oath, subscription, the ceremonies and the iniquities of the ecclesiastical courts. There was to be a new puritan visitation of the Church and its ministry, more thorough and exact than the survey of the ministry of 1584-6.[13]

The response to this directive provides sufficient evidence that the organized puritan movement of Elizabeth's reign, far from dissolving in 1590, had held itself in quiet readiness for just such an opportunity. The conferences had already revived in some districts, if indeed they had ever entirely lapsed, and the 'advices' recommended that 'the opinion of the brethren is by speedy and convenient means to be made known from one conference to another, specially from and to the brethren at London.' To Northamptonshire Egerton wrote on July 14th: 'That only county of Northampton is sufficient to stop the mouths of them that say there are not above some ten or twelve factious persons that desire reformation of these things.' A week later a conference of sixteen ministers met in Northamptonshire. Seven of those present had been active in the *classes* of the 'eighties, and of the co-ordinating committee of three, two – Thomas Stone and John Barbon – had been prominent in the earlier movement. The decisions taken were a repetition in detail of the Northamptonshire campaign of 1584-9: a survey of the ministry, by deaneries, to be summarized by a central committee; two ministers to be sent up to London at parliament time 'by common advice and consent, their places supplied, their charges borne'; petitions to Parliament and to Convocation 'according to the pattern of a supplication of Mr Dudley Fenner's' of 1584. There was to be a petition to the king from 'the justices and gentlemen of the country', and the aged Thomas Cartwright was appointed to ask Sir Christopher Yelverton 'as the principal wether of the flock, to go before the rest' in drafting the petition and canvassing for signatures. It must have been the very last public act of the veteran leader.[14]

We owe our knowledge of these decisions to the chance survival of the letter-book of one of the ministers involved, Robert Smarte of Preston Capes,[15] and although we should expect Northamptonshire to be 'forward', there is no reason to doubt that similar developments were taking place in other counties. In Sussex the preparation of threefold petitions from gentlemen, ministers and commonalty was in the hands of an

453

elaborate organization for which, so far as this county was concerned, there was probably no Elizabethan precedent. The leaders were Samuel Norden, the most radical minister of his shire in the 'eighties, and Henry Jacob, who went down from London to procure signatures. The Sussex puritans had their 'travellers to the Court about the business', their meetings to draft petitions, their 'carriers and procurers of subscriptions to the same', all concealed by a 'covenant' of 'silence with everyone they deal with'. The campaign was organized locally from 'conventicles' of ministers and active laymen held in ministers' houses. Signatures were gathered 'sometimes at meeting at sermons, sometimes after evening prayers in church, where the petition was read unto the people, much by private solicitation, sometimes by a constable, and at one time by an officer or sergeant.'[16] There were petitions from the gentlemen of Suffolk and from the ministers of Oxfordshire,[17] the new surveys of the ministry for Essex and Staffordshire and part of Yorkshire.[18] Action was looked for in Lancashire, and it was thought that Edward Fleetwood of Wigan, still the leading spirit in that hostile country as he had been fifteen years before, would 'take order for all these parts about him.'[19] Three Elizabethan veterans, Melanchthon Jewel, John Travers and Edmund Snape were still the managers of the campaign in the West Country.[20]

A royal proclamation of October 24th which contained complaints of 'tumult, sedition and violence' is evidence that this agitation tarnished the image of orderly submission which the puritans had displayed in the Millenary Petition.[21] Equally provocative were the more flagrant acts of nonconformity of those few extremists who refused to have anything to do with the Book of Common Prayer. When Egerton heard of this, he expressed lively concern, 'for his Majesty willeth that such be repressed as use new forms.' Legal opinion was to be taken to test the validity of the distinction between employing an alternative liturgy and the more normal puritan practice of using the established Book 'saving only some omissions'.[22] Those who were unwilling to temper their nonconformity according to the need of the hour would be unlikely to hide under a bushel their equally radical rejection of the episcopal polity of the Anglican Church. By the end of June, Henry Jacob had communicated to some of his friends a new form of petition which contained a patently presbyterian formula, the request 'that the present state of our Church be further reformed in all things needful according to the rule of God's holy word, and agreeably to the example of other reformed churches, which have restored both the doctrine and discipline, as it was delivered by our Saviour Christ and His holy apostles.' In early June this petition was scrutinized by a general conference in which both wings of the movement seem to have been represented with near parity. When it was distributed on July 14th by 'the brethren in London', it was with the proviso that petitioners might, if they so pleased, stop short of 'the example of other churches', or descend at this point into a recital of specific abuses. 'Herein we leave every man.' In Oxfordshire, the ministers chose the moderate alternative, while Northamptonshire, as we should expect, adopted the petition in its original presbyterian form.[23]

If the puritan conferences had been invited to appoint representatives for the forthcoming conference, both the moderate and the more extreme voices might have been heard. But the spokesmen at Hampton Court were to be government nominees. There was no intention on the side of the king and his advisers of according them the status of delegates for organized constituencies. Indeed, those leaders who were known to have been implicated in the agitation of the summer seem to have been excluded from the conference for that very reason. In August the Council warned nine bishops and twelve other divines to present themselves at Court on November 1st, the date originally assigned to the conference. This was a single, undivided list which took no account of the two main parties, let alone of distinct positions within the puritan movement. John Knewstub here jostled with his old friend Lancelot Andrewes, who had by now advanced well beyond his early puritanism. But the four ministers who would ultimately appear as the plaintiffs at Hampton Court were all named in this first list. In Northamptonshire, it was thought in August that the puritan representation would consist of Walter Travers, John Reynolds of Oxford and Laurence Chaderton of Cambridge, with Knewstub from Suffolk and John Ireton and Arthur Hildersham from Leicestershire.[24] A later list, apparently composed by Patrick Galloway, names Reynolds, Hildersham, Chaderton and Knewstub, but substitutes Humfrey Fen of Coventry for Ireton and adds the name of Cartwright, who would be dead by the time that the postponed conference met in mid-January. (His old antagonist, Whitgift, was to survive the conference by a month.) And Travers here gives place to Dr Thomas Sparke of Bletchley. Sparke had stood with Travers in defence of the cause at that earlier and analogous disputation which the earl of Leicester had staged at Lambeth in December 1584, but he was no presbyterian.[25] The two surviving extremists, Fen and Hildersham, were later dropped from the list, and in the event, only four spokesmen appeared to state the puritan case at Hampton Court. Two of them were so near the middle of the road as scarcely to merit the name of puritan: Reynolds, 'the foreman' as Dr

Barlow calls him in his semi-official account, and Sparke. The other two were responsible, senior men, who, if presbyterians by conviction, were conscious of the need for realistic moderation: Chaderton and Knewstub.

Before the king received these four principals on the second day of the conference, another and much larger assembly of puritan ministers had held private meetings not far away, at the conference 'but not in place' as the record of their decisions explains. Their meeting implies the presumption on the puritan side that they were to be represented at the conference by delegates, and the thirty ministers who attended represented their own 'countries'. Moreover, many of them were the very same men who would have appeared for their local conferences in the 'eighties: Snape for Exeter, Nichols for Kent, Fleetwood for Lancashire, Hildersham for Leicestershire, Norden, amongst others, for Sussex and Dyke for Hertfordshire. London was represented by Egerton, Jacob – and Thomas Wilcox. In this list there is striking confirmation of both continuity and progress through the hidden years. Some districts were represented which so far as we know played little or no part in the Elizabethan general conferences: Oxfordshire (represented by the great John Dod), Wiltshire, Portsmouth, Salisbury, Surrey, Middlesex and Buckinghamshire. Amongst these names there may have been about as many radicals as moderates, and there were certainly at least a dozen delegates who stood well to the left of any of the official spokesmen at the conference proper. Three of these, Hildersham, Egerton and Fleetwood, headed the delegation which communicated the instructions of this body to the principals.[26]

Yet there was no suggestion in these formal demands that any radical change was looked for in the organization or government of the Church, or in its public worship. This can hardly be insisted upon too strongly, for all too many (and notably the late Roland Green Usher) have indulged in the unwarranted assumption that full-blooded presbyterianism was implied and even openly advocated in the presentation of the puritan case at Hampton Court. The 'earnest suit' of the puritan delegates, addressed to those 'chosen to deal for the cause', was first, that they should ask for the establishment of a sound, resident teaching ministry, and for the raising of a 'competent maintenance' by such means as the uniting of small parishes and the redemption of impropriate tithes. (Here, as previously in the Millenary Petition, was a recognition of the economic problems of the Church which had been conspicuously absent under Elizabeth.) After this, they were to request a revision of the Articles of Religion and the restriction of subscription to such of the Articles as were of the nature of 'the confession of the faith of our churches'. The proposed revision was in assertion of the Calvinist doctrine of grace, and it reflects the renewed interest of recent months in the theological issues contested between the strict Calvinists and their opponents. At the conference itself, Reynolds gave doctrinal reform pride of place, which it would never have enjoyed in the high Elizabethan days. The spokesmen were further instructed to desire the abolition of offensive ceremonies, or at least the allowance of some latitude in their use, and the correction of the liturgy 'according to the word' (but not the abolition of the Prayer Book or its replacement by some 'new form'). They were to ask for the restitution of prophesying in both universities and parishes, the revision of the canons and ecclesiastical laws according to the declared intention of the Henrician Act for the Submission of the Clergy, and the redress of abuses in the church courts, including the *ex officio* oath. They were to demand the better regulation of the Sabbath, the abolition of other holy days, and the authorization of a new short catechism.[27]

That the moderates were far from dominating these deliberations is indicated in a lengthy assertion, buttressed with an array of syllogisms, that such ceremonies as the surplice and the ring in marriage were not indifferent but 'simply unlawful'. This opinion had always been the shibboleth of the more extreme brethren. It was emphasized here because Reynolds, for one, did not hold it and was consequently reluctant to express it at the conference.[28] Nevertheless, the assembled ministers came no closer to demanding any significant change in church government than the request that 'the ministers' right in the exercise of the church censures and ordination of ministers may be restored.' The admission of the parish clergy to some share in discipline and ordination would not necessarily have entailed the replacement of episcopal by presbyterian government. What may well be another version of these instructions explains in detail the kind of reform that seems to have been intended. The conduct of instance causes (civil actions, between parties) was to remain with the officials of the bishops' and archdeacons' courts, and excommunication was not to be used in this branch of the Church's jurisdiction. On the other hand, 'matters criminal', the office causes brought against both ministers and people, were to be reserved to the bishop or archdeacon in person, or to their deputy in each deanery. This resident, preaching dean was to hold a quarterly court, assisted by six or more of the preaching clergy of the division. Ordinations were to be upon the testimonials either of the university or of the dean and other preachers of the deanery, and they were to be conducted with the assistance of the same 'six grave preachers'.[29] Some of the king's pronouncements at the conference suggest that these proposals were not widely divergent from his own views on the proper conduct of spiritual government.

The four spokesmen deviated from these instructions only in their moderation and reticence. One hostile account has it that Sparke 'spake very sparingly' and that Chaderton was 'mute as any fish'. Reynolds, in effect, played a solo part. James's celebrated outburst against the presbytery and his insistence on its incompatibility with monarchy was occasioned not by any demand for the removal of bishops but by Reynolds's comparatively innocuous request that in the exercise of episcopal discipline there should be more reliance on synodical procedures and less on the agency of lay officials. The parochial clergy should be encouraged to meet every fortnight or three weeks in rural chapters, from which matters were to be referred to the archdeacon, and from him to the episcopal synod, where the bishop was to sit 'with his presbytery'. Reynolds had in mind a system of episcopacy in presbytery, not a purely presbyterian polity, and even the unsympathetic Dr Barlow implies that James was too hasty in 'thinking that they aimed at a Scottish presbytery.'[30] The king himself, in private conference with the bishops on the first day, had asked why excommunications were performed by laymen, and why the bishops were not assisted in this and other functions such as ordination by the dean and chapter or other ministers 'of gravity and account'. On the last day, James made an explicit recommendation to this effect, and proposed that excommunication should be reformed 'both in name and nature', and that as the civil penalty imposed by lay judges for contempt of court, it should be replaced by a writ out of Chancery. These instructions have left some mark on the Constitutions and Canons of 1604, where in ordination provision is made for the bishop to be assisted 'at the imposition of hands' by members of his chapter, 'or other sufficient preachers' of the diocese to the number of three at the least; and where pronouncement of sentences of deprivation or deposition is limited to the bishop in person, assisted, when the court was held in the country, by at least two 'grave ministers and preachers'.[31]

As for Prayer Book matters, Reynolds and Knewstub followed their brief in protesting that the sign of the cross and the surplice were 'teaching ceremonies', and so more than mere 'matters indifferent', but this was not Reynolds's own view of the matter, and it was stated with little conviction, as an argument for the toleration of nonconformity rather than as a justification for any radical surgery in the text of the Prayer Book. No more time seems to have been devoted to these major *gravamina* than to minor, textual errors, and less than had been earlier spent on a number of faults in the Articles of Religion and in the translation of the Bishops' Bible. Dr Reynolds was presumably responsible for the heavy concentration on points of theological difficulty, as for the tendency to descend into scholarly particulars. His indictment of the established religion was not very impressive. At least, it failed to impress the royal governor. 'If these be the greatest matters you be grieved with,' James is reported to have said, after a prolonged discussion of faulty points of translation, 'I need not have been troubled with such importunities and complaints as have been made unto me; some other more private course might have been taken for your satisfaction.' 'And withal, looking upon the lords, he shook his head, smiling.'[32]

All this, as we shall see, was damaging and even fatal to the militant puritan cause which we have now traced through forty years of frustrated expectation. Yet the Hampton Court conference and its outcome are not to be over-simplified, still less to be over-dramatized. These are the dangers of attempting to sum the matter up in the more intemperate and quotable royal outbursts, as reported in Barlow's *Summe and substance of the conference*. These three days of argument in the royal presence chamber must have appeared a little more like a round-table conference, and a little less like the once-for-all confrontation of two embattled parties which most accounts convey, and which the radical puritans had fondly expected. No more than the godly preachers were the bishops a monolithic group with but one voice, and that the voice of Bancroft. Babington of Worcester, Rudd of St David's, Robinson of Carlisle and Matthew of Durham were all Calvinists in their theology and they were not willing opponents of the puritan ministers. Stephen Egerton could even report in the months before the conference that the first three had 'turned puritans, to whom I doubt not but Durham will join.'[33] These four, who were all present at the conference, were in closer sympathy with Reynolds and Sparke than they were with their episcopal colleagues, Bancroft and Bilson, just as these two moderate puritan spokesmen held a position closer to the moderate bishops than to the radicals who regarded them as their delegates. Reynolds and Robinson had spent many years together in the same college, and were at least as closely allied in the Oxford of the 1590s as were the leading Calvinist divines of Cambridge, Whitaker and Chaderton.[34] As for the king himself, Dr Curtis has rightly insisted in his recent reassessment of the conference that he was very far from ranging himself unreservedly with the bishops against the puritan representatives, as Barlow's heavily biassed account would suggest: so much is clear from some of the other surviving memoranda of the occasion, and in particular from one important though anonymous account which has not received as much attention as it deserves.[35] But neither was James a very correct or impartial chairman. His interventions were made almost as if he were a third party to the discussions.

Such decisions as were made at Hampton Court were more indicative of a round-table conference than of the disputations which changed the faith of other parts of Europe in the years of the Reformation. Some of the matters on which the king agreed to act were not at all controversial in their nature, such as the planting of ministers in Ireland, and the new procedure for the presentment of non-communicants. Others were, in effect, neutralized by royal orders made at or after the conference, notably the authorization of a new English Bible. As Dr Curtis has reminded us, the Authorised Version was not the only reform to which the king consented at Hampton Court, although it was to prove the only enduring monument to the conference. Indeed, more was actually carried through, at least on paper, than Dr Curtis seems to be aware of. As we have seen, the Canons of 1604 incorporate some modest limitation of episcopal government in line with the notions shared by Reynolds and the king. And the Prayer Book, as printed after Hampton Court, removed a substantial puritan grievance in appearing to exclude lay persons from the administration of private baptism by twice referring in the rubric to 'the lawful minister'. This was a compromise, agreed to at the first day's conference in the absence of the puritan spokesmen, and 'not so much stuck at by the bishops', who were themselves divided on the question.[36]

Of wider significance than these small accommodations was James's ecclesiastical policy as it unfolded in the years after Hampton Court, and which can be witnessed both in his activities as a royal theologian, and in his episcopal appointments and promotions. Bancroft became archbishop of Canterbury in 1604 and proceeded to crush nonconformity with his campaign of subscription to the new Canons. But if we can put out of our minds the Laudian advance of later decades, which was hardly to be foreseen before the death of James, it will appear that Bancroft's achievement was limited and partly illusory. With the succession of George Abbot in 1611 there was to be no continuity in archiepiscopal policy, while at York Calvinist followed Calvinist, Matthew Hutton giving place to Toby Matthew. As Dr Marchant's researches have suggested, the promotion of Richard Neile in 1632 marked the first real watershed in the history of the diocese of York since the appointment of Grindal in 1570.[37] Usher was no doubt justified in representing the years of Bancroft's primacy as an age of ecclesiastical reconstruction, but they were not a total departure from those Elizabethan conditions which had for so long contained puritan religion within the Church. Calvinism was anything but a declining cause in England for as long as James I lived, and these were lean years for the English 'Arminians'. Evidently Hampton Court was very far from marking a total repudiation of puritanism in the broader sense.[38]

Yet such modest reforms as the king conceded – not all of which took effect[39] – were not calculated to meet the aspirations of the more radical puritans for whom Reynolds had spoken. Viewed from the position which they held, Hampton Court was an almost total irrelevance. A case which had been deliberately understated in the brief prepared for the four spokesmen was subjected by them to still further attenuation, and even so was for the most part rejected. The ice had cracked and stirred, but there was no sign of the general thaw which these puritans had hoped to see. James brought a fresh mind to bear on the English Church, and as an observer he was not uncritical, yet he had no deep objection to the substance of the existing church settlement, and his concern was only 'to amend abuses, as natural to bodies politic.' His active interest in church reform, unlike his enduring concern with theology, scarcely survived the conference itself. James was not the man to pursue political and administrative tasks to their conclusion, and the programme of reconstruction which followed Hampton Court was Bancroft's rather than the king's.[40]

Far from achieving what was hoped of it, the conference did the puritan cause positive harm. It was now clear, if it had not been so before, that James was as hostile to the very principles of dissent and nonconformity as ever Elizabeth had been. A lifetime's acquaintance with the pertinacity of the puritan conscience in Scotland had taught him to make no concessions whatsoever to this spirit. It is true that when, on the last day of the conference, Laurence Chaderton made a special plea that the preachers of Lancashire should not be pressed to use the surplice and the sign of the cross, James was prepared to grant a strictly temporary toleration. But this, which was less than had been asked for, served merely to accentuate his general resolve to enforce obedience.[41] In this resolve there was an element of contempt as well as of hostility. In Scotland, militant Calvinism was a force which James was obliged to respect while he opposed it, but a number of his pronouncements at Hampton Court suggest surprise that the case presented by the English puritans was so weak, and commended with such mildness and deference. When Reynolds raised no objection to the square cap (shades of William Turner, the puritan dean of Wells!) the king is supposed to have turned to the bishops to say: 'Well then, you may now safely wear your caps. But I shall tell you, if you should walk in one street in Scotland with such a cap on your head, if I were not with you, you should be stoned to death with your cap.' Whether or not, as one account has it, 'Dr Reynolds and his brethren' were 'utterly condemned for seely men', their performance evidently offended the king without convincing him that they were a force to be seriously reckoned with.[42]

As with the Jansenists of the France of Louis XIV, it was the singularity of the puritans and their very existence as a disaffected party within the Church which provoked alarm and offence more than any of their doctrines. In the agitation which had continued throughout James's first year, as in the concerted resistance which Bancroft would later provoke, there was what Samuel Rawson Gardiner called 'a presumption of a presbyterian temper',[43] whether or not presbyterian principles were openly advocated. Yet at Hampton Court James was confronted with a paper tiger. Dr Reynolds was a pale shadow of Andrew Melville, and what he had to say failed to justify in the king's mind the schismatic and implicitly disloyal posture which his constituents had adopted. The mistake of understating the puritan case was one which John Field, or, for that matter, Edmund Snape, would not have made, but in the light of Elizabethan experience, James's misleading promises, and the awe of the Englishman in the face of monarchy, it was wholly understandable, and it is not likely that in English political conditions any other course of action would have proved more successful. The puritans were nevertheless the victims of their own strategy, and unfortunately they were not the only victims. Hampton Court can only have confirmed the king's grave underestimation of the strength and potentiality of English puritanism, and this error on his side was to have damaging consequences for the whole Church and nation.

As soon as it became clear that the new reign was to see not a new settlement of the Church but a closer definition and more active enforcement of the old, the solidarity of the puritan movement on the carefully modulated programme of 1603 showed signs of foundering, with the radicals complaining that their representatives had failed to convey the true gravity of the case. According to Henry Jacob, the matters in controversy were 'but nakedly propounded, and some not at all touched.' Moreover, he alleged that the four ministers of the conference were no true representatives. 'Most of the persons appointed to speak for the ministers' were 'not of their choosing, nor nomination, nor of their judgment in the matters then and now in question, but of a clean contrary.' Humfrey Fen, himself a possible contender at Hampton Court, shared this conspiratorial view of 'that show of a dispute'. He is said to have written to Chaderton at the time with a plea 'not to betray their cause', and almost thirty years later he could record the conviction that the spokesmen had merely acted a part, like stage-players. They were men 'purposely chosen', who, 'excepting one reverend father, never took the question about ceremonies to heart.' Some were not afraid to hint at the most sinister reasons for the fiasco. Demanding a genuine disputation with a free choice of the spokesmen, Jacob alleged that the 'whole managing' of the conference implied that it had been 'underhand plotted and procured by the prelates themselves', and that Galloway had been their 'instrument'. 'What sincerity was there meant,' asked the Scottish Calderwood, 'when for the sincere party were nominated two that were very corrupt? Apparently they were nominated only to be spies, and to prevaricate.'[44]

In support of these wild charges it could be said that all four spokesmen at Hampton Court had then and there promised in general terms to conform, and that one of them, Dr Sparke, soon became an open apologist for conformity and subscription with the publication in 1607 of his *Brotherly perswasion to unitie and uniformitie*. Sparke, it was said, had failed to speak out against the corruptions of the Church 'though he were well provided for it, and promised faithfully to have done it.' Now he professed himself entirely satisfied with his reception by the king (which had included a private audience) and he urged his brethren to follow his example and conform as the only course open to those who respected the royal supremacy. Moreover, he explained that even before the conference he had publicly declared his reluctance 'to be drawn to stand in any opposition or contention with the reverend fathers about any of these matters.'[45]

Throughout this account of the puritan movement we have noticed that two divergent views of the nature of the Prayer Book ceremonies and of episcopacy – whether these things were indifferent or inherently evil – identified the two wings of the party, which at times of crisis were held together with some difficulty. This cleavage was now to become an open fissure, for while moderate puritans could find no sufficient reason for indefinitely withholding conformity, those who believed that the Anglican liturgy and polity were actually repugnant in God's sight had now, as never before, to consider how in conscience they could remain in full fellowship with the established Church. As for Sparke, his *Brotherly perswasion* declared that his opinion had always been that the ceremonies, 'being but of the nature they are', were to be yielded unto rather than that a man should be deprived of his ministry on their account. And nothing that he had read in thirty-four years – that is, since the publication of the earliest presbyterian manifestoes – had convinced him that the presbyterian polity was scriptural, or that it was 'so answerable or conformable to the perpetual government used by God for and in his Church' as was episcopacy. 'Perpetual government' was the phrase invoked by Bishop Bilson in defence of the highest doctrine of episcopacy yet asserted in the post-Reformation Church, and Sparke publicly associated himself with the bishop's opinion. Certainly if the unity of the Church was to be conserved and an end put to 'all show of schism', episcopacy and ceremonial matters of indifference had to be swallowed. Evidently Sparke now found radical puritanism and sectarianism a more serious threat to the Church's true interests than royal and episcopal policy.[46]

The greater part of the puritan ministry, after showing some will to resist Archbishop Bancroft's renewed campaign for uniformity, was to agree with Sparke, if reluctantly and without his gratuitous display of changing sides. So much for the 'many hundred worthy ministers' who John Burgess thought would 'surely die' rather than submit to the ceremonies.[47] Of the thousand and more ministers who were supposed to have consented to the Millenary Petition, and of the seven hundred and forty-six signatories whose names were attached to the *Apologye* of the ministers of Lincoln diocese against Bancroft's proceedings of 1604, Dr Babbage believes that not more than ninety beneficed clergy preferred deprivation to subscription and conformity.[48]

The subscribing majority could still be described as puritans, although, like the ministers of Baxter's youth, relatively few of them were nonconformists. Life for many of them was far from intolerable. A number of bishops were still sympathetic, and under their indulgent rule the conversion of England continued, especially as the ranks of parish and market-town lecturers continued to swell. Some presbyterian veterans, like 'old Mr Fen of Coventry', retained their vision unimpaired. In the preamble to a will which proved too hot for the bishop's court to handle, he reaffirmed his faith in the discipline of the Church in detail, and roundly declared that the Church of England maintained 'a shameful schism against all the reformed churches of the gospel'. 'Yet I do not hold it lawful for these corruptions to separate from communion of the churches of England, if therein a Christian may enjoy true doctrine, with the sacraments, from a minister able to teach the truth', and where it was not possible to avoid subscription.[49] That was an authentically Elizabethan sentiment, written in 1631. But for most church puritans, the presbyterian polity, or any other scheme for the extensive reparation of the Church's structure, institutions and ministry, became a remote and irrelevant idea. By 'reformation' they tended to mean the pursuit of a piety and a moral order of the puritan type, not the establishment of the external forms and symbols of a reformed church. Only when Bishop Wren ruled in Norwich and Archbishop Neile in York and Laud over all in Canterbury, and when, after 1640, the opportunity arrived to reverse the policies of prelacy, only then were these church puritans encouraged to consider once again the relation of outward forms to godliness. And by that time the puritans of the Long Parliament and of the Westminster Assembly of Divines were inclined to work out their own salvation, preferring to renew the search for scriptural principles, rather than to accept ready-made the prescriptions of the Elizabethan puritans or of the Scottish Church. Previous history would at that time be reflected in the wide appeal of the presbyterian polity, but equally in the conspicuous failure of the presbyterians to command anything like universal assent.

And what of the radical puritans in the aftermath of Hampton Court? Those who held that the ceremonies and the polity of the Elizabethan settlement were actually unlawful had never found it easy to justify their participation in the sacraments and fellowship of the parish churches. With characteristic Elizabethan pragmatism, their presence in the national Church implied the optimistic presumption that further reformation and the removal of offence would not be long delayed. They could not prolong indefinitely the acceptance of an alien system which they had no power to alter, especially when the inconclusive arrangements of the Elizabethan Church were replaced with the uncompromising symmetry of Bancroft's new Canons. After 1604 they had either to choose the separatist way or to assimilate the subtle thinking of the non-separating congregationalists who denied that the ecclesiastical laws of the realm either made or unmade the churches of God in England in their true essence. To our eyes – if not as yet to theirs – it may seem apparent that both paths led to independency and the fading of the bright Elizabethan vision of a godly commonwealth, instructed in one doctrine from the pulpit of every parish church, and corrected by one uniform and wholesome discipline. The convictions of the independents were among the factors which would later frustrate the work of the Westminster Assembly and deprive English presbyterianism of its long-delayed hour of triumph.

For us 1604, a moment of disillusionment and confusion, is the end of the story. Although Bancroft's campaign for subscription was to arouse a resistance more impressive even than that which had greeted Whitgift's

465

first onslaught twenty years before, the puritans were never again to confront the government as a reasonably united and cohesive party with a single programme for the purification of the English Church. It was now virtually inevitable, as it had not been before, that protestant dissent in England would develop as a fragmented sectarianism, agreed as to the *delenda* but not as to the *agenda* of the further reformation.[50] Hampton Court is therefore the proper place at which to conclude an account of the Elizabethan puritan movement, within months of the almost symbolical demise of both Thomas Cartwright and John Whitgift. The historian who pursues the history of puritanism into the decades that follow will be concerned with a persistent tradition, and yet with something more diffuse, lacking in specific and short-term objectives, no longer a movement in the strictest sense.

We are left at the end with unanswerable questions. Would there have been a national schism in the mid-seventeenth century if James had embraced the programme of the millenary petition? Could the early Stuarts by accommodating the broadly based centre of the puritan movement have avoided those major and permanent divisions in English protestant Christianity which have denied to the Church of England the wide national assent enjoyed for much of its history by the Church of Scotland or by the Lutheran state churches of Scandinavia? How much rosier the prospects might have been for reform of the familiar and almost perennial abuses of the English Church if James I had not forfeited the confidence of the many puritans in the responsible and creative classes! Some will feel that the repulsion of some sections of society was not too great a price to pay for the exclusion from the national Church of an unwelcome puritan spirit. Others will value the contribution to English civilization of large and vigorous nonconformist bodies outside the establishment, and will argue that our history would have been the poorer without the correction and stimulus of the dissenting tradition.

These are imponderables, and, as an Elizabethan might say, such speculations are likely to be ruled more by our affections than by our learning. However, this much can perhaps be said. That in 1603-4 the puritan movement had profited from earlier failure and had come close to solving its internal problems. That the proposals with which it confronted James I contained no revolutionary threat to the monarchical-episcopal constitution of the Church and were consistent with that generously protestant interpretation of the Elizabethan settlement which in fact prevailed in some dioceses and under certain bishops from the time of Grindal to the rise of Laud sixty years later. And that it would not have been beyond the ingenuity of statesmanship for James I to have escaped the fatal antagonism of the puritan conscience. This, at least, was the consistent opinion of the greatest mind of the age, Francis Bacon. The concessions required, if large, were not fundamental, and they were in effect granted for some parts of the country as the consequence of a number of James's own episcopal appointments. To say all this is not to forget the contribution of an intransigent minority of puritan extremists to the wrecking of any such moderate settlement of the Church. But if this book has contributed anything to the understanding of English church history, I should like to think that it has helped to establish this: that surrender to the drastic prescriptions of the presbyterians on the one hand, and exclusion from an interest in the national Church of the great and growing body of religious opinion and experience which we know as puritanism on the other, were never in this period the simple alternatives open to the government of the Church of England. That our modern conception of Anglicanism commonly excludes puritanism is both a distortion of a part of our religious history and a memorial to one of its more regrettable episodes.

Abbreviations

A.P.C.	*Acts of the Privy Council of England*, n.s., ed. J. R. Dasent, 1890–1907
BL	Bodleian Library
BM	British Museum:
	MS. Add. Additional Manuscripts
	MS. Harl. Harleian Manuscripts
	MS. Lansd. Lansdowne Manuscripts
'Classical Movement'	Patrick Collinson, 'The Puritan Classical Movement in the Reign of Elizabeth I', unpubl. London Ph.D. thesis, 1957
CS	Camden Society
C.S.P.	Calendars of State Papers (Foreign, Scottish, Spanish, Venetian), Rolls Series
CUL	Cambridge University Library
Daungerous positions	Richard Bancroft, *Daungerous positions and proceedings, published and practised within this iland of Brytaine*, 1593 (1344)
Dedham Minutes	R. G. Usher (ed.), *The Presbyterian Movement in the Reign of Queen Elizabeth, as Illustrated by the Minute Book of the Dedham Classis, 1582–1589*, CS 3rd ser. viii. 1905
D'Ewes	Sir Simon D'Ewes (ed.), *The Journals of all the Parliaments during the Reign of Queen Elizabeth, both of the House of Lords and House of Commons*, 1682

DNB	*Dictionary of National Biography*
DWL	Dr Williams's Library
E.H.R.	*English Historical Review*
ENT	Elizabethan Nonconformist Texts
ERO	Essex Record Office:
	D/ACA Act-Books of the Archdeaconry of Colchester
	D/AEA Act-Books of the Archdeaconry of Essex
	QSR Quarter-Sessions Rolls
GLRO	Greater London Record Office, London Division
Grindal,	*The Remains of Edmund Grindal, D.D.*, ed. W. Nicholson,
Remains	PS, 1843
HMC	Reports of the Historical Manuscripts Commission
HRO	Hertfordshire Record Office
ITL	Inner Temple Library
J.E.H.	*Journal of Ecclesiastical History*
Letters of	Patrick Collinson (ed.), *Letters of Thomas Wood, Puritan,*
Thomas	*1566–1577*, Bulletin of the Institute of Historical Research,
Wood	Special Supplement v. 1960
LPL	Lambeth Palace Library
Neale, i	J. E. Neale, *Elizabeth I & her Parliaments, 1559–1581*, 1953
Neale, ii	,, ,, *Elizabeth I & her Parliaments, 1584–1601*, 1957
NNRO	Norfolk & Norwich Record Office
Parker	*Correspondence of Matthew Parker, D.D.*, ed. Bruce and
Correspon-	Perowne, PS, 1853
dence	
PRO	Public Record Office:
	S.P. 12 State Papers, Domestic, Eliz. I
	S.P. 14 ,, ,, , ,, , Jas. I
	S.P. 15 ,, ,, , ,, , Addenda, Ed. VI to
	Jas. I
	S.P. 16 ,, ,, , ,, , Chas. I
	S.P. 52 ,, ,, , Scotland, Eliz. I
	S.P. 59 Border Papers
	S.P. 83 State Papers, Foreign, Holland and Flanders
	Sta. Cha. 5 Records of the Court of Star Chamber, Eliz.
A parte	*A parte of a register, contayninge sundrie memorable matters, written by divers godly and learned in our time, which stande for and desire the reformation of our Church, in discipline and ceremonies, according to the pure worde of God, and the lawe of our lande*, Edinburgh or Middleburg (?) 1593 (10400)

PS	Parker Society
Puritan Manifestoes	W. H. Frere & C. E. Douglas (eds.), *Puritan Manifestoes: A study of the Origin of the Puritan Revolt. With a Reprint of the Admonition to the Parliament and Kindred Documents, 1572*, repr. 1954
Scott Pearson	A. F. Scott Pearson, *Thomas Cartwright & Elizabethan Puritanism, 1535–1603*, 1925
Seconde Parte	A. Peel (ed.), *The Seconde Parte of a Register; Being a Calendar of Manuscripts under that title intended for publication by the Puritans about 1593, and now in Dr Williams's Library, London*, 2 vols. 1915
Survay	Richard Bancroft, *A survay of the pretended holy discipline, contayning the beginninges, successe, parts, proceedings, authority and doctrine of it*, 1593 (1352)
Z.L., i	*The Zurich Letters, 1558–1579*, ed. H. Robinson, PS, 1842
Z.L., ii	*The Zurich Letters (Second Series), 1558–1602*, ed. H. Robinson, PS, 1845

The numbers quoted in brackets after the titles of English books printed before 1641 refer to the entries in *A Short-Title Catalogue of Books … , 1475–1640*, ed. A. W. Pollard & G. R. Redgrave, 1926.

All references to the works of John Strype are to the Oxford edition of 1821–4.

Notes and References

Part 1 Chapter 1

1. BM, MS. Lansd. 377, fols. 8ᵛ–28ʳ.
2. Laurence Humphrey, *The nobles, or of nobility*, 1563 (13964), Sig. l. vi.
3. Quoted, G. F. A. Best, *Temporal Pillars*, p. 168.
4. Dedication to the earl of Leicester of Robert Fyll's translation of Theodore Beza, *A briefe and piththie [sic] sum of the Christian faith*, 1563 (2007), Sig.★ iiiʳ.
5. Quoted in my *A Mirror of Elizabethan Puritanism: The Life and Letters of 'Godly Master Dering'*, Friends of Dr Williams's Library 17th Lecture, 1963 (pub. 1964), p. 4.
6. BM, MS. Add. 27632, fol. 48ʳ.
7. George Gifford, *A dialogue betweene a papist and a protestant*, 1582 (11849), fol. 38ʳ.
8. Most of our knowledge of these congregations depends upon the eighth volume (in Cattley and Townshend's edn) of John Foxe's *Acts and Monuments*. See also a letter from Thomas Lever to Bullinger, Aug. 8th, 1559, *Z.L.*, ii. 28–31. For evidence of a concealed movement of protestant refugees within England, see D. M. Loades in *Bull. Inst. Hist. Research*, xxxv. 87–97.
9. PRO, S.P. 12/2/10; *Writings of Henry Barrow, 1587–1590*, ed. Carlson, ENT iii. 283; Humphrey, op. cit., Epistle, Sig. A ii; W. Haller, *Foxe's Book of Martyrs & the Elect Nation*, 1963.
10. *Writings of Barrow*, ENT iii. 558.
11. For some of these expressions, see George Gifford, *A briefe discourse of... the countrie divinitie*, 1582 (11845).
12. *A dialogue concerning the strife of our Church*, 1584 (10396), p. 49.
13. Bartimaeus Andrewes, *Certaine verie worthie godlie and profitable sermons*, 1583 (585), p. 185.
14. Percival Wiburn, *A checke or reproofe of M. Howlet's untimely schreeching*, 1581 (25586), fol. 15ᵛ.
15. Quoted, H. C. Porter, in *Trans. Royal Hist. Socy*, 5th ser. xiv. 162–3.
16. *An answere for the tyme to the examination put in print*, 1566 (10388), pp. 28–9.
17. Quoted, R. Thomas, 'The Break-up of Nonconformity', in *The Beginnings of Nonconformity*, Hibbert Lectures 1962 (1964), p. 33.
18. Henry Parker?, *A discourse concerning puritans*, 1641, Sig. 2.

Chapter 2

1. 'The Elizabethan Acts of Supremacy and Uniformity', *E.H.R.*, lxv. 304–32; Neale, i. 51–84.
2. *Z.L.*, ii. 5, 11; PRO, S.P.12/3/9; *Seconde Parte*, ii. 58.
3. I am obliged to the History of Parliament Trust and to Sir John Neale as editor of the Elizabethan section of the *History of Parliament* for allowing me to refer to a transcript of this list (PRO, E371/402(1)).
4. *Z.L.*, ii. 13.
5. This suggestion, which was Professor Neale's, has been scouted by Fr Philip Hughes (*Reformation in England*, 1963 edn, iii. 26, n.4). But see the reports of the clerical party sent to their continental friends and their later recollections (*Z.L.*, i. 10, 18; ii. 19). See also a comment of the Venetian ambassador (*C.S.P., Venice*, vii. 52–3).
6. *The Diary of Henry Machyn*, ed. Nichols, CS, xlii. 189–90; *Z.L.*, i. 10–11, 18.
7. *Cambridge Modern History*, ii. 569–70, 587–9, cf. *E.H.R.*, xviii. 517–32. For the Confession of Augsburg in French politics, see Evennett, *The Cardinal of Lorraine & the Council of Trent*.
8. *A Brief Discourse of the Troubles at Frankfort*, ed. Arber, 1908.
9. ITL, MS. Petyt 538/47, fols. 380, 380x.
10. *Original Letters*, PS, ii. 753–5; *Z.L.*, i. 169.
11. Mr Peter Kirk (Gravesend), Dec. 14th, 1962; Hansard, *Parliamentary Debates*, 5th ser., vol. 669, col. 783.
12. Cardwell, *History of Conferences*, p. 176.
13. *C.S.P., Span.*, i. 105; *Parker Correspondence*, pp. 79–95, 105; *Z.L.*, i. 55, 63–4, 68, 73–4. 85; *Diary of Henry Machyn*, pp. 226, 229; *C.S.P., For. 1561–2*, 86.
14. *Seconde Parte*, ii. 60.
15. Among other schedules of abuses in the Prayer Book see Humphrey and Sampson's and Percival Wiburn's lists of 1566 (*Z.L.*, i. 163–5; ibid., ii. 358–62) and John Field's objections of 1583 (recensions in *Seconde Parte*, i. 256–7, 284–6; PRO, S.P.12/164/11).
16. H. C. Porter, *Reformation & Reaction in Tudor Cambridge*, pp. 323–90.
17. For a study of the implicit differences, see J. F. H. New, *Anglican & Puritan: The Basis of their Opposition, 1558–1640*, 1964. Mr New seems to me to go too far in his suggestion that these differences, apart from the historical circumstances of conflict, constituted 'the basis' of the quarrel. See my comments in *E.H.R.*, lxxx. 592–3.
18. ITL, MS. Petyt 538/47, fols. 526–7; Gifford, *A briefe discourse*, fols. 7ʳ, 24ᵛ; Josias Nichols, *The plea of the innocent*, 1602 (1854¹). pp. 212–14; *Puritan Manifestoes*, p. 29.
19. *Z.L.*, i. 84. For a further discussion of part of the programme of the *Reformatio Legum*, see pp. 102–3. Helpful guides to the complexities of English ecclesiastical law are provided in the Report of the Archbishops' Commission on Canon Law, *The Canon Law of the Church of England*, 1947, and E. W. Kemp, *An Introduction to Canon Law in the Church of England*, 1957.
20. F. D. Price, 'The Abuses of Excommunication & the Decline of Ecclesiastical Discipline under Queen Elizabeth', *E.H.R.*, lvii. 106–15; CUL, Ely Diocesan Records, B 2/9.
21. Neale, i. 209; *Z.L.*, i. 164; ibid., ii. 149–50; Beza, *Epistolae*, 2nd edn, Geneva 1575, pp. 94–103.
22. This follows some suggestions of Dr Ronald A. Marchant in an unpublished work, 'Church Courts & Administration in the Diocese of York, 1559–1640', to which he has kindly allowed me to refer.
23. *Economic Problems of the Church*, p. 162 and almost *passim*. Cf. the early pages of G. F. A. Best, *Temporal Pillars*.
24. *Z.L.*, i. 29; ibid., ii. 84–90, 94.
25. Ibid., ii. 128.
26. *The Life off the 70. archbishopp of Canterbury presentlye sittinge Englished*, Heidelberg 1574 (19292ᵃ), Sigs. C viiʳ, E iiʳ, E viᵛ–viiᵛ.
27. B. J. Kidd, *History of the Counter-Reformation*, p. 9.

Chapter 3

1. *Seconde Parte*, ii. 57–60; Knox, *Works*, ed. Laing, vi. 83–5; Calvin, *Opera*, xviii, in *Corpus Reformatorum*, xlvi. cols. 341, 364–5.

2. Undated list of 'bishops elect', PRO, S.P.12/11/12; *Z.L.*, i. 63; A. F. Pollard in *DNB*, art. Whitehead; PRO, S.P.12/19/48; CUL, MS. Mm. 1. 43, p. 447.

3. *Z.L.*, i. 61–2, 169; LPL, MS. 2010, 'Epistolae virorum doctorum', no. 73, fol. 114. Strype (*Grindal*, pp. 41–4) mistakenly attributed to Grindal the correspondence with Peter Martyr which in the *Zurich Letters* is correctly assigned to Sampson.

4. *Z.L.*, i. 51, 61; Birt, *Elizabethan Religious Settlement*, p. 229; Mozley, *John Foxe & his Book*, p. 137.

5. *Z.L.*, i. 1–2, 62–5, 75–6.

6. 1 Eliz., cap. 19, IV. For the implications of this statute, see Christopher Hill, *Economic Problems of the Church*, pp. 14–15.

7. *Parker Correspondence*, pp. 97–102; BM, MS. Cotton, Vespasian F XII, fol. 129ᵛ; PRO, S.P.12/14/47; LPL, MS. 2010, nos. 82–3, fols. 133–5ʳ.

8. Magdalene College, Cambridge, Pepysian Library, 'Papers of State', ii. 701. For the dating of this document, see a note in 'Classical Movement', p. 24, n. 1.

9. That is, if James Pilkington and not his brother Leonard is meant. Biographical information for this paragraph from Garrett, *Marian Exiles*.

10. *Z.L.*, ii. 161; *An answere for the tyme*, 1566 (10388), B.M. pressmark 702.a.37, MS. marginalia on Sigs. A iiᵛ, iiiᵛ, p. 22; *Letters of Thomas Wood*, p. 19; BM, MS. Add. 22473, fol. 12.

11. *Z.L.*, i. 86, 93; Mozley, op. cit., p. 66. The puritan preachers are viewed as the successors of the medieval friars by I. Morgan in his *The Godly Preachers of the Elizabethan Church*, 1965.

12. *HMC*, *Ancaster MSS*, p. 459; J. F. Mozley, *Coverdale and his Bibles*, pp. 23, 316–17; Mozley, *John Foxe*, pp. 65, 74–6; Corpus Christi College, Oxford, MS. 297, p. 18; Essex Archaeol. Socy Archives, C. 41, p. 115.

13. *Pace* many authorities, including Nichols (*History of Leicestershire*, III. ii. 619) there seems to be no evidence that Gilby was ever vicar of Ashby. Thomas Wydowes, who may have been his son-in-law, was inducted in 1569 (M. Claire Cross in *Historical Journal*, iii. 5).

14. See *Letters of Thomas Wood*, p. xii.

15. For Coventry, *Z.L.*, i. 86–7; for Colchester, Essex Archaeol. Socy Archives, C. 41, pp. 115, 117; for Ipswich, Ipswich & E. Suffolk Record Office, Ipswich Borough Records, numerous refs. in Great Court Book, 1572–1634, Assembly Books, Book of Enrolment of Apprenticeship Indentures and Rate Assessments, Treasurer's Accounts; and accounts of sums collected for preachers' wages, 1587–8, BM, MS. Stowe 881, fol. 6ʳ; for Leicester, *Records of Leicester*, ed. Bateson, iii. 101, Cross in *Historical Journal*, iii. 1–2.

16. *Z.L.*, i. 86–7.

17. *History of the Church of England*, vi. 42.

18. Mozley, *Coverdale*, pp. 316–17.

19. *Corpus Reformatorum*, xlvi. col. 341; Huntington Libr., San Marino, MS. Hastings 8373 (a reference I owe to the kindness of Dr M. Claire Cross); *Letters of Thomas Wood*, pp. v–vi, ix, 6–9; 'Life of Whittingham', *Camden Miscellany*, vi. 10–19.

20. PRO, S.P.12/6/17; Garret, op. cit., pp. 275–7; *Z.L.*, ii. 36–8, 54–5, 63–4, 74–5; *Corpus Reformatorum*, xlvi. cols. 75–6, 141–2, 341, 505; *Review of English Studies*, vii. 385–405; Conyers Read, *Mr. Secretary Cecil*, p. 241.

21. See W. T. MacCaffrey, 'Elizabethan Politics; the first Decade, 1558–68', *Past & Present*, xxiv.

22. *Letters of Thomas Wood*, pp. xx, xxiii–xxv.

23. PRO, Baschet Transcripts 31/3/26, fol. 207. I owe this reference to the kindness of Professor W. T. MacCaffrey.

24. The doctrine of the 'inferior magistrates' was given an English interpretation in Laurence Humphrey's tract *Optimates*, 1559, English tr. *The nobles*, 1563.

25. *Parker Correspondence*, p. 240.

26. Dr M. Claire Cross hopes to publish Sir Francis Hastings's letters. See her essay, 'An Example of Lay Intervention in the Elizabethan Church', *Studies in Church History*, ii. 273–82.

27. Humphrey, op. cit., Sig. A iii.

28. 'Collection of Original Letters from the Bishops to the Privy Council, 1564', ed. Bateson, *Camden Miscellany*, ix; A. H. Smith, 'The Elizabethan Gentry of Norfolk: Office-Holding & Faction', unpubl. London Ph.D. thesis, 1959, pp. 72–4.

R *

Part 2 Chapter 1

1. On Jewel, see J. E. Booty's introduction to his edn of the *Apology* (in the series 'Folger Documents of Tudor & Stuart Civilisation') and his *John Jewel as Apologist of the Church of England*, both 1963; and W. M. Southgate, *John Jewel and the Problem of Doctrinal Authority*, 1962.
2. *Parker Correspondence*, p. 125.
3. *Z.L.*, i. 21, 23; *Parker Correspondence*, p. 65.
4. There are contemporary memoranda of the revenues of the bishoprics in PRO, S.P.12/4/38&39, 12/2.
5. Grindal, *Remains*, p. 402; *Parker Correspondence*, pp. 49–63; *D.N.B.*, art. Bacon.
6. I am not concerned here with the dates of consecration and confirmation, or even with the issue of the *congé d'élire* where an earlier date can tentatively be established at which a bishop 'emerged'. The dates are based on Rymer, *Foedera*; Le Neve, *Fasti*; *Diary of Henry Machyn*, pp. 200–1; *Z.L.*, i. 21, 23, 63; *C.S.P., For.*, *1558–9*, 287; ibid. *1559–60*, 138; and a number of domestic state papers. H. N. Birt, *Elizabethan Religious Settlement*, collects some of the evidence, but is misleading in his suggestion that the sees are assigned to prospective occupants in a list of bishoprics and spiritual persons in PRO, S.P.12/4/39 (May 1559?). On the other hand Birt neglects a list of 'bishops elect', S.P.12/11/12. This may have been drawn up before June 22nd, the date when Scory's *congé d'élire* for Hereford was issued, since Sampson has been substituted for Scory at Norwich and Scory for Sampson at Hereford with the marginal note 'despatched'. The earliest reference to the substitution of Horne for Pilkington at Winchester and Pilkington's nomination for Durham seems to be in a draft of the queen's letter missive to the dean and chapter of Winchester, corrected by Cecil, Nov. 25th, 1560, S.P.12/14/47.
7. De L'Isle & Dudley papers, consulted in Baskerville transcripts, National Register of Archives; *Letters of Thomas Wood*, pp. xxi–xxii, 9, 13, 19.
8. H. G. Owen, 'The London Parish Clergy in the Reign of Elizabeth I', unpubl. London Ph.D. thesis, 1957, pp. 469–76; details of the puritan stake in the diocese of Durham will be found in my 'Classical Movement', p. 31.
9. *Z.L.*, i. 23, 100, 52, 149; Jewel, *Works*, PS, iii. 339; *Parker Correspondence*, pp. 215–16.
10. *Letters of Thomas Wood*, p. xxxv; *Parker Correspondence*, p. 65; W. M. Kennedy, *The 'Interpretations' of the Bishops*, Alcuin Club Tracts, viii. 1908.
11. *Z.L.*, i. 179, 248; BL, MS. Tanner 50, no. 10, fol. 83; Sandys, *Sermons*, PS, pp. 448–9.
12. *Z.L.*, i. 108; Sandys, op. cit., p. 433.
13. Neale, i. 165–70.
14. HMC, Hatfield MSS, ii. 73; *Z.L.*, ii. 161; Corpus Christi College, Oxford, MS. 297, fol. 17; *Parker Correspondence*, p. 284.
15. Corpus Christi College, Oxford, MS. 297, fol. 18.
16. Dixon, *History of the Church*, vi. 77; *Letters of Thomas Wood*, p. 20; *Seconde Parte*, i. 72; BM, MS. Harl. 6990, fol. 64.
17. *Z.L.*, i. 229–30; *Parker Correspondence*, pp. 148–9, 237; ITL, MS. Petyt 538/47, fols. 526–7.
18. Ibid.; *Parker Correspondence*, pp. 158, 125.
19. *Z.L.*, i. 134.
20. 'Bishop Hooper's "Notes" to the King's Council', ed. C. Hopf, *Journ. Theol. Studies*, xliv. 194–9.
21. Dixon, op. cit., vi. 39–42.
22. *Parker Correspondence*, pp. 223–7; Dixon, op. cit., vi. 44–6, 56; *Letters of Thomas Wood*, pp. 1–2.
23. The Advertisements are printed in Gee and Hardy, *Documents Illustrative of English Church History*, pp. 467–75.

Chapter 2

1. *Corpus Reformatorum*, xliv (Calvin, *Opera*, xviii), col. 144.
2. *Z.L.*, i. 52.
3. *Journ. Theol. Studies*, xliv. 194–9; Ridley's reply in *Writings of John Bradford*, PS, pp. 373–95.
4. *Brief Discourse of the Troubles at Frankfort*, ed. Arber, pp. 54, 42,

224–7; Knox, *Works*, vi. 84, 124.

5. *C.S.P., Span.*, *1558–67*, p. 406; *Z.L.*, ii. 151; PRO, S.P.15/12/68.

6. But see also my 'The "nott conformytye" of the young John Whitgift', *J.E.H.*, xv. 192–200.

7. There is also a published doctoral thesis, J. H. Primus, *The Vestments Controversy*, Kampen 1960.

8. *Z.L.*, i. 141–3, 168–70, 175–82; Grindal, *Remains*, p. 211; *J.E.H.*, xv. 195.

9. *Z.L.*, i. 142; CUL, MS. Mm. 1. 29, fol. 2ʳ; *Z.L.*, ii. 150.

10. The copy is in BM, MS. Lansd. 8, fols. 17–18. The original until recently formed item no. 119 of the volume 'Epistolae virorum doctorum', a Laud-Selden-Fairhurst MS. now at LPL, MS. 2010. It has been detached and is in private hands. Since going to press I learn that it is to be restored to LPL, where it will form part of MS. 2019.

11. In establishing the most probable chronology for the vestments controversy in London and for several details I am dependent upon Dr Owen's thesis, 'The London Parish Clergy', pp. 468–514.

12. *Parker Correspondence*, pp. 270, 233–41; Owen, op. cit., pp. 492–4; *An answere for the tyme*, 1566 (10388), Sig. A iiiiᵛ; BL, MS. Tanner 50, no. 10, fols. 23ʳ, 33ᵛ–4ʳ.

13. CUL, MS. Mm. 1. 29, fols. 1–3; *Parker Correspondence*, pp. 262–4, 267–70; Dixon, *History of the Church*, vi. 93–8; *Z.L.*, ii. 148; Coverdale, *Remains*, PS, p. 532; Owen, op. cit., pp. 497–500, 506–7; Mozley, *John Foxe & his Book*, p. 74.

14. *Parker Correspondence*, pp. 271–9; Grindal, *Remains*, pp. 288–9; John Stow, 'Memoranda', printed, *Three Fifteenth-Century Chronicles*, ed. Gairdner, CS n.s. xxviii. 135–6, 138–40.

15. *Letters of Thomas Wood*, pp. 1–2; Stow, 'Memoranda', pp. 138–40; *A briefe discourse against the outwarde apparrell*, 1566 (6078), Sigs. A iiᵛ, B iiiᵛ, Cv; *An answere for the tyme*, Sig. A viᵛ; *Parker Correspondence*, p. 285; *A briefe examination of a certaine declaration*, 1566 (10387), Sig. * 4ᵛ.

16. *To my lovynge brethren*, 1566 (10390); Gilby, *Pleasaunt dialogue*, 1581 edn (11888) Sigs. B 2, 3ᵛ, C 6ᵛ, 7ᵛ, F 4, L7–M5; *Letters of Thomas Wood*, p. 25. Knappen has a valuable account of the pamphlets discussed here, *Tudor Puritanism*, pp. 200–3.

17. *Z.L.*, i. 130–1, 133–4, 151–5, 341–4.

18. Bullinger's original letter is in LPL, MS. 2010, no. 91, fols. 146–7ᵛ; copy in *Z.L.*, i. 345–55.

19. Ibid., 356–7, 168–9, 175–82, 162–5; ibid., ii. 121–7.

20. *Ecclesiae Londino-Batavae Archivum*, ed. Hessels, 1899, ii. 618–20; Neale, i. 90; *Z.L.*, ii. 127–35, 358–62, 136–40; ibid., i. 187–91, 357–60.

21. Ibid., ii. 140–2, 226–7; ibid., i. 234–8, 362–5, 279–80; *Puritan Manifestoes*, pp. 41–3.

22. *Z.L.*, ii. 146–51, 154–64.

23. Beza, *Epistolae*, 2nd edn Geneva 1575, pp. 68–80, 94–103; *Puritan Manifestoes*, pp. 43–55; Hessels, op. cit., ii. 280–90; *Z.L.*, ii. 127–36, 153–4.

24. *Parker Correspondence*, p. 285; Stow, 'Memoranda', pp. 139–40; E. Rosenberg, *Leicester, Patron of Letters*, pp. 211–212; *Z.L.*, ii. 119.

25. *Parker Correspondence*, p. 272; CUL, MS. Mm. 1. 29, fol. 1ᵛ; Owen, op. cit., pp. 505–8; refs. to deprivations and resignations in Henessy, *Novum Repertorium*; Stow, 'Memoranda', p. 140; CUL, MS. Mm. 1. 43, p. 446.

Chapter 3

1. Much of the evidence for this chapter is gathered in Albert Peel, *The First Congregational Churches*, correcting and amplifying Champlin Burrage, *Early English Dissenters*, i. 79–93, ii. 9–18. I again owe many insights to Dr Owen, 'The London Parish Clergy', pp. 516–525.

2. BL, MS. Tanner 50, no. 10, fols. 18–93.

3. PRO, S.P.12/176/68.

4. *Letters of Thomas Wood*, p. 1.

5. I am grateful to Miss Helen Miller for this information, supplied from the Orders of Court of the Clothworkers' Company and unknown to me when I published 'John Field & Elizabethan Puritanism', *Elizabethan Government and Society*, ed. Bindoff, Hurstfield & Williams. Other references occur in that essay, pp. 129–34.

6. Wilcox, *An exposition upon the booke of Canticles*, 1585 (25622), Sigs. A 3–4, *A short, yet sound commentarie ... on ... Proverbes*, 1589 (25627), Sigs. A 2–4; account of Wilcox's spiritual letters in DWL, MS. Morrice I, pp. 617 (2), (4).

7. Stow, 'Memoranda', p. 143; ITL, MS. Petyt 538/47, fols. 380, 380x; E. M. Tomlinson, *History of the Minories*, esp. pp. 161–7, 190–225; Owen, op. cit., pp. 517–21; *Parker Correspondence*, p. 279; Peel, op. cit., p. 8; 'A short replye to a smale treatise', LPL, MS. 2007, fols. 145–6^r. I owe the reference to Jackson's will to Dr Owen's article, 'A Nursery of Elizabethan Nonconformity, 1569–72', *J.E.H.*, xvii. 65–76, which he allowed me to read in typescript. Cf. his 'The Liberty of the Minories: a study in Elizabethan religious radicalism', *East London Papers*, viii. (2).

8. Stow, 'Memoranda', p. 143; *Writings of John Greenwood*, ed. Carlson, ENT, iv. 294, 301–2. The summer houses or 'garden houses' where the separatists met are illustrated on the engraved copper plate of Moorfields from the earliest surviving map of London; see M. R. Holmes, *Moorfields in 1559*, H.M.S.O. 1963.

9. Peel, op. cit., pp. 6–8, 10–11; Burrage, op. cit., ii. 9–11; Owen, op. cit., pp. 523–5; P. Lorimer, *John Knox and the Church of England*, 1875, p. 300.

10. *A parte*, pp. 23–37; reprinted, Grindal, *Remains*, pp. 199–216.

11. Lorimer, op. cit., p. 300.

12. Peel, op. cit., pp. 22–6, 31–3; *Seconde Parte*, i. 59–61; Burrage, op. cit., ii. 9–18; Garret, *Marian Exiles*, pp. 94–5.

13. *Seconde Parte*, i. 56–7, 153; ITL, MS. Petyt 538/47, fol. 511; PRO, S.P.15/20/107 I, II. The last reference is to the 'Order of the privye churche in London', printed in black-letter, and subscribed 'Richarde Fytz, minister'.

14. *Z.L.*, i. 201–5; *Seconde Parte*, i. 53–64; Lorimer, op. cit., pp. 298–300.

15. Ibid., p. 300.

Chapter 4

1. *Letters of Thomas Wood*, pp. xxiv–xxv.

2. Collinson, *A Mirror of Elizabethan Puritanism*, Friends of DWL 17th lecture, 1963 (1964), p. 4.

3. Romier, *Le Royaume de Catherine de Medicis*, ii. 240; Grindal, *Remains*, p. 288; John Stow, 'Memoranda', p. 140; Burrage, *Early English Dissenters*, ii. 9–11.

4. K. Thomas, 'Women & the Civil War Sects', *Past & Present*, xiii. 42–62, repr., *Crisis in Europe, 1560–1660*, pp. 317–40.

5. Grindal, *Remains*, p. 203; Humphrey, *The nobles, or of nobility*, 1563 (13964), Sig. B vii^v; *Letters of Thomas Wood*, p. 23.

6. H. G. Koenigsberger, 'The Organisation of Revolutionary Parties in France and the Netherlands during the Six-teenth Century', *Journal of Modern History*, xxvii. 335–51.

7. *Parker Correspondence*, p. 149. The writer is Cecil.

8. *Z.L.*, i. 168, 23; *A briefe discourse against the outwarde apparell*, Sig. C i; Parker, 'The Problem of Uniformity, 1559–1604', in *The English Prayer Book, 1549–1662*, Alcuin Club 1963, pp. 49–50.

9. BL, MS. Tanner 79, fol. 16; Gilby, *A pleasaunt dialogue*, Sig. C 5; *A briefe discourse*, Sig. C ii^v.

10. Corpus Christi College, Oxford, MS. 297, fol. 17; ITL, MS. Petyt 538/47, fol. 320; DWL, MS. Morrice B II, fols. 11^v, 18^v.

11. *Seconde Parte*, i. 224; *Writings of Harrison & Browne*, ed. Carlson & Peel, ENT, ii. 52–3.

Part 3 Chapter 1

1. Stubbs, *Second part of the anatomie of abuses*, ed. Furnivall, New Shakespeare Socy, pp. 100–2.

2. CUL:, MS. Mm. 1. 43, p. 445; *A parte*, p. 530.

3. What follows is partly dependent upon Norman F. Sykes, *Old Priest, New Presbyter*, esp. pp. 1–48; and upon Prof. Gordon Donaldson in his unpublished doctoral thesis, 'The Relations between the English and Scottish Presbyterian Movements to 1604', London, 1938.

4. The differences between them and their Anglican opponents, in so far as they have concerned 'intention' rather than the 'form' of the Ordinal itself, would seem to lie in the capacity of a defective intention to invalidate a sacrament.

5. *Reformation of the Ecclesiastical Laws*, ed. Cardwell, p. 103; Bucer, *De regno Christi* and *De ordinatione legitima* in *Scripta Anglicana*, Basle 1577, pp. 67–9, 259; cf. R. T. Smith, *We Ought Not to Alter the Ordinal*, 1872; and E. C. Messenger, *The Lutheran Origin of the Anglican Ordinal*, 1934.

6. Jewel, *Works*, PS, i. 340, 379, 439; Pilkington, *Works*, PS, p. 493.

7. Whitgift, *Works*, PS, ii. 265, iii. 535–6, 166, 175–8; Sandys, *Sermons*, PS, p. 448.

8. See his introduction to the Oxford edn of Hooker's *Works*, 1888, i. lix.

9. Calvin, *Institutes*, bk. IV, cap. iii; Reyburn, *John Calvin*, pp. 259–60; Calvin, *Lettres Anglaises, 1548–61*, ed. Schmidt, Paris 1959; Whitgift, op. cit., i. 243–8; Calvin, *Institutes*, tr. Norton, 1562, B.M. pressmark 3557.h.4, fol. 371ᵛ.

10. Ibid., fol. 355.

11. Jewel, *Works*, PS, iii. 103–4, 348; *Z.L.*, i. 50–1; Strype, *Ecclesiastical Memorials*, II. ii. 141–3.

12. e.g. William Harrison, *Description of England*, ed. Furnivall, pt. 1, p. 16.

13. BM, MS. Add. 27632, fols. 47–8ʳ; Gilby, *A pleasaunt dialogue*, 1581 (11888), Sig. B 6ʳ; CUL, MS. Mm. 1. 43, p. 434.

14. Travers, *A full and plaine declaration*, tr. Cartwright (?), Heidelberg 1574 (24184), p. 13.

15. Thomas Cartwright, *The rest of the second replie*, Basle 1577 (4715), p. 30; Dering, *A briefe and necessarie catechisme*, in *Workes*, 1597 (6677), Sig. A 3ᵛ.

16. John Field, *Godly prayers and meditations*, 1601 (10846), fols. 83ᵛ, 89ʳ. On the political doctrines of the Elizabethan presbyterians, see A. F. Scott Pearson, *Church and State*, 1928.

17. Field, op. cit., Sig. A 7ʳ.

18. *A full and plaine declaration*, esp. pp. 177–179; *A briefe and plaine declaration*, 1584 (10395), esp. pp. 77–90; CUL, MS. Mm. 1. 43, p. 447.

19. DWL, MS. Morrice B II, p. 184.

Chapter 2

1. Beza, *A briefe and piththie* [sic] *summe*, tr. R[obert] F[yll], 1565? (2007), Sigs. N viii–P viiiʳ; Beza, *Epistolae*, 2nd edn Geneva 1575, nos. VIII, XII, XXIII; *Puritan Manifestoes*, pp. 43–55; *Brief Discourse of the Troubles at Frankfort*, ed. Arber, pp. 239–50; *Z.L.*, ii. 127–35, 153–4.

2. Beza, *Epistolae*, no. LXXIX; CUL, MS. Mm. 1. 43, p. 441; *The judgement of a most reverend and learned man from beyond the seas concerning a threefold order of bishops*, 1580? (2021); Gordon Donaldson, *The Scottish Reformation*, pp. 187–191.

3. Charles Bourgeaud, 'Cartwright and Melville at the University of Geneva, 1569–74', *Amer. Hist. Rev.*, v. 284–90; Scott Pearson, pp. 46–51; Donaldson, *Scottish Reformation*, pp. 190–1.

4. *Z.L.*, i. 312, 364; LPL, MS. 2010, nos. 55, 59, fols. 83, 90–1; Scott Pearson, pp. 133–5.

5. See especially a letter of April 1572 from Petrus Dathenus, representing the *classis* of Dutch refugee churches in the Palatinate, which reminds the Dutch congregation in London of the decisions taken at the national synod at Emden in 1571 and asks them to notify their assent to the French Church, 'de qua nos nihil dubitare Domino Bezae et Sijnodo Gallicanarum Ecclesiarum proximo mense Maijo habendae, ante hoc tempus non nihil scripsimus.' (Hessels, *Ecclesiae Londino-Batavae Archivum*, ii. 1889, 394–6.)

6. Neale, ii. 151.

7. *Puritan Manifestoes*, p. 45; Scott Pearson, *Church and State*, pp. 119–23; Donaldson, *Scottish Reformation*, pp. 194–200.

8. Scott Pearson, pp. 1–46. Cartwright's part in the vestments controversy is established from a letter in the State Papers unnoticed by Scott Pearson, PRO, S.P.12/38/10.

9. Cartwright prepared a summary of his more controversial doctrines at the request of the vice-chancellor; copies in PRO, S.P.12/74/29i, 30.

10. L. J. Trinterud, 'The Origins of Puritanism', *Church History*, xx. 37–57; Turner, *The huntynge of the Romyshe vuolfe*, Zurich 1554 (24356), Sigs. B vii, E viii; BM, MS. Lansd. 8, fol. 6.

11. What follows is based on my article,

'The Elizabethan Puritans & the Foreign Reformed Churches in London', *Procs. Hug. Socy*, xx. 525–55, where full documentation will be found.

12. CUL, MS. Mm. 1. 29, fol. 2ʳ; *Puritan Manifestoes*, p. 19.

13. *An answere for the tyme*, 1566 (10388), p. 94; I[ohn] B[artlett], *The fortresse of fathers*, 1566 (1040), Sig. a 4; my 'John Field & Elizabethan Puritanism', *Elizabethan Government & Society*, ed. Bindoff, Hurstfield & Williams, p. 130.

14. *Seconde Parte*, i. 56, 64, 97–8, 79–83; Grindal, *Remains*, p. 205; Albert Peel, 'William White, an Elizabethan Puritan', *Trans. Cong. Hist. Socy*, vi. 4–19.

15. Neale, i. 165–70; Gilby, *A pleasant dialogue*, Sig. A viiᵛ.

16. Neale, i. 191–217 and his 'Parliament & the Articles of Religion, 1571', *E.H.R.*, lxvii. 510–21.

17. *Seconde Parte*, i. 79–82. The presence of a copy of this reply in a letter-book of Bishop Parkhurst of Norwich (CUL, MS. Ee. 11. 34, fols. 15–18) has led to the erroneous impression that he had shared in this attack on the puritans.

18. Cardwell, *Synodalia*, i. 126–7; *Parker Correspondence*, pp. 381–6; *Seconde Parte*, i. 82; *Troubles at Frankfort*, p. 245.

19. *Seconde Parte*, i. 82; CUL, MS. Mm. 1. 43; p. 447.

20. Neale, i. 241–2; Scott Pearson, p. 57; *Survay*, pp. 54–5; CUL, MS. Mm. 1. 43, pp. 445–7, 442–3.

21. Neale, i. 291–304; text of the earlier and later forms of the bill in *Puritan Manifestoes*, pp. 149–51.

22. Whitgift alleged that it was published after the prorogation of Parliament on June 30th. But Field and Wilcox were already prisoners in Newgate before the last week of June (Whitgift, *Works*, i. 39, 80, iii. 521; CUL, MS. Mm. 1. 43, pp. 442–4). It is just possible that the *Admonition* appeared even earlier. As an appendix, Field printed a letter from Gualter of Zürich to Parkhurst of Sept. 11th, 1566, which was critical of the bishops for their handling of the nonconformists. As early as June 9th Gualter knew that this letter had been 'published far and wide'. However, he was replying to a complaint from Cox who had come across a MS. copy of the letter in February. (*Z.L.*, i. 362–365, 234–8.)

23. *Puritan Manifestoes*, p. 30.

24. The 2nd edn has 'scarce' and this alteration is made in MS. in the three extant copies of the 1st edn.

25. *Seconde Parte*, i. 89; *Puritan Manifestoes*, pp. 21–2, 29, 33.

26. Ibid., p. 61.

27. ITL, MS. Petyt 538/38, fol. 66ʳ.

28. Ibid., MS. Petyt 538/47, fol. 481; CUL, MS. Mm. 1. 43, pp. 431–2; Huntington Library, San Marino, MS. Hastings 13766 (a reference I owe to the kindness of Dr M. Claire Cross); BM, MS. Lansd. 24, fol. 52; BL, MS. Rawlinson C 167, fol. 18ʳ, MS. Rawlinson C 849, fol. 390ᵛ.

29. CUL, MS. Mm. 1. 43, p. 433.

30. Mozley, *John Foxe & his Book*, pp. 111–112; CUL, MS. Mm. 1. 43, p. 446; my 'The Authorship of *A brief discours off the troubles begonne at Franckford*', *J.E.H.*, ix. 188–208.

31. ITL, MS. Petyt 538/38, fol. 65; Hessels, op. cit., ii. 426–7.

Chapter 3

1. *Seconde Parte*, i. 71.

2. Strype, *Whitgift*, i. 50–1; Porter, *Reformation & Reaction in Tudor Cambridge*, pp. 213–15.

3. BL, MS. Tanner 50, no. 10, fol. 18.

4. Full references will be found in my article 'The "nott conformytye" of the young John Whitgift', *J.E.H.*, xv. 192–200.

5. Mullinger, *History of the University of Cambridge*, pp. 121–6; Porter, op. cit., pp. 163–73, 213–15.

6. Scott Pearson, pp. 42–3; G. Paule, *Life of Whitgift*, 1612 (19484), p. 9; Porter, op. cit., p. 141; *Parker Correspondence*, pp. 427, 429.

7. Curtis, *Oxford & Cambridge in Transition*, pp. 80, 107; Porter, op. cit., pp. 237–8.

8. Ibid., pp. 237–41; Haller, *The Rise of Puritanism*, 1957 edn, pp. 54–5; Pembroke College, Cambridge, MS. 2.19.

9. CUL, MS. Mm. 1. 43, pp. 437–8.

10. [Travers], *A full and plaine declaration*, p. 144; 'Life of Carter', Samuel Clarke, *A general Martyrologie*, 1677, pt. 2, p. 133.

11. See Part 4, Chapter 2.

12. *Dedham Minutes*, p. 30.
13. Erasmus, *Seven dialogues*, tr. William Burton, 1606 (10457), Sig. A2.
14. An explanation of how these rough statistics have been compiled will be found in my 'Classical Movement', pp. 123–6; cf. J. A. Venn, *Oxford and Cambridge Matriculations, 1544–1906*, 1908.
15. Haller, op. cit., *passim*; Porter, op. cit., pp. 215–73.
16. *Church History*, 1845 edn, v. 192.
17. Dering's *Godly and comfortable letters* in *Workes*, 1597; Wilcox's letters, no longer extant, described by Roger Morrice, DWL, MS. Morrice I, pp.

617 (2), (4). Both collections relate to the 'seventies.
18. As Professor Curtis notes, op. cit., pp. 191–3.
19. 'Classical Movement', pp. 126–8.
20. J. T. Gillespie, 'Presbyterianism in Devon and Cornwall in the 17th Century', unpublished M.A. thesis (Durham), DWL, MS. 201.30, pp. 2, 4.
21. For Cambridge, see Porter, op. cit., pp. 119–35, 183–94, 236; for Magdalen, PRO, S.P.12/105 (many papers), 12/125/38.
22. *Seconde Parte*, ii. 241–8.

Chapter 4

1. PRO, Sta. Cha. 5 A 49/34; Whitgift, *Works*, i. 102.
2. *Writings of Harrison and Browne*, ed. Peel & Carlson, ENT ii. 401.
3. *Letters of Thomas Wood*, pp. 7–8, iv–ix, 24–5; BM, MS. Add. 29546, fol. 28; *Beds. Hist. Record Socy*, viii. 155; *Seconde Parte*, ii. 49–64; my 'The Role of Women in the English Reformation Illustrated by the Life and Friendships of Anne Lock', *Studies in Church History*, ii. 1965.
4. PRO, Sta. Cha. 5 A 49/34; *A parte of a register* and the MSS calendared in *The Seconde Parte of a Register, passim*.
5. *A parte*, pp. 94–118; *DNB*, art. Penny; Grindal, *Remains*, p. 348; my *A Mirror of Elizabethan Puritanism*, Friends of DWL 17th lecture, 1963 (1964).
6. Scott Pearson, pp. 69–71; CUL, MS. Mm. 1. 43, p. 448; *Dangerous positions*, p. 119.
7. Both in Oxford: one in BL (pressmark Douce C.388), the other in Christ Church. They were noted by Bishop Paget in the Oxford edn of Hooker's *Works* (i. 151n.).
8. CUL, MS. Mm. 1. 43, pp. 442–4; Whitgift, op. cit., i. 101; ITL, MS. Petyt 538/38, fol. 65v.
9. Theodore Beza & Nicolas des Gallars (?), *Histoire ecclésiastique*, Antwerp 1580, i. 172–3; CUL, MS. Mm. 1. 43, pp. 444–5; ITL, MS. Petyt 538/47, fol. 481.
10. *Dangerous positions*, p. 43 (*sic, recte* 67); Scott Pearson, pp. 74–81; DWL, MS. Morrice I, p. 617(2); J. N. McCorkle, 'A Note Concerning "Mistress Crane" and the Marprelate Controversy', *Library*, 4th ser. xii. 276–83.

11. *Seconde Parte*, ii. 69–70, i. 68–74. Peel's date of 1570 for this conference between Axton and Bentham is too early. Axton was elected to a fellowship at Trinity in 1573. The likelihood is that he was forced out of Cambridge and came to Shropshire later in the same year, and that this examination belongs to the 'inquisition' of that autumn.
12. Scott Pearson, pp. 83–100, 73–4, 109–114; CUL, MS. Mm. 1. 43, p. 447; *Puritan Manifestoes*, pp. xxvii–xxix, 148, 135, 155; Grindal, *Remains*, pp. 347–8; *Seconde Parte*, i. 108–20; *Transcript of the Stationers' Register*, ed. Arber, i. 467; DWL, MS. Morrice B II, fols. 8–25; A. F. Johnson, 'Books printed at Heidelberg for Thomas Cartwright', *Library*, 5th ser. ii. 284–6.
13. *Seconde Parte*, i. 114–16; DWL, MS. Morrice L, no. V, pp. 8–11, MS. Morrice I, pp. 617(2), (4); Wilcox, *A very godly and learned exposition upon the ... Psalmes*, 1591, Sigs. A 2–3; Dering, *Certain godly and comfortable letters* in *Workes*, Sigs. C 7–8.
14. *Seconde Parte*, i. 68–74; University College, Oxford, MS. E 152, fol. 1v; *A.P.C.* viii. 140; Library of the French Protestant Church, Soho Square, MS. Deacons' Accounts, 1572–3, fol. 41v; Erasmus, tr. Burton, *Seven Dialogues*, Sig. A 2; *Parker Correspondence*, pp. 449–50; CUL, MS. Mm. 1. 43, p. 448; *Letters of Thomas Wood*, p. vii.
15. *Victoria County History of Northants.*, ii. 38–9; G. Anstruther, *Vaux of Harrowden*, Newport Mon. 1953, *passim*; PRO, S.P.12/78/38; *Marprelate Tracts*, ed. Pierce, p. 62; *An answer at*

large to a most hereticall, trayterous, and papisticall byll, repr. Northampton 1881.

16. Magdalene College Cambridge, Pepysian Library, MS. 'Papers of State', ii. 389–90, 647–8; MS. Bath II, Dudley ii, no. 160 in Baskerville transcripts, National Register of Archives; Neale i. 181–3, 294–5; Pierce, *Historical Introduction to the Marprelate Tracts*, *passim*; Westminster Abbey Muniments, index no. 38956; *Seconde Parte*, i. 121–3; *DNB*, art. Paget; Paget, *A godly sermon*

preached at Detford, 1586 (19105), Sig. B 4ᵛ. I am indebted to Miss K. M. Longley, of the Minster Library, York, for the Westminster Abbey reference and for some verbal communications.

17. Peterborough Diocesan Records, *comperta* of 1572–3 visitation, transcribed by Miss Edna Bibby; Scott Pearson, p. 162; BM, MS. Lansd. 17, fol. 55; *Letters of Thomas Wood*, p. xxviii.
18. P.C.C. wills, 23 Martyn.
19. PRO, S.P.15/21/121.

Chapter 5

1. CUL, MS. Mm. 1. 43, p. 448.
2. Versions of the incident in *HMC, Hatfield MSS*, ii. 64, ITL, MS. Petyt 538/38, fol. 68 +; Dering's explanation in BM, MS. Lansd. 17, fol. 204.
3. The tract (19292ᵃ) has been linked with the name of John Stubbs, who later wrote *The gaping gulf* (see p. 199). I suspect that it may have been the *jeu d'esprit* of a group of young men at the Inns of Court, which may have included Stubbs.
4. *Parker Correspondence*, pp. 418–19, 453–455. A further statement of Parker's yearly expenses, and an apology for such abused institutions as the Court of Faculties, is in BM, MS. Lansd. 17, fols. 206–7.
5. *Parker Correspondence*, p. 427, misreads this as 'displeasing'.
6. BM, MS. Lansd. 17, fols. 69, 96, 48.
7. *Letters of Thomas Wood*, pp. xxix–xxxi, xxv, xxvii; *Parker Correspondence*, pp. 406, 408, 439, 472–4; *Puritan Manifestoes*, p. 153.
8. One of these presentation copies, given to the earl of Arundel, is in the BM, pressmark C. 24.b.7.
9. *Parker Correspondence*, pp. 425–6; Humphrey, *The nobles, or of nobility*, 1563 (13964), Sig. F vʳ.
10. Thomas Münzer, one of the earliest 'anabaptist' leaders, identified the cause of radical religious reform with the Peasants' Revolt and was executed in the aftermath of the battle of Frankenhausen (1525).
11. *Parker Correspondence*, p. 437.
12. ITL, MS. Petyt 538/47, fols. 479–80; my *Mirror of Elizabethan Puritanism*, pp. 21–4.
13. Steele, *Tudor & Stuart Proclamations*, i. no. 687; *Puritan Manifestoes*, pp. 153–5;

BM, MS. Lansd. 17, fol. 96ᵛ; CUL, MS. Ee.11.34, no. 4; PRO, S.P.46/16, fols. 39ᵛ–40ʳ, 42ʳ; ibid., S.P.12/124/19.
14. *A parte*, pp. 371–81; ITL, MS. Petyt 538/47, fol. 476; BM, MS. Lansd. 17, fol. 96.
15. Ibid.; *Seconde Parte*, i. 90; *Puritan Manifestoes*, pp. 152–3, 154–5.
16. Steele, op. cit., i. no. 689; Strype, *Parker*, ii. 327–8; Strype, *Annals*, II. i. 426–7; *Parker Correspondence*, pp. 449, 445–6; BM, MS. Lansd. 16, fols. 191–198ᵛ.
17. BM, MS. Lansd. 17, fol. 49; *A.P.C.*, viii. 140, 171; Conyers Read, *Lord Burghley & Queen Elizabeth*, pp. 117–8; ITL, MS. Petyt 538/47, fol. 510; Scott Pearson, pp. 120–1.
18. *Seconde Parte*, i. 97, 121–3, 137; *Letters of Thomas Wood*, p. 7; CUL, MS. Ee. 11. 34, nos. 176, 180, 186, 191, 195; BM, MS. Add. 29546, fols. 56ᵛ–7ʳ; Scott Pearson, pp. 161–2.
19. CUL, MS. Mm. 1. 43, pp. 441, 439; Dering, *Godly and comfortable letters* in *Workes*, Sig. A 4; *Letters of Thomas Wood*, pp. 6–9; *Seconde Parte*, i. 92–7, 124, 99; *A parte*, pp. 94–119.
20. *Z.L.*, i. 312–13; LPL, MS. 2010, nos. 55, 59, fols. 90–1.
21. Scott Pearson, pp. 130–46; BM, MS. Lansd. 18, fol. 35; C.-P. Clasen, *The Palatinate in European History, 1559–1660*, 1963; *Library*, 5th ser. ii. 284–6; my article 'The Authorship of *A Brieff Discours off the Troubles Begonne at Franckfort*', *J.E.H.*, ix. 188–208.
22. My 'John Field & Elizabethan Puritanism', *Eliz. Govt & Society*, pp. 139–140; Clasen, op. cit., pp. 33–9; Neale, i. 313–17; CUL, MS. Mm. 1. 43, p. 448.
23. Ibid., p. 442; *Seconde Parte*, i. 101–2, 92–7; *Letters of Thomas Wood*, pp. 6–9.

24. The forged letters, originally in a bundle, are in PRO, S.P.12/93/4. 'See also Sta. Cha. 5 B 6/3 (bill of complaint of Bedford against Wenslowe, Needham and 'Undertree'); BM, MS. Add. 48116, fol. 281ᵛ, MS. Add. 48039,

fol. 49ᵛ; *Parker Correspondence*, pp. 460-465; *HMC, Hatfield MSS* iv. 48-9; *A.P.C.*, viii. 261, 319, 322, 340, ix. 53. Scott Pearson has a full account of the affair, pp. 124-9.

Part 4 Chapter 1

1. ITL, MS. Petyt 538/47, fol. 336.
2. I hope to substantiate some of these assertions in my biography of Grindal, to be published in the Thomas Nelson series, 'Leaders of Religion in Britain'.
3. See the congratulatory letters on his elevation from Johann Sturm of Strasbourg (BM, MS. Add. 32092, fol. 1) and Hierom Zanchi of Heidelberg (*Z.L.*, ii. 271-2); and Conrad Hubert's dedicatory epistle in Bucer's *Scripta Anglicana*, Basle 1577.
4. PRO, S.P.12/103/48; Knappen, *Tudor Puritanism*, p. 251.
5. At the end of his life, Grindal acknowledged to Burghley that 'your lordship hath been, next unto her Majesty, the principal procurer of all my preferments' (*Remains*, p. 402).
6. Strype, *Grindal*, pp. 282-3; PRO, S.P.12/103/48, 49; PRO, S.P.59/19, fol. 248ᵛ; Gonville & Caius College, Cambridge, MS. 30/53, fols. 42ᵛ, 54.
7. PRO, S.P.59/19, fol. 248ᵛ; calendared, *C. S.P. For.*, 1575-7, pp. 468-9.
8. Neale, i. 349-53, 398-406; BM, MS. Add. 48039, fols. 66ᵛ-7ʳ; ibid., MS. Add. 48023, fols. 27ᵛ, 32ᵛ-3ᵛ; ITL, MS. Petyt 538/54, fols. 247-62; Cardwell, *Synodalia*, i. 132-8.
9. Neale, i. 209; PRO, S.P.12/107/41; Strype, *Grindal*, pp. 324-5, 300-9, 542; *A.P.C.*, ix. 16-20; BM, MS. Stowe 570, fols. 96-8.
10. Surveys for archdeaconries of Middlesex and Leicester, and the dioceses of

Hereford and Gloucester, LPL, MS. Carte Misc. XII, nos. 1, 4, 5, 7; Leicester survey printed, *The State of the Church*, ed. Foster, Lincoln Record Socy, xxiii. 33-46.

11. ITL, MS. Petyt 538/54, fols. 265, 268, 282, 284.
12. Neale, i. 192-3, 212-16, 304, 394; Spedding, *Letters & Life of Francis Bacon*, i. 97-8; F. X. Walker, 'The Implementation of the Elizabethan Statutes against Recusants, 1581-1603', unpubl. London Ph. D. thesis, 1961, pp. 36-118.
13. Pollard, *Records of the English Bible*, pp. 39-43; *Elizabethan Liturgical Services*, PS, pp. xv-xvii; A. E. Peaston, *The Prayer Book Tradition in the Free Churches*, 1964, pp. 21-34.
14. My 'John Field & Elizabethan Puritanism' in *Eliz. Govt & Society*, ed. Bindoff, Hurstfield & Williams, pp. 142-3; *Seconde Parte*, i. 190-1; HRO, MS. Gorhambury VIII/B/143, fol. 43ᵛ; Josias Nichols, *The plea of the innocent*, 1602 (18541), pp. 9-10, 216-217.
15. Neale, ii. 429.
16. Conyers Read, 'Walsingham & Burghley in Queen Elizabeth's Privy Council', *E.H.R.*, xxviii. 34-58; cf., at large, the same author's *Walsingham* (3 vols.), and *Mr Secretary Cecil & Queen Elizabeth* and *Lord Burghley & Queen Elizabeth*.
17. *Letters of Thomas Wood*, p. 23.

Chapter 2

1. Samuel Harsnet, *A discovery of the fraudulent practises of John Darrel*, 1599 (12883), pp. 270-1; my 'The Beginnings of English Sabbatarianism', *Studies in Church History*, i. 219; 'Life of Hildersham', Samuel Clarke, *A General Martyrologie*, 1677, pt. 2, p. 117.
2. R. A. Marchant, *Puritans and the Church Courts in the Diocese of York, 1560-1642*,

pp. 30-1; BM, MSS. Add. 4933, A & B.
3. In 1614 at least seventy preachers were associated in six exercises in the diocese of Lincoln alone (CUL, MS. Baumgartner 8, double fols. 199-202).
4. 1 Cor. xiv, vv. 29, 31.
5. *Documents Illustrative of the Continental Reformation*, ed. Kidd, pp. 442, 448-50, 592; W.M.S. West, 'John Hooper & the

Origins of Puritanism', *Baptist Quarterly*, xv. 353–4; *Zwingli & Bullinger: Selected Translations*, ed. Bromiley, Libr. of Christian Classics, xxxiv. 27; LPL, MS. 2003, fol. 10ᵛ.

6. J. G. Macgregor, *The Scottish Presbyterian Polity*, pp. 53–4; Joannis à Lasco, *Opera*, ed. Kuyper, Amsterdam 1866, ii. 101–5; W. D. Maxwell, *John Knox's Genevan Service Book, 1556*, p. 104.

7. *Letters of Thomas Wood*, p. 1; Burrage, *Early English Dissenters*, ii. 176–7.

8. See Part 7, Chapter 4.

9. *Visitation Articles & Injunctions*, ed. Frere, ii. 122–3, iii. 13–14, 178; Cardwell, *Synodalia*, i. 117; Hooper, *Later Writings*, PS, pp. 132–3; LPL, MS. 2003, fol. 23; BM, MS. Lansd. 27, fol. 20; *Ecclesiastical Proceedings of Bishop Barnes*, Surtees Socy, xxii. 70–9; Peck, *Desiderata Curiosa*, I. iii. 28–9, iv. 33; Cardwell, *Documentary Annals*, i. 389–91.

10. LPL, MS. 2003, fol. 17ᵛ; *Elizabethan Episcopal Administration*, ed. Kennedy, ii. 45–6; Usher, *Reconstruction of the English Church*, i. 383; *The State of the Church*, ed. Foster, xx; *Records of the Old Archdeaconry of St. Alban's*, ed. Wilton Hall, St Albans & Herts. Arch. and Archaeol. Socy, 1908, pp. 49–50; LPL, Whitgift's Register, i. fol. 131. For a fuller account of these clergy exercises, see my 'Classical Movement', pp. 244–60.

11. LPL, MS. 2003, fols. 12, 4.

12. Ibid., fols. 16–18.

13. PRO, S.P.15/12/27; LPL, MS. 2003, fols. 5, 30; *Letters of Thomas Wood*, pp. xvii–xviii; for Wiburn's Northampton orders, see Part 3, Chapter 4; BM, MS. Add. 27632, fol. 49.

14. LPL, MS. 2003, fols. 29–30, 8, 4; BM, MS. 27632, fol. 48ᵛ; *Lincoln Episcopal Records*, ed. Foster, Lincoln Record Socy ii. 114; BM, MS. Lansd. 21, fol. 4; Marchant, op. cit., pp. 134–6; *Trans. Shropshire Arch. & Nat. Hist. Socy*, iii. 273.

15. CUL, MS. Ee. 11. 34, no. 114; ibid., MS. Ff. 5. 14, fols. 85–7ʳ; LPL, MS. 2007, fols. 108–9, 106–7; Strype, *Annals*, II. i. 473–7. The Herts. order has been printed in the article noted in n. 16, pp. 93–7.

16. Original letters in LPL, MS. 2003; copies made by the 18th-century nonjuror George Harbin in BM, MS. Add. 29546, fols. 36–57; Grindal's abstracts of these and further letters, ibid., MS. Add. 21565, fol. 26. Most of the docs. in LPL, MS. 2003, together with a few other relevant papers from the Laud-Selden-Fairhurst MSS at Lambeth, have been printed by S. E. Lehmberg, 'Archbishop Grindal & the Prophesyings', *Historical Magazine of the Prot. Episcopal Church*, xxxiv. 1965, 87–145.

17. LPL, MS. 2003, fol. 8.

18. The source in most cases is the body of letters cited in n. 16. See also Marchant, op. cit., pp. 134–6, 169 (Notts.); *Lincoln Episcopal Records*, 114 (Grantham); MS. Bath II, Dudley ii. no. 160 in Baskerville transcripts, National Register of Archives (Rutland, Stamford); ITL, MS. Petyt 538/47, fol. 28; *Stiffkey Papers*, ed. Saunders, CS 3rd ser. xxvi. 189 (Norfolk); CUL, MS. Ee. 11. 34, no. 114 (Bury St Edmunds); BM, MS. Lansd. 15, fol. 95 (Farnham district of Surrey).

19. Additional information from *Letters of Thomas Wood*, p. 17; Macgregor, op. cit., pp. 53–4; *Troubles of our Catholic Forefathers*, ed. Morris, 2nd ser., p. 241.

20. *Letters of Thomas Wood*, p. 22; LPL, MS. 2003, fols. 8, 30, 17; ERO, Maldon Borough Records, D/B/3/258.

21. Huntington Library, Hastings MS. 8012 (a reference I owe to Dr M. Claire Cross); *Letters of Thomas Wood*, pp. 18, xxviii; LPL, MS. 2003, fol. 5; Erasmus, *Seven Dialogues*, tr. William Burton, 1606 (10457), Sig. A 2ᵛ.

Chapter 3

1. Macgregor, *The Scottish Polity*, pp. 53, 115–16; Jaques Courvoisier, *La Notion d'Eglise chez Bucer*, pp. 33, 139; Kidd, *Documents*, p. 592; Nash, *Works*, ed. McKerrow, i. 61; *Tracts Ascribed to Richard Bancroft*, ed. Peel, pp. 11–12; Donaldson, *Scottish Reformation*, pp. 204–8.

2. *Puritan Manifestoes*, pp. 107–8; *Seconde Parte*, ii. 217.

3. A fuller discussion of the ideals and practice of Elizabethan pastoral oversight will be found in my 'Classical Movement', pp. 218–25, and in my paper 'Episcopacy and Reform in England in the later Sixteenth Century',

in *Studies in Church History*, iii. The evidence for St Albans comes from *Records of the Old Archdeaconry of St. Alban's*, ed. Wilton Hall, the act books and miscellaneous papers of the archdeaconry deposited in HRO, and R. Peters's study based on this material, *Oculus Episcopi*, Manchester 1963. *Libri synodorum* for Ely in CUL, Ely Diocesan Records, B2/1, 7, 8, D2/14, 16. Cf. much relevant information in Marchant, *Puritans and the Church Courts in the Diocese of York, 1560–1642*.

4. Aylmer, *An harborowe for faithfull and trewe subjects*, Strasbourg 1559 (1005), Sig. O 4; Knox, *Works*, v. 518–19; Turner, *Huntyng of the Romishe vuolfe*, Zürich 1554 (23318), Sig. Fi; BM, MS. Add. 48066, fols. 2–15; Stoughton, *An assertion for true and Christian church-policie*, Middelburg 1604 (24356), epistle, pp. 13–14.

5. Hooper, *Later Writings*, PS, pp. xix, 132; Foxe, *Acts & Monuments*, ed. Pratt, vi. 610.

6. William Dansey, *Horae Decanicae Rurales*, 2 vols., 1835; A. Hamilton Thompson, *Diocesan Organisation in the Middle Ages: Archdeacons & Rural Deans*.

7. Bucer, *De Regno Christi*, ed. Wendel, in *Opera Latina*, xv. 129; *Reformation of the Ecclesiastical Laws*, ed. Cardwell, pp. 100–1; PRO, S.P.12/36/41; Cardwell, *Synodalia*, i. 117; D'Ewes, *Journals*, p. 193a.

8. CUL, MS. Ee. 11. 34, no. 114.

9. HMC, *Hatfield MSS*, ii. 195–8; Strype, *Annals*, II. ii. 695–701.

10. Thomas Norton's 'devices', BM, MS. Add. 48023, fol. 56ʳ; PRO, S.P.12/282/71; ITL, MS. Petyt 538/54, fols. 247–62; Kennedy, *Elizabethan Episcopal Administration*, iii. 161–74. For Overton, Leicester and Becon, see my 'Classical Movement', pp. 982–3; Lever's notes, ITL, MS. Petyt 538/38, fols. 71–4.

11. BM, MS. Egerton 1693, fol. 118; *Seconde Parte*, i. 260–7.

12. NNRO, Norwich Diocesan Records, ACT/31, fols. 63ᵛ–4ʳ; Wilton Hall, op. cit., pp. 46–7; *Victoria County History of Derbyshire*, ii. 21–2.

13. *Liber Visitationis*, 1586, Guildhall Library, MS. 9537/6, fols. 108ʳ, 115ʳ, 173–83; LPL, Whitgift's Register, i. fol. 131; ERO, D/ACA/14, fols. 124ʳ, 264ᵛ, ACA/16, fol. 79ᵛ, ACA/19, fols. 12ʳ, 435ᵛ, ACA/11, fol. 103ᵛ; NNRO, Norwich Diocesan Records, SUN/3, fol. 186.

14. *DNB*, arts. More, Bownd; Blomfield, *History of Norfolk*, iv. 301; *Stiffkey Papers*, p. 185; More, *Three godly and fruitful sermons*, ed. Bownd, 1594, epistle, pp. 66–9; BM, MS. Egerton 2713, fols. 210–11; ibid., MS. Add. 41140, fol. 9; HMC, *Hatfield MSS.*, ii. 228–9; Folger Shakespeare Libr., Washington D.C., MS. Bacon I.T. 10 (a reference to More's catechizing which I owe to Dr A. H. Smith); my *A Mirror of Elizabethan Puritanism*, Friends of DWL 17th Lecture 1963 (1964), pp. 9–10, 33–4; PRO, S.P. 15/25/119, fol. 282ᵛ.

15. HMC, *Hatfield MSS.*, ii. 198, 195; PRO, S.P.12/282/71. For the political context of Becon's proposals, see my 'Classical Movement', pp. 883–5; and the allegations of Freke's opponents, PRO, S.P.15/25/119.

16. I have dealt with religion and faction in West Suffolk in Bishop Freke's time in my 'Classical Movement', chapter 9, pp. 860–930, where full references will be found. Also *Tracts Ascribed to Richard Bancroft*, pp. 71–3; Erasmus, tr. Burton, *Seven dialogues*, Sig. A2.

17. *Letters of Thomas Wood*, pp. 11, 14.

18. Dering, *A collection of speeches… in matter of religion*, 1642, pp. 155–61; A. M. Everitt, 'Kent & its Gentry, 1640–60: A Political Study', unpublished London Ph.D. thesis, 1957, p. 105.

19. BM, MS. Add. 48039, fols. 49ᵛ, 67ᵛ.

Chapter 4

1. Grindal, *Remains*, pp. 378–9; Neale, ii. 71.

2. CUL, MS. Ee. 11. 34, fols. 151–61 (correspondence of Bishop Parkhurst, partly printed in G. C. Gorham, *Reformation Gleanings*, 1857, and *Parker Correspondence*, pp. 457–8, 459–60);

J. Browne, *History of Congregationalism in Norfolk & Suffolk*, 1877, pp. 18–20; BM, MS. Add. 21565, fol. 26; Sandys to the Council, July 13th, 1574, LPL, MS. 2003, fol. 27. Lehmberg ('Archbishop Grindal', chapter 2, n. 16) misdates this letter 1576, which creates confusion in that it appears to provide evidence that Grindal (rather than Parker) passed on the queen's order 'that such exercises should cease.'

3. LPL, MS. 2003, fols. 29, 10; BM, MS. Add. 29546, fol. 56ʳ.

4. Grindal, *Remains*, p. 471; *Letters of Thomas Wood*, pp. 14, xvii–xviii, 18, 11; BM, MS. Add. 29546, fols. 51ᵛ–2ᵛ; ibid., MS. Lansd. 23, fol. 7.

5. *HMC, Hastings MSS*, i. 433.

6. *Letters of Thomas Wood*, pp. xviii–xix, 10–11, 12–16; PRO, S.P.83/6/54.

7. Grindal, *Remains*, pp. 376–9, 471–2.

8. For the provenance of these letters, see Chapter 2, n. 16.

9. LPL, MS. 2003, fols. 8, 35; BM, MS. Add. 29546, fols. 56ᵛ–7ᵛ.

10. LPL, MS. 2007, fols. 126–44; ibid., MS. 2014, fols. 22–30; BM, MS. Lansd. 109, fol. 3.

11. The date of Dec. 20th on most of the surviving copies is wrong. The letter is to be dated about Dec. 8th, from a reference in Grindal's letter to Burghley of Dec. 16th (*Remains*, p. 391).

12. *Remains*, pp. 376–90; Frere, *History of the Church in the Reigns of Elizabeth & James I*, p. 192.

13. LPL, MS. 2003, fol. 39, printed, Lehmberg, loc. cit., 141–2; *Remains*, pp. 391, 472; BM, MS. Lansd. 25, fols. 92–5; *Seconde Parte*, i. 135.

14. BM, MS. Add. 5935, fol. 68; R. E. Head, *Royal Supremacy & the Trials of Bishops, 1558–1725*, pp. 16–23; LPL, MS. 2004, fol. 1; PRO, S.P. 15/25/30, 35, 71, 74; *Hutton Correspondence*, Surtees Socy, xvii. 58–60; BM, MS. Lansd. 25, fols. 163–4, 161–2, 61; Grindal, *Remains*, pp. 469–73; BM, MS. Harl. 398, fol. 12; PRO, S.P. 12/122/15.

15. Charles Arundel (?), *The copie of a leter*, Antwerp 1584 (19399), pp. 26–7; Camden, *Elizabeth*, 4th edn 1688, pp. 287–8; John Harington, *A briefe view of the state of the Church of England* (1608), 1653, pp. 5–6.

16. Burghley wrote to Walsingham on May 31st, 1577: 'In the evening after that we had delivered to the archbishop her Majesty's message, I understood that Mr Julio had that morning told a doctor of the law what should be done. So as I see he was more of her Majesty's counsel than two or three that are of present counsel.' (BM, MS. Add. 5935, fol. 68.)

17. What follows is based on Read,

Walsingham, i. 263–422, ii. *passim*; Read, *Lord Burghley & Queen Elizabeth*, pp. 173–255; Neale, *Queen Elizabeth*, pp. 234–56; J. A. Bossy, 'English Catholics & the French Marriage, 1577–81,' *Recusant History*, v. 2–16.

18. Read, *Burghley*, p. 180.

19. Ibid., p. 210.

20. *Letters of Thomas Wood*, p. xxviii; *A.P.C.*, xi. 132–3, 218–19.

21. BM, MS. Harl. 6992, fol. 89.

22. P. E. McLane, *Spenser's Shepheardes Calendar*, Notre Dame, Indiana 1961.

23. White, *Lives of the Elizabethan Bishops*, p. 251; Harris Nicolas, *Hatton*, pp. 58–9, 240; PRO, S.P. 12/126/4.

24. Nicolas, op. cit., p. 56; Strype, *Aylmer*, pp. 62–8, 36–7, *Annals*, III. i. 79–80; ITL, MS. 'Letters to Benchers and Treasurer, 1570–1679', no. 5; H. G. Owen, 'The London Parish Clergy in the Reign of Elizabeth I', unpubl. London Ph.D. thesis, 1957, pp. 542–7; Kennedy, *Eliz. Episcopal Admin.*, ii. 106–7; CUL, MS, Mm. 1. 43, p. 446; my 'John Field & Eliz. Puritanism', *Eliz. Govt. & Society*, pp. 143–4.

25. *Seconde Parte*, i. 143; PRO, S.P. 15/25/119, fol. 282ᵛ.

26. I have told the story of Bishop Freke's struggle with the puritan gentry in Chapter 9 of my 'Classical Movement'. For the specific points made here, see *Seconde Parte*, i. 157–60; PRO, S.P. 15/25/119, fols. 278ᵛ, 280ᵛ.

27. *A parte*, pp. 393–400; *Seconde Parte*, i. 143–6; BM, MS. Add. 48101, fols. 132–4; *Stiffkey Papers*, pp. 185–6; *A.P.C.*, xi. 437–8; BM, MS. Add., 48023, fol. 373; PRO, S.P. 12/126/45, S.P. 15/25/113; *Relations Politiques des Pays-Bas et de l'Angleterre*, Brussels 1900, xi. 55.

28. *A parte*, pp. 393–400; *Seconde Parte*, i. 137; Strype, *Aylmer*, p. 36; for the movements of Chapman, Crick and Dow, see pp. 223–7; Great Yarmouth Borough Records, Assembly Book 1570–9, fol. 211 (I owe this ref. to the kindness of Miss N. M. Fuidge).

29. A. Peel, *The Brownists in Norwich & Norfolk about 1580*, Cambridge 1920; *Writings of Harrison & Browne*, ed. Peel & Carlson, ENT, ii. 151, 404, 60.

30. Full documentation will be found in my 'Classical Movement', pp. 887–930.

31. Strype, *Aylmer*, pp. 60–2; Usher, *Rise and Fall of the High Commission*, pp. 42–120, *passim*.

32. Grindal, *Remains*, p. 413; BM, MS. Add. 48039, fol. 20ᵛ; Strype, *Grindal*, p. 381; BM, MS. Harl. 6992, fol. 92.

33. Harington, op. cit., p. 8; Neale, i. 398–406; ITL, MS. Petyt 538/54, fols. 247–62; BM, MS. Add. 48039, fols. 66ᵛ–7, 42.

34. *Archaeologia*, xxxvi. 109–15.

Chapter 5

1. *Letters of Thomas Wood*, p. 15.

2. Stephen Gosson, *A schoole of abuse, containing a pleasant invective against poets, pipers, plaiers, jesters, and such like caterpillers of a commonwealth*, 1579 (12097); Philip Stubbs, *Anatomy of abuses*, 1583 (23376–80). Cf. John Northbrooke, *A treatise wherein dicing, dauncing, vaine plaies or enterludes, with other idle pastimes etc., commonly used on the Sabbath Day are reproved*, 1579 (18671); Gilbert Walker, *A manifest detection of diceplay*, 1580? (24961).

3. CUL, MS. Mm. 1.43, p. 438; BM, MS. Add. 27632, fol. 51.

4. BM, MS. Add. 48023, fol. 56ʳ; ibid., MS. Add. 48064, fol. 102; ibid., MS. Lansd. 72, fols. 137ᵛ–8.

5. BM, MS. Add. 48064, fol. 221; CUL, MS. Baumgartner 8, double fols. 199–202; *Leicester Borough Records*, ed. Stocks, iv. 115; Anthony Cade, *Saint Paules agonie*, 1618 (4328), Sig. A 4ᵛ. I owe the last reference to the Rev. Dr G. J. Cuming.

6. *The Registrum Vagum of Anthony Harison*, i. Norfolk Record Socy xxii. 1963, 96–103; *Procs. Suffolk Inst. Archaeol.*, ii, 1859, 40; Rogers's letter to Archdeacon Still on a fly-leaf of Rogers's own copy of his tract *Miles Christianus*, 1590 (21238), BM, pressmark C.124.c.7 (lately 4103.bbb.26); my essay 'The Beginnings of English Sabbatarianism', *Studies in Church History*, i. 219; BL, MS. Tanner 75, fols. 126–7.

7. BM, MS. Lansd. 27, fol. 20; Peck, *Desiderata Curiosa*, I. iii. 29, I. iv. 33; Gonville & Caius Coll., Cambridge, MS. 197/103, pp. 175–84; *HMC, 14th Report, App. IV, Kenyon MSS*, p. 15; Marchant, *Puritans & the Church Courts*, pp. 29–39, 115, 134–5, 169; J. A. Newton, 'Puritanism in the Diocese of York, Excluding Nottinghamshire, 1604–1640', unpubl. London Ph.D. thesis, 1956, pp. 218–38, 234, 236–8; BM, MS. Add. 4933, A & B; Huntington Library, Hastings MS. 8012 (a reference I owe to Dr M. Claire Cross).

8. *A.P.C.*, xi. 306; BM, MS. Lansd. 82, fol. 111ᵛ.

9. *Writings of Harrison & Browne*, pp. 64–5; *Seconde Parte*, i. 231; BM, MS. Add. 48064, fol. 81.

10. LPL, MS. 2003, fol. 4; PRO, S.P. 12/159/14. Dr R. B. Manning discusses this affair in his study of the enforcement of the Elizabethan settlement in Sussex, which he kindly allowed me to read in typescript.

11. DWL, MS. Morrice B I, pp. 268–70; printed, Browne, *History of Congregationalism in Norfolk & Suffolk*, pp. 18–20.

12. Percival Wiburn, *A checke or reproofe of Mr. Howlets untimely schreeching in her Majesties eares*, 1581 (25586), fol. 58; George Gifford, *A dialogue betweene a papist and a protestant*, 1582 (11849), fol. 43ᵛ.

13. Printed in *Cartwrightiana*, ed. Peel & Carlson, ENT, i. 127–42. This work has been attributed to the Cambridge schoolmaster William Wilkinson, but Dr Peel argues persuasively for Cartwright's authorship.

14. PRO, S.P. 12/29/56; *Parker Correspondence*, p. 154; *Elizabethan Liturgical Services*, PS, pp. 475–512; Grindal, *Remains*, pp. 79–80, 258–9; BM, MS. Lansd. 15, fol. 79; Knewstub, *A confutation of monstrous and horrible heresies*, 1579 (15040), Sig. * * 6ʳ.

15. BM, MS. Add. 27632, fol. 47ʳ; G. M. Doe, 'North Devon in Elizabethan Times', *Trans. Devon Assoc.*, lviii. 241; Norfolk & Norwich Archaeol. Socy, Frere MSS, Box K. 12(A), deposited in NNRO; *Troubles of our Catholic Forefathers*, ed. Morris, ii. 240–1 (this account also to be found in *William Weston: Autobiography of an Elizabethan*, tr. Caraman, pp. 164–5).

16. Wiburn, op. cit., fol. 57ᵛ; Samuel Bird, *Lectures . . . upon the 11 chapter of . . . Hebrews*, Cambridge 1598 (3088) pp. 77–8; *A.P.C.*, xi. 450; LPL, Grindal's Register, fol. 197ᵛ; BM, MS. Lansd. 30, fol. 145.

17. Printed at Douai, 1580, under the name of 'J. Howlet'. According to Field, Parsons's informant was Everard Hans, alias Dunket, who lived near Stamford before his 'going over to Douai'.

18. Field, *A caveat for Parsons*, 1581 (10844); Wiburn, op. cit.

19. Field, op. cit., Sigs. Gi^v–x; BM, MS. Lansd. 102, fol. 185; HMC, *Hatfield MSS*, ii. 332; Wiburn, op. cit., fols. 56^v–7^r; Parsons, *A brief discours* . . ., Sig. ‡ ‡ i^v.

20. Neale, i. 378–9; BM, MS. Add. 48119, fol. 167^v.

21. Paget, *A godly sermon preached at Detford*, 1586 (19105), Sig. C6; *Cartwrightiana*, pp. 129–30, 140–3; Matthew Sutcliffe, *An answere unto a certaine calumnious letter*, 1595 (23451), fol. 48^v; *Two Elizabethan Puritan Diaries*, ed. Knappen, p. 69; 'Necessary causes to us

of humiliation at this present', BM, MS. Add. 38492, fol. 98; *Daungerous positions*, pp. 112–13; Peck, op. cit., I. iii. 29.

22. *Daungerous positions*, p. 44 (*sic, recte* 68).

23. He dates his *Comfortable treatise upon the latter part of the fourth chapter of Saint Peter* (19915) from London, April 6th, 1582.

24. *Daungerous positions*, p. 45 (*sic, recte* 69).

25. Printed by Knappen in *Two Elizabethan Puritan Diaries*.

26. ERO, QSR 84/33, 43; HMC, *Hatfield MSS*, ii. 509; BM, MS. Harl. 6993, fol. 61; PRO, S.P. 12/155/5.

27. *The Presbyterian Movement in the Reign of Queen Elizabeth as Illustrated by the Minute Book of the Dedham Classis, 1582–1589*, CS 3rd. ser. viii. 1905, cited as *Dedham Minutes*.

28. Rylands English MS. 874.

Chapter 6

1. All material in this chapter not otherwise referred to is drawn from Usher's edition of the Dedham conference papers, cited immediately above. The original papers are referred to as 'Rylands English MS. 874' for some items not printed by Usher, or mistranscribed.

2. Copinger, *Manors of Suffolk*, vi. 18, 21; *Dedham Minutes*, p. xxxvii; H. Rendall, *Dedham in History*, Colchester 1937, pp. 58, 69; GLRO, Records of the Consistory Court of London, DL/C/333, Vicar-General's Book, Hamond, fol. 242^r; Newcourt, *Repertorium*, ii. 210; T. F. Paterson, *East Bergholt in Suffolk*, Cambridge 1923, p. 47; Ipswich Borough Record Office, Chamberlain's Account no. 18, 1580; Ipswich Public Libr., manuscript transcript of Stratford St Mary baptismal register.

3. Harold Smith, *Ecclesiastical History of Essex under the Long Parliament & Commonwealth*, Colchester [1933], pp. 6–8; ERO, QSR 2/15.

4. See pp. 213–14.

5. This analysis is made in greater detail and with supporting references in my 'Classical Movement', pp. 357–60.

6. See pp. 317–18.

7. JRL, Rylands English MS. 874, fol. 2^r; for an account of the plays and their subsequent suppression by the Charity Commissioners, see *Essex Review*, xv. 153–5.

8. JRL, Rylands English MS. 874, fols. 33^v–4^r.

9. Ibid., fol. 37.

10. Great Yarmouth Borough Records, Assembly Book 1579–98, fol. 85^v. I owe this reference to Miss N. M. Fuidge.

11. JRL, Rylands English MS. 874, fol. 55^r.

12. *Two Elizabethan Puritan Diaries*, p. 53.

13. *Daungerous positions*, pp. 44–5 (*sic, recte* 68–9).

14. PRO, Sta. Cha. 5 A 56/1.

15. *Warrender Papers*, ed. Cameron & Rait, i. 203–4.

16. PRO, Sta. Cha. 5 A 49/34; *A parte*, pp. 401–8; *Seconde Parte*, i. 136–43; PRO, S.P. 15/25/71, 74, S.P. 83/4/38, 6/29/54; Scott Pearson, pp. 170–90; S. J. Knox, *Walter Travers*, 1962, p. 44.

17. Printed (from National Library of Scotland MS. 6/1/13, fol. 42) in R. M. Gillon, *John Davidson of Prestonpans*, 1938, pp. 262–3; cf. G. Donaldson, 'The Relations Between the English & Scottish Presbyterian Movements to 1604', unpubl. London Ph.D. thesis, 1938, pp. 157–9.

18. Scott Pearson, pp. 198–210.

19. Conyers Read's statement (*Walsingham*, ii. 261 n.3) that this was done 'by the queen's command' seems to lack foundation.

20. Cartwright, *A confutation of the Rhemist translation*, 1618 (4709), Sigs. A2–4^r; Nashe, *Works*, ed. McKerrow, iii. 368.

21. Porter, *Reformation & Reaction in Tudor Cambridge*, pp. 376–8; Baro, *Fower sermons and two questions*, in Andreas Gerardus, *A speciall treatise of Gods providence*, 1588? (11760); J. H. Hessels, *Ecclesiae Londino-Batavae Archivum*, ii. Cambridge 1889, 648–56, 667–75; Strype, *Whitgift*, ii. 310; Rogers, *The Catholic Doctrine of the Church of England*, PS, p. 10.

22. PRO, Sta. Cha. 5 A 49/34; *Daungerous positions*, pp. 45 (*sic, recte* 69)–73.

23. Knox, op. cit., p. 55.

24. See pp. 327–8.

25. CUL, MS. Mm. 1. 43, p. 446; *Dedham Minutes*, p. 96; *Daungerous positions*, pp. 118–19.

Part 5 Chapter 1

1. Paule, *Life of Whitgift*, 1612 (19484), p. 35; LPL, MS. 647, fols. 151ᵛ, 162ᵛ.

2. Paule, op. cit., p. 21; BM, MS. Add. 48039, fols. 2ʳ, 86ʳ; *Seconde Parte*, i. 215–16; *Dedham Minutes*, pp. 31, 96.

3. Whitgift, *Works*, PS, iii. 586–96; Strype, *Whitgift*, iii. 70–81; LPL, MS. 647, fol. 162ᵛ; BM, MS. Add. 48039, fol. 2ʳ.

4. Strype prints the articles from Whitgift's Register, grouped under twelve headings (*Whitgift*, i. 220–32), as do Gee & Hardy, *Docs. Illustrative of English Church History*, pp. 481–4. They exist as sixteen articles in the puritan 'register' (*Seconde Parte*, i. 172–4). See also PRO, S.P. 12/163/31.

5. *Lincoln Episcopal Records*, ed. Foster, Lincoln Record Socy ii. 108; Cardwell, *Synodalia*, i. 126–7; Rogers, *The English Creede*, 1585–7 (21226–7), preface dated Febr. 6th, 1585(6), Sig. * iiᵛ.

6. Essex Archaeol. Socy Archives, C 45, pp. 82, 91, 107.

7. *A parte*, p. 282; *A dialogue concerning the strife of our Church*, 1584 (10396), p. 96; PRO, S.P. 12/171/23; NNRO, MS. 20387; BM, MS. Add. 48039, fols. 43ᵛ–4ᵛ, MS. Add. 48064, fol. 26.

8. Dudley Fenner, *A counterpoyson*, 1584 (10770), Sigs. A 6ᵛ–7ʳ; HRO, MS. Gorhambury VIII/B/143, fol. 44; *A dialogue concerning the strife of our Church*, p. 124; Nichols, *The plea of the innocent*, 1602 (18541), pp. 9–10; *Dedham Minutes*, p. 96.

Chapter 2

1. *Seconde Parte*, i. 209–20; DWL, MS. Morrice B II, fols. 39ᵛ–47ʳ; PRO, S.P. 12/163/67; JRL, Rylands English MS. 874, fols. 37ᵛ–8ʳ (a copy of the Sussex subscription incorrectly ascribed to 'the ministers of London'); Strype, *Whitgift*, i. 259.

2. HRO, MS. Gorhambury VIII/B/143, fol. 44; *Dedham Minutes*, pp. 95–6; JRL, Rylands English MS. 874; *Seconde Parte*, i. 174–286.

3. *Dedham Minutes*, pp. 96, 35; DWL, MS. Morrice B II, fol. 46ʳ.

4. NNRO, MS. 20387.

5. There are three versions of Field's views extant: an 'abstract of Mr. Field's opinions', endorsed by Burghley (PRO, S.P. 12/164/11); 'Mr. Field and Mr. Egerton their toleration', apparently prepared for consumption by other ministers and the Puritan laity (DWL, MS. Morrice B II, fols. 94–5, calendared, *Seconde Parte*, i. 284–6); and 'the generall inconveniences of the Booke of Common Prayer' (DWL, MS. Morrice B II, fols. 111–14, calendared *Seconde Parte*, i. 256–7).

6. BM, MS. Lansd. 99, fol. 10; *Seconde Parte*, i. 146–7, 242, 226; JRL, Rylands English MS. 874, fols. 38, 42, 39; BM, MS. Add. 28571, fol. 51; *A parte*, pp. 388–9; ITL, MS. Petyt 538/52, fol. 8; BM, MS. Stowe 159, fols. 151–3ᵛ; Foster, *State of the Church*, Lincoln Record Socy, xxiii. xxvi, 47–51, 53–61.

7. *Seconde Parte*, i. 221, ii. 219, i. 283–4; *Dedham Minutes*, p. 34; ERO, Cal. Q.S.R. XII/89/8, 9; for the total suspended in Essex, see the evidence collected in my 'Classical Movement', p. 432, n. 2; HRO, Archdeaconry of St Albans Records, ASA 5/5/47, 80.

8. *Seconde Parte*, i. 227–8, 241, ii. 165–74, i. 248–51; BM, MS. Lansd. 109, fols. 46–7; CUL, MS. Mm.1.43, p. 437.

9. *Wodrow Miscellany*, ed. Laing, 432–6, 440–4; HRO, MS. Gorhambury VIII/B/143, fol. 43ᵛ.

10. BM, MS. Add. 48064, fols. 167–9, 170–2; ITL, MS. Petyt 538/42, fols. 8–10ᵛ; *Seconde Parte*, i. 230–41; *A parte*, pp. 388–91; Sheffield City Libr., Wentworth Woodhouse MSS, Tracts 32, no. 16; BM, MS. Add. 48039, fol. 52ᵛ.

11. ITL, MS. Petyt 538/52, fols. 8–10; LPL, Whitgift's Register, i. fol. 91; NNRO, MS. 20387; *HMC, 12th Report, App. IV, Rutland MSS*, pp. 160, 162; BM, MS. Add. 48038, fols. 55ᵛ, 1–49, 42. For the argument that the Prayer Book to which subscription was urged had not been authorized by Parliament, see my note in *Notes & Queries*, cc. 362–3.

12. ITL, MS. Petyt 538–52, fols. 8–10.

13. *Seconde Parte*, i. 223–30, 241; JRL, Rylands English MS. 874, fol. 32ᵛ; BM, MS. Lansd. 40, fol. 44.

14. *Seconde Parte*, ii. 187–8, i. 228, 225; *A parte*, pp. 295–6; Colchester & Essex Museum, Essex Archaeol. Socy Archives, C 43, p. 117, C 45 *passim*; PRO, S.P. 12/169/12; LPL, MS. 647, fol. 145.

15. Some's 'certaine points', Hammond's address and Norton's answer (in that order, not identified by editor) in *Seconde Parte*, i. 174–95. Further copies, or variants, of all three in BM, MS.

Stowe 159, fols. 128–9, 135, 145ᵛ. Another copy of Hammond in BM, MS. Add. 48064, fols. 25–9; of Some in JRL, Rylands English MS. 874, fols. 40–2ʳ. 'The copie of a letter, written by a gentleman in the countrey unto a Londoner, touching an answere to the archb. articles', evidently a variant of Norton, in *A parte*, 132–200. Foxe's letter (Latin) known only from a copy in LPL, MS. 2010, no. 75, fols. 117–21.

16. BM, MS. Cotton Vespasian C XIV, ii. fol. 244.

17. Ibid., MS. Add. 48039, fols. 48–56ʳ, 44; ibid., MS. Lansd. 396, fols. 30–2; *HMC, Bath MSS*, ii. 23–4.

18. DWL, MS. Morrice L, no. V, pp. 8–11; BM, MS. Lansd. 43, fol. 7.

19. BM, MS. Add. 15891, fol. 129; ibid., MS. Lansd. 396, fol 31ʳ; ibid., MS. Add. 48039, fol. 43ᵛ.

20. *HMC, Bath MSS*, ii. 24–6; HRO, MS Gorhambury VIII/B/143, fol. 45.

21. *Dedham Minutes*, pp. 35, 94.

22. Ibid., p. 81.

23. JRL, Rylands English MS. 874, fol. 29. Usher mistakenly attributes this letter to Mr Tye, another member of the conference.

24. *Dedham Minutes*, p. 87; Jude, vv. 4, 8.

25. *Dedham Minutes*, pp. 36–7; JRL, Rylands English MS. 874, fols. 33–4.

Chapter 3

1. *Seconde Parte*, i. 221; PRO, S.P. 12/93/8.

2. BM, MS. Lansd. 42, fol. 107, MS. Lansd. 109, fols. 46–7.

3. *A parte*, p. 296; BM, MS. Add. 22473, fols. 23ᵛ, 20ᵛ.

4. DWL, MS. Morrice I, 589(10); *A parte*, p. 297.

5. JRL, Rylands English MS. 874, fol. 39.

6. *Seconde Parte*, i. 252; *Dedham Minutes*, p. 91; Gee & Hardy, *Documents . . .*, p. 509. There is further evidence of the Suffolk and Warwickshire subscriptions in Dudley Fenner, *A defence of the godlie ministers*, 1587 (10771), Sig. G. 3ʳ.

7. *State of the Church*, ed. Foster, xxv; *Dedham Minutes*, *passim*; LPL, MS. Carte Misc. XII, no. 19; *Seconde Parte*, ii. 261–2.

8. Strype, *Whitgift*, iii. 81–7; Prothero, *Constitutional Documents*, 4th edn, pp. 472ᵃ⁻ʰ. For the early resistance of

recusants to the *ex officio* oath, see P. Tyler, *The Ecclesiastical Commission & Catholicism in the North, 1562–77*, 1960, p. 124.

9. *HMC, Bath MSS*, ii. 23–4; BM, MS. Lansd. 42, fol. 105; Strype, *Whitgift*, i. 277; *Dedham Minutes*, pp. 37–8.

10. Rogers, *The English Creede*, Sig. ✶ iiiʳ.

11. Originally published early in 1585 and reprinted in *A parte*, pp. 280–303.

12. Ibid., pp. 294–300; Udall, *The State of the Church of England*, (1588), ed. Arber, 1879, p. 21. Cf. a very similar analysis in Field's preface to *A briefe and plaine declaration*, 1584 (10395), Sig. A4.

13. See the prefaces, both possibly of Field's authorship, to the pamphlets printed by Waldegrave in 1584, *A briefe and plaine declaration* and *A dialogue concerning the strife of our Church*.

14. Copies of Travers's account in *Seconde Parte*, i. 275–83 and BM, MS. Add.

48064, fols. 49–63. The date is supplied from Paule, *Whitgift*, p. 30.

15. *A parte*, p. 295.

16. Paule, op. cit., p. 31; M. C. Curtis, 'Hampton Court Conference & its Aftermath', *History*, xlvi. 1–16; Neale, ii. 81.

17. *HMC, Hatfield MSS* iii. 35–6; *HMC, Bath MSS*, ii. 26–7; BM, MS. Lansd. 396, fols. 49–56; PRO, S.P. 12/171/23.

18. PRO, S.P. 12/172/1; BM, MS. Add. 48039, fols. 49ᵛ–50ʳ.

19. Ibid., MS. Add. 22473, fols. 20–1, 12; PRO, S.P. 12/173/15.

20. BM, MS. Add. 22473, fols. 14–15.

21. See a discussion of the puritan 'survey of the ministry' for Essex, pp. 280–82.

22. BM, MS. Add. 48064, fols. 76–81ʳ, 85–7.

Chapter 4

1. Thomas Rogers, *A sermon upon the 6, 7 and 8 verses of the 12. chapter of . . . Romanes*, 1590 (21240), p. 2.

2. W. J. Couper, *Robert Waldegrave*, Glasgow 1916; Pierce, *Historical Introduction to the Marprelate Tracts*, p. 151.

3. Matthew Sutcliffe, *An answere to a certaine libel supplicatorie*, 1592 (23450), p. 41.

4. *Amendment of Life*, *Obedience to the gospell*, *Peters fall*, all printed in 1584 (24489, 24501, 24503); reprinted in 1596 in *Certaine sermons* (24491). In 1588 Waldegrave printed Udall's famous tract, *The state of the Church of Englande* (24505).

5. *Marprelate Tracts*, ed. Pierce, pp. 272–6; *Transcript of the Stationers' Register*, ed. Arber, ii. 810; Arber, *Introductory Sketch to the Martin Marprelate Controversy*, pp. 51–2; J. Dover Wilson, 'Richard Schilders & the English Puritans', *Trans. Bibliog. Socy*, xi. 65–134.

6. *Survay*, p. 366; *Dedham Minutes*, pp. 35, 94; *Daungerous positions*, pp. 73–4.

7. This account is based on Gordon Donaldson, 'Scottish Presbyterian Exiles in England, 1584–8', *Records of the Scottish Church History Socy*, xiv. 67–80.

8. Whitgift and Adamson's correspondence in BM, MS. Add. 32092, fols. 75ᵛ–6ᵛ, 78ᵛ–80; Robert Beale's comments in MS. Add. 48039, fols. 44ᵛ–5, 53; Walsingham's correspondence in C.S.P., *Scottish*, iii. no. 161, vii. nos. 138, 146, 149, 240.

9. Donaldson, loc. cit., 70.

10. Paget, *A godlie and fruitefull sermon*, 1580? (19102), Sig. A5ᵛ; PRO, S.P. 12/153/55.

11. *Warrender Papers*, ed. Cameron & Rait, i. 203–5; LPL, MS. Carte Misc. XII, nos. 15, 16; Sir Francis Hastings to Sir Richard Grenville, Sept. 2nd, 1583,

Huntington Library, Hastings MS. 5087. I am indebted to Dr M. Claire Cross for this last reference.

12. Donaldson, loc. cit., 72–4; *Seconde Parte*, i. 284; *Wodrow Miscellany*, pp. 449–52; BM, MS. Add. 4736, fol. 166ᵛ.

13. *A parte*, p. 299.

14. Neale, ii. 13–18, 48–51.

15. *Survay*, p. 369.

16. Neale, ii. 23–5; R. C. Gabriel, 'Members of the House of Commons, 1586–7', unpublished London M.A. thesis, 1954, p. 10.

17. *Dedham Minutes*, pp. 40–2; *Daungerous positions*, p. 75; Fuller, *Church History*, 1845 edn v. 83; *Survay*, p. 366; BM, MS. Add. 38492, fols. 68–9.

18. DWL, MS. Morrice B II, fol. 91ᵛ.

19. BM, MS. Add. 38492, fols. 89–91, 107–8, 68–9, 37–8.

20. If one takes the parliamentary documentation, with the internal evidence of the surveys themselves, chiefly biographical, the position seems to be as follows: Some sort of surveys for Warwickshire, Lincolnshire and Essex were ready by Dec. 1584, when they were brought into the Commons in support of petitions from those counties. But the Lincolnshire document must have been an early draft, since the survey as we have it dates from the first two months of 1585, while the Essex survey in its final form contains references to Bishop Aylmer's visitation of 1586. By Feb. 1585, the surveys seem to have been received for parts of Leicestershire, Sussex, Kent, Suffolk, Rutland and Buckinghamshire. The Oxfordshire and Berkshire surveys also date from this Parliament. But the arrangement of the full survey in the *Seconde Parte of a Register* dates from the Parliament of 1586. (D'Ewes, pp. 345b,

349a; *State of the Church*, ed. Foster, xxxiv; *Seconde Parte*, ii. 88–184; BM, MS. Add. 38492, fols. 90–1. Oxon. & Berks. surveys dated from biographical data in *Oxfordshire Archaeol. Socy Report*, 1910; Phillimore, *Calendar of Berkshire Wills*, Oxford Hist. Socy, 1893.)

21. *Seconde Parte*, ii. 161, 153, 109, 166–7; *Daungerous positions*, p. 81; *State of the Church*, ed. Foster, xxxiii–vii.

22. Ibid., xxiv; evidence of the preparation of the Northants. surveys of 1588 and 1603, PRO, Sta. Cha. 5 A 49/34 (deposition of John Johnson), BM, MS. Sloane 271, fols. 20ᵛ–1ʳ; Essex evidence, *Seconde Parte*, ii. 156–65.

23. *A dialogue concerning the strife of our Church*, Sig. A4ʳ; BM, MS. Lansd. 104, fol. 128ᵛ; ibid., MS. Add. 22473, fols. 14–15; *Seconde Parte*, ii. 88.

24. BM, MS. Add. 48038, fols. 56ᵛ–61; Conyers Read, *Mr. Secretary Walsingham*, ii. 261n.; PRO, S.P. 12/175/2.

25. The petition printed in D'Ewes, pp.

357–9 and in Strype, *Whitgift*, iii. 118–24.

26. This paragraph and those that follow for the most part merely digest Neale's definitive account of this Parliament, ii. 58–101.

27. BM, MS. Add. 38492, fols. 37–8.

28. Ibid., MS. Add. 48039, fol. 67ʳ.

29. D'Ewes, p. 339a.

30. I am assuming, with Neale, that we have the text of Turner's Bill in a document in *Seconde Parte*, ii. 215–18.

31. D'Ewes, p. 339a; Neale, ii. 62–3.

32. In his famous *Sermon preached at Paules Crosse* on Feb. 9th, 1589 (1346), Bancroft alluded to three distinct recent editions of the *Booke of the forme of common prayers*. Of these the first, printed 'about four years since', can be identified from a quotation with the edition printed by Waldegrave (16567). It is therefore a strong presumption that Turner's 'Book' was a copy of this same edition.

33. *Dedham Minutes*, p. 59.

Part 6 Chapter 1

1. *Daungerous positions*, pp. 73–4.

2. *Dedham Minutes*, p. 45.

3. *Seconde Parte*, ii. 216.

4. BM, MS. Add. 38492, fol. 37ᵛ.

5. PRO, Sta. Cha. 5 A 49/34.

6. M. G. Campbell, *Discipline, or Book of Order of the Reformed Churches of France*, 1924. Field's 'register' contained a copy of the revised form of 1571 (*Seconde Parte*, i. 77–8).

7. Donaldson, *Scottish Reformation*, pp. 198–9, 203–4.

8. Scott Pearson, pp. 161–3.

9. *Daungerous positions*, pp. 74–5.

10. See my paper, 'The Elizabethan Puritans & the Foreign Reformed Churches in London', *Procs. Hug. Socy*, xx. 549.

11. There are contemporary English translations of the Acts of this synod, BM, MS. Add. 48014, fols. 193–9; BL, MS. Tanner 78, fols. 155–8.

12. *Daungerous positions*, p. 76; *Survay*, p. 366.

13. LPL, MS. Carte Misc. IV, no. 190.

14. S. J. Knox, *Walter Travers*, 1962, *passim*.

15. Reprinted in facsimile by Peter Lorimer, 1872.

16. Scott Pearson, p. 392.

17. Ibid., pp. 227–33, 290–4; *Survay*, pp. 377, 375; *Daungerous positions*, p. 73.

18. Ibid., p. 76.

19. See above, p. 108.

20. When I first saw the BM copy of this edn in 1954 (pressmark C.111.b.6) this leaf was lightly attached to the inside back cover and was so described in my 'John Field & Elizabethan Puritanism', *Eliz. Govt & Socy*, ed. Bindoff, Hurstfield & Williams, p. 156. Since rebinding it occupies the position of Sig. E 7, and it is now apparent that it belongs to that gathering. This is confirmed by the LPL copy (pressmark 1598.27.(3)), where the leaf is paginated, p. 77, but left untrimmed.

21. *Seconde Parte*, ii. 215–18.

22. Corpus Christi College, Oxford, MS. 294, pp. 1–11; LPL, MS. 113, fols. 180–6; Baker's copy, BM, MS. Harl. 7029, fols. 58–63.

23. The three MSS cited above and two copies in Trinity College, Dublin, noted by Knox, op. cit., p. 101. Bishop Francis Paget collated the Harley and Lambeth texts in his *Introduction to the Fifth Book of Hooker's Laws of Ecclesiastical Polity* (1907), and A. F. Scott Pearson printed the Oxford text in his

Alteste Englische Presbyterianismus (1912).

24. BM, MS. Harl. 6539, fols. 76–86 agrees with the 1644 text. Queen's College, Oxford, MS. 280, fols. 163ʳ–9ʳ is an independent translation. Neither was known to Bancroft who makes his own translation from the Latin. Yet the Harleian MS. embodies the form of approbation, and both texts lack the additions made in September 1587. It is therefore possible that the Discipline was circulated in English. I am not able to date precisely the hands in which these two MSS are written, but they are not much later than the late 16th century.

25. *A directory*, Sigs. C4ʳ, A3ᵛ.

26. Mrs W. W. D. Campbell (M. G. Campbell) noted points of agreement with and divergence from the French Discipline in her paper, 'Early English Presbyterianism and the Reformed Church of France', *Journ. of the Presbyt. Hist. Socy of England*, ii. 123–33. Cf. her *Discipline or Book of Order*, pp. v–xii.

The French Discipline stresses the parity of minister and elder, where the English Discipline assumes the presidency of the pastor. The French *colloque* met twice yearly or quarterly, the English conference once every six weeks.

27. See pp. 159–77 and 185 of Cartwright's translation, *A full and plaine declaration*, (24184).

28. *Puritan Manifestoes*, p. 119.

29. This question is discussed by J. M. Ross, 'The Elizabethan Elder', *Journ. of the Presbyt. Hist. Socy of England*, x. 59–70, 126–38.

30. *Puritan Manifestoes*, p. 98; *A full and plaine declaration*, pp. 73–158.

31. *A booke of the form of common prayers*, 1584 (16567), p. 18.

32. *A directory*, Sigs. A2ᵛ–3ʳ.

33. Ibid., Sig. A4ʳ.

34. *A full and plaine declaration*, pp. 178–9.

35. Pp. 111–45.

36. *A directory*, Sigs. A 3, C 1–4ʳ.

37. *A booke of the forme of common prayers*, Middelburg 1586 (16568), Sigs. E 3–4ʳ.

Chapter 2

1. *Dedham Minutes*, p. 92.

2. Neale, ii. 104. Once again, this account of the puritan campaign in Parliament follows Neale's narrative closely.

3. *Seconde Parte*, ii. 72.

4. Ibid., ii. 89–97, 70–87.

5. Ibid., ii. 174–7, 185–7.

6. For the evidence on which this calculation is based, see my 'Classical Movement', p. 557, n. 1. All but twelve of the names will be found in a list in *Seconde Parte*, ii. 260–1.

7. *Dedham Minutes*, p. 58.

8. *Seconde Parte*, ii. 188–90, 191–2, i. 274–5.

9. *Dedham Minutes*, pp. 50–1, 59.

10. *Survay*, p. 369; Neale, ii. 104–5, 147; R. C. Gabriel, 'Members of the House of Commons, 1586–7', unpubl. London M.A. thesis, 1954, pp. 6–8.

11. *The Black Book of Warwick*, ed. Kemp, Warwick 1898, pp. 386–97; Scott Pearson, pp. 295–7.

12. Neale, ii. 147–8, 151, 161; Neale, 'Peter Wentworth', *E.H.R.*, xxxix. 50; *Dedham Minutes*, p. 98; *Daungerous positions*, pp. 76, 122; *A petition made to the Convocation house, 1586*, reprinted, *A parte*, pp. 323–33.

13. *Seconde Parte*, ii. 212–15; Neale, ii. 149.

14. There were altogether three edns of the 'Middelburg Book', in 1586, 1587, 1602; a conflated text in *Reliquiae Liturgicae*, ed. Hall, 1847, i. 1–107.

15. *A sermon preached at Paules Crosse*, 1588 [1589] (1346), pp. 62–4.

16. *A booke of the forme of common prayers*, Sigs. E 2ᵛ–4ʳ, 8; 1584 edn, pp. 13–17.

17. Neale, ii. 104.

18. Ibid., 106–44.

19. Ibid., 166–81, 148.

20. Ibid., 149–54. Penry's *Aequity of an humble supplication* is reprinted in a modern edn of his *Treatises Concerning Wales*, ed. D. Williams, 1959. Cf. Downlee's 'Letter to the lord chancellor, being put out of the commission of the peace', BM, MS. Add. 48064, fols. 144ʳ–5ʳ.

21. Neale, ii. 154–7, 174; cf. his 'Peter Wentworth', loc. cit., 47–54.

22. Pierpoint Morgan Library, New York, MS. 276, pp. 13–27. Sir John Neale kindly allowed me to use his transcript of Throckmorton's speeches.

23. D'Ewes, p. 410; BM, MS. Harley 7188, fol. 92ᵛ.

24. Neale, ii. 157–62; the anonymous

diarist's account of these speeches, BM.
MS. Harley 7188, fols. 95^v–9^v; 'Mr.
Solicitor's Notes', PRO, S.P. 12/199/2.

25. See the *Tracts Ascribed to Richard Ban-croft*, embodying material collected c. 1583–5, ed. A. Peel, Cambridge 1953.
26. Ibid., p. xviii.
27. PRO, S.P. 12/199/1; All Souls College, Oxford, MS. 204, p. 59.
28. LPL, MS. 178, fols. 48–51.
29. Ibid., fol. 52.
30. Ibid., fol. 59^v.

31. *Tracts Ascribed to Richard Bancroft*, pp. 58–9.
32. LPL, MS. 178, fols. 85^r–7^v.
33. Neale, ii. 162–4. The queen's message is in LPL, MS. 178, fol. 88^r.
34. BM, MS. Add. 48064, fol. 148^v. The bishop was Cooper of Winchester, and the tale is repeated in the para-Martinist tract, *A dialogue, wherein is plainly laide open the tyrannical dealing of L. Bishopps against Gods children*, 1589?, Sig. D^v.

Chapter 3

1. This survives appended to the LPL text of the Book (MS. 113, fol. 186); attached to a copy seized by the authorities in Warwickshire, bearing the names of twelve subscribers (BM, MS. Harl. 6849, fol. 222, whence transcribed in MS. Harl. 7042, fol. 41^r, printed by Strype in *Whitgift*, i. 502–3 and by Lorimer in his facsimile edn of the *Directory*); in the depositions of two ministers in the Star Chamber, 1591 (PRO, Sta. Cha. 5 A 49/34); and in the Dedham papers (*Dedham Minutes*, pp. 92–3). These versions vary in significant details but agree in substance. A shorter formula is appended to the text in MS. Harl. 6539 (fol. 86^v) and to the printed *Directory* of 1645.
2. PRO, Sta. Cha. 5 A 56/1.
3. *Dedham Minutes*, pp. 92–3.
4. This complicates the dating of the articles of approbation, since it was also agreed that provincial meetings should be held every half-year. It is possible that this advice was circulated before the Parliament of Nov. 1586.
5. 1822 edn i. 387, n.
6. *Dedham Minutes*, pp. 98, 60–1; JRL, Rylands English MS. 874, fol. 37.
7. *Daungerous positions*, p. 76; *Survay*, p. 366; *Dedham Minutes*, p. 70.
8. Ibid., pp. 61–7. Usher's transcription omits from the June meeting Tay's renewed motion and its deferment (JRL, Rylands English MS. 874, fol. 10^r).
9. PRO, Sta. Cha. 5 A 49/34.
10. *Two Elizabethan Puritan Diaries*, ed. Knappen, pp. 55–6, 58–9. Cf. the diary of Samuel Willingham, parson of Stone, Lincs., and Walter Newton, Hunts.: 'September 10, 11, 1587: At the rising of the moon I went to Stourbridge before midnight. 13, 14: I came

home from Stourbridge at night, being Wednesday.' (PRO, S.P. 9/42/(2).)
11. *Dedham Minutes*, p. 66.
12. Transcribed by Thomas Baker from a manuscript in the possession of John Laughton, a late 17th-century librarian of Trinity College, Cambridge (BM, MS. Harl. 7029, fol. 64). Printed by Strype in *Annals*, III. ii. 477–9. Bancroft knew of this meeting from the Warwickshire *Acta* of the following spring (*Daungerous positions*, pp. 85–6), but efforts to obtain further information from the Puritan defendants and witnesses in the Star Chamber in 1591 proved unproductive.
13. *Dedham Minutes*, p. 66.
14. *Daungerous positions*, p. 76.
15. PRO, Sta. Cha. 5 A 49/34, depositions of Johnson and Stone.
16. BM, MS. Add. 29546, fol. 56^v.
17. PRO, S.P. 12/225/67–70; H. I. Longden, *Northants. & Rutland Clergy from 1500*, v. 71; BM, MS. Harl. 7029, fol. 64^v; PRO, Sta. Cha. 5 A 49/34, depositions of Johnson, Stone and Thomas Barber; ibid., S.P. 12/168/1; Principal Probate Registry, Somerset House, P.C.C. wills, 2 Drury; *Writings of Greenwood, 1587–90*, ed. Carlson, ENT, iv. 97–102; Payne's letter, reconstructed from fragments in *Daungerous positions*, pp. 133–4, BM, MS. Lansd. 120, fol. 75, MS. Harl. 6866, fol. 318; William Ames, *A second manuduction for Mr. Robinson*, 1615 (556), pp. 3–4.
18. *Daungerous positions*, p. 88.
19. Gellibrand was temporarily resident at Southam at this time. (W. I. Smith, *Historical Notices . . . Relating to . . . Southam*, 1894, baptismal register, p. 11, marriage register, p. 4.)
20. The subscriptions of the Warwicks. ministers, BM, MS. Harl. 6849, fol.

222; responses of Fen, Lord, Wight and Cartwright, PRO, Sta. Cha. 5 A 56/1. Questioned about the synod in which they seem to have subscribed, all denied knowledge of a meeting 'in or near the town of Warwick'; while two Warwicks. witnesses, Hercules Cleveley and Anthony Nutter, referred to meetings in 1588 to deal with the Discipline 'in the town of Warwick and Coventry'. Lord confessed that he subscribed 'at his own house at Wolston'.

21. Pierce, *Historical Introduction to the Marprelate Tracts*, pp. 188–9, 206–8.
22. BM, MS. Harl. 7029, fol. 64ᵛ.
23. *Daungerous positions*, pp. 86–7. Substantially the same rendering will be found in 'the proceedinges of certayne

undutifull ministers, tending to innovation, soe farr as is hetherto disclosed by certain papers and letters founde amongst them', BM, MS. Harl. 6866, fols. 321ᵛ–2ʳ.

24. This is the more likely rendering of the original sense (*dato occasione?*) than Bancroft's 'upon every occasion'.
25. BM, MS. Harl. 7042, fol. 42ʳ; PRO, Sta. Cha. 5 A 27/33.
26. Printed by Bancroft, 'faithfully translated word for word, out of their own Latin copy', which was 'extant, to be seen, under Master Wight's hand'; *Daungerous positions*, pp. 46–8 (*sic, recte* 70–2).
27. *Church History*, 1845 edn v. 7.

Part 7 Chapter 1

1. PRO, Sta. Cha. 5 A 49/34.
2. *Writings of John Greenwood, 1587–90*, ed. Carlson, ENT, iv. 194.
3. *Puritan Manifestoes*, p. 98.
4. *Writings of Henry Barrow, 1587–90*, ed. Carlson, ENT, iii. 233; *Writings of Greenwood*, 191, 242–3, 249–51, 189.
5. For the details on which this assessment is based, see my 'Classical Movement', pp. 656–7.
6. *Seconde Parte*, i. 71–2.
7. BM, MS. Add. 41655, fols. 23, 24.
8. *Dedham Minutes*, pp. 37, 47, 44, 69.
9. Folger Shakespeare Libr., Washington D.C., MS. Box 1472, Bacon V. folder 11. I owe this reference to Dr A. H. Smith.
10. BM, MS. Egerton 2713, fols. 210–11, 220–3.
11. Ibid., MS. Egerton 1693, fol. 98ʳ.
12. *Dedham Minutes*, pp. 27–8, 42–7, 51.
13. *Daungerous positions*, pp. 113–14; BM, MS. Lansd. 64, fol. 54; ibid., MS. Harl. 6849, fol. 233ᵛ.
14. For much relevant information on the question of impropriations, see Christopher Hill, *Economic Problems of the Church from Whitgift to the Long Parliament*, pp. 132–67.
15. An estimate of 1617; BM, MS. Add. 21054, fol. 71ᵛ.
16. *Dedham Minutes*, pp. 61–7; JRL, Rylands English MS. 874, fol. 10ʳ (supplying a sentence missing in Usher's transcript of the Dedham minutes); Muskett, *Suffolk Manorial Families*, i. 111–12.

17. *Seconde Parte*, ii. 28–35; NNRO, Norwich Diocesan Archives, DEP/24, fols. 251ᵛ–7ᵛ.
18. Typescript notes on ecclesiastical disturbances in Ipswich in 1637, compiled from material in the PRO, and deposited in Ipswich Public Libr.
19. Blomefield, *History of Norfolk*, iv. 300–1.
20. 'Life of Gouge', Samuel Clarke, *A general Martyrologie*, 1677, pt. 2, p. 239; *Diary of John Manningham*, ed. Bruce, CS, xcix. 74–5, 101; *Daungerous positions*, p. 124.
21. See above pp. 86–8.
22. *Daungerous positions*, p. 84; Corpus Christi College, Oxford, MS. 318, fol. 143.
23. *Writings of Greenwood*, p. 248; *Dedham Minutes*, pp. 45, 83–4; *Daungerous positions*, p. 103; CUL, MS. Mm.1.43, p. 446; *Seconde Parte*, i. 132.
24. *Sophronistes: a dialogue, perswading the people to reverence and attend the ordinance of God, in the ministerie of their owne pastors*, 1589 (22930), p. 55.
25. BM, MS. Add. 38492, fol. 107; Ipswich Borough Record Office, Assembly Book 20–30 Eliz., meetings of July 19th, 1585, March 19th, 1586.
26. BM, MS. Lansd. 61, fol. 76; *State Trials*, 1730 edn, I. xiv.
27. *Daungerous positions*, pp. 120, 122–3; *Survay*, p. 369; BM, MS. Harl. 6849, fol. 220ʳ.
28. Ibid., MS. Add. 6394, fol. 107ʳ; Strype,

Annals, III. 1. 178–9; BM, MS. Lansd. 33, fol. 48; T. W. Davids, *Annals of Evangelical Nonconformity in Essex*, pp. 69–72.

29. *Seconde Parte*, ii. 70.
30. *Daungerous positions*, pp. 46–8 (*sic*, *recte* 70–2); *Seconde Parte*, i. 71.
31. *Daungerous positions*, pp. 86–7; BM, MS. Harl. 6849, fol. 222ᵛ; PRO, Sta. Cha. 5 A 27/33, deposition of Richard

Hawgar; *Writings of Greenwood*, pp. 190, 203.
32. *Daungerous positions*, pp. 113–14; BM, MS. Lansd. 64, fols. 53–4. The evidence digested in this material was that of Richard Hawgar, who was also one of the Crown witnesses in the Star Chamber. Johnson's evidence in PRO, Sta. Cha. 5 A 49/34.
33. *Writings of Barrow*, p. 54.

Chapter 2

1. *Writings of Greenwood*, pp. 183–5.
2. PRO, Sta. Cha. 5 A 49/34.
3. *Writings of Greenwood*, pp. 185, 201.
4. *Dedham Minutes*, pp. 69–73, 49–50; Josias Nichols, *Plea of the innocent*, 1602 (18541), pp. 212–14; JRL, Rylands English MS. 524, fol. 2ʳ. For Scottish practice, see G. B. Burnet, *The Holy Communion in the Reformed Church of Scotland, 1560–1960*, 1960, pp. 35–63.
5. ERO, D/AEA/12, 13, 14, 15, numerous refs. of which details will be found in my 'Classical Movement', pp. 798–800; further information in BM, MS. Add. 48064, fols. 85–7.
6. *Writings of Greenwood*, p. 184.
7. BM, MS. Harl. 6866, fol. 320.
8. See p. 138.
9. *Daungerous positions*, p. 87.
10. Ibid., pp. 113–15; PRO, Sta. Cha. 5 A

49/34, 27/33; *Writings of Greenwood*, p. 213.
11. *Daungerous positions*, p. 47 (*sic, recte* 71); PRO, Sta. Cha. 5 A 49/34.
12. PRO, S.P. 12/78/38.
13. *Writings of Greenwood*, pp. 201–2.
14. *The Reconstruction of the English Church*, i. 249–67; and in *Church Quarterly Review*, lviii. 107–14.
15. BM, MS. Add. 38492, fol. 34ʳ.
16. Richard Rogers, *Seaven treatises*, 1605 (21216ᵃ), pp. 497–8; PRO, Sta. Cha. 5 A 27/33, 49/34; Richard Hooker, *Works*, i. 150 n. 1.
17. PRO, Sta. Cha. 5 A 49/34.
18. *Daungerous positions*, pp. 116–17; *Dedham Minutes*, pp. 99–101, 47, 50.
19. The history of this activity, still largely unwritten, will provide another dimension for the study of the social history of the English Reformation.

Chapter 3

1. John Geree, *The character of an old English puritane, or nonconformist*, 1646, p. 1.
2. Robert Parsons, *A brief discours contayning certayne reasons why catholiques refuse to goe to church*, Douai 1580 (19394), Sig. ‡ iiiiʳ.
3. *Tracts Ascribed to Richard Bancroft*, ed. Peel, p. 10; *Puritan Manifestoes*, p. 11; Horton Davies, *The Worship of the English Puritans*, pp. 38, 81; *Writings of John Greenwood*, pp. 57–8, 75.
4. *Laws of Ecclesiastical Polity*, V. xxvii. 1.
5. McMillan, *The Worship of the Scottish Reformed Church, 1550–1638*. See also W. D. Maxwell, *Worship in the Church of Scotland*, pp. 67–73, G. Donaldson, *The Making of the Scottish Prayer Book of 1637*, pp. 13–18. The element of freedom in Scottish worship receives

more emphasis in Burnet, *The Holy Communion . . .*, pp. 11–12.
6. *A brief apologie of Thomas Cartwright*, 1596 (4706), Sigs. C2ᵛ–3.
7. Op. cit., p. 98. However Davies later concedes (p. 116) that 'the main stream of the Puritan tradition was in favour of liturgical prayer, provided that this did not exclude free prayer.' The argument seems to be confused by uncertainties of nomenclature.
8. *Puritan Manifestoes*, p. 22; University College, Oxford, MS. E. 152, fol. 1ᵛ; ERO, D/AEA/12, fol. 90ᵛ.
9. PRO, S.P. 12/164/11; E. C. Ratcliff, 'Puritan Alternatives to the Prayer Book', in *The English Prayer Book, 1549–1662*, Alcuin Club, 1963, esp. pp. 75–9.
10. There is an example of this practice in

Arthur Hildersham's memoir of Richard Greenham, JRL, Rylands English MS. 524, fol. 11.

11. DWL, MS. Morrice A, fol. 160ʳ; ERO, Maldon Borough Records, D/B/3/3/ 155/5; *Sophronistes, A Dialogue*, p. 42.

12. *Seconde Parte*, ii. 216–17; *The Life and Death of William Bedell*, CS, n.s. iv. 5; Field, *Godly prayers and meditations* (described in the following note), Sig. A2ᵛ; my *A Mirror of Elizabethan Puritanism*, Friends of DWL 17th lecture 1963 (1964), pp. 33–5.

13. 'John Field's Prayers', as they are described in a catalogue of books appended to a will of 1592 (George Tenacre, P.C.C. 58 Harrington), survive only in the edn of 1601 (10846), of which Sion College Library possesses an almost unique copy. From the preface it is clear that the collection was first published with *Praiers of Maister John Calvin* (ent. Apr. 12th, 1583, Arber, *Stationers' Register*, ii. 194b) and subsequently reissued, possibly as a contribution to the polemics of 1584.

14. Cartwright, *A brief apologie*, Sig. C3ʳ; 'Life of Bradshaw', Samuel Clarke, *A general Martyrologie*, pt. 2, p. 52; *Surrey Archaeol. Colls.* xvii. 174; BM, MS. Add. 19794, fols. 83ʳ, 51ᵛ–64ʳ, 81ᵛ–2ʳ; Geree, op. cit., pp. 1–2.

15. *Tracts Ascribed to Richard Bancroft*, pp. 71, 52–3, 77–8; *Dedham Minutes*, pp. 33, 50, 66, 48; PRO, Sta. Cha. 5 A 56/1.

16. *Institutes*, IV. xvii. 43.

17. *Dedham Minutes*, pp. 99, 48, 55.

18. See the analyses of successive versions of the Geneva Book in W. D. Maxwell, *John Knox's Genevan Service Book, 1556*, and Horton Davies, op. cit., pp. 261–7.

19. *Dedham Minutes*, p. 93; *Writings of Henry Barrow*, pp. 130–1; references to the purchase of 'Geneva books' noted by Dr H. G. Owen in his unpublished London Ph.D. thesis, 'The London Parish Clergy in the Reign of Elizabeth I', 1957, p. 478; Grindal, *Remains*, pp. 203–4. No evidence of any kind exists to support Maxwell's statement (*John Knox's Genevan Service Book*, p. 75) that 'many other editions' of the *Forme of prayers* 'must have appeared for the use of the Puritans' of which 'all trace has since been lost.'

20. CUL, MS. Ee. 11. 34, nos. 224–6, 191; BM, MS. Egerton 1693, fol. 89ʳ; CUL, Ely Diocesan Records, B 2/10, fol. 110ᵛ; ERO, D/ACA/19, fol. 5ᵛ.

21. *Puritan Manifestoes*, pp. 149–50.

22. Procter & Frere, *History of the Book of Common Prayer*, pp. 115, 133–5; A. E. Peaston, *The Prayer Book Tradition in the Free Churches*, 1964, pp. 21–34.

23. CUL, Ely Diocesan Records, B 2/10, fols. 77, 74ᵛ; BM, MS. Lansd. 42, fol. 187; NNRO, Norwich Diocesan Archives, DEP/24, fols. 260ʳ, 251ᵛ–4ʳ, 10ʳ–11ʳ; Corpus Christi College, Oxford, MS. E. 297, no. 8, fol. 18; Canon XIV.

24. BM, MS. Lansd. 8, fol. 16.

25. Peaston, op. cit., pp. 31–2.

26. GLRO, Consistory Court of London Records, DL/C/213, depositions relating to Philip Gilgate, vicar of Boxted, June 1st, 1590.

27. Ibid.

28. William Pond of Laindon Hills, Essex, was said to have refused to kneel at the communion and for the general confession, but 'most commonly leaneth his back to a pew.' He admitted having 'set with his hat on.' (ERO, D/ACA/12, fol. 199ʳ.)

29. *Seconde Parte*, i. 289–91; BM, MS. Lansd. 42, fol. 187.

30. ERO, D/AEA/12, fols. 40ʳ, 160ᵛ; BM, MS. Lansd. 42, fol. 187; P. Tyler, *The Ecclesiastical Commission & Catholicism in the North, 1562–77*, 1960, pp. 76–7; DWL, MS. Morrice A, fol. 16ᵛ; HRO, St Albans Archdeaconry Records, ASA 5/5/523; Hooker, *Works*, iii. 573; PRO, S.P. 12/78/38. For the Scottish practice, see Burnet, op. cit., pp. 25–8.

31. *Puritan Manifestoes*, p. 26; *Dedham Minutes*, p. 39; JRL, Rylands English MS. 524, fol. 11ʳ.

32. For a discussion of such bizarre Christian names, see P. A. Scholes, *The Puritans & Music*, pp. 113–16. Scholes probably underestimates this phenomenon. For an example of scrupulosity in this respect, see *Daungerous positions*, p. 105.

33. *Puritan Manifestoes*, pp. 28, 143; *The forme of prayers*, 1584 edn (16567), Sig. E4ᵛ.

34. LPL, MS. Carte. Misc. XII, no. 16; GLRO, Consistory Court of London Records, DL/C/334, Vicar-General's Book, Stanhope Pt. I, fol. 343ʳ; BM, MS. Add. 4736, fol. 166ᵛ; *Daungerous positions*, p. 104; will of Richard Cox, Guildhall Library, MS. 9051/4, fol. 90ᵛ. I owe two of these references to Dr H. G. Owen.

Chapter 4

1. For an account of the non-separating congregationalists, see Perry Miller, *Orthodoxy in Massachusetts, 1630–50*, pp. 75–101.
2. See especially *A manuduction for M. Robinson*, 1614 (no S.T.C. entry), and *A second manuduction (sic)*, 1615 (556).
3. *A manuduction*, Sig. Q4ʳ.
4. Gifford, *A briefe discourse of . . . the countrie divinitie*, 1582 (11845), fol. 43ᵛ; BM, MS. Add. 48064, fol. 79ᵛ.
5. PRO, S.P. 12/159/27; BM, MS. Lansd. 61, fol. 73ʳ; ERO, D/AEA/13, 14, courts of Jan. 19th, 1587, Dec. 12th, 1588.
6. Bartimaeus Andrewes, *Certaine verie worthie godlie and profitable sermons*, 1583 (585), p. 186; GLRO, Consistory Court of London Records, DL/C/213, depositions relating to Philip Gilgate, vicar of Boxted, Nov. 3rd, 1589; BM, MS. Lansd. 61, fol. 73ʳ; ERO, D/AEA/9, fol. 13ᵛ, 9/12, fols. 89ʳ, 93ᵛ–4ʳ.
7. Bullock, *Voluntary Religious Societies, 1520–1799*, 1963, esp. pp. 114–19.
8. Andrewes, op. cit., p. 141; Richard Baxter, *Works*, 1830 edn, xiii. 444.
9. Strype, *Aylmer*, p. 71.
10. Geree, *The character of an old English puritane*, p. 5; for the place of 'repetition' in the godly household, see *The Diary of Lady Margaret Hoby*, ed. Meads, esp. pp. 65, 244–5, n. 188.
11. PRO, S.P. 12/176/68.
12. Whitgift for Chichester, *sede vacante*, 1585, Kennedy, *Elizabethan Episcopal Administration*, iii. 182; cf. Aylmer for London, 1586, ibid., 205.
13. ERO, Maldon Borough Records, D/B/3/3/178, D/B/3/3/422/2; ibid., D/AEA/12, fol. 89ʳ.
14. John Udall, *Two sermons of obedience to the gospell*, in *Certaine sermons*, 1596 (24491), Sig. I i iiijʳ.
15. ERO, Maldon Borough Records, D/B/3/3/178, D/B/3/3/397/13, D/B/3/3/422/2.
16. Rogers, *Seaven treatises*, p. 497.
17. Geree, op. cit., p. 3; Nicholas Bownd, *The doctrine of the Sabbath*, 1595 (3436), pp. 210–22, 235–46; Udall, op. cit., Sig. I i iiij.
18. ERO, D/AEA/12, fol. 199ʳ; Nicholas Bownd, *The holy exercise of fasting*, 1604 (3438), pp. 212–13.
19. LPL, MS. Carte Misc. XII, no. 19; Settle, *A catechisme*, c. 1587 (22267), epistle; *Seconde Parte*, ii. 39, 262.
20. ITL, MS. Petyt 538/47, fols. 492–3; BM, MS. Lansd. 157, fol. 186; ERO, D/AEA/12, fols. 103–4ʳ, 115ᵛ, 266, 92ᵛ–3ʳ; BM, MS. Add. 48064, fol. 85ʳ.
21. Dedham Minutes, p. 35; *Troubles of our Catholic Forefathers*, ed. Morris, ii. 240–1, 250–1; George Gifford, *A sermon on the parable of the sower*, 1583 (11863), Sig. Avii;ʳ DWL, MS. Morrice B II, fol. 8ᵛ. For the participation of women in the puritan sects, see K. Thomas, 'Women & the Civil War Sects', *Past & Present*, xiii. 42–62, repr. *Crisis in Europe: 1560–1660*, pp. 317–40.
22. *A manudiction*, Sigs. P4ᵛ, Q1ʳ.
23. *Daungerous positions*, pp. 123–4.
24. Miller, op. cit., p. 87.
25. Rogers, op. cit., pp. 497–8.
26. *Dedham Minutes*, pp. 30, 28.
27. The short title of this tract is *Sophronistes*.

Part 8 Chapter 1

1. Quoted, Neale, *Queen Elizabeth*, p. 300.
2. *The plea of the innocent*, 1602 (18541), pp. 31–2.
3. BM, MS. Lansd. 66, fol. 150.
4. References will be found in my *Letters of Thomas Wood*, pp. xxxvii–xl.
5. DWL, MS. Morrice I, p. 417(8).
6. A volume in LPL, MS. 178, is suggestive of this political grouping; it is a collection of Whitgift, Hatton and Bancroft papers, transcribed by Whitgift's secretary and household steward, Michael Murgatroyd, and inscribed 'Memorials of affairs in church and state in Archbishop Whitgift's time'. See also a volume of commemorative verses for Cosin, edited by his pupil William Barlow in 1598, *Vita et obitus . . . Richardi Cosin* (1460).
7. Udall, *The state of the Church of England*, ed. Arber, p. 10; Digges, *Humble motives for association to maintaine religion established*, 1601 (6873), pp. 24–5.

8. See my 'John Field & Elizabeth Puritanism', *Elizabethan Government & Society*, ed. Bindoff, Hurstfield & Williams, pp. 161–2; CUL, MS. Mm.1.29, fol. 59ᵛ.

9. Nichols, op. cit., pp. 31–2; *Writings of John Greenwood, 1587–90*, ed. Carlson, ENT iv. 197, 241–4.

10. Nichols, op. cit., p. 31; BM, MS. Harl. 7042, fol. 42, MS. Harl. 6849, fol. 220, MS. Harl. 6866, fols. 323–5ᵛ, MS. Lansd. 120, fol. 76ʳ; *Daungerous positions*, pp. 57, 127–8.

11. BM, MS. Lansd. 120, fol. 76ʳ, MS. Harl. 7042, fol. 42ᵛ; Arber, *Introductory Sketch to the Marprelate Controversy*, p. 83; PRO, Sta. Cha. 5 A 27/33, deposition of Richard Holmes, 49/34, Edmunds's deposition.

12. Ibid., 27/33, deposition of Richard Hawgar; *Two Elizabethan Puritan Diaries*, ed. Knappen, pp. 78, 99, 98.

13. What follows is based on the standard studies of the Marprelate problem: E. Arber, *An Introductory Sketch*, 1879; W. Pierce, *An Historical Introduction to the Marprelate Tracts*, 1908; G. Bonnard, *La Controverse de Martin Marprelate*, Geneva 1916; also on J. Dover Wilson in *Cambridge Hist. Eng. Lit.*, iii and *Martin Marprelate & Shakespeare's Fluellen*, 1912. The tracts are quoted from Pierce's edn, 1911.

14. Penry's *Exhortation* reprinted in D. Williams's edn of the *Three Treatises Concerning Wales*, 1960. His complete writings are about to appear in the series, Elizabethan Nonconformist Texts, ed. Leland H. Carlson.

15. Some of these items are usually stated to have been printed at Kingston, presumably in Udall's house. But East Molesey was a chapelry in the parish of Kingston, and Mrs Crane's house may well have been the only premises in the district which Waldegrave used.

16. The phrase is Matthew Sutcliffe's, *An answere unto a certaine calumnious letter published by M. Iob Throkmorton*, 1595 (23451), fol. 56ʳ. Sutcliffe mentions other Martinist libels which are no longer extant, *Martins interim* and *The crops and flowers of Bridges garden* (ibid., fol. 72ᵛ). Add to these 'More worke for Cooper', which was on the press when Hodgkins and his men were taken.

17. *Tracts*, p. 122.

18. Ibid., pp. 238–9, 304; Arber, op. cit., pp. 122, 149, 99; Scott Pearson, p. 451;

19. Nichols, op. cit., pp. 32–3; Brightman, *Workes*, 1644, pp. 149–50.

Mrs Crane's identity was established by J. N. McCorkle, 'A Note Concerning "Mistress Crane" and the Martin Marprelate Controversy', *Library*, 4th ser. xii. 276–83. Miss K. M. Longley, of the Minster Library, York, in an unpublished paper, 'A New Approach to the Marprelate Tracts', has dated her marriage to Carleton between Feb. and Nov. 1589. For her part in the Marprelate affair and for her contempt of court, Mrs Crane was heavily fined and imprisoned (PRO, Sta. Cha. 5 A 30/22; BM, MS. Harl. 2143, fols. 48ᵛ–9ʳ).

20. Northants. Record Office, K. CI. 1017. I owe this reference to Miss Longley.

21. Pierce, op. cit., p. 207.

22. *Cambr. Hist. of Engl. Lit.*, iii. 377.

23. Arber, op. cit., p. 94; *Tracts*, pp. 82–3.

24. Ibid., p. 246.

25. The case against Throckmorton rests largely on Sutcliffe's *Answere unto a certaine calumnious letter*, together with the examinations of the printers Hodgkins, Simms and Thomlyn, printed by Pierce, op. cit., pp. 333–9. For the parliamentary speeches and Neale's view, see Neale ii. 109–11, 150–2, 169–73, 220.

26. *Notebook of John Penry, 1593*, ed. Peel, CS 3rd ser. lxvii. pp. 62–7, 69–71; *The defence of Iob Throkmorton*, Middelburg 1594 (24055), Sig. E ii.

27. *Tracts*, pp. 322–3. Pierce took the evidence of the *Theses* to refer to Throckmorton's authorship. But his case really rests on the assumption that the *Protestatyon*, printed at Wolston in September 1589, belongs to the primary series. The author of this last of the tracts claimed to 'go under the name of Martin Marprelate.' This surely points to an assumption of the pseudonym by Throckmorton rather than to the original Martin.

28. I am indebted to Miss Longley for many helpful suggestions communicated in conversation some years ago, and to Sir John Neale for allowing me to see a copy of her essay, 'A New Approach to the Marprelate Tracts', which is in his possession.

29. PRO, S.P. 12/168/1.

30. Neale, ii. 194–201; Sutcliffe, op. cit., fol. 30ᵛ.

31. *A sermon preached at Paules Crosse*, 1588 [1589] (1346), pp. 24, 86–7.

32. Chiefly Sir Francis Knollys, who made

it his 'chiefest study' to preserve the queen's safety against the pretensions of the bishops to an authority other than that granted in the statute of 25 Hen. VIII. Thanks to Knollys's pertinacity, Dr John Reynolds, Dr John Hammond, and Whitgift himself were drawn into a public declaration of their opinions of the theological and legal status of episcopacy. (PRO, S.P. 12/223/23; BM, MS. Lansd. 61, fols. 78–80, 151–2, MS. Add. 48064, fols. 94–5, 226–38; HMC, Hatfield MSS, iii. 412–13.) The late Dr Norman Sykes was strictly correct in his statement (Old Priest & New Presbyter, pp. 25–6) that Bancroft did not advance beyond the accepted Elizabethan doctrine of episcopacy in this sermon. Yet as Reynolds pointed out (MS. Lansd. 61, fol. 78) he did imply that to call in question the superiority of bishops was heresy. Cf.

W. D. J. Cargill Thompson, 'Anthony Marten and the Elizabethan Debate on Episcopacy', Essays in Modern English Church History, ed. Bennett & Walsh, 1966, pp. 44–75.

33. Tracts Ascribed to Richard Bancroft, ed. Peel, p. xix; BM, MS. Egerton 2598, fol. 242; Sutcliffe, op. cit., fol. 30ᵛ.

34. PRO, Sta. Cha. 5 A 49/34.

35. What follows is based on Neale, ii. 216–39.

36. Whitgift's annotated copy of the 'motions' is at Longleat House, MS. Thynne lxxvi, fols. 5–12.

37. BM, MS. Add. 48064, fols. 72–3, 48.

38. BM, MS. Lansd. 63, fols. 221, 223–4, 225, 229.

39. PRO, Sta. Cha. 5 A 49/34, depositions of Thomas Stone, Henry Alvey, William Perkins, Thomas Barber.

40. BM, MS. Lansd. 78, fols. 170, 156, 154–5ʳ, 160.

Chapter 2

1. The just censure and reproofe of Martin Iunior, in Marprelate Tracts, ed. Pierce, pp. 352–60.

2. BM, MS. Lansd. 64, fol. 53ʳ.

3. These papers were bound up, or transcribed, into a volume of supporting documents for the use of the prosecution in the Star Chamber case against the nine ministers. This collection is no longer extant, but its contents can be partially reconstructed by comparing the page (or folio) numbers mentioned in the Star Chamber proceedings with the briefs prepared for the prosecution and the papers amassed by the queen's counsel in his oversight of the case (BM, MSS Harl. 6849, Harl. 6866, MS. Lansd. 120). I hope to publish an account of the missing volume elsewhere.

4. Copies in ITL, MS. Petyt 538/38, fol. 155, CUL, MS. Mm. 1. 47, pp. 333–5; printed Usher, Reconstruction of the English Church, ii. 366–9; Tracts Ascribed to Richard Bancroft, ed. Peel, pp. xvii–xx.

5. 'Richard Bancroft's Submission', J.E.H., iii. 58–73.

6. See his careful endorsement of a letter incriminating Humfrey Newman, distributor of the tracts, BM, MS. Add. 28571, fols. 165–6.

7. This was alleged by 'Martin' in The iust censure and reproofe (Tracts, p. 355). It is

confirmed from proceedings in the consistory court of London against Lionel Foster, vicar of Great Tey, Essex; GRLO, Consistory Court of London Records, DL/C/213, deposition of Lionel Foster, Apr. 19th, 1589.

8. ERO, D/P/135/1/1 (parish book of Heydon), fol. 137ᵛ; Seconde Parte, ii. 231–2.

9. Porter, Reformation & Reaction in Tudor Cambridge, pp. 157–63; BM, MS. Add. 48064, fols. 148–51ᵛ, MS. Lansd. 68, fol. 173, MS. Lansd. 64, fol. 86.

10. Ibid., MS. Lansd. 68, fols. 110, 133, 196–7; Two Elizabethan Puritan Diaries, ed. Knappen, pp. 90–102.

11. Urwick, Nonconformity in Herts., pp. 110–13.

12. BM, MS. Add. 48064, fols. 90–1.

13. Nichols, History of Leicestershire, III. ii. 626; DWL, MS. Morrice M, no. viii.

14. There is a fully documented account of the Lancashire preachers and their unusual status in my 'Classical Movement', pp. 1069–85.

15. Cardwell, History of Conferences, p. 210; Usher, op. cit., ii. 353.

16. This account is based on the materials collected in Chetham Miscellanies, v. ed. Raines, Chetham Socy, O.S., xcvi; HMC 14th Report, App. IV. Kenyon MSS, pp. 598–602; and Miss Edna Bibby's notes of the records of the

visitation (now deposited in the Borth-
wick Institute of Historical Research,
York).

17. BM, MS. Add. 48064, fols. 68–9;
D.N.B., art. Walmesley; *Kenyon MSS*,
p. 602; S. L. Ware, *The Elizabethan
Parish in its Ecclesiastical and Financial
Aspects*, Baltimore 1908, p. 25; HMC,
Hatfield MSS, xii. 142; PRO, S.P.
15/31/154.

18. *State Trials*, edn 1730, I. xiv. 161–72.

19. The speech contains echoes of Bancroft's distinctive polemic, and a
reference to the papers seized in the
Midlands. Moreover Puckering's papers
include the draft of a further speech
intended for use at this trial which
connects Udall's case with the recently
discovered Book of Discipline and
bears a few insertions in Bancroft's
hand (BM, MS. Harl. 6849, fols.
235–6).

20. *State Trials*, I. xiv. 172–81.

21. Beale's account in a letter to Burghley,
BM, MS. Add. 48064, fol. 110; copies
of the articles, ibid., fol. 88, ITL, MS.
Petyt 538/38, fols. 167ᵛ–70 (whence
printed, Strype, *Whitgift*, iii. 261–2),
BM, MS. Harl. 6849, fol. 179 (Puckering's copy), HMC, *Hatfield MSS*, iv.
94–5 (Burghley's copy with critical
comments by Beale); cf. Bancroft, *A
sermon preached at Paules Crosse*, p. 49.

22. *Daungerous positions*, pp. 84, 92.

23. PRO, Sta. Cha. A 5 56/1; *Daungerous
positions*, p. 92.

24. *Stiffkey Papers*, ed. Saunders, CS 3rd
ser. xxxvi. 186–9 (misdated); PRO,
S.P. 12/238/75.

25. Collections of arguments against the
oath, apparently connected with this
case, in Corpus Christi College,
Oxford, MS. 294, pp. 381–423, including a treatise also found (with many
variant readings) in HMC, *Hastings
MSS*, i. 433–46, and printed from the
Hastings MSS in *Cartwrightiana*, ed.
Peel, ENT i. 31–46 (although not
necessarily the work of Cartwright).
Another statement in the name of all
the ministers, BM, MS. Add. 48064,
fols. 180–1 (printed *Cartwrightiana*, pp.
28–30) and further relevant documents
in BL, MS. Tanner 84, fols, 25–31.
Fen's and Snape's arguments in LPL,
MS. 2004, nos. 56, 58, fols. 83–7, with
many other documents relating to the
oath and to this case.

26. BM, MS. Lansd. 119, fol. 106ʳ; PRO,
Sta. Cha. 5 A 56/1, 39/23.

27. *Daungerous positions*, pp. 91–3, and 43
(sic, recte 67)–128, passim.

28. Scott Pearson, pp. 315–20, 445–57;
Cartwrightiana, p. 63; articles printed in
Fuller, *Church History*, 1845 edn v.
142–54. Fuller's date of Sept 1st,
generally thought to be a mistake,
persists in two other copies of the
articles: Corpus Christi College, Oxford, MS. 294, pp. 217–27; CUL, MS.
Baumgartner 6, fol. 794 (Strype's
papers).

29. BM, MS. Lansd. 63, fol. 203, MS.
Lansd. 103, fol. 206; Scott Pearson,
pp. 455–6.

30. PRO, Sta. Cha. 5 A 49/34, Stone's
deposition; *Daungerous positions*, pp.
93–4.

31. PRO, Sta. Cha. 5 A 56/1; BM, MS.
Harl. 6849, fol. 176; Scott Pearson,
pp. 467–70.

32. Queen's College, Oxford, MS. 280,
fols. 173ᵛ–5ʳ. Reynolds's letter dated
Nov. 30th, Fen's letter undated.

33. BM, MS. Lansd. 68, fols. 98–100,
Lansd. 72, fols. 140–1, MS. Harl. 6849,
fols. 220, 229ᵛ, 176, 175; PRO, Sta.
Cha. 5 A 56/1; A.P.C., xx. 270, 304,
313–14.

34. PRO, Sta. Cha. 5 A 56/1; BM, MS.
Add. 48039, fols. 74–5, MS. Add.
48064, fols. 158–9, MS. Lansd. 72, fols.
137–41.

35. Corpus Christi College, Oxford, MS.
294, pp. 205–7, 269.

36. Draft in pencil of a report from Whitgift to the queen, commenting on
parliamentary proceedings of Feb. 27th,
1593. The document is quoted in
Neale ii. 273–4 as St Paul's Add. MS.
VII. 6 (38). I am grateful to Mr Robin
Howard of the Gore Restaurant &
Elizabethan Rooms, in whose possession it now is, for permission to
refer to it. Since going to press it has
been recovered by LPL and forms part
of MS. 2019.

37. BM MS. Lansd. 72, fols. 140–1;
Daungerous positions, p. 93.

38. BM, MS. Harl. 6849, fol. 176, MS.
Add. 48064, fols. 220–2, printed,
Cartwrightiana, pp. 21–7.

39. Scott Pearson, pp. 458–63. This
appearance is misdated in *Cartwrightiana*, p. 27.

Chapter 3

1. BM, MS. Lansd. 68, fol. 97. The writer was probably Sir Francis Knollys.
2. Copies in BM, MS. Lansd. 120, fols. 29–41, MS. Harl. 6866, fols. 316–27, 136.
3. Ibid., MS. Lansd. 120, fols. 43–6, 77ʳ, MS. Lansd. 119, fols. 104–7. There is evidence in Strype's correspondence that Whitgift submitted these documents, with two books of extracts from the ministers' letters, to Sir John Boys of Canterbury, who was both a Middle Temple lawyer and his steward. (CUL, MS. Baumgartner 6, fol. 794.)
4. BM, MS. Lansd. 119, fol. 106, MS. Lansd. 120, fol. 78ʳ.
5. Arber, *Introductory Sketch*, pp. 121–36; Pierce, *Historical Introduction*, pp. 205–8.
6. McCorkle, ' "Mistress Crane" ', 276–283; Mrs Crane's sentence, unknown to Miss McCorkle, is reported in BM, MS. Harl. 2143, fols. 48ᵛ–9ʳ.
7. Ibid., MS. Lansd. 68, fol. 190.
8. *A briefe view of the state of the Church of England*, 1653, p. 13.
9. See many refs. to Fuller in the later Elizabethan *A.P.C.*; *State Trials*, I. xiv. 163, 169; *DNB*, art. Fuller.
10. According to Knollys, to 'join with the judges for their information.' The correction is made from a later account of this occasion, also probably by Knollys, BM, MS. Lansd. 68, fol. 97.
11. Ibid.
12. Ibid., MS. Lansd. 68, fols. 119, 98–101; Scott Pearson, p. 466. Other abstracts, BM, MS. Add. 32092, fols. 126–33 (in Whitgift's hand), MS. Harl. 6849, fols. 227–8 (Puckering's digest), PRO, S.P. 12/238/102.
13. BM, MS. Lansd. 68, fol. 121, MS. Harl. 6849, fols. 225–6, MS. Harl. 7042, fol. 40; Richard Cosin, *Conspiracie for pretended reformation*, 1592 (5823), p. 23; *Daungerous positions*, p. 156.
14. PRO, Sta. Cha. 5 A 56/1 (interrogatories ministered to defendants on the queen's behalf, and depositions); Sta. Cha. 5 A 39/23 (interrogatories put to these witnesses on behalf of the defendants, and depositions); Sta. Cha. 5 A 27/33 (interrogatories ministered to witnesses produced against Snape, and depositions).
15. BM, MS. Lansd. 68, fol. 121.
16. *Daungerous positions*, p. 161.

17. BM, MS. Harl. 6849, the latter part of the volume, *passim*.
18. Ibid., MS. Lansd. 68, fols. 98–100.
19. 'Touching the proceeding against the ministers'; copies in BM, MS. Add. 48064, fols. 134ʳ–43ʳ, MS. Add. 48039, fols. 78–86.
20. Ibid., MS. Add. 48064, fols. 102–3.
21. See Chapter 2, n. 3.
22. He was later to be charged before the High Commissioners, on the sole evidence of the Field-Gellibrand correspondence (LPL, MS. Carte Misc. IV, no. 190).
23. There is a contemporary manuscript catalogue of much of the material, BM, MS. Harl. 360, fols. 85–7. The register later came into the possession of the Suffolk puritan gentleman, Sir John Higham (DWL, MS. Morrice I, p. 617(8)).
24. BM, MS. Lansd. 72, fol. 197ᵛ, MS. Harl. 6866, fol. 318ᵛ.
     sin, op. cit., *passim*; *Daungerous positions*, pp. 144–83. See also Matthew Sutcliffe, *An Answere unto a certaine calumnious letter*, *passim*.
26. Nichols, *Plea of the innocent*, pp. 32–3; Fuller, *Church History*, v. 162–3; Scott Pearson, pp. 463–4; *State Trials*, I. xiv. 180; *A.P.C.* xxi. 299, 300, 343, 376, 392–3.
27. Stone's letters and papers, no longer extant, were seen and partly transcribed by Thomas Fuller, op. cit., v. 163–9.
28. BM, MS. Lansd. 120, fols. 84–8; cf. Scott Pearson, pp. 476–7.
29. BM, MS. Harl. 6849, fols. 173–4, 176–8, 220–1, 228ᵛ–9ᵛ, 237ʳ.
30. Ibid., MS. Lansd. 68, fol. 43.
31. Ibid., fol. 97, MS. Lansd. 66, fol. 150.
32. Nichols, *Leicestershire*, III. ii. 626.
33. LPL, MS. 2004, fol. 7.
34. Paule, *Life of Whitgift* 1612 (19484), pp. 54–8; Neale, ii. 280–97.
35. Scott Pearson, pp. 473–4; *State Trials*, I. xiv. 180; Strype, *Whitgift*, iii. 265–7.
36. Scott Pearson, pp. 470–3; BM, MS. Lansd. 109, fols. 25, 31; LPL, MS. Carte Misc. iv. nos. 193, 188.
37. Not, I think, Fen, as the catalogue would suggest, but possibly Prowdlove. There may have been some confusion of these documents in binding.
38. Scott Pearson, pp. 473–9; BM, MS.

Lansd. 68, fol. 102; LPL, MS. Carte Misc. iv. no. 185.

39. ITL, MS. Petyt 538/38, fols. 167ᵛ–70; BM, MS. Lansd. 68, fols. 139–41; LPL, MS. Carte Misc. iv. nos. 185, 187, 189, 194–5, 196. Payne and Jewel were not required to answer these interrogatories, presumably because it was now recognized that they had played no significant part in the conference movement.

40. Scott Pearson, p. 479; LPL, MS. Carte Misc. iv. nos. 197–8, 184, 186, 192; ibid., MS. 577, fol. 237.

41. The London separatist Christopher Bowman, at his examination in the spring of 1593, attributed his views in

part to the teaching of Snape and King (BM, MS. Harl. 7042, fol. 61).

42. PRO, S.P. 14/10A/81.

43. An examination of M. Thomas Cartwrights late apologie, 1596 (23463), fol. 44.

44. For a realistic assessment of Hooker's immediate impact, see C. J. Sisson, The Judicious Marriage of Mr. Hooker.

45. Neale, ii. 267–97; NNRO, Norwich Diocesan Archives, ACT/31 (Act Book of the Consistory Court, containing some Acts of the Ecclesiastical Commissioners for the diocese, 1595–8), fols. 66ᵛ, 69ᵛ; Correspondence of Matthew Hutton, Surtees Socy, xvii. 117.

Chapter 4

1. Dedham Minutes, pp. 77–8; Fuller, Church History, v. 252.

2. This is suggested by the confessions of some London separatists, BM, MS. Harl. 7042, fols. 35–8, 59–60, 204ᵛ–5.

3. Bradshaw, English puritanisme, 1640 edn (3517), p. 2; Paget, A defence of church-government, 1641, p. 106.

4. See Christopher Hill, Society & Puritanism in Pre-Revolutionary England, passim, but esp. pp. 501–6.

5. A parte, pp. 381–6; Pierce, Historical Introduction, pp. 281–2; BM, MS. Lansd. 82, fol. 111ʳ.

6. For the early Cambridge 'Arminians', see Porter, Reformation & Reaction in Tudor Cambridge, pp. 323–413. An early instance of the attack on double predestination as a puritan doctrine is the Paul's Cross sermon preached on Oct. 27th, 1584 by Samuel Harsnet, printed with Three sermons preached by the reverend and learned Dr. Richard Stuart, 1658. Probably the best account of Perkins's theology, especially in its European reformed context, is in the Manchester Ph.D. thesis by Prof. I. Breward, 'The Life and Theology of William Perkins', 1963.

7. Perkins, Works, 1608 (19649), i. 32a.

8. For 'covenant theology', see Perry Miller, The New England Mind, and the important corrections of J. G. Møller, J.E.H., xiv. 46–67.

9. Two Elizabethan Puritan Diaries, ed. Knappen.

10. I. Breward, 'William Perkins & the Origins of Puritan Casuistry', Faith & a

Good Conscience, Puritan & Reformed Studies Conference Papers for 1962 (1963), pp. 5–17. Cf. G. L. Mosse, The Holy Pretence, 1957.

11. For an interpretation of the social 'uses' of puritanism, see C. Hill, 'William Perkins & the Poor', Puritanism & Revolution, pp. 215–38; and his Society & Puritanism, passim.

12. Mosse, The arraignment and conviction of usury, 1595 (18207).

13. Hill, 'The uses of the Sabbath', Society & Puritanism, pp. 145–218; my 'The Beginnings of English Sabbatarianism', Studies in Church History, i. 207–21.

14. Thomas Rogers, The faith, doctrine and religion professed ... in ... England, 1607 (21228), Sig. ¶¶¶ 3ᵛ.

15. Canon LXXII of 1604 is directed against the practice.

16. Samuel Harsnet, A discovery of the fraudulent practises of John Darrell, 1599 (12883), pp. 270–1, 293; Darrell, A true narration, 1600 (6288), pp. 8–13; An apologie or defence of the possession of William Sommers, 1599? (6282), fol. 1ʳ; A detection of the sinnful, shamful, lying, and ridiculous discours of Samuel Harsnet, 1600 (6283), p. 89.

17. Dedham Minutes, p. 74.

18. He wrote in a letter of Feb. 17th of that year of 'this lewd woman that is the ground of my troubles'; ibid., p. 84.

19. GLRO, Consistory Court of London Records, DL/C/213, depositions of May 10th, May 14th, July 4th, 1590; ERO, D/ACA/19, fols. 57ᵛ, 89ᵛ; Guildhall Library, MS. 9531/13

(Bishop of London's Register, 1560–1617), fol. 251ʳ. I owe my knowledge of the first source to Dr H. G. Owen.

20. LPL, MS. 649, no. 233. That Faunt's host at Bergholt was Cardinal is inferred from the evidence of other letters in the Bacon papers that he was a friend of the family.

21. LPL, MS. 648, nos. 103, 109, 176, MS. 649, nos. 24, 79, MS. 650, nos. 69, 169; Wilcox, *A short, yet sound commentarie ... on ... the proverbes of Salomon*, 1589 (25627), Sig. A3.

22. Urwick, *Nonconformity in Herts.*, p. 86; *Seconde Parte*, i. 13.

23. Urwick, op. cit., pp. 106–15; LPL, MS. 650, nos. 192, 14; R. Peters, *Oculus Episcopi*, 1963, p. 85.

24. HRO, St Albans Archdeaconry Records, ASA 5/5/291, 305; Urwick, op. cit., pp. 117–18; Stow, *Annals*, 1631 edn, p. 766.

25. LPL, MS. 649, no. 71, MS. 650, no. 232; Pierce, *John Penry*, pp. 383–4; Urwick, op. cit., p. 93.

26. HRO, ASA 5/5/291; Urwick, op. cit., p. 93.

27. Scott Pearson, pp. 373–86; Schickler, *Les Églises du Refuge en Angleterre*, ii. 447; *HMC, Hatfield MSS*, vi. 265–6; PRO, S.P. 14/12/68.

28. *HMC, Hatfield MSS*, xvii. 623, x. 450–1; PRO, S.P. 14/10A/81; ITL, MS, Petyt 538/38, fols. 40, 62; BM, MS. Add. 38492, fol. 43.

29. Corpus Christi College, Oxford, MS. 294, pp. 205–7, 269–73; City of Exeter Muniments, Act Book V, fol. 502 (a reference I owe to Mr J. C. Roberts); *HMC, City of Exeter MSS*, p. 40; PRO, S.P. 12/282/49; BM, MS. Add. 38492, fol. 36, MS. Sloane 271, fol. 24ʳ.

30. GLRO, P/92/SAV/450, St Saviour's Vestry Minutes ii. pp. 373, 381, 391 (a reference I owe to Dr H. G. Owen); Edward Philips, *Certaine godly and learned sermons*, ed. Henry Yelverton,

1605 (19853), Sig. A4ᵛ; *Diary of Walter Yonge*, ed. Roberts, CS xli. 4.

31. *HMC, Hatfield MSS*, iv. 460–1; Neale, ii. 267–79, 326, 251–66.

32. Huntington Library, Hastings. MS., 5090. I owe this reference to Dr M. Claire Cross.

33. These words, missing from the printed text in *State Trials*, were supplied to me from Longleat House, MS. Devereux vii. fol. 142, by Miss Carolyn Merion.

34. J. Dover Wilson, *Martin Marprelate & Shakespeare's Fluellen*; PRO, S.P. 12/238/82; *State Trials*, I. xiv. 177–9; *Notebook of John Penry*, op. cit., pp. 70, 85–95.

35. Paule, *Life of Whitgift*, pp. 54–5; *Reliquiae Wottonianae*, 1651, p. 22; Scott Pearson, pp. 384–6; *HMC, Hatfield MSS*, vi. 477–8; Nichols, *An order of household instruction*, 1596 (18540), Sigs. A2–B2.

36. An account of Essex's puritan chaplains and of the books dedicated to him by puritan authors will be found in my 'Classical Movement', pp. 1206–9.

37. BM, MS. Add. 48064, fols. 148–51; *HMC, Hatfield MSS*, vi. 317, xi. 154.

38. PRO, S.P. 12/273/55, 59, 274/1; *HMC, Hatfield MSS*, xi. 154; Birch, *Memoirs*, ii. 464; *Records of the English Province of the Socy of Jesus*, i. ed. Foley, 7–8.

39. *HMC, Hatfield MSS*, xi. 154–5, 148; PRO, S.P. 12/278/63; Calderwood, *History of the Kirk of Scotland*, ed. Thomson, vi. 130–1, 135, 194.

40. The expression belongs to the divine Hugh Broughton; PRO, S.P. 52/64/2.

41. *James VI and I*, p. 149.

42. *HMC, Hatfield MSS*, xi. 148, 157–8, 161, 506.

43. Gee & Hardy, *Documents Illustrative of English Church History*, p. 511. Fuller reports that the petition was drafted by Egerton and Arthur Hildersham (op. cit., v. 265).

Chapter 5

1. Nichols, *Plea of the innocent*, p. 35; J. E. Neale, 'Peter Wentworth', *EHR*, xxxix. 198–200; Wentworth, *A pithie exhortation*, Edinburgh 1598 (25245); PRO, S.P. 52/64/2; *DNB*, art. Broughton; Sparke, *A brotherly perswasion to unitie*, 1607 (23020), Sig. A4; Hatfield House, MS. 191, fol. 44, a reference I owe to the papers of the

late Miss Bibby. For further evidence of James's acceptability, see Miles Mosse, *Scotlands welcome*, a sermon preached at Needham Market, Suffolk, on Apr. 5th, 1603 (18210); and Andrew Willet, *Ecclesia triumphans: that is the joy of the English Church for the happie coronation of the most vertuous and pious prince James*, 1603 (25676).

2. D. H .Willson, *King James VI and I*, pp. 197, 135–6, 200–2; Βαδιλικὸν Δῶρον, (14350), Sigs. A4ᵛ–6ʳ; BM, MS. Add. 38492, fol. 9ʳ, MS. Sloane 271, fol. 20ᵛ; *The Registrum Vagum of Anthony Harison*, i. Norfolk Record Socy, xxxii. 34–6, 156–7, 158–9.

3. Curtis, 'Hampton Court Conference & its Aftermath', *History*, xlvi. 1–16.

4. Quoted, Willson, op. cit., p. 250.

5. Usher, *Reconstruction of the English Church*, i. 294.

6. Wilkins, *Concilia*, iv. 369; PRO, S.P. 14/2/38.

7. Wilkins, op. cit., iv. 368–9; *Registrum Vagum*, i. 20–3. For the episcopal returns, see BM, MS. Harl. 280, fols. 157–72 (digest of the complete returns for both provinces, partly in Whitgift's hand), MS. Harl. 595, fols. 94–194 (detailed archdeacons' returns for Norwich), 195–266 (episcopal returns for Salisbury, Worcester, Winchester).

8. *Registrum Vagum*, i. 24–34, 40–50.

9. G. Donaldson, 'Scottish Presbyterian Exiles in England, 1584–8', *Records of the Scottish Church History Socy*, xiv. 67–80; Calderwood, *History of the Kirk of Scotland*, vi. 235; PRO, S.P. 14/2/39, 14/6/21; BM, MS. Sloane 271, fols. 23–4ʳ; Henry Jacob, *A Christian and modest offer of a most indifferent conference*, Middelburg 1606 (14329), p. 20. Mosse's *Scotlands Welcome* was dedicated to Mar, whom he had known as a presbyterian exile in Norwich in 1584.

10. Calderwood, op. cit., vi. 235; Nichols, *Plea of the innocent*, p. 77; Gee & Hardy, *Documents*, p. 508.

11. Principal Probate Registry, Somerset House, P.C.C. wills, 38 Rutland. Egerton's signature is clear in the original will, whereas in the register the initial 'S.' is likely to be read as an 'F.' or a 'J.'.

12. 'Life of Hildersham', Samuel Clarke, *General Martyrologie*, 1677, pt. 2, p. 116.

13. The better and fuller copy of the 'Advices' is in BM, MS. Add. 38492, fol. 62ʳ; Usher prints MS. Add. 28571, fol. 199, op. cit., ii. 358–9. Cf. Calderwood, op. cit., vi. 234–5.

14. BM, MS. Add. 38492, fol. 62ʳ, MS. Sloane 271, fols. 20ᵛ–2; Cartwright's letter printed, Scott Pearson, pp. 481–2.

15. MS. Sloane 271.

16. *HMC, Hatfield MSS*, xv. 262–3; PRO, S.P. 14/3/83.

17. BM, MS. Add. 38492, fols. 71–2, MS. Sloane 271, fol. 20.

18. Essex survey printed from Manchester MSS (*vide, HMC VIIIth Report, App. 2*, p. 4) in quasi-facsimile, *A viewe of the state of the clargie within the countie of Essex*, 1894?; Staffs. survey printed by A. Peel from DWL, MS. Morrice M, no. V, *EHR*, xxvi. 338–52; survey for deanery of Doncaster 'out of Mr. Hildersham's papers – paper 9th', in BM, MS. Add. 4293, fol. 41, reproduced in Dr J. A. Newton's unpubl. London Ph.D. thesis, 'Puritanism in the Diocese of York (excluding Nottinghamshire), 1603–40', App. 1, pp. 413–419. Cf. Marchant, *Puritans & the Church Courts in the Diocese of York, 1560–1642*, pp. 27–8, 221. The Staffs. survey can be dated between Jan. and March 1604 and the Essex and Doncaster surveys probably both belong to 1604, which suggests that, as in 1584, the project took longer to complete than the time available.

19. Calderwood, op. cit., vi. 235.

20. PRO, S.P. 14/10A/81.

21. Steele, *Tudor & Stuart Proclamations*, i. no. 974. Curtis gives an account of an earlier draft of this proclamation, loc. cit., 5–6.

22. BM, MS. Sloane 271, fols. 24ᵛ–5ʳ.

23. Burrage, *Early English Dissenters*, ii. 146–8; *The answere of the ... universitie of Oxford*, 1603 (19010), pp. 6–7; BM, MS. Sloane 271, fol. 20.

24. PRO, S.P. 14/3/48; BM, MS. Sloane 271, fol. 21ᵛ. Ireton appears in the Northants. list as 'Jerton'. Usher, op. cit., i. 312–13, reads this as (Stephen) Egerton, who is not named in any of the extant lists. For evidence that Fen was substituted for Ireton, see MS. Sloane 271, fol. 23ʳ.

25. PRO, S.P. 14/6/15. Hildersham is named only as a possible substitute, apparently for Dr Richard Field. Field was one of several members of the conference who cannot be placed easily in either camp. He is listed by the puritans as a 'minister of the conference' (*HMC, Montagu of Beaulieu MSS*, p. 34) and he went into the conference with the four ministers, but only to speak 'but once, and that altogether against them' (BM, MS. Harl. 3795, fol. 7ᵛ). For the 1584 conference see p. 269.

26. *HMC, Beaulieu MSS*, pp. 32–4; 'Life of Hildersham', Clarke, op. cit., p. 116.

27. *HMC, Beaulieu MSS*, pp. 32–40. For the Calvinist assertion in 1603, see

especially Andrew Willet's works, *An antilogie or counter plea to an apologeticall epistle* (25672), and *Ecclesia triumphans.*

28. For Reynolds's opinion of the matter in 1590, see p. 413. Henry Jacob explains the difference between the four spokesmen and the larger puritan conference in his *Christian and modest offer*, pp. 29–30.

29. BM, MS. Add. 38492, fol. 11.

30. Usher, op. cit., ii. 337.

31. Cardwell, *History of Conferences*, pp. 201–2, 172, 208–9; Usher, op. cit., ii. 351–2; PRO, S.P. 14/6/16–20; BM, MS. Lansd. 89, fol. 29; Canons XXXV, CXXII.

32. Cardwell, op. cit., p. 188.

33. BM, MS. Sloane 271, fol. 23[v].

34. Bancroft called Robinson Reynolds's 'especial and most familiar friend' (*Survay*, pp. 389–92). Reynolds's letter to Edward Fleetwood of Nov. 30th, 1590 (see p. 413) conveyed their common opinion of the ceremonies. Cf. *DNB*, arts. Reynolds, Robinson.

35. Curtis, loc. cit. The anon. account printed by Usher, op. cit., ii. 341–54, from BM, MS. Harl. 828, fols. 32–8. Another and better copy, MS. Add. 38492, fols. 82–5.

36. Cardwell, op. cit., p. 176.

37. Op. cit., pp. 29–68.

38. The last three paragraphs owe much to Mr N. R. N. Tyacke, who allowed me to read a draft of part of his unpublished

Oxford D. Phil. thesis, 'Arminianism in England in Religion & Politics, 1604–1640'.

39. Information about some of the reforms recommended but not implemented can be gathered from PRO, S.P. 14/6/18–20, 99, and BM, MS. Add. 28571, fols. 187–92.

40. Cardwell, op. cit., p. 178. In support of this view, see the king's declaration of July 3rd, 1604; PRO, S.P. 15/36/49.

41. Cardwell, op. cit., pp. 210–11.

42. Ibid., p. 201; BM, MS. 38492, fol. 81[v].

43. *History of England*, i. (1886), 198.

44. Jacob, op. cit., pp. 29–30, 3; notes on Chaderton, LPL, MS. 933, no. 41; PRO, S.P. 16/260/83; Calderwood, op. cit., vi. 236.

45. Reynolds's explanation of the undertaking he entered into at Hampton Court, sent to Salisbury, Hatfield House, MS. 191, no. 46; *A defence of the ministers reasons*, 1607 (13395), Sig. 4[r]; Sparke, op. cit., Sigs. A3–4, B4, pp. 2–5.

46. Ibid., Sigs. B1, 3, pp. 18–22, 74–8, 81.

47. Quoted, S. B. Babbage, *Puritanism & Richard Bancroft*, pp. 167–8.

48. Ibid., pp. 147–219.

49. PRO, S.P. 16/260/83; printed, *The last will and testament … of Humfrey Fen*, 1641.

50. Horton Davies, *The Worship of the English Puritans*, p. 130.

Index

INDEX

Cheyney, Richard, bishop of Gloucester, 40, 61, 192, 206
Chichester, bishop of, *see* Barlow, William (1559–69); Curteys, Richard (1570–82)
——, diocese of, 209, 249
——, Sir John, 22, 52
Chillingworth, William, 28
Cholmeley, Mr, of Antwerp, 237–8
Christian names used by puritans, 370, 495 n
Churchwardens, 299, 334, 351–2, 354, 355, 369
Civil War, the English, 27
Clark, John, 440
Clarke, Samuel, 436
   Lives of eminent divines, 128
——, Mr, of Warwick, 414
Cleeve, Glos., 47, 68
Cleveley, Hercules, 426, 493 n
Clothiers, 222–3, 226, 227, 374
Clothworkers' Company, 85–6, 475 n
Cobham, Lord, *see* Brooke, William
Cockfield, Suff., 218–20, 224, 232, 321, 338, 339
Coggeshall, Essex, 185, 225, 260, 319, 321
Colchester, 50, 168, 174, 222, 225, 246, 256–7, 267, 275, 278, 279, 321, 382, 399
——, archdeaconry of, 67, 185, 232
Cold Norton, Essex, 376
Cole, Thomas, archdeacon of Essex, 68, 74
——, William, 48, 50, 52, 67, 257, 366
Coligny, Gaspard de, sieur de Châtillon, 53
Colset, Mr, of Easton-on-the-Hill, Northants., 266
Commissary's Court, 120, 183, 187–8
Commons, House of, 27, 30–34, 116–19, 162–3, 183, 200, 206–7, 217–18, 273, 280, 282–8, 296, 306–9, 310–16, 317, 363, 398–400, 428, 431, 443, 444, 489 n; *see also* Parliament
Condé, prince of, *see* Bourbon, Louis
Conference or *classis*, the theory of, 177–9, 296–7, 299–301, 329, 338, 350, 421–2
——, general refs to, 106, 111, 177–9, 231–4, 275, 292–3, 305, 318, 322–7, 333, 336, 338, 350, 396, 402, 404, 415, 420, 421–2, 429, 437, 438, 453, 456
——, specific refs to, 134, 139, 224–31, 260–262, 276–7, 305–6, 319–20, 323–7, 338–9, 343, 389–90, 398, 408–9, 410, 438–9, 441; *see also* under Dedham conference; Daventry *classis*; Kettering *classis*; London; Northampton; Northamptonshire; Synods

——, the great, of the shire, 296–7, 301, 323–326, 398; *see also* under Northampton; Northamptonshire
Confession of faith, project for a puritan, 136, 137, 154, 292
Congregationalism or independency, 229–231, 333–4, 372
Consistory or congregational presbytery, 105–6, 107–8, 286, 299, 308, 335, 340–41, 350–54
Constable, John, 222–3
Convocation: **1559**, 31–2; **1563**, 34, 65–6; **1566**, 74; **1571**, 118, 182, 245; **1576**, 163; **1581**, 205; **1584–5**, 277, 284, 453; **1586–1587**, 171, 185, 307, 315; **1603**, 453; other refs, 22, 30, 39, 180
Cooke, Sir Anthony, 31, 53
——, Erasmus, 440
Cooper, Martin or Robert, 336, 341
Cooper, Thomas, bishop of Lincoln, 105, 152, 171, 173, 174, 175, 192, 193, 196, 201, 209, 211, 217, 252, 260, 392, 400, 492 n
Cope, Sir Anthony, 142–3, 193, 306, 307, 310, 311, 312, 314, 315, 317, 362, 363, 407, 443
Copinger, Edmund, 419–20, 424–5
Corbet, Sir Andrew, 139, 337
Cornwall, 149, 233, 276, 280, 304, 370, 441
Cosin, Richard, 274, 387, 404, 415, 417, 419, 420, 421, 423–4, 430, 496 n
   An answer to the ... abstract, 274
   Conspiracie for pretended reformation, 424
Cotton, John, 125
——, William, bishop of Exeter, 441, 442
Council, Privy, 72, 76, 77, 93, 140, 147–9, 151, 154, 155, 161, 162, 163, 186, 187, 192, 196–7, 198, 200, 203–6, 211, 216, 217, 237, 249–50, 251, 254–7, 258, 263, 268, 271–2, 281–2, 292, 303, 305, 306, 312, 386–7, 401, 406, 413, 414, 418–19, 428, 429, 430, 442, 443, 452, 455
Council in the North, 211
Council in the Welsh Marches, 139, 176
Court, the, 53–4, 75, 93, 147, 161, 162, 167, 192–4, 196–7, 198–201, 247, 249–50, 257, 258, 272, 277, 284, 313, 387, 443–4, 450, 452, 454, 455
Covenant, puritan concept and practice of, 353, 381–2
——, separatist, 90, 381
—— or federal theology, 434–5
Coventry, 35, 49, 51, 153, 168, 172, 174, 185, 196, 233, 321, 327, 343, 394, 397, 403, 414, 455, 464, 493 n

510

INDEX

Dorchester, Dorset, 278

Dorset, 150–51

Douai, 486 n

Douglas, James, earl of Morton, 199

Dow, Richard, 204, 223–4, 226–7, 339, 408

Downham, William, bishop of Chester, 206–7

Downlee, Edward, 311, 491 n

Dry Drayton, Cambs., 128, 349, 369, 436

Dudley, Ambrose, earl of Warwick, 52, 63, 94, 166, 189, 243, 257, 387, 444

——, Ann, countess of Warwick, 442, 443

——, John, duke of Northumberland, 38, 189

——, Robert, earl of Leicester: ecclesiastical patronage of, 62–3, 201; patron of puritans in early years of reign, 48, 49, 52–3, 74; committed to puritan and Calvinist cause, 53, 92–3; supports preachers in Northampton, 142–3, 147–8, 151–2; reaction to *Admonition*, 147; Archbishop Parker's enemy, 147; and Elizabethan policy, 166, 198–200; attends preaching exercises in Midlands, 176; allied to puritan gentry, 193, 199, 205; but averse to puritan spirit, 185; blamed for suppression of prophesyings, 193–4; warns puritans of dangers of extremism, 194, 208; helps Grindal in disgrace, 196–7; but said to be responsible for his troubles, 198; marries countess of Essex, 200; patron of Field, 202; relations with Archbishop Whitgift, 243–4, 270, 285, 386–7; supports puritans in 1584, 257; convenes Lambeth conference, 1584, 269, 455; in the Netherlands, 294; with puritan chaplains, 343, 386; patron of Cartwright, 295, 306; death, 386, 388; other refs, 64–5, 94, 184, 235, 397, 444, 445, 471 n

Dugmore, Prof. C. W., 16

Dunmow, Essex, 305

Durham, 52

Durham, bishop of, *see* Pilkington, James (1561–76); Barnes, Richard (1577–87); Matthew, Toby (1595–1606)

——, bishopric of, 49, 343, 474 n

——, diocese of, 64

Dutch church in London, 91, 113–15, 119, 477 n

Dutch Reformed Church, 134, 298

Dyke, William, 321, 373–4, 405, 440, 446, 456

EAST ANGLIA, 54, 187, 202–5, 210, 212, 218–220, 222–33, 253, 263, 337–8, 378, 401, 409

East Bergholt, Suff., 223, 226, 230–31, 319, 338, 339, 348, 439, 502 n

East Hanningfield, Essex, 349–50, 352–3, 379

East Molesey, Surrey, 138, 391–2, 394, 497 n

Easton-on-the-Hill, Northants., 266

East Peckham, Kent, 141

Eastwell, Kent, 321, 368

Ecclesiastical Commissioners (or the Court of High Commission), 65, 74–5, 76, 82, 85, 88–9, 118, 140, 152, 164, 205, 251, 260, 266, 267–8, 270–71, 273, 276, 326, 345, 351, 370–71, 396, 402, 405, 407, 408–11, 412, 414, 415–16, 417, 418, 423, 428, 431, 438, 440, 446, 450, 500 n

Ecclesiastical courts, 38–42, 164, 183, 187–8, 189, 285, 305, 346, 348, 349–50, 409–10, 444, 450–51, 453, 457

Ecclesiastical patronage of nobility and gentry, 22, 51–5, 186–8, 336

Economic problems of the Church, 42, 48, 314, 456

Edinburgh, 273, 276, 370, 397, 448, 449

Edmunds, Thomas, 132, 134, 152, 233, 237, 351, 390, 410–11, 426

Edward VI, King, 23, 33, 34, 46, 49, 50, 62, 69, 96, 103, 170, 181

Edwin, John, 138

Egerton, Stephen, 320, 321, 341, 351, 397, 412, 446–7, 449, 452, 453, 454, 456, 459, 487 n, 502 n, 593 n

——, Sir Thomas, 312–13

Elders and the eldership, 101, 102, 108, 114, 138, 178, 226, 286, 298–9, 308, 317–18, 329, 334, 346, 347, 350–55, 360, 420

Election, doctrine of, 25, 68, 456–7; *see also* Predestination

Election and ordination procedures, 114, 138–9, 178–9, 299, 301, 308–9, 328–9, 333, 335–45, 350

Elizabeth I, Queen: accession, 72; religious views and attitudes, 29–30, 32, 60; and the religious settlement of 1559, 29–36, 307; and marriage, 35–6, 198–9; ecclesiastical policy, 60, 201–2; ecclesiastical appointments, 61–2, 201; relationship with Leicester, 62; and vestments controversy, 69–70, 72–6; harangued by Edward Dering, 135; issues proclamations against puritans, 1573, 148–51; reluctant to promote Grindal, 160–61; refers Commons petition of 1576 to Convocation, 163; and articles of 1581 to bishops, 206; and penal laws against catholics, 164; and Elizabethan policy, 166–7; orders sup-

Geneva, 24, 31, 33, 40, 41, 43, 45–6, 48–9, 72, 73, 79–82, 91, 103, 104, 109–11, 118, 124, 135, 141, 153, 169, 180, 298, 354, 368, 422, 434
—— Academy, 109–10
—— Bible, *see* Bible, Geneva version
—— Book (recensions of *The forme of prayers*), 89, 143, 169, 215, 274, 276, 286–8, 292, 296–7, 298, 299, 301, 303, 307–9, 310–313, 315, 317, 318, 324, 333, 334, 356, 360, 361–5, 367, 370–71, 490 n, 495 n; *see also The forme of prayers*
—— Consistory, 110
——, Ecclesiastical ordinances of, 40, 114, 354
——, English congregation at, 31, 45–6, 48–49, 52, 63–4, 72, 89, 90, 113, 133–4, 153, 169, 286, 296
Gentlemen's houses, puritan assemblies in, 143, 199, 202
Gentry, puritanism among the, 54–5, 160, 166, 186–8, 192–3, 201, 203–5, 210, 217–218, 256–7, 258–9, 268, 277–8, 283, 305, 312, 337
Geree, John, *The character of an old English puritane*, 361, 375
Germany, 23, 66, 67, 95, 306
Gesner, Conrad, 135
Gifford, George, 265, 267, 279, 321, 357, 359, 363, 373, 374, 376, 377, 378, 401–2, 405, 408, 412
    The countrie divinitie, 373
Gilby, Anthony, 48–50, 52, 78, 95, 105, 108, 116, 118, 121, 126, 131, 135, 136–7, 141, 152, 153–4, 173, 185, 209, 238, 473 n
    A pleasaunt dialogue, 78, 208
    Two short and comfortable epistles, 78
——, Nathaniel, 126
Gilgate, Philip, 495 n
Glibery, William, 373
Gloucester, bishop of, *see* Hooper, John (1550–53); Cheyney, Richard (1562–79)
——, diocese of, 192, 481 n
Gloucestershire, 47, 174, 181
Goad, Roger, 235–7
Golding, Dame Elizabeth, 141
Goldsborough, Godfrey, bishop of Gloucester, 130
Goodman, Christopher, archdeacon of Richmond, 46, 52, 92, 118, 133, 139, 147, 210–11, 298
    How superior powers oght to be obeyed, 46, 150
——, Gabriel, dean of Westminster, 249

Goodwin, Vincent, 204
Gorhambury, Herts., 171, 439–40
Gosson, Stephen, 208
Gouge, Richard, 128
Gough, John, 74, 75, 77–8, 82, 93
Grantham, Lincs., 174, 211
Great Billing, Northants., 143
Great Bromley, Essex, 223
Great Tey, Essex, 498 n
Great Wakering, Essex, 379
Greenaway, Samuel, 215
Greenham, Richard, 128, 349, 369, 436, 495 n
Greenwich Palace, 143, 285
Greenwood, John, 336, 341, 354, 357, 388, 405, 412, 428
Grenville, Sir Richard, 276
Greville, Sir Fulke (later Lord Brooke), 86
Grey, Lady Catharine, 53
——, Lady Jane, 63, 141, 149
——, Lady Mary, 86, 149
——, Lord Henry, of Pirgo, 269
——, Ursula, 379–80
Grindal, Edmund, bishop of London (1559–1570), archbishop of York (1570–75), archbishop of Canterbury (1576–83): character and reputation, 159–60, 481 n; and the religious settlement of 1559, 33; hesitates to accept episcopal office, 47, 437 n; made bishop of London, 63; owes preferments to Cecil, 62, 481 n; tolerant of puritans and nonconformity, 66–7, 96, 366; and the vestments controversy, 70, 71, 73–6, 80–81, 84; examines Plumbers' Hall leaders, 88–9, 116; admonished by Theodore Beza, 110; superintendent of strangers' churches in London, 114; archbishop of York, 173, 211, 460; archbishop of Canterbury, 155, 159, 161; reforms projected in his primacy, 161–7, 181–90; the prophesyings and his letter to the queen, 60, 191–6, 207, 484 n; disgrace and suspension, 196–8, 205; political implications of his disgrace, 167, 198–201; reputation of his archiepiscopate, 166, 248; death, 243; other refs, 59, 61, 86, 90, 92, 93, 94, 109, 118, 134, 166, 187, 188, 208, 215, 238, 273, 466, 484 n
Groby, Leics., 141
Gualter, Rodolph, 30, 80–81, 110–11, 153, 478 n
Guernsey, 430, 441
Guest, Edmund, bishop of Rochester (1560–1571), Salisbury (1571–7), 61, 206
Gurney, family of, 220

DATE DUE

DEC 1 3 '89		
OCT 2 4 '90		
NOV 2 2 '90		
1 8 '90		
DEC 1 8 '90		
DEC 2 7 '91		
DEC 2 8 1994		
JAN 1 0 1996		
JAN 0 4 1997		
DEC 0 1 2001		
FEB 1 7 2006		